Metabolomics Data Processing and Data Analysis—Current Best Practices

Metabolomics Data Processing and Data Analysis—Current Best Practices

Editors

Justin J.J. van der Hooft
Kati Hanhineva

MDPI • Basel • Beijing • Wuhan • Barcelona • Belgrade • Manchester • Tokyo • Cluj • Tianjin

Editors
Justin J.J. van der Hooft
Wageningen University
The Netherlands

Kati Hanhineva
University of Eastern Finland
Finland

Editorial Office
MDPI
St. Alban-Anlage 66
4052 Basel, Switzerland

This is a reprint of articles from the Special Issue published online in the open access journal *Metabolites* (ISSN 2218-1989) (available at: https://www.mdpi.com/journal/metabolites/special_issues/data_analysis).

For citation purposes, cite each article independently as indicated on the article page online and as indicated below:

LastName, A.A.; LastName, B.B.; LastName, C.C. Article Title. *Journal Name* **Year**, *Volume Number*, Page Range.

ISBN 978-3-0365-1194-8 (Hbk)
ISBN 978-3-0365-1195-5 (PDF)

© 2021 by the authors. Articles in this book are Open Access and distributed under the Creative Commons Attribution (CC BY) license, which allows users to download, copy and build upon published articles, as long as the author and publisher are properly credited, which ensures maximum dissemination and a wider impact of our publications.

The book as a whole is distributed by MDPI under the terms and conditions of the Creative Commons license CC BY-NC-ND.

Contents

About the Editors vii

Preface to "Metabolomics Data Processing and Data Analysis—Current Best Practices" ix

Julijana Ivanisevic and Elizabeth J. Want
From Samples to Insights into Metabolism: Uncovering Biologically Relevant Information in LC-HRMS Metabolomics Data
Reprinted from: *Metabolites* **2019**, *9*, 308, doi:10.3390/metabo9120308 1

Jasmine Chong, Mai Yamamoto and Jianguo Xia
MetaboAnalystR 2.0: From Raw Spectra to Biological Insights
Reprinted from: *Metabolites* **2019**, *9*, 57, doi:10.3390/metabo9030057 31

Partho Sen and Matej Orešič
Metabolic Modeling of Human Gut Microbiota on a Genome Scale: An Overview
Reprinted from: *Metabolites* **2019**, *9*, 22, doi:10.3390/metabo9020022 41

Anton Klåvus, Marietta Kokla, Stefania Noerman, Ville M. Koistinen, Marjo Tuomainen, Iman Zarei, Topi Meuronen, Merja R. Häkkinen, Soile Rummukainen, Ambrin Farizah Babu, Taisa Sallinen, Olli Kärkkäinen, Jussi Paananen, David Broadhurst, Carl Brunius and Kati Hanhineva
"Notame": Workflow for Non-Targeted LC–MS Metabolic Profiling
Reprinted from: *Metabolites* **2020**, *10*, 135, doi:10.3390/metabo10040135 57

Yannick Djoumbou-Feunang, Allison Pon, Naama Karu, Jiamin Zheng, Carin Li, David Arndt, Maheswor Gautam, Felicity Allen and David S. Wishart
CFM-ID 3.0: Significantly Improved ESI-MS/MS Prediction and Compound Identification
Reprinted from: *Metabolites* **2019**, *9*, 72, doi:10.3390/metabo9040072 93

Manuel D. Peris-Díaz, Shannon R. Sweeney, Olga Rodak, Enrique Sentandreu and Stefano Tiziani
R-MetaboList 2: A Flexible Tool for Metabolite Annotation from High-Resolution Data-Independent Acquisition Mass Spectrometry Analysis
Reprinted from: *Metabolites* **2019**, *9*, 187, doi:10.3390/metabo9090187 117

Madeleine Ernst, Kyo Bin Kang, Andrés Mauricio Caraballo-Rodríguez, Louis-Felix Nothias, Joe Wandy, Christopher Chen, Mingxun Wang, Simon Rogers, Marnix H. Medema, Pieter C. Dorrestein and Justin J.J. van der Hooft
MolNetEnhancer: Enhanced Molecular Networks by Integrating Metabolome Mining and Annotation Tools
Reprinted from: *Metabolites* **2019**, *9*, 144, doi:10.3390/metabo9070144 133

Joe Wandy, Vinny Davies, Justin J.J. van der Hooft, Rónán Daly, Simon Rogers
In Silico Optimization of Mass Spectrometry Fragmentation Strategies in Metabolomics
Reprinted from: *Metabolites* **2019**, *9*, 219, doi:10.3390/metabo9100219 159

Herbert Oberacher, Vera Reinstadler, Marco Kreidl, Michael A. Stravs, Juliane Hollender and Emma L. Schymanski
Annotating Nontargeted LC-HRMS/MS Data with Two Complementary Tandem Mass Spectral Libraries
Reprinted from: *Metabolites* **2019**, *9*, 3, doi:10.3390/metabo9010003 175

Clement Frainay, Emma L. Schymanski, Steffen Neumann, Benjamin Merlet, Reza M. Salek, Fabien Jourdan and Oscar Yanes
Mind the Gap: Mapping Mass Spectral Databases in Genome-Scale Metabolic Networks Reveals Poorly Covered Areas
Reprinted from: *Metabolites* **2018**, *8*, 51, doi:10.3390/metabo8030051 . . . . **191**

Hiroshi Tsugawa, Aya Satoh, Haruki Uchino, Tomas Cajka, Makoto Arita and Masanori Arita
Mass Spectrometry Data Repository Enhances Novel Metabolite Discoveries with Advances in Computational Metabolomics
Reprinted from: *Metabolites* **2019**, *9*, 119, doi:10.3390/metabo9060119 . . . . **205**

Tessa Schillemans, Lin Shi, Xin Liu, Agneta Åkesson, Rikard Landberg and Carl Brunius
Visualization and Interpretation of Multivariate Associations with Disease Risk Markers and Disease Risk—The Triplot
Reprinted from: *Metabolites* **2019**, *9*, 133, doi:10.3390/metabo9070133 . . . . **221**

Qian Gao, Lars O. Dragsted and Timothy Ebbels
Comparison of Bi- and Tri-Linear PLS Models for Variable Selection in Metabolomic Time-Series Experiments
Reprinted from: *Metabolites* **2019**, *9*, 92, doi:10.3390/metabo9050092 . . . . **233**

Esteban del Castillo, Lluc Sementé, Sònia Torres, Pere Ràfols, Noelia Ramírez, Manuela Martins-Green, Manel Santafe and Xavier Correig
rMSIKeyIon: An Ion Filtering R Package for Untargeted Analysis of Metabolomic LDI-MS Images
Reprinted from: *Metabolites* **2019**, *9*, 162, doi:10.3390/metabo9080162 . . . . **251**

About the Editors

Justin J.J. van der Hooft is Assistant Professor of Bioinformatics at Wageningen University, The Netherlands, and an author of over 60 peer-reviewed articles in the metabolomics field. His main expertise lies in metabolite annotation and identification using mass spectrometry-based and NMR-based spectral data and the application and development of computational metabolomics workflows to support this key bottleneck in metabolomics studies, in particular aimed toward natural product discovery. He obtained a BSc (2004) and MSc (2007) in Molecular Sciences (Wageningen University, NL). In 2012, he obtained his PhD at the Biochemistry and Bioscience groups in Wageningen. He then moved to Glasgow, UK, for postdoctoral positions with Prof. Alan Crozier and Prof. Michael Barrett, subsequently, where he coined MS2LDA substructure discovery with Dr Simon Rogers – thereby combining the field of natural language processing (NLP) with metabolomics analysis. In 2017, he took up a shared postdoctoral position between Dr Marnix Medema and Prof. Pieter Dorrestein on linking metabolome and genome mining workflows. In January 2020, he started his own group in Wageningen that will develop computational metabolomics methodologies to decompose complex metabolite mixtures into their (sub)structures and apply these workflows to study plant and microbiome-associated metabolites and the food metabolome. For example, Justin is pioneering the use of word-embedding NLP approaches to aid in metabolomics analyses, which resulted in the first machine learning-based mass spectral similarity score Spec2Vec. Another example is MolNetEnhancer, that combines the output of various mining and annotation tools to facilitate chemical exploration and analysis – as described in this book. Furthermore, this led to the establishment of Paired Omics Data Platform under his leadership, which will facilitate the combined analysis of genome and metabolome mining. Complex metabolite mixtures are still full of yet unknown metabolic matter that, once elucidated, will boost our insights in molecular mechanisms underpinning the regulation of growth, development, and health.

Kati Hanhineva is Professor of food development with a special focus on Nordic foods and health effects at the University of Turku, Department of Life Technologies, Food Chemistry and Food Development Unit, since the beginning of 2020. She also holds a Research Director position at the School of Public Health and Clinical Nutrition at the University of Eastern Finland and is a visiting scientist (Marie Curie MoRE2020 Fellow) at the Division of Food and Nutrition Science, Department of Biology and Biological Engineering at the Chalmers University of Technology, Gothenburg, Sweden. Hanhineva completed PhD her in Biotechnology at the University of Kuopio 2008. During years 2008–2014, she conducted postdoctoral research at the Department of Public Health and Clinical Nutrition at the University of Eastern Finland, with several research visits to the Weizmann Institute of Science in Israel. Since 2014, she has been the principal investigator in the food and nutritional metabolomics research group and led and participated in several national and EU-funded research projects, including Academy Researcher fellowship 2014–2019. Her main research focus is within the biochemistry of foods, especially phytochemical compounds and the effect of food processing such as fermentation on their composition. Likewise, molecular level understanding of the role of nutrition in maintaining good health and food–microbiota interaction are within the core of the research. The key analytical technology at the different stages of research is the mass spectrometry-based metabolic profiling that her group has developed and utilized for various food- and nutrition-related applications, in particular, within projects related to the beneficial health effect of whole grain-rich diets.

Preface to "Metabolomics Data Processing and Data Analysis—Current Best Practices"

Metabolomics analysis has taken its place as a staple tool in all research areas across the bioscience and medical scientific fields where chemical matter is involved. While technical developments on the instruments used for metabolomics analytics allow for deeper than ever chemical exploration of biological samples, the importance of appropriate data-analytical approaches to treat, analyze, and interpret the vast metabolomics data is increasingly highlighted. The data-analytical workflow required for metabolomics study is a multi-step procedure necessitating different software and algorithm approaches for different steps that include but are not limited to peak picking, data preprocessing, and metabolite annotation and identification as well as visualization. In this book, we present a collection of papers focusing on practices and resources for various aspects of the metabolomics data-analytical workflows, starting from data collection all the way to the presentation of publication-ready metabolomics results, including both reviews on the current best practices as well as reports describing novel, innovative approaches for aspects such as in silico prediction of metabolite structures. Any metabolomics study is a multidisciplinary effort necessitating expertise across areas of, e.g., analytical chemistry, biochemistry, bioinformatics, and data-analytics. Therefore, fluent combination of the various steps involved in the workflow involves various challenges and factors to be taken into consideration. Here, current practices are reviewed, from samples to biochemical interpretation (Ivanisevic and Want, 2019), advances in metabolic modeling on a genomic scale (Sen and Orešič, 2019), as well as possibilities for open-source algorithms for data-analysis (Klåvus et al. 2020). In addition, is the presentation of a web-based interface that fosters many parts of the metabolomics statistical workflow (Chong et al. 2019). As described by Ivanisevic and Want, metabolite identification remains as one of the pitfalls of metabolomics analysis, and it is therefore essential that advanced procedures are developed for both data acquisition (DIA and DDA) as well as MSMS annotation and metabolite identification. In this book, novel strategies for the computational prediction of mass fragmentation spectra (Djoumbou-Feunang et al. 2019), the integration of computational predictions provided by various algorithms to foster the in silico prediction of metabolite structures (Ernst et al. 2019), handling of DIA MS/MS spectra (Peris-Díaz et al. 2019), as well as an in silico framework to optimize the acquisition of mass fragmentation data (Wandy et al. 2019) are presented. Databases and data repositories are an inevitable part of an efficient metabolomics analysis workflow. Curated databases of spectral libraries encompassing both experimental and in silico predicted fragmentation spectra are a prerequisite for efficient metabolite identification. This book contains a section where databases were reviewed and gaps in coverage in terms of different metabolite classes were identified (Oberacher et al. 2018; Frainay et al. 2018). Repositories holding raw metabolomics data enable further utilization of data collections and enable efficient collaborative attempts as described in Tsugawa et al. 2019. Within metabolomics data-analysis an essential element is the efficient strategy for feature selection benefitting especially from the multivariate nature of metabolomics data. Therefore, both advanced methods for the chemometric processing of the data, as well as visualization of the results with ease of interpretation of the biological significance are focus areas requiring further development, as described in the final three papers of this book (Schillemans et al. 2019; Gao et al. 2019; del Castillo et al. 2019). We hope the book will serve as useful resource for anyone entering the field of metabolomics and, especially, the data-analytical part of the technology. Likewise, the book presents various novel algorithms and combined pipelines that may well be utilized by experienced researchers in the field, as well as be further developed owing to the open-source nature of all the presented resources.

Justin J.J. van der Hooft, Kati Hanhineva
Editors

 *metabolites*

Review

From Samples to Insights into Metabolism: Uncovering Biologically Relevant Information in LC-HRMS Metabolomics Data

Julijana Ivanisevic [1,*] **and Elizabeth J. Want** [2,*]

[1] Metabolomics Platform, Faculty of Biology and Medicine, University of Lausanne, Rue du Bugnon 19, 1005 Lausanne, Switzerland
[2] Section of Biomolecular Medicine, Department of Metabolism, Digestion and Reproduction, Faculty of Medicine, Imperial College London, London SW7 2AZ, UK
* Correspondence: julijana.ivanisevic@unil.ch (J.I.); e.want@imperial.ac.uk (E.J.W.)

Received: 4 November 2019; Accepted: 12 December 2019; Published: 17 December 2019

Abstract: Untargeted metabolomics (including lipidomics) is a holistic approach to biomarker discovery and mechanistic insights into disease onset and progression, and response to intervention. Each step of the analytical and statistical pipeline is crucial for the generation of high-quality, robust data. Metabolite identification remains the bottleneck in these studies; therefore, confidence in the data produced is paramount in order to maximize the biological output. Here, we outline the key steps of the metabolomics workflow and provide details on important parameters and considerations. Studies should be designed carefully to ensure appropriate statistical power and adequate controls. Subsequent sample handling and preparation should avoid the introduction of bias, which can significantly affect downstream data interpretation. It is not possible to cover the entire metabolome with a single platform; therefore, the analytical platform should reflect the biological sample under investigation and the question(s) under consideration. The large, complex datasets produced need to be pre-processed in order to extract meaningful information. Finally, the most time-consuming steps are metabolite identification, as well as metabolic pathway and network analysis. Here we discuss some widely used tools and the pitfalls of each step of the workflow, with the ultimate aim of guiding the reader towards the most efficient pipeline for their metabolomics studies.

Keywords: untargeted metabolomics; liquid chromatography–mass spectrometry (LC-MS); metabolism; experimental design; sample preparation; data processing; metabolite identification; univariate and multivariate statistics; metabolic pathway and network analysis

1. Introduction

It is assumed that metabolite identification remains a major challenge in untargeted mass spectrometry (MS)-based metabolomics. Is this indeed true? Should there be greater effort to design experiments in a smarter, more streamlined way, and to know how to reduce noise and redundancy in untargeted metabolomics datasets? For example, a meta-analysis comparative strategy can be used, where several pairwise comparisons are performed (with the same control group), followed by second-order or meta-analysis to prioritize the identification of the shared deregulated metabolites [1,2]. Here, we provide tips on how to design metabolomics experiments in an optimal way, considering sample size, confounders, and bias. We discuss important factors in sample preparation and describe how preparation approaches should be tailored to each biofluid or tissue. Methods should be simple, reproducible, and inexpensive, while preparation steps should not be biased for or against specific analytes, in order to maximize metabolome and/or lipidome coverage. We also summarize different liquid chromatography–mass spectrometry (LC-MS) strategies in order to acquire high quality MS and MS/MS data (reversed phase (RP) LC and hydrophilic interaction liquid chromatography (HILIC) coupled to full scan high resolution (HR) MS data-dependent and data-independent acquisition (DDA and DIA)), while maximizing the metabolome and lipidome coverage, parameters to pay attention to for data pre-processing, and, specifically, feature annotation. Also covered are which criteria to use for data filtering (quality control, chemical and informatic noise removal, etc.), how to apply statistical analysis in the best way, how to facilitate metabolite identification (using computational approaches) and how to translate the results in a biochemically relevant context (metabolite set enrichment analysis (MSEA), overrepresentation analysis (ORA), metabolic network analysis). We emphasize the importance in metabolomics studies of employing quality control (QC) strategies. QC samples, typically a pool of all study samples, can be used to both condition the analytical column and to monitor stability throughout the run. Expanding the polar metabolome and lipidome coverage, removal of noise and redundancy, and consideration of metabolic capacities of a model organism (i.e., biochemical reactions that can be performed by the specific organism, species, genus, etc.) are essential for generation of well-founded hypotheses from untargeted assays. We show how the mass analyzer for untargeted assays should harness high mass accuracy and resolution, and the ability to perform fragmentation or MS/MS experiments for structural elucidation. Many different software exist for the extraction of peaks (metabolite features) from the data, the deconvolution of such data, and the subsequent analysis in both multivariate and univariate ways. There are many statistical tools available, which aim to streamline and aid interpretation, of which we endeavor to summarize and evaluate some of the most commonly used. Finally, we highlight the lack of quantitative data and the need to validate these data-driven hypotheses using targeted quantification, with a focus on identified biochemical pathways associated with phenotype. These analyses will allow to go towards more mechanistic insights and, most importantly, allow for cross-laboratory and -study comparisons for intelligent data re-usage.

2. Results

2.1. Considerations for Experimental Design

Before starting any metabolomics study, it is important to consider the question(s) being asked. Many metabolomics studies are complex in design and may incorporate several classes, e.g., control subjects versus those receiving low and high dose of a drug (Figure 1), healthy subjects versus those with a benign condition and cancer (maybe several stages). It is vital that the study is designed to maximize useful information, whilst keeping costs and animal usage to a minimum. Ideally, you are aiming for the smallest number of experiments needed to produce the maximum amount of data and achieve precision, whilst addressing power and effect size, and accounting for confounding factors [3]. However, it is challenging to calculate the appropriate sample size for untargeted metabolomics studies, as metabolite changes are typically unknown and may be numerous. Further, the high dimensionality of the data and the large degree of correlation between the variables (metabolite features) adds to the complexity of the issue. Ideally, a pilot study should be conducted in order to gain an understanding of the expected effects; however, these are rarely performed due to logistical reasons (sample availability, cost, animal usage, ethics, etc.). Software such as MetaboAnalyst can aid in these calculations if pilot data are available [4]. Recently, Ebbels, et al. [5] proposed an approach to circumvent the need for obtaining preliminary data by using a multivariate simulation approach. Also publicly available is MetSizeR, which uses information from both the metabolomics experiment and the data analysis technique to simulate pilot data from a statistical model (where two groups are present). In order to estimate the required sample size, permutation-based techniques are applied to these simulated data [6]. Also important to consider is the nature of the experiment and the type of samples being analyzed. For instance, when using cell models, conditions can be tightly controlled, and thus sample numbers kept to a minimum (e.g., five replicates). Animal studies are also subject to fairly tight control in terms of age, housing, diet, underlying disease, etc. Therefore, for ethical and practical reasons, sample numbers can also be kept low. However, humans prove to be much more challenging subjects. Except in a small number of situations, factors such as diet, exercise, and medication cannot be controlled, and so a much larger number of subjects is needed in order to be able to determine a "normal" range for metabolite levels, account for inter-individual variation, and be able to detect changes above baseline.

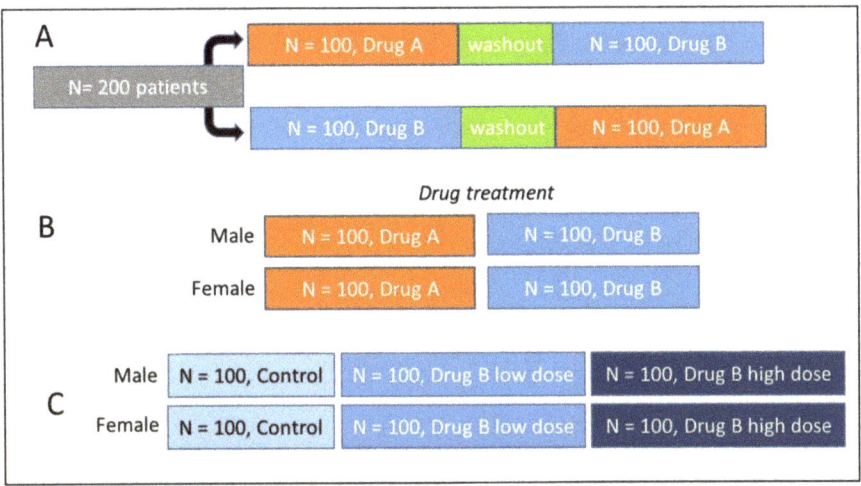

Figure 1. Common experimental designs. (**A**) Cross-over design involving a large patient cohort. Two drugs are administered sequentially to each patient, with a crucial washout period between each drug to enable the effects of each drug to be elucidated. (**B**) Factorial design, where both the gender of the subject and effect of the drug are being studied. (**C**) Common cross-sectional design in metabolomics studies, comparing controls and two drug dose levels in both genders.

2.1.1. The Importance of Controls

It is extremely important to design an experiment containing the correct controls, in order to be able to associate observed metabolite changes with the condition being investigated [7,8]. The main types of controls to consider including are:

(a) Positive controls, where changes are expected. These can be used to check that experimental methods are working correctly, and could include a group of subjects (human or animal model) with a known disease, or a specific cell line.
(b) Negative controls, where no change is expected. These can be used to check that unknown variables are not affecting the experiments, which could result in a false-positive conclusion.
(c) Sham controls. These can be used to check effects induced by the procedure or treatment without actual use of the procedure (e.g., gastric bypass) or substance (e.g., drug).
(d) Vehicle controls. These can be used to check effects induced by a solution of the experimental compound, e.g., when a drug is administered in dimethyl sulfoxide (DMSO), the effect of DMSO on its own should be studied.
(e) Comparative controls. These act as a reference which is commonly accepted or an internal control/disease control. In cases where there is a drug treatment, it is important to test a sample of the drug to assess which (if any) signals observed in the metabolic profile arise from the drug, drug metabolites, or degradation products. Extraction blanks enable artefacts and contaminants to be assigned (e.g., from plastic tubes), and are particularly useful when extracting tissue samples.

2.1.2. Confounding Factors and Variables

There are several sources of variation in metabolomics studies. Firstly, there is the biological variation in the samples themselves. Factors which can affect the metabolic profile of individuals include diet, age, medication, underlying disease, and environmental factors [9]. These are a particular issue for human subjects, as many are difficult to control, but some will be pertinent to animal models as well. When considering cell models, fluctuations in metabolite levels over time must be considered, e.g., as the cells grow and cell density changes (different cell lines grow at different rates). It is important to measure both intra- and extracellular metabolite levels to ensure that the effects observed are due to the treatment and not natural fluctuations. Also important to consider is the time of sampling, as many metabolites are subject to circadian rhythm in human and animal models, particularly hormones in blood and urine. When considering blood samples, whether the subject is in a fasting or non-fasting state should be considered, as blood glucose, amino acid, and lipid levels will be affected dramatically. There is also the variability introduced through sample collection and handling. a large body of work is available in the literature considering these factors [10,11], which is beyond the scope of this review. In summary, blood collection tubes can impact the metabolite profile due, in part, to ion suppression from anticoagulants, e.g., ethylenediaminetetraacetic acid (EDTA) [12,13]. Some serum collection tubes contain polymers such as polyethylene glycol (PEG), which is detrimental to LC-MS analysis, masking the signals from potentially important metabolites. Another consideration if collecting serum samples is the time left to clot, as metabolites such as lactate are known to change as clotting time increases, thus changing the metabolite profile [14]. When collecting urine samples, the type of preservative used, e.g., sodium azide or boric acid, may impact upon the metabolite profile [15]. The storage temperature and number of freeze–thaw cycles that the samples undergo are also important, as metabolites may degrade [16,17]. Lastly, the metabolite extraction approach (e.g., liquid extraction versus solid phase extraction; Section 2.2), extraction solvents used, and diluent also impact the metabolite profile hugely. Although some approaches may be favored over others, it is still largely subjective and will vary between research groups. The key to reproducible metabolomics data is to maintain consistency between samples as much as possible and keep the number of sampling handling steps to a minimum.

2.1.3. Which Experimental Design to Choose?

There are several different experimental design types to consider. Amongst the more common are completely randomized, crossover, and factorial designs [18–21]. Although commonly used due to their fairly simple nature, completely randomized designs are limited in the fact that they study the effect of one primary factor without considering other factors. This approach would not be recommended in a metabolomics study, due to likely confounding factors (see Section 2.1.2), which may have a large impact on the metabolite profile. However, in reality, randomized studies are conducted and the confounders considered at the data analysis steps. a solution to this may be to employ a crossover design, where there could be sequential application of several treatments to the same individual (Figure 1). This means that a subject acts as its own control, thus providing smaller within-individual variation. However, the following factors need to be considered: "carryover effect", "time-related effect", "reversible treatment", and "wash out period". Factorial designs investigate the effect of more than one factor simultaneously, such as gender of the subject and response to a treatment, and so have the potential to increase information obtained from single study.

2.2. Sample Preparation Approaches

Crucial to obtaining high quality metabolomics data is how the samples are prepared. There are many excellent papers in the literature concerning sample preparation for metabolomics studies [22–29] and individual methodologies are beyond the scope of this review. However, it is important to consider some key factors when designing the sample preparation approaches most appropriate for the biofluid or tissue of interest. These include (a) ease of method, i.e., it should be easily reproduced by different operators within the same laboratory and across laboratories; (b) there should be a minimal number of steps, so that technical/analytical variability is kept to a minimum; and (c) cost—a less expensive method will be favorable, so that it can be scaled up to larger sample numbers, such as in the case of epidemiological studies [30,31]. For untargeted metabolomics, it is desirable to use methods which do not bias for or against specific classes of analytes, so that as broad metabolite coverage as possible can be achieved [30,31]. However, it may be practical to prepare sample extracts for polar and non-polar metabolites separately, such as in the case of tissue samples [31]. In general, urine is a straightforward biofluid to prepare, as unless collected from subjects with proteinuria (or rodents), it will largely be free from protein, and so a simple centrifugation and dilution approach can be taken [30]. Be sure to ensure that the diluent used is compatible with the mode of chromatography to be subsequently employed. Plasma/serum and tissue samples require protein to be removed, which can be performed through the addition of cold organic solvent, often methanol, acetonitrile, isopropanol, or a butanol and methanol solution (BuMe), in a one-step approach [32–35]. Tissue samples require homogenization prior to protein precipitation, often using a bead beater [31]. For both blood and tissue samples, a biphasic extraction approach, such as the Bligh-Dyer or a variation (e.g., MTBE:MeOH:H_2O), can be used [36]. Alternatively a two-step approach can be utilized, where sequential extraction of polar and non-polar metabolites is performed [37]. Particular care needs to be taken in the case of preparation of cell samples, where quenching is a crucial step in order to arrest metabolism [26,28]. It is also important to be aware of the stability of analytes, as some such as adenosine triphosphate (ATP) will degrade rapidly [26], and it may not be possible to measure these accurately. It is also important to randomize the sample preparation order, particularly in the case of large sample numbers, and to ensure that this preparation order is not the same as the analytical run order (Figure 2), so that systematic bias is minimized.

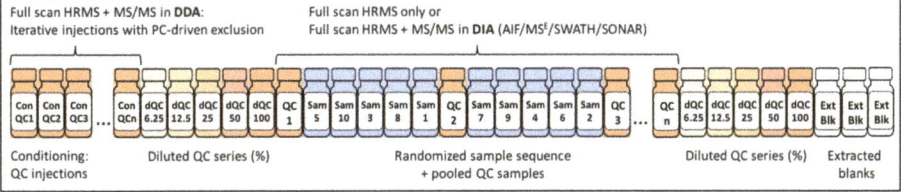

Figure 2. Setting up the data acquisition worklist to facilitate metabolite quantification and identification. Prior to batch run, the instrument should be conditioned (or "passivated") using the pooled quality control (QC) of biological samples. During the conditioning, high-quality MS/MS data can be acquired in a data-dependent acquisition (DDA) mode by taking advantage of iterative injections through the application of PC-driven exclusion (of ions for which the MS/MS data have already been acquired). In this way, the amount of acquired high-quality MS/MS data will be maximized. The batch run can start (and end) with the analysis of diluted QC series that will serve to remove the features whose response is not linear; however, this removal should be performed carefully by evaluating low abundance features and those with saturation issues. Finally, samples should be run in a randomized fashion (considering the most important confounding factors, such as disease, sex, age, etc., depending on the experiment) with pooled QCs every 4–10 samples (depending on the size of the batch). Extracted blanks can be analyzed after the sample run and used for the removal of background (chemical and informatic) noise. Abbreviations: MS/MS data—fragmentation pattern, HRMS—high-resolution mass spectrometry, DDA—data-dependent acquisition, DIA—data-independent acquisition, AIF—all ion fragmentation (on Agilent or Thermo systems), MS^E—all ion fragmentation on Waters systems¯, SWATH—sequential window acquisition of all theoretical mass spectra or DIA strategy on Sciex systems, SONAR—scanning quadrupole DIA or DIA strategy on Waters systems.

2.3. Data Acquisition Strategies to Facilitate Metabolite Quantification and Identification

The choice of technological platform and analytical strategy for sample analysis will be guided by the objective of the study, the metabolites of interest and the approach—untargeted or targeted—deemed most appropriate to answer the biological question. While Nuclear Magnetic Resonance (NMR) spectroscopy is endowed with high reproducibility and accuracy for metabolite measurement, MS-based technologies have made the most significant imprint in metabolomics following the introduction of electrospray ionization (ESI), which has considerably enhanced measurement sensitivity and thus promoted "omics scale" metabolite analysis [38,39]. Direct injection analytical strategies, such as flow-injection analysis (FIA), that do not apply any analyte separation have already provided an increased coverage of up to 200–300 metabolites. While this direct ionization strategy can be of particular interest in studies where high-throughput is essential, for example, in real-time metabolite profiling [40,41], it suffers from ion suppression, poor reproducibility, matrix effects, etc., allowing for only a small fraction of the polar metabolome to be putatively annotated based on accurate mass. As opposed to polar metabolites, a large body of evidence has demonstrated the value of direct infusion-based shotgun analysis for lipid identification. The latest strategies applied in shotgun lipidomics take advantage of the selective ionization of different classes of lipids in the ion source (i.e., intra-source separation under different conditions) and continuous direct injection of the sample, allowing for multi-dimensional MS analysis (i.e., multiple acquisitions in full scan and MS/MS scan modes), and thus, the unambiguous identification (including isobaric/isomeric species) and accurate quantification of lipid species (in two steps) [42,43]. Although the multi-dimensional mass spectrometry-shotgun lipidomics (MDMS-SL) improves most of the limitations related to classical shotgun lipidomics, it is relatively low-throughput and still suffers from ion-suppression, thus limiting the analysis of low abundant lipid species (unless they are derivatized) [43].

Among different hyphenated techniques, such as LC-MS, GC-MS, and CE-MS, that are complementary in their attempt to resolve chemical diversity, LC-ESI MS allows for the most comprehensive coverage of the polar metabolome and lipidome [44,45]. It allows for the simultaneous measurement of several hundred to thousands of metabolites (comprising lipids) from only minimal amounts of a biological sample in a single analysis. This coverage capacity is a benefit of LC separation that minimizes ion-suppression and maximizes measurement specificity by the separation of isobars and isomers and by providing retention time (RT) identifiers [46]. LC represents the best compromise with limited MS acquisition (scanning) speeds; by improving the specificity, and thus, S/N ratio, it enhances the quantity and the quality (i.e., purity) of acquired MS/MS data, essential for metabolite identification (in untargeted assays) and quantification (in targeted analysis) [47].

Due to inherent chemical diversity and the large size of the metabolome, there is no universal technique that can be used to assess the entire metabolome, i.e., "one size does not fit all". The choice of LC-MS analytical strategy, including the LC and MS modes of analysis, will depend on the type of metabolites to be measured (polar vs. nonpolar) and limitations with respect to time and sample amount, which will determine how many analysis modes could be combined to expand the metabolome and/or lipidome coverage [37,48].

2.3.1. LC Techniques

The most commonly used LC techniques in metabolomics include Reversed-Phase Liquid Chromatography (RPLC), ion pairing RPLC, and HILIC. Stationary phase (hydrophobic or hydrophilic), mobile phase modifiers (formic acid, acetic acid, ammonium acetate or formate, ammonium fluoride, etc.), elution gradient (from highly aqueous to highly organic and vice versa), and sample diluent will vary depending on the chromatographic mode applied. Recognized for its reproducibility and broad applicability, RPLC is predominantly used in untargeted metabolomic assays. While RPLC can be used for profiling of mid-polar and non-polar metabolites, including complex lipids, recently, the major challenge in metabolomics has been the separation of highly hydrophilic central carbon metabolites [49], specifically to understand the metabolic shifts in cellular metabolism under different conditions. To enhance the poor retention of hydrophilic metabolites by RPLC, ion pairing agents (e.g., alkyl sulfonates or heptafluorobutyric acid in positive mode, and long chain tertiary/quaternary amines such as tributylamine in negative mode) can be added into the mobile phase, where they combine with the analyte (i.e., cations or anions) to form an ion pair that can be efficiently retained by the reversed phase packing [50]. Yet, this strategy is not MS friendly, with the background signal of ion pairing agent causing system contamination and resulting in notable ion suppression and reduced sensitivity, thus demanding a dedicated LC-MS system. Alternative strategies, such as multimode C18 columns that contain cation and anion ligands (e.g., HSS T3 Waters, Milford, MA, US, Scherzo SM-C18 Imtakt USA) and, in particular, HILIC, have been developed and have become increasingly robust and popular for polar compound retention [51,52]. Indeed, stationary phases with derivatized silica, including diol, amine, and amide, have proven their efficiency and robustness in the separation of polar molecules through multiple mechanisms, such as partitioning between the mobile phase and enriched water layer on the stationary phase, hydrogen bonding, dipole–dipole interactions, etc. In addition, the stationary phases with zwitterionic functional groups (with the polymeric support, e.g., ZIC-HILIC and ZIC-pHILIC, ZIC stands for zwitterionic stationary phase) offer excellent performance in the retention of highly polar metabolites (e.g., di- and tri-carboxylic acids, phosphorylated energy currency metabolites) via ion exchange, and wide pH range stability (from 2 to 10) [51,53]. Besides polar metabolite separation, HILIC has also been increasingly used for complex lipid separation by class, according to polar head groups [54,55].

For an untargeted metabolomics experiment, one would ideally maximize data acquisition and metabolome coverage by combining HILIC and RPLC in both positive and negative ionization modes. Analysis using HILIC in acidic conditions in positive ionization mode would allow for the assessment of amino acid and acylcarnitine metabolism [56], while the analysis in basic conditions in negative ionization mode would provide insight into glycolysis, tricarboxylic acid cycle (TCA) cycle, purine and pyrimidine metabolism, etc [51]. Analysis using RPLC and non-polar eluents (often a combination of isopropanol (IPA) and acetonitrile would allow for comprehensive lipid profiling, including glycerolipids (TAGs—triacylglycerols, DAGs—diacylglycerols, and MAGs—monoacylglycerols), cholesterol esters (CEs), sphingolipids (sphingomyelins, ceramides), glycerophospholipids (PCs—phosphatidylcholines, PEs—phosphatidylethanolamines, PSs—phosphatidylserines, PIs—phosphatidylinositols, PGs—phosphatidylglycerols), and free fatty acids [57]. These analyses can be performed following two-phase extraction (e.g., MTBE/MeOH/H_2O) or single step extraction using isopropanol or butanol and methanol solution (BuMe). When time and sample amount are limited, the researcher should decide depending on which metabolite classes are of the utmost relevance to answer the specific biological question.

2.3.2. Mass Spectrometry Acquisition Modes

Following LC separation, MS detection must be performed in optimized conditions to acquire maximal high-quality MS and MS/MS data for metabolite quantification and identification (Figure 2). Optimal MS acquisition conditions are instrumentation-dependent and comprise ion source and analyzer parameters. For an untargeted experiment, data are usually acquired in full scan mode, where the instrument is set to scan the complete mass range from 50 to 1200 Da. Despite the fact that increasing mass-resolving power is beneficial to resolve co-eluting isobaric compounds and we may say that *"the higher the resolution the better, there may never be enough resolution to separate all the metabolites present in complex biological matrices"*, in the small molecule "world", many compounds have the exact same accurate mass [58]. From this point of view, resolution becomes less important when compared to instrument scanning speed and sensitivity, essential for acquisition of maximum high-quality MS/MS data necessary to translate putative hits into metabolite identities [47,53]. During sample analysis, HRMS data acquisition can be followed by sequential acquisition of MS/MS data using data-independent acquisition (DIA; such as all-ion-fragmentation (AIF) in Agilent Q-TOF, MS^E in Waters Q-TOF, or SWATH in Sciex TripleTOF, and BASIC DIA in Orbitrap) with a minimal loss of sensitivity (approximately two times), or MS/MS data can be acquired only on pooled QC samples at the end of the run, in DIA or in data-dependent acquisition mode (DDA with a focus on top "n" ions, Table 1). In data-independent acquisition (DIA), all fragment ions for all precursors are acquired simultaneously, while in data-dependent acquisition (DDA) the ions for MS/MS acquisition are selected in real-time based on threshold intensity [59]. Finally, the filtered metabolite features of interest (i.e., those that vary significantly between two or more analyzed conditions) can be targeted for MS/MS data acquisition in selective or targeted MS/MS mode, a posteriori, following data processing, filtering, and statistical analysis. The pitfall of this strategy is the time lapse (and thus possible sample alterations) between the first batch of analyses in MS mode only, for relative quantification, and the targeted run to acquire MS/MS data on ions of interest for their identification.

Table 1. MS/MS data acquisition modes with their advantages and disadvantages.

MS/MS Data Acquisition Mode	Selection of Precursor Ions	Advantage	Pitfall
1-4 Selective or targeted MS/MS	Only selected ions specified on an inclusion list will be targeted	Highest quality MS/MS data	a posteriori acquisition, in a separate batch of analyses
Data-Dependent Acquisition (DDA)	Ions are selected for MS/MS acquisition in real-time based on threshold intensity: Top «n» ions are «picked» in each scan Preferred list and exclusion list	High-quality MS/MS data and established link between precursor and product ions	High acquisition rates required. Selection of the most highly abundant ions each time, across multiple scans, resulting in low MS/MS coverage
Data-Independent Acquisition (DIA)	All fragment ions for all precursors are acquired simultaneously: All-ion-fragmentation (Q1 transmits the full mass range, 50-1700 Da of precursor ions in the collision cell: AIF, MS^E) or with sequential mass windows (Q1 transmits several increments of 20–50 amu across the mass range in the collision cell: SWATH, SONAR, BASIC DIA—see Figure 2)	Improved coverage for low abundant precursor ions	High acquisition rates required. Difficulty of MS/MS data deconvolution to re-establish the link between the precursor and product ions

Although DDA is still the most popular simultaneous MS/MS acquisition mode used, DIA is gaining attention following the development of MS/MS data deconvolution algorithms (to link precursor and product ions) and improved coverage for low abundant precursor ions [60–62]. In general, the quality and the amount of acquired MS/MS data depend on instrument acquisition speed and sensitivity (also related to metabolite ionization efficiency). With regards to instrument scanning speed, in DDA, attention should be paid to the m/z resolution window (wide vs. medium vs. narrow), the accumulation times, and the number of targeted precursor ions per scan [47]. To avoid the selection of the most highly abundant ions each time, across multiple scans, a preferred list of ions of interest can be defined and contaminant ions placed on the exclusion list. Data can also be acquired in a time-staggered fashion through a set of iterative injections (of pooled QC samples) with PC-driven exclusion (of ions on which the data has already been acquired in previous runs), which will significantly enhance the amount of acquired MS/MS data [63,64].

DIA can be applied in an all-ion-fragmentation mode (AIF, MS^E) where the first quadrupole (Q1) transmits the full mass range (m/z 50–1700) of precursor ions in the collision cell, or with sequential windows (SWATH and SONAR on Q-TOFs or BASIC-DIA on Orbitrap), where the Q1 will transmit several increments (20–50 amu) across the mass range of interest sequentially in the collision cell (Table 1) [59]. Here, again, the number and the size of mass windows will depend on the instrument acquisition speed. a major challenge related to DIA is to re-establish the direct link between the precursors and their fragment ions or to correctly deconvolute the MS/MS spectra. The wider the isolation window for precursor ion selection, the higher the contamination is of MS/MS spectra, making their deconvolution more difficult. Several algorithms have already been successfully implemented proving their efficiency in MS/MS data deconvolution (MS-DIAL [62], MetDIA [65], DecoMetDIA [66]), with a major limitation being the comprehensiveness of experimentally acquired spectral databases (e.g., METLIN [67], NIST, MoNA, MassBank [68], mzCloud, GNPS [69], etc.). Due to time-consuming standard characterization to expand these experimentally-derived spectral databases, considerable efforts were put towards the development of computational tools for in silico generation of mass spectra used for MS/MS data matching and metabolite annotation (e.g., iMet [70], LipidBlast [71], MetFrag [72], MetDNA [60], CSI:FingerID coupled to Sirius [73]; see section on metabolite identification below; Figure 3).

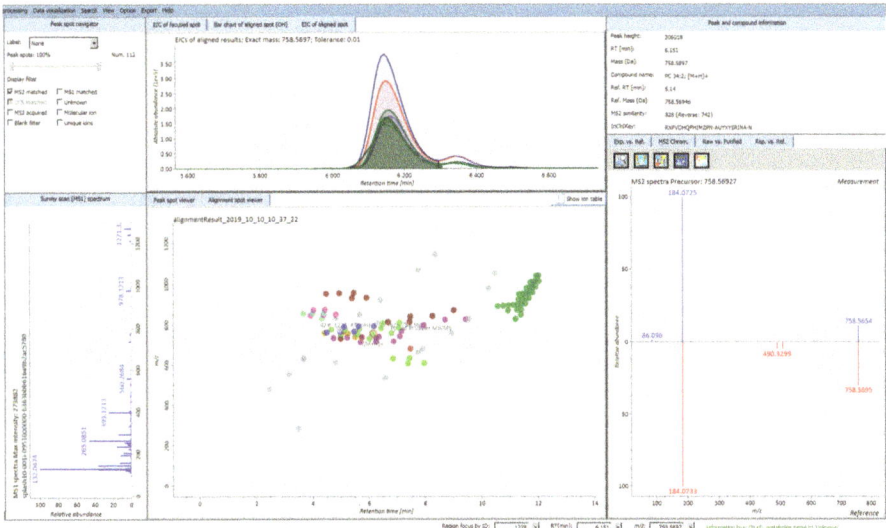

Figure 3. Overview of lipidomic data analysis (acquired by DDA) using MS-DIAL, the open-access software designed for simultaneous metabolite quantification and identification. Displayed are the MS/MS matched peaks (each lipid class is differently colored) with the example of phosphatidylcholine annotation using MS/MS matching against LipidBlast.

It should be emphasized here that coupling of ion mobility (IM) analyzers, as an additional separation technique to conventional LC-MS/MS analysis, can markedly facilitate metabolite identification, and even resolve stereoisomers [74]. The separation of ions according to their size and conformation prior to MS/MS data acquisition will also enhance spectral clarity and fragmentation specificity. Importantly, experimental collision cross-section (CCS) values can be computed (using drift tube ion mobility MS or DTIMS and traveling wave ion mobility MS or TWIMS) with very high reproducibility (Relative standard deviation or RSD < 2%) [75]. FAIMS (high-field asymmetric waveform ion mobility MS) is atmospheric pressure IM technology that can also be used as an orthogonal separation approach (also known as DMS or differential mobility spectrometry), although it does not allow for the acquisition of CCS values.

In an untargeted metabolomics experiment, one would ideally acquire as many MS and MS/MS data as possible, simultaneously, or at least within the same analysis batch. This would allow for the simultaneous metabolite quantification and identification (via MS/MS matching against spectral libraries and using computational tools like Sirius [73]) in an automated fashion. To reach optimal metabolome coverage and annotation, there is room for improvement on the instrumentation side (i.e., limited acquisition speeds, and sensitivity related to ionization efficiency and ion transmission), the need to enhance the comprehensiveness of spectral libraries (taking into consideration the exposome), and to improve the computational approaches for annotation of unknown metabolites.

It is worth noting that the fastidious metabolite identification process in untargeted experiments often yields the identification of *"known (un)knowns"*, as a consequence of the above-specified remaining challenges. This bias encouraged the development of high-coverage targeted methods for quantification of polar metabolites and lipids to bridge the gap between untargeted and targeted approaches. These methods can be strategically derived from DIA methods, such as SWATH, capable of acquiring MS/MS data for all detectable metabolites in a biological sample [76]. As a library of Multiple Reaction Monitoring (MRM) transitions, acquired on different instruments, the METLIN-MRM can be particularly useful to accelerate the development of broad-scale MRM methods [77].

2.4. Data (Pre)Processing: from Peak Detection to Profile Alignment

2.4.1. Software for Data Pre-processing

The amount of raw data generated from an untargeted metabolomics study using mass spectrometry is often huge, with large file sizes (possibly up to 1–2 GB per sample) depending on the instrumentation used. Therefore, there is a need for large computational power or use of computational clusters or clouds for data processing. The data pre-processing pipeline consists of several important steps in order to extract the maximum useful information from the data, whilst eliminating redundancy. The many different software available for performing these data pre-processing steps range from MS vendor software to freely available scripts and software. Some examples of freeware are XCMS [78,79], MZmine2 [80], and MSDial [62] There is also the XCMS online platform [81,82], where you can upload your data and the processing will be performed for you, employing parameters set within the software.

2.4.2. Important Steps in Data Pre-Processing

The first, crucial step is peak detection (or extraction). At this stage, the files are uploaded (read) into the software, and using a selected algorithm, the software will search for any peaks in the samples. a peak (or metabolite feature) may be defined as a distinct ion species with a unique m/z ratio and retention time (RT). It is important to note that one metabolite can be represented by multiple peaks or distinct ion species, namely, isotopes, adducts, in-source fragments, or multiple charged species. This peak detection is normally split into two steps: (1) Separation of mass traces and (2) filtering or detection of chromatographic features. The parameter settings at this stage will be important, such as signal to noise ratio (S/N) and width of the chromatographic peak, in order to enable the detection of peaks with very low S/N ratios while simultaneously filtering out random noise. These parameters, as well as maximal m/z deviation, can be calculated by looking at the raw data files of QC samples across the analytical run or similar (e.g., selected study samples across the run) and specified in the pre-processing parameters. Peak width range should be calculated using the narrowest and widest peaks in the chromatograms, again determined visually from QC samples or similar. Extracted ion chromatograms can be constructed to aid determination of these parameters. Similarly, S/N and m/z deviation should be calculated across the elution profile using high and low intensity peaks to ensure an accurate calculation. Typically m/z deviation is ~5 ppm for Orbitrap data and ~25 ppm for Q-ToF data. Once these peaks have been extracted, they need to be grouped, or matched, across all the samples in the dataset. This is to enable peak areas (or, in some cases, peak heights) to be compared across the samples in a semi-quantitative fashion. Untargeted metabolomics experiments can be large, particularly in the case of epidemiological studies where thousands of samples may be analyzed in a single run or across batches. Usually, retention time alignment is needed, as there may be peak shifting across the analytical run (due to changes in pH or temperature, column aging or build-up on the column). However, this is less frequent since the advent of U(H)PLC, and the authors have found that in the case of small datasets, retention time correction may no longer be required. Nonetheless, it is important to assess each dataset individually, and as most software performs this retention time alignment, it is generally advisable to do so. The output at this stage will be a peak table containing m/z, RT, and abundance for each metabolite feature (peak) in every sample [83–85]. Depending on the software employed, grouping of isotopes/adducts, etc., may have been performed—if it has not, then software such as CAMERA, AStream, RAMClust, and the recently developed METLIN In-source fragment Annotation (MISA) [86,87] exist within the R environment to assist with this grouping and, therefore, data reduction [88–90]. Further, peak annotation may have been performed in some instances through linking with databases, such as with XCMSOnline. This peak table can then be further analyzed, either within the same software or using dedicated software such as SIMCA (Umetrics). Freeware available includes Metaboanalyst [91], a multipurpose software which can also provide pathway analysis tools.

2.4.3. Dealing with Artefacts

The output from the data pre-processing software can be very large and complex, depending on the peak picking parameters, as described in the previous section. As instrument sensitivity increases, so does the likelihood of picking up noise and artefacts in the data. Artefacts can include solvent clusters, contaminants (from the column, vials, or solvents), and other spurious signals. These inflate the data and so need to be removed; thus, there are several approaches to tackling this challenge. a widely used approach in the metabolomics community since 2006 is the employment of QC samples [92]. These generally take the form of a pooled samples comprised of aliquots of all study samples, but may be a subset of samples if the size of the study is large [93]. Occasionally, a "surrogate" QC sample could be used, such as the NIST reference plasma material [94].

2.4.4. The Importance of Quality Control

QC samples play a crucial role in untargeted metabolomics studies, in terms of monitoring system stability and data quality (summarized in Table 2). The QC sample will be injected at the start of the analytical batch in order to condition the column and assess instrument stability; the number of injections required may be sample- and column-dependent, but is often in the region of 10 injections [95,96]. Then, the same QC sample can be injected every 4–10 samples, making up to ~10% of the sample injections. This within-run QC can be used to assess stability within the run, e.g., retention time and signal intensity drifts. Importantly, a QC dilution series can be employed; this takes the form of serial dilutions from the QC sample [93]. The purpose of this dilution series is to identify and remove peaks (metabolite features) that do not respond to dilution in a linear manner (as determined by calculating coefficient of determination (r^2 or R^2) values), as they are likely to be noise, or at least non-biological in origin. Additionally, the coefficient of variation (CV) can be calculated for every metabolite feature in the within-run QC samples. Features with a CV above a certain threshold, e.g., > 30% can be removed from the dataset, as they are unlikely to be reliable biomarkers [30]. In some cases, metabolite features which appear in below a certain proportion of the QC samples (e.g., in < 75% of samples) could also be removed from the data. Lastly, the analysis of blank samples, such as blank mobile phases and also extraction blanks (where the sample preparation procedure has been followed but in the absence of biological sample), can provide valuable insight into the origin of many of the metabolite features reported. Those that appear in the blank samples are again likely to be non-biological in origin and so can be removed from further processing steps [93]. These data filtering and reduction steps can dramatically reduce the size of the dataset and streamline the subsequent data analysis procedure.

Table 2. Criteria for feature filtering using QC and blank samples in order to reduce data complexity and remove redundancy.

Parameter	Criteria	Outcome	Notes
1-4 Coefficient of variation (CV)	Choose threshold of variation, e.g., of metabolite peak area in repeated injections of QC sample	Remove metabolite features, e.g., with CV > 30% in QC samples *	CV cut-off values may be dependent on sample type, chromatography, or instrument parameters
Presence in study samples	Metabolite feature/peak must be present in a certain proportion of the study samples (and/or QCs)	Remove metabolite features present in only a low proportion of study samples	Certain peaks may only be present in one class of samples—adjust threshold accordingly
Presence in blank samples	Metabolite feature/peak must not be present in study samples/at very low levels	Remove metabolite features present in blank samples	Some metabolite features may be present in blank samples due to carryover—ensure multiple blanks have been run to address this
Response to dilution	Metabolite feature/peak must respond to dilution series with r2 > 0.8**	Remove metabolite features with r2 < 0.8 **	Some metabolite features may be saturated at higher concentrations and so do not behave linearly—check raw data

* Some groups recommend a lower cut-off, e.g., 20% [97]; ** this removal should be performed carefully by evaluating the features whose response may not be linear due to their low abundance.

2.5. Univariate and Multivariate Statistical Data Analysis

Untargeted metabolomics studies generate a wealth of data, from which meaningful biological interpretations are desired. Statistical analysis of the data is another hugely important step in the metabolomics pipeline; therefore, there are many important parameters which must be considered. The most typical workflow is to perform multivariate analysis followed by univariate analysis in order to elucidate and validate potentially discriminatory metabolites [98,99].

2.5.1. Multivariate Approaches

Multivariate analysis encompasses methods to reduce the complexity of data, such as that generated from a metabolomics study, where the number of variables (in this case, metabolite features) is greater than the number of samples. Multivariate analysis can be performed using vendor software, programming platforms such as R and Metaboanalyst, or commercial software such as MATLAB® (MathWorks) or SIMCA (Umetrics).

2.5.2. Principal Components Analysis

The first step is generally an unsupervised approach, such as principal components analysis (PCA), which can be used to visualize data structure, class differences, and outliers (Figure 4). PCA can be considered as to be finding *maximal variation* between the groups of interest. Importantly with unsupervised approaches, no class information is given, and so an unbiased view of class separation can be obtained. When visualizing a PCA scores plot, the first principal component (PC1) explains the largest variation in the data, followed by PC2, PC3, etc. Multiple classes can be viewed on the scores plot, in two or three dimensions, and so group separation can be observed, e.g., over time. The loadings plot provides an indication of which metabolite features are responsible for any observed separation, e.g., between classes, and can be mapped onto the scores plot if desired, in what is known as a bi-plot.

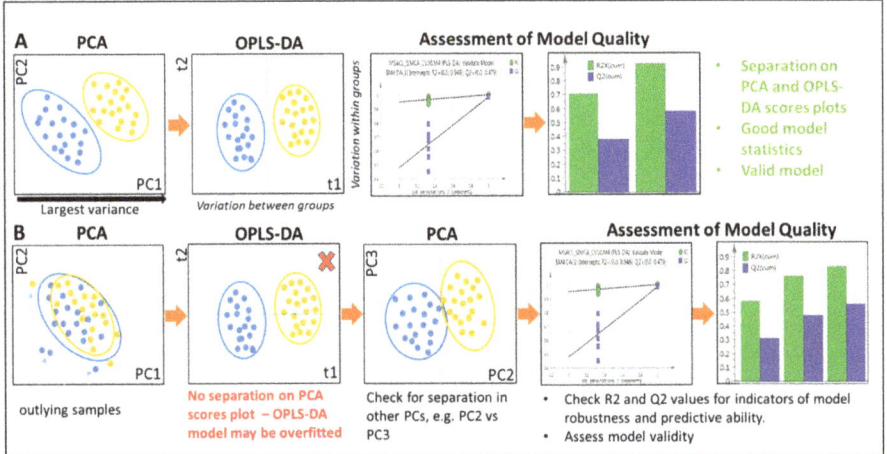

Figure 4. Simplified overview of PCA and OPLS-DA showing (**A**) good separation on PCA and OPLS-DA scores plots. High R2 and Q2 values indicate good model robustness and predictive capability. Permutation test indicates a valid model. (**B**) No separation on the PCA scores plot of PC1 vs. PC2, but separation is still achieved using OPLS-DA. In this instance, the model could be overfitted and unreliable. It is advisable to check for separation in other components, e.g, PC2 vs. PC3, as well as to assess R2 and Q2 and perform permutation tests. CV-ANOVA can also be used to assess model validity (not shown).

2.5.3. Supervised Approaches

Once separation has been assessed, supervised analyses can be performed, such as partial least squares discriminant analysis (PLS-DA) and its orthogonal counterpart, OPLS-DA. These approaches incorporate class information and so find a way to achieve the maximal separation between the classes of interest. In the scores plots, the x-axis shows the variation *between* the groups, while the y-axis shows variation *within* the groups. These methods can suffer from the risk of over-fitting the data—they can produce class separation even with random data—and must be interpreted with caution (Figure 4) [100]. This can have detrimental downstream impacts on biomarker discovery and validation as results may not be reliable or reproducible. R2 and Q2 values can be used to assess the model robustness and predictive power; these values will be low—particularly the Q2—in an overfitted model. a low Q2 indicates that new data would not be predicted accurately in the model. Further, machine learning-based model validation approaches, such as CV-ANOVA (based on ANOVA of the cross-validated residuals), can assess model validity [101]. Permutation tests can also be used to assess the significance of a classification. The class assignment is permuted repeatedly, with a model between the data and the permuted class-assignment built for each permutation. These models are then compared with the original multivariate model [102]. Variable Importance for the Projection (VIP) scores can be used to identify the metabolite features contributing most to any class separation; VIP scores > 1 are suggested to be important, whilst those < 1 are suggested to be unimportant for the model. The range of VIP scores will vary with each dataset and, in some studies, there may be hundreds of metabolite features with a VIP score around 1, meaning that the cut-off applied is much higher. OPLS-DA S plots can also be used to identify discriminatory metabolite features warranting further investigation.

2.5.4. Univariate Methods

Even though multivariate analysis tools can be useful for exploring metabolomics data and guiding researchers towards potential discriminatory biomarkers, there are several pitfalls to these approaches.

As discussed above, supervised models suffer from the risk of overfitting. Datasets containing a large amount of sparse data (in terms of the number of input variables) or missing data (which can occur with some pre-processing tools) may compromise model performance [103]. To this end, features which have been proposed as discriminatory from multivariate analyses can be further validated using appropriate univariate statistics [81]. However, univariate tools are also not without their challenges, and it is easy to inadvertently apply the wrong statistical test to a dataset. It is important to assess the data at the start to ensure the correct test is being performed, e.g., whether to use a parametric or non-parametric test. a rule of thumb is that if the data are normally distributed, then a parametric test, such as a t-test, can be used. Normality can be tested using, e.g., the Shapiro–Wilk test, which is good when the sample size is < 50. Note that it is not possible to assess normality of the distribution if the sample size is small, and some tests do not cope well with small sample sizes. Parametric tests are considered to be more powerful than non-parametric tests, with less risk of a false negative (i.e., non-significant) result than with a non-parametric test. However, when dealing with populations that are non-normally distributed, with unequal variances and/or unequal small sample sizes—all possible in untargeted metabolomics—often a non-parametric test can perform better [81]. an additional complication is that univariate tests applied separately to numerous variables will overlook correlations within metabolite features, which may be important in elucidating related metabolites and interpreting biological pathways.

2.5.5. Multiple Comparison Testing

In untargeted metabolomics studies, it is likely that the number of metabolite features (variables) is greater than the number of samples analyzed [104,105]. If univariate tests were performed on each of these variables, the false discovery rate (the chance of significance being found) is high. These are known as Type I errors (false positives) and must be addressed if valid metabolite markers and meaningful biological conclusions are to be found. To combat this issue, multiple comparison testing can be performed. Commonly used approaches for false discovery rate correction (FDR) are the Bonferroni correction (a conservative method) or the less conservative Benjamini–Hochberg or Benjamini–Yukatelli corrections. These will adjust the p-value cut-off, meaning that fewer variables will reach significance and, therefore, there will be fewer false positive results. Using a combination of multivariate and univariate testing, a potential biomarker should have a VIP > 1 and a p-value < 0.05 (or the corrected value after FDR—false discovery rate correction) [106].

2.6. Metabolite Identification: From Spectral Database Matching to Computational Approaches for Unknown Metabolite Annotation

Following feature filtering using QC-based estimates (see Table 2) and statistical criteria to extract the metabolite features of interest, the next challenge constitutes assigning the identity to these features and placing them in a biochemically relevant context for data interpretation. As specified in Section 3, LC-MS is not only the most versatile and comprehensive methodology with respect to metabolome and lipidome coverage, but also provides important information for metabolite structure elucidation, including RT, accurate mass, isotope distribution, and MS/MS fragmentation pattern, in addition to IMS (and/or CCS value). Despite this, the majority of metabolite features in untargeted metabolomic datasets (approximately 80%, so-called "dark matter") remain un-annotated or misidentified [75,107,108], hiding many unknown metabolites, but also high levels of chemical and informatic noise (artefacts of peak detection algorithms) and redundancy (due to defects in feature annotation and grouping algorithms). We distinguish two main bottlenecks, one associated with known metabolite misidentification and another one related to unknown or novel metabolite identification (see Table 3).

Table 3. Major problems and solutions associated with metabolite identification in metabolomic datasets. The references for different tools are cited in the main text.

Bottleneck	Cause	Solutions
1-3 *Known metabolite (mis)identification*	Isomers or metabolites with identical mass (and molecular formula) but different structures	• Chromatographic resolution (i.e., separation by RT, chiral columns for stereoisomers) • Ion mobility MS (IMS and/or cross-collision section—CCS values) • MS/MS fragmentation pattern matching against experimentally acquired or in silico generated MS/MS databases (i.e., METLIN, mzCloud, NIST, MassBank, LipidBlast, LipidMaps, GNPS)
	Isobars or compounds of similar molecular weight produce interferences	• MS resolution (HRMS using TOF or Orbitrap mass analyzer) • Chromatographic resolution (i.e., separation by RT) • MS/MS fragmentation pattern matching as specified above • Ion mobility MS (IMS and/or cross-collision section—CCS values)
	In-source fragments—due to production of ions (by loss of H_2O, CO_2, H_3PO_4) that have the same mass and/or structure as the molecular ions of other metabolites	• Chromatographic resolution (i.e., separation by RT) • MS source with reduced in-source fragmentation
Unknown metabolite identification	"*Known unknowns*"—metabolites listed in molecular structure databases but without recorded reference MS/MS spectra in spectral libraries	• In silico fragmentation tools and derived databases (e.g., CSI:FingerID coupled to Sirius, MetFrag, iMet, MS2LDA, MS-FINDER, etc.) and similarity matching (of experimentally acquired and in silico generated MS/MS) and network analysis (e.g., GNPS) • RT prediction models (limited to specific columns and LC conditions) • CCS prediction models and databases (e.g., MetCCS, LipidCCS) • Multiple-stage tandem MS (MS^n)
	"*Unknown unknowns*"—new metabolites not listed in any database	• Metabolite isolation and NMR analysis for structural elucidation • LC-MS/MS analysis (RT, accurate mass, MS/MS) combined with above indicated tools for "*known unknowns*" • Multiple-stage tandem MS (MS^n)

Metabolite identification starts, in general, by database searching using accurate mass (m/z) measurements (up to 4 decimal places) and prediction of elemental composition (i.e., molecular formula). Accurate mass searches yield many putative hits, including potentially false matches due to the presence of isomers, interferences between the metabolites of similar molecular weight (i.e., isobars), and mis-annotation of in-source fragments and even certain adducts (see Table 3) [26]. In most cases, the MS/MS fragmentation pattern, defined by the product ion masses and their relative abundances, will provide sufficiently specific data to confirm the metabolite identity with a high level of confidence. The exceptions are structural and/or stereoisomers (i.e., L- and D-serine, for example, or complex lipids differing only in positions of unsaturations), which can be distinguished only with the additional chromatographic resolution (RT, chiral columns) and/or IMS (and CCS values) data.

MS/MS spectra acquired from samples will be matched against spectral databases containing experimentally acquired spectra on pure standards (e.g., METLIN [67,109], NIST, mzCloud) or any annotated structures (community databases such as MassBank [68], including European MassBank, MassBank of North America, and GNPS based on crowd sourcing [69]). The content of these databases has been extensively reviewed in several recent publications [75,110]. MS/MS spectra matching is usually followed by the similarity score calculations for matches (e.g., METLIN online database) and ranking of candidates based on the similarity to the reference spectra [47,111]. While five different levels of reporting confidence in metabolite identification have been established by the Metabolomics Standards Initiative [75], absolute identity can only be made when an authentic commercially available standard has been compared to the analyte of interest and found to match all applicable measurements (accurate m/z, MS/MS, RT, etc.). When standards are not available, the unknown metabolite of interest needs to be isolated from the biological matrix (e.g., plant, fungi, sponge extract) using LC, and the combined LC-HRMS and NMR analysis will allow for structural elucidation. The novel metabolite identity needs to be confirmed by custom synthesis of standard and its analysis under the same analytical conditions.

To facilitate and automatize metabolite identification, significant efforts were made to further expand the experimentally-derived spectral libraries by MS/MS data acquisition (on different instruments, collision energies, and ionization modes) and sharing. However, compared to the size and diversity of endogenous and exogenous metabolome, this conventional method of metabolite annotation by matching the experimentally acquired MS/MS spectra to standard spectral databases remains limited by the size of databases and the lack of commercially available standards for many cellular metabolites. To address this problem, recently, the computational metabolomics community has grown to develop and improve computational approaches for known and unknown metabolite identification (Table 3). These computational metabolomic approaches employ two main strategies: (1) In silico prediction of fragmentation MS/MS spectra from chemical structures of known compounds, and (2) in silico prediction of molecular substructures (i.e., molecular fingerprints or feature vectors that encode the structure of a molecule) and general chemical properties of the unknowns from experimentally acquired MS/MS spectra [112]. With the in silico fragmentation methods, the experimentally acquired spectra of an unknown metabolite (for which reference spectra are not available) can be matched against in silico theoretically predicted spectra simulated on known candidate structures retrieved from databases (Human Metabolome Database (HMDB), PubChem, KEGG, etc.) [113]. In silico fragmentation from chemical structures of known compounds can be computed by rule- (e.g., MS-FINDER, LipidBlast), combinatorial- (e.g., MetFrag), and machine learning-based methods (e.g., CFM-ID) [75]. Rule-based generation of specific fragmentation patterns and heuristic modeling of ion abundances is efficient for classes that have consistent and predicative fragmentation patterns, such as lipids (e.g., LipidBlast).

The in silico prediction of molecular substructures are machine learning-based methods that can translate the MS/MS spectra to metabolite structure information. To learn the mapping of an MS/MS spectrum to a molecule structure, these methods need to be trained on spectral databases of known metabolites. In general, machine learning methods can be divided in two groups, supervised learning for substructure prediction (e.g., CSI:FingerID) and unsupervised learning for substructure annotation and grouping of metabolites based on shared, biochemically relevant substructures (e.g., MS2LDA) [112,114–116]. The main objective of supervised methods, such as CSI:FingerID integrated in Sirius tool, is to determine, using a database of molecular structures, the structure that best fits the experimental data. In Sirius 4, the assessment of molecular structures from MS/MS data can be performed automatically for the entire LC-MS dataset (rather than per spectrum) and MS data-driven annotations can be obtained for all detected features [73]. These machine learning approaches were essential for the recent progress in metabolite identification and will pave the future of metabolite structural identification.

Data sharing will also be key to advance these computational approaches. There are two main repositories that can be used for metabolomics data sharing, the Metabolomics Workbench (US, [117]) and MetaboLights (EU, [118]). There is space for the improvement of data upload, which demands fastidious data preparation due to considerable requirements on sample and method related metadata.

2.7. Metabolite Features and/or Metabolites to Pathways and Metabolic Networks

2.7.1. Metabolic Networking for Metabolite Identification

While pathway and network analysis are mainly used to facilitate metabolite data visualization and interpretation, the biochemical knowledge about chemical reactions (i.e., metabolite conversions via enzymes) and metabolic pathways integrated within a metabolic network (to sustain cellular function) can also be used to facilitate metabolite identification. As an alternative to the above-described tools relying only on the spectral data and information related to molecular (chemical) structure, several approaches, such as Mummichog [119], PIUMet [120], and MetDNA [120], based on the *"features to pathways"* principle, have been developed to facilitate and speed up metabolite identification using reference metabolic network models. This biochemically relevant information can guide with respect to the metabolites that the organism of interest is able to produce and thus increase the confidence of metabolite annotations (see Table 3) [121]. Both Mummichog and PIUMet rely on the assumptions that locally enriched metabolite matches within the metabolic network are true, while false matches will distribute randomly. Both tools will infer metabolically active pathways without requiring metabolite identification. Finally, metabolite identities will be predicted and chemical information on annotated isotopes and adducts will be used to evaluate the prediction confidence level. Metabolite annotation and Dysregulated Network Analysis, or MetDNA, uses the metabolic network knowledge for the annotation of known metabolites (from highly conserved primary metabolism) detected in untargeted experiments. Annotation starts from the set of identified "seed" metabolites by predicting their reaction-paired neighbor metabolites on the assumption of their structural similarities. Through the reiterated application of this recursive algorithm, the number of annotated metabolites will be progressively propagated and significantly enhanced (to up to 2000 metabolites from one untargeted experiment) [60]. Using a similar principle, the GNPS or Global Natural Products Social Molecular Networking will construct the molecular similarity network based on the similarity of MS/MS spectra (two metabolites share similar MS/MS data due to their structural similarity) with the aim to annotate the unknown natural products using already annotated metabolites (by the community) within the same sub-network. While these networking approaches are fast and valuable for the reduction of metabolomic datasets, however, annotation remains ambiguous and should be validated through more specific targeted MS/MS analysis.

2.7.2. Metabolic Networking to Visualize and Interpret Metabolite Changes

In general, changes at the metabolite level cannot be looked at independently outside of the context (of their interactions with other metabolites, proteins, and genes), and meaningful changes can be missed by relying only on the arbitrary significance threshold (or p-value). It is thus of the utmost importance to interpret identified alterations at the metabolite level within the metabolic networks, especially when it comes to the discovery and understanding of subtle (fold change < 2) but coordinated and physiologically relevant changes, often the case in biomedical and human population studies. Metabolic networks, derived from genome-scale metabolic network models (GSMNM) are the most accurate ways to describe and represent metabolism, as compared to discrete pathways [122]. Multiple metabolic pathways share metabolites, and the synthesis of one metabolite can require the integrated cooperation of more than one pathway. The reconstructed GSMNM from annotated gene–protein reaction (GPR) associations can define the metabolic capacity of a model organism(s), in any specified condition. While the primary metabolic pathways are highly conserved across model organisms, they can be differentially regulated, in an organism-specific manner, as a function of genetic effects (i.e., mutations in different genotypes) and environmental exposures. Efforts are needed for systematic characterization of the model organism metabolomes (across different conditions, using quantitative information), and to develop compartmentalized models for different organs and host–microbiome metabolic interactions [123–126].

To interpret data from metabolomics experiments and gather biologically meaningful information, one would ideally perform two types of analysis: (1) Mapping and visualization of metabolite changes in the graphical representation of cell metabolism, i.e., metabolic network; and (2) statistical analysis to determine the overrepresented pathways, known as metabolite set enrichment analysis (MSEA). Most of the open access tools designed for pathway and network analysis provide both of these functionalities, visualization to assess if metabolites are involved in the same pathways and how they are connected within a metabolic network and enrichment analysis to highlight the pathways associated with the examined phenotype. The open access software that provide these functionalities in the interactive fashion are listed in Table 4. For the computational community, the recently assembled MetaRbolomics toolbox provides an extensive resume of R packages that can be used for data processing, metabolite annotation, and biochemical network and pathway analysis [127].

Table 4. List of selected open access web servers for interactive pathway visualization, metabolite mapping, and visualization in the context of pathways and metabolic networks, and metabolite set enrichment and overrepresentation analysis (MSEA, ORA).

Tool	Functionalities
1-2 MeTexplore web server [128]	• Metabolite mapping on metabolic pathways and networks • Visualizing networks • Mining and editing networks based on data and network structure (identify sub-networks connecting identified metabolites) • Pathway enrichment analysis • Mapping polyomics data • Computing fluxes
Pathvisio [129]	• Metabolite mapping on the pathways • Pathway editing, drawing, and analysis • Overrepresentation analysis
iPath—Interactive Pathways Explorer [130]	• Metabolite mapping on the pathways • Pathway editing and analysis
MetaboAnalyst* web server [91]	• Metabolite ID conversion • Enrichment analysis (ORA, MSEA) • Pathway topology analysis • Joint pathway analysis (genes and metabolites) • MS peaks to pathways
PathBank [131]	• Interactive database for visualizing metabolic pathways in different model organisms • Metabolite (as well as gene, protein, drug) search and mapping • Detailed description and references are provided for each pathway from energy metabolism, associated with metabolic diseases, drug-action pathways, drug metabolism pathways, signaling pathways
LION/web [132]	• Web platform for lipid ontology enrichment analysis • Lipid classification by chemical data (LIPIDMAPS), biophysical data, lipid functions and organelle associations
XCMS online* [133]	• Activity network analysis i.e., "MS peaks to metabolic network" (integrated *Mummichog* tool) • Integrated pathway analysis (using genome and proteome data, in addition to metabolome data)

* Features relevant to pathway and network analysis have been listed here, MetaboAnalyst and XCMS online servers provide plenty of other functionalities related to data processing and analysis.

In order to map the identified metabolite changes in the biochemically relevant context, one first needs to convert the metabolite identities into the relevant metabolite identifiers (e.g., KEGG, HMDB, Recon, etc.) that can be used for mapping to metabolic networks derived from genome-scale models (as a product of genome sequencing, annotation, and, finally, metabolic model reconstruction). The conversion to different metabolite identifiers can be executed in batches using a chemical translation service, provided by UC Davis [134] or MetaboAnalyst [91]. Users should consider that a portion of identifiers may be missing and/or incorrectly matched (approximately 10%), thus manual curation may be necessary prior to the upload to pathway or network analysis tools for further analysis and visualization. Metabolite mapping would ideally be based on InChIs or InChIKeys, requiring that these identifiers are specified in both databases and networks [126]. There is an important challenge here regarding lipids, due to the ambiguous identification given by sum composition (i.e., PC 34:2) that can correspond to many similar lipid species having different fatty acid composition (16:1/18:1, 16:0/18:2, etc.) [132].

Visualization of metabolite changes in the context of metabolic networks brings together chemical reactions (of which metabolites are the products or substrates), and the genes coding for the enzymes making these reactions possible. MetExplore is among the most comprehensive tools that allows for the construction of tailored networks and collaborative curation and annotation of metabolic models, in addition to the interactive network visualization, from the entire network down to detailed sub-networks (build from selected network elements—a pathway or a set of genes) [128,135]. In addition to visual inspection, flux consistency is checked for the metabolic model, i.e., network, validation. MetExplore integrates a large panel of metabolic models (called "biosources" in MetExplore) depending on the model organism, and each metabolic network can be exported as an SBML or Excel file. Mapping of metabolites can be achieved using their network identifiers (KEGG, Recon, etc.) and, further on, smart filters can be applied to select the reactions involved in a combination of pathways (e.g., enriched pathways) of interest to be visualized—through the MetExploreViz web module (Figure 5). The MSEA is integrated and performed using hypergeometric tests (corrected with Bonferroni or Benjamini–Hochberg methods). Specific metabolites and pathways can be highlighted, edited, and exported, and the shortest paths between the metabolites of interest can be automatically extracted to reduce visual complexity, thus allowing for data mining.

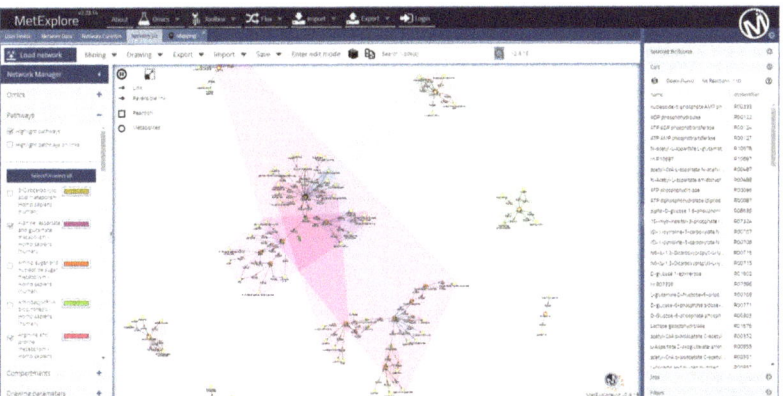

Figure 5. Metabolite mapping on the metabolic networks—an overview of MetExplore network Viz functionalities. The projected network has been created from the list of chemical reactions (in the cart on the right side of the figure)—derived from the list of identified metabolites whose levels varied significantly (as a result of brain cell profiling). The extent of each pathway has been encircled and colored for visualization. Alanine, aspartate and glutamate metabolism, and arginine biosynthesis have been highlighted as enriched (using integrated ORA).

As mentioned above, in addition to metabolic (sub)network visualization, metabolite set enrichment analysis (MSEA) as a metabolomic counterpart of the gene set enrichment analysis (GSEA) and/or over-representation analysis (ORA) are used to investigate the metabolic pathways whose activity differs among analyzed conditions (e.g., CTRL vs. disease). MSEA takes into consideration the quantitative measure associated with each metabolite (i.e., abundance or concentration, and fold change) [121]. MSEA firstly assigns metabolites to pre-defined groups of functionally related metabolites (or metabolite sets) based on references databases (e.g., KEGG, HMDB; Table 5). The metabolite sets can be defined as biochemical or signaling pathways (i.e., metabolites involved in the same biological process), pathways associated with a metabolic disease (i.e., metabolites that vary significantly under the same pathological conditions, suggested by HMDB, [136,137]), pathways active in specific organs, tissues, or organelles (i.e., metabolites present in the same location, suggested by HMDB, [137]), etc. MSEA then applies *Globaltest* [138] to detect the subtle but consistent and coordinated changes (i.e., differences) among the group of metabolites (i.e., pathway) between two conditions, and thus identifies the affected (or deregulated) biochemical pathway associated with the analyzed outcome or phenotype [91,121]. The obtained *p*-value gives the probability that none of the matched compounds in the group of metabolites is associated with the phenotype. a closely related approach to MSEA, an over-representation analysis (ORA), is used to evaluate the probability that the particular set of metabolites (e.g., biochemical pathway) is represented, within a defined list of metabolites of interest, more than expected by random chance. For ORA, a user can provide only a list of metabolite identifiers, corresponding to metabolites that vary significantly between two analyzed conditions. Several probability tests, such as Fisher's exact test, binomial probability, or hypergeometric distribution test, can be applied, followed by the correction for multiple testing. Here, the reference metabolome should comprise the metabolite sets that can be detected in the analytical conditions used, thus reflecting the analytical method coverage. If the entire library of metabolite sets is used for ORA by default, the observed enrichment may be a consequence of applied analytical platform bias instead of being biologically relevant. ORA and/or MSEA are integrated in many different pathway and/or metabolic network analysis software, such as MetaboAnalyst, MetExplore, Pathvisio, etc. Finally, MetaboAnalyst allows also for the combined MSEA and pathway topology analysis that will display pathway impact values based on centrality measure—local quantitative measure of the position of a node (or a «key» position) relative to the other nodes in the network.

Although the tools for metabolic network analysis are being steadily improved by the computational community, there are still a number of challenges, related to metabolome coverage bias of the experiment (i.e., analytical limitations), scarcity of well-annotated metabolomics data (number of unknowns or non-annotated metabolite(s) (features) remains high), and, finally, the lack of knowledge about network regulation. It is also important to consider that the metabolome cannot be computed directly from the genome, and that many metabolites still need to be integrated into our current metabolic networks, thus making use of the wealth of data generated in metabolomic experiments.

Table 5. List of open access knowledge databases (used in the above listed web servers). Some databases have been extended into pathway browsers for interactive metabolite mapping. Although some databases are gene-centric, all of them are searchable for metabolites and represent a great source of biochemical knowledge for metabolite data interpretation.

Database	Functionalities
1-2 KEGG database and pathway browser [139]	• Metabolite mapping on metabolic pathways (with annotation of the direction of changes)
Reactome database and pathway browser [140,141]	• Visualization of known biological processes and pathways from intermediary metabolism, signaling, transcriptional regulation, apoptosis, disease • Metabolite mapping and pathway and network visualization and analysis • Pathway enrichment analysis
Cyc databases (EcoCyc, HumanCyc, MetaCyc, BioCyc) [142]	• Curated database of experimentally elucidated metabolic pathways from many different model organisms • Metabolite, protein, reaction, and pathway search • Comparison of specific pathway and metabolic networks of different organisms
Recon database [143,144] Virtual metabolic human	• Largest database of human and gut microbiome metabolism • Searchable by metabolic reaction, metabolites and genes, by microorganism species, by disease, and by diet • Organelle maps
WikiPathways database [145]	• Pathway database maintained by scientific community • Pathway browsing and editing

2.8. From Untargeted to Targeted Assays

Global or untargeted metabolomics provides the opportunity for biomarker discovery and hypothesis generation. Potentially, it can enable the elucidation of the involvement of previously unknown or unsuspected pathways in disease states or in response to therapy. Inherently, this untargeted approach does not bias for or against specific analyte classes and provides a wide view of the metabolome. Sample preparation and analytical methods are somewhat generic and are usually optimized for sample type. However, with this approach comes the bottleneck of metabolite feature annotation and metabolite identification, as described in this review. Therefore, high-coverage targeted assays are becoming more prominent in the field of metabolomics. With targeted assays, tandem or triple quadrupole mass spectrometers are employed, with lower mass resolution than the Orbitrap or Q-ToF mass spectrometers used for untargeted analyses. However, these have the advantages of lower cost, higher sensitivity, linearity, and specificity. By employing isotopically labelled standards of the analytes of interest, which are spiked into each study sample, absolute quantification can be achieved. Furthermore, as the analytes being measured are known upfront, and the chromatographic and mass spectrometric methods are optimized at the start, run times can be much shorter than for untargeted analyses. There are guidelines which can be followed for ensuring accuracy and precision of the assay, such as those laid out by the FDA [146]. Software exist for the analysis of targeted data, either vendor provided or freeware such as Skyline [147]. It is likely that as this field of research advances, more targeted assays will be incorporated into the metabolomics workflow.

3. Conclusions

Untargeted metabolomics is a powerful approach to understanding changes due to disease, drug treatment, or environmental factors in a multitude of human, animal, and cell models. However, as metabolism is complex, so are the data produced in these studies. It is therefore crucial to be vigilant at every stage of the experiment. If the study has not been designed correctly, it will be hard to elucidate biologically relevant information, as confounding factors may overwhelm any biological changes. To maximize the metabolome coverage, it is necessary to acquire data in several chromatographic and ionization modes, ideally HILIC for polar metabolites and RPLC for complex lipids (using non-polar solvents for elution). MS/MS data—of high quality and volume—can be acquired in DDA mode using iterative injections with PC-driven exclusion and/or in DIA mode with sequential mass windows (e.g., SWATH, SONAR). Furthermore, it is of the utmost importance to pre-process the data correctly, as there will inherently be redundancy in the data. As metabolite identification remains the bottleneck in metabolomics studies, so stringent approaches are needed to ensure that models have been validated and only the strongest candidates are pursued through the identification pipeline. The comprehensiveness of experimentally generated and in silico-derived spectral databases has grown significantly, and their integration into the data processing workflow, together with the improvement of computational approaches (for in silico prediction of MS/MS data), are paving the way towards automated MS/MS data matching to facilitate metabolite annotation. Finally, the advancements in metabolic network analysis tools are enabling more mechanistic insights, beyond the biomarker discovery. Here, metabolite data provide crucial complementary information on "what has indeed happened", as the phenotype readout at the molecular level, thus representing the "missing piece" of puzzle towards multi-scale omics data integration for more accurate interpretation of biological processes.

Author Contributions: J.I. and E.J.W. contributed equally to the preparation of this manuscript.

Funding: This research received no external funding.

Acknowledgments: The authors acknowledge all of the members of their respective teams, from the University of Lausanne and Imperial College London, as well as their collaborators (fundamentalist and clinicians), for their support and interaction during many years of involvement with metabolomics.

Conflicts of Interest: The authors declare no conflicts of interest.

References

1. Patti, G.J.; Tautenhahn, R.; Siuzdak, G. Meta-analysis of untargeted metabolomic data from multiple profiling experiments. *Nat. Protoc.* **2012**, *7*, 508–516. [CrossRef] [PubMed]
2. Mills, E.L.; Pierce, K.A.; Jedrychowski, M.P.; Garrity, R.; Winther, S.; Vidoni, S.; Yoneshiro, T.; Spinelli, J.B.; Lu, G.Z.; Kazak, L.; et al. Accumulation of succinate controls activation of adipose tissue thermogenesis. *Nature* **2018**, *560*, 102–106. [CrossRef] [PubMed]
3. Hayton, S.; Maker, G.L.; Mullaney, I.; Trengove, R.D. Experimental design and reporting standards for metabolomics studies of mammalian cell lines. *Cell. Mol. Life Sci.* **2017**, *74*, 4421–4441. [CrossRef] [PubMed]
4. Chong, J.; Wishart, D.S.; Xia, J. Using MetaboAnalyst 4.0 for Comprehensive and Integrative Metabolomics Data Analysis. *Curr. Protoc. Bioinformatics* **2019**, *68*, e86.
5. Blaise, B.J.; Correia, G.; Tin, A.; Young, J.H.; Vergnaud, A.-C.; Lewis, M.; Pearce, J.T.M.; Elliott, P.; Nicholson, J.K.; Holmes, E.; et al. Power Analysis and Sample Size Determination in Metabolic Phenotyping. *Anal. Chem.* **2016**, *88*, 5179–5188. [CrossRef] [PubMed]
6. Nyamundanda, G.; Gormley, I.C.; Fan, Y.; Gallagher, W.M.; Brennan, L. MetSizeR: Selecting the optimal sample size for metabolomic studies using an analysis based approach. *BMC Bioinform.* **2013**, *14*, 338. [CrossRef]
7. Leon, Z.; Garcia-Canaveras, J.C.; Donato, M.T.; Lahoz, A. Mammalian cell metabolomics: Experimental design and sample preparation. *Electrophoresis* **2013**, *34*, 2762–2775. [CrossRef]
8. Jacyna, J.; Kordalewska, M.; Markuszewski, M.J. Design of Experiments in metabolomics-related studies: an overview. *J. Pharm. Biomed. Anal.* **2019**, *164*, 598–606. [CrossRef]

9. Martins, M.C.M.; Caldana, C.; Wolf, L.D.; de Abreu, L.G.F. The Importance of Experimental Design, Quality Assurance, and Control in Plant Metabolomics Experiments. *Methods Mol. Biol.* **2018**, *1778*, 3–17. [CrossRef]
10. Cruickshank-Quinn, C.; Zheng, L.K.; Quinn, K.; Bowler, R.; Reisdorph, R.; Reisdorph, N. Impact of Blood Collection Tubes and Sample Handling Time on Serum and Plasma Metabolome and Lipidome. *Metabolites* **2018**, *8*, 88. [CrossRef]
11. Hernandes, V.V.; Barbas, C.; Dudzik, D. a review of blood sample handling and pre-processing for metabolomics studies. *Electrophoresis* **2017**, *38*, 2232–2241. [CrossRef] [PubMed]
12. Khadka, M.; Todor, A.; Maner-Smith, K.M.; Colucci, J.K.; Tran, V.; Gaul, D.A.; Anderson, E.J.; Natrajan, M.S.; Rouphael, N.; Mulligan, M.J.; et al. The Effect of Anticoagulants, Temperature, and Time on the Human Plasma Metabolome and Lipidome from Healthy Donors as Determined by Liquid Chromatography-Mass Spectrometry. *Biomolecules* **2019**, *9*, 200. [CrossRef] [PubMed]
13. Nishiumi, S.; Suzuki, M.; Kobayashi, T.; Yoshida, M. Differences in metabolite profiles caused by pre-analytical blood processing procedures. *J. Biosci. Bioeng.* **2018**, *125*, 613–618. [CrossRef] [PubMed]
14. Teahan, O.; Gamble, S.; Holmes, E.; Waxman, J.; Nicholson, J.K.; Bevan, C.; Keun, H.C. Impact of analytical bias in metabonomic studies of human blood serum and plasma. *Anal. Chem.* **2006**, *78*, 4307–4318. [CrossRef] [PubMed]
15. Smith, L.M.; Maher, A.D.; Want, E.J.; Elliott, P.; Stamler, J.; Hawkes, G.E.; Holmes, E.; Lindon, J.C.; Nicholson, J.K. Large-scale human metabolic phenotyping and molecular epidemiological studies via 1H NMR spectroscopy of urine: Investigation of borate preservation. *Anal. Chem.* **2009**, *81*, 4847–4856. [CrossRef] [PubMed]
16. La Frano, M.R.; Carmichael, S.L.; Ma, C.; Hardley, M.; Shen, T.; Wong, R.; Rosales, L.; Borkowski, K.; Pedersen, T.L.; Shaw, G.M.; et al. Impact of post-collection freezing delay on the reliability of serum metabolomics in samples reflecting the California mid-term pregnancy biobank. *Metabolomics* **2018**, *14*, 151. [CrossRef]
17. Jonasdottir, H.S.; Brouwers, H.; Toes, R.E.M.; Ioan-Facsinay, A.; Giera, M. Effects of anticoagulants and storage conditions on clinical oxylipid levels in human plasma. *Biochim. Biophys. Acta (BBA) Mol. Cell Biol. Lipids* **2018**, *1863*, 1511–1522. [CrossRef]
18. Gibon, Y.; Rolin, D. Aspects of experimental design for plant metabolomics experiments and guidelines for growth of plant material. *Methods Mol. Biol.* **2012**, *860*, 13–30. [CrossRef]
19. DeBoer, M.D.; Platts-Mills, J.A.; Scharf, R.J.; McDermid, J.M.; Wanjuhi, A.W.; Gratz, J.; Svensen, E.; Swann, J.R.; Donowitz, J.R.; Jatosh, S.; et al. Early Life Interventions for Childhood Growth and Development in Tanzania (ELICIT): a protocol for a randomised factorial, double-blind, placebo-controlled trial of azithromycin, nitazoxanide and nicotinamide. *BMJ Open* **2018**, *8*, e021817. [CrossRef]
20. Khan, S.R.; Whiteman, D.C.; Kimlin, M.G.; Janda, M.; Clarke, M.W.; Lucas, R.M.; Neale, R.E. Effect of solar ultraviolet radiation exposure on serum 25(OH)D concentration: a pilot randomised controlled trial. *Photochem. Photobiol. Sci.* **2018**, *17*, 570–577. [CrossRef]
21. Roager, H.M.; Vogt, J.K.; Kristensen, M.; Hansen, L.B.S.; Ibrugger, S.; Maerkedahl, R.B.; Bahl, M.I.; Lind, M.V.; Nielsen, R.L.; Frokiaer, H.; et al. Whole grain-rich diet reduces body weight and systemic low-grade inflammation without inducing major changes of the gut microbiome: a randomised cross-over trial. *Gut* **2019**, *68*, 83–93. [CrossRef] [PubMed]
22. Gong, Z.G.; Hu, J.; Wu, X.; Xu, Y.J. The Recent Developments in Sample Preparation for Mass Spectrometry-Based Metabolomics. *Crit. Rev. Anal. Chem.* **2017**, *47*, 325–331. [CrossRef] [PubMed]
23. Patejko, M.; Jacyna, J.; Markuszewski, M.J. Sample preparation procedures utilized in microbial metabolomics: an overview. *J. Chromatogr. B Anal. Technol. Biomed. Life Sci.* **2017**, *1043*, 150–157. [CrossRef] [PubMed]
24. Deda, O.; Chatziioannou, A.C.; Fasoula, S.; Palachanis, D.; Raikos, N.; Theodoridis, G.A.; Gika, H.G. Sample preparation optimization in fecal metabolic profiling. *J. Chromatogr. B Anal. Technol. Biomed. Life Sci.* **2017**, *1047*, 115–123. [CrossRef] [PubMed]
25. Drouin, N.; Rudaz, S.; Schappler, J. Sample preparation for polar metabolites in bioanalysis. *Analyst* **2017**, *143*, 16–20. [CrossRef] [PubMed]
26. Lu, W.; Su, X.; Klein, M.S.; Lewis, I.A.; Fiehn, O.; Rabinowitz, J.D. Metabolite Measurement: Pitfalls to Avoid and Practices to Follow. *Annu. Rev. Biochem.* **2017**, *86*, 277–304. [CrossRef]

27. Li, N.; Song, Y.; Tang, H.; Wang, Y. Recent developments in sample preparation and data pre-treatment in metabonomics research. *Arch. Biochem. Biophys.* **2016**, *589*, 4–9. [CrossRef]
28. Chetwynd, A.J.; Dunn, W.B.; Rodriguez-Blanco, G. Collection and Preparation of Clinical Samples for Metabolomics. *Adv. Exp. Med. Biol.* **2017**, *965*, 19–44. [CrossRef]
29. Masson, P.; Alves, A.C.; Ebbels, T.M.; Nicholson, J.K.; Want, E.J. Optimization and evaluation of metabolite extraction protocols for untargeted metabolic profiling of liver samples by UPLC-MS. *Anal. Chem.* **2010**, *82*, 7779–7786. [CrossRef]
30. Want, E.J.; Wilson, I.D.; Gika, H.; Theodoridis, G.; Plumb, R.S.; Shockcor, J.; Holmes, E.; Nicholson, J.K. Global metabolic profiling procedures for urine using UPLC-MS. *Nat. Protoc.* **2010**, *5*, 1005–1018. [CrossRef]
31. Want, E.J.; Masson, P.; Michopoulos, F.; Wilson, I.D.; Theodoridis, G.; Plumb, R.S.; Shockcor, J.; Loftus, N.; Holmes, E.; Nicholson, J.K. Global metabolic profiling of animal and human tissues via UPLC-MS. *Nat. Protoc.* **2013**, *8*, 17–32. [CrossRef] [PubMed]
32. Lofgren, L.; Stahlman, M.; Forsberg, G.B.; Saarinen, S.; Nilsson, R.; Hansson, G.I. The BUME method: a novel automated chloroform-free 96-well total lipid extraction method for blood plasma. *J. Lipid Res.* **2012**, *53*, 1690–1700. [CrossRef] [PubMed]
33. Löfgren, L.; Forsberg, G.-B.; Ståhlman, M. The BUME method: a new rapid and simple chloroform-free method for total lipid extraction of animal tissue. *Sci. Rep.* **2016**, *6*. [CrossRef] [PubMed]
34. Gil, A.; Zhang, W.; Wolters, J.C.; Permentier, H.; Boer, T.; Horvatovich, P.; Heiner-Fokkema, M.R.; Reijngoud, D.-J.; Bischoff, R. One- vs two-phase extraction: Re-evaluation of sample preparation procedures for untargeted lipidomics in plasma samples. *Anal. Bioanal. Chem.* **2018**, *410*, 5859–5870. [CrossRef] [PubMed]
35. Sarafian, M.H.; Gaudin, M.; Lewis, M.R.; Martin, F.-P.; Holmes, E.; Nicholson, J.K.; Dumas, M.-E. Objective Set of Criteria for Optimization of Sample Preparation Procedures for Ultra-High Throughput Untargeted Blood Plasma Lipid Profiling by Ultra Performance Liquid Chromatography–Mass Spectrometry. *Anal. Chem.* **2014**, *86*, 5766–5774. [CrossRef] [PubMed]
36. Cajka, T.; Fiehn, O. Comprehensive analysis of lipids in biological systems by liquid chromatography-mass spectrometry. *Trends Anal. Chem.* **2014**, *61*, 192–206. [CrossRef]
37. Vorkas, P.A.; Isaac, G.; Anwar, M.A.; Davies, A.H.; Want, E.J.; Nicholson, J.K.; Holmes, E. Untargeted UPLC-MS Profiling Pipeline to Expand Tissue Metabolome Coverage: Application to Cardiovascular Disease. *Anal. Chem.* **2015**, *87*, 4184–4193. [CrossRef]
38. Want, E.J.; Nordstrom, A.; Morita, H.; Siuzdak, G. From exogenous to endogenous: The inevitable imprint of mass spectrometry in metabolomics. *J. Proteom. Res.* **2007**, *6*, 459–468. [CrossRef]
39. Johnson, C.H.; Ivanisevic, J.; Siuzdak, G. Metabolomics: Beyond biomarkers and towards mechanisms. *Nat. Rev. Mol. Cell Biol.* **2016**. [CrossRef]
40. Fuhrer, T.; Heer, D.; Begemann, B.; Zamboni, N. High-Throughput, Accurate Mass Metabolome Profiling of Cellular Extracts by Flow Injection–Time-of-Flight Mass Spectrometry. *Anal. Chem.* **2011**, *83*, 7074–7080. [CrossRef]
41. Zamboni, N.; Saghatelian, A.; Patti, G.J. Defining the Metabolome: Size, Flux, and Regulation. *Mol. Cell* **2015**, *58*, 699–706. [CrossRef] [PubMed]
42. Wang, J.; Wang, C.; Han, X. Tutorial on lipidomics. *Anal. Chim. Acta* **2019**, *1061*, 28–41. [CrossRef] [PubMed]
43. Hu, C.; Duan, Q.; Han, X. Strategies to Improve/Eliminate the Limitations in Shotgun Lipidomics. *Proteomics* **2019**. [CrossRef] [PubMed]
44. Patti, G.J.; Yanes, O.; Siuzdak, G. Innovation: Metabolomics: The apogee of the omics trilogy. *Nat. Rev. Mol. Cell Biol.* **2012**, *13*, 263–269. [CrossRef] [PubMed]
45. Cajka, T.; Smilowitz, J.T.; Fiehn, O. Validating Quantitative Untargeted Lipidomics Across Nine Liquid Chromatography-High-Resolution Mass Spectrometry Platforms. *Anal. Chem.* **2017**, *89*, 12360–12368. [CrossRef] [PubMed]
46. Patti, G.J. Separation strategies for untargeted metabolomics. *J. Sep. Sci.* **2011**, *34*, 3460–3469. [CrossRef]
47. Benton, H.P.; Ivanisevic, J.; Mahieu, N.G.; Kurczy, M.E.; Johnson, C.H.; Franco, L.; Rinehart, D.; Valentine, E.; Gowda, H.; Ubhi, B.K.; et al. Autonomous Metabolomics for Rapid Metabolite Identification in Global Profiling. *Anal. Chem.* **2015**, *87*, 884–891. [CrossRef]

48. Ivanisevic, J.; Zhu, Z.-J.; Plate, L.; Tautenhahn, R.; Chen, S.; O'Brien, P.J.; Johnson, C.H.; Marletta, M.A.; Patti, G.J.; Siuzdak, G. Toward Omic Scale Metabolite Profiling: a Dual Separation—Mass Spectrometry Approach for Coverage of Lipid and Central Carbon Metabolism. *Anal. Chem.* **2013**, *85*, 6876–6884. [CrossRef]
49. Yanes, O.; Tautenhahn, R.; Patti, G.J.; Siuzdak, G. Expanding Coverage of the Metabolome for Global Metabolite Profiling. *Anal. Chem.* **2011**, *83*, 2152–2161. [CrossRef]
50. Lu, W.; Clasquin, M.F.; Melamud, E.; Amador-Noguez, D.; Caudy, A.A.; Rabinowitz, J.D. Metabolomic Analysis via Reversed-Phase Ion-Pairing Liquid Chromatography Coupled to a Stand Alone Orbitrap Mass Spectrometer. *Anal. Chem.* **2010**, *82*, 3212–3221. [CrossRef]
51. Gallart-Ayala, H.; Konz, I.; Mehl, F.; Teav, T.; Oikonomidi, A.; Peyratout, G.; van der Velpen, V.; Popp, J.; Ivanisevic, J. a global HILIC-MS approach to measure polar human cerebrospinal fluid metabolome: Exploring gender-associated variation in a cohort of elderly cognitively healthy subjects. *Anal. Chim. Acta* **2018**, *1037*, 327–337. [CrossRef]
52. Wernisch, S.; Pennathur, S. Evaluation of coverage, retention patterns, and selectivity of seven liquid chromatographic methods for metabolomics. *Anal. Bioanal. Chem.* **2016**, *408*, 6079–6091. [CrossRef]
53. Naz, S.; Gallart-Ayala, H.; Reinke, S.N.; Mathon, C.; Blankley, R.; Chaleckis, R.; Wheelock, C.E. Development of a Liquid Chromatography-High Resolution Mass Spectrometry Metabolomics Method with High Specificity for Metabolite Identification Using All Ion Fragmentation Acquisition. *Anal. Chem.* **2017**, *89*, 7933–7942. [CrossRef]
54. Cífková, E.; Holčapek, M.; Lísa, M.; Ovčačíková, M.; Lyčka, A.; Lynen, F.; Sandra, P. Nontargeted Quantitation of Lipid Classes Using Hydrophilic Interaction Liquid Chromatography–Electrospray Ionization Mass Spectrometry with Single Internal Standard and Response Factor Approach. *Anal. Chem.* **2012**, *84*, 10064–10070. [CrossRef]
55. Fei, F.; Bowdish, D.M.; McCarry, B.E. Comprehensive and simultaneous coverage of lipid and polar metabolites for endogenous cellular metabolomics using HILIC-TOF-MS. *Anal. Bioanal. Chem.* **2014**, *406*, 3723–3733. [CrossRef]
56. Teav, T.; Gallart-Ayala, H.; van der Velpen, V.; Mehl, F.; Henry, H.; Ivanisevic, J. Merged Targeted Quantification and Untargeted Profiling for Comprehensive Assessment of Acylcarnitine and Amino Acid Metabolism. *Anal. Chem.* **2019**, *91*, 11757–11769. [CrossRef]
57. Cajka, T.; Fiehn, O. LC-MS-Based Lipidomics and Automated Identification of Lipids Using the LipidBlast In-Silico MS/MS Library. *Methods Mol. Biol.* **2017**, *1609*, 149–170. [CrossRef]
58. Rinehart, D.; Johnson, C.H.; Nguyen, T.; Ivanisevic, J.; Benton, H.P.; Lloyd, J.; Arkin, A.P.; Deutschbauer, A.M.; Patti, G.J.; Siuzdak, G. Metabolomic data streaming for biology-dependent data acquisition. *Nat. Biotech.* **2014**, *32*, 524–527. [CrossRef]
59. Cajka, T.; Fiehn, O. Toward Merging Untargeted and Targeted Methods in Mass Spectrometry-Based Metabolomics and Lipidomics. *Anal. Chem.* **2016**, *88*, 524–545. [CrossRef]
60. Shen, X.; Wang, R.; Xiong, X.; Yin, Y.; Cai, Y.; Ma, Z.; Liu, N.; Zhu, Z.J. Metabolic reaction network-based recursive metabolite annotation for untargeted metabolomics. *Nat. Commun.* **2019**, *10*, 1516. [CrossRef]
61. Hu, Y.; Cai, B.; Huan, T. Enhancing metabolome coverage in data-dependent LC-MS/MS analysis through an integrated feature extraction strategy. *Anal. Chem.* **2019**, *91*, 14433–14441. [CrossRef]
62. Tsugawa, H.; Cajka, T.; Kind, T.; Ma, Y.; Higgins, B.; Ikeda, K.; Kanazawa, M.; VanderGheynst, J.; Fiehn, O.; Arita, M. MS-DIAL: Data-independent MS/MS deconvolution for comprehensive metabolome analysis. *Nat. Meth.* **2015**, *12*, 523–526. [CrossRef]
63. Koelmel, J.P.; Kroeger, N.M.; Gill, E.L.; Ulmer, C.Z.; Bowden, J.A.; Patterson, R.E.; Yost, R.A.; Garrett, T.J. Expanding Lipidome Coverage Using LC-MS/MS Data-Dependent Acquisition with Automated Exclusion List Generation. *J. Am. Soc. Mass Spectrom.* **2017**, *28*, 908–917. [CrossRef]
64. Wang, Y.; Feng, R.; Wang, R.; Yang, F.; Li, P.; Wan, J.B. Enhanced MS/MS coverage for metabolite identification in LC-MS-based untargeted metabolomics by target-directed data dependent acquisition with time-staggered precursor ion list. *Anal. Chim. Acta* **2017**, *992*, 67–75. [CrossRef]
65. Li, H.; Cai, Y.; Guo, Y.; Chen, F.; Zhu, Z.J. MetDIA: Targeted Metabolite Extraction of Multiplexed MS/MS Spectra Generated by Data-Independent Acquisition. *Anal. Chem.* **2016**, *88*, 8757–8764. [CrossRef]
66. Yin, Y.; Wang, R.; Cai, Y.; Wang, Z.; Zhu, Z.J. DecoMetDIA: Deconvolution of Multiplexed MS/MS Spectra for Metabolite Identification in SWATH-MS-Based Untargeted Metabolomics. *Anal. Chem.* **2019**, *91*, 11897–11904. [CrossRef]

67. Guijas, C.; Montenegro-Burke, J.R.; Domingo-Almenara, X.; Palermo, A.; Warth, B.; Hermann, G.; Koellensperger, G.; Huan, T.; Uritboonthai, W.; Aisporna, A.E.; et al. METLIN: a Technology Platform for Identifying Knowns and Unknowns. *Anal. Chem.* **2018**, *90*, 3156–3164. [CrossRef]
68. Horai, H.; Arita, M.; Kanaya, S.; Nihei, Y.; Ikeda, T.; Suwa, K.; Ojima, Y.; Tanaka, K.; Tanaka, S.; Aoshima, K.; et al. MassBank: a public repository for sharing mass spectral data for life sciences. *J. Mass Spectrom.* **2010**, *45*, 703–714. [CrossRef]
69. Wang, M.; Carver, J.J.; Phelan, V.V.; Sanchez, L.M.; Garg, N.; Peng, Y.; Nguyen, D.D.; Watrous, J.; Kapono, C.A.; Luzzatto-Knaan, T.; et al. Sharing and community curation of mass spectrometry data with Global Natural Products Social Molecular Networking. *Nat. Biotechnol.* **2016**, *34*, 828. [CrossRef]
70. Aguilar-Mogas, A.; Sales-Pardo, M.; Navarro, M.; Guimera, R.; Yanes, O. iMet: a Network-Based Computational Tool To Assist in the Annotation of Metabolites from Tandem Mass Spectra. *Anal. Chem.* **2017**, *89*, 3474–3482. [CrossRef]
71. Kind, T.; Liu, K.H.; Lee, D.Y.; DeFelice, B.; Meissen, J.K.; Fiehn, O. LipidBlast in silico tandem mass spectrometry database for lipid identification. *Nat. Methods* **2013**, *10*, 755–758. [CrossRef] [PubMed]
72. Ruttkies, C.; Schymanski, E.L.; Wolf, S.; Hollender, J.; Neumann, S. MetFrag relaunched: Incorporating strategies beyond in silico fragmentation. *J. Cheminform.* **2016**, *8*, 3. [CrossRef] [PubMed]
73. Duhrkop, K.; Fleischauer, M.; Ludwig, M.; Aksenov, A.A.; Melnik, A.V.; Meusel, M.; Dorrestein, P.C.; Rousu, J.; Bocker, S. SIRIUS 4: a rapid tool for turning tandem mass spectra into metabolite structure information. *Nat. Methods* **2019**, *16*, 299–302. [CrossRef]
74. Paglia, G.; Astarita, G. Metabolomics and lipidomics using traveling-wave ion mobility mass spectrometry. *Nat. Protoc.* **2017**, *12*, 797–813. [CrossRef]
75. Blazenovic, I.; Kind, T.; Ji, J.; Fiehn, O. Software Tools and Approaches for Compound Identification of LC-MS/MS Data in Metabolomics. *Metabolites* **2018**, *8*, 31. [CrossRef]
76. Zha, H.; Cai, Y.; Yin, Y.; Wang, Z.; Li, K.; Zhu, Z.J. SWATHtoMRM: Development of High-Coverage Targeted Metabolomics Method Using SWATH Technology for Biomarker Discovery. *Anal. Chem.* **2018**, *90*, 4062–4070. [CrossRef]
77. Domingo-Almenara, X.; Montenegro-Burke, J.R.; Ivanisevic, J.; Thomas, A.; Sidibé, J.; Teav, T.; Guijas, C.; Aisporna, A.E.; Rinehart, D.; Hoang, L.; et al. XCMS-MRM and METLIN-MRM: a cloud library and public resource for targeted analysis of small molecules. *Nat. Methods* **2018**, *15*, 681–684. [CrossRef]
78. Smith, C.A.; Want, E.J.; O'Maille, G.; Abagyan, R.; Siuzdak, G. XCMS: Processing mass spectrometry data for metabolite profiling using nonlinear peak alignment, matching, and identification. *Anal. Chem.* **2006**, *78*, 779–787. [CrossRef]
79. Tautenhahn, R.; Bottcher, C.; Neumann, S. Highly sensitive feature detection for high resolution LC/MS. *BMC Bioinform.* **2008**, *9*, 504. [CrossRef]
80. Pluskal, T.; Castillo, S.; Villar-Briones, A.; Oresic, M. MZmine 2: Modular framework for processing, visualizing, and analyzing mass spectrometry-based molecular profile data. *BMC Bioinform.* **2010**, *11*, 395. [CrossRef]
81. Gowda, H.; Ivanisevic, J.; Johnson, C.H.; Kurczy, M.E.; Benton, H.P.; Rinehart, D.; Nguyen, T.; Ray, J.; Kuehl, J.; Arevalo, B.; et al. Interactive XCMS Online: Simplifying Advanced Metabolomic Data Processing and Subsequent Statistical Analyses. *Anal. Chem.* **2014**, *86*, 6931–6939. [CrossRef] [PubMed]
82. Tautenhahn, R.; Patti, G.J.; Rinehart, D.; Siuzdak, G. XCMS Online: a Web-Based Platform to Process Untargeted Metabolomic Data. *Anal. Chem.* **2012**, *84*, 5035–5039. [CrossRef] [PubMed]
83. Tugizimana, F.; Steenkamp, P.A.; Piater, L.A.; Dubery, I.A. a Conversation on Data Mining Strategies in LC-MS Untargeted Metabolomics: Pre-Processing and Pre-Treatment Steps. *Metabolites* **2016**, *6*, 40. [CrossRef] [PubMed]
84. Gross, T.; Mapstone, M.; Miramontes, R.; Padilla, R.; Cheema, A.K.; Macciardi, F.; Federoff, H.J.; Fiandaca, M.S. Toward Reproducible Results from Targeted Metabolomic Studies: Perspectives for Data Pre-processing and a Basis for Analytic Pipeline Development. *Curr. Top. Med. Chem.* **2018**, *18*, 883–895. [CrossRef]
85. Myers, O.D.; Sumner, S.J.; Li, S.; Barnes, S.; Du, X. Detailed Investigation and Comparison of the XCMS and MZmine 2 Chromatogram Construction and Chromatographic Peak Detection Methods for Preprocessing Mass Spectrometry Metabolomics Data. *Anal. Chem.* **2017**, *89*, 8689–8695. [CrossRef]
86. Domingo-Almenara, X.; Montenegro-Burke, J.R.; Benton, H.P.; Siuzdak, G. Annotation: a Computational Solution for Streamlining Metabolomics Analysis. *Anal. Chem.* **2018**, *90*, 480–489. [CrossRef]

87. Domingo-Almenara, X.; Montenegro-Burke, J.R.; Guijas, C.; Majumder, E.L.W.; Benton, H.P.; Siuzdak, G. Autonomous METLIN-Guided In-source Fragment Annotation for Untargeted Metabolomics. *Anal. Chem.* **2019**, *91*, 3246–3253. [CrossRef]
88. Kuhl, C.; Tautenhahn, R.; Böttcher, C.; Larson, T.R.; Neumann, S. CAMERA: an Integrated Strategy for Compound Spectra Extraction and Annotation of Liquid Chromatography/Mass Spectrometry Data Sets. *Anal. Chem.* **2011**, *84*, 283–289. [CrossRef]
89. Alonso, A.; Julia, A.; Beltran, A.; Vinaixa, M.; Diaz, M.; Ibanez, L.; Correig, X.; Marsal, S. AStream: an R package for annotating LC/MS metabolomic data. *Bioinformatics* **2011**, *27*, 1339–1340. [CrossRef]
90. Broeckling, C.D.; Afsar, F.A.; Neumann, S.; Ben-Hur, A.; Prenni, J.E. RAMClust: a novel feature clustering method enables spectral-matching-based annotation for metabolomics data. *Anal. Chem.* **2014**, *86*, 6812–6817. [CrossRef]
91. Chong, J.; Soufan, O.; Li, C.; Caraus, I.; Li, S.; Bourque, G.; Wishart, D.S.; Xia, J. MetaboAnalyst 4.0: Towards more transparent and integrative metabolomics analysis. *Nucleic Acids Res.* **2018**, *46*, W486–W494. [CrossRef] [PubMed]
92. Sangster, T.; Major, H.; Plumb, R.; Wilson, A.J.; Wilson, I.D. a pragmatic and readily implemented quality control strategy for HPLC-MS and GC-MS-based metabonomic analysis. *Analyst* **2006**, *131*, 1075–1078. [CrossRef] [PubMed]
93. Broadhurst, D.; Goodacre, R.; Reinke, S.N.; Kuligowski, J.; Wilson, I.D.; Lewis, M.R.; Dunn, W.B. Guidelines and considerations for the use of system suitability and quality control samples in mass spectrometry assays applied in untargeted clinical metabolomic studies. *Metabolomics* **2018**, *14*, 72. [CrossRef] [PubMed]
94. Bowden, J.A.; Heckert, A.; Ulmer, C.Z.; Jones, C.M.; Koelmel, J.P.; Abdullah, L.; Ahonen, L.; Alnouti, Y.; Armando, A.M.; Asara, J.M.; et al. Harmonizing lipidomics: NIST interlaboratory comparison exercise for lipidomics using SRM 1950-Metabolites in Frozen Human Plasma. *J. Lipid Res.* **2017**, *58*, 2275–2288. [CrossRef] [PubMed]
95. Beger, R.D.; Dunn, W.B.; Bandukwala, A.; Bethan, B.; Broadhurst, D.; Clish, C.B.; Dasari, S.; Derr, L.; Evans, A.; Fischer, S.; et al. Towards quality assurance and quality control in untargeted metabolomics studies. *Metabolomics* **2019**, *15*, 4. [CrossRef] [PubMed]
96. Dudzik, D.; Barbas-Bernardos, C.; Garcia, A.; Barbas, C. Quality assurance procedures for mass spectrometry untargeted metabolomics. a review. *J. Pharm. Biomed. Anal.* **2018**, *147*, 149–173. [CrossRef]
97. Dunn, W.B.; Broadhurst, D.; Begley, P.; Zelena, E.; Francis-McIntyre, S.; Anderson, N.; Brown, M.; Knowles, J.D.; Halsall, A.; Haselden, J.N.; et al. Procedures for large-scale metabolic profiling of serum and plasma using gas chromatography and liquid chromatography coupled to mass spectrometry. *Nat. Protoc.* **2011**, *6*, 1060–1083. [CrossRef]
98. Worley, B.; Powers, R. Multivariate Analysis in Metabolomics. *Curr Metab.* **2013**, *1*, 92–107. [CrossRef]
99. Liland, K.H. Multivariate methods in metabolomics—From pre-processing to dimension reduction and statistical analysis. *TrAC Trends Anal. Chem.* **2011**, *30*, 827–841. [CrossRef]
100. Kjeldahl, K.; Bro, R. Some common misunderstandings in chemometrics. *J. Chemom.* **2010**, *24*, 558–564. [CrossRef]
101. Eriksson, L.; Trygg, J.; Wold, S. CV-ANOVA for significance testing of PLS and OPLS®models. *J. Chemom.* **2008**, *22*, 594–600. [CrossRef]
102. Rubingh, C.M.; Bijlsma, S.; Derks, E.P.; Bobeldijk, I.; Verheij, E.R.; Kochhar, S.; Smilde, A.K. Assessing the performance of statistical validation tools for megavariate metabolomics data. *Metabolomics* **2006**, *2*, 53–61. [CrossRef] [PubMed]
103. Do, K.T.; Wahl, S.; Raffler, J.; Molnos, S.; Laimighofer, M.; Adamski, J.; Suhre, K.; Strauch, K.; Peters, A.; Gieger, C.; et al. Characterization of missing values in untargeted MS-based metabolomics data and evaluation of missing data handling strategies. *Metabolomics* **2018**, *14*, 128. [CrossRef] [PubMed]
104. Hendriks, M.M.W.B.; Eeuwijk, F.A.V.; Jellema, R.H.; Westerhuis, J.A.; Reijmers, T.H.; Hoefsloot, H.C.J.; Smilde, A.K. Data-processing strategies for metabolomics studies. *TrAC Trends Anal. Chem.* **2011**, *30*, 1685–1698. [CrossRef]
105. Tzoulaki, I.; Ebbels, T.M.; Valdes, A.; Elliott, P.; Ioannidis, J.P. Design and analysis of metabolomics studies in epidemiologic research: a primer on -omic technologies. *Am. J. Epidemiol.* **2014**, *180*, 129–139. [CrossRef]
106. Vinaixa, M.; Samino, S.; Saez, I.; Duran, J.; Guinovart, J.J.; Yanes, O. a Guideline to Univariate Statistical Analysis for LC/MS-Based Untargeted Metabolomics-Derived Data. *Metabolites* **2012**, *2*, 775–795. [CrossRef]

107. Da Silva, R.R.; Dorrestein, P.C.; Quinn, R.A. Illuminating the dark matter in metabolomics. *Proc. Natl. Acad. Sci. USA* **2015**, *112*, 12549–12550. [CrossRef]
108. Dias, D.A.; Jones, O.A.; Beale, D.J.; Boughton, B.A.; Benheim, D.; Kouremenos, K.A.; Wolfender, J.L.; Wishart, D.S. Current and Future Perspectives on the Structural Identification of Small Molecules in Biological Systems. *Metabolites* **2016**, *6*, 46. [CrossRef]
109. Tautenhahn, R.; Cho, K.; Uritboonthai, W.; Zhu, Z.; Patti, G.J.; Siuzdak, G. an accelerated workflow for untargeted metabolomics using the METLIN database. *Nat. Biotechnol.* **2012**, *30*, 826–828. [CrossRef]
110. Vinaixa, M.; Schymanski, E.L.; Neumann, S.; Navarro, M.; Salek, R.M.; Yanes, O. Mass spectral databases for LC/MS- and GC/MS-based metabolomics: State of the field and future prospects. *TrAC Trends Anal. Chem.* **2016**, *78*, 23–35. [CrossRef]
111. Mylonas, R.; Mauron, Y.; Masselot, A.; Binz, P.A.; Budin, N.; Fathi, M.; Viette, V.; Hochstrasser, D.F.; Lisacek, F. X-Rank: a robust algorithm for small molecule identification using tandem mass spectrometry. *Anal. Chem.* **2009**, *81*, 7604–7610. [CrossRef] [PubMed]
112. Nguyen, D.H.; Nguyen, C.H.; Mamitsuka, H. Recent advances and prospects of computational methods for metabolite identification: a review with emphasis on machine learning approaches. *Brief. Bioinform.* **2018**. [CrossRef] [PubMed]
113. Ruttkies, C.; Neumann, S.; Posch, S. Improving MetFrag with statistical learning of fragment annotations. *BMC Bioinform.* **2019**, *20*, 376. [CrossRef] [PubMed]
114. Blazenovic, I.; Kind, T.; Sa, M.R.; Ji, J.; Vaniya, A.; Wancewicz, B.; Roberts, B.S.; Torbasinovic, H.; Lee, T.; Mehta, S.S.; et al. Structure Annotation of All Mass Spectra in Untargeted Metabolomics. *Anal. Chem.* **2019**, *91*, 2155–2162. [CrossRef] [PubMed]
115. Van der Hooft, J.J.J.; Wandy, J.; Barrett, M.P.; Burgess, K.E.V.; Rogers, S. Topic modeling for untargeted substructure exploration in metabolomics. *Proc. Natl. Acad. Sci. USA* **2016**, *113*, 13738–13743. [CrossRef] [PubMed]
116. Van der Hooft, J.J.J.; Wandy, J.; Young, F.; Padmanabhan, S.; Gerasimidis, K.; Burgess, K.E.V.; Barrett, M.P.; Rogers, S. Unsupervised Discovery and Comparison of Structural Families Across Multiple Samples in Untargeted Metabolomics. *Anal. Chem.* **2017**, *89*, 7569–7577. [CrossRef] [PubMed]
117. Sud, M.; Fahy, E.; Cotter, D.; Azam, K.; Vadivelu, I.; Burant, C.; Edison, A.; Fiehn, O.; Higashi, R.; Nair, K.S.; et al. Metabolomics Workbench: an international repository for metabolomics data and metadata, metabolite standards, protocols, tutorials and training, and analysis tools. *Nucleic Acids Res.* **2016**, *44*, D463–D470. [CrossRef]
118. Steinbeck, C.; Conesa, P.; Haug, K.; Mahendraker, T.; Williams, M.; Maguire, E.; Rocca-Serra, P.; Sansone, S.A.; Salek, R.M.; Griffin, J.L. MetaboLights: towards a new COSMOS of metabolomics data management. *Metabolomics* **2012**, *8*, 757–760. [CrossRef]
119. Li, S.; Park, Y.; Duraisingham, S.; Strobel, F.H.; Khan, N.; Soltow, Q.A.; Jones, D.P.; Pulendran, B. Predicting network activity from high throughput metabolomics. *PLoS Comput. Biol.* **2013**, *9*, e1003123. [CrossRef]
120. Pirhaji, L.; Milani, P.; Leidl, M.; Curran, T.; Avila-Pacheco, J.; Clish, C.B.; White, F.M.; Saghatelian, A.; Fraenkel, E. Revealing disease-associated pathways by network integration of untargeted metabolomics. *Nat. Methods* **2016**, *13*, 770–776. [CrossRef]
121. Rosato, A.; Tenori, L.; Cascante, M.; De Atauri Carulla, P.R.; Martins dos Santos, V.A.P.; Saccenti, E. From correlation to causation: Analysis of metabolomics data using systems biology approaches. *Metabolomics* **2018**, *14*, 37. [CrossRef] [PubMed]
122. Frainay, C.; Schymanski, E.L.; Neumann, S.; Merlet, B.; Salek, R.M.; Jourdan, F.; Yanes, O. Mind the Gap: Mapping Mass Spectral Databases in Genome-Scale Metabolic Networks Reveals Poorly Covered Areas. *Metabolites* **2018**, *8*, 51. [CrossRef] [PubMed]
123. Edison, A.S.; Hall, R.D.; Junot, C.; Karp, P.D.; Kurland, I.J.; Mistrik, R.; Reed, L.K.; Saito, K.; Salek, R.M.; Steinbeck, C.; et al. The Time Is Right to Focus on Model Organism Metabolomes. *Metabolites* **2016**, *6*, 8. [CrossRef] [PubMed]
124. Reed, L.K.; Baer, C.F.; Edison, A.S. Considerations when choosing a genetic model organism for metabolomics studies. *Curr. Opin. Chem. Biol.* **2017**, *36*, 7–14. [CrossRef]
125. Yilmaz, L.S.; Walhout, A.J.M. Metabolic network modeling with model organisms. *Curr. Opin. Chem. Biol.* **2017**, *36*, 32–39. [CrossRef]

126. Milreu, P.V.; Klein, C.C.; Cottret, L.; Acuna, V.; Birmele, E.; Borassi, M.; Junot, C.; Marchetti-Spaccamela, A.; Marino, A.; Stougie, L.; et al. Telling metabolic stories to explore metabolomics data: a case study on the yeast response to cadmium exposure. *Bioinformatics* **2014**, *30*, 61–70. [CrossRef]
127. Stanstrup, J.; Broeckling, C.D.; Helmus, R.; Hoffmann, N.; Mathe, E.; Naake, T.; Nicolotti, L.; Peters, K.; Rainer, J.; Salek, R.M.; et al. The metaRbolomics Toolbox in Bioconductor and beyond. *Metabolites* **2019**, *9*, 200. [CrossRef]
128. Cottret, L.; Frainay, C.; Chazalviel, M.; Cabanettes, F.; Gloaguen, Y.; Camenen, E.; Merlet, B.; Heux, S.; Portais, J.C.; Poupin, N.; et al. MetExplore: Collaborative edition and exploration of metabolic networks. *Nucleic Acids Res.* **2018**, *46*, W495–W502. [CrossRef]
129. Kutmon, M.; van Iersel, M.P.; Bohler, A.; Kelder, T.; Nunes, N.; Pico, A.R.; Evelo, C.T. PathVisio 3: an extendable pathway analysis toolbox. *PLoS Comput. Biol.* **2015**, *11*, e1004085. [CrossRef]
130. Yamada, T.; Letunic, I.; Okuda, S.; Kanehisa, M.; Bork, P. iPath2.0: Interactive pathway explorer. *Nucleic Acids Res.* **2011**, *39*, W412–W415. [CrossRef]
131. Wishart, D.S.; Li, C.; Marcu, A.; Badran, H.; Pon, A.; Budinski, Z.; Patron, J.; Lipton, D.; Cao, X.; Oler, E.; et al. PathBank: a comprehensive pathway database for model organisms. *Nucleic Acids Res.* **2019**. [CrossRef] [PubMed]
132. Molenaar, M.R.; Jeucken, A.; Wassenaar, T.A.; van de Lest, C.H.A.; Brouwers, J.F.; Helms, J.B. LION/web: a web-based ontology enrichment tool for lipidomic data analysis. *GigaScience* **2019**, *8*. [CrossRef] [PubMed]
133. Huan, T.; Forsberg, E.M.; Rinehart, D.; Johnson, C.H.; Ivanisevic, J.; Benton, H.P.; Fang, M.; Aisporna, A.; Hilmers, B.; Poole, F.L.; et al. Systems biology guided by XCMS Online metabolomics. *Nat. Methods* **2017**, *14*, 461. [CrossRef] [PubMed]
134. Wohlgemuth, G.; Haldiya, P.K.; Willighagen, E.; Kind, T.; Fiehn, O. The Chemical Translation Service–a web-based tool to improve standardization of metabolomic reports. *Bioinformatics* **2010**, *26*, 2647–2648. [CrossRef]
135. Cottret, L.; Wildridge, D.; Vinson, F.; Barrett, M.P.; Charles, H.; Sagot, M.F.; Jourdan, F. MetExplore: a web server to link metabolomic experiments and genome-scale metabolic networks. *Nucleic Acids Res.* **2010**, *38*, W132–W137. [CrossRef]
136. Wishart, D.S.; Knox, C.; Guo, A.C.; Eisner, R.; Young, N.; Gautam, B.; Hau, D.D.; Psychogios, N.; Dong, E.; Bouatra, S.; et al. HMDB: a knowledgebase for the human metabolome. *Nucleic Acids Res.* **2009**, *37*, 25. [CrossRef]
137. Wishart, D.S.; Feunang, Y.D.; Marcu, A.; Guo, A.C.; Liang, K.; Vázquez-Fresno, R.; Sajed, T.; Johnson, D.; Li, C.; Karu, N.; et al. HMDB 4.0: The human metabolome database for 2018. *Nucleic Acids Res.* **2018**, *46*, D608–D617. [CrossRef]
138. Goeman, J.; van de Geer, S.; Kort, F.; van Houwelingen, J. a global test for groups of genes: Testing association with a clinical outcome. *Bioinformatics* **2004**, *20*, 93–99. [CrossRef]
139. Kanehisa, M.; Furumichi, M.; Tanabe, M.; Sato, Y.; Morishima, K. KEGG: New perspectives on genomes, pathways, diseases and drugs. *Nucleic Acids Res.* **2017**, *45*, D353–D361. [CrossRef]
140. Fabregat, A.; Korninger, F.; Viteri, G.; Sidiropoulos, K.; Marin-Garcia, P.; Ping, P.; Wu, G.; Stein, L.; D'Eustachio, P.; Hermjakob, H. Reactome graph database: Efficient access to complex pathway data. *PLoS Comput. Biol.* **2018**, *14*, e1005968. [CrossRef]
141. Bohler, A.; Wu, G.; Kutmon, M.; Pradhana, L.A.; Coort, S.L.; Hanspers, K.; Haw, R.; Pico, A.R.; Evelo, C.T. Reactome from a WikiPathways Perspective. *PLoS Comput. Biol.* **2016**, *12*, e1004941. [CrossRef] [PubMed]
142. Caspi, R.; Billington, R.; Keseler, I.M.; Kothari, A.; Krummenacker, M.; Midford, P.E.; Ong, W.K.; Paley, S.; Subhraveti, P.; Karp, P.D. The MetaCyc database of metabolic pathways and enzymes-a 2019 update. *Nucleic Acids Res.* **2019**. [CrossRef] [PubMed]
143. Noronha, A.; Danielsdottir, A.D.; Gawron, P.; Johannsson, F.; Jonsdottir, S.; Jarlsson, S.; Gunnarsson, J.P.; Brynjolfsson, S.; Schneider, R.; Thiele, I.; et al. ReconMap: an interactive visualization of human metabolism. *Bioinformatics* **2017**, *33*, 605–607. [CrossRef] [PubMed]
144. Noronha, A.; Modamio, J.; Jarosz, Y.; Guerard, E.; Sompairac, N.; Preciat, G.; Daníelsdóttir, A.D.; Krecke, M.; Merten, D.; Haraldsdóttir, H.S.; et al. The Virtual Metabolic Human database: Integrating human and gut microbiome metabolism with nutrition and disease. *Nucleic Acids Res.* **2019**, *47*, D614–D624. [CrossRef]

145. Slenter, D.N.; Kutmon, M.; Hanspers, K.; Riutta, A.; Windsor, J.; Nunes, N.; Mélius, J.; Cirillo, E.; Coort, S.L.; Digles, D.; et al. WikiPathways: a multifaceted pathway database bridging metabolomics to other omics research. *Nucleic Acids Res.* **2018**, *46*, D661–D667. [CrossRef]
146. Kaza, M.; Karaźniewicz-Łada, M.; Kosicka, K.; Siemiątkowska, A.; Rudzki, P.J. Bioanalytical method validation: new FDA guidance vs. EMA guideline. Better or worse? *J. Pharm. Biomed. Anal.* **2019**, *165*, 381–385. [CrossRef]
147. Egertson, J.D.; MacLean, B.; Johnson, R.; Xuan, Y.; MacCoss, M.J. Multiplexed peptide analysis using data-independent acquisition and Skyline. *Nat. Protoc.* **2015**, *10*, 887–903. [CrossRef]

© 2019 by the authors. Licensee MDPI, Basel, Switzerland. This article is an open access article distributed under the terms and conditions of the Creative Commons Attribution (CC BY) license (http://creativecommons.org/licenses/by/4.0/).

Article

MetaboAnalystR 2.0: From Raw Spectra to Biological Insights

Jasmine Chong [1], Mai Yamamoto [1] and Jianguo Xia [1,2,*]

1. Institute of Parasitology, McGill University, Montreal, QC H3A 0G4, Canada; jasmine.chong@mail.mcgill.ca (J.C.); mai.yamamoto@mail.mcgill.ca (M.Y.)
2. Department of Animal Science, McGill University, Montreal, QC H3A 0G4, Canada
* Correspondence: jeff.xia@mcgill.ca; Tel.: +1-514-398-8668

Received: 5 March 2019; Accepted: 21 March 2019; Published: 22 March 2019

Abstract: Global metabolomics based on high-resolution liquid chromatography mass spectrometry (LC-MS) has been increasingly employed in recent large-scale multi-omics studies. Processing and interpretation of these complex metabolomics datasets have become a key challenge in current computational metabolomics. Here, we introduce MetaboAnalystR 2.0 for comprehensive LC-MS data processing, statistical analysis, and functional interpretation. Compared to the previous version, this new release seamlessly integrates XCMS and CAMERA to support raw spectral processing and peak annotation, and also features high-performance implementations of mummichog and GSEA approaches for predictions of pathway activities. The application and utility of the MetaboAnalystR 2.0 workflow were demonstrated using a synthetic benchmark dataset and a clinical dataset. In summary, MetaboAnalystR 2.0 offers a unified and flexible workflow that enables end-to-end analysis of LC-MS metabolomics data within the open-source R environment.

Keywords: global metabolomics; LC-MS; spectra processing; pathway analysis; enrichment analysis

1. Introduction

Metabolomics is the comprehensive study of all small molecule metabolites (<1500 Da) detected within a biological system. An individual's metabolic profile represents the functional product of interactions among genetics, lifestyle, environment, diet, and native microbiota, which closely reflects his or her health status [1,2]. The metabolome thus serves as the link between genotype and phenotype, and metabolomics will play a critical role in the development and implementation of precision medicine [3,4].

There are two general approaches in conducting metabolomics. Targeted metabolomics aim to study a predefined set of metabolites, requiring familiarity with the system [3]. Untargeted metabolomics, also known as global metabolomics, aim to measure the global set of metabolites within a sample without a prior knowledge of the system. A typical metabolomics analysis workflow involves three main steps: raw data processing, statistical analysis, and functional interpretation (Figure 1). Global metabolomics requires more sensitive analytics platforms to achieve comprehensive measurement. High-resolution liquid chromatography-mass spectrometry (LC-MS) systems is currently the main workhorse for global metabolomics. The platform often generates thousands of signals, including true biological signals from metabolites, their adducts, fragments, and isotopes, as well as noise signals from contaminants and artifacts [5]. Computational tools able to significantly reduce noise in MS spectra are crucial for more meaningful downstream analyses [6].

There are several powerful computational workflows including commercial tools such as Mass Profiler (Agilent Technologies) and Compound Discoverer (Thermo Scientific), cloud-based software such as XCMS Online [7] and Workflow4Metabolomics [8], desktop software such as MZmine2 [9], MS-DIAL [10], and Open-MS [11], and finally R packages such as MAIT [12] and metaX [13]. Most of these software focus on addressing one of the two main tasks: spectral processing or statistical analysis. Consequently, users must often learn several tools to meet their data analysis needs. Due to compatibility issues, users often have to write scripts to convert outputs from one tool in order to use another tool.

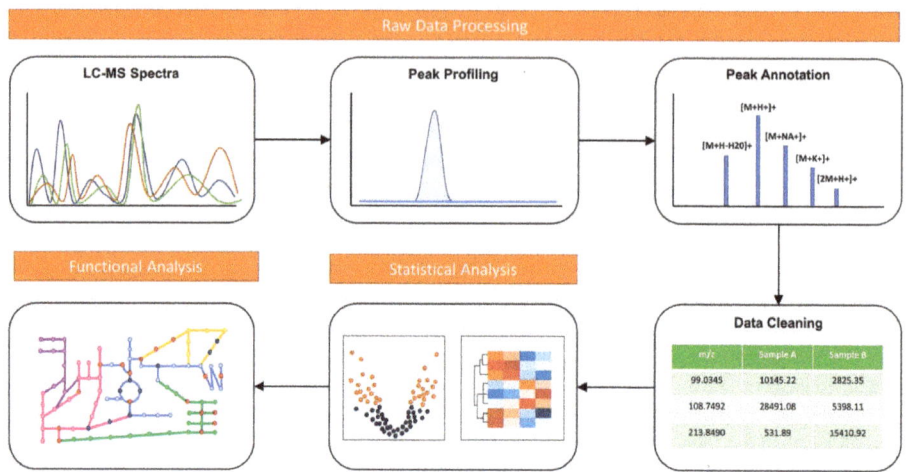

Figure 1. A typical metabolomics data analysis workflow including raw data processing, statistical analysis and functional interpretation.

Tools for functional interpretation of global metabolomics data is in general lacking or poorly addressed [14,15]. A prerequisite for metabolomics data interpretation is metabolite identification, thereby permitting the contextualization of annotated peaks in metabolic pathways and their integration with other omics data. However, even with high mass accuracy afforded by the current high-resolution MS platforms, it is often impossible to uniquely identify a given peak based on its mass alone [16]. Researchers usually need to manually search compound databases and then perform further experimental validations such as tandem MS. Novel bioinformatics tools are urgently needed to enable researchers to gain biological insights with a minimum amount of manual efforts. To get around this bottleneck, a key concept is to shift the unit of analysis from individual compounds to individual pathways or a group of functionally related compounds (i.e., metabolite sets [17]). The general assumption is that the collective behavior of a group is more robust against a certain degree of random errors of individuals. The mummichog algorithm is the first implementation of this concept to infer pathway activities from a ranked MS peaks [18]. The original algorithm implements an over-representation analysis (ORA) method to evaluate pathway-level enrichment based on significant peaks. An alternative approach is the Gene Set Enrichment Analysis (GSEA) method, which is widely used to test enriched functions from ranked gene lists [19]. Unlike ORA, GSEA considers the overall ranks of features without using a significance cutoff. It can detect subtle and consistent changes which could be missed from using ORA methods. Despite its widespread applications in gene expression profiling, it has not yet been applied to global metabolomics.

MetaboAnalyst is one of the most widely used tools for statistical and functional analysis of metabolomics data [20–23]. It was initially designed for targeted metabolomics, and subsequent releases gradually introduced many statistical methods applicable to both targeted and untargeted metabolomics. Due to its web-based implementation, there is very limited support for raw spectra processing and peak annotation. The most recent update (version 4.0) was released with a companion R package, MetaboAnalystR (v1.0), to help tackle issues associated with workflow customization, reproducibility, and handling large datasets [24].

Here, we present MetaboAnalystR (v2.0) to address the two important gaps left in its previous version: (1) raw spectral processing - we have implemented comprehensive support for raw LC-MS spectral data processing including peak picking, peak alignment, and peak annotations; and (2) functional interpretation directly from m/z peaks - in addition to an efficient implementation of the mummichog algorithm [18], we have added a new method to support pathway activity prediction based on the well-established GSEA algorithm [19]. We showcase the performance of these new functions through two case studies.

2. Results

MetaboAnalystR 2.0 consists of a series of flexible R functions that can take a variety of user-supplied data and parameters to perform end-to-end metabolomics data analysis. The source code is freely available at the GitHub repository (https://github.com/xia-lab/MetaboAnalystR). Detailed instructions, tutorials, troubleshooting tips, example datasets, and analyses discussed in this paper are also available in this repository.

To demonstrate the utility of MetaboAnalystR 2.0 workflow, we present the results from two case studies: (i) a synthetic benchmark dataset to evaluate the raw MS spectra processing functions, with a focus on its peak detection and quantification performance; and (ii) a clinical pediatric inflammatory bowel disease (IBD) dataset to showcase the overall workflow, with a focus on its capacity to provide biological insights. All R scripts to perform the entire metabolomics data analysis pipeline are available from the MetaboAnalystR GitHub repository under the section "Case Studies". The accompanying vignette ("The MetaboAnalystR 2.0 Workflow") provides a step-by-step tutorial to demonstrate how to use MetaboAnalystR 2.0 to perform an end-to-end metabolomics data analysis on a subset of 12 of the 48 clinical IBD samples. This tutorial was created on a Dell XPS 9570 laptop running Ubuntu 16.04 with 16 GB of memory. The total running time of the tutorial was 14 min, averaging ~1.25 min per sample, using 6 cores in parallel and 10.5 GB of memory.

2.1. Benchmark Case Study

We first demonstrate the accuracy of the raw data preprocessing module using a benchmark dataset comprised of a mixture of 1100 known compounds ranging in size from 100 to 1300 Da [25]. The original study used a targeted analysis to obtain their benchmark feature list, which we used as the ground truth to evaluate our workflow. As shown in Table 1, the original study detected 35,215 peaks using XCMS Online, with 820 classified as true features. Using the same data preprocessing parameters as published, MetaboAnalystR 2.0 detected 21,013 peaks from the benchmark data. Among them, 732 matched the true features based on m/z and retention time (10 ppm and 0.3 min RT tolerance). Next, we compared the number of accurately quantified true features using MetaboAnalystR 2.0 to those from the original manuscript using XCMS Online (Table 1). Features were accurately quantified if their fold changes had a <20% relative error as compared to the benchmark data. MetaboAnalystR 2.0 accurately quantified 632 features and identified 45 truly discriminating features.

Table 1. Comparison of peak identification and quantification accuracies using the benchmark dataset between MetaboAnalystR 2.0 and the original manuscript using XCMS Online.

	Methods	Features Detected	True Features		
			Total	Accurately Quantified	Discriminating
Li et al. 2018 [25]	Targeted	-	836	836	-
	Untargeted (XCMS Online)	35215	820	731	45
MetaboAnalystR 2.0	Untargeted	21013	732	632	45

2.2. IBD Case Study

The 48 fecal samples were obtained from 24 pediatric Crohn's Disease (CD) patients and 24 pediatric healthy controls (Table S1). Our workflow detected 8187 features which were further reduced to 6930 features after filtering out isotopes and features missing in >50% of samples. After exclusion of low-variance features, a total of 4113 features were analyzed using the standard MetaboAnalystR functions.

Mann–Whitney U test and fold change analysis detected 59 features that were significantly different between CD and healthy controls. Differences between CD and healthy controls were evaluated using PCA, PLS-DA, and OPLS-DA. The PCA showed an overlapping of clusters along the first two components, with CD exhibiting a wider data distribution (Figure S1). This indicates an overall similarity of the metabolic profiles between CD and healthy controls but larger heterogeneity within CD patients. The PLS-DA score plot showed a clear separation between the two groups (Figure S2). Ten-fold cross validation of two PLS-DA components gave an $R2$ of 0.912 and $Q2$ of 0.424 (Figure S3). The OPLS-DA score plot shows a clear separation between CD and healthy controls (Figure 2) with an R2Y of 0.979 and Q2 of 0.522, respectively. To further evaluate the model, we performed permutation tests ($n = 1000$). The empirical p values were 0.026 for R2Y and <0.001 for Q2. Altogether, a clear distinction between the metabolome of CD and healthy controls was observed.

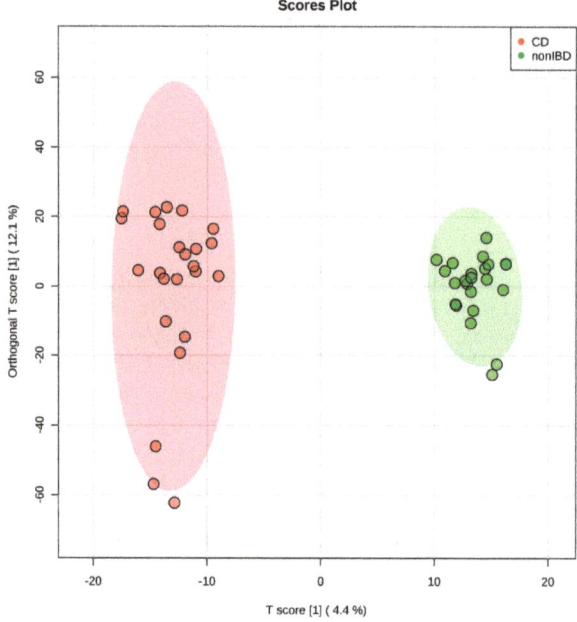

Figure 2. The OPLS-DA score plot based on the stool metabolome of 24 pediatric Crohn's disease patients and 24 healthy children

To gain potential biological insights from the global metabolomics data, we applied both mummichog and GSEA algorithms and integrated their results (Figure 3). Mummichog suggested that differentially abundant features between CD and healthy patients were associated with perturbations in bile acid biosynthesis and fatty acid activation, as well as vitamin E, fatty acid, and vitamin D3 metabolism. The GSEA algorithm also identified alterations in bile acid biosynthesis. Moreover, it identified differences in androgen and estrogen biosynthesis and metabolism, squalene and cholesterol biosynthesis, biopterin metabolism, and butyrate metabolism. More details of the top 5 enriched pathways from both methods are given in Table 2.

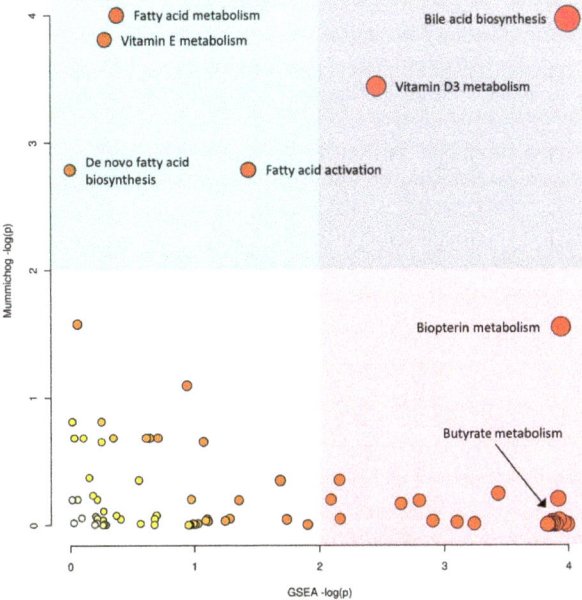

Figure 3. The scatter plot integrating GSEA (x-axis) and mummichog (y-axis) pathway analysis results. The size and color of the circles correspond to their transformed combined *p*-values. The blue and pink areas highlight significant pathways based on either GSEA (pink) or mummichog (blue).

Table 2. The top five enriched metabolic pathways identified using the mummichog algorithm (*PerformMummichog*) and GSEA (*PerformGSEA*) in MetaboAnalystR 2.0.

	Mummichog			GSEA		
Pathway Name	Compound Hits *	*p*-Value	Pathway Name	Compound Hits	*p*-Value
Bile acid biosynthesis	29/52	0.00282	Bile acid biosynthesis	52	0.001761
Vitamin E metabolism	20/33	0.00356	Androgen and estrogen biosynthesis and metabolism	10	0.01465
Fatty acid metabolism	9/11	0.00268	Squalene and cholesterol biosynthesis	7	0.02214
Vitamin D3 metabolism	8/10	0.00616	Biopterin metabolism	14	0.07806
Fatty acid activation	10/15	0.01620	Butyrate metabolism	11	0.08318

* The mummichog compound hits represent the number of significant compounds divided by the total number of compound hits per pathway.

Interestingly, the GSEA algorithm identified Butyrate metabolism as a significantly enriched pathway, whereas the mummichog algorithm did not. Further inspection (Figure S4) indicated that the mummichog algorithm only utilized the three significant *m/z* features to calculate the enrichment score; while GSEA utilized all 20 compound hits (corresponding to 38 *m/z* features). Of these features, 145.04962 *m/z* was putatively annotated as (S)-2-Aceto-2-hydroxybutanoate (a deprotonated ion), as was 205.07102 *m/z* (a formic acid adduct). Furthermore, 124.03917 *m/z* corresponded to 2-Butynoate.

This demonstrates the ability of GSEA to pick up on subtle changes, such as perturbations in Butyrate metabolism, and the utility of using both algorithms to gain biological insights.

We further examined the 17 features that overlap between the putatively annotated features in the pathway analysis and the important features found in univariate statistical analysis. Notably, 431.3164 m/z was putatively annotated as a deprotonated ion of 3-β, 7-α-dihydroxy-5-cholestenoate based on its correspondence to the exact mass of C17336 from the KEGG database [26]. This compound is found in the primary bile acid pathway. Additionally, the same mass also corresponds to a deprotonated ion of 23S, 25, 26-trihydroxyvitamin D3 (CE2202). Exact identification of this feature requires further experiments, which is beyond the scope of this manuscript. In addition to this compound, five additional compounds out of the 17 have been previously found as stool metabolites in the context of IBD [27]. Representative EICs, boxplots, and corresponding information, such as m/z, retention time, and p-values, are highlighted in the Supplemental Materials (Figure S5).

3. Discussion

In this paper, we have described the new functions introduced in MetaboAnalystR 2.0 to support global metabolomics data analysis, covering raw LC-MS spectra processing to generation of biological insights. These functions were showcased through two case studies.

For the benchmark dataset, despite applying the same parameters used by Li et al. [25], we were unable to reproduce the identification and quantification performance obtained by the original authors using XCMS Online. Their setup detected >14,000 (68%) more features compared to those obtained using our pipeline. We tried several options, including the suggested parameters for a HPLC or UPLC coupled with a Q Exactive HF mass spectrometer. We posit this incongruity arose because the authors did not specify the exact peak width used, which is a critical parameter for peak picking. Additionally, the data conversion step from .RAW to mzML used in our workflow may have resulted in a slight difference in the input data when compared to the data conversion used in XCMS Online. It is also important to note that our workflow integrated the latest version of XCMS (version 3.4.4), which has introduced many new functionalities and updates in existing functions. Overall, our preprocessing workflow performed well, executing peak picking, annotation, and filtering on the eight benchmark samples in less than twenty minutes.

For the IBD case study, we observed a clear separation in the metabolomic profiles between pediatric CD patients and healthy controls using either PLS-DA or OPLS-DA. Furthermore, our analysis highlighted several metabolic pathways associated with CD, without performing accurate metabolite identification. For instance, alterations in bile acid biosynthesis and short-chain fatty acids metabolism are well known among IBD patients [28,29]. Combining the results of pathway analysis and statistical analysis also putatively identified some promising metabolic features that could be used to as potential biomarkers. In addition to bile acids, vitamin D has been shown to play an immunomodulatory role in IBD pathogenesis [30]. Taken together, this use case demonstrates the ease of which MetaboAnalystR 2.0 can be utilized to gain mechanistic insights and generate hypotheses for future experimental validation.

MetaboAnalystR 2.0 has addressed the needs for high throughput raw spectra processing and inferring pathway dysregulation directly from high-resolution MS1 data. A future direction of our workflow includes the integration of MS2 data to support targeted annotations for important peaks assigned to pathways of interest. The function will be developed in coordination with the MetaboAnalyst web server to provide online visual analytics support for molecular networking [31].

4. Conclusions

The previous version (v1.0) of MetaboAnalystR features comprehensive normalization and statistical methods inherited from the MetaboAnalyst web server. The version 2.0 not only integrates XCMS and CAMERA to support raw MS spectral processing and peak annotation, but also implements mummichog and GSEA methods for prediction of pathway activities. The performance of this workflow was evaluated on a published benchmark dataset as well as a recent clinical study on IBD. The MetaboAnalystR package is maintained in conjunction with the cloud-based MetaboAnalyst web application and is under continuous development based on the community feedback. Our next focus is on integration with MS2 data as well as development of a Galaxy-based platform for raw data processing [32].

5. Materials and Methods

5.1. Spectral Processing

Three main wrapper functions have been implemented for metabolomics data processing based on XCMS (version 3.4.4) and CAMERA (version 1.38.1) [33–35] including: (i) the *ImportRawMSData* function for reading in raw data files, (ii) the *PerformPeakProfiling* function for peak picking and alignment, and (iii) the *PerformPeakAnnotation* function for annotating isotopes and adducts in processed m/z data. These functions are described below in further detail.

The *ImportRawMSData* function reads in raw MS data files and saves it as an *OnDiskMSnExp* object. To avoid potential memory issues on a user's desktop/laptop, the function will limit the number of cores used to half of the available number of cores. The function outputs two plots: the Total Ion Chromatogram (TIC), which provides an overview of the entire spectra, and the Base Peak Chromatogram (BPC), which is a cleaner profile of the spectra based on the most abundant signals. These plots are useful to inform the setting of parameters downstream. For users who wish to view a peak of interest, an Extracted Ion Chromatogram (EIC) can be generated using the *PlotEIC* function.

The *PerformPeakProfiling* function is a wrapper of several XCMS R functions that performs peak detection, alignment, and grouping in a single step. The resulting peaks are outputted as a *XCMSnExp* object. The function also generates two diagnostic plots including a retention time adjustment map, and a PCA plot showing the overall sample clustering prior to data cleaning and statistical analysis. Users can specify several parameters such as the mass accuracy, peak width, and retention time range using the *SetPeakParam* function to optimize the peak picking function. A detailed table of suggested parameters for common LC-MS platforms is provided in Table S2.

The *PerformPeakAnnotation* function annotates isotope and adduct peaks using the CAMERA package [35]. CAMERA matches m/z features to potential isotopes and adducts based on mass using a dynamic rule set. It does not utilize any spectral databases to perform annotation. It outputs the result as a CSV file ("annotated_peaklist.csv") and saves the annotated peaks as an *xsAnnotate* object. Finally, the peak list is formatted to the correct structure for MetaboAnalystR and filtered based upon user's specifications using the *FormatPeakList* function. This function permits the filtering of adducts (i.e., removal of all adducts except for $[M + H]^+/[M - H]^-$) and filtering of isotopes (i.e., removal of all isotopes except for monoisotopic peaks). The goal of filtering peaks is to remove degenerative signals and to reduce the file size.

5.2. Prediction of Pathway Activities

Several metabolic databases are supported at the moment including KEGG [26], BioCyc [36], etc. The main mummichog algorithm is available in the *PerformMummichog* function. Users need to specify a pre-defined cutoff based on either t-statistics or fold changes. The *PerformGSEA* function contains the GSEA implementation based on the high-performance *fgsea* R package [37].

5.3. Benchmark Case Studies

The benchmark data created by Li et al. 2018 [25] is comprised of two standard mixtures (A and B) consisting of 1100 known compounds, with four replicates per mixture. The link to this raw dataset is available in Table S3. For this manuscript, we selected the dataset that was generated from a Q Exactive HF mass spectrometry (Thermo Fisher Scientific) in positive ion mode, coupled with a Dionex UltiMate 3000 HPLC equipped with a ZORBAX Eclipse Plus C18 column (Agilent Technologies). Parameters for our workflow were selected based on the default values provided for HPLC-Q Exactive Orbitrap data on XCMS Online (mass error: 5 ppm and peak width: 10-60 s).

The second dataset consists of pediatric IBD stool samples obtained from the Integrative Human Microbiome Project Consortium (iHMP) [38]. The original study included samples longitudinally collected from IBD patients and non-IBD controls over 50 weeks. The link to this raw dataset is provided in Table S3. For our evaluation purpose, we collected samples that met the following criteria for the diseased group: (i) age between 6 and 19, and (ii) diagnosed with Crohn's disease. Samples obtained at the earliest clinical visit of each patient who met criteria (i) and (ii) were included in our study. For the healthy control, samples of non-IBD individuals between age 6 and 19 collected during their first and second clinical visits were included. The dataset was generated from a Q-Exactive Plus Orbitrap mass spectrometer (Thermo Fisher Scientific) in negative ion mode, coupled with a Nexera X2-U-HPLC system (Shimadzu Scientific Instruments) equipped with an ACQUITY BEH C18 column (Waters).

All raw data in .RAW format were converted into .mzML format using ProteoWizard 3.0 MSConvert [39] with parameters summarized in the supplemental Materials (Table S4). Following the spectral processing described earlier, data cleaning and statistical analysis were performed on the clinical data using various functions within MetaboAnalystR. Firstly, missing value imputation was performed by replacing them with half of the minimum value found for each feature. Features containing more than 50% missing values across all samples were excluded. Features with nearly constant values across samples were also filtered out based on the inter quantile range (IQR), which removed approximately 25% of total features. Subsequently, value of each feature was normalized with the median value of all features per sample to account for variable water content of stool samples. Finally, generalized log-transformation and auto-scaling were applied to data prior to multivariate statistical analysis. For univariate analysis, non-parametric methods (i.e., Mann–Whitney U test and fold change calculation) were applied to untransformed data to avoid false positives due to data manipulation [40]. A minimum fold change >2 and <0.5, and a false discovery rate (FDR) adjusted p-value of 0.05 were used as cut-off values. To infer pathway activities, we applied both mummichog and GSEA to predict pathway activities. The human BiGG and Edinburgh Model (hsa_mfn) library was selected as the pathway database, with the p-value cutoff set to 0.05 and the instrumentation accuracy set to 5 ppm.

Supplementary Materials: The following are available online at http://www.mdpi.com/2218-1989/9/3/57/s1, Table S1: Characteristics of pediatric IBD patients and healthy controls included in this study; Table S2: Suggested peak picking parameters for commonly used LC-MS platforms; Table S3: Raw datasets used in the Case Studies; Table S4: Parameters used to convert .RAW files to mzML format on ProteoWizard MSConvert; Figure S1: PCA plot of pediatric IBD stool metabolome. Data including 4113 features were median-normalized, log-transformed, and auto-scaled; Figure S2: PLS-DA plot of pediatric IBD stool metabolome. Data including 4113 features were median-normalized, log-transformed, and auto-scaled; Figure S3: Ten-fold cross validation of PLS-DA model (Figure S3) generated from the pediatric IBD stool metabolome data; Figure S4: Boxplots of m/z features used for functional interpretation; Figure S5: Representative EICs and boxplots of compounds differentially excreted in stool samples of healthy children and pediatric CD patients based on pathway analysis and Mann–Whitney U test (FDR adjusted p-value < 0.05).

Author Contributions: Conceptualization, J.X.; Data curation, M.Y.; Formal analysis, J.C. and M.Y.; Funding acquisition, J.X.; Methodology, J.C., M.Y. and J.X.; Supervision, J.X.; Writing—original draft, J.C. and M.Y.; Writing—review & editing, J.X.

Funding: This research was funded by Genome Canada, Génome Québec, Natural Sciences and Engineering Research Council of Canada (NSERC), and Canada Research Chairs (CRC) Program.

Acknowledgments: We gratefully acknowledge the developers of XCMS and CAMERA, Steffen Neumann and Johannes Rainer, for their valuable contribution to the metabolomics community.

Conflicts of Interest: The authors declare no conflicts of interests.

References

1. Beger, R.D.; Dunn, W.; Schmidt, M.A.; Gross, S.S.; Kirwan, J.A.; Cascante, M.; Brennan, L.; Wishart, D.S.; Oresic, M.; Hankemeier, T. Metabolomics enables precision medicine: "A white paper, community perspective". *Metabolomics* **2016**, *12*, 149. [CrossRef] [PubMed]
2. Wishart, D.S. Emerging applications of metabolomics in drug discovery and precision medicine. *Nat. Rev. Drug Discov.* **2016**, *15*, 473. [CrossRef] [PubMed]
3. Johnson, C.H.; Ivanisevic, J.; Siuzdak, G. Metabolomics: Beyond biomarkers and towards mechanisms. *Nat. Rev. Mol. Cell biol.* **2016**, *17*, 451. [CrossRef] [PubMed]
4. Fiehn, O. Metabolomics—The link between genotypes and phenotypes. In *Functional Genomics*; Springer: Berlin/Heidelberg, Germany, 2002; pp. 155–171.
5. Nash, W.J.; Dunn, W.B. From mass to metabolite in human untargeted metabolomics: Recent advances in annotation of metabolites applying liquid chromatography-mass spectrometry data. *TrAC Trends Anal. Chem.* **2018**. [CrossRef]
6. Uppal, K.; Walker, D.I.; Liu, K.; Li, S.; Go, Y.-M.; Jones, D.P. Computational metabolomics: A framework for the million metabolome. *Chem. Res. Toxicol.* **2016**, *29*, 1956–1975. [CrossRef]
7. Forsberg, E.M.; Huan, T.; Rinehart, D.; Benton, H.P.; Warth, B.; Hilmers, B.; Siuzdak, G. Data processing, multi-omic pathway mapping, and metabolite activity analysis using XCMS Online. *Nat. Protoc.* **2018**, *13*, 633. [CrossRef] [PubMed]
8. Giacomoni, F.; Le Corguillé, G.; Monsoor, M.; Landi, M.; Pericard, P.; Pétéra, M.; Duperier, C.; Tremblay-Franco, M.; Martin, J.-F.; Jacob, D. Workflow4Metabolomics: A collaborative research infrastructure for computational metabolomics. *Bioinformatics* **2014**, *31*, 1493–1495. [CrossRef]
9. Pluskal, T.; Castillo, S.; Villar-Briones, A.; Oresic, M. MZmine 2: Modular framework for processing, visualizing, and analyzing mass spectrometry-based molecular profile data. *BMC Bioinform.* **2010**, *11*, 395. [CrossRef] [PubMed]
10. Tsugawa, H.; Cajka, T.; Kind, T.; Ma, Y.; Higgins, B.; Ikeda, K.; Kanazawa, M.; VanderGheynst, J.; Fiehn, O.; Arita, M. MS-DIAL: Data-independent MS/MS deconvolution for comprehensive metabolome analysis. *Nat. Methods* **2015**, *12*, 523–526. [CrossRef]
11. Rost, H.L.; Sachsenberg, T.; Aiche, S.; Bielow, C.; Weisser, H.; Aicheler, F.; Andreotti, S.; Ehrlich, H.C.; Gutenbrunner, P.; Kenar, E.; et al. OpenMS: A flexible open-source software platform for mass spectrometry data analysis. *Nat. Methods* **2016**, *13*, 741–748. [CrossRef]
12. Fernández-Albert, F.; Llorach, R.; Andrés-Lacueva, C.; Perera, A. An R package to analyse LC/MS metabolomic data: MAIT (Metabolite Automatic Identification Toolkit). *Bioinformatics* **2014**, *30*, 1937–1939. [CrossRef] [PubMed]
13. Wen, B.; Mei, Z.; Zeng, C.; Liu, S. metaX: A flexible and comprehensive software for processing metabolomics data. *BMC Bioinform.* **2017**, *18*, 183. [CrossRef] [PubMed]
14. Xia, J. Computational Strategies for Biological Interpretation of Metabolomics Data. *Adv. Exp. Med. Biol.* **2017**, *965*, 191–206. [CrossRef] [PubMed]
15. Gardinassi, L.G.; Xia, J.; Safo, S.E.; Li, S. Bioinformatics Tools for the Interpretation of Metabolomics Data. *Curr. Pharmacol. Rep.* **2017**, *3*, 374–383. [CrossRef]
16. Kind, T.; Fiehn, O. Seven Golden Rules for heuristic filtering of molecular formulas obtained by accurate mass spectrometry. *BMC Bioinform.* **2007**, *8*, 105. [CrossRef] [PubMed]
17. Xia, J.; Wishart, D.S. MSEA: A web-based tool to identify biologically meaningful patterns in quantitative metabolomic data. *Nucleic Acids Res.* **2010**, *38*, W71–W77. [CrossRef]
18. Li, S.; Park, Y.; Duraisingham, S.; Strobel, F.H.; Khan, N.; Soltow, Q.A.; Jones, D.P.; Pulendran, B. Predicting network activity from high throughput metabolomics. *PLoS Comput. Biol.* **2013**, *9*, e1003123. [CrossRef] [PubMed]
19. Subramanian, A.; Tamayo, P.; Mootha, V.K.; Mukherjee, S.; Ebert, B.L.; Gillette, M.A.; Paulovich, A.; Pomeroy, S.L.; Golub, T.R.; Lander, E.S.; et al. Gene set enrichment analysis: A knowledge-based approach for interpreting genome-wide expression profiles. *Proc. Natl. Acad. Sci. USA* **2005**, *102*, 15545–15550. [CrossRef]
20. Xia, J.; Psychogios, N.; Young, N.; Wishart, D.S. MetaboAnalyst: A web server for metabolomic data analysis and interpretation. *Nucleic Acids Res.* **2009**, *37*, W652–W660. [CrossRef]
21. Xia, J.; Mandal, R.; Sinelnikov, I.V.; Broadhurst, D.; Wishart, D.S. MetaboAnalyst 2.0—A comprehensive server for metabolomic data analysis. *Nucleic Acids Res.* **2012**, *40*, W127–W133. [CrossRef]

22. Xia, J.; Sinelnikov, I.V.; Han, B.; Wishart, D.S. MetaboAnalyst 3.0—making metabolomics more meaningful. *Nucleic Acids Res.* **2015**, *43*, W251–W257. [CrossRef]
23. Chong, J.; Soufan, O.; Li, C.; Caraus, I.; Li, S.; Bourque, G.; Wishart, D.S.; Xia, J. MetaboAnalyst 4.0: Towards more transparent and integrative metabolomics analysis. *Nucleic Acids Res.* **2018**, *46*, W486–W494. [CrossRef]
24. Chong, J.; Xia, J. MetaboAnalystR: An R package for flexible and reproducible analysis of metabolomics data. *Bioinformatics* **2018**, *34*, 4313–4314. [CrossRef]
25. Li, Z.; Lu, Y.; Guo, Y.; Cao, H.; Wang, Q.; Shui, W. Comprehensive evaluation of untargeted metabolomics data processing software in feature detection, quantification and discriminating marker selection. *Anal. Chim. Acta* **2018**, *1029*, 50–57. [CrossRef] [PubMed]
26. Kanehisa, M.; Goto, S.; Sato, Y.; Furumichi, M.; Tanabe, M. KEGG for integration and interpretation of large-scale molecular data sets. *Nucleic Acids Res.* **2011**, *40*, D109–D114. [CrossRef]
27. Franzosa, E.A.; Sirota-Madi, A.; Avila-Pacheco, J.; Fornelos, N.; Haiser, H.J.; Reinker, S.; Vatanen, T.; Hall, A.B.; Mallick, H.; McIver, L.J.; et al. Gut microbiome structure and metabolic activity in inflammatory bowel disease. *Nat. Microbiol.* **2019**, *4*, 293–305. [CrossRef]
28. Duboc, H.; Rajca, S.; Rainteau, D.; Benarous, D.; Maubert, M.-A.; Quervain, E.; Thomas, G.; Barbu, V.; Humbert, L.; Despras, G. Connecting dysbiosis, bile-acid dysmetabolism and gut inflammation in inflammatory bowel diseases. *Gut* **2013**, *62*, 531–539. [CrossRef]
29. Hofmann, A.; Hagey, L. Bile acids: Chemistry, pathochemistry, biology, pathobiology, and therapeutics. *Cell. Mol. Life Sci.* **2008**, *65*, 2461–2483. [CrossRef]
30. Limketkai, B.N.; Mullin, G.E.; Limsui, D.; Parian, A.M. Role of vitamin D in inflammatory bowel disease. *Nutr. Clin. Pract.* **2017**, *32*, 337–345. [CrossRef]
31. Wang, M.; Carver, J.J.; Phelan, V.V.; Sanchez, L.M.; Garg, N.; Peng, Y.; Nguyen, D.D.; Watrous, J.; Kapono, C.A.; Luzzatto-Knaan, T.; et al. Sharing and community curation of mass spectrometry data with Global Natural Products Social Molecular Networking. *Nat. Biotechnol.* **2016**, *34*, 828–837. [CrossRef]
32. Afgan, E.; Baker, D.; Batut, B.; van den Beek, M.; Bouvier, D.; Cech, M.; Chilton, J.; Clements, D.; Coraor, N.; Gruning, B.A.; et al. The Galaxy platform for accessible, reproducible and collaborative biomedical analyses: 2018 update. *Nucleic Acids Res.* **2018**, *46*, W537–W544. [CrossRef] [PubMed]
33. Tautenhahn, R.; Boettcher, C.; Neumann, S. Highly sensitive feature detection for high resolution LC/MS. *BMC Bioinform.* **2008**, *9*, 504. [CrossRef] [PubMed]
34. Benton, H.P.; Want, E.J.; Ebbels, T.M. Correction of mass calibration gaps in liquid chromatography-mass spectrometry metabolomics data. *Bioinformatics* **2010**, *26*, 2488–2489. [CrossRef]
35. Kuhl, C.; Tautenhahn, R.; Bottcher, C.; Larson, T.R.; Neumann, S. CAMERA: An integrated strategy for compound spectra extraction and annotation of liquid chromatography/mass spectrometry data sets. *Anal. Chem.* **2011**, *84*, 283–289. [CrossRef] [PubMed]
36. Karp, P.D.; Billington, R.; Caspi, R.; Fulcher, C.A.; Latendresse, M.; Kothari, A.; Keseler, I.M.; Krummenacker, M.; Midford, P.E.; Ong, Q.; et al. The BioCyc collection of microbial genomes and metabolic pathways. *Brief. Bioinform.* **2017**. [CrossRef] [PubMed]
37. Sergushichev, A. An algorithm for fast preranked gene set enrichment analysis using cumulative statistic calculation. *BioRxiv* **2016**. [CrossRef]
38. Consortium, I.H.i.R.N. The Integrative Human Microbiome Project: Dynamic analysis of microbiome-host omics profiles during periods of human health and disease. *Cell Host Microbe* **2014**, *16*, 276.
39. Holman, J.D.; Tabb, D.L.; Mallick, P. Employing ProteoWizard to convert raw mass spectrometry data. *Curr. Protoc. Bioinform.* **2014**, *46*, 13.24.1–13.24.9.
40. Di Guida, R.; Engel, J.; Allwood, J.W.; Weber, R.J.; Jones, M.R.; Sommer, U.; Viant, M.R.; Dunn, W.B. Non-targeted UHPLC-MS metabolomic data processing methods: A comparative investigation of normalisation, missing value imputation, transformation and scaling. *Metabolomics* **2016**, *12*, 93. [CrossRef]

© 2019 by the authors. Licensee MDPI, Basel, Switzerland. This article is an open access article distributed under the terms and conditions of the Creative Commons Attribution (CC BY) license (http://creativecommons.org/licenses/by/4.0/).

Review

Metabolic Modeling of Human Gut Microbiota on a Genome Scale: An Overview

Partho Sen [1,2,*] and Matej Orešič [1,2]

1. Turku Centre for Biotechnology, University of Turku and Åbo Akademi University, FI-20520 Turku, Finland; matej.oresic@utu.fi
2. School of Medical Sciences, Örebro University, 702 81 Örebro, Sweden
* Correspondence: partho.sen@utu.fi; Tel.: +358-469608145

Received: 25 November 2018; Accepted: 24 January 2019; Published: 28 January 2019

Abstract: There is growing interest in the metabolic interplay between the gut microbiome and host metabolism. Taxonomic and functional profiling of the gut microbiome by next-generation sequencing (NGS) has unveiled substantial richness and diversity. However, the mechanisms underlying interactions between diet, gut microbiome and host metabolism are still poorly understood. Genome-scale metabolic modeling (GSMM) is an emerging approach that has been increasingly applied to infer diet–microbiome, microbe–microbe and host–microbe interactions under physiological conditions. GSMM can, for example, be applied to estimate the metabolic capabilities of microbes in the gut. Here, we discuss how meta-omics datasets such as shotgun metagenomics, can be processed and integrated to develop large-scale, condition-specific, personalized microbiota models in healthy and disease states. Furthermore, we summarize various tools and resources available for metagenomic data processing and GSMM, highlighting the experimental approaches needed to validate the model predictions.

Keywords: gut microbiome; meta-omics; metagenomics; metabolomics; metabolic reconstructions; genome-scale metabolic modeling; constraint-based modeling; flux balance; host–microbiome; metabolism

---

1. Introduction

The human gut microbiome consists of trillions of microorganisms such as bacteria, archaea, and unicellular eukaryotes [1,2]. Most gut microbes are facultative obligate anaerobes spanning between five different phyla (Bacteriodetes, Firmicutes, Proteobacteria, Verrumicrobia, and Actinobacteria), with over 1000 species already identified [3]. Several collaborative studies and large consortia such as MetaHIT [4,5], the Human Microbiome Project (HMP) [6,7], and American Gut [8] have taxonomically and functionally profiled the gut microbiome in healthy and various disease states. The composition of the gut microbiota is relatively simple at birth, it undergoes a series of changes in composition, metabolic functions and eventually matures between 3–5 years of age [9]. For any one individual, the composition of the gut microbiome tends to be stable over time. Interestingly, there is a difference in the composition of the gut microbiome within a human population [10–12]. Several genetic and environmental factors such as diet, lifestyle, geography, mode of delivery, infection, infant feeding modality (e.g. formula versus breastfed) and medication attribute to these differences, and thereby, shape the gut microbiota during the early stages of life [2,9,13].

The gut microbiome acts as an auxiliary metabolic organ. Several complex carbohydrates, not digested by the host intestinal enzymes, are passed to the microbial community, which are then metabolized in the large intestine [14,15]. The gut microbiota is involved in metabolism of short-chain fatty acid (SCFAs), branched chain fatty acids (BCFAs), branched chain amino acids (BCAAs), biogenic amines, vitamins, bile acids (BAs), and xenobiotics, as well as the production of gases (e.g., CO_2, CH_4) [16–18]. Gut microbes also affect the host immune system, such as by regulating immune homeostasis versus autoimmunity [19]. Studies in germ-free mice suggest that gut microbiota can induce toll-like receptor (TLR) expression, antigen presenting cells (APCs), and differentiated $CD4^+$ T cells [20]. It also maintains the stability of the immune system by providing resistance against pathogens.

Our understanding of the gut microbiome and its role in health and disease has considerably improved with the advent of high-throughput meta-omics technologies. The wealth of data generated by the gut microbiome research, however, begs the development of novel computational tools and mathematical models. Such tools have already enabled researchers to begin exploring complexities of the gut microbiome (Table 1). Several approaches, such as 16S rRNA amplicon sequencing and whole genome shotgun metagenomics sequencing (WGS) have already been used for profiling gut microbes [21]. However, such genome-centric approaches are themselves unable to provide mechanistic insights at the level of individual species, their interactions with other gut flora, and their impact on host metabolism [14,22,23].

Genome-scale metabolic modeling (GSMM), a constraint-based mathematical modeling approach has been increasingly used to study gut ecosystems, attempting to elucidate the microbial metabolic interactions with each other and their host [15,24–26]. Recently, genome-scale models (GEMs) of catalogued human gut microbes [4,27], based on their metabolic functions, were developed. GEMs can integrate multiple type of biological information within a computational framework [28–31]. The complex interplay of genes, enzymes, and metabolites provides a scaffold for the integration of multi-omics datasets such as transcriptomics, proteomics, metagenomics, metabolomics and fluxomics (Figure 1). A GEM framework allows researchers to decipher, postulate and test hypotheses linking genotype to phenotype [28–30]. Overall, it provides a comprehensive systems biology platform for modeling and analyzing biological systems.

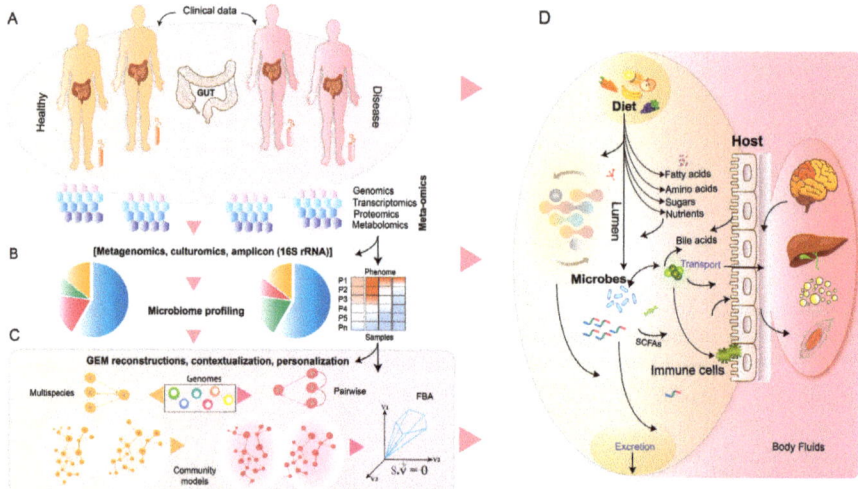

Figure 1. Overview of meta-omics profiling, annotation and genome-scale metabolic reconstructions. (**A**) Fecal, plasma and/or serum samples are taken from healthy and diseased subjects and meta-omics data is generated from these. (**B**) Taxonomic and functional profiling of gut microbes. (**C**) Reconstruction of microbial GEMs. Contextualization and personalization of GEMs with meta-omics datasets. (**D**) Summary of host-microbial interactions in the human gut. GEM simulations to study and understand the intricate relationship among diet, host and microbiota under healthy and disease states.

Herein, we review the role of GSMM in understanding microbial metabolism in the human gut, with a focus on how GEMs have been used to infer diet–microbiome, microbe–microbe and host–microbiome interactions under physiological conditions. We discuss metagenomics profiling, and how meta-omics datasets can be used for building condition-specific personalized community models of gut microbiota. We further summarize the available tools for metagenomic profiling and GSMM. Finally, we highlight and emphasize the experimental techniques and data required to validate the GEM-based predictions.

2. Colonization and Shaping of the Gut Ecosystem

Early colonization of the gut microbiota in infants is vital for shaping of the intestinal ecosystem at a later age [2,32]. These processes are driven by multiple factors such as mode of delivery, gestational age, maternal diet, environment and host genetics. Additionally, geography, life style, age, certain diseases and drug usage can all affect the gut microbial composition and function [2,33].

The distribution of microbes along the gastrointestinal (GI) tract is non-random, in that, certain species of microbes are co-localizing. *Lactobacillacea*, *Veilonellaceae* and *Helicobacterceae* co-occur in stomach, *Bacillaceae* and *Streptococcaceae* in the small intestine, and *Bacteroidaceae*, *Clostridium*, *Lactobacillaceae* and *Bifidobacterium* in the colon [34]. Dysbiosis in the intestinal ecosystem has been both directly and indirectly linked to autoimmune diseases (e.g., type 1 diabetes (T1D), rheumatoid arthritis (RA)) [35,36], colon cancer [37], type 2 diabetes (T2D) and obesity [5,25], cardiovascular disorders [38], non-alcoholic fatty liver disease (NAFLD) [39,40] as well as inflammatory bowel disease (IDB) [41].

3. Gut Microbiome Profiling and Functional Annotation

Metagenomics shotgun sequencing [42] and 16S rRNA amplicon sequencing [43] have been used for profiling gut microbiota from fecal (stool) samples. An appropriately annotated shotgun metagenomics dataset can be used for accurately mapping and predicting microbiota-affected metabolic pathways. These approaches also have proven potential for novel gene discovery [44] and identification of essential functions. Annotation of metagenomics datasets is primarily carried out in two ways: (a) by assembling nucleotide sequences from NGS reads of appropriate length and subsequently predicting the protein coding sequences (called CDS) [45], and (b) by mapping the reads to genome or non-redundant marker gene sets of the relevant organisms guided by the taxonomic profiling [46]. These genes can be clustered, catalogued and aligned against reference database(s) of annotated gene/protein families (e.g., KEGG Orthology [47]), and/or they can be linked to metabolic pathways (e.g., MetaCyc [48]).

Various computational tools and pipelines have been developed for these sorts of purposes. MOCAT2, for example, provides automated annotation of non-redundant reference catalogues from 18 databases covering various functional categories [45]. HMP Unified Metabolic Analysis Network (HUMAnN2) is a pipeline for profiling the relative abundances of microbes and the activity of their metabolic pathways from metagenomics data [46,49]. MEtaGenome ANalyzer (MEGAN) is an interactive and comprehensive microbiome analysis toolbox, that allows researchers to explore and analyze large-scale metagenomics datasets both from taxonomic and functional perspectives [50]. Metagenomics Rast (MG-RAST), is a RAST (Rapid Annotation using Subsystem Technology) server for automated annotation of metagenomics datasets [51]. Integrated Microbial Genomes & Microbiomes (IMG/M) is another server-based system that supports the annotation and analysis of microbiome datasets [52]. There is a plethora of tools for sequence assembly, gene prediction and phylogenetic classification which underpin many of these processes, and these tools are extensively reviewed elsewhere [53].

Functional annotation of metagenomics datasets poses several challenges in itself [53,54]. Although metagenomics data categorizes microbial functions at the community level, it fails to suggest a mechanistic explanation for how these functions arise. To understand the intricate relationship between microbial components, such as genes, proteins and metabolites, and their influence on host metabolism via different biochemical pathways, microbe-specific metabolic models need to be developed at the genome scale.

4. A Constraint-Based Strategy and Tools for Genome-Scale Metabolic Modeling of Gut Microbiota

A rapid increase in use of shotgun metagenomics, the availability of model organisms, and the number of meta-omics datasets in public repositories, gives an opportunity to develop metabolic reconstructions of human gut microbes. These reconstructions can be converted into quantitative mathematical models that can be used to study metabolism at the genome scale [28,55–58]. Current tools and resources for gut microbiome modeling are listed in Table 1.

Table 1. Tools and resources for genome-scale metabolic modeling.

Toolboxes	Short Description	Source or Reference
Modeling Tools		
COBRA (Microbiome Modeling Toolbox)	A MATLAB suite for constraint-based modeling (CBM), includes tools and methods for pairwise and community modeling of microbiota. COBRA can be used for GEM reconstruction and analysis.	[59–61]
RAVEN (CASINO)	A MATLAB suite for CBM, includes tools for modeling diet-microbiota interactions. It can be used for GEM reconstruction and analysis.	[62]
Kbase	A web-based tool for systems biology and metabolic modeling. It can be used for automatic GEM reconstruction and analysis.	[63]
BacArena	An R-package for individual-based and CBM of microbes in a gut community.	[64]
COMETS	A software platform for stoichiometric modeling of individual microbial species using dynamic flux balance analysis (FBA).	[65]
MCM	A tool for CBM of microbial community model, based on conventional FBA.	[66]
DyMMM	A tool for CBM that integrates multiple microbial species into a dynamic community model.	[67]
OptCom	A modeling framework to perform FBA of microbial communities.	[68]
SteadyCom	A toolbox that can be used to predict the changes in microbial species abundance in response to the dietary changes.	[69]
MetExplore	An open access web-server for integrative analysis of metabolomic datasets and genome-scale metabolic networks.	[70]
MMinte	An integrated pipeline for modeling the pairwise interactions within a microbial network.	[71]
jQMM library	An open-source, Python-based framework for modeling internal metabolic fluxes. The toolbox can be used for FBA and 13C Metabolic Flux Analysis (MFA).	[72]
Model repositories and databases		
BiGG database	An open access database for gold standard GEMs.	[73]
Virtual Metabolic Human (VMH)	An open access database for human and gut microbial metabolism (GEMs).	[74]
ModelSEED	A web-based resource for metabolic modeling.	[75]
Human Metabolic Atlas (HMA)	An open access web-based resource for human metabolism.	[76]
Metabolic Pathways and Enzyme databases		
MetaCyc/HumanCyc	A curated database of experimentally validated metabolic pathways. HumanCyc is a database of curated human metabolic pathways.	[48]
KEGG	A resource comprised of databases including large-scale molecular datasets and detailed pathway information.	[77,78]
BRENDA	An information retrieval system focusing on enzymes and their ligands.	[79]
REACTOME	An open access database of biological pathways.	[80]
UniProt.	An open access database of curated protein information.	[81]

In a GEM, uptake or secretion of certain metabolites over time (denoted as their 'flux'), enzymes/transcript abundances and ON/OFF gene expression can be constrained using information from datasets generated by quantitative fluxomic, metabolomic, transcriptomic and proteomic experiments. By applying these constraints, GEMs can be contextualized to a particular state or condition. These condition-specific/contextualized models can provide information about the activity of metabolic pathways, metabolite flux, cellular growth, and provide estimates of the overall metabolic capacities of these gut microbes. GSMM use FBA [28], a constraint-based approach (CBA), to predict organisms' phenotypes [28]. A tutorial on linear programming and FBA is available in [28].

GSMM has been applied to study gut microbial metabolism and its interactions with the host. Recently, AGORA (Assembly of Gut Organisms through Reconstruction and Analysis) was published, which carried out semi-automatic metabolic reconstruction of 773 human gut bacteria (205 genera, 605 species) [26]. The authors modeled metabolic interactions among microbial species based on their metabolic potential and availability of nutrients. This approach has identified and defined growth medium for *Bacteroides caccae* ATCC 34185. Moreover, these metabolic reconstructions have been used to infer metabolic diversity of microbial communities. The AGORA framework can be coupled with, for example Recon 2, a generic reconstruction of human metabolism, which in turn can be used to study host–microbiome interactions. AGORA reconstructions are publicly available via the Virtual Metabolic Human (VMH) [74] database (https://vmh.life/). In addition, BiGG Models [73] (http://bigg.ucsd.edu/) and the Human Metabolic Atlas [76] (http://metabolicatlas.org/) are other open access knowledge bases for metabolic reconstructions.

Kbase [63] (https://kbase.us/) and ModelSEED [75] (http://modelseed.org/) are the web-based servers for automatic reconstruction of microbial GEMs by integrating genome sequences and/or metagenomics datasets. The COnstraint-Based Reconstruction and Analysis (COBRA) [59–61] and RAVEN (Reconstruction, Analysis, and Visualization of Metabolic Networks) [62] toolboxes are stand-alone MATLAB software suites with collections of basic and advanced functions for genome-scale reconstructions and modeling. The Microbiome Modeling Toolbox [82] extends the functionality of the COBRA toolbox to use metagenomic data for modeling microbe–microbe/host–microbe metabolic interactions and modeling personalized microbial communities. Draft GEMs generated by these platforms are then curated for the occurrence of genes, metabolites, reactions and their associations based on evidence from the literature and expert knowledge of metabolism. Quality control checks, which are performed to eliminate false positives, also enhance the predictability of GEMs [55].

5. Reconstruction of Condition-Specific Personalized Gut Microbiota Models

In a metabolic model, numerous genes and metabolites are associated by way of metabolic pathways deemed to be thermodynamically feasible. These models are formalized and applied over the entire microbiota community model [82]. Various efforts have already been made to integrate metagenomic data with a genome-scale framework [26,83]. However, approaches to integrate other kinds of meta-omics data are still in the early phases of development.

Shotgun metagenomics and 16S rRNA data have guided the selection of representative microbes (species or strains) in a community [24]. Integration of meta-omics datasets such as metatranscriptomics, metaproteomics together with fecal metabolomics with the microbiota metabolic modeling framework can constrain the model, improving the accuracy of its representation of the biological system. Moreover, meta-omics data can be applied to develop condition-specific microbiota models (Figure 1) such as metabolic reconstruction of gut microbiota in lean vs. obese subjects. Likewise, a microbiota model can be personalized for an individual subject by combining the metagenomics information with other phenomics datasets. Metagenomics, metatranscriptomics and metaproteomics data can provide an estimate for enzymatic and pathway activities in the gut [49], which approximate the metabolic activity in the gut of an individual under specified conditions.

Context-based, personalized microbiota models have already been used to study various conditions [28,55,56,61,84]. An array of analysis can be performed with these models. Flux Variability Analysis (FVA) [28,85] can estimate the maximal and minimal possible flux differences (flux span) for a specific metabolic exchange reaction of a specific microbial strain, pair of strains, or community as a whole. It determines the potential of a reaction to carry out flux under the applied constraints/conditions. FVA can thus be used to compute strain-specific exchange fluxes for a particular metabolite that can be compared with the net metabolite exchanges in the community. Moreover, it can evaluate the role of individual microbe for metabolite production. On the other hand, shadow price (SP) of a metabolite determines whether it is limiting for an optimal objective function (growth or biomass production) [28,61]. A negative SP suggests that flux through the objective function would increase with the increase in the concentration of the metabolite. As an example, SP analysis has already identified several microbial strains that decrease ursodeoxycholate (UDCA) biosynthesis by limiting its precursors [83].

Food metabolomics datasets detailing dietary constituents have been used to constrain the nutrient uptake rates of microbiota models [58]. Diet acts as a 'spooning media' for the microbiome. Several diets such as a typical Western diet, high fiber diet [26], average European diet [26], breast milk [58], and Ready-to-Use Therapeutic Foods (RUTFs) [24], have been designed. The diet designer tool included as part of the aforementioned [74] can be used to calculate range of dietary fluxes, given the metabolite concentrations. On the other hand, fecal, serum and plasma metabolomics data can be used to confirm the identity of microbial metabolites produced by the models [24,25].

6. Modeling the Effect of Diet on Gut Microbiome

Diet is the direct regulator of microbial metabolism in the gut ecosystem; dietary patterns have profound effect on gut colonization and the shaping of the gut microbiome during the early stages of life [9]. Western diets are associated with a *Bacteroides* enterotype whereas plant-based polysaccharides are associated with a *Prevotella* enterotype [86]. Mostly, three primary macronutrients such carbohydrates, proteins, and fats are known to affect the gut microbial composition [18].

GSMM has already begun to be used to help improve mechanistic understanding of gut microbial metabolism and its dietary interactions [24–26]. Computational tools such as COMET [65], BacArena [64], dOptCom [68], MatNet [87], DyMMM [67], MCM [66], and CASINO [25] were designed to study diet–microbiome interactions. CASINO was able to predict the interactions along the diet-microbiota-host axis in 45 obese and overweight individuals [25]. Furthermore, this study estimated the metabolic capabilities of microbes in the lumen of obese and overweight individuals. The model predicted a significant change in the amino acids and SCFAs levels in response to dietary intervention. The model predictions were further validated by fecal and blood metabolomics data. In another study, GSMM was used to predict and elucidate the underlying interactions between *Bacteroides thetaiotamicron*, *Eubacterium rectale* and *Methanobrevibacter smithii*, when subjected to different gut ecosystems [15,22]. Recently, GEM-based predictions were used to evaluate the effect of RUTFs on gut microbiome of healthy and malnourished children from Bangladesh and Malawi [24]. This methodology can be further extended to study the effect of health supplements, prebiotics and probiotics on the human gut microbiota.

7. Multispecies Modeling and Interactions in the Gut Community

Microbial species or strains with high abundances in samples are often selected for pairwise or community modeling [24,26]. Two or more microbial GEMs are joined together along their extracellular compartments to build a community model [82]. The community model is linked to a "common compartment" mimicking the human gut, through which exchange of metabolites takes place. A community biomass, i.e., the sum of biomasses estimated for each microbe, and coupling constraints are added [82].

Pairwise analysis of microbes in the community has determined their metabolic relationships when introduced to different types of diets [24,26,83]. However, in vitro screening of microbial pairs can be laborious and expensive. When subjected to Western and high fiber diets under aerobic and anaerobic conditions, pairwise modeling has predicted six different interactions between gut microbes such as competition, parasitism, amensalism, neutralism, commensalism and mutualism [26].

Furthermore, pairwise models developed from personalized gut microbiomes have been interrogated for single, cooperative, and community-wide bile acid production potential [83]. This strategy has identified several microbe pairs producing secondary BAs. For instance, *Bacteroides spp.* and *R. gnavus* can cooperatively produce UDCA [83]. In another study, the rate of butyrate production increased by pairs of microbes as compared to a single species, when studied in the gut communities of healthy Bangladeshi and Malawian children [24].

Alternatively, correlation-based co-occurrence topological networks looking at abundant metagenomic species can be developed [88,89]. Such a network can predict positive or negative associations between the microbes. Microbe–microbe co-occurrence pairs of interest can be selected and evaluated by in vitro co-culture experiments [90]. Interestingly, co-occurring species compete strongly for metabolic resources, which are required for cellular growth and maintenance. In this context, the network analysis can be extended to incorporate different metrics such as competition and complementarity indices, which can be used to further characterize/quantify the degree of metabolic interactions between the selected pairs of microbes.

8. Metabolic Modeling of Host–Microbiome Interactions

Gut microbiota can harvest nutrients and energy from the diet. During these processes, small molecules (metabolites) are produced. Some of these metabolites can be beneficial for host and microbial symbionts [16,18,84]. One such metabolite is butyrate, a bacterial fermentation product that fuels the colonic epithelium [22]. In fact, butyrate is the primary energy source for colonocytes. In mammals, the production of cresols from tyrosine have been linked to various species of *Clostridium*, *Bifidobacterium*, and *Bacteroides*, and altered 4-cresol levels in human urine have been associated with weight loss in IBD [17]. The primary conjugated BAs produced by liver are deconjugated and biotransformed by gut microbes, affecting host signaling and metabolism [83]. Also, BAs can activate the innate immune genes which in turns alters the gut microbial composition. It also inhibits the growth of pathogens in the gut.

GEMs have been expanded to study metabolism in humans. Human generic metabolic reconstructions such as Recon 1 [91] and the Edinburgh Human Metabolic Network (EHMN) [92] were developed with a vision to integrate and analyze biological datasets. Similarly, Recon 2 [56,93] and Recon 3D [94], and Human Metabolic Reaction (HMR) [95,96], were designed, that comprehensively captured human metabolism. A metabolic reconstruction of human small intestinal epithelial cells (sIECs) was assembled and manually curated [97]. sIECs were used to study the physiological functionality of the small intestine and their overall role in human metabolism. These models incorporate transporters present in the human gut [94,97,98], while some of them are putatively identified. Furthermore, several functional cell or tissue-specific GEMs have been generated for the liver [96], brain [99], adipocytes [95] and myocytes [100], using semi-automated approaches [101]. In addition, a gender-specific, whole-body metabolism (WBM) reconstruction was developed to capture and characterize the metabolism of 20 human organs [102]. A WBM framework can be constrained with dietary, physiological parameters and omics datasets. Such a framework was used to link organ-level metabolic processes in 149 subjects induced by their gut microbiota.

The Microbiome Modeling Toolbox [82], deployed under the COBRA suite, includes several functions for modeling complex metabolic interactions between the host and gut microbiota. It can integrate microbe (AGORA [26], BiGG [73]) and host (Recon [56,91,94]) metabolic reconstructions. Similarly, a common compartment mimicking the human gut is added, which enables pooling and exchange of metabolites between the microbes, lumen and the host cells.

In a different context, the microbiome-induced immune response is currently well established. An imbalance in gut microbial composition has been linked to inflammatory and autoimmune diseases [103–106]. Various immune cells including CD4$^+$ effector T cells (particularly Th1, Th2, Th17 and iTreg), CD8$^+$ T cells (cytotoxic) and macrophages undergo metabolic reprogramming during proliferation and differentiation processes [107]. The macrophage (RAW 264.7 cell line) model was developed to study immunoactivation and immunosuppression [108]. Metabolic reconstructions of immune cells are currently unavailable. By developing GEMs for host immune cells [57], might guide us to study, the microbiome-mediated immunometabolic responses under various health/disease conditions.

9. Model Predictions and Experimental Validation

To establish the biological relevance of metabolic models, the congruence between model predictions and experimental data is of utmost importance. GEM-based predictions can be validated by existing data, knowledge and bibliographical evidence. For instance, metabolites secreted by gut microbiota can be compared with the concentrations of metabolites found in fecal and blood samples [24,25]. Furthermore, blood metabolomics data can be used for validation of metabolites predicted as being transported across the human gut. Meta-omics datasets [109] can be used to estimate the abundances of gut enzymes and microbial pathways for an individual species or strain [49]. The pathway abundances can be compared with the enrichment and usage (flux) of GEM-predicted pathway(s). GSMM can be applied to quantify dietary nutrient uptake of gut microbes and their metabolic interactions with the host. To understand the regulation of host metabolism by gut microbes, germ-free (GF) and conventionally raised (CONV-R) mice are usually used [110]. These mice can be raised on different diets and then euthanized, with samples analyzed by meta-omics analyses. The generated datasets can be used for contextualization and validation of GEMs. Furthermore, the theoretical growth rate of a microbe can be validated by culturing species in a specific media [25,26]. In addition, the predicted metabolic interactions between microbes, regulation of co-occurrence network, and dietary cross-feeding can be validated by mono- and co-culture experiments [90].

10. Concluding Remarks and Future Perspectives

Integration of meta-omics datasets and genome-wide metabolic reconstructions provide a framework for interrogating and suggesting mechanistic workings of diet-microbe-host metabolic interaction. However, such integrative methods are still evolving and require extensive and robust experimental validation.

Profiling and culturing gut microbes at the strain level, under controlled conditions, remains challenging. Recently, an integrated approach involving targeted phenotypic culturing, WGS, phylogenetic analysis and computational modeling has succeeded in culturing a substantial portion of bacteria previously declared to be 'unculturable' under laboratory conditions. This approach identified 137 bacterial species, including novel species isolated from pure cultures [111]. Furthermore, the culturomics techniques are currently used for filling the gap by isolating the unknown or novel members of the gut community [111,112].

In studies of gut microbial communities, there is increasing interest in mechanistic approaches, in contrast to solely genome-centric approaches. Correspondingly, GSMM is widely used as a preferred computational method for studying gut microbial metabolism and its interaction with the host. Additionally, GEMs can be contextualized and personalized using longitudinal meta-omics datasets, providing a snapshot of metabolic processes over time. Personalized microbiota models may help to reduce the costs of clinical studies, predict markers and contribute to the development of potential treatments at either the individual patient level, or for a defined patient group [83,113]. Many efforts are ongoing, aiming to couple pharmacokinetic and constraint-based models to study drug-microbe-diet interactions [114]. However, a limitation of GSMM approach is that GEMs are stoichiometric models, and cannot, in their current form at least, incorporate metabolite concentrations or enzyme kinetics (V_{max}, K_m, K_{cat}) [115,116]. Albeit more limited in scope, kinetic modeling [116] may help improve understanding of the dynamics of metabolic pathways in the human gut.

As indicated in this review, GSMM and CBA have provided computational tools and frameworks to study metabolism of gut microbiota. These tools guided researchers to study and identify the metabolic functions of individual microbes in the gut community. It also helped to infer their spatial dynamics, environmental interactions and metabolic resource allocations under a certain condition. We believe that, a combination of several computational and experimental approaches, may reveal the complex and diverse structure of the human gut microbiome and its underlying interactions with the host metabolic machinery. It might bridge the gaps in gut microbiome research and thereby, enhance our knowledge of human gut microbiota under health/disease conditions.

Author Contributions: P.S. drafted the manuscript. M.O. provided critical comments and edited the manuscript. Both authors approved the final version of the manuscript.

Funding: This work was supported by the Academy of Finland (Centre of Excellence in Molecular Systems Immunology and Physiology Research 2012–2017, Decision No. 250114, to M.O.) and the Juvenile Diabetes Research Foundation (2-SRA-2014-159-Q-R to M.O.) and the European Union Horizon 2020 project 'Elucidating Pathways of Steatohepatitis – EpoS' (Grant Agreement 634413).

Acknowledgments: We thank to Alex Dickens and Santosh Lamichhane for helpful scientific discussions. We also thank Aidan McGlinchey for editing the manuscript.

Conflicts of Interest: The authors declare no conflict of interest.

Abbreviations

NGS	Next-Generation Sequencing
GSMM	Genome-Scale Metabolic Modeling
HMP	Human Microbiome Project
SCFAs	Short-Chain Fatty Acids
BCFAs	Branched Chain Fatty Acids
BCAAs	Branched Chain Amino Acids
BAs	Bile Acids
TLR	Toll-Like Receptor
APCs	Antigen Presenting Cells
WGS	Whole Genomes Shotgun metagenomics sequencing
GEMs	Genome-Scale Models
T1D	Type 1 Diabetes
RA	Rheumatoid Arthritis
T2D	Type 2 Diabetes
NAFLD	Non-Alcoholic Fatty Liver Disease
IDB	Bowel Disease
CDS	Protein Coding Sequences
KEGG	Kyoto Encyclopedia of Genes and Genomes
HUMAnN2	HMP Unified Metabolic Analysis Network
MEGAN	MEtaGenome ANalyzer
MG-RAST	Metagenomics Rast
RAST	Rapid Annotation using Subsystem Technology
IMG/M	Integrated Microbial Genomes and Microbiomes
FBA	Flux Balance Analysis
CBA	Constraint-Based Approach
AGORA	Assembly of Gut Organisms through Reconstruction and Analysis
VMH	Virtual Metabolic Human
COBRA	COnstraint-Based Reconstruction and Analysis
RAVEN	Reconstruction, Analysis, and Visualization of Metabolic Networks
FVA	Flux Variability Analysis
SP	Shadow Price
UDCA	Ursodeoxycholate
RUTFs	Ready-to-Use Therapeutic Foods
EHMN	Edinburgh Human Metabolic Network
HMR	Human Metabolic Reaction

sIECs   small Intestinal Epithelial Cells
WBM   Whole-Body Metabolism
GF   Germ-Free
CONV-R   Conventionally Raised

References

1. Thursby, E.; Juge, N. Introduction to the human gut microbiota. *Biochem. J.* **2017**, *474*, 1823–1836. [CrossRef]
2. Schmidt, T.S.B.; Raes, J.; Bork, P. The Human Gut Microbiome: From Association to Modulation. *Cell* **2018**, *172*, 1198–1215. [CrossRef]
3. Hugon, P.; Dufour, J.C.; Colson, P.; Fournier, P.E.; Sallah, K.; Raoult, D. A comprehensive repertoire of prokaryotic species identified in human beings. *Lancet Infect. Dis.* **2015**, *15*, 1211–1219. [CrossRef]
4. Li, J.; Jia, H.; Cai, X.; Zhong, H.; Feng, Q.; Sunagawa, S.; Arumugam, M.; Kultima, J.R.; Prifti, E.; Nielsen, T.; et al. An integrated catalog of reference genes in the human gut microbiome. *Nat. Biotechnol.* **2014**, *32*, 834–841. [CrossRef]
5. Pedersen, H.K.; Gudmundsdottir, V.; Nielsen, H.B.; Hyotylainen, T.; Nielsen, T.; Jensen, B.A.; Forslund, K.; Hildebrand, F.; Prifti, E.; Falony, G.; et al. Human gut microbes impact host serum metabolome and insulin sensitivity. *Nature* **2016**, *535*, 376–381. [CrossRef]
6. Gevers, D.; Knight, R.; Petrosino, J.F.; Huang, K.; McGuire, A.L.; Birren, B.W.; Nelson, K.E.; White, O.; Methe, B.A.; Huttenhower, C. The Human Microbiome Project: A community resource for the healthy human microbiome. *PLoS Biol.* **2012**, *10*, e1001377. [CrossRef]
7. Integrative, H. The Integrative Human Microbiome Project: Dynamic analysis of microbiome-host omics profiles during periods of human health and disease. *Cell Host Microbe* **2014**, *16*, 276.
8. McDonald, D.; Hyde, E.; Debelius, J.W.; Morton, J.T.; Gonzalez, A.; Ackermann, G.; Aksenov, A.A.; Behsaz, B.; Brennan, C.; Chen, Y.; et al. American Gut: An Open Platform for Citizen Science Microbiome Research. *mSystems* **2018**, *3*. [CrossRef]
9. Rodriguez, J.M.; Murphy, K.; Stanton, C.; Ross, R.P.; Kober, O.I.; Juge, N.; Avershina, E.; Rudi, K.; Narbad, A.; Jenmalm, M.C.; et al. The composition of the gut microbiota throughout life, with an emphasis on early life. *Microb. Ecol. Health Dis.* **2015**, *26*, 26050. [CrossRef]
10. Faith, J.J.; Guruge, J.L.; Charbonneau, M.; Subramanian, S.; Seedorf, H.; Goodman, A.L.; Clemente, J.C.; Knight, R.; Heath, A.C.; Leibel, R.L.; et al. The long-term stability of the human gut microbiota. *Science* **2013**, *341*, 1237439. [CrossRef]
11. Costea, P.I.; Coelho, L.P.; Sunagawa, S.; Munch, R.; Huerta-Cepas, J.; Forslund, K.; Hildebrand, F.; Kushugulova, A.; Zeller, G.; Bork, P. Subspecies in the global human gut microbiome. *Mol. Syst. Biol.* **2017**, *13*, 960. [CrossRef]
12. Hisada, T.; Endoh, K.; Kuriki, K. Inter- and intra-individual variations in seasonal and daily stabilities of the human gut microbiota in Japanese. *Arch. Microbiol.* **2015**, *197*, 919–934. [CrossRef]
13. Wen, L.; Duffy, A. Factors influencing the gut microbiota, inflammation, and type 2 diabetes. *J. Nutr.* **2017**, *147*, 1468S–1475S. [CrossRef]
14. Ji, B.; Nielsen, J. New insight into the gut microbiome through metagenomics. *Adv. Genom. Genet.* **2015**, *5*, 77–91.
15. Shoaie, S.; Karlsson, F.; Mardinoglu, A.; Nookaew, I.; Bordel, S.; Nielsen, J. Understanding the interactions between bacteria in the human gut through metabolic modeling. *Sci. Rep.* **2013**, *3*, 2532. [CrossRef]
16. Lamichhane, S.; Sen, P.; Dickens, A.M.; Oresic, M.; Bertram, H.C. Gut metabolome meets microbiome: A methodological perspective to understand the relationship between host and microbe. *Methods* **2018**. [CrossRef]
17. Nicholson, J.K.; Holmes, E.; Kinross, J.; Burcelin, R.; Gibson, G.; Jia, W.; Pettersson, S. Host-gut microbiota metabolic interactions. *Science* **2012**, *336*, 1262–1267. [CrossRef]
18. Rowland, I.; Gibson, G.; Heinken, A.; Scott, K.; Swann, J.; Thiele, I.; Tuohy, K. Gut microbiota functions: Metabolism of nutrients and other food components. *Eur. J. Nutr.* **2018**, *57*, 1–24. [CrossRef] [PubMed]
19. Molloy, M.J.; Bouladoux, N.; Belkaid, Y. Intestinal microbiota: Shaping local and systemic immune responses. *Semin. Immunol.* **2012**, *24*, 58–66. [CrossRef]

20. Valentini, M.; Piermattei, A.; Di Sante, G.; Migliara, G.; Delogu, G.; Ria, F. Immunomodulation by gut microbiota: Role of Toll-like receptor expressed by T cells. *J. Immunol. Res.* **2014**, *2014*, 586939. [CrossRef]
21. Hamady, M.; Knight, R. Microbial community profiling for human microbiome projects: Tools, techniques, and challenges. *Genome Res.* **2009**, *19*, 1141–1152. [CrossRef] [PubMed]
22. Shoaie, S.; Nielsen, J. Elucidating the interactions between the human gut microbiota and its host through metabolic modeling. *Front. Genet.* **2014**, *5*, 86. [CrossRef] [PubMed]
23. Bauer, E.; Thiele, I. From Network Analysis to Functional Metabolic Modeling of the Human Gut Microbiota. *mSystems* **2018**, *3*. [CrossRef] [PubMed]
24. Kumar, M.; Ji, B.; Babaei, P.; Das, P.; Lappa, D.; Ramakrishnan, G.; Fox, T.E.; Haque, R.; Petri, W.A., Jr.; Bäckhed, F. Gut microbiota dysbiosis is associated with malnutrition and reduced plasma amino acid levels: Lessons from genome-scale metabolic modeling. *Metab. Eng.* **2018**, *49*, 128–142. [CrossRef] [PubMed]
25. Shoaie, S.; Ghaffari, P.; Kovatcheva-Datchary, P.; Mardinoglu, A.; Sen, P.; Pujos-Guillot, E.; de Wouters, T.; Juste, C.; Rizkalla, S.; Chilloux, J. Quantifying diet-induced metabolic changes of the human gut microbiome. *Cell Metab.* **2015**, *22*, 320–331. [CrossRef] [PubMed]
26. Magnúsdóttir, S.; Heinken, A.; Kutt, L.; Ravcheev, D.A.; Bauer, E.; Noronha, A.; Greenhalgh, K.; Jäger, C.; Baginska, J.; Wilmes, P. Generation of genome-scale metabolic reconstructions for 773 members of the human gut microbiota. *Nat. Biotechnol.* **2017**, *35*, 81–89. [CrossRef] [PubMed]
27. Qin, J.; Li, R.; Raes, J.; Arumugam, M.; Burgdorf, K.S.; Manichanh, C.; Nielsen, T.; Pons, N.; Levenez, F.; Yamada, T. A human gut microbial gene catalog established by metagenomic sequencing. *Nature* **2010**, *464*, 59. [CrossRef]
28. Orth, J.D.; Thiele, I.; Palsson, B.Ø. What is flux balance analysis? *Nat. Biotechnol.* **2010**, *28*, 245–248. [CrossRef] [PubMed]
29. Price, N.D.; Reed, J.L.; Palsson, B.Ø. Genome-scale models of microbial cells: Evaluating the consequences of constraints. *Nat. Rev. Microbiol.* **2004**, *2*, 886–897. [CrossRef] [PubMed]
30. O'Brien, E.J.; Monk, J.M.; Palsson, B.O. Using genome-scale models to predict biological capabilities. *Cell* **2015**, *161*, 971–987. [CrossRef] [PubMed]
31. Bordbar, A.; Monk, J.M.; King, Z.A.; Palsson, B.O. Constraint-based models predict metabolic and associated cellular functions. *Nat. Rev. Genet.* **2014**, *15*, 107–120. [CrossRef] [PubMed]
32. Backhed, F.; Roswall, J.; Peng, Y.; Feng, Q.; Jia, H.; Kovatcheva-Datchary, P.; Li, Y.; Xia, Y.; Xie, H.; Zhong, H.; et al. Dynamics and Stabilization of the Human Gut Microbiome during the First Year of Life. *Cell Host Microbe* **2015**, *17*, 852. [CrossRef] [PubMed]
33. Milani, C.; Duranti, S.; Bottacini, F.; Casey, E.; Turroni, F.; Mahony, J.; Belzer, C.; Delgado Palacio, S.; Arboleya Montes, S.; Mancabelli, L.; et al. The First Microbial Colonizers of the Human Gut: Composition, Activities, and Health Implications of the Infant Gut Microbiota. *Microbiol. Mol. Biol. Rev.* **2017**, *81*. [CrossRef] [PubMed]
34. Zhang, Z.; Geng, J.; Tang, X.; Fan, H.; Xu, J.; Wen, X.; Ma, Z.S.; Shi, P. Spatial heterogeneity and co-occurrence patterns of human mucosal-associated intestinal microbiota. *ISME J.* **2014**, *8*, 881–893. [CrossRef] [PubMed]
35. Boerner, B.P.; Sarvetnick, N.E. Type 1 diabetes: Role of intestinal microbiome in humans and mice. *Ann. N. Y. Acad. Sci.* **2011**, *1243*, 103–118. [CrossRef] [PubMed]
36. Abdollahi-Roodsaz, S.; Abramson, S.B.; Scher, J.U. The metabolic role of the gut microbiota in health and rheumatic disease: Mechanisms and interventions. *Nat. Rev. Rheumatol.* **2016**, *12*, 446–455. [CrossRef]
37. Sears, C.L.; Garrett, W.S. Microbes, microbiota, and colon cancer. *Cell Host Microbe* **2014**, *15*, 317–328. [CrossRef] [PubMed]
38. Jonsson, A.L.; Backhed, F. Role of gut microbiota in atherosclerosis. *Nat. Rev. Cardiol.* **2017**, *14*, 79–87. [CrossRef]
39. Spencer, M.D.; Hamp, T.J.; Reid, R.W.; Fischer, L.M.; Zeisel, S.H.; Fodor, A.A. Association between composition of the human gastrointestinal microbiome and development of fatty liver with choline deficiency. *Gastroenterology* **2011**, *140*, 976–986. [CrossRef]
40. He, X.; Ji, G.; Jia, W.; Li, H. Gut Microbiota and Nonalcoholic Fatty Liver Disease: Insights on Mechanism and Application of Metabolomics. *Int. J. Mol. Sci.* **2016**, *17*, 300. [CrossRef]
41. Wlodarska, M.; Kostic, A.D.; Xavier, R.J. An integrative view of microbiome-host interactions in inflammatory bowel diseases. *Cell Host Microbe* **2015**, *17*, 577–591. [CrossRef] [PubMed]

42. Simon, C.; Daniel, R. Metagenomic analyses: Past and future trends. *Appl. Environ. Microbiol.* **2011**, *77*, 1153–1161. [CrossRef] [PubMed]
43. Carlos, N.; Tang, Y.W.; Pei, Z. Pearls and pitfalls of genomics-based microbiome analysis. *Emerg. Microbes Infect.* **2012**, *1*, e45. [CrossRef] [PubMed]
44. Sharma, V.K.; Kumar, N.; Prakash, T.; Taylor, T.D. MetaBioME: A database to explore commercially useful enzymes in metagenomic datasets. *Nucleic Acids Res.* **2010**, *38*, D468–D472. [CrossRef] [PubMed]
45. Kultima, J.R.; Coelho, L.P.; Forslund, K.; Huerta-Cepas, J.; Li, S.S.; Driessen, M.; Voigt, A.Y.; Zeller, G.; Sunagawa, S.; Bork, P. MOCAT2: A metagenomic assembly, annotation and profiling framework. *Bioinformatics* **2016**, *32*, 2520–2523. [CrossRef] [PubMed]
46. Abubucker, S.; Segata, N.; Goll, J.; Schubert, A.M.; Izard, J.; Cantarel, B.L.; Rodriguez-Mueller, B.; Zucker, J.; Thiagarajan, M.; Henrissat, B.; et al. Metabolic reconstruction for metagenomic data and its application to the human microbiome. *PLoS Comput. Biol.* **2012**, *8*, e1002358. [CrossRef]
47. Kanehisa, M.; Sato, Y.; Kawashima, M.; Furumichi, M.; Tanabe, M. KEGG as a reference resource for gene and protein annotation. *Nucleic Acids Res.* **2015**, *44*, D457–D462. [CrossRef]
48. Caspi, R.; Billington, R.; Ferrer, L.; Foerster, H.; Fulcher, C.A.; Keseler, I.M.; Kothari, A.; Krummenacker, M.; Latendresse, M.; Mueller, L.A.; et al. The MetaCyc database of metabolic pathways and enzymes and the BioCyc collection of pathway/genome databases. *Nucleic Acids Res.* **2016**, *44*, D471–D480. [CrossRef]
49. Franzosa, E.A.; McIver, L.J.; Rahnavard, G.; Thompson, L.R.; Schirmer, M.; Weingart, G.; Lipson, K.S.; Knight, R.; Caporaso, J.G.; Segata, N.; et al. Species-level functional profiling of metagenomes and metatranscriptomes. *Nat. Methods* **2018**, *15*, 962–968. [CrossRef]
50. Huson, D.H.; Auch, A.F.; Qi, J.; Schuster, S.C. MEGAN analysis of metagenomic data. *Genome Res.* **2007**, *17*, 377–386. [CrossRef]
51. Glass, E.M.; Wilkening, J.; Wilke, A.; Antonopoulos, D.; Meyer, F. Using the metagenomics RAST server (MG-RAST) for analyzing shotgun metagenomes. *Cold Spring Harbor Protocols* **2010**, *2010*. [CrossRef] [PubMed]
52. Chen, I.A.; Markowitz, V.M.; Chu, K.; Palaniappan, K.; Szeto, E.; Pillay, M.; Ratner, A.; Huang, J.; Andersen, E.; Huntemann, M.; et al. IMG/M: Integrated genome and metagenome comparative data analysis system. *Nucleic Acids Res.* **2017**, *45*, D507–D516. [CrossRef] [PubMed]
53. Prakash, T.; Taylor, T.D. Functional assignment of metagenomic data: Challenges and applications. *Brief. Bioinform.* **2012**, *13*, 711–727. [CrossRef] [PubMed]
54. Gilbert, J.A.; Field, D.; Swift, P.; Thomas, S.; Cummings, D.; Temperton, B.; Weynberg, K.; Huse, S.; Hughes, M.; Joint, I. The taxonomic and functional diversity of microbes at a temperate coastal site: A 'multi-omic'study of seasonal and diel temporal variation. *PLoS ONE* **2010**, *5*, e15545. [CrossRef]
55. Thiele, I.; Palsson, B.Ø. A protocol for generating a high-quality genome-scale metabolic reconstruction. *Nat. Protocols* **2010**, *5*, 93. [CrossRef]
56. Thiele, I.; Swainston, N.; Fleming, R.M.; Hoppe, A.; Sahoo, S.; Aurich, M.K.; Haraldsdottir, H.; Mo, M.L.; Rolfsson, O.; Stobbe, M.D.; et al. A community-driven global reconstruction of human metabolism. *Nat. Biotechnol.* **2013**, *31*, 419–425. [CrossRef]
57. Sen, P.; Kemppainen, E.; Orešič, M. Perspectives on Systems Modeling of Human Peripheral Blood Mononuclear Cells. *Front. Mol. Biosci.* **2018**, *4*, 96. [CrossRef]
58. Sen, P.; Mardinogulu, A.; Nielsen, J. Selection of complementary foods based on optimal nutritional values. *Sci. Rep.* **2017**, *7*, 5413. [CrossRef]
59. Becker, S.A.; Feist, A.M.; Mo, M.L.; Hannum, G.; Palsson, B.O.; Herrgard, M.J. Quantitative prediction of cellular metabolism with constraint-based models: The COBRA Toolbox. *Nat. Protoc.* **2007**, *2*, 727–738. [CrossRef]
60. Heirendt, L.; Arreckx, S.; Pfau, T.; Mendoza, S.N.; Richelle, A.; Heinken, A.; Haraldsdottir, H.S.; Keating, S.M.; Vlasov, V.; Wachowiak, J. Creation and analysis of biochemical constraint-based models: The COBRA Toolbox v3.0. *arXiv* **2017**, arXiv:1710.04038.
61. Schellenberger, J.; Que, R.; Fleming, R.M.; Thiele, I.; Orth, J.D.; Feist, A.M.; Zielinski, D.C.; Bordbar, A.; Lewis, N.E.; Rahmanian, S.; et al. Quantitative prediction of cellular metabolism with constraint-based models: The COBRA Toolbox v2.0. *Nat. Protoc.* **2011**, *6*, 1290–1307. [CrossRef] [PubMed]

62. Agren, R.; Liu, L.; Shoaie, S.; Vongsangnak, W.; Nookaew, I.; Nielsen, J. The RAVEN toolbox and its use for generating a genome-scale metabolic model for Penicillium chrysogenum. *PLoS Comput. Biol.* **2013**, *9*, e1002980. [CrossRef] [PubMed]
63. Arkin, A.P.; Stevens, R.L.; Cottingham, R.W.; Maslov, S.; Henry, C.S.; Dehal, P.; Ware, D.; Perez, F.; Harris, N.L.; Canon, S. The DOE Systems Biology Knowledgebase (KBase). *bioRxiv* **2016**. [CrossRef]
64. Bauer, E.; Zimmermann, J.; Baldini, F.; Thiele, I.; Kaleta, C. BacArena: Individual-based metabolic modeling of heterogeneous microbes in complex communities. *PLoS Comput. Biol.* **2017**, *13*, e1005544. [CrossRef] [PubMed]
65. Harcombe, W.R.; Riehl, W.J.; Dukovski, I.; Granger, B.R.; Betts, A.; Lang, A.H.; Bonilla, G.; Kar, A.; Leiby, N.; Mehta, P.; et al. Metabolic resource allocation in individual microbes determines ecosystem interactions and spatial dynamics. *Cell Rep.* **2014**, *7*, 1104–1115. [CrossRef] [PubMed]
66. Louca, S.; Doebeli, M. Calibration and analysis of genome-based models for microbial ecology. *eLife* **2015**, *4*, e08208. [CrossRef] [PubMed]
67. Zhuang, K.; Izallalen, M.; Mouser, P.; Richter, H.; Risso, C.; Mahadevan, R.; Lovley, D.R. Genome-scale dynamic modeling of the competition between Rhodoferax and Geobacter in anoxic subsurface environments. *ISME J.* **2011**, *5*, 305. [CrossRef] [PubMed]
68. Zomorrodi, A.R.; Islam, M.M.; Maranas, C.D. d-OptCom: Dynamic multi-level and multi-objective metabolic modeling of microbial communities. *ACS Synth. Biol.* **2014**, *3*, 247–257. [CrossRef] [PubMed]
69. Chan, S.H.J.; Simons, M.N.; Maranas, C.D. SteadyCom: Predicting microbial abundances while ensuring community stability. *PLoS Comput. Biol.* **2017**, *13*, e1005539. [CrossRef] [PubMed]
70. Cottret, L.; Wildridge, D.; Vinson, F.; Barrett, M.P.; Charles, H.; Sagot, M.F.; Jourdan, F. MetExplore: A web server to link metabolomic experiments and genome-scale metabolic networks. *Nucleic Acids Res.* **2010**, *38*, W132–W137. [CrossRef] [PubMed]
71. Mendes-Soares, H.; Mundy, M.; Soares, L.M.; Chia, N. MMinte: An application for predicting metabolic interactions among the microbial species in a community. *BMC Bioinform.* **2016**, *17*, 343. [CrossRef] [PubMed]
72. Birkel, G.W.; Ghosh, A.; Kumar, V.S.; Weaver, D.; Ando, D.; Backman, T.W.H.; Arkin, A.P.; Keasling, J.D.; Martin, H.G. The JBEI quantitative metabolic modeling library (jQMM): A python library for modeling microbial metabolism. *BMC Bioinform.* **2017**, *18*, 205. [CrossRef]
73. King, Z.A.; Lu, J.; Dräger, A.; Miller, P.; Federowicz, S.; Lerman, J.A.; Ebrahim, A.; Palsson, B.O.; Lewis, N.E. BiGG Models: A platform for integrating, standardizing and sharing genome-scale models. *Nucleic Acids Res.* **2015**, *44*, D515–D522. [CrossRef] [PubMed]
74. Noronha, A.; Modamio, J.; Jarosz, Y.; Sompairac, N.; Gonzalez, G.P.; Danielsdottir, A.D.; Krecke, M.; Merten, D.; Haraldsdottir, H.S.; Heinken, A. The Virtual Metabolic Human database: Integrating human and gut microbiome metabolism with nutrition and disease. *bioRxiv* **2018**. [CrossRef]
75. Henry, C.S.; DeJongh, M.; Best, A.A.; Frybarger, P.M.; Linsay, B.; Stevens, R.L. High-throughput generation, optimization and analysis of genome-scale metabolic models. *Nat Biotechnol* **2010**, *28*, 977–982. [CrossRef] [PubMed]
76. Pornputtapong, N.; Nookaew, I.; Nielsen, J. Human metabolic atlas: An online resource for human metabolism. *Database* **2015**, *2015*, bav068. [CrossRef]
77. Kanehisa, M.; Goto, S.; Sato, Y.; Furumichi, M.; Tanabe, M. KEGG for integration and interpretation of large-scale molecular data sets. *Nucleic Acids Res.* **2012**, *40*, D109–D114. [CrossRef]
78. Kanehisa, M.; Goto, S.; Sato, Y.; Kawashima, M.; Furumichi, M.; Tanabe, M. Data, information, knowledge and principle: Back to metabolism in KEGG. *Nucleic Acids Res.* **2013**, *42*, D199–D205. [CrossRef]
79. Schomburg, I.; Jeske, L.; Ulbrich, M.; Placzek, S.; Chang, A.; Schomburg, D. The BRENDA enzyme information system-From a database to an expert system. *J. Biotechnol.* **2017**, *261*, 194–206. [CrossRef]
80. D'Eustachio, P. Reactome knowledgebase of human biological pathways and processes. *Methods Mol. Biol.* **2011**, *694*, 49–61. [CrossRef]
81. UniProt Consortium, T. UniProt: The universal protein knowledgebase. *Nucleic Acids Res.* **2018**, *46*, 2699. [CrossRef] [PubMed]
82. Baldini, F.; Heinken, A.; Heirendt, L.; Magnusdottir, S.; Fleming, R.M.; Thiele, I. The Microbiome Modeling Toolbox: From microbial interactions to personalized microbial communities. *bioRxiv* **2018**. [CrossRef] [PubMed]

83. Heinken, A.; Ravcheev, D.A.; Baldini, F.; Heirendt, L.; Fleming, R.M.; Thiele, I. Personalized modeling of the human gut microbiome reveals distinct bile acid deconjugation and biotransformation potential in healthy and IBD individuals. *bioRxiv* **2017**. [CrossRef]
84. Heinken, A.; Sahoo, S.; Fleming, R.M.; Thiele, I. Systems-level characterization of a host-microbe metabolic symbiosis in the mammalian gut. *Gut Microbes* **2013**, *4*, 28–40. [CrossRef] [PubMed]
85. Gudmundsson, S.; Thiele, I. Computationally efficient flux variability analysis. *BMC Bioinform.* **2010**, *11*, 489. [CrossRef] [PubMed]
86. Gorvitovskaia, A.; Holmes, S.P.; Huse, S.M. Interpreting Prevotella and Bacteroides as biomarkers of diet and lifestyle. *Microbiome* **2016**, *4*, 15. [CrossRef] [PubMed]
87. Biggs, M.B.; Papin, J.A. Novel multiscale modeling tool applied to Pseudomonas aeruginosa biofilm formation. *PLoS ONE* **2013**, *8*, e78011. [CrossRef] [PubMed]
88. Weiss, S.; Van Treuren, W.; Lozupone, C.; Faust, K.; Friedman, J.; Deng, Y.; Xia, L.C.; Xu, Z.Z.; Ursell, L.; Alm, E.J.; et al. Correlation detection strategies in microbial data sets vary widely in sensitivity and precision. *ISME J.* **2016**, *10*, 1669–1681. [CrossRef]
89. Kurtz, Z.D.; Muller, C.L.; Miraldi, E.R.; Littman, D.R.; Blaser, M.J.; Bonneau, R.A. Sparse and compositionally robust inference of microbial ecological networks. *PLoS Comput. Biol.* **2015**, *11*, e1004226. [CrossRef]
90. Das, P.; Ji, B.; Kovatcheva-Datchary, P.; Bäckhed, F.; Nielsen, J. In vitro co-cultures of human gut bacterial species as predicted from co-occurrence network analysis. *PLoS ONE* **2018**, *13*, e0195161. [CrossRef]
91. Duarte, N.C.; Becker, S.A.; Jamshidi, N.; Thiele, I.; Mo, M.L.; Vo, T.D.; Srivas, R.; Palsson, B.O. Global reconstruction of the human metabolic network based on genomic and bibliomic data. *Proc. Natl. Acad. Sci. USA* **2007**, *104*, 1777–1782. [CrossRef] [PubMed]
92. Ma, H.; Sorokin, A.; Mazein, A.; Selkov, A.; Selkov, E.; Demin, O.; Goryanin, I. The Edinburgh human metabolic network reconstruction and its functional analysis. *Mol. Syst. Biol.* **2007**, *3*, 135. [CrossRef] [PubMed]
93. Swainston, N.; Smallbone, K.; Hefzi, H.; Dobson, P.D.; Brewer, J.; Hanscho, M.; Zielinski, D.C.; Ang, K.S.; Gardiner, N.J.; Gutierrez, J.M. Recon 2.2: From reconstruction to model of human metabolism. *Metabolomics* **2016**, *12*, 1–7. [CrossRef] [PubMed]
94. Brunk, E.; Sahoo, S.; Zielinski, D.C.; Altunkaya, A.; Dräger, A.; Mih, N.; Gatto, F.; Nilsson, A.; Gonzalez, G.A.P.; Aurich, M.K.; et al. Recon3D enables a three-dimensional view of gene variation in human metabolism. *Nat. Biotechnol.* **2018**, *36*, 272–281. [CrossRef] [PubMed]
95. Mardinoglu, A.; Agren, R.; Kampf, C.; Asplund, A.; Nookaew, I.; Jacobson, P.; Walley, A.J.; Froguel, P.; Carlsson, L.M.; Uhlen, M.; et al. Integration of clinical data with a genome-scale metabolic model of the human adipocyte. *Mol. Syst. Biol.* **2013**, *9*, 649. [CrossRef] [PubMed]
96. Mardinoglu, A.; Agren, R.; Kampf, C.; Asplund, A.; Uhlen, M.; Nielsen, J. Genome-scale metabolic modelling of hepatocytes reveals serine deficiency in patients with non-alcoholic fatty liver disease. *Nat. Commun.* **2014**, *5*, 3083. [CrossRef] [PubMed]
97. Sahoo, S.; Thiele, I. Predicting the impact of diet and enzymopathies on human small intestinal epithelial cells. *Hum. Mol. Genet.* **2013**, *22*, 2705–2722. [CrossRef]
98. Sahoo, S.; Aurich, M.K.; Jonsson, J.J.; Thiele, I. Membrane transporters in a human genome-scale metabolic knowledgebase and their implications for disease. *Front. Physiol.* **2014**, *5*, 91. [CrossRef]
99. Lewis, N.E.; Schramm, G.; Bordbar, A.; Schellenberger, J.; Andersen, M.P.; Cheng, J.K.; Patel, N.; Yee, A.; Lewis, R.A.; Eils, R. Large-scale in silico modeling of metabolic interactions between cell types in the human brain. *Nat. Biotechnol.* **2010**, *28*, 1279. [CrossRef]
100. Väremo, L.; Scheele, C.; Broholm, C.; Mardinoglu, A.; Kampf, C.; Asplund, A.; Nookaew, I.; Uhlén, M.; Pedersen, B.K.; Nielsen, J. Proteome-and Transcriptome-Driven Reconstruction of the Human Myocyte Metabolic Network and Its Use for Identification of Markers for Diabetes. *Cell Rep.* **2016**, *14*, 1567. [CrossRef]
101. Agren, R.; Bordel, S.; Mardinoglu, A.; Pornputtapong, N.; Nookaew, I.; Nielsen, J. Reconstruction of genome-scale active metabolic networks for 69 human cell types and 16 cancer types using INIT. *PLoS Comput. Biol.* **2012**, *8*, e1002518. [CrossRef] [PubMed]
102. Thiele, I.; Sahoo, S.; Heinken, A.; Heirendt, L.; Aurich, M.K.; Noronha, A.; Fleming, R.M. When metabolism meets physiology: Harvey and Harvetta. *bioRxiv* **2018**. [CrossRef]

103. Roesch, L.F.; Lorca, G.L.; Casella, G.; Giongo, A.; Naranjo, A.; Pionzio, A.M.; Li, N.; Mai, V.; Wasserfall, C.H.; Schatz, D.; et al. Culture-independent identification of gut bacteria correlated with the onset of diabetes in a rat model. *ISME J.* **2009**, *3*, 536–548. [CrossRef] [PubMed]
104. Wen, L.; Ley, R.E.; Volchkov, P.Y.; Stranges, P.B.; Avanesyan, L.; Stonebraker, A.C.; Hu, C.; Wong, F.S.; Szot, G.L.; Bluestone, J.A.; et al. Innate immunity and intestinal microbiota in the development of Type 1 diabetes. *Nature* **2008**, *455*, 1109–1113. [CrossRef]
105. Brugman, S.; Klatter, F.; Visser, J.; Wildeboer-Veloo, A.; Harmsen, H.; Rozing, J.; Bos, N. Antibiotic treatment partially protects against type 1 diabetes in the Bio-Breeding diabetes-prone rat. Is the gut flora involved in the development of type 1 diabetes? *Diabetologia* **2006**, *49*, 2105–2108. [CrossRef]
106. Kostic, A.D.; Gevers, D.; Siljander, H.; Vatanen, T.; Hyötyläinen, T.; Hämäläinen, A.-M.; Peet, A.; Tillmann, V.; Pöhö, P.; Mattila, I. The dynamics of the human infant gut microbiome in development and in progression toward type 1 diabetes. *Cell Host Microbe* **2015**, *17*, 260–273. [CrossRef]
107. Dimeloe, S.; Burgener, A.V.; Grahlert, J.; Hess, C. T-cell metabolism governing activation, proliferation and differentiation; a modular view. *Immunology* **2017**, *150*, 35–44. [CrossRef]
108. Bordbar, A.; Mo, M.L.; Nakayasu, E.S.; Schrimpe-Rutledge, A.C.; Kim, Y.M.; Metz, T.O.; Jones, M.B.; Frank, B.C.; Smith, R.D.; Peterson, S.N.; et al. Model-driven multi-omic data analysis elucidates metabolic immunomodulators of macrophage activation. *Mol. Syst. Biol.* **2012**, *8*, 558. [CrossRef]
109. Segata, N.; Boernigen, D.; Tickle, T.L.; Morgan, X.C.; Garrett, W.S.; Huttenhower, C. Computational meta'omics for microbial community studies. *Mol. Syst. Biol.* **2013**, *9*, 666. [CrossRef]
110. Mardinoglu, A.; Shoaie, S.; Bergentall, M.; Ghaffari, P.; Zhang, C.; Larsson, E.; Bäckhed, F.; Nielsen, J. The gut microbiota modulates host amino acid and glutathione metabolism in mice. *Mol. Syst. Biol.* **2015**, *11*, 834. [CrossRef]
111. Lagier, J.C.; Khelaifia, S.; Alou, M.T.; Ndongo, S.; Dione, N.; Hugon, P.; Caputo, A.; Cadoret, F.; Traore, S.I.; Seck, E.H.; et al. Culture of previously uncultured members of the human gut microbiota by culturomics. *Nat. Microbiol.* **2016**, *1*, 16203. [CrossRef] [PubMed]
112. Lagier, J.-C.; Hugon, P.; Khelaifia, S.; Fournier, P.-E.; La Scola, B.; Raoult, D. The rebirth of culture in microbiology through the example of culturomics to study human gut microbiota. *Clin. Microbiol. Rev.* **2015**, *28*, 237–264. [CrossRef] [PubMed]
113. David, L.A. Toward Personalized Control of Human Gut Bacterial Communities. *mSystems* **2018**, *3*. [CrossRef] [PubMed]
114. Thiele, I.; Clancy, C.M.; Heinken, A.; Fleming, R.M. Quantitative systems pharmacology and the personalized drug–microbiota–diet axis. *Curr. Opin. Syst. Biol.* **2017**, *4*, 43–52. [CrossRef]
115. Sen, P.; Vial, H.J.; Radulescu, O. Mathematical modeling and omic data integration to understand dynamic adaptation of Apicomplexan parasites and identify pharmaceutical targets. *Compr. Anal. Parasite Biol. Metab. Drug Discov.* **2016**, *7*, 457.
116. Sen, P.; Vial, H.J.; Radulescu, O. Kinetic modelling of phospholipid synthesis in Plasmodium knowlesi unravels crucial steps and relative importance of multiple pathways. *BMC Syst. Biol.* **2013**, *7*, 123. [CrossRef]

© 2019 by the authors. Licensee MDPI, Basel, Switzerland. This article is an open access article distributed under the terms and conditions of the Creative Commons Attribution (CC BY) license (http://creativecommons.org/licenses/by/4.0/).

Protocol

"Notame": Workflow for Non-Targeted LC–MS Metabolic Profiling

Anton Klåvus [1,*,†], Marietta Kokla [1,*,†], Stefania Noerman [1], Ville M. Koistinen [1], Marjo Tuomainen [1], Iman Zarei [1], Topi Meuronen [1], Merja R. Häkkinen [2], Soile Rummukainen [2], Ambrin Farizah Babu [1], Taisa Sallinen [1,2], Olli Kärkkäinen [2], Jussi Paananen [3], David Broadhurst [4], Carl Brunius [5,6] and Kati Hanhineva [1,5,7,*]

1. Department of Clinical Nutrition and Public Health, University of Eastern Finland, 70210 Kuopio, Finland; stefania.noerman@uef.fi (S.N.); ville.m.koistinen@uef.fi (V.M.K.); marjo.tuomainen@uef.fi (M.T.); iman.zarei@uef.fi (I.Z.); topi.meuronen@uef.fi (T.M.); ambbab@student.uef.fi (A.F.B.); taisa.sallinen@uef.fi (T.S.)
2. School of Pharmacy, University of Eastern Finland, 70210 Kuopio, Finland; merja.hakkinen@uef.fi (M.R.H.); soile.rummukainen@uef.fi (S.R.); olli.karkkainen@uef.fi (O.K.)
3. Institute of Biomedicine, University of Eastern Finland, 70210 Kuopio, Finland; jussi.paananen@uef.fi
4. Centre for Integrative Metabolomics & Computational Biology, School of Science, Edith Cowan University, Joondalup, WA 6027, Australia; d.broadhurst@ecu.edu.au
5. Department of Biology and Biological Engineering, Chalmers University of Technology, 41296 Gothenburg, Sweden; carl.brunius@chalmers.se
6. Chalmers Mass Spectrometry Infrastructure, Chalmers University of Technology, 41296 Gothenburg, Sweden
7. Department of Biochemistry, Food Chemistry and Food Development unit, University of Turku, 20014 Turun yliopisto, Finland
* Correspondence: anton.klavus@uef.fi (A.K.); marietta.kokla@uef.fi (M.K.); kati.hanhineva@uef.fi (K.H.)
† These authors have contributed equally to this work.

Received: 2 March 2020; Accepted: 28 March 2020; Published: 31 March 2020

Abstract: Metabolomics analysis generates vast arrays of data, necessitating comprehensive workflows involving expertise in analytics, biochemistry and bioinformatics in order to provide coherent and high-quality data that enable discovery of robust and biologically significant metabolic findings. In this protocol article, we introduce notame, an analytical workflow for non-targeted metabolic profiling approaches, utilizing liquid chromatography–mass spectrometry analysis. We provide an overview of lab protocols and statistical methods that we commonly practice for the analysis of nutritional metabolomics data. The paper is divided into three main sections: the first and second sections introducing the background and the study designs available for metabolomics research and the third section describing in detail the steps of the main methods and protocols used to produce, preprocess and statistically analyze metabolomics data and, finally, to identify and interpret the compounds that have emerged as interesting.

Keywords: metabolomics; LC–MS; mass spectrometry; metabolic profiling; computational statistical; unsupervised learning; supervised learning; pathway analysis

1. Introduction

The rapid technical development of instrumentation for biomolecule analysis has led to a wide application of metabolomics in biological and biomedical research. Due to its very high sensitivity and the ability to concomitantly assess thousands of molecular features, liquid chromatography coupled with mass spectrometry (LC–MS) is making its way as the key analytical tool in the field of discovery-driven metabolic profiling [1–3]. The LC–MS platform generates large amounts of signals—biological signals from metabolites, their adducts, fragments, isotopes and instrument noise, thereby necessitating adequate computational tools to process, analyze and interpret the data [4,5]. Although the data processing solutions for complex metabolomics data are accumulating with increasing speed, they continue to be the bottleneck within the analysis, especially the metabolite identification process [6–8]. Starting from the acquisition of data to the identification of metabolites, the metabolic profiling workflow involves numerous steps that require expertise in analytical chemistry, biochemistry, bioinformatics and data analysis—click-and-go online tools may therefore not provide adequate reliability. To guarantee high quality output from metabolomics experiments, cooperation of scientists with various backgrounds and expertise is needed.

First, the production of high-quality metabolomics data requires high quality samples originating from studies with meaningful research questions, adequate sample preparation and know-how in operating MS instruments in order to get out the maximum performance of the sensitive measurements. The acquired data needs to undergo several preprocessing steps, starting from data collection (peak picking), where it is imperative to understand the detection threshold and signal-to-noise ratios of the measurement. This is then followed by a multi-step processing phase involving imputation, normalization, data reduction and clean-up, which determines the quality of the data that is used in downstream data-analysis, metabolite identification and biological interpretation of the results. All of these steps need to follow necessary quality assurance and quality control procedures for reliable outcome of the metabolomics analysis [9,10]. Finally, the compounds that have emerged as interesting in the given study setup need to be identified using a combination of automated metabolite identification algorithms and exploration of the raw LC–MS/MS spectral data.

Although the currently proposed non-targeted metabolic profiling workflow is applicable on basically any metabolomics study, it has been developed and utilized mainly on food and nutritional approaches. Therefore, examples provided here on the presentation of results are from studies within that field. In fact, food and nutrition sciences encompass a versatile array of research fields, which have adopted metabolomics as one of the most important analytical tools during the past decade [9]. For example, metabolic profiling allows a comprehensive analysis of the chemical composition of food and estimating the impact of industrial processing and modifications by gut microbiota [11,12]. Likewise, when assessing the actual health outcomes of certain diets or specific foods, metabolic profiling enables pointing out the areas of metabolism that are reflecting the dietary differences; especially when data are correlated with other, traditional clinical variables, they may raise novel hypotheses on the molecular-level linkage between diet and health [13–15].

Here, we present analytical workflows suitable for any non-targeted metabolic profiling study in a systematic manner (Figure 1), with a major focus on data-analysis challenges. We also present a new R package: notame (version 0.0.1, https://github.com/antonvsdata/notame), where we have bundled many of the data-analysis tools used in our lab so that they are easy to adopt for other scientists working in the field of metabolic profiling. This includes the pre-processing steps and visualizations in Section 3.2.2, Section 3.2.3, Section 3.2.4, Section 3.2.5, statistical tests and multivariate models in Section 3.3, as well as the visualizations in Section 3.4. The package documentation contains extensive instructions for using the package, along with a template script for preprocessing and analyzing data from a single-batch LC–MS experiment as well as a small example dataset.

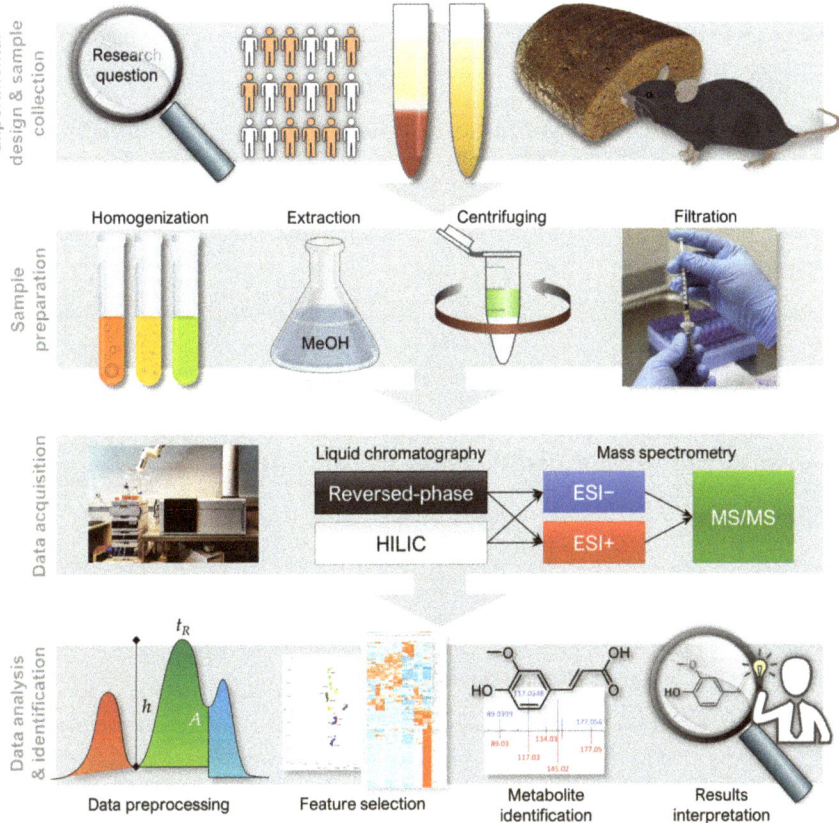

Figure 1. A general overview of notame workflow containing four important stages; 1. Experimental designs and sample collection, 2. sample preparation, 3. data acquisition, 4. data analysis and biomarker identification analysis.

2. Experimental Design

The non-targeted metabolic profiling analytical workflow presented here includes steps from sample preparation and LC–MS analysis all the way to metabolite identification (Figure 1). It is noteworthy to mention, however, that the study design and careful planning for the sampling are very important part of the study governing the quality of the results and therefore require special attention [9]. Herein, we focus on metabolomics analysis performed in one batch (where the number of samples typically reaches 200–300 samples). However, the procedures are in general applicable for larger, multi-batch experiments, although extra procedures for quality control are in order [10,16].

2.1. Materials

Sample preparation materials:

a. 96-well plate (Thermo Scientific, Rochester, NY, USA, Cat.No. 260252),
b. Filter plate (Agilent, Santa Clara, CA, USA, Cat.No. A5969002)
c. 96-Well cap mats (Thermo Scientific, Roskilde, Denmark, Cat.No. 276002)
d. Syringe filters (PALL Corporation, Ann Arbor, MI, USA, Cat.No. 4552T)
e. Syringe Norm-Ject® tuberculin 1 mL (Henke Sass Wolf, Tuttlingen, Germany, Cat.No 4010-200V0)

f. Wide orifice pipette tips (Thermo Scientific, Vantaa, Finland, Cat.No. 9405050)
g. Homogenizer microtubes (OMNI International, Kennesaw, GA, USA, Cat.No 19-620)

LC–MS materials:

h. Reversed-phase chromatography (RP) column: Zorbax Eclipse XDB-C18, particle size 1.8 µm, 2.1 × 100 mm (Agilent Technologies, Santa Clara, CA, USA, Cat.No. 981758-902).
i. Hydrophilic interaction chromatography (HILIC) column: Acquity UPLC BEH Amide 1.7 µm, 2.1 × 100 mm (Waters Corporation, Milford, MA, USA, Cat.No. 186004801).

Reagents:

a. Acetonitrile, ACN (HiPerSolv CHROMANORM, VWR Chemicals, Fontenay-sous-Bois, France, Cat.No. 83640.320)
b. Methanol, MeOH (CHROMASOLV™ LC–MS Ultra, Riedel-de Haën™, Honeywell, Seelze, Germany, Cat.No. 14262-2L)
c. Formic acid (Optima LC/MS, Fisher Chemical, Geel, Belgium, Cat.No. A117-50)
d. Ammonium formate (CHROMASOLV™ LC–MS Ultra, Honeywell Fluka, Seelze, Germany, Cat.No. 14266-25G)
e. Ultra-pure water (Class 1, ELGA PURELAB Ultra Analytical, Lane End, UK)

2.2. Equipment

The current workflow is demonstrated with one suitable LC–MS instrumentation and software combination but can likewise employ any other high-accuracy LC–MS setup.

Sample preparation and LC–MS instruments:

a. Centrifuges: For 96-well plates: Heraus Megafuge 40R (ThermoFisher Scientific, Osterode, Germany), for microcentrifuge tubes: Centrifuge 5804R (Eppendorf, Hamburg, Germany)
b. Vortex: Vortex Genie 2 (Scientific Industries, Bohemia, NY, USA)
c. Homogenizer: Bead Ruptor 24 Elite with OMNI BR CRYO unit (OMNI International, Kennesaw, GA, USA)
d. Shaker: Multi Reax (Heidolph, Schwabach, Germany)
e. 1290 Infinity Binary UPLC system (Agilent Technologies, Waldbronn, Karlsruhe, Germany)
f. 6540 UHD accurate-mass quadrupole-time-of-flight mass spectrometer (qTOF-MS) with Jetstream ESI source (Agilent Technologies, Santa Clara, CA, USA)

Software:

g. Agilent MassHunter Acquisition B.07.00 (Agilent Technologies),
h. MS-DIAL version 3.70 [17],
i. MS-FINDER version 3.24 [18],
j. R version 3.5.0 [19]
k. Multiple Experiment Viewer (MeV) version 4.9.0 (http://mev.tm4.org/).

3. Analytical Procedure and Results

3.1. LC–MS Analysis

3.1.1. Sample Preparation

Sample preparation for the non-targeted metabolite profiling work aimed to extract in a single attempt as wide range of metabolites as possible with, in general, minimal sample workup. Therefore, straightforward, simple extraction protocols were preferred. Protocol 1 was designed for extracting plasma/serum samples at a ratio of 1:5 with ACN and Protocol 2 for extracting homogenized tissue samples at a ratio of 1:6 with 80% methanol.

Protocol 1: Plasma/Serum Samples

1. Thaw plasma/serum samples in ice water and keep them on wet ice during all the waiting periods.
2. Place the 96-well plate on wet ice for sample preparation and set the filter plate on it.
3. Add 400 µL of cold ACN to the filter plate well.
4. Vortex a plasma/serum sample 10 s at the maximum speed.
5. Add 100 µL of plasma/serum sample to the same well as ACN.
6. To prepare the pooled quality control (QC) samples, collect 10 µL aliquots of each sample and add them to the same clean microcentrifuge tube and finally, mix properly.
7. Mix ACN and sample by pipetting four times. Use wide orifice Finn Pipette tips to avoid tip clogging.
8. Repeat steps 1–5 for all samples. Lastly, use the same procedure for the QC sample. For the extraction blank, perform step 3 (cold ACN without sample) and use the same procedure thereon.
9. Filter the precipitated samples by centrifuging the plate for 5 min at 700× g at 4 °C.
10. Remove the filter plate and seal the 96-well plate tightly with the 96-well cap mat to avoid sample evaporation.
11. Analyze the samples immediately or store the plate at +4 °C for a maximum of 1 day or at −20 °C until analysis.

Protocol 2: Tissue Samples

12. Weigh a maximum of 300 mg frozen tissue into 2-mL OMNI microtube with beads. Keep the samples on dry ice.
13. Add ice cold 80% methanol in a ratio of 500 µL solvent per 100 mg tissue and keep the tubes on wet ice. Include an extraction blank with solvent only.
14. **Optional step:** In the case of metabolite-dense sample material (e.g., plants), it might be necessary to use a more diluted solvent/sample ratio to avoid analytical problems, such as saturation of the detector or overloading of the column.
15. Homogenize samples with a Bead Ruptor 24 Elite homogenizer. For soft tissues, perform one homogenization cycle at the speed 6 m/s at +/− 2 °C for 30 s.
16. **Optional step:** In case a homogenizer instrument is not available, manual tissue disruption can be performed using mortar and pestle with liquid nitrogen.
17. Extract the homogenized samples in a shaker for 5 min at RT.
18. Centrifuge samples for 10 min at 20,000× g at +4 °C.
19. Collect the supernatants on a 96-well filter plate and centrifuge for 5 min at 700× g at 4 °C.
20. **Optional step:** Filter the samples using solvent resistant syringes and PTFE filters into the HPLC vials.
21. Take aliquots (5–25 µL) of filtered samples and combine into one vial to be used as QC sample in the analysis.
22. Analyze the samples immediately or store the plate at +4 °C maximum of 1 day or −20 °C until analysis.

3.1.2. LC–MS Measurement

The most commonly applied analytical technique in non-targeted metabolic profiling is mass spectrometry, often combined with liquid or gas chromatographic separation at the front end. In order to cover a wide range of polarities among the analyzable metabolites, different chromatographic methods may be utilized, e.g., reversed-phase chromatography (RP) and hydrophilic interaction chromatography (HILIC). MS data can then be acquired in both positive (+) and negative (−) electrospray ionization (ESI) polarities.

23. Use the following conditions for RP chromatography: Column oven temperature 50 °C, flow rate 0.4 mL/min, gradient elution with water (eluent A) and methanol (eluent B) both containing 0.1% (v/v) of formic acid. Gradient profile for RP separations: 0–10 min: 2 → 100% B; 10–14.5 min: 100% B; 14.5–14.51 min: 100 → 2% B; 14.51–16.5 min: 2% B. Needle wash with 50% ACN. Set the injection volume at 2 µL and sample tray at 10 °C.

24. Use the following conditions for HILIC: Column oven temperature 45 °C, flow rate 0.6 mL/min, gradient elution with 50% v/v ACN in water (eluent A) and 90% v/v ACN in water (eluent B), both containing 20 mM ammonium formate (pH 3). The gradient profile for HILIC separations: 0–2.5 min: 100% B, 2.5–10 min: 100% B → 0% B; 10–10.01 min: 0% B → 100% B; 10.01–12.5 min: 100% B. Needle wash with 50% ACN. Set the injection volume at 2 µL and sample tray at 10 °C.

25. To operate at high mass accuracy (<2 ppm), calibrate the MS daily and use the continuous mass axis calibration by monitoring two reference ions from an infusion solution throughout the analytical runs. Examples of reference ions in ESI+ mode: m/z 121.050873 and m/z 922.009798, and reference ions in ESI− mode m/z 112.985587 and m/z 966.000725. These reference ions are coming from the compounds in the infusion solution. m/z 121 is purine, m/z 112 is trifluoroacetic acid and m/z 922 and 966 are HP-0921 (Hexakis (1H,1H,3H-tetrafluoropropoxy) phosphazine) [20,21]

26. Use the following conditions for Jetstream ESI source: drying gas temperature 325 °C and flow 10 L/min, sheath gas temperature 350 °C with a flow of 11 L/min, nebulizer pressure 45 psi, capillary voltage 3500 V, nozzle voltage 1000 V, fragmentor voltage 100 V and skimmer 45 V. Use nitrogen as the instrument gas.

27. For data acquisition, use a 2 GHz extended dynamic range mode in both ESI + and ESI - ionization modes from m/z 50 to 1600 (may be adjusted according to sample matrix). Collect the data in the centroid mode at an acquisition rate of 1.67 spectra/s (i.e., 600 ms/spectrum) with an abundance threshold of 150. For automatic data dependent MS/MS analyses, set the precursor isolation width to 1.3 Da. From every precursor scan cycle, 4 most abundant ions are selected for fragmentation. These ions are excluded after two product ion spectra and released again for fragmentation after a 0.25 min hold. Product ion scan time is based on precursor ion intensity, ending at 25,000 counts or after 300 ms. Use collision-induced dissociation voltage 10, 20 and 40 V in subsequent runs.

28. Generate the worklist containing analytical samples. Inject quality control samples after every 12 samples and before and after the sample sequence. To monitor contamination during sample preparation and liquid chromatography, inject extraction blanks in the beginning (before the QC samples) and end of the analysis. The injection order of samples should be randomized. If the study contains samples from multiple matrices, such as samples from different organs, it is recommended that all the samples of a matrix be injected consecutively, for example first inject all heart samples, followed by all liver samples. If there are multiple samples from the same individual, it is recommended that the samples of an individual are run consecutively. We use an in-house developed software called Wranglr (github.com/antonvsdata/wranglr) to automate the generation of sample worklists by automatically randomizing the sample order and adding QC and MS/MS samples. Wranglr is an open-source web application developed with the Shiny package for R [22].

29. Inject 2 blanks and then 15–20 QC samples at the beginning of each run for column conditioning. Inject a QC sample after every 12 samples during the analysis. At the end of each run, include 4 QC samples: 1 for MS analysis, 3 for MS/MS analysis from 3 different collision energies and finally, 2 blanks. If the run contains samples from different tissues or species (i.e., different expected metabolite profiles), it is recommended to run the MS/MS analysis additionally from one sample per different sample type to increase the coverage of available MS/MS data.

3.2. Data Collection and Preprocessing

The data collection (peak picking) and subsequent preprocessing of the raw data are critical steps in non-targeted metabolomics data-analysis since they determine the quality of the data for all the remaining steps (Figure 2). Various peak picking algorithms exist, utilized by vendor-specific and open-source software as well as freely available online services. Widely used examples of open-source software include XCMS (and XCMS Online), MZmine and MS-DIAL. In this workflow, MS-DIAL (http://prime.psc.riken.jp/Metabolomics_Software/MS-DIAL/) [17] is used for the peak picking; it has user-friendly interphase and contains advanced tools for signal filtering, metabolite annotation, chromatogram curation and visualization. After collection of the raw data, pre-processing is required to monitor the quality of the data, make any required transformations/corrections to the data, as well as reduce/merge the number of features originating from the same metabolite.

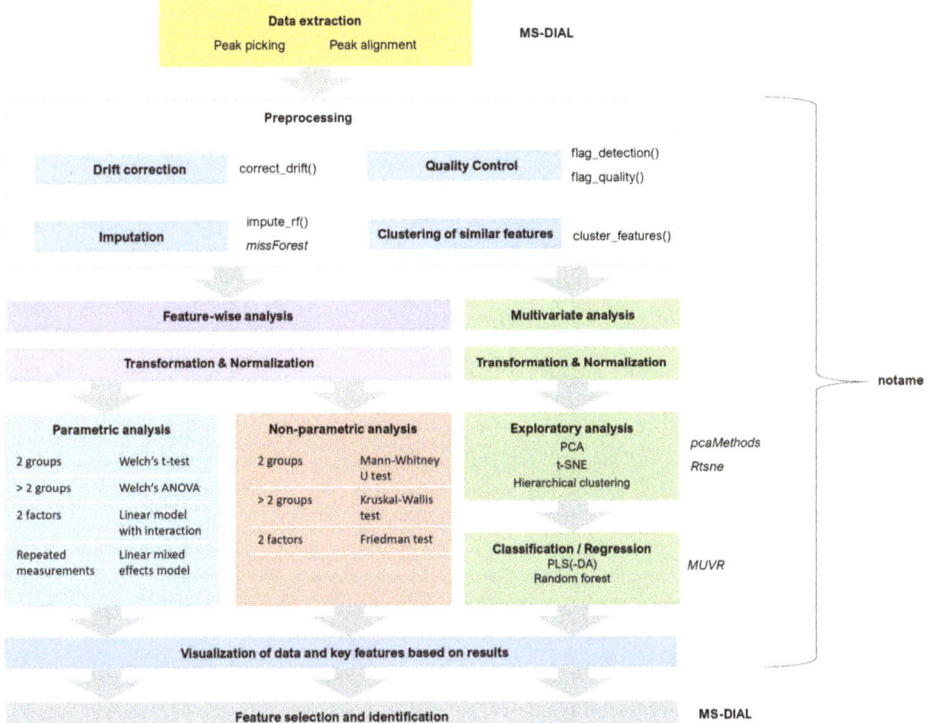

Figure 2. Workflow of the statistical analysis after the peak-picking step. The choices depend on the type of data, the research question and the study design. The tools used for specific steps are listed on the right side of the respective steps. Italicized names are names of external R packages, names ending with () are major functions from the notame package. For more details, see the package documentation.

3.2.1. Peak Picking and Alignment

30. Before the peak picking, convert the raw instrumental data (i.e., *.d) to ABF format using Reifycs Abf Converter (https://www.reifycs.com/AbfConverter). Follow the vendor-specific instructions on the website.
31. For the peak picking in MS-DIAL (version 3.70), choose the following parameters:

a. m/z tolerance according to the instrument mass accuracy; however, it is advisable to set a bit higher tolerance to avoid screening out peaks close to the threshold, e.g., for QTOF we have used tolerance of 0.01 Da or 10 ppm.
b. minimum peak height 2000 signal counts for QTOF (or at least 5 times the typical noise level of the instrument; 3000 signal counts for highly concentrated plant samples).
c. mass slice width 0.1 Da (suitable for QTOF and other instruments with high mass accuracy).
d. linear weighted moving average as the smoothing method (smoothing level 3 scans and minimum peak width 5 scans, according to developer recommendations).
e. in positive mode, select $[M + H]^+$, $[M + NH_4]^+$, $[M + Na]^+$, $[M + K]^+$, $[M + CH_3OH + H]^+$ and $[M - NH_3 + H]^+$ as the most typical adducts and in-source fragments; in negative mode, select $[M - H]^-$, $[M - H2O - H]^-$, $[M + Cl]^-$, $[M + HCOOH - H]^-$ and $[2M - H]^-$ as the adducts and in-source fragments. Depending on previous knowledge, more adducts may be determined.

32. For the peak alignment, set the retention time tolerance according to method accuracy (for the present method we have used 0.05 min and MS1 tolerance at 0.015 Da. Set the detection filter (detected in at least one sample group) at 50%. Unselect the "detected in all QCs" option and select gap filling by compulsion.

33. Once the peak picking is finished, export the alignment result as peak areas into a raw data matrix as a tab-separated text file. Transform the data matrix into a datasheet in a spreadsheet software, such as Excel. Insert additional columns to each datasheet specifying the chromatography and the ionization mode before combining the datasheets into a single file. Remove columns containing peak areas from auto-MS/MS data files.

3.2.2. Drift Correction and Flagging Low-Quality Features

LC–MS-based metabolomics suffers from systematic intensity drift during an LC–MS run. This means that the signal intensity of a molecular feature either decreases or increases systematically throughout the experiment. Removing this drift increases the quality of LC–MS data and allows estimating the true biological effects more accurately. Unfortunately, some molecular features show too much variation in the QC intensities even after drift correction. We use here different quality metrics defined by Broadhurst et al. [10] for measuring the quality of a molecular feature before and after drift correction. Low-quality features are flagged and not included in downstream data analysis. Note that we do not recommend removing low-quality features completely, as they are sometimes needed in the metabolite identification phase when searching for specific ions or fragments of known molecules.

34. Make sure that missing values are correctly represented. A peak picking software might use a numerical value (such as 0, 1 or -999) to represent missing values, while other software such as R have specific ways of representing missing values. For more information on handling missing values, see Section 3.2.4.

35. Molecular features with too low detection rate in the QC samples should be flagged. We recommend a threshold is 70%, meaning that a molecular feature needs to be detected in at least 70% of the QC samples.

36. Log-transform the features prior to drift correction. Log-transformed data normally conform better with the assumptions of the regression model used to model the drift. We use the natural logarithm. Replace zeroes with a value slightly above one (e.g., 1.1) to make sure that all log-transformed values are > 0.

37. The drift correction should then be performed by repeating steps 38–40 for each molecular feature. These procedures are included in notame (function correct_drift()).

38. Model the drift function (f_{drift}) by fitting a smoothed cubic spline [23] to the QC samples, where the abundance of the molecular feature is predicted by the injection order Figure 3a. Smoothed cubic spline regression has one hyperparameter: a smoothing parameter, which controls the

overall curvature of the drift function. The smoothing prevents the spline from overfitting the drift function in the presence of a few deviating QC samples (see Figure 4). A suitable value for the smoothing parameter is chosen by leave-one-out cross validation. For the R function smooth.spline, [24] we recommend the smoothing parameter to be between 0.5 and 1.5.

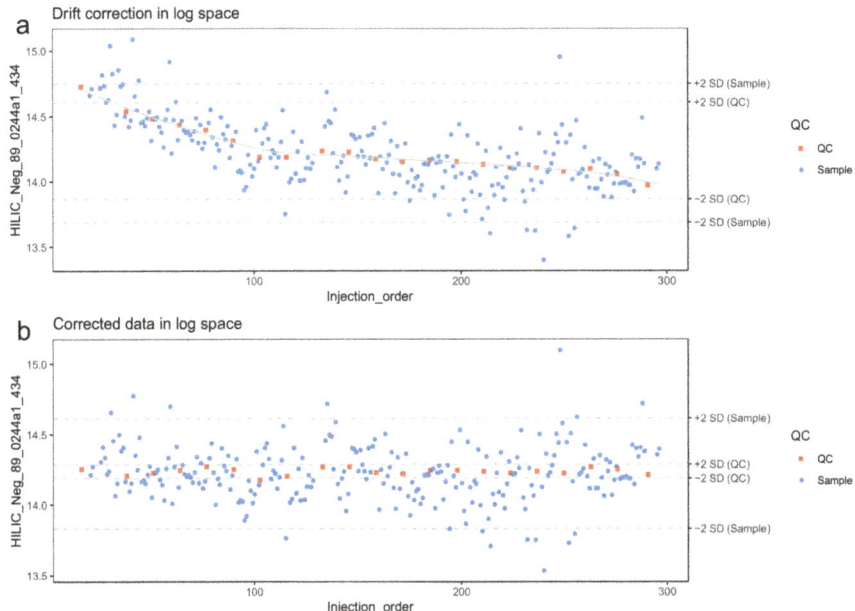

Figure 3. A molecular feature before (**a**) and after (**b**) drift correction by smoothed cubic spline regression. The horizontal lines represent 2 standard deviations from the mean of quality control (QC) samples and biological samples, respectively. The systematic effect of the drift is reduced upon correction.

39. Correct the abundance of each sample using the following formula (for a sample with injection order i):

$$x_{corrected}(i) = x_{original}(i) + mean(x_{QC}) - f_{drift}(i) \quad (1)$$

40. Reverse the log transformation by applying the corresponding exponential function.
41. The drift correction procedure is visualized (Figures 3 and 4) by drawing a scatter plot of the abundances against the injection order before and after drift correction. A line representing the drift function should be added to the scatter plot before correction. To reduce the amount of manual inspection, we usually only inspect potential candidate molecular features selected from downstream statistical tests.
42. **Optional step:** Compute the quality metrics after drift correction and keep only the drift-corrected values for the molecular features where the change in quality metrics indicate that the data quality has been improved. For the other molecular features, retain the original values.
43. Flag or remove low-quality features. As recommended by Broadhurst et al. [10], only the molecular features with RSD < 0.2 and D-ratio < 0.4 should be retained. In notame, this can be done with the function flag_quality().

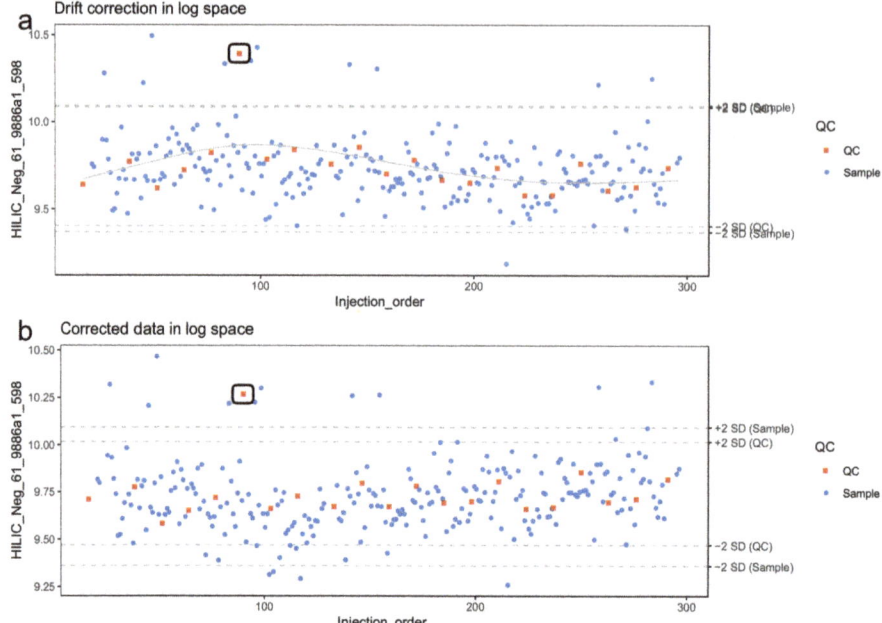

Figure 4. A molecular feature in the presence of an outlying quality control (QC) sample (circled) before (**a**) and after (**b**) drift correction by smoothed cubic spline regression. The horizontal lines represent 2 standard deviations from the mean of QC samples and biological samples, respectively. Due to the smoothing, the correction method is robust against the deviating QC sample and adjusts seemingly adequately for the global drift trend.

3.2.3. Quality Control

The raw data obtained from the peak picking software requires careful examination to estimate the need for additional preprocessing such as drift correction (see 3.2.2.). In the now proposed workflow, the data quality is monitored at each step of the preprocessing with a set of visualizations. Example figures are based on RP positive data from a dietary intervention study [25], before and after drift correction and removal of low-quality features. All the visualizations described in this section are available in notame (see the visualizations vignette for details).

44. Draw the visualizations in steps 46-52 before drift and after drift correction.
45. Flag low-quality features to monitor data quality and the effect of preprocessing.
46. Apply a linear model to each feature, where the feature levels are predicted by injection order. Fit the model separately for QC samples, biological samples and all samples. Then visualize the effect of drift correction to individual features by drawing histograms of the p-values for the regression coefficient of injection order (Figure 5). We represent the expected uniform distribution by a horizontal line. Ideally, the p-values should roughly follow the expected uniform distribution, which would mean that there is no systematic dependency between feature abundances and injection order [26]. Unfortunately, this is rarely the case, but the closer the distribution is to uniform, the better. It is recommended to apply this procedure separately on QC samples and biological samples, which allows observing the drift patterns in both parts of the dataset.

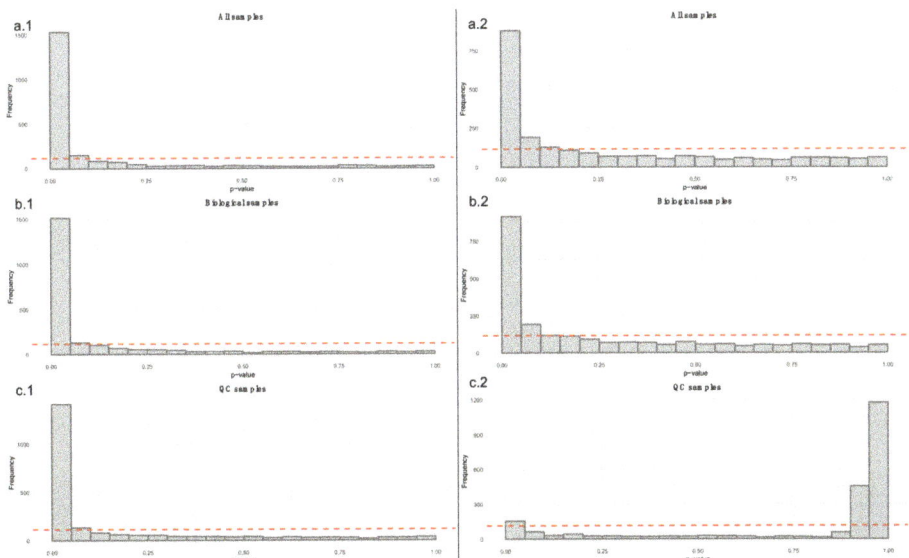

Figure 5. The six histograms illustrate *p*-values from linear regression models between each feature and injection order. The dashed red lines represent the uniform distribution. The a.1 and a.2 histograms show the *p*-values from before (**a.1**) and after (**a.2**) drift correction in all the samples. The b.1 and b.2 histograms focus only in the biological samples before (**b.1**) and after (**b.2**) drift correction. Finally, the c.1 and c.2 histograms show only the *p*-values from the quality control (QC) samples before and after drift correction. In this case, we have a strong drift in the LC–MS data because the *p*-values of the QCs (**c.1**) tend to gather close to zero. After the drift correction, (**c.2**), *p*-values for the QCs are increased.

47. Draw boxplots (Figure 6) where each individual boxplot represents the distribution of all feature levels in a sample: in the first boxplot order the samples by study group (a.1, a.2) (and possibly time point). This can reveal systematic changes in the global feature levels across samples. In the second type (b.1, b.2) order the samples by injection order, highlighting the QC samples. This allows us to observe any systematic drift across the feature levels in the samples.
48. Before subsequent visualizations, mean center the features and divide by standard deviation.
49. Visualize the distribution of the Euclidean distances between samples using a density plot. The plot should feature two distributions, the distribution of distances between QC samples and the distances between biological samples. Ideally, the distribution of QC sample distances should be narrow and well separated from the distribution of study samples (Figure 7).

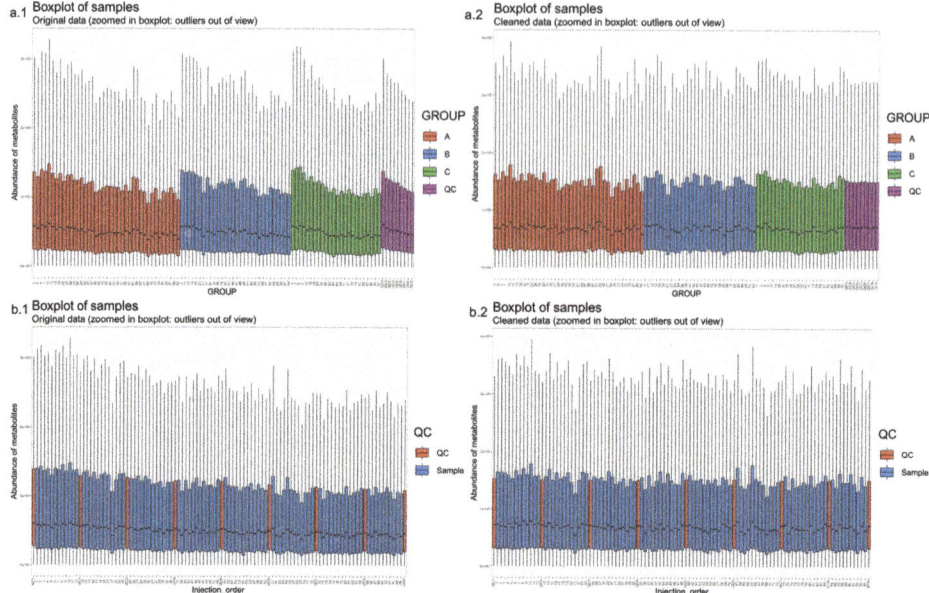

Figure 6. Boxplots of feature intensities per sample. The boxplots (**a.1**), where the samples are ordered by study group (**a.1**) and (**b.1**), where the samples are ordered by injection order and quality control (QC) samples are colored distinctly (**b.1**), show a clear systematic decrease in signal intensity during the injection sequence. After the drift correction, the drift pattern is no longer observable (in boxplots **a.2** and **b.2**).

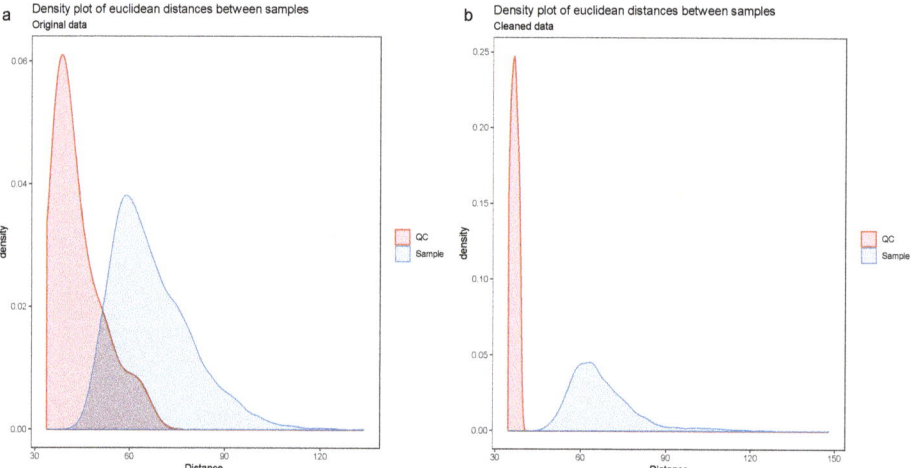

Figure 7. The density plot (**a**) shows a clear overlap between the distribution of quality control (QC) samples and the biological samples, which indicates poor data quality. After drift correction and quality control (**b**), the distributions are no longer overlapping.

Principal component analysis (PCA) [27–29] or t-distributed stochastic neighbor embedding (t-SNE) [30] can be used for observing patterns in the data by drawing scatter plots of the samples in a low-dimensional space (Figures 8 and 9). PCA is a linear method, while t-SNE can also reveal non-linear patterns. Unlike t-SNE, PCA offers information on loadings, i.e., on how the principal components are constructed from original features. For these reasons, we consider PCA and t-SNE as complementary methods. For conciseness we only show t-SNE figures here.

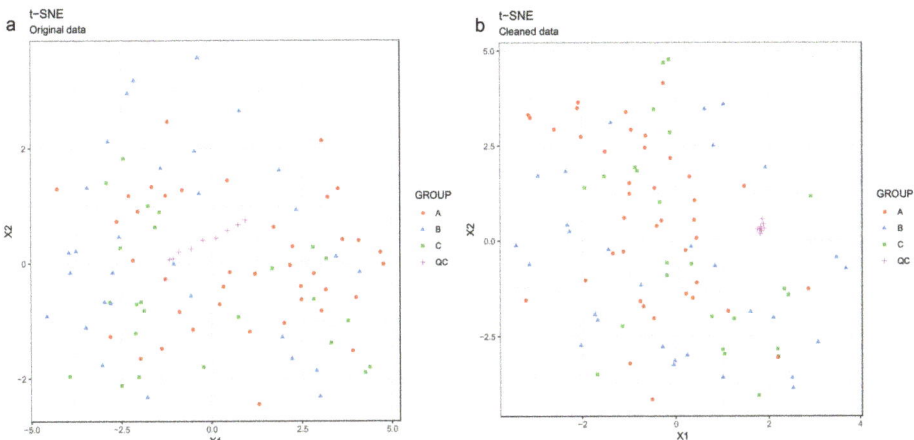

Figure 8. Investigating drift correction patterns using the t-SNE method. The quality control (QC) samples are shifting systematically before drift correction (the line trend of the purple crosses symbol) (**a**), whereas after the drift correction (**b**), the line trend of the QCs is gone and the QCs are now group nicely.

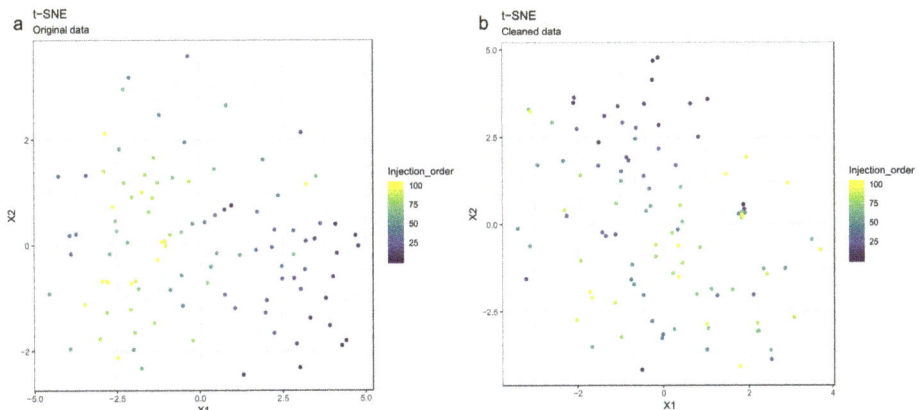

Figure 9. The drift pattern in the injection order (the color trend) using the t-distributed stochastic neighbor embedding (t-SNE) method is visible before drift correction (**a**), whereas after drift correction (**b**), the samples are more randomly scattered.

50. Draw scatterplots of the data points using PCA and t-SNE. Samples can be highlighted by coloring the points in the scatter plot with a study factor (e.g., treatment groups or time points) to observe trends in the data. Ideally, QC samples should cluster together (Figure 8). We also draw separate plots where the samples are colored by injection order to observe drift patterns (Figure 9). If the data quality is high, there should be no visible patterns according to injection order (Figure 9b).
51. **Optional step:** If there is a large number of samples and the points in the t-SNE plots tend to overlap, draw a hexbin version of t-SNE scatter plots colored by injection order (Figure 10), where the plot area is divided into hexagons and each hexagon is colored by the mean of the injection orders of the points inside that hexagon. As before, in an ideal case, there should be no visible drift patterns.

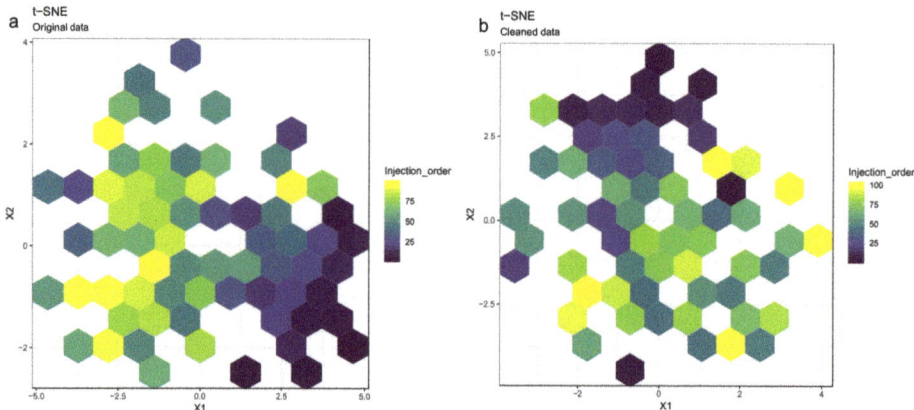

Figure 10. The hexbin plots show similar patterns as the scatterplots in Figure 9: The drift pattern in the injection order (the color trend) using the t-distributed stochastic neighbor embedding (t-SNE) method is visible before drift correction (**a**), whereas after drift correction (**b**), the samples are more randomly scattered. The color of each hexagon corresponds to the mean injection order of the data points in that hexagon.

52. Apply hierarchical clustering [31,32] to the samples and visualize the result in a dendrogram (Figure 11a,b). The QC samples should cluster together early. We also draw a heatmap (Figure 11c,d) representing pairwise distances between samples, where samples on the x and y axes are ordered by hierarchical clustering. The QC samples should have smaller inter-sample distances than other samples. Several techniques can be used for clustering. However, we have consistently achieved good results with hierarchical clustering using Euclidean distances and Ward's criterion for linking clusters [32].

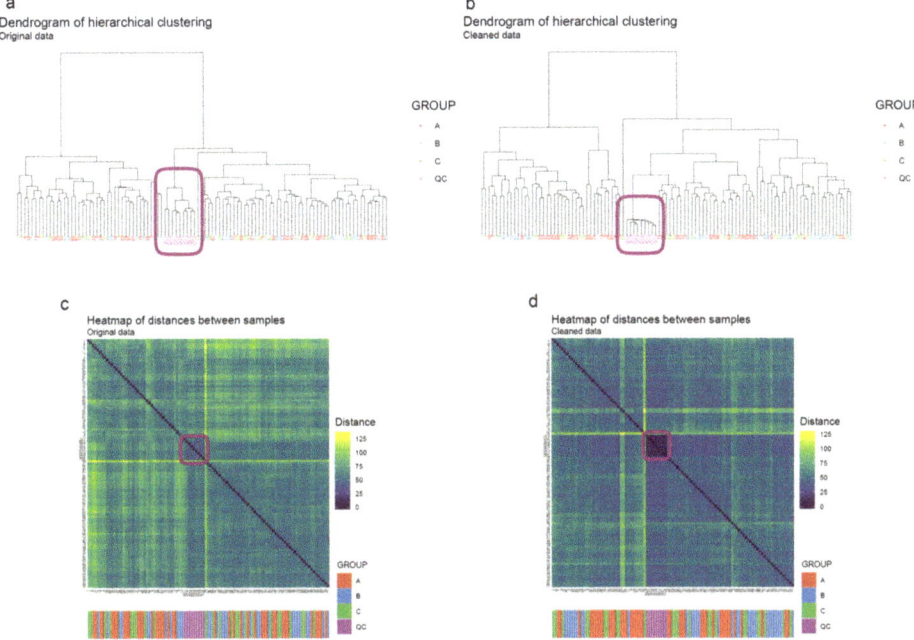

Figure 11. The hierarchical clustering algorithm clusters quality control (QC) samples together even before drift correction (**a**) whereas, after performing drift correction (**b**), the QC samples cluster more clearly together. In the heatmap after the drift correction (**d**) a QC "block" pattern (purple color code), is more clearly visible than in the heatmap before drift correction (**c**).

3.2.4. Imputation, Transformation, Normalization and Scaling

Missing data occur in metabolomics datasets for various reasons and managing this missingness is highly challenging [33]. Imputation is the procedure of replacing missing data with reasonable values using a priori knowledge or information available from the existing data. In this workflow, we perform random forest (RF)-based imputation using the missForest package [33,34], although several other procedures are available [35,36]. Data distributions can affect statistical analysis, especially for variance-based models [37]. Consequently, transformation and normalization can be used to adjust for data heteroscedasticity and skewed distributions among the molecular features. Depending on the type of multivariate analysis chosen we will proceed with different normalization and transformation approaches [38], however in the case of the feature-wise univariate analysis (Section 3.3.1) only imputation is performed. All the preprocessing methods mentioned here are provided in notame (see the preprocessing vignette for details).

53. Impute missing values using random forest imputation. QC samples should be removed prior to imputation to ensure that the imputation is based on patterns in the biological data.
54. Transform the data using either natural logarithmic (nlog) or the generalized logarithmic (glog) function when the data are heavily skewed [38].
55. Normalize the data by probabilistic quotient normalization (PQN) [38,39].
56. Perform mean centering and scaling by standard deviation (autoscaling), before multivariate analysis; this is necessary with GLM-based methods as well as PCA and PLS-DA. However, this is not required for scale invariant techniques such as RF [40].

3.2.5. Clustering Molecular Features Originating from Same Metabolite

Now used peak picking software can detect isotopes, most common adducts and some in-source fragments and combine those features into one entry in the data matrix. However, in LC–MS analysis, unpredictable adduct behavior and neutral loss formation occurs frequently, resulting in the same metabolite being redundantly represented in the data matrix, causing problems not only for the identification of the compounds but also potentially in the data-analysis step due to multiple collinearities.

We present here a method for clustering and combining these features. This approach was developed bespoke to our workflow [41]. Partially similar methods to tackle this problem have been published also elsewhere [42–44]. Features originating from the same compound are assumed to be strongly correlated and have a small difference in their retention time. Thus, the algorithm initially identifies pairs of correlated features within a specified retention time window. The user specifies both the correlation threshold and the size of the retention time window. For illustration, a correlation coefficient threshold of 0.9 and a retention time window of ±1 s are used. Spearman's correlation coefficient is used, as the relationship between features originating from the same compound is assumed linear. However, this assumption may not hold true if some measured features are close to lower or upper limit of quantification (LLOQ and ULOQ) of the instrument.

Next, an undirected graph of all the connections between the features is generated, where each node represents a feature and each edge represents the corresponding correlation coefficient under the retention time constraint (Figure 12a). The algorithm recursively identifies clusters presumed to reflect the same analyte. In brief, this is achieved using a connectivity criterion, i.e., that the features within a cluster should have strong correlation to a sufficient number of the other features within the cluster. A detailed explanation of the algorithm is beyond the scope of this paper and has been included in the Supplementary Materials (Section 1: Clustering features originating from the same compound) for more advanced (bio) computational scientists.

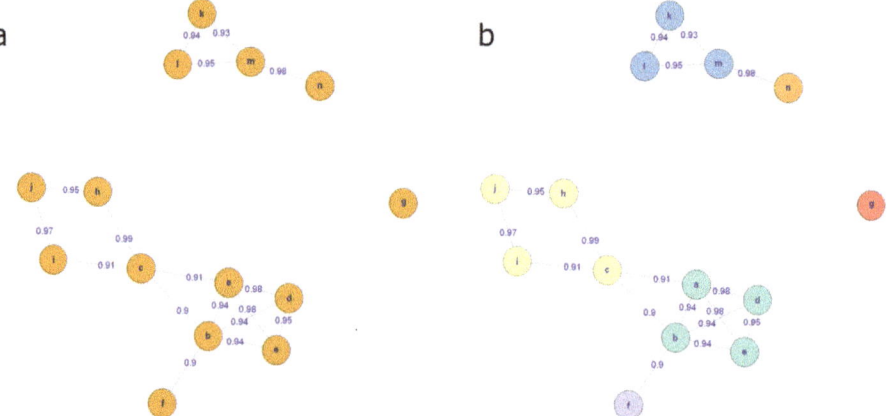

Figure 12. (**a**) An example graph, where every node is a molecular feature and every edge represents a high correlation coefficient and a small retention time difference between the features. (**b**) The graph after the clustering procedure. Each color corresponds to a distinct cluster of features.

After clustering, the feature with the largest median peak area per cluster is retained. All the features that are clustered together are recorded for future reference. Figure 12b shows the state of the graph from Figure 12a after clustering, with each final cluster colored differently.

57. Cluster the molecular features from each analytical mode separately using the algorithm described above. Represent each cluster with the feature with the highest median abundance. Use these features for multivariate analysis and the clustering information for metabolite identification. The algorithm is provided in notame through the cluster_features() function.

3.3. Data Analysis

Once the raw data are checked for quality and analytical drift and the features originating from same metabolites merged to reduce the data matrix, the next phase is to utilize data analytical methods to discover the metabolites of biological importance within the taken study set-up. Preferably, a combination of feature-wise and multivariate analyses can be applied (Figure 2). Notame provides an interface for all the statistical tools mentioned in this section (see the statistics vignette for details).

58. Combine the features from the different analytical modes to a single data matrix. In notame, this is achieved with the function merge_metabosets, which simply concatenates the data matrices and feature information tables row-wise (each row corresponds to a feature) and preserves the sample information unchanged. Note that combining analytical modes inevitably results in increased redundancy in the data matrix, as many compounds are detected in multiple analytical modes. However, combining the analytical modes is necessary so that all available information is available for multivariate analysis methods.

3.3.1. Feature-Wise (Univariate) Analysis

In feature-wise analysis, two types of testing may be used depending on the data: parametric and non-parametric test [45]. The choice of the test statistical depends on the data and the biological questions of the study. Most typically parametric tests are used, but if the features do not satisfy the assumptions of parametric tests, they may be replaced with non-parametric alternatives. Non-parametric methods perform better when dealing with non-normal populations, unequal variances and unequal small sample sizes.

59. For study designs with two groups and no covariates, such as case versus control studies, use a simple Welch's t-test, i.e., the extension of Student's t-test to manage unequal variances between groups. For a non-parametric alternative, consider a Mann-Whitney U test.
60. For studies with multiple groups, first apply Welch's one-way analysis of variance (ANOVA), which can manage unequal variances between groups, to select interesting features based on overall p-value. To investigate differences between groups, conduct post-hoc pairwise Welch's t-tests.
61. For studies with two categorical study factors, apply two-way ANOVA, which allows examining the main effect of each factor and their interaction. If one or both factors have multiple levels, select interesting features based on overall p-values and conduct post-hoc pairwise t-tests as above (bullet 59). For a non-parametric alternative, consider Friedman test.
62. For studies with repeated measurements, use a linear mixed effects model with the time point, group and their interaction factors as fixed effects and the subjects as a random effect. If there are no more than two groups or time points, use t-tests on the regression coefficients to assess the significance of the effects. In the case of multiple groups and/or time points, use type III F-tests for ANOVA-like tables, e.g., with the help of the R packages lme4 and lmerTest that provide all the necessary tests [46,47].

63. To test the strength of association between molecular features or between molecular features and other variables, use Pearson correlation or Spearman correlation as a non-parametric alternative. This can also be done post-hoc, after identification of key metabolites [14].
64. After performing feature-wise tests, *p*-values should be adjusted for multiple testing. We recommend using the Benjamini–Hochberg false discovery rate (FDR) approach. Note that FDR-adjusted *p*-values are frequently referred to as q-values. [45,48,49].

3.3.2. Multivariate Analysis

There are several powerful multivariate tools for analysis of metabolomics data. Dimensionality reduction methods like PCA or t-SNE enable us to explore the data to identify outliers and patterns among samples. Unsupervised clustering methods, such as hierarchical clustering are useful for validating findings from dimensionality reduction methods, as they allow us to observe clustering patterns in high-dimensional space.

Supervised learning techniques, such as partial least squares (PLS) and random forest (RF) are useful for identifying the most interesting molecular features [50,51]. Both the PLS and RF algorithms can be used for both regression and classification purposes. In the case of classification, the PLS model is normally referred to as partial least squares discriminant analysis (PLS-DA). Contrary to the unsupervised methods, supervised methods rely on known outcome or response (e.g., class membership) of each sample and can be used for predictive and descriptive modeling as well as for discriminative variable selection. RF is highly flexible with 3 main advantages over PLS: RF does not assume Gaussian distribution of the variables; RF does not assume linear relationships between response and (latent) predictor variables; Finally, RF is scale invariant, which circumvents issues with scaling and transformations of metabolomics data. On the other hand, it should be noted that PLS can produce stronger models if model assumptions are met. Both PLS and RF offer statistics for evaluating the importance of individual features, such as the variable importance in projection (VIP) values in PLS and Gini index or mean increased error in RF.

65. Apply multivariate algorithms for prediction and variable selection. We employ the MUVR package in R which includes both RF and PLS [50]. For each analysis, three different models are obtained: the minimal-optimal ('min'), 'mid' and all-relevant ('max') models (Figure 13). The 'max' model corresponds to maximum information content once the non-informative features have been removed and includes the highest numbers of relevant molecular features, thought it may include some redundant features or highly correlated features. This model is normally selected when e.g., pathway analysis will be applied afterwards. The 'min' model corresponds to the minimal-optimal set of molecular features where the strongest biomarker candidates are likely to be found. The 'mid' model corresponds to a compromise (geometric mean) between the 'min' and 'max' options, representing and with some redundancy between molecular features. In the end, the selection of the model depends on the research interest and study question, such as pathway analysis ('max'), best prediction ('mid') or biomarker discovery ('min').
66. **Optional Step**: Follow this step if the MUVR package is not available (for example if other software than R is used). Evaluate performance of the multivariate model. Use cross-validation for PLS and out-of-bag error estimate for RF (for more information see [51])If the model performance is satisfactory, record variable importance metric (VIP value for PLS and rise in error rate for RF) for each feature.

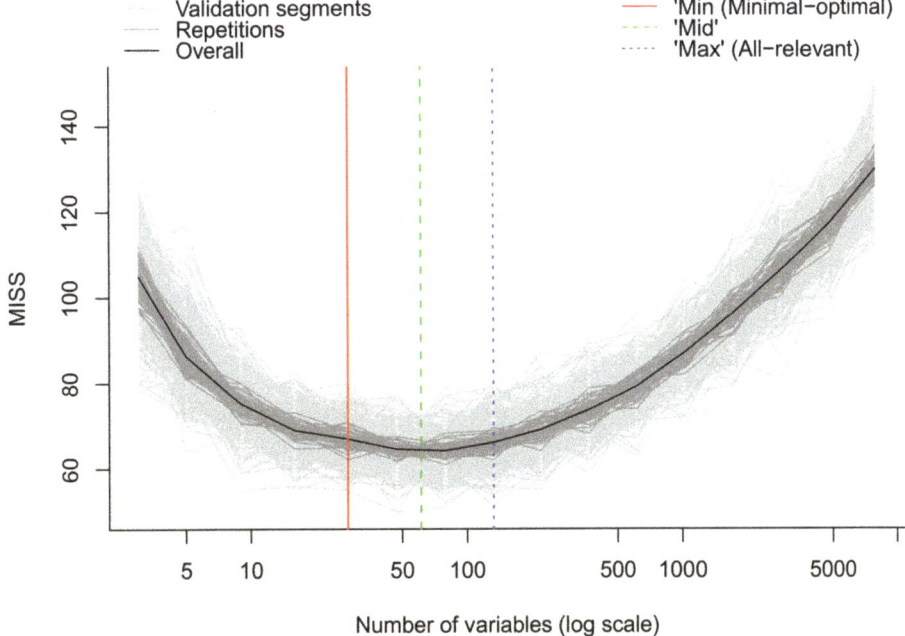

Figure 13. Modelling error measured as the number of miss-classification during internal cross-validation in MUVR. The overall modelling error (black curve) initially decreases when removing noisy variables until the 'max' model. Further removal of variables until the 'min' model removes redundant features while keeping modeling error almost constant. The 'mid' model represents a compromise between the 'min' and 'max' models and a theoretical optimum model. Light and dark grey lines represent higher level of detail in the validation procedure and we refer to Shi et al. [50] for details.

3.3.3. Ranking and Filtering for Variable Selection

After the completion of both feature-wise and multivariate analysis, results are combined via a ranking method in order to determine the most robust and presumably biologically relevant metabolic features to undergo identification.

67. The first step is to sort the molecular features according to their ranks that received though the variable selection process, with the lowest rank or the most important rank (depending on the software) being the 1st rank and the biggest rank or the least important rank being the nth rank (n here is equal to the total number of molecular features available from the variable selection method). In the MUVR package, the output from the 'min', 'mid' or' max' models provides the ranks for each of the molecular features already sorted by the smallest rank. The smallest rank represents that this particular molecular feature is the most important one.
68. Similarly, for each univariate model, the molecular features are sorted based on their q. The 1st rank is given for the feature with the lowest q-values from the FDR correction and the nth rank for the largest one.
69. Then, the rank from the RF model e.g., 'mid' model for each molecular feature is added together with the rank from the same molecular feature for the feature-wise model creating a new column with the Final Ranks.
70. The choice of the total number of the molecular features that are selected in the end for further analysis e.g., identification or pathway analysis is dependent strictly on the user.

71. **Optional Step**: In case the MUVR package is not used for variable selection, the procedure of ranking the molecular features stays the same for any type variable selection is chosen.

3.4. Visualization of Results

After feature-wise and multivariate analysis, we recommend visualization of patterns of the dataset, both on a feature level and a global level as well as visualization of the p-values and effect size measures, to offer a broad view of the results. All the visualizations in this section are provided in notame unless stated otherwise (see the visualizations vignette for details).

3.4.1. Feature-Wise Graphs

While t-SNE figures (Figures 8 and 9) provide a solid overview of the overall patterns in the data, visualizing effects of study factors on a molecular feature level is useful when interpreting the results. The visualization type used depends on study design.

72. If the study has multiple study groups, the differences between groups can be illustrated by beeswarm boxplots separately for each group (Figure 14).

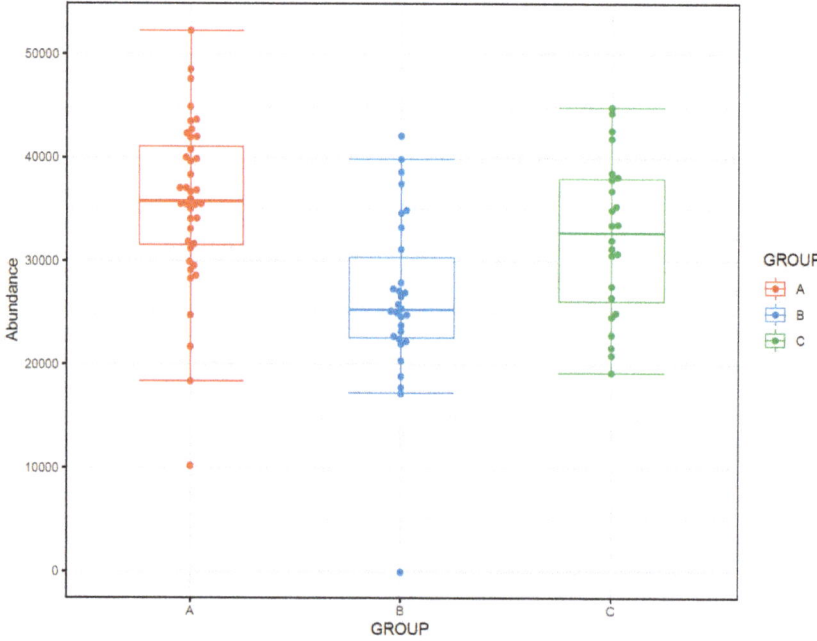

Figure 14. Beeswarm boxplots for a molecular feature subdivided into study group.

73. If the study contains samples from multiple time points, the effect of time can be visualized with a line plot using one line per subject together with a thicker line representing the mean at every time point (Figure 15).

If the study contains both multiple groups and multiple time points, consider the following visualizations:

For repeated measures data, plot least square means from the repeated measures model for each study group. You should also add whiskers around the points representing 95% confidence intervals, standard deviation or other measure of variability (Figure 16).

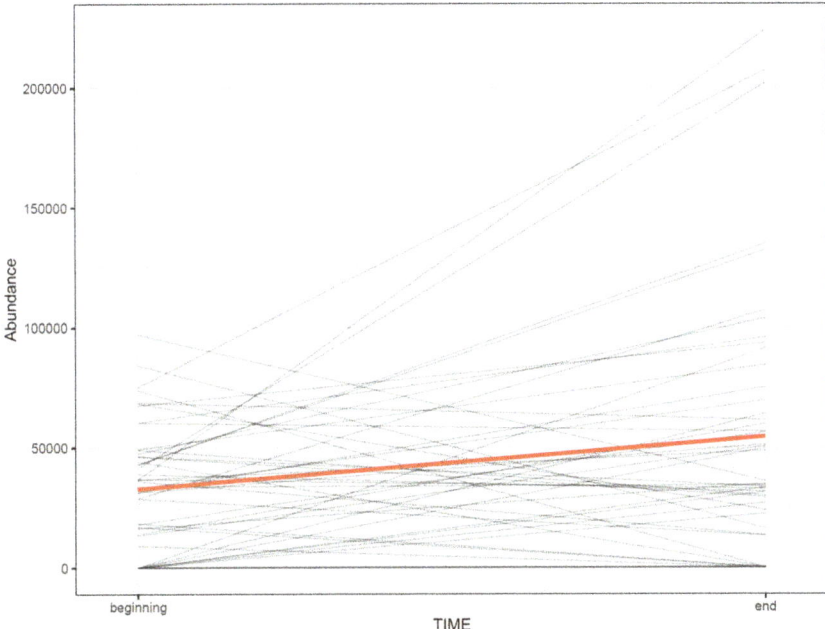

Figure 15. The change in the abundance of a molecular feature as a function of time in each subject. The thick red line represents the sample mean.

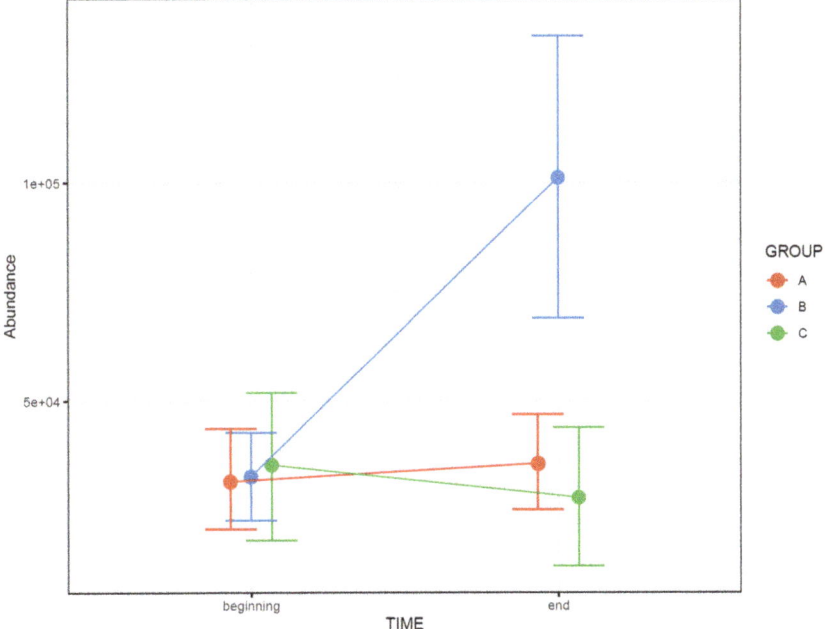

Figure 16. The change in the abundance of a molecular feature as a function of time in each study group. The whiskers depict 95% confidence intervals.

74. Draw a line plot similar to the one in step 73, but color the subject lines according to group and draw separate mean lines for each group (Figure 17a). If the figure gets too cluttered, consider plotting each group separately in small multiples, with a common y-axis (Figure 17b).

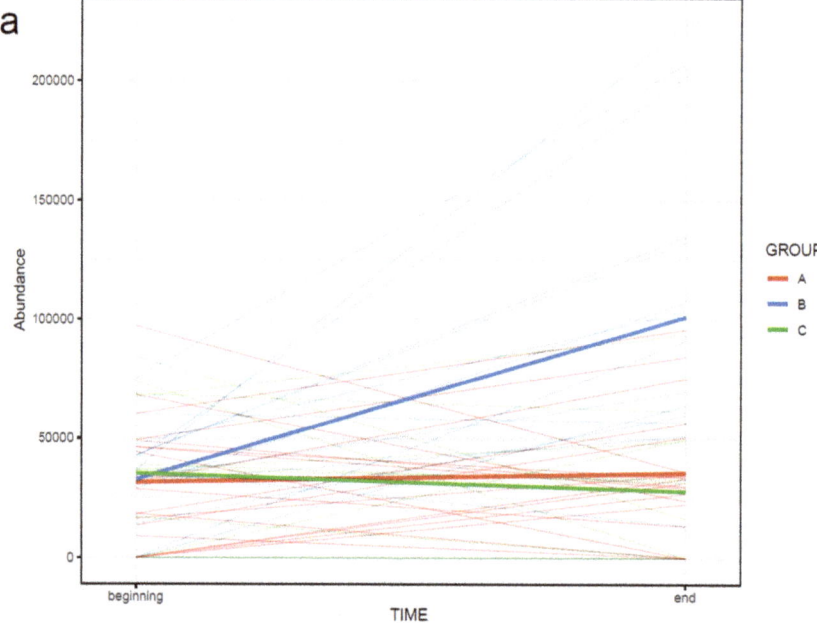

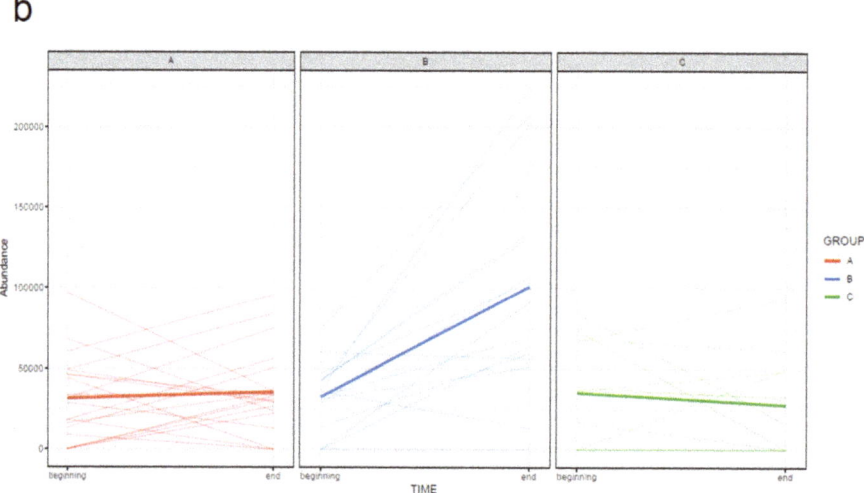

Figure 17. The change in abundance of a molecular feature between two time points in each subject, colored by group (**a**). Data with time series from multiple groups is easier to read when divided to small multiples (**b**). The bold lines represent group means. Note that the bold mean lines do not necessarily reflect an overall trend present in each subject.

3.4.2. Comprehensive Visualization of Results

Here, we present ways of visualizing results from both feature-wise and multivariate analysis. For illustration, we use a simple case from the RP positive mode of an intervention study, where the samples were taken from two time points, before and after an intervention. For feature-wise analysis, we used a linear model with individual molecular feature as the dependent variable and the time point as the independent variable. We also calculated fold change between the two time points for a scale-free measure of effect size. For multivariate analysis we fit a PLS-DA model predicting the time point from the features.

75. Visualize the patterns in the final dataset using unsupervised dimensionality reduction techniques such as PCA [28] (Figure 18) and t-SNE. If the PCA score plot reveals interesting patterns, use a PCA loadings plot to reveal which features contribute the most to the visualized components.

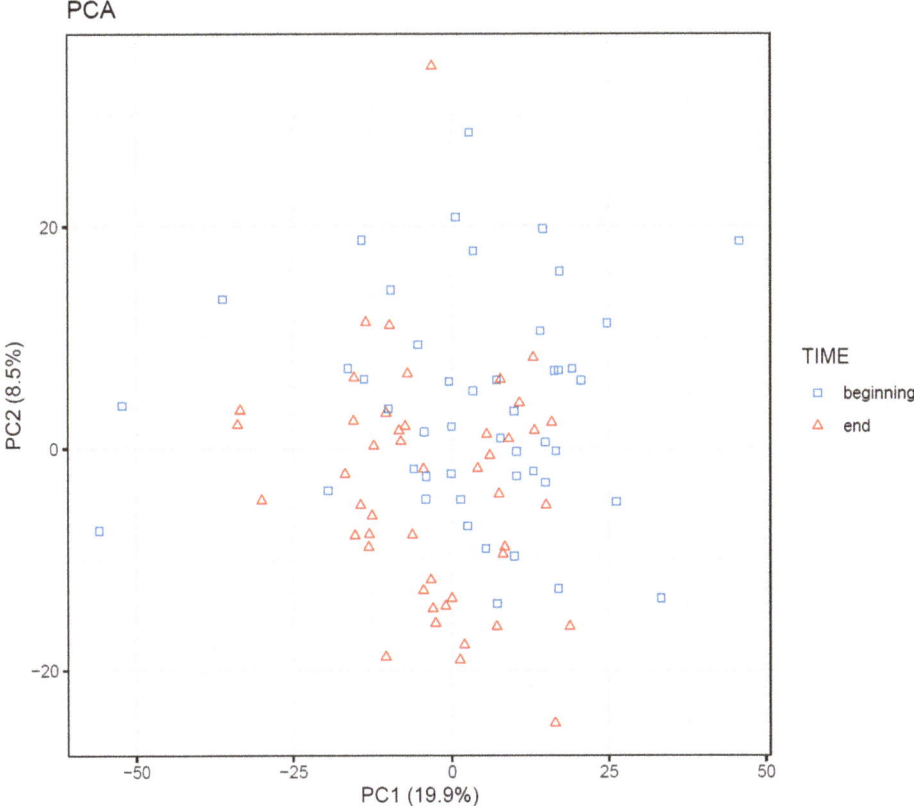

Figure 18. Principal component analysis (PCA) plot of samples from an intervention study, before and after the intervention. The time points are somewhat separated, but no clear clusters or outliers are visible.

76. If PLS(-DA) is used, visualize the samples in a PLS score plot (see Figure 19).

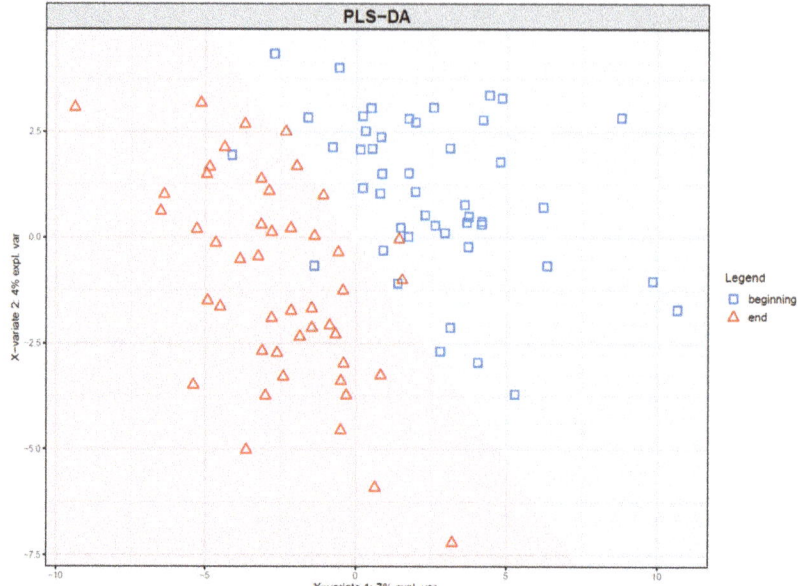

Figure 19. Score plot of the first two components of a partial least squares-discriminant analysis (PLS-DA) model trained to predict the time point of samples from an intervention study. The background color indicates the prediction of the model: samples in the blue area are classified to time point "beginning" and samples in the red area to time point "end". Note that the time points are clearly more separated than in the corresponding principal component analysis (PCA) plot (Figure 18). This is to be expected, as PLS-DA finds components that specifically separate the two time points.

77. To visualize overall changes with respect to time in studies with multiple time points, use PCA and t-SNE figures with arrows depicting change in each individual. The arrows should start at the first time point and end at the last time point for each individual. We recommend plotting each study group separately, as the plot can get crowded since the arrows occupy significantly more space than points (Figure 20).

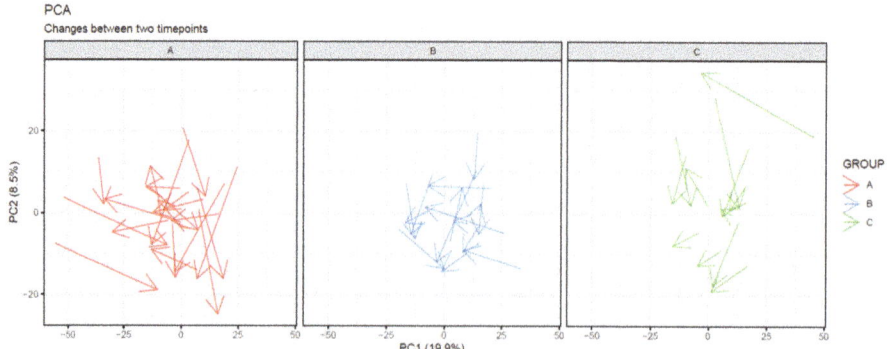

Figure 20. Changes in each subject between two time points visualized as arrows between points in a principal component analysis (PCA) plot. Samples in different groups are separated into subplots. While no group shows a systematic direction of change, we can observe that the subjects in group A show greater overall change that subjects in the other groups.

78. Visualize the distribution of *p*-values from feature-wise analysis in a histogram. Use a line to depict the expected uniform distribution (under null hypothesis). If the distribution of the *p*-values deviates from the line as in Figure 21, it can be argued that we are observing a real effect.

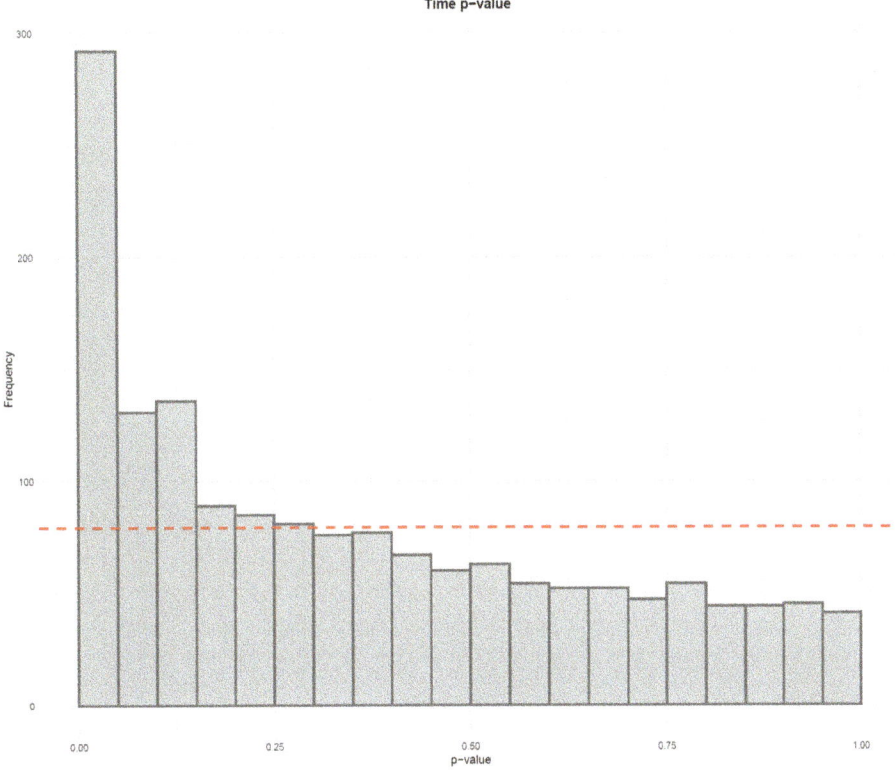

Figure 21. The distribution of *p*-values from linear models testing the difference in feature abundance between two time points. Since the distribution clearly deviates from the uniform distribution depicted by the red line, it can be argued that there is a true difference between the two time points.

79. Visualize the results of feature-wise tests in a volcano plot. Volcano plots are scatter plots with *p*-values on the y axis and effect size (such as fold change) on the x-axis. Add a horizontal line representing the significance threshold for FDR-adjusted q-values. To co-visualize multivariate results, the features can be colored by their relevance score in the multivariate prediction (Figure 22).

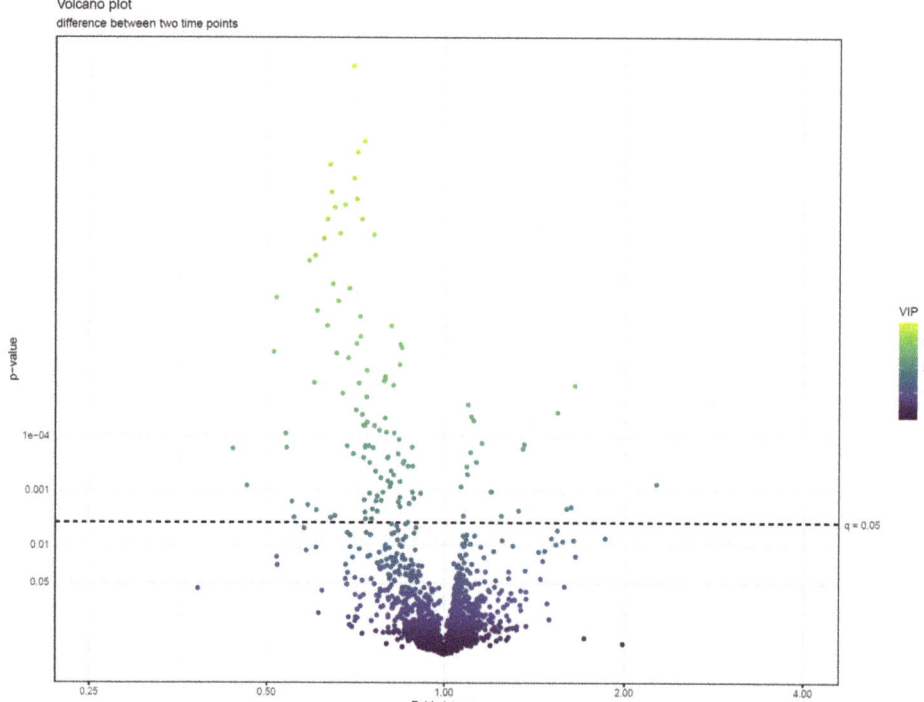

Figure 22. A volcano plot of *p*-values (negative log10 scale) from linear models testing the difference of feature abundances between two time points against fold changes between samples taken before and after a dietary intervention (log2 scale). The features are colored by variable importance in projection (VIP)-value from a partial least squares-discriminant analysis (PLS-DA) model trained to separate the two time points. We can observe that the features with the smallest *p*-values tend to have fold changes below 1, indicating that they are less abundant at the end of the intervention. Other metrics of effect size, like Cohen's d values, can also be used in volcano plots.

Manhattan plots are commonly used in genome-wide association studies (GWAS) to visualize the location of the most significant single nucleotide polymorphisms on the genome. Manhattan plots can be applied in metabolomics by using mass-to-charge ratio or retention time on the x-axis. In addition, in cases where direction of effect can be determined, we can multiply the y-axis by the sign of the effect to create so-called directed Manhattan plots. The Manhattan analogy is not lost since the downward points represent the reflection of the skyline on the Hudson River. Note that Manhattan plots should always be drawn separately for each column and ionization mode, as the metabolite classes corresponding to certain *m/z* and retention time values depend on the column and ionization mode used.

80. Use a Manhattan plot to connect the results of statistics to biochemical properties of the molecular features. The Manhattan plot should have either retention time or mass-to-charge ratio as the x-axis and −log10(*p*-value) on the y-axis. For a directed Manhattan plot, multiply −log10(*p*-value) by the sign of the effect. The points in the Manhattan plot can be colored by the respective VIP value from PLS-DA or another similar metric. Similar to volcano plots, add a horizontal line to represent the significance threshold for FDR-adjusted q-values. Figure 23a,b show Manhattan plots with mass-to-charge ratio and retention time on the x-axis, respectively.

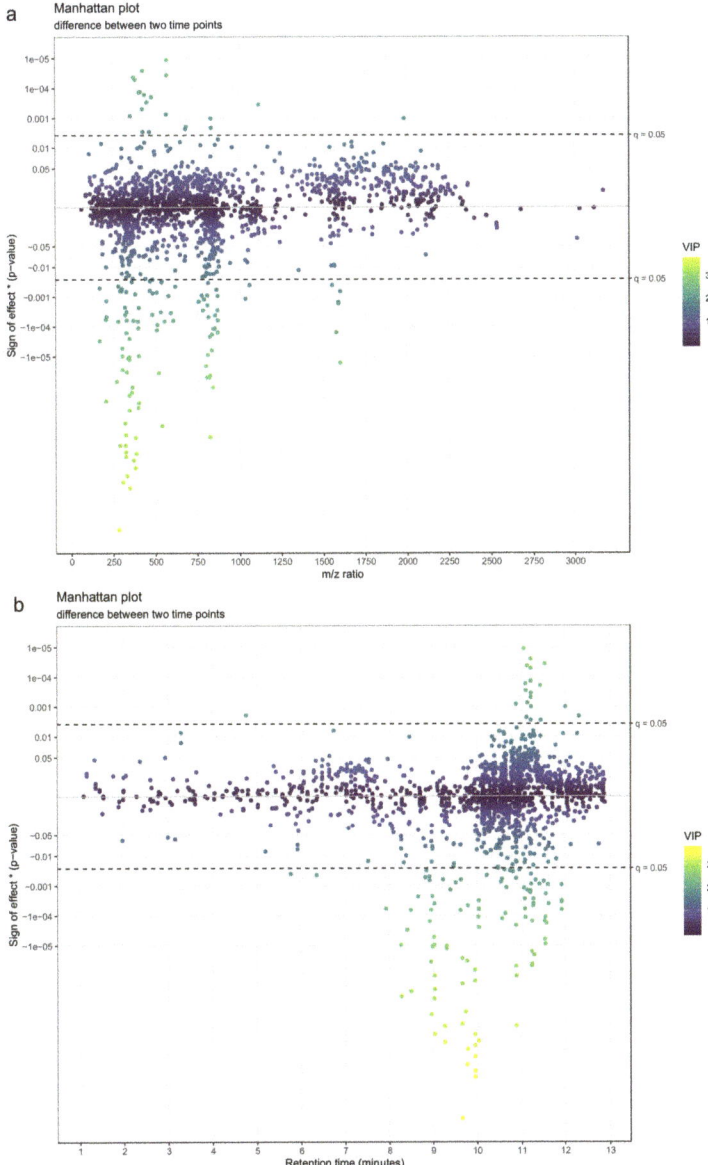

Figure 23. (a) A directed Manhattan plot of *p*-values from linear models testing the difference of feature abundances between two time points with mass-to-charge ratio of the features as x-axis. The points are colored by variable importance in projection (VIP)-value from a partial least squares-discriminant analysis (PLS-DA) model trained to separate the two time points. The most interesting groups of molecular features seem to have *m/z* ratios around 350 and around 800. Both groups are predominantly lower in the end of the intervention. (b) A similar directed Manhattan plot, only with retention time of the features as y-axis. The most interesting groups of molecular features seem to have retention times around 9–10 min and around 11 min. The first group is predominantly lower in the end of the intervention, while the features in the second group have mixed associations.

81. To combine the information of both Manhattan plots, consider a scatter plot with *m/z* and retention time on the x- and y-axis, with the size of the point reflecting *p*-value and potentially colored by variable importance from multivariate modelling (e.g., VIP; Figure 24) or by effect size (e.g., fold change; not shown). While size is not an accurate metric in visualizations, this visualization combines mass and retention time so that the most interesting metabolite classes can be identified. As with Manhattan plots, these plots should be drawn separately for each column and ionization mode.

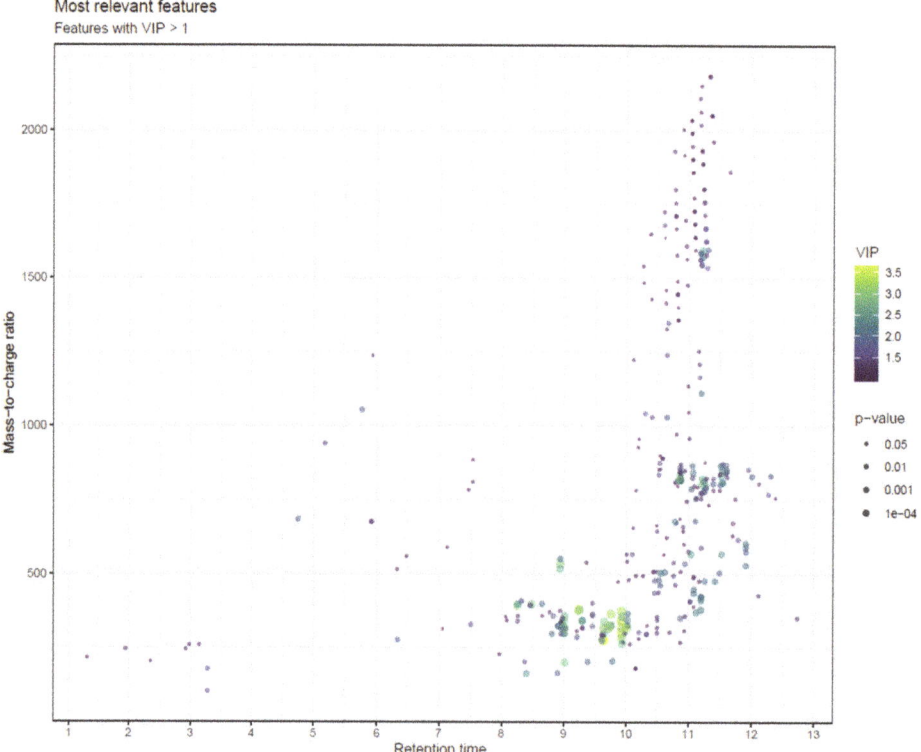

Figure 24. Scatter plot of molecular features in *m/z* vs retention time space, with the size of the points reflecting *p*-values from linear models testing the difference in feature abundances between two time points. The points are colored by variable importance in projection (VIP)-value from a partial least squares-discriminant analysis (PLS-DA) model trained to separate the two time points. To avoid too many overlapping points, only points with VIP value > 1 are drawn. We can observe that the most interesting group of features has retention times around 9–10 min and *m/z* ratios around 350.

We utilize Multiple Experiment Viewer (http://mev.tm4.org/) for *k*-means clustering and hierarchical clustering analyses, which group metabolites into separate clusters or into a hierarchy tree, respectively. Multiple Experiment Viewer is a useful option for post-hoc analysis as it requires no programming expertise. Readers familiar with programming can use other tools for similar results.

The heat maps produced from the analyses can be used to assess the impact of the intervention and the number and proportion of metabolites behaving in a certain manner (Figure 25). We also use the notame R package to produce heat maps of the identified metabolites and their associations with e.g., clinical markers, in which case additional information may be added to each cell, such as the statistical significance with circles, where a larger circle represents a lower *p*-value.

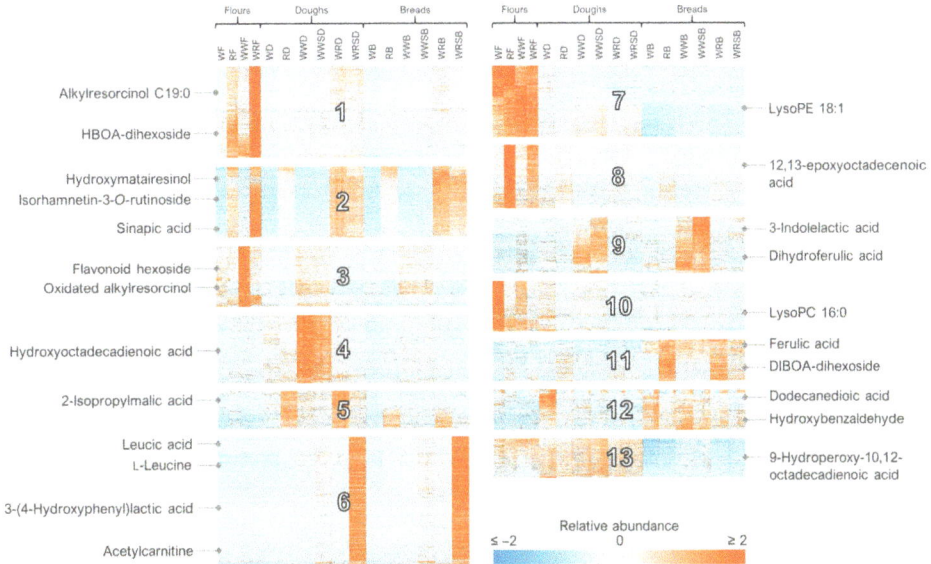

Figure 25. Heat map of all the 12,579 molecular features detected in reversed phase negative mode from cereal samples with some of the annotated compounds highlighted. *k*-Means clustering was applied to the dataset, dividing it into distinct clusters (n = 13) based on the relative abundance of the features across samples.

82. For the clustering in Multiple Experiment Viewer, first normalize the rows (signal abundances) and select appropriate color scale limits for the normalized abundances (0 to 10% of features can be off limits). For hierarchical clustering, choose whether to cluster only the features or samples as well. Use Pearson correlation and average linkage clustering. For k-means clustering, choose cluster genes, use Pearson correlation, calculate k-means and choose a low number of clusters (e.g., 4) for the initial run. Repeat the procedure by increasing the number of clusters until no more clusters with a unique pattern emerge and choose the highest number of clusters based on this visual optimization.

3.5. Identification of Metabolites

The identification and annotation of metabolites is a critical step in any metabolomics study to attribute biological meaning to the data analytical results and to enable further hypotheses to be developed for subsequent studies. In recent years, the development of new software and online tools as well as the emergence and expansion of publicly available spectral databases of metabolites have greatly facilitated the identification process [52,53]. Nevertheless, metabolite identification remains perhaps the most time-consuming task where manual curation is necessary and where not all detected molecular features can be identified, leaving knowledge gaps for the interpretation of the results. Alongside with the challenges related to the instrumental differences and matching the obtained MS/MS data to databases, a key bottleneck restricting the level and number of identifications is the lack of reference data for the vast number of metabolites produced by living organisms, estimated up to one million for the plant kingdom [54] and more than 40,000 for humans [55]. Likewise, matching the obtained MS/MS data to existing databases is not straightforward due to differences in experimental conditions used for collecting the reference data. Other limitations may be related to poor quality or lack of mass spectra from metabolites with low abundance in the sample.

We utilize MS-DIAL [18] in the initial semi-automated step of metabolite identification, where the experimental characteristics (exact m/z, retention time where applicable and MS/MS spectra in CID voltages 10, 20 and 40 V) are compared with those in databases available in NIST MSP format. These databases include MassBank [53], MoNA [56] and others available from the RIKEN Center for Sustainable Resource Science website (http://prime.psc.riken.jp/Metabolomics_Software/) combined in single files for the positive and negative ionization mode. Additionally, we have included our in-house spectral library in the MSP files. The semi-automated identification process annotates metabolites with similarity score 80% or above, after which the annotations are manually curated by assessing the similarity of the MS/MS spectra and the alternative annotations proposed by the software.

After the curation of the metabolites annotated by MS-DIAL, the remaining unknown metabolites undergo additional searches in databases that are primarily available online, including METLIN [52] for small metabolites and LIPID MAPS [57] for unknown metabolites with RP retention time in the lipid region (> 9 min). Additional attempts to characterize the unknowns are made utilizing MS-FINDER [18], which 1) calculates and scores the possible molecular formulas based on the exact mass and isotopic pattern, 2) searches for compounds corresponding to the likely molecular formulas from non-spectral chemical libraries and 3) compares the experimental MS/MS spectrum of the unknowns with *in silico*-generated MS/MS spectra of the candidate structures.

3.5.1. Comparison with Pure Standard Compounds (MSI Level 1)

83. For the identification of metabolites (identification level 1 according to the Metabolomics Standards Initiative) [58], compare the molecular features against an in-house library (i.e., a reference standard analyzed previously with the same platform in the same chromatographic conditions). Apply the following criteria:

    a. matching m/z (within 10 ppm or according to instrument mass accuracy);
    b. similar retention time ($\Delta RT < 0.2$–0.5 min), taking into consideration any possible near-eluting isomers.
    c. MS/MS spectra (main fragments matching within 0.02 Da in one or more CID voltage)

3.5.2. MS/MS Fragmentation and Database Comparison (MSI levels 2–3)

84. For the putative annotation of metabolites (ID level 2), compare the mol features against publicly available spectral databases, including a database file (compiled in MSP format for using within MS-DIAL) and online databases. The annotation has acceptable reliability if the main fragments (excluding the molecular ion) match between the experimental and reference MS/MS spectra in only one proposed metabolite. In case several alternatives exist with similar MS/MS, the common denominator of all the alternatives (e.g., a compound class, ID level 3) is given as the annotation instead. Apply the following criteria:

    a. matching m/z (within 10 ppm or according to instrument mass accuracy)
    b. MS/MS spectra (main fragments matching within 0.02 Da)

85. For the putative characterization of compound class (ID level 3), use the following approaches to obtain characteristic information of the metabolite:

    a. Compare the experimental MS/MS with in-silico generated spectra in MS-FINDER;
    b. Use the calculated molecular formula, retention time and diagnostic MS/MS fragments to determine the compound class.

3.5.3. Pathway Analysis

Once molecular features are annotated as metabolites, pathway analysis may be conducted to better understand the biological relevance of the metabolites, as well as their involvement in metabolic pathways, e.g., related to intervention effects of disease etiology [1,3]. We consider identification of metabolites until level 2 (putative annotation) to be essential prior to pathway analysis. Of the several pathway analysis tools that are freely available, we use predominantly MetaboAnalyst and Cytoscape. For both tools, conversion of metabolite name to HMDB or KEGG ID that are generally recognizable by the pathway analysis software is essential, since one molecule can have multiple names according to the preference of each research group.

86. Option 1: In MetaboAnalyst [59] (https://www.metaboanalyst.ca/) use Enrichment or Pathway Analysis which enables enrichment and visualization of metabolic pathways in which the metabolites could potentially be involved. For more detailed information about metabolic regulation, the Network Explorer enables inclusion of fold change data, along with gene expression data.
87. Option 2: Cytoscape [60] (https://cytoscape.org/) is a powerful stand-alone tool that is used by biomedical researchers to visualize and dynamically analyze gene/protein/metabolite interaction networks. The strength of Cytoscape is even more apparent when linked to databases, e.g., MetScape [61], which allows for visualizing and interpreting metabolomic data in the context of human metabolic networks.

A step-by-step instruction to use the software is listed in the Supplementary Materials (Section 2: Tutorial on Pathway Analyses Tools). It is worth to mention that pathway analysis may not be helpful for lipids, due to i) the limitation of the non-targeted LC–MS metabolomics platform to differentiate the position of the double bonds within the lipid molecule, which impairs the translation of lipid identity to KEGG or HMDB ID and; ii) that most pathway analysis tools would group certain lipid classes that vary greatly based on their fatty acid composition to one node, which may not be biologically meaningful. As an example, phosphatidylcholines with different acyl composition, will be grouped into one node of phosphatidylcholine regardless of the acyl composition, which may not accurately represent acyl transfer in vivo. This gap hence emphasizes the need of pathway analysis tool specialized for lipid molecules.

3.6. Biological Interpretation of the Results

The analytical procedure described above is aimed to identify metabolites and metabolic pathways that are affected in the chosen study design e.g., differences in circulating metabolites after dietary or other interventions or processing-induced alterations to the phytochemical composition of a certain food. While the described workflow is efficient in elucidating such metabolites, the ultimate value lies in the demonstration of biological significance. The findings need to be related to the scientific context and interpreted in the light of existing biological knowledge. Optimally, findings can be validated e.g., in subsequent studies, where the most interesting/important metabolite species may be chosen for additional analysis, often encompassing development of targeted, quantitative analytical approaches and analyzed in different study populations. An example of such approach is the recent discovery of various trimethylated compounds related to whole grain consumption [62] and the establishment of a quantitative method within another cohort [63].

4. Conclusions

Non-targeted metabolic profiling analysis employing liquid chromatography and mass spectrometry analysis has proven its usefulness in various fields of natural and medical sciences during the last couple of decades and has greatly improved our capabilities to explore and understand the chemical space in biological samples. Notame workflow encompasses all the essential steps in metabolic profiling studies, from generation of samples to the interpretation of the results and is aimed to serve as a general guideline for setting up and executing metabolomics studies, as well as support users with an in-housed developed R package (notame, version 0.0.1 https://github.com/antonvsdata/notame).

Supplementary Materials: The following are available online at http://www.mdpi.com/2218-1989/10/4/135/s1, Section 1: Clustering features originating from the same compound, Section 2: Tutorial on Pathway Analyses Tools.

Author Contributions: M.K. wrote chapters of imputation and multivariate analysis, writing, review and editing the manuscript. A.K. wrote the chapters on quality control, drift correction, feature clustering algorithm, feature-wise analysis and visualizations, is the main author of the notame R package and Wranglr web application and reviewed and edited the manuscript. S.N., M.T. and T.M. wrote the chapter on study design. S.N. and I.Z. described pathway analysis. J.P. conceived the original idea of the statistical and visualization pipeline and contributed to content of the manuscript. V.M.K. wrote the chapter on the identification of metabolites and prepared illustrations; A.F.B. and T.S. wrote the introduction. S.R. and M.R.H. wrote, reviewed and edited the section with LC–MS analysis; K.H. is main responsible for the structure of the workflow and supervision of the scientists, wrote introduction, review and participated in editing; O.K., J.P., D.B. and C.B. participated in writing—Reviewing, editing and supervision. All authors read, reviewed and accepted the final manuscript.

Funding: Academy of Finland, Biocenter Finland, EU Horizon 2020, Finnish Cultural Foundation, Lantmännen Research Foundation.

Acknowledgments: Development of the R package and Wranglr as well as data analyses were carried out with the support of Bioinformatics Center, University of Eastern Finland, Finland. Miia Reponen is thanked for the preparation of samples and LC–MS operation.

Conflicts of Interest: The authors declare no conflict of interest. The funders had no role in the design of the study; in the collection, analyses or interpretation of data; in the writing of the manuscript; or in the decision to publish the results. K.H., O.K., V.M.K., A.K. and J.P. are owners of a spin-off company providing metabolomics services, Afekta Technologies Ltd.

References

1. Johnson, C.H.; Ivanisevic, J.; Siuzdak, G. Metabolomics: Beyond biomarkers and towards mechanisms. *Nat. Rev. Mol. Cell Biol.* **2016**, *17*, 451–459. [CrossRef]
2. Manach, C.; Hubert, J.; Llorach, R.; Scalbert, A. The complex links between dietary phytochemicals and human health deciphered by metabolomics. *Mol. Nutr. Food Res.* **2009**, *53*, 1303–1315. [CrossRef] [PubMed]
3. Gika, H.; Virgiliou, C.; Theodoridis, G.; Plumb, R.S.; Wilson, I.D. Untargeted LC/MS-based metabolic phenotyping (metabonomics/metabolomics): The state of the art. *J. Chromatogr.* **2019**, *1117*, 136–147. [CrossRef]
4. Nash, W.J.; Dunn, W.B. From mass to metabolite in human untargeted metabolomics: Recent advances in annotation of metabolites applying liquid chromatography-mass spectrometry data. *TrAC Trends Anal. Chem.* **2019**, *120*, 115324. [CrossRef]
5. Johnson, C.H.; Ivanisevic, J.; Benton, H.P.; Siuzdak, G. Bioinformatics: The Next Frontier of Metabolomics. *Anal. Chem.* **2015**, *87*, 147–156. [CrossRef]
6. Chaleckis, R.; Meister, I.; Zhang, P.; Wheelock, C.E. Challenges, progress and promises of metabolite annotation for LC–MS-based metabolomics. *Curr. Opin. Biotechnol.* **2019**, *55*, 44–50. [CrossRef] [PubMed]
7. Misra, B.B.; Mohapatra, S. Tools and resources for metabolomics research community: A 2017–2018 update. *Electrophoresis* **2019**, *40*, 227–246. [CrossRef]
8. Dias, D.A.; Jones, O.A.H.; Beale, D.J.; Boughton, B.A.; Benheim, D.; Kouremenos, K.A.; Wolfender, J.; Wishart, D.S. Current and future perspectives on the structural identification of small molecules in biological systems. *Metabolites* **2016**, *6*, 46. [CrossRef]
9. Ulaszewska, M.M.; Weinert, C.H.; Trimigno, A.; Portmann, R.; Lacueva, C.A.; Badertscher, R.; Brennan, L.; Brunius, C.; Bub, A.; Capozzi, F.; et al. Nutrimetabolomics: An Integrative Action for Metabolomic Analyses in Human Nutritional Studies. *Mol. Nutr. Food Res.* **2019**, *63*, 1800384. [CrossRef]
10. Broadhurst, D.; Goodacre, R.; Reinke, S.N.; Kuligowski, J.; Wilson, I.D.; Lewis, M.R.; Dunn, W.B. Guidelines and considerations for the use of system suitability and quality control samples in mass spectrometry assays applied in untargeted clinical metabolomic studies. *Metabolomics* **2018**, *14*, 72. [CrossRef]
11. Koistinen, V.M.; Hanhineva, K. Microbial and endogenous metabolic conversions of rye phytochemicals. *Mol. Nutr. Food Res.* **2017**, *61*, 1600627. [CrossRef] [PubMed]
12. Koistinen, V.M.; Hanhineva, K. Mass spectrometry-based analysis of whole-grain phytochemicals. *Crit. Rev. Food Sci. Nutr.* **2017**, *57*, 1688–1709. [CrossRef] [PubMed]

13. De Mello, V.D.; Paananen, J.; Lindström, J.; Lankinen, M.A.; Shi, L.; Kuusisto, J.; Pihlajamäki, J.; Auriola, S.; Lehtonen, M.; Rolandsson, O.; et al. Indolepropionic acid and novel lipid metabolites are associated with a lower risk of type 2 diabetes in the Finnish Diabetes Prevention Study. *Sci. Rep.* **2017**, *7*, 46337. [CrossRef] [PubMed]
14. Noerman, S.; Kärkkäinen, O.; Mattsson, A.; Paananen, J.; Lehtonen, M.; Nurmi, T.; Tuomainen, T.; Voutilainen, S.; Hanhineva, K.; Virtanen, J.K. Metabolic Profiling of High Egg Consumption and the Associated Lower Risk of Type 2 Diabetes in Middle-Aged Finnish Men. *Mol. Nutr. Food Res.* **2019**, *63*, 1800605. [CrossRef]
15. Rothwell, J.A.; Keski-Rahkonen, P.; Robinot, N.; Assi, N.; Casagrande, C.; Jenab, M.; Ferrari, P.; Boutron-Ruault, M.; Mahamat-Saleh, Y.; Mancini, F.R.; et al. A Metabolomic Study of Biomarkers of Habitual Coffee Intake in Four European Countries. *Mol. Nutr. Food Res.* **2019**, *63*, 1900659. [CrossRef]
16. Brunius, C.; Shi, L.; Landberg, R. Large-scale untargeted LC-MS metabolomics data correction using between-batch feature alignment and cluster-based within-batch signal intensity drift correction. *Metabolomics* **2016**, *12*, 173. [CrossRef]
17. Tsugawa, H.; Cajka, T.; Kind, T.; Ma, Y.; Higgins, B.; Ikeda, K.; Kanazawa, M.; VanderGheynst, J.; Fiehn, O.; Arita, M. MS-DIAL: Data-independent MS/MS deconvolution for comprehensive metabolome analysis. *Nat. Methods* **2015**, *12*, 523–526. [CrossRef]
18. Tsugawa, H.; Kind, T.; Nakabayashi, R.; Yukihira, D.; Tanaka, W.; Cajka, T.; Saito, K.; Fiehn, O.; Arita, M. Hydrogen Rearrangement Rules: Computational MS/MS Fragmentation and Structure Elucidation Using MS-FINDER Software. *Anal. Chem.* **2016**, *88*, 7946–7958. [CrossRef]
19. R: The R Project for Statistical Computing. Available online: https://www.r-project.org/ (accessed on 19 December 2019).
20. Agilent Technologies Agilent 6500 Series Q-TOF LC/MS system Maintenance Guide Research Use Only. Not for use in Diagnostic Procedures. Available online: https://www.crawfordscientific.com/media/wysiwyg/Literature/CMS/Tech_Pages/Agilent_Maintenance_Docs/6500%20Series%20QTOF/6500_Q-TOF_Maintenance%20Guide.pdf (accessed on 30 March 2020).
21. Certificate of Analysis API-TOF Reference Mass Solution Kit Agilent Part Number: G1969-85001. Available online: https://www.agilent.com/cs/library/certificateofanalysis/G1969-85001cofa872024U-LB25990.pdf (accessed on 30 March 2020).
22. Chang, W.; Cheng, J.; Allaire, J.J.; Xie, Y.; McPherson, J.; RStudio; jQuery Foundation; jQuery contributors; jQuery UI contributors; Otto, M.; et al. shiny: Web Application Framework for R. R package version 1.2.0. Available online: https://CRAN.R-project.org/package=shiny (accessed on 30 March 2020).
23. Kirwan, J.A.; Broadhurst, D.I.; Davidson, R.L.; Viant, M.R. Characterising and correcting batch variation in an automated direct infusion mass spectrometry (DIMS) metabolomics workflow. *Anal. Bioanal. Chem.* **2013**, *405*, 5147–5157. [CrossRef]
24. R: Fit a Smoothing Spline. Available online: https://stat.ethz.ch/R-manual/R-devel/library/stats/html/smooth.spline.html (accessed on 30 March 2020).
25. Puupponen-Pimiä, R.; Seppänen-Laakso, T.; Kankainen, M.; Maukonen, J.; Törrönen, R.; Kolehmainen, M.; Leppänen, T.; Moilanen, E.; Nohynek, L.; Aura, A.-M.; et al. Effects of ellagitannin-rich berries on blood lipids, gut microbiota, and urolithin production in human subjects with symptoms of metabolic syndrome. *Mol. Nutr. Food Res.* **2013**, *57*, 2258–2263. [CrossRef]
26. Breheny, P.; Stromberg, A.; Lambert, J. P-Value histograms: Inference and diagnostics. *High-Throughput* **2018**, *7*, 23. [CrossRef] [PubMed]
27. Hotelling, H. Relations Between Two Sets of Variates. *Biometrika* **1936**, *28*, 321. [CrossRef]
28. Bro, R.; Smilde, A.K. Principal component analysis. *Anal. Methods* **2014**, *6*, 2812–2831. [CrossRef]
29. Pearson, K. LIII. On lines and planes of closest fit to systems of points in space. *London Edinburgh Dublin Philos. Mag. J. Sci.* **1901**, *2*, 559–572. [CrossRef]
30. van der Maaten, L.; Hinton, G. Visualizing Data using t-SNE. *J. Mach. Learn. Res.* **2008**, *9*, 2579–2605.
31. Rokach, L.; Maimon, O. Clustering Methods. In *Data Mining and Knowledge Discovery Handbook*; Springer: New York, NY, USA, 2005; pp. 321–352.
32. Murtagh, F.; Legendre, P. Ward's Hierarchical Agglomerative Clustering Method: Which Algorithms Implement Ward's Criterion? *J. Classif.* **2014**, *31*, 274–295. [CrossRef]

33. Kokla, M.; Virtanen, J.; Kolehmainen, M.; Paananen, J.; Hanhineva, K. Random forest-based imputation outperforms other methods for imputing LC-MS metabolomics data: A comparative study. *BMC Bioinform.* **2019**, *20*, 1–11. [CrossRef]
34. Stekhoven, D.J.; Bühlmann, P. Data and text mining MissForest-non-parametric missing value imputation for mixed-type data. *Bioinformatics* **2012**, *28*, 112–118. [CrossRef]
35. Armitage, E.G.; Godzien, J.; Alonso-Herranz, V.; López-González, Á.; Barbas, C. Missing value imputation strategies for metabolomics data. *Electrophoresis* **2015**, *36*, 3050–3060. [CrossRef]
36. Beretta, L.; Santaniello, A. Nearest neighbor imputation algorithms: A critical evaluation. *BMC Med. Inform. Decis. Mak.* **2016**, *16*, 74. [CrossRef]
37. Sysi-Aho, M.; Katajamaa, M.; Yetukuri, L.; Orešič, M. Normalization method for metabolomics data using optimal selection of multiple internal standards. *BMC Bioinform.* **2007**, *8*, 93. [CrossRef] [PubMed]
38. di Guida, R.; Engel, J.; Allwood, J.W.; Weber, R.J.M.; Jones, M.R.; Sommer, U.; Viant, M.R.; Dunn, W.B. Non-targeted UHPLC-MS metabolomic data processing methods: A comparative investigation of normalisation, missing value imputation, transformation and scaling. *Metabolomics* **2016**, *12*, 93. [CrossRef] [PubMed]
39. Kohl, S.M.; Klein, M.S.; Hochrein, J.; Oefner, P.J.; Spang, R.; Gronwald, W. State-of-the art data normalization methods improve NMR-based metabolomic analysis. *Metabolomics* **2012**, *8*, 146–160. [CrossRef] [PubMed]
40. Tyralis, H.; Papacharalampous, G.; Langousis, A. A Brief Review of Random Forests for Water Scientists and Practitioners and Their Recent History in Water Resources. *Water* **2019**, *11*, 910. [CrossRef]
41. Mattsson, A. Analysis of LC-MS Data in Untargeted Nutritional Metabolomics. Master's Thesis, Aalto University, Espoo, Finland, August 2019. Available online: https://aaltodoc.aalto.fi/handle/123456789/39870 (accessed on 31 March 2020).
42. Senan, O.; Aguilar-Mogas, A.; Navarro, M.; Capellades, J.; Noon, L.; Burks, D.; Yanes, O.; Guimerà, R.; Sales-Pardo, M. CliqueMS: A computational tool for annotating in-source metabolite ions from LC-MS untargeted metabolomics data based on a coelution similarity network. *Bioinformatics* **2019**, *35*, 4089–4097. [CrossRef]
43. Kachman, M.; Habra, H.; Duren, W.; Wigginton, J.; Sajjakulnukit, P.; Michailidis, G.; Burant, C.; Karnovsky, A. Deep annotation of untargeted LC-MS metabolomics data with Binner. *Bioinformatics* **2020**, *36*, 1801–1806. [CrossRef]
44. Kouřil, Š.; de Sousa, J.; Václavík, J.; Friedecký, D.; Adam, T. CROP: Correlation-based reduction of feature multiplicities in untargeted metabolomic data. *Bioinformatics* **2020**. [CrossRef]
45. Vinaixa, M.; Samino, S.; Saez, I.; Duran, J.; Guinovart, J.J.; Yanes, O. A Guideline to Univariate Statistical Analysis for LC/MS-Based Untargeted Metabolomics-Derived Data. *Metabolites* **2012**, *2*, 775–795. [CrossRef]
46. Kuznetsova, A.; Brockhoff, P.B.; Christensen, R.H.B. lmerTest Package: Tests in Linear Mixed Effects Models. *J. Stat. Softw.* **2017**, *82*. [CrossRef]
47. Bates, D.; Mächler, M.; Bolker, B.; Walker, S. Fitting Linear Mixed-Effects Models using lme4. *arXiv* **2014**, arXiv:1406.5823. Available online: https://arxiv.org/abs/1406.5823 (accessed on 30 March 2020).
48. Claggett, B.L.; Antonelli, J.; Henglin, M.; Watrous, J.D.; Lehmann, K.A.; Musso, G.; Correia, A.; Jonnalagadda, S.; Demler, O.V.; Vasan, R.S.; et al. Quantitative Comparison of Statistical Methods for Analyzing Human Metabolomics Data. *arXiv* **2017**, arXiv:1710.03443. Available online: https://arxiv.org/abs/1710.03443 (accessed on 30 March 2020).
49. Stoessel, D.; Stellmann, J.; Willing, A.; Behrens, B.; Rosenkranz, S.C.; Hodecker, S.C.; Stürner, K.H.; Reinhardt, S.; Fleischer, S.; Deuschle, C.; et al. Metabolomic Profiles for Primary Progressive Multiple Sclerosis Stratification and Disease Course Monitoring. *Front. Hum. Neurosci.* **2018**, *12*, 226. [CrossRef] [PubMed]
50. Shi, L.; Westerhuis, J.A.; Rosén, J.; Landberg, R.; Brunius, C. Variable selection and validation in multivariate modelling. *Bioinformatics* **2019**, *35*, 972–980. [CrossRef] [PubMed]
51. Breiman, L.; Cutler, A. Random Forests. *Mach. Learn.* **2001**, *45*, 5–32. [CrossRef]
52. Smith, C.A.; Maille, G.O.; Want, E.J.; Qin, C.; Trauger, S.A.; Brandon, T.R.; Custodio, D.E.; Abagyan, R.; Siuzdak, G. METLIN: A metabolite mass spectral database. *Ther. Drug Monit.* **2005**, *27*, 747–751. [CrossRef]
53. Horai, H.; Arita, M.; Kanaya, S.; Nihei, Y.; Ikeda, T.; Suwa, K.; Ojima, Y.; Tanaka, K.; Tanaka, S.; Aoshima, K.; et al. MassBank: A public repository for sharing mass spectral data for life sciences. *J. Mass Spectrom.* **2010**, *45*, 703–714. [CrossRef]

54. Afendi, F.M.; Okada, T.; Yamazaki, M.; Hirai-Morita, A.; Nakamura, Y.; Nakamura, K.; Ikeda, S.; Takahashi, H.; Altaf-Ul-Amin, M.; Darusman, L.K.; et al. KNApSAcK Family Databases: Integrated Metabolite–Plant Species Databases for Multifaceted Plant Research. *Plant Cell Physiol.* **2012**, *53*, e1. [CrossRef]
55. Wishart, D.S.; Jewison, T.; Guo, A.C.; Wilson, M.; Knox, C.; Liu, Y.; Djoumbou, Y.; Mandal, R.; Aziat, F.; Dong, E.; et al. HMDB 3.0—The Human Metabolome Database in 2013. *Nucleic Acids Res.* **2012**, *41*, D801–D807. [CrossRef]
56. MassBank of North America. Available online: https://mona.fiehnlab.ucdavis.edu/ (accessed on 8 October 2019).
57. Fahy, E.; Sud, M.; Cotter, D.; Subramaniam, S. LIPID MAPS online tools for lipid research. *Nucleic Acids Res.* **2007**, *35*, W606–W612. [CrossRef] [PubMed]
58. Sumner, L.W.; Amberg, A.; Barrett, D.; Beale, M.H.; Beger, R.; Daykin, C.A.; Fan, T.W.-M.; Fiehn, O.; Goodacre, R.; Griffin, J.L.; et al. Proposed minimum reporting standards for chemical analysis. *Metabolomics* **2007**, *3*, 211–221. [CrossRef] [PubMed]
59. Chong, J.; Yamamoto, M.; Xia, J. MetaboAnalystR 2.0: From Raw Spectra to Biological Insights. *Metabolites* **2019**, *9*, 57. [CrossRef] [PubMed]
60. Shannon, P.; Markiel, A.; Ozier, O.; Baliga, N.S.; Wang, J.T.; Ramage, D.; Amin, N.; Schwikowski, B.; Ideker, T. Cytoscape: A software Environment for integrated models of biomolecular interaction networks. *Genome Res.* **2003**, *13*, 2498–2504. [CrossRef]
61. Gao, J.; Tarcea, V.G.; Karnovsky, A.; Mirel, B.R.; Weymouth, T.E.; Beecher, C.W.; Cavalcoli, J.D.; Athey, B.D.; Omenn, G.S.; Burant, C.F.; et al. Metscape: A Cytoscape plug-in for visualizing and interpreting metabolomic data in the context of human metabolic networks. *Bioinformatics.* **2010**, *26*, 971–973. [CrossRef] [PubMed]
62. Kärkkäinen, O.; Lankinen, M.A.; Vitale, M.; Jokkala, J.; Leppänen, J.; Koistinen, V.; Lehtonen, M.; Giacco, R.; Rosa-Sibakov, N.; Micard, V.; et al. Diets rich in whole grains increase betainized compounds associated with glucose metabolism. *Am. J. Clin. Nutr.* **2018**, *108*, 971–979. [CrossRef] [PubMed]
63. Tuomainen, M.; Kärkkäinen, O.; Leppänen, J.; Auriola, S.; Lehtonen, M.; Savolainen, M.J.; Hermansen, K.; Risérus, U.; Åkesson, B.; Thorsdottir, I.; et al. Quantitative assessment of betainized compounds and associations with dietary and metabolic biomarkers in the randomized study of the healthy Nordic diet (SYSDIET). *Am. J. Clin. Nutr.* **2019**, *110*, 1108–1118. [CrossRef]

© 2020 by the authors. Licensee MDPI, Basel, Switzerland. This article is an open access article distributed under the terms and conditions of the Creative Commons Attribution (CC BY) license (http://creativecommons.org/licenses/by/4.0/).

 *metabolites*

Article

CFM-ID 3.0: Significantly Improved ESI-MS/MS Prediction and Compound Identification

Yannick Djoumbou-Feunang [1,†], Allison Pon [2], Naama Karu [1,‡], Jiamin Zheng [1], Carin Li [1], David Arndt [1], Maheswor Gautam [1], Felicity Allen [3] and David S. Wishart [1,4,*]

1. Department of Biological Sciences, University of Alberta, Edmonton, AB T6G 2E9, Canada; djoumbou@ualberta.ca (Y.D.-F.); n.karu@lacdr.leidenuniv.nl (N.K.); jiamin3@ualberta.ca (J.Z.); cbli@ualberta.ca (C.L.); darndt@ualberta.ca (D.A.); maheswor@ualberta.ca (M.G.)
2. OMx Personal Health Analytics, Edmonton, AB T5J 1B9, Canada; allisonpon@gmail.com
3. Wellcome Sanger Institute, Wellcome Trust Genome Campus, Hinxton CB10 1SA, UK; felicity.allen@sanger.ac.uk
4. Department of Computing Science, University of Alberta, Edmonton, AB T6G 2E8, Canada
* Correspondence: david.wishart@ualberta.ca; Tel.: +1-780-492-0383
† Current address: Corteva Agriscience, 9300 Zionsville Road, Indianapolis, IN 46268, USA.
‡ Current address: Leiden Academic Centre for Drug Research, Leiden University, 2300RA Leiden, The Netherlands.

Received: 4 March 2019; Accepted: 8 April 2019; Published: 13 April 2019

Abstract: Metabolite identification for untargeted metabolomics is often hampered by the lack of experimentally collected reference spectra from tandem mass spectrometry (MS/MS). To circumvent this problem, Competitive Fragmentation Modeling-ID (CFM-ID) was developed to accurately predict electrospray ionization-MS/MS (ESI-MS/MS) spectra from chemical structures and to aid in compound identification via MS/MS spectral matching. While earlier versions of CFM-ID performed very well, CFM-ID's performance for predicting the MS/MS spectra of certain classes of compounds, including many lipids, was quite poor. Furthermore, CFM-ID's compound identification capabilities were limited because it did not use experimentally available MS/MS spectra nor did it exploit metadata in its spectral matching algorithm. Here, we describe significant improvements to CFM-ID's performance and speed. These include (1) the implementation of a rule-based fragmentation approach for lipid MS/MS spectral prediction, which greatly improves the speed and accuracy of CFM-ID; (2) the inclusion of experimental MS/MS spectra and other metadata to enhance CFM-ID's compound identification abilities; (3) the development of new scoring functions that improves CFM-ID's accuracy by 21.1%; and (4) the implementation of a chemical classification algorithm that correctly classifies unknown chemicals (based on their MS/MS spectra) in >80% of the cases. This improved version called CFM-ID 3.0 is freely available as a web server. Its source code is also accessible online.

Keywords: mass spectrometry; liquid chromatography; MS spectral prediction; metabolite identification; structure-based chemical classification; rule-based fragmentation; combinatorial fragmentation

1. Introduction

Liquid chromatography (LC) coupled to mass spectrometry (MS) or tandem mass spectrometry (MS/MS) has become one of the leading techniques for compound identification in organic chemistry, natural product chemistry, and metabolomics [1,2]. In the field of metabolomics, LC-MS/MS is widely used to identify and quantify individual chemicals in complex biological or environmental mixtures. For untargeted MS-based metabolomics, high performance or ultrahigh performance liquid chromatography (HPLC or UHPLC) is first performed to separate compounds in the sample and then electrospray ionization (ESI) mass spectrometry (MS and MS/MS) is used to collect the mass spectra of each chromatographic peak. In order to identify individual compounds, the resulting MS/MS spectra, along with the chromatographic retention time and parent ion masses of the compound of interest, are then (ideally) compared to the MS/MS spectra and retention time of authentic standards to confirm the compound's identity.

Because of the limited availability of many authentic chemical standards in most metabolomics labs, putative metabolite identification is more commonly performed [3]. Putative identification (MSI level 2) is achieved by comparing the MS/MS spectra to experimentally collected reference spectra found in various MS/MS spectral databases. Key to the success of this putative identification process is the availability of a large, comprehensive database containing experimentally collected MS/MS spectra of pure compounds that covers a large portion of "chemical space". Unfortunately, publicly available databases of experimental MS/MS spectra currently cover a total of only ~20,000 unique compounds [4]. Consequently, as reported in many large-scale metabolomic studies [5,6], the percentage of MS spectral features that can be confidently assigned to known compounds is often less than 2%. As a result, the compound identification step continues to be the central bottleneck in almost all untargeted MS-based metabolomic studies.

Given the cost of synthesizing or acquiring the 100,000's of chemicals needed to create the required experimental MS/MS spectral libraries, a growing number of scientists are turning to in silico metabolomic methods to facilitate compound identification. Over the last decade, a number of computational MS approaches have been developed for this purpose. Some of the more popular software tools use MS/MS fragmentation trees and spectral fingerprints (e.g., CSI:FingerID [7]) of an observed ESI-MS/MS spectrum to rank the likelihood that a given chemical structure could produce such a spectrum. Other tools arrange substructures of a candidate molecule into a format that best explains the fragmentation pattern observed in a given experimental MS^n spectral tree (MAGMA [8]). Still others, such as MetFrag [9] use in silico fragmentation of candidate molecules, based on a given mass spectrum and mass of a precursor molecule to identify its structure. Competitive Fragmentation Modeling-ID (CFM-ID) [10–12] use in silico fragmentation techniques to predict ESI-MS/MS (for LC-MS) or EI-MS (for GC-MS) spectra for a given structure. By matching the observed MS/MS spectrum to a library of predicted MS/MS spectra, it is possible to identify or rank which compound is being observed. It is widely believed that increasing the number (and accuracy) of in silico-predicted spectra should increase the likelihood of successfully identifying compounds from newly acquired MS/MS spectra [13].

The two main in silico MS fragmentation techniques are rule-based approaches and combinatorial approaches. Rule-based "fragmenters" use hand-made rules based on experimentally observed fragmentation patterns that are specific to one or more structural features or chemical classes. These rules are typically extracted from analyzing the scientific literature or, preferably, learned from in-house experimental data. Mass Frontier™ (ThermoFisher, CA; HighChem, Bratislava, Slovakia) is an example of a software tool that uses hand-made fragmentation rules. Once the rules are implemented, this approach can be very fast, consistent, and accurate. However, a major disadvantage to this approach is that the design of fragmentation rules requires considerable expert curation. Furthermore, these rules cannot be applied to novel classes of molecules. For these reasons, much more emphasis has recently been put toward the implementation of computational combinatorial fragmentation approaches. Combinatorial fragmentation approaches iteratively cleave chemical bonds within a molecule in a combinatorial fashion, and use (or learn) penalty scores that favor the cleavage events that are most likely to occur at each step. Examples of tools that implement combinatorial fragmentation include CFM-ID [10–12], MetFrag [9], and FiD [14].

CFM-ID is a publicly available software tool and web server that can be used for MS/MS spectral prediction, MS/MS spectrum peak assignment, as well as MS-based compound identification. It implements a technique known as Competitive Fragmentation Modeling (CFM). CFM is a probabilistic generative modeling method that uses a customized cost function to take into account the structural composition of a molecule to predict its electrospray ESI-MS/MS spectrum. The original version of

CFM-ID was used to generate a reference MS/MS spectral library of over 51,000 known compounds from the HMDB [15] and KEGG [16] databases at 3 different collision energies (10, 20, and 40 eV). This spectral library was used by CFM-ID (version 1.0 and version 2.0) to suggest candidate molecules that match input experimental MS/MS spectra. In 2015, the original version of CFM-ID was shown to outperform FingerID and an earlier version of MetFrag in various identification tasks from ESI-MS/MS spectra [11]. However, subsequent tests and studies that further assessed the performance of CFM-ID have shown that a number of improvements could be made to the program and its spectral database [11,12].

For instance, one well-known limitation of CFM-ID is its very slow and relatively poor performance for predicting MS/MS spectra of lipids and other large "segmented" or modular metabolites. This is primarily due to the length of the fatty acids or attached head-group segments, leading to a combinatorial explosion of the possible fragments at each step of the in silico fragmentation process. As demonstrated by Kind et al. [17], who developed LipidBlast, and Tsugawa et al. [18], who studied sphingolipid fragmentation, the use of structure-based fragmentation rules appears to be much better at handling lipids and other large segmented or modular molecules (such as carbohydrates) than combinatorial fragmentation. However, it is important to note that LipidBlast also has some limitations. For instance, it does not provide a well-defined set of fragmentation rules or algorithms that can be incorporated into other computational MS spectral prediction tools. Furthermore, while LipidBlast does provide m/z values and heuristically modeled static relative abundances for fragment ions, the annotation of fragment ion peaks is limited to formulas and does not include actual structures. Moreover, LipidBlast predict consensus mass spectra, and does not distinguish between different collision energies. These are the kinds of output that are typically found with most in silico fragmenters, and these shortcomings have been addressed in this update to CFM-ID.

In addition to the incorporation of compound-specific fragmentation rules, it has also been shown that significant improvements in MS-based compound identification can be achieved by including metadata or other forms of external data in the spectral matching and scoring functions [9]. In particular, the inclusion of citation frequency (the number of times a given compound is mentioned in the literature), along with the incorporation of experimentally collected MS/MS spectra in the reference spectral database can often improve compound identification performance by a factor of 2 or more [19]. When taking into account the chemical similarity or the distribution of structural features or chemical classes (via ClassyFire [20]) among candidates, it is often possible to improve the performance even further [7]. Based on these and other developments in the field of in silico metabolomics and in silico mass spectrometry, we have implemented a number of modifications to CFM-ID. These modifications have helped in a number of important ways, including (1) achieving faster and more accurate prediction of MS/MS-spectra for 21 classes of lipids, (2) enabling the expansion of CFM-ID's reference spectral library to include both experimental and predicted MS/MS spectra, (3) enhancing CFM-ID's ability to incorporate metadata and chemical similarity, (4) improving CFM-ID's compound identification rates, and (5) enhancing CFM-ID's ability to predict the structural class of compounds for query spectra that could not be matched in CFM-ID's spectral database. The improved version of CFM-ID is called CFM-ID 3.0. It is freely available as a web server at http://cfmid3.wishartlab.com. Its source code is accessible at https://sourceforge.net/p/cfm-id/wiki/Home (combinatorial fragmentation tool) and https://bitbucket.org/wishartlab/msrb-fragmenter/ (rule-based fragmentation tool).

2. Results

2.1. Encoding Lipid Fragmentation Rules

Our manual analysis of experimentally acquired lipid MS/MS spectra provided a basis for the generation of 344 unique fragmentation rules covering 21 lipid classes and 7 adducts, for a total of 50 combinations of lipid classes and adduct types. Each rule describes a chemical reaction that fragments the precursor molecule to generate a specific fragment. The structure and mass-to-charge ratio of the fragment can be easily computed based on the encoded pattern. For each lipid class, an ESI-MS/MS spectrum can be simulated by CFM-ID 3.0 at collision energies of 10, 20, and 40 eV. In general, almost all ESI-MS/MS spectra of lipids show similar fragmentation patterns with characteristic losses of the polar head group, and the acyl or alkyl chains, with relatively little fragmentation within the acyl or alkyl chains. For example, in choline-containing glycerophospholipids, the most commonly observed fragments include phosphocholine ($C_5H_{14}NO_4P+$ ion; neutral mass = 184.0733 Da) and the cyclic 1,2-cyclic phosphate diester ($C_2H_6O_4P+$ ion; neutral mass = 125.0003 Da). Figure 1 illustrates consensus fragmentation patterns for phosphatidylcholines from their [M+H]$^+$ precursor ions. The number of rules for each lipid class and the number of covered adduct types per lipid class are shown in Table 1. These fragmentation rules are also available at https://bitbucket.org/wishartlab/msrb-fragmenter/.

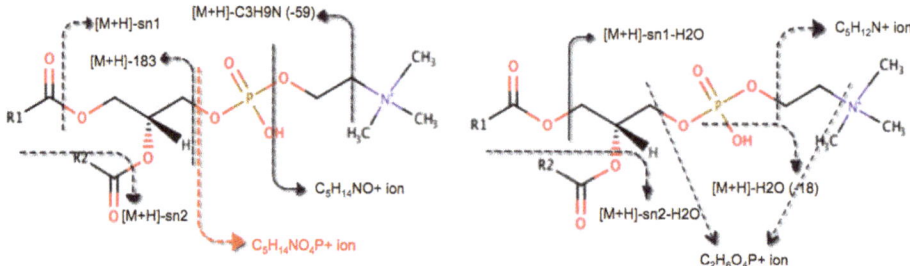

Figure 1. Fragmentation patterns of phosphatidylcholines obtained from their [M+H]$^+$ precursor ions. Among all resulting fragments, only the precursor ion is observed at each of the three energy levels. The ion fragment $C_5H_{14}NO_4P+$ (red arrow) corresponding to phosphocholine is observed at 20 and 40 eV, and the remaining fragments were observed only at 40 eV.

Table 1. Number of fragmentation rules and adduct types covered for each chemical category.

Lipid Class	Number of Covered Rules	Number of Covered Adduct Types
1-Monoacylglycerols	8	[M+Li]$^+$; [M+NH4]$^+$
2-Monoacylglycerols	11	[M+H]$^+$; [M+NH4]$^+$; [M+Na]$^+$
1,2-Diacylglycerols	10	[M+NH4]$^+$; [M+Na]$^+$
Triacylglycerols	19	[M+Na]$^+$; [M+NH4]$^+$; [M+Li]$^+$
Phosphatidic acids	22	[M+H]$^+$; [M+Na]$^+$; [M−H]$^-$
Phosphatidylcholines	41	[M+H]$^+$; [M+Na]$^+$; [M+Li]$^+$; [M+Cl]$^-$
Phosphatidylethanolamines	24	[M+H]$^+$; [M+Na]$^+$; [M−H]$^-$
Lysophosphatidylcholines	29	[M+H]$^+$; [M+Na]$^+$; [M+Li]$^+$; [M+Cl]$^-$
Lysophosphatidic acids	12	[M+H]$^+$; [M−H]$^-$
Phosphatidylserines	28	[M+H]$^+$; [M+Li]$^+$; [M+Na]$^+$; [M−H]$^-$
Ceramides	17	[M+H]$^+$; [M+Li]$^+$; [M−H]$^-$
Sphingomyelins	13	[M+H]$^+$; [M+Li]$^+$; [M+Na]$^+$
Cardiolipins	13	[M−2H](2H)$^-$
Phosphatidylglycerols	11	[M−H]$^-$
Lysophosphatidylglycerols	7	[M−H]$^-$
Plasmanyl-PC (1-alkyl,2-acylglycero-3-phosphocholines)	17	[M+H]$^+$; [M+Cl]$^-$
Plasmenyl-PC (1-(1Z-alkenyl)-glycero-3-phosphocholines)	17	[M+H]$^+$; [M+Cl]$^-$
1-Alkanylglycerophosphocholines (Monoalkylglycerophosphocholines)	15	[M+H]$^+$; [M+Cl]$^-$; [M+Na]$^+$
1-Alkenylglycerophosphocholines (1-(1Z-alkenyl)-glycero-3-phosphocholines)	13	[M+H]$^+$; [M+Cl]$^-$
Phosphatidylinositols	9	[M−H]$^-$
Lysophosphatidylinositols	8	[M−H]$^-$
Total	344	50

2.2. The New CFM-ID 3.0 Spectral Library

The original CFM-ID 2.0 spectral library contained 102,153 unique computationally generated ESI-MS/MS spectra (from 51,635 compounds). Because of improvements in the spectral prediction performance, additions of new compounds, and the decision to add experimental spectra, the new CFM-ID 3.0 spectral library has been expanded by a factor of 2.6 over the original CFM-ID 2.0 spectral library (as of February 2019). In particular, the new library now contains a total of 167,547 computationally generated ESI-MS/MS spectra (generated via CFM-ID 3.0) from 108,972 compounds in the HMDB [15]; 22,914 computationally generated ESI-MS/MS spectra from 11,685 compounds in KEGG [16]; and 83,049 experimentally collected ESI-MS/MS spectra from 21,904 compounds. The compounds in CFM-ID 3.0's experimental MS/MS spectral library are structurally and functionally diverse, and originate from various databases/libraries including HMDB (human metabolites) [15], DrugBank (drugs and drug metabolite) [21], KEGG (metabolites and drugs) [16], PhytoHub (dietary phytochemicals and their metabolites) [22], GNPS (natural products) [23], and MoNA [24]. In addition, 568 spectra from the CASMI 2014 [25] and CASMI 2016 [19] challenges were imported into the database. Moreover, 3953 spectra that were experimentally acquired at the Metabolomics Innovation Center (TMIC, Edmonton, AB, Canada) were also added. Each of the 229,084 compounds in the new spectral library was assigned a citation score (described below) that is used as metadata in compound identification tasks. Each compound in the spectral library has two or more citations. A summary of the library's statistics is displayed in Table 2.

Table 2. Statistics for the Competitive Fragmentation Modeling-ID (CFM-ID) 3.0 spectral database.

Feature	Value
Total number of unique compounds	229,084
Total number of unique ESI-MS/MS spectra	397,679
Total number of experimental ESI-MS/MS spectra	87,570
Total number of predicted ESI-MS/MS spectra	310,109
Number of compounds with ≥1 experimental ESI-MS/MS spectra	13,537
Number of compounds with ≥1 predicted ESI-MS/MS spectra	108,972
Number of compounds with ≥2 citations	229,084
Average number of citations per compound	272
Number of compounds with chemical classification assignments	229,084
Average number of chemical category assignments/compound	25

In our effort to improve the identification rates, a full chemical classification was computed for all 229,084 unique compounds using the computational chemical classifier called ClassyFire [20]. An average of ~25 chemical categories were assigned per compound. The chemical classification was used to adjust CFM-ID's original scoring system, to take into account the chemical composition and chemical similarity among candidate molecules. This compound classification process also served as a basis to predict the chemical class of any new compound corresponding to the query spectrum in identification tasks.

2.3. Performance Testing

2.3.1. Lipid ESI-MS/MS Spectral Prediction

Two tests were performed to assess CFM-ID 3.0's lipid spectral prediction performance. One was for speed while the other was for accuracy. In terms of speed, CFM-ID 3.0 averaged 0.395 ± 0.03 s of computation time to predict each of the 120 lipid ESI-MS/MS spectra in the test set, while CFM-ID 2.0 averaged 68.58 ± 0.21 s for the same task. This represents a speed-up of 173.6X. Clearly, the rule-based approach for lipid analysis used in CFM-ID 3.0 is significantly faster than the combinatorial approach used in CFM-ID 2.0. For most other kinds of molecules, the average processing time for CFM-ID (3.0 and 2.0) is about 23.75 ± 0.2 s. Clearly, the computational slow-down for lipid spectral calculation (due to the many potential fragmentation combinations) is quite significant, which largely motivated us to develop a faster rule-based approach.

In terms of spectral prediction performance, the average spectral similarity score (measured using the dot product) between the experimental lipid ESI-MS/MS spectra (collected on a QTOF at multiple collision energies) and the CFM-ID 3.0-predicted ESI-MS/MS spectra was 0.85 ± 0.2. On the other hand, the average spectral similarity score between the CFM-ID 2.0-predicted ESI-MS/MS spectra and the experimental ESI-MS/MS spectra was 0.09 ± 0.1. This suggests that the accuracy of CFM-ID 3.0 for lipid spectral prediction is 11X better than that of CFM-ID 2.0, which is highly significant. It is worth mentioning that CFM-ID predicts ESI-MS/MS spectra at three different collision energies while other programs, such as LipidBlast, generate a consensus MS/MS spectrum that essentially merges the MS/MS spectra over all collision energies. Therefore, during our comparative analysis, only one LipidBlast-generated consensus ESI-MS/MS spectrum was used for each unique compound and compared against the experimental spectrum, independent of the energy level. The average spectral similarity score between the LipidBlast-predicted ESI-MS/MS spectra and the experimental ESI-MS/MS spectra was 0.34 ± 0.4. Figure 2 shows head-to-tail plots comparing the experimental ESI-MS/MS spectrum of dipalmitoyl phosphatidylcholine (PC(16:0/16:0)) collected at a 40 eV collision energy with the corresponding in silico spectra predicted with CFM-ID 2.0 [11] (Figure 2a), CFM-ID 3.0 (Figure 2b), and LipidBlast [17] (Figure 2c), respectively. The experimental spectrum was measured in positive ion mode ([M+H]$^+$), with a collision energy of 40 eV.

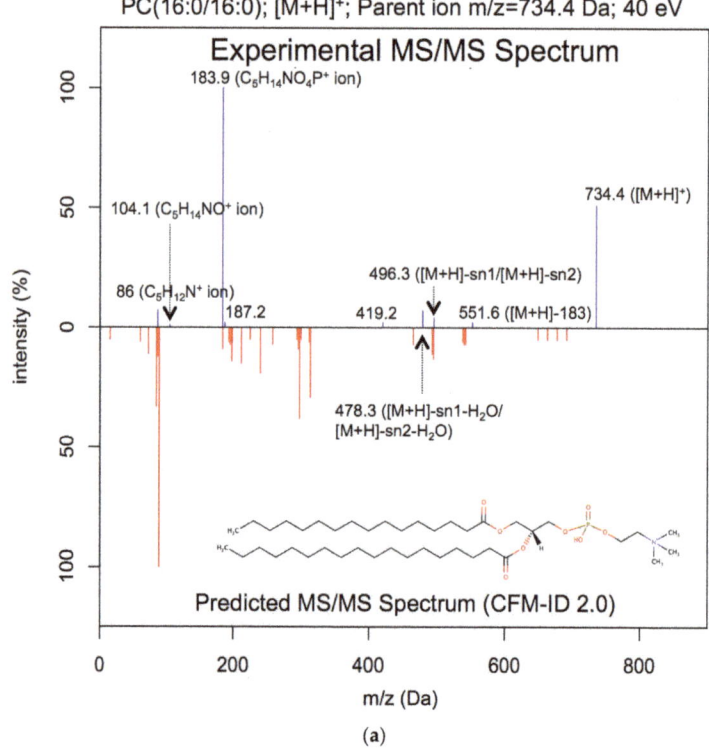

(a)

Figure 2. *Cont.*

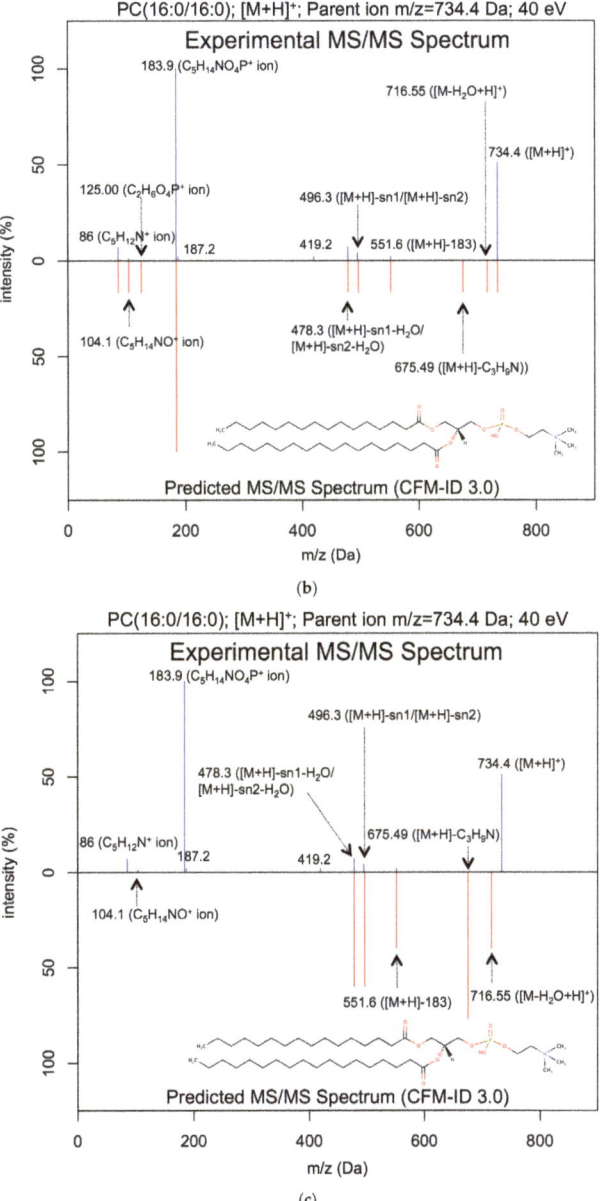

Figure 2. Head-to-tail plot of experimental and predicted electrospray ionization-tandem mass spectroscopy (ESI-MS/MS) spectra of PC(16:0/16:0). (**a**) Head-to-tail plot showing an experimental ESI-MS/MS spectrum of dipalmitoyl phosphatidylcholine (PC(16:0/16:0)) measured at 40 eV, and the matching ESI-MS/MS spectrum predicted by CFM-ID 2.0. The computed spectral similarity score is 0.07. (**b**) Head-to-tail plot showing an experimental of ESI-MS/MS spectrum of dipalmitoyl phosphatidylcholine measured in positive ion mode ([M+H]$^+$) at 40 eV, and the matching ESI-MS/MS spectrum predicted by CFM-ID 3.0. The computed spectral similarity score is 0.88. (**c**) Head-to-tail plot showing an experimental of ESI-MS/MS spectrum of dipalmitoyl phosphatidylcholine measured in positive ion mode ([M+H]$^+$) at 40 eV, and the matching ESI-MS/MS spectrum predicted by LipidBlast. The computed spectral similarity score is 0.13.

As seen in Figure 2, the spectral similarity between the CFM-ID 2.0-generated spectrum and the experimental ESI-MS/MS spectrum was 0.07, with CFM-ID 2.0 being able to predict only two fragments that were observed in the experimental spectrum (namely, the C5H12N+ and C5H14NO4P+ ion fragments). For this particular example, CFM-ID 2.0 predicted 31 fragments (Figure 2a) while CFM-ID 3.0 predicted 10 fragments (Figure 2b), 7 of which were observed in the experimental ESI-MS/MS spectrum. It is worth noting that the remaining three fragments result from fragmentations that were observed in experimentally measured ESI-MS/MS spectra of phosphatidylcholines obtained for [M+H]$^+$ adducts at 40 eV. For this example, the spectral similarity score was 0.88 when comparing the experimental ESI-MS/MS spectrum with the CFM-ID 3.0-predicted spectrum. Surprisingly, the dot product score was only 0.13 when compared with the LipidBlast-predicted ESI-MS/MS spectrum to the experimental ESI-MS/MS spectrum. Figure 3 shows comparisons between experimental and predicted ESI-MS/MS spectra for 1-palmitoyl-2-oleoyl-sn-glycero-3-phospho-L-serine (PS(16:0/18:1(9Z))) in the negative ([M−H]$^−$) ion mode at a collision energy of 40 eV. The measured spectral similarity scores between the experimental and the in silico-generated spectra are 0.10, 0.92, and 0.91 with CFM-ID 2.0 (Figure 3a), CFM-ID 3.0 (Figure 3b), and LipidBlast (Figure 3c), respectively.

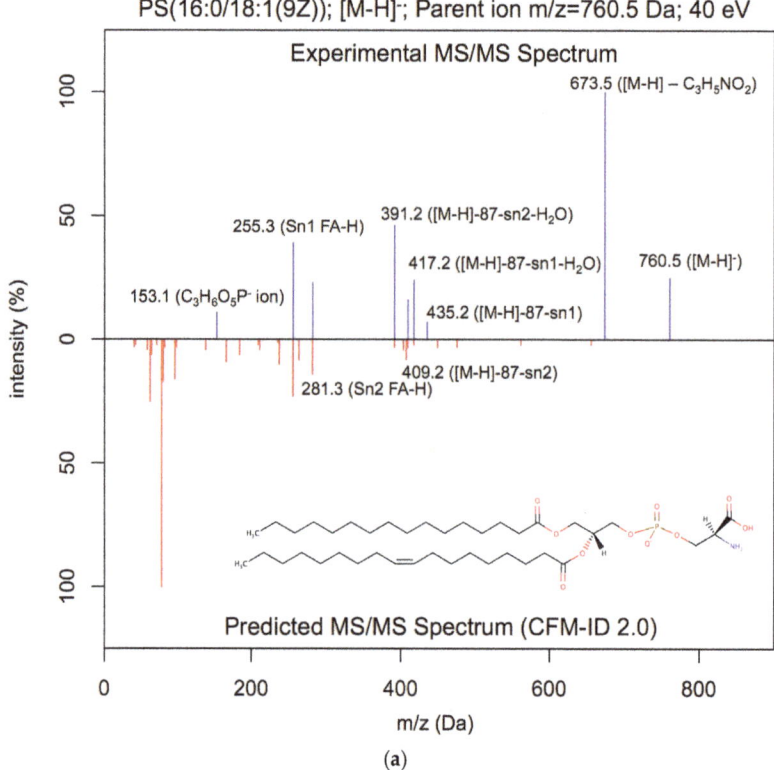

Figure 3. *Cont.*

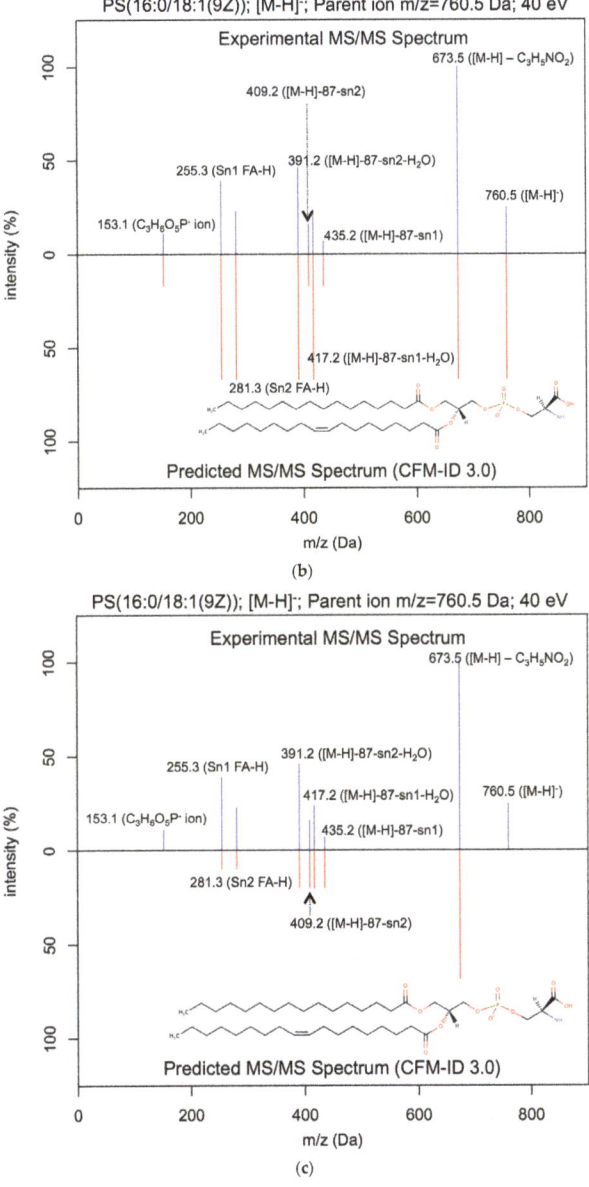

Figure 3. Head-to-tail plot of experimental and predicted ESI-MS/MS spectra of (PS(16:0/18:1(9Z))). (**a**) Head-to-tail plot showing an experimental of ESI-MS/MS spectrum of 1-palmitoyl-2-oleoyl-sn-glycero-3-phospho-L-serine (PS(16:0/18:1(9Z))) measured at 40 eV, and the matching ESI-MS/MS spectrum predicted by CFM-ID 2.0. The computed spectral similarity score is 0.10. (**b**) Head-to-tail plot showing an experimental ESI-MS/MS spectrum of 1-palmitoyl-2-oleoyl-sn- glycero-3-phospho-L-serine (PS(16:0/18:1(9Z))) measured at 40 eV, and the matching ESI-MS/MS spectrum predicted by CFM-ID 3.0. The computed similarity score is 0.92. (**c**) Head-to-tail plot showing an experimental ESI-MS/MS spectrum of 1-palmitoyl-2-oleoyl-sn-glycero-3-phospho-L-serine (PS(16:0/18:1(9Z))) measured at 40 eV, and the matching ESI-MS/MS spectrum predicted by LipidBlast. The computed similarity score is 0.91.

As highlighted in Table 3, CFM-ID 3.0 significantly outperforms CFM-ID 2.0 in terms of lipid spectral prediction performance (average score of 0.85 versus 0.09) and CFM-ID 3.0 generally outperforms LipidBlast (average score of 0.85 versus 0.34). Another important advantage of CFM-ID 3.0 over LipidBlast is the fact that it generates spectral predictions for multiple collision energies (10, 20, and 40 eV) whereas LipidBlast only provides a single spectrum at an undefined collision energy. Furthermore, all spectral predictions generated by CFM-ID 3.0 include information about not only the *m/z* values and their relative intensities but also the structure of the predicted fragments (expressed as InChI and SMILES strings) for every predicted peak. LipidBlast only provides the *m/z* values and intensities.

Table 3. Computed spectral similarity scores between experimental and predicted ESI-MS/MS spectra at three energy levels (10, 20, and 40 eV). The results show higher similarities, and thus an improvement when using a rule-based approach (CFM-ID 3.0) over a combinatorial one (CFM-ID 2.0) for the prediction of lipid ESI-MS/MS spectra. The spectral similarities of the LipidBlast-generated consensus spectra further illustrate this trend. When available, the same LipidBlast-generated consensus spectrum was used for comparisons at each energy level. N/A corresponds to cases where (1) the adduct type was not covered by CFM-ID 2.0 at all, or (2) the adduct type was not covered by LipidBlast for the chemical class to which the test compound belongs.

Compound	Adduct	Energy (eV)	CFM-ID 3.0 (Score)	CFM-ID 2.0 (Score)	LipidBlast (Score)
PA(16:0/18:1(9Z))	[M−H]−	10	1.00	0.36	0.00
PS(16:0/18:1(9Z))	[M−H]−	10	1.00	0.31	0.00
CL(18:0/18:0/18:0/18:0)	[M−2H](2H)	10	0.98	N/A	0.00
DG(18:0/20:4/0:0)	[M+Na]+	10	0.92	0.00	N/A
PA(16:0/18:1(9Z))	[M−H]−	20	0.55	0.02	0.00
PS(16:0/18:1(9Z))	[M−H]−	20	0.98	0.03	0.00
CL(18:0/18:0/18:0/18:0)	[M−2H](2H)	20	0.97	N/A	0.12
DG(18:0/20:4/0:0)	[M+Na]+	20	0.93	0.00	N/A
PA(16:0/18:1(9Z))	[M−H]−	40	0.96	0.03	0.90
PS(16:0/18:1(9Z))	[M−H]−	40	0.92	0.10	0.91
CL(18:0/18:0/18:0/18:0)	[M−2H](2H)	40	0.91	N/A	0.89
DG(18:0/20:4/0:0)	[M+Na]+	40	0.18	0.00	N/A
PC(16:0/16:0)	[M+H]+	40	0.88	0.07	0.13
TG(18:1/18:1/18:2)	[M+NH4]+	40	0.78	0.01	0.84

2.3.2. Compound Identification Using the New Scoring Functions

A set of 1,000 compounds was used to train a new and improved scoring function for ESI-MS/MS-based compound identification (see Section 4.5). This function was developed in order to optimize CFM-ID 3.0's compound identification performance using spectral matching scores, compound classification information from high-scoring hits, and compound metadata (citations). The models were obtained using 5X cross-validation, and tested on different sets. Table 4 compares the performance of CFM-ID 3.0 versus CFM-ID 2.0 (2016 and 2019) and MS-FINDER [26] for compound identification based on 208 ESI-MS/MS spectra from 185 unique compounds. The test involving CFM-ID 2.0 for 2016 and 2019 used the same algorithm and scoring functions. However, the 2019 version mentioned here uses the expanded spectral library, compared to the in silico spectral library of 2016. The test spectra correspond to those provided for the CASMI 2016 contest (category 3). To establish a baseline and ensure the spectral similarity matching method worked, we first queried the 208 experimental spectra against the full spectral database (with those same 208 spectra included). In this case, both CFM-ID 2.0-2019 and CFM-ID 3.0 correctly identified all 208 query compounds with perfect spectral similarity scores. The 208 experimental spectra were then removed from the CFM-ID 3.0's spectral library and the queries were run again. As illustrated in Table 4, CFM-ID 3.0 was able to correctly identify the query compound in 149 out of 208 challenges, compared to only 123 by CFM-ID 2.0-2019 or 120 by CFM-ID 2.0-2016. This represents an improvement of 21.1%

over CFM-ID 2.0. The query compound was generally ranked higher (average rank = 1.8) by CFM-ID 3.0 compared to CFM-ID 2.0-2019 (average rank = 2.4). CFM-ID 3.0 also achieved a better medal score (848) compared to CFM-ID 2.0-2019 (718). A medal score is calculated as the sum of weighted top 1 ranks with 5 points (gold medal), top 2 ranks with 3 points (silver), and top 3 ranks (bronze) with 1 [19]. CFM-ID 2.0-2016 and MS-FINDER [26] were also evaluated in the CASMI 2016 contest (category 3). As the original winner of the CASMI 2016 contest, MS-FINDER correctly identified the query compound in 146 cases [19]. However, as shown in Table 4, MS-FINDER scored 20% fewer top 3 hits compared to CFM-ID 3.0. Moreover, MS-FINDER achieved a lower medal score (766 versus 848), and had a much lower average "hit" rank (6.4 versus 1.8) compared to CFM-ID 3.0. It is also worth noting that CFM-ID 2.0-2016 scored the lowest in terms of top 1 hits, had the lowest average "hit" rank (13.6), and the lowest medal score (just 600).

Table 4. Comparison of CFM-ID 3.0, CFM-ID 2.0, and MS-FINDER scoring functions upon identification of 185 compounds from 208 ESI-MS/MS spectra. Reported are the total number of challenges in which the corresponding implementation of the scoring function ranked the query compound in the top 1, top 3, and top 10. The average and median ranks for the query compound are also reported. A chemical classification is assessed as correct if the predicted category matches a category originally assigned by ClassyFire. N/A, not applicable; * performance when applied over the expanded spectral library database including the 208 experimental ESI-MS/MS from the CASMI 2016 contest (category 3).

Version	# Top 1	# Top 3	# Top 10	Average Rank	Median Rank	# Correct Classifications
CFM-ID 3.0	149	194	204	1.8	1	168
CFM-ID 2.0-2019	123	171	201	2.4	1	N/A
CFM-ID 2.0-2016	120	160	182	13.64	1	N/A
MS-FINDER	146	162	174	6.4	1	N/A
CFM-ID 3.0 *	208	208	208	1	1	N/A
CFM-ID 2.0-2019 *	208	208	208	1	1	N/A

2.3.3. Compound Chemical Classification

For this assessment, the 208 challenge MS/MS spectra (corresponding to 185 distinct compounds) from the 2016 CASMI competition were used as queries. CFM-ID 3.0 was used to predict the chemical class of the query compound with the predicted class being the direct parent (according to ClassyFire [20]) of the highest-ranked compound. The direct parent is the parental or broader chemical class in the ClassyFire hierarchy to which a compound belongs. It typically corresponds to the largest identifiable chemical skeleton or most dominant feature of the classified compound [20]. In case of a tie, the predicted class was identified as the most frequently occurring chemical class among the direct and alternative parents of all compounds with the highest score. Alternative parents are categories in the ClassyFire ontology that describe the classified compound and do not display a parent–child relationship to each other or to the direct parent [20]. When using ESI-MS/MS spectra as input, CFM-ID 3.0 correctly predicted the chemical class in 168 out of 208 challenges. Interestingly, in 19 out of the 168 challenges, the corresponding query compound could not be correctly identified. These results suggest that CFM-ID 3.0 was still able to capture key structural features that characterize the fragmentations observed in the corresponding input MS/MS spectra. These findings also demonstrate the importance of using a diverse set of compounds and MS/MS spectra to assist with compound identification or classification. In particular, they highlight the need for large compound/spectral databases for proper compound identification.

3. Discussion

3.1. ESI-MS/MS Lipid Spectra Prediction

The much better performance for lipid spectra prediction via rule-based fragmentation approaches (CFM-ID 3.0) relative to combinatorial fragmentation approaches (CFM-ID 2.0) is likely due to two factors. First, lipids are modular molecules and so the MS fragmentation patterns seen under most collision energies are easily understood and relatively simple to describe. On the other hand, combinatorial fragmenters have no knowledge of molecular structure and so they cannot recognize modular structures. Instead, they view lipids as molecules with dozens of breakable bonds, all of which could potentially be fragmented. This leads to a substantial over-prediction of MS peaks. The second reason why combinatorial fragmenters do not perform well on lipids is that they have generally not been "trained" on lipid spectra. For example, CFM-ID 2.0 was only trained on ~1000 experimental MS/MS spectra, none of which included lipid MS/MS spectra. Similarly, MetFrag [9], another combinatorial fragmenter, was also not originally programmed to handle lipid MS/MS spectra (although a later version was [27]). By expanding CFM-ID's training set and including lipid spectra as well as other modular compound classes in that training set, CFM-ID could potentially improve its performance to match even the rule-based fragmenter.

Overall, our results show that CFM-ID 3.0 was able to reproduce most lipid fragments with accurate m/z ratios and reasonably accurate relative intensities. Characteristic fragment ion losses (e.g., loss of polar head, or side chains) were also well reproduced. CFM-ID 3.0's spectral predictions also include many ion fragments that are independent of the acyl or alkyl chain(s) of the molecular ion, including the cyclic 1,2-cyclic phosphate diester (neutral m/z = 125.0003) fragment, which is often observed in ESI-MS/MS spectra of various choline glycerophospholipids. Interestingly, most of these kinds of fragments are not reported in LipidBlast-generated spectra. On average, the spectral similarity score between experimental ESI-MS/MS spectra and LipidBlast-generated spectra was 0.34 ± 0.4. One of the reasons for the lower similarity scores for LipidBlast has to do with the fact that it generates only one consensus spectrum per compound, which tends to more closely match with experimental ESI-MS/MS spectra collected at 40 eV. As a result, the average spectral similarities for LipidBlast-generated spectra to experimental spectra obtained at 10 and 20 eV are very low.

As expected, some discrepancies were observed when comparing predicted MS/MS spectra with the corresponding experimental MS/MS spectra. First, the relative peak intensities were generally found to be higher in the predicted MS/MS spectra than the experimental spectra. Second, the peak lists are often not identical. MS/MS spectral peak intensities are very difficult to predict and vary considerably depending on the instrument, the instrument parameters, and experimental design. For instance, phosphatidylcholines, when analyzed by Q-TOF instruments, tend to lose the molecular ion even at medium collision energies. On the other hand, when phosphatidylcholines were analyzed on ion-trap MS instruments, the molecular ion was still highly abundant at medium collision energies, and was significantly fragmented only at high energies [28–30]. In addition to instrument differences, the type of solvent being used can affect the extent to which a compound is fragmented. However, rather than focusing on these subtleties, we chose to focus on selecting (and annotating) the most abundant or most characteristic fragments, which were generally reproducible on different instruments, and reported in multiple studies.

While CFM-ID 2.0 predicts fragmentation probabilities and numeric peak intensities for all query compounds, CFM-ID 3.0 does not predict numeric peak intensities for lipid spectra (however, it still predicts numeric peak intensities for all other classes of molecules). Instead, CFM-ID 3.0 predicts categorical peak intensities for lipid spectra (low, medium, high, and maximum abundance). This simple categorization partly explains why, in many cases, the relative peak intensity is higher in predicted lipid spectra compared to experimental spectra. We believe that a larger lipid MS spectral training set (at least 10+ spectra per chemical class and adduct type) would help to improve the prediction of numeric intensities and simulate their variation between collision energies more accurately. Another limitation of CFM-ID 3.0's rule-based approach for lipid prediction is that the current fragmentation rules do not take the information about the stereochemistry and the position of double/triple bonds into consideration. Therefore, the existing rules do not allow one to distinguish between stereoisomers or regiomers. This is a common problem for rule-based "fragmenters", since the incorporation of such distinctions would require the acquisition of a much more diverse and larger set of high-resolution MS^n spectra.

CFM-ID 3.0 returns the structure (in InChI or SMILES strings) for all predicted fragments. This helps to provide a rationale for nearly all observed peaks. Additionally, this linkage simplifies the lipid ESI-MS/MS spectral annotation process. Because CFM-ID 3.0 provides MS/MS spectra at three energy levels (10, 20, and 40 eV), it means that the predicted MS/MS spectra can be matched more closely to real experimental conditions and real experimental MS/MS spectra. Many other spectral libraries (LipidBlast, NIST) only provide consensus MS/MS spectra for lipids, which makes it difficult to relate experimental data to the predictions.

3.2. Compound Identification and Chemical Class Prediction

The incorporation of citation counts in MS-based compound identification protocols has been consistently shown to improve identification rates in recent studies on spectral/compound identification [19,31]. However, an obvious limitation of this approach is that it reduces the probability of identifying novel or rare compounds that have never been cited. Citation counts can also bias the ranking scheme to select one very similar structure (and therefore a very similar MS spectrum) over another purely on the basis of one having slightly more citations than another. To help balance the influence of citation counts, we incorporated chemical classification into our new scoring system. In this way, the scientific relevance or approximate abundance (in terms of citations) as well as the structural features among candidates could be taken into consideration. Using this approach, a new scoring function was developed for compound identification in CFM-ID 3.0. This new function helped to improve MS-based compound identification quite significantly (see Table 4). When applied to 208 identification challenges on a CFM-ID spectral library containing the 208 ESI-MS/MS spectra, both CFM-ID 2.0 and CFM-ID 3.0 were able to identify all 208 compounds based on spectral similarity. However, as pointed out earlier, it can be expected that most spectral libraries, including CFM-ID 3.0's, will not include (the same) experimental spectra corresponding to a compound of interest. Thus, the use of metadata (i.e., citations) in addition to spectral similarity can help improve identification rates. In particular, when applied to 208 identification challenges, CFM-ID 3.0's ESI-MS/MS scoring function achieved an improvement in overall ranking and identification rate (21.1%) over CFM-ID 2.0's original scoring function. We believe the use of diverse training sets of compounds, representing widely varying structures and structural classes was critical to achieving this improved performance. Our work in this area also confirmed the notion that more work needs to go into expanding spectral databases with experimental data and that this will ultimately improve spectral/compound identification performance.

CFM-ID 3.0 was also assessed with regard to its performance in chemical class prediction. While it may not be possible to identify the exact compound via MS/MS spectral matching, the ability to use MS/MS spectra to narrow down the correct chemical class or chemical family for a given query spectrum or compound can be very valuable for many applications in metabolomics or natural product de-replication. In assessing the performance of CFM-ID's chemical class prediction, the same scoring system introduced here was used to rank the individual candidates. However, in order to perform a formal chemical class identification, the query compound was predicted to belong to the "direct parent" class of the highest-ranked candidate. In cases of a tie, the predicted chemical class was predicted to be the most frequently occurring among all the direct and alternative parents among all the compounds with the highest score. Upon testing the new ESI-MS/MS scoring function on 208 challenges, the correct class was predicted in 80.8% of the challenges (compared to 71.6% for correct compound identification). This result indicates that even when a compound was not identified correctly, the correct class prediction could still be made (in 19 cases). This suggests that CFM-ID 3.0 is still able to identify structural features that characterize the MS/MS fragmentation patterns of certain classes of compounds. These results also demonstrate the importance of using a diverse set of compounds and spectra, as well as the need of having a sufficiently large database to enable compound (or compound class) identification via spectral matching. Structurally similar compounds tend to produce similar spectra. Therefore, even if the compound (and its corresponding MS/MS spectrum) is not in the database (or is poorly ranked), a large number of compounds/spectra from related compound classes could still help to identify the correct compound class. We believe that this helped CFM-ID 3.0 achieve its relatively good performance in the class prediction task.

The inclusion of additional data (citation frequency and chemical class information) in the CFM-ID scoring functions clearly improved compound identification performance. We also believe these improvements were partially aided by the much-improved quality of lipid MS/MS spectra predicted by CFM-ID 3.0. While we made substantive improvements to the quality of CFM-ID's lipid spectra prediction, more work still needs to be done in CFM-ID to better predict the MS/MS fragmentation of other classes of compounds (such as alkaloids, polyphenols, terpenes, and steroids) and to increase the quality of other predicted MS/MS spectra. The addition of many more experimental ESI-MS/MS spectra, measured with various MS instruments, and under different conditions, is also expected to help capture spectral patterns that are not yet accurately predicted by CFM-ID's algorithm, and thus, improve its overall compound identification performance.

4. Materials and Methods

To improve CFM-ID's overall performance for MS/MS analysis, we pursued several algorithmic and database enhancements such as (1) encoding and validating rules for ESI-induced fragmentation of 21 classes of lipids; (2) implementing an automated chemical classification schema (via ClassyFire) for both CFM-ID's database and its query compounds; (3) redesigning, expanding, and improving CFM-ID's MS/MS spectral library (by including experimental MS/MS spectra and adding many thousands of predicted ESI-MS/MS spectra, as well as metadata); (4) collecting citation information from various sources for all of the compounds in CFM-ID's MS/MS spectral library; and (5) modifying CFM-ID's scoring function to incorporate the above changes and improve its overall performance.

The encoding of the lipid rule-based fragmentation approaches was added to improve the speed and accuracy of CFM-ID's lipid ESI-MS/MS predictions, as well as to cover a larger pool of experimental conditions as reflected by different adduct types. The use of ClassyFire's chemical classification method [20] was implemented to automate the rule-based/combinatorial-based decisions for CFM-ID and to improve CFM-ID's ability to identify or re-rank potential MS/MS spectral matches based on structural similarity. The redesign and expansion of the CFM-ID's spectral database was performed to accelerate search speeds, reduce the memory requirements, and to grow the spectral database size (of both predicted and known MS/MS spectra) by a factor of 2.6 so as to improve the likelihood of user query spectral matches. The inclusion of citation data was intended to enhance the scoring accuracy of potential MS/MS spectral matches, while the modification of CFM-ID's scoring function was intended to improve its overall performance. Details regarding how all of these changes were implemented are described below.

4.1. Encoding Lipid Fragmentation Rules

Our analysis of numerous databases and the literature indicated that there are 21 major classes of lipids for which MS/MS spectra are best predicted using hand-made fragmentation rules. The encoding of these hand-made lipid fragmentation rules involved several steps: (1) experimentally measuring or compiling (via literature) characteristic MS/MS fragment ions observed at each of three collision energy levels (10, 20, and 40 eV) for each lipid class, (2) determining the relative abundance of each fragment ion at each energy level, (3) accurately determining the chemical structure and m/z values of each of the fragment ions, (4) including more MS/MS experimental conditions (and adduct ions) by expanding the list of adduct types covered by previous versions of CFM-ID, and (5) implementing these rules using standardized cheminformatics languages (SMARTS [32] and SMIRKS [33]) in order to rapidly and accurately predict and annotate ESI-MS/MS spectra for lipids.

4.1.1. Acquisition of Reference Lipid MS/MS Spectra

The generation of the lipid fragmentation rules required the acquisition of experimental ESI-MS/MS spectra for a number of lipids and lipid classes. The acquired spectra were collected at several collision energies, for various adduct types (e.g., [M+H]$^+$, [M−H]$^−$), and, if possible, from various MS instruments. This was used to help capture fluctuations or biases that can be introduced by the different parameters. A total of 533 experimental MS/MS spectra were collected for 16 standard lipids (purchased from Avanti Polar Lipids Alabaster, AL) from 15 lipid classes at various collision energies (10 to 60 eV), in both positive and negative mode using an AB Sciex QTrap 4000 MS instrument. For each lipid standard, an enhanced MS (EMS) scan was first collected to identify precursor ions with high abundance in either ionization mode. Enhanced product ion (EPI) scans were then collected for each precursor ion to generate the MS/MS spectra with different collision energy levels ranging from 10 to 60 eV, with the supervision of a mass spectrometry expert. For more information about the collection of spectra for the 16 standard lipids, see Supplementary Material. In addition to the MS/MS spectra collected in our laboratory, published lipid MS/MS spectral data were compiled from the LIPID MAPS [28] and the MoNA [24] databases. For the LIPID MAPS spectra, only annotated spectral images were available. Therefore, MS/MS peak lists were generated by annotating the peaks using a semi-automated approach. This approach consisted of computing the relative abundance of each peak, and manually mapping it to the m/z list provided in the LIPID MAPS spectrum. In addition to the experimental spectra, the LipidBlast and FAHFA 26 libraries, as well as MassBank [34], mzCloud [35], and the sphingolipid library of Tsugawa et al. [18] served as references that provided additional information for lipid classes not covered by our experiments. In total, 844 lipid MS/MS spectra from 21 lipid classes were collected and analyzed.

4.1.2. Annotation of Reference Lipid MS/MS Spectra

With the lipid MS/MS spectra in hand, we proceeded to manually annotate each spectrum. This consisted of assigning each fragment ion peak to a specific structure and a specific reaction or fragmentation event (e.g., the loss of a water molecule from a [M+H]$^+$ precursor ion, the loss of a side chain, or the presence of a specific fragment). The annotation of spectra was limited to the in-house generated MS/MS spectra and the LIPID MAPS set, as both were measured with the same model of instrument (AB Sciex QTrap 4000). The annotation process was largely guided by the information provided in LIPID MAPS, LipidBlast, and other scientific reports [17,28,29,36]. In a number of cases, the same compound had MS/MS spectra in at least two of the data sets (including the LipidBlast database), and the corresponding spectra were available for the same adducts or ions. In these cases, we annotated the spectra by direct comparison of the peak lists. Among the 21 lipid classes, 11 were not covered by our in-house experimental data. For this reason, the MS/MS spectra of these missing lipid classes were extracted from the LIPID MAPS (experimental) and/or LipidBlast (in silico) library. Since the experimental and theoretical spectra acquired from other sources (LipidBlast, LIPID MAPS) did not always cover all three collision energy levels (10, 20, and 40 eV), the generation of consensus fragmentation patterns was done by comparing standards to corresponding experimental spectra obtained under the same conditions (adduct type and collision energy). Moreover, when applicable, experimental MS/MS spectra collected from other sources (e.g., MoNA) and obtained under similar experimental conditions were compared to one another, as well as to theoretical spectra. In particular, theoretical spectra from LipidBlast helped in the spectral annotation. The fragmentation and spectral annotation rules were further validated by mining the scientific literature and acquiring/confirming additional spectral data from published papers. Once the energy-specific fragmentation patterns were generated, the relative abundance of each peak was assigned to one of the four intensity levels: low (1–15%), medium (15–60%), high (60–90%), or maximum (90–100%) abundance level. The assigned intensity was based on observed relative abundances from our experimental spectra. The maximum level of abundance was assigned to the base peak, typically when no fragmentation was observed (usually at a low collision energy). Additional feedback from local MS experts combined with an extensive review of the lipid MS/MS literature helped to complete the spectral annotation process. This effort led to the near-complete annotation of all observed fragment ions, their precise m/z values, and the corresponding fragmentation reactions for a total of 610 peaks from 21 lipid classes at each of 3 collision energies (10, 20, and 40 eV).

4.1.3. Implementation of Lipid Fragmentation Rules

The annotated fragment ions along with their structures and reactions provided the basis for the creation of fragmentation rules. All of the fragmentation rules were implemented in the Java programming language through a new "lipid fragmenter module" in CFM-ID. The structural backbone of each lipid or lipid fragment class was represented using the Daylight SMARTS language [32]. This is a module implemented in ClassyFire (version 2.1), a software tool for automating structure-based hierarchical annotation of chemicals [20]. To accelerate the lipid classification process, a sub-ontology from the ChemOnt [20] ontology was used. For each lipid or lipid fragment class, one set of fragmentation patterns is encoded for each of the applicable adducts as chemical reactions. The chemical reactions are represented using the Daylight SMIRKS language [33]. Moreover, SMARTS strings are used to select the appropriate fragments [32]. Additionally, a number of transformation rules were encoded to standardize the structures of all the query compounds. The standardization of the fragmentation reactions using well-developed cheminformatics languages ensures that the structural representations are consistent for all query compounds, structural classes, and chemical reactions. Without adhering to these standards many chemicals classes could be misidentified or invalid fragments could be returned.

The new CFM-ID lipid fragmenter program has been fully integrated into the existing spectral prediction workflow of the previous version of CFM-ID [12]. In CFM-ID 3.0, the lipid MS/MS prediction tasks require a lipid structure (submitted as a SMILES string or SDF file) and an adduct or an ion as input. Upon submission, the compound is classified based on its structure via ClassyFire. If the compound is identified by ClassyFire as a lipid molecule belonging to any of the covered classes and if the fragmentation patterns applicable to the selected adduct exist in the lipid fragmentation library, then the compound is fragmented accordingly. The fragmentation operation is executed using the AMBIT library [37]. After the in silico fragmentation step is completed, the relative abundance of each peak is assigned (using the fragmentation rules described above), and three ESI-MS/MS spectra are generated (at 10, 20, and 40 eV). Relative intensities are assigned using a set of pre-calculated intensities based on the chemical class, the adduct type, and the collision energy. The fragmentation patterns, as well as the relative intensities of the resulting peaks, are the same for all compounds from the same chemical class, under the same experimental conditions (i.e., adduct type and collision energy). If no set of fragmentation patterns is applicable to the compound and/or the selected adduct, and the compound is not a glycero-, phospho- or sphingolipid, then the ESI-MS/MS spectra are predicted using the original CFM-ID algorithm as implemented in CFM-ID 2.0. However, if the compound is a glycero-, phospho- or sphingolipid, the computation is stopped, and an error message is returned. This is done to ensure that CFM-ID does not use the combinatorial fragmentation algorithm, which, as mentioned, does not perform well for such compounds. The resulting ESI-MS/MS spectra are then returned with each peak annotated by its m/z value, its relative abundance, and the chemical structure of the corresponding fragment encoded in a standard SMILES format. Additionally, any available experimental MS spectra in the CFM-ID spectral database matching the query compound are also displayed in the results alongside the predicted spectra.

4.2. Integration of Chemical Classification

Similar structures tend to undergo similar MS fragmentation events under the same conditions. For this reason, a number of in silico MS fragmentation algorithms now take the chemical structure of query molecules into consideration for improved MS-spectra prediction and compound identification tasks. For the prediction of EI-MS/MS spectra, CFM's scoring function partly relies on a list that describes the presence or absence of 107 functional groups and 86 fragment descriptors. These groups and fragment descriptors are provided by ClassyFire [20] and RDKit [38], respectively. Other computational tools such as CSI:FingerID [7] rely on models that can predict the presence of functional groups and fragments based on a given compound or a given MS-spectrum. For this reason, it might be expected that for compound identification tasks, the highest-ranked candidates would likely share a significant number of functional groups or possibly share a maximum common substructure. This information would be particularly helpful in cases where it is very difficult to discriminate between the highest-ranked candidates. More specifically, the presence of one or more common structural backbones (e.g., diterpene, ceramide, phosphatidylglycerol, etc.) could significantly impact the ranking, when very structurally similar candidates are prioritized among those that have a high spectral similarity to the query compound.

Therefore, a chemical classification was assigned to each compound in CFM-ID 3.0's database. The chemical classification was computed by ClassyFire and retrieved using the ClassyFire API [20]. As will be described later in this section, the chemical class assigned to candidate molecules was taken into account along with other metadata to improve the original CFM scoring method (dot product or Jaccard score). In addition to the adjustment of the scoring function, chemical classification was also used to predict the chemical class(es) to which the query compound belonged. Formally, the predicted chemical class corresponds to the direct parent of the highest-ranked candidate. In case of a tie, the predicted chemical category is the most frequently occurring direct or alternative parent among all candidates that has the highest score.

4.3. Collection of Compound Citations

Several studies have demonstrated that the integration of metadata can significantly improve compound identification rates with spectral library searches [7,9,19]. In particular, the frequency with which a compound is mentioned in the literature could serve as a proxy for the likelihood that the compound is sufficiently abundant for detection via MS/MS methods. Therefore, every compound in the CFM-ID spectral library was assigned a citation score. An initial set of citation counts was obtained using DataWrangler. DataWrangler is an in-house tool that automatically mines PubChem [39], HMDB [15], ChemSpider [40], and ChEBI [41], and returns a unique list of scientific reference citations for a given compound. A second set containing PubMed citation counts (without PubMed IDs) was obtained by mining the EPA's CompTox dashboard [42]. This set was computed and generously provided to us by the CompTox dashboard's development team. The two sets were merged by comparing each compound's InChI keys. More specifically, when a compound had a citation count in only one set, the corresponding citation count was assigned to that compound. For compounds that had citation counts both from DataWrangler and CompTox, the largest count was assigned, as it was expected that both counts could include many of the same citations. A total of 140,379 compounds were assigned a citation count of 1 or more. For the remaining compounds, DataWrangler assigned a custom citation count of 1, if and only if, they were found in at least one of the following databases: HMDB [15], DrugBank [21], T3DB [43], ContaminantDB [44], FooDB [45], ECMDB [46], YMDB [47], and PhytoHub [22].

4.4. Redesigning and Expanding of CFM-ID's Spectral Library

The original reference spectral library in CFM-ID 2.0 contained unique computationally generated ESI-MS/MS spectra for ~51,000 compounds from the HMDB and KEGG databases. These in silico ESI-MS/MS spectra were computed in positive ([M+H]$^+$) and negative ([M−H]$^-$) ionization modes, one for each of three collision energies (10, 20, and 40 eV). In order to significantly improve identification rates, the new CFM-ID library was updated as described below.

4.4.1. Collection of Experimental MS/MS Spectra from External Sources

While the accuracy of computationally predicted MS spectra is often quite good, the accuracy of experimentally collected MS spectra is obviously much better. Therefore, the inclusion of experimentally determined ESI-MS/MS spectra would be expected to improve the match scores for query spectra/compounds that have previously been analyzed by ESI-MS/MS. Experimentally determined ESI-MS/MS spectra were downloaded from the MassBank of North America's (MoNA) online repository [24]. As of February 2019, MoNA contained 89,861 experimental LC-MS/MS spectra for 12,799 compounds. The spectra and compounds in MoNA originate from several databases, including the HMDB database [15], MassBank [18], the GNPS database [23], and the ReSpect database [48], among others. Only experimental spectra were collected from MoNA. An additional 915 ESI-MS/MS spectra were manually regenerated for 523 compounds from information contained in the NIST 14 database.

Since CFM-ID uses models trained on MS/MS spectral data sets that use specific collision energy and mass accuracy criteria, the HMDB, MoNA, and NIST spectra were further filtered to match these criteria. Specifically, experimental MS spectra were required to have a known ionization type, a known compound neutral mass, and to have been analyzed with high-resolution MS instruments (e.g., Q-TOF instruments) in the case of LC-MS spectra. After filtering, there were 72,678 usable experimental MS/MS spectra remaining from the MoNA dataset. These experimental MS/MS spectra were converted into the peak list format required for CFM-ID and uploaded into CFM-ID's online spectral library. In addition, the complete library of experimental MS/MS spectra from the HMDB was obtained from our in-house repository, and filtered. Upon filtering, this library contained 1152 unique ESI-MS/MS spectra for 239 unique compounds.

4.4.2. Compilation of Predicted ESI-MS/MS Spectra

The original CFM-ID 2.0 database contained 102,153 unique computationally generated ESI-MS/MS spectra (from 51,635 compounds). Among the 102,153 ESI-MS/MS spectra, 36,746 were previously computed for 18,373 unique compounds belonging to the 21 lipid classes covered by the rule-based fragmenter, and transferred to the CFM-ID 3.0 database. The remaining 65,407 mass spectra computed by CFM-ID 2.0 were also moved to the CFM-ID 3.0 database. In total, ~36,900 spectra were generated for 18,438 lipids. To this database, another ~207,956 ESI-MS/MS spectra were computed for another ~80,000 lipids and 7288 other metabolites obtained from new versions of HMDB, DrugBank, and PhytoHub. These compounds were added to the CFM-ID 3.0 database. These predicted ESI-MS/MS spectra were generated for both positive and negative ion mode as well as at three different collision energies (10, 20, and 40 eV). In total, the CFM-ID 3.0 database now contains 310,109 computationally generated ESI-MS/MS spectra (from 155,544 compounds). If the experimental ESI-MS/MS spectra are added to this total, the CFM-ID 3.0 spectral database now contains a grand total of 393,158 ESI-MS/MS spectra.

4.5. Modifying CFM-ID's Scoring Function and Ranking Schema

The results of the Critical Assessment of Small Molecular Identification (CASMI) 2016 contest showed that the integration of additional data (i.e., citation frequency of compounds and structure similarity) into the original scoring function for CFM-ID improved compound identification rates [19]. This trend was also observed for several other tools during the contest and in separate studies [9,19]. To create a combined score, the original dot product spectral similarity score computed by CFM-ID was combined with a citation score and a chemical classification score. The citation score is based on the number of citations that a given compound has in the scientific literature. More highly cited compounds are typically those that are more commonly detected, studied, or used. Therefore, the citation score serves as a proxy of the general abundance or concentration of a compound and is intended to favor more abundant compounds over extremely rare or compounds at very low biological concentrations.

The chemical classification score is based on the number of chemical categories to which a compound is assigned (by ClassyFire), relative to the total pool of chemical classes assigned to all candidate molecules. The chemical classification score was added to help re-rank or cluster structurally similar molecules (and MS spectra) closer together. Each of the three scores was normalized by dividing its computed score by the maximum score across the candidate list. The general formula for the total candidate score is:

$$S_{TOTAL}(C) = a_{CFM_{ORIG}} * S_{CFM_{ORIG}}(C) + a_{CLASS} * S_{CLASS}(C) + a_{REF} * S_{REF}(C)$$

where $S_{TOTAL}(C)$, $S_{CFM\_ORIG}(C)$, $S_{CLASS}(C)$, and $S_{REF}(C)$ are the total score, the normalized spectral matching CFM-ID score, the normalized ClassyFire score, and the normalized reference score for candidate C, respectively. Each of the three scores are weighted by the coefficients a_{CFM_ORIG}, a_{CLAS_S}, and a_{REF}, respectively, where:

$$a_{CFM\_ORIG}, a_{CLASS}, a_{REF} \geq 0$$

and

$$a_{CFM\_ORIG} + a_{CLASS} + a_{REF} = 1$$

This scoring function was then iteratively optimized on a training data set to maximize its metabolite identification potential. In particular, the optimal set of coefficients was determined through a grid search using a manually selected set of 1000 spectral/compound identification tasks (for 1000 unique compounds ranging from drugs to lipids). Each of the selected molecules had one or more experimental spectra at one of three level energies (10, 20, and 40 eV), in addition to the predicted ESI-MS/MS spectra. The data set was divided into five equally sized subsets. Several models (with a unique combination of coefficients) were trained on 800 compounds (4/5 of the data set) and tested on the remaining 200 (1/5 of the data set). This process was repeated four more times, using a different test set of 200 compounds for each iteration. Experimental spectra were used as input for each identification test, and upon testing, only the best model was selected. A consensus model was built based on the five selected models, and further tested using a smaller test set. The final coefficient values for the ESI-MS/MS scoring function were $a_{CFM\_ORIG} = 0.6$, $a_{CLAS_S} = 0.1$, and $a_{REF} = 0.3$.

This function was further refined to improve its performance and to deal with certain extreme or rare situations. In particular, we observed certain cases in which the spectral similarity between a query and a database match is so close that applying the citation and chemical classification scores causes such strong matches to be unfairly penalized. In order to prevent this, we implemented a 95% similarity threshold, above which only the original spectral similarity score is applied, and the citation and classification information is disregarded. Moreover, our training showed that the enormous discrepancy between citation counts (from 2 to >30,000) could negatively impact the identification rate. For instance, a compound that would be correctly identified using spectral similarity (with or without metadata) could be easily ranked much lower, in favor of a similar compound with a significantly high citation score. Thus, the citation count was adjusted to have a ceiling corresponding to 156 (2 × average citation count) for every compound that has over 156 citations.

4.6. Performance Testing

Three types of performance tests were conducted. The first assessed the performance of the lipid ESI-MS/MS spectral prediction method, the second assessed the performance of the new scoring function in exact compound identification, and the third assessed CFM-ID's performance in identifying a compound's correct chemical class. To test the lipid ESI-MS/MS spectral prediction method, a benchmark analysis was performed on 20 randomly chosen lipids from each of the 21 known lipid classes for which fragmentation rules were derived. The computation was performed on a 2.7 GHz Intel Core i5 running macOS with 16 GB (1867 MHz DDR3) of memory. A total of 120 ESI-MS/MS spectral predictions were generated for both CFM-ID 2.0 and CFM-ID 3.0 at 3 different energies and 2 different ionization modes with various adduct types. The average execution time was determined for each spectral prediction. In addition to the execution time comparison, an additional performance comparison was conducted to assess the quality of the predicted MS/MS spectra. For this task, a set of 5 experimental ESI-MS/MS spectra measured in positive ion mode, and 9 experimental ESI-MS/MS spectra measured in negative ion mode were selected. The selected spectra were measured under conditions that can be simulated by CFM-ID 3.0's lipid fragmentation rules (same energy levels, same adducts). For each experimental MS/MS spectrum, CFM-ID 2.0 and CFM-ID 3.0 were used to predict a corresponding MS/MS spectrum under the same conditions. The performance was assessed by measuring the average pairwise spectral similarity between experimental and predicted spectra using a standard dot product score as implemented in the OrgMassSpecR package [49]. Moreover, they were also compared to LipidBlast, as the selected lipids and corresponding predicted spectra were also contained in the LipidBlast library.

The ESI-MS/MS scoring function was tested on a set of 208 experimental ESI-MS/MS spectra (for 185 unique compounds) generated on a Q Exactive Plus Orbitrap (Thermo Scientific), and used for the CASMI 2016 contest (Category 3) [19]. These spectra were used as input for compound identification. One-hundred and twelve of the 185 compounds were included in the database and had at least one experimental ESI-MS/MS spectrum in addition to the pre-computed ones. For each of the remaining compounds, ESI-MS/MS spectra were predicted using CFM-ID and stored in the spectral library. To assess the performance, we used CFM-ID 2.0 and CFM-ID 3.0 scoring functions, separately, to attempt to identify the query compounds. The evaluation was performed in two steps. The first consisted of identifying compounds by searching them in the CFM-ID spectral library that included the 208 experimental ESI-MS/MS spectra from the CASMI. In a second step, the search was performed after excluding the 208 experimentally acquired spectra in the searchable portion of the database. The required mapping between OrbiTrap collision energies and Q-TOF collision energies (which are used by CFM-ID) is described in the Supplementary Material.

For the third assessment, CFM-ID 3.0 was evaluated on its performance in chemical class prediction/identification. This particular task assessment was included because in many situations involving MS-based metabolomics or MS-based natural product identification, it may not be possible to identify the exact compound via MS/MS spectral matching. Therefore, the ability to use MS/MS spectra to reduce the candidate list and to predict the correct chemical class or correct chemical family for a given query spectrum or compound can be very valuable. In assessing the performance of CFM-ID's chemical class prediction, the query compound was predicted to belong to the "direct parent" class of the highest-ranked candidate. In cases of a tie, the chemical class was predicted to be the most frequently occurring among all the direct and alternative parents among all the compounds with the highest score.

5. Conclusions

We have shown that it is possible to substantially improve CFM-ID's performance in both spectral prediction and compound identification tasks. This was achieved through a number of ways including (1) integrating a rule-based fragmentation approach that currently applies 344 manually curated rules to predict the ESI-MS/MS spectra for 21 classes of common, biologically important lipids, (2) modifying the structure of CFM-ID's spectral database, and increasing its size by a factor of 2.6, (3) designing new scoring functions that take into account both compound citation frequency and chemical classification features of candidate molecules, and (4) implementing a chemical classification algorithm based on spectral similarity.

In particular, the implementation of a rule-based approach for fragment ion prediction was shown to improve the speed by a factor of 200X and the accuracy of the lipid ESI-MS/MS spectra prediction by a factor of 10X. The success of using rule-based fragmentation patterns encoded in standard chemical representations (SMILES, SMARTS, and SMIRKS) suggests that this concept could be successfully applied to other classes of modular molecules such as carnitines, polyphenols, terpenes, and carbohydrates. The construction and expansion of CFM-ID's spectral library has also helped CFM-ID's overall performance. The most recent spectral library has been expanded by a factor of 2.6 over the previously released spectral library. This expansion process is still ongoing, and we plan to include ~500,000 more compounds including drugs, lipids, environmental pollutants, phytochemicals, food compounds, as well as their predicted metabolites generated by BioTransformer [50]. The new scoring function, which already showed an improvement over CFM-ID 2.0's scoring function, could potentially be further improved by using machine learning techniques and training over a much larger set of MS/MS spectra. Moreover, the acquisition and incorporation of other metadata, such as retention time or collisional cross section information, could help further increase the compound identification rates, as demonstrated in several recent studies [9,19].

The fields of in silico metabolomics and in silico mass spectrometry are rapidly evolving. Thanks to the many excellent ideas emerging in many labs around the world and the willingness of many researchers to share their code and their databases, it is likely that these fields will continue to grow and continue to inspire others to make MS spectral analysis, MS spectral prediction, and MS-based compound identification better, faster, and even more informative.

Supplementary Materials: The following are available online at http://www.mdpi.com/2218-1989/9/4/72/s1.

Author Contributions: Conceptualization, Y.D.-F., and D.S.W.; methodology, Y.D.-F., D.S.W., and J.Z.; standard acquisition, J.Z. and Y.D.-F.; MS data interpretation, Y.D.-F., N.K., and J.Z.; generation of fragmentation rules, Y.D.-F.; validation of fragmentation rules, Y.D.-F., N.K., and J.Z.; spectral library expansion, Y.D.-F., A.P., C.L., D.A., and M.G.; scoring function learning and evaluation, Y.D.-F. and A.P.; software, Y.D.-F., A.P., and C.L.; writing—original draft preparation, Y.D.-F., J.Z., A.P., and D.S.W.; writing—review and editing, Y.D.-F., J.Z., A.P., C.L., N.K., D.A., F.A., M.G., and D.S.W.

Funding: This research was funded by Genome Canada and Genome Alberta.

Acknowledgments: The authors would like to acknowledge Tanvir Sajed (University of Alberta, Edmonton, AB, Canada) for providing spectral data from the Human Metabolome Database, Fei Wang (University of Alberta) for helping with the semi-automated annotation of peak list from the LIPID MAPS set of standards, and Antony J Williams (U.S. Environmental Protection Agency) for providing citation metadata from the chemical dashboard.

Conflicts of Interest: The authors declare no conflict of interest.

References

1. Lynn, K.S.; Cheng, M.L.; Chen, Y.R.; Hsu, C.; Chen, A.; Lih, T.M.; Chang, H.Y.; Huang, C.J.; Shiao, M.S.; Pan, W.H.; et al. Metabolite identification for mass spectrometry-based metabolomics using multiple types of correlated ion information. *Anal. Chem.* **2015**, *87*, 2143–2151. [CrossRef] [PubMed]
2. Allard, P.M.; Péresse, T.; Bisson, J.; Gindro, K.; Marcourt, L.; Pham, V.C.; Roussi, F.; Litaudon, M.; Wolfender, J.L. Integration of Molecular Networking and In-Silico MS/MS Fragmentation for Natural Products Dereplication. *Anal. Chem.* **2016**, *88*, 3317–3323. [CrossRef] [PubMed]
3. Sumner, L.W.; Amberg, A.; Barrett, D.; Beale, M.H.; Beger, R.; Daykin, C.A.; Fan, T.W.; Fiehn, O.; Goodacre, R.; Griffin, J.L.; et al. Proposed minimum reporting standards for chemical analysis Chemical Analysis Working Group (CAWG) Metabolomics Standards Initiative (MSI). *Metabolomics* **2007**, *3*, 211. [CrossRef] [PubMed]
4. Dias, D.A.; Jones, O.A.H.; Beale, D.J.; Boughton, B.A.; Benheim, D.; Kouremenos, K.A.; Wolfender, J.L.; Wishart, D.S. Current and future perspectives on the structural identification of small molecules in biological systems. *Metabolites* **2016**, *6*, 46. [CrossRef]
5. Schymanski, E.L.; Singer, H.P.; Longrée, P.; Loos, M.; Ruff, M.; Stravs, M.A.; Ripollés Vidal, C.; Hollender, J. Strategies to characterize polar organic contamination in wastewater: Exploring the capability of high resolution mass spectrometry. *Environ. Sci. Technol.* **2014**, *48*, 1811–1818. [CrossRef] [PubMed]
6. Da Silva, R.R.; Dorrestein, P.C.; Quinn, R.A. Illuminating the dark matter in metabolomics. *Proc. Natl. Acad. Sci. USA* **2015**, *112*, 12549–12550. [CrossRef]
7. Dührkop, K.; Shen, H.; Meusel, M.; Rousu, J.; Böcker, S. Searching molecular structure databases with tandem mass spectra using CSI:FingerID. *Proc. Natl. Acad. Sci. USA* **2015**, *112*, 12580–12585. [CrossRef] [PubMed]
8. Ridder, L.; Van Der Hooft, J.J.J.; Verhoeven, S.; De Vos, R.C.H.; Van Schaik, R.; Vervoort, J. Substructure-based annotation of high-resolution multistage MSn spectral trees. *Rapid Commun. Mass Spectrom.* **2012**, *26*, 2461–2471. [CrossRef] [PubMed]
9. Ruttkies, C.; Schymanski, E.L.; Wolf, S.; Hollender, J.; Neumann, S. MetFrag relaunched: Incorporating strategies beyond in silico fragmentation. *J. Cheminform.* **2016**, *8*. [CrossRef] [PubMed]
10. Allen, F.; Pon, A.; Wilson, M.; Greiner, R.; Wishart, D. CFM-ID: A web server for annotation, spectrum prediction and metabolite identification from tandem mass spectra. *Nucleic Acids Res.* **2014**, *42*, W94–W99. [CrossRef]

11. Allen, F.; Greiner, R.; Wishart, D. Competitive fragmentation modeling of ESI-MS/MS spectra for putative metabolite identification. *Metabolomics* **2014**, *11*, 98–110. [CrossRef]
12. Allen, F.; Pon, A.; Greiner, R.; Wishart, D. Computational Prediction of Electron Ionization Mass Spectra to Assist in GC/MS Compound Identification. *Anal. Chem.* **2016**, *88*, 7689–7697. [CrossRef]
13. Hufsky, F.; Böcker, S. Mining molecular structure databases: Identification of small molecules based on fragmentation mass spectrometry data. *Mass Spectrom. Rev.* **2017**, *36*, 624–633. [CrossRef]
14. Heinonen, M.; Rantanen, A.; Mielikäinen, T.; Kokkonen, J.; Kiuru, J.; Ketola, R.A.; Rousu, J. FiD: A software for ab initio structural identification of product ions from tandem mass spectrometric data. *Rapid Commun. Mass Spectrom.* **2008**, *22*, 3043–3052. [CrossRef]
15. Wishart, D.S.; Feunang, Y.D.; Marcu, A.; Guo, A.C.; Liang, K.; Vázquez-Fresno, R.; Sajed, T.; Johnson, D.; Li, C.; Karu, N.; et al. HMDB 4.0: The human metabolome database for 2018. *Nucleic Acids Res.* **2018**, *46*, D608–D617. [CrossRef]
16. Kanehisa, M.; Furumichi, M.; Tanabe, M.; Sato, Y.; Morishima, K. KEGG: New perspectives on genomes, pathways, diseases and drugs. *Nucleic Acids Res.* **2017**, *45*, D353–D361. [CrossRef]
17. Kind, T.; Liu, K.H.; Lee, D.Y.; Defelice, B.; Meissen, J.K.; Fiehn, O. LipidBlast in silico tandem mass spectrometry database for lipid identification. *Nat. Methods* **2013**, *10*, 755–758. [CrossRef] [PubMed]
18. Tsugawa, H.; Ikeda, K.; Tanaka, W.; Senoo, Y.; Arita, M.; Arita, M. Comprehensive identification of sphingolipid species by in silico retention time and tandem mass spectral library. *J. Cheminform.* **2017**, *9*. [CrossRef]
19. Schymanski, E.L.; Ruttkies, C.; Krauss, M.; Brouard, C.; Kind, T.; Dührkop, K.; Allen, F.; Vaniya, A.; Verdegem, D.; Böcker, S.; et al. Critical Assessment of Small Molecule Identification 2016: Automated methods. *J. Cheminform.* **2017**, *9*. [CrossRef]
20. Djoumbou Feunang, Y.; Eisner, R.; Knox, C.; Chepelev, L.; Hastings, J.; Owen, G.; Fahy, E.; Steinbeck, C.; Subramanian, S.; Bolton, E.; et al. ClassyFire: Automated chemical classification with a comprehensive, computable taxonomy. *J. Cheminform.* **2016**, *8*, 1–20. [CrossRef]
21. Wishart, D.S.; Feunang, Y.D.; Guo, A.C.; Lo, E.J.; Marcu, A.; Grant, J.R.; Sajed, T.; Johnson, D.; Li, C.; Sayeeda, Z.; et al. DrugBank 5.0: A major update to the DrugBank database for 2018. *Nucleic Acids Res.* **2018**, *46*, D1074–D1082. [CrossRef]
22. Phytohub v1.4. Available online: http://phytohub.eu/ (accessed on 10 February 2018).
23. Wang, M.; Carver, J.J.; Phelan, V.V.; Sanchez, L.M.; Garg, N.; Peng, Y.; Nguyen, D.D.; Watrous, J.; Kapono, C.A.; Luzzatto-Knaan, T.; et al. Sharing and community curation of mass spectrometry data with Global Natural Products Social Molecular Networking. *Nat. Biotechnol.* **2016**, *34*, 828–837. [CrossRef] [PubMed]
24. MassBank of North America (MoNA), Fiehn Lab, UC Davis, CA 95618. Available online: http://mona.fiehnlab.ucdavis.edu/ (accessed on 26 February 2019).
25. Nikolic, D.; Jones, M.; Sumner, L.; Dunn, W. CASMI 2014: Challenges, solutions and results. *Curr. Metab.* **2017**, *5*, 5–17. [CrossRef]
26. Tsugawa, H.; Kind, T.; Nakabayashi, R.; Yukihira, D.; Tanaka, W.; Cajka, T.; Saito, K.; Fiehn, O.; Arita, M. Hydrogen rearrangement rules: Computational MS/MS fragmentation and structure elucidation using MS-FINDER software. *Anal. Chem.* **2016**, *88*, 7946. [CrossRef] [PubMed]
27. Witting, M.; Ruttkies, C.; Neumann, S.; Schmitt-Kopplin, P. LipidFrag: Improving reliability of in silico fragmentation of lipids and application to the Caenorhabditis elegans lipidome. *PLoS ONE* **2017**, *12*, e0172311. [CrossRef] [PubMed]
28. Fahy, E.; Subramaniam, S.; Murphy, R.C.; Nishijima, M.; Raetz, C.R.H.; Shimizu, T.; Spener, F.; Van Meer, G.; Wakelam, M.J.O.; Dennis, E.A. Update of the LIPID MAPS comprehensive classification system for lipids. *J. Lipid Res.* **2009**, *50*, S9–S14. [CrossRef]
29. Pi, J.; Wu, X.; Feng, Y. Fragmentation patterns of five types of phospholipids by ultra-high-performance liquid chromatography electrospray ionization quadrupole time-of-flight tandem mass spectrometry. *Anal. Methods* **2016**, *8*, 1319–1332. [CrossRef]
30. Murphy, R.C. *Tandem Mass Spectrometry of Lipids: Molecular Analysis of Complex Lipids*; Royal Society of Chemistry: London, UK, 2014. [CrossRef]
31. Blaženović, I.; Kind, T.; Torbašinović, H.; Obrenović, S.; Mehta, S.S.; Tsugawa, H.; Wermuth, T.; Schauer, N.; Jahn, M.; Biedendieck, R. Comprehensive comparison of in silico MS/MS fragmentation tools of the CASMI contest: Database boosting is needed to achieve 93% accuracy. *J. Cheminform.* **2017**, *9*, 32. [CrossRef]

32. SMARTS Theory Manual, Daylight Chemical Information Systems, Inc., Laguna Niguel, CA 92677. Available online: http://www.daylight.com/dayhtml/doc/theory/theory.smarts.html (accessed on 20 December 2018).
33. SMIRKS Theory Manual, Daylight Chemical Information Systems, Inc., Laguna Niguel, CA 92677. Available online: http://www.daylight.com/dayhtml/doc/theory/theory.smirks.html (accessed on 29 October 2018).
34. Horai, H.; Arita, M.; Kanaya, S.; Nihei, Y.; Ikeda, T.; Suwa, K.; Ojima, Y.; Tanaka, K.; Tanaka, S.; Aoshima, K.; et al. MassBank: A public repository for sharing mass spectral data for life sciences. *J. Mass Spectrom.* **2010**, *45*, 703–714. [CrossRef]
35. mzCloud—Advanced Mass Spectral Database, HighChem, Bratislava, Slovakia. Available online: https://www.mzcloud.org/ (accessed on 18 December 2018).
36. Han, X. *Lipidomics: Comprehensive Mass Spectrometry of Lipids*; John Wiley & Sons: Hoboken, NJ, USA, 2016.
37. Jeliazkova, N.; Kochev, N. AMBIT-SMARTS: Efficient searching of chemical structures and fragments. *Mol. Inform.* **2011**, *30*, 707–720. [CrossRef]
38. RDKit: Open-Source Cheminformatics Software. Available online: https://www.rdkit.org/ (accessed on 6 September 2018).
39. Kim, S.; Thiessen, P.A.; Bolton, E.E.; Chen, J.; Fu, G.; Gindulyte, A.; Han, L.; He, J.; He, S.; Shoemaker, B.A.; et al. PubChem substance and compound databases. *Nucleic Acids Res.* **2016**, *44*, D1202–D1213. [CrossRef] [PubMed]
40. Pence, H.E.; Williams, A. Chemspider: An online chemical information resource. *J. Chem. Educ.* **2010**, *87*, 1123–1124. [CrossRef]
41. Hastings, J.; Owen, G.; Dekker, A.; Ennis, M.; Kale, N.; Muthukrishnan, V.; Turner, S.; Swainston, N.; Mendes, P.; Steinbeck, C. ChEBI in 2016: Improved services and an expanding collection of metabolites. *Nucleic Acids Res.* **2016**, *44*, D1214–D1219. [CrossRef] [PubMed]
42. McEachran, A.D.; Sobus, J.R.; Williams, A.J. Identifying known unknowns using the US EPA's CompTox Chemistry Dashboard. *Anal. Bioanal. Chem.* **2017**, *409*, 1729–1735. [CrossRef] [PubMed]
43. Wishart, D.; Arndt, D.; Pon, A.; Sajed, T.; Guo, A.C.; Djoumbou, Y.; Knox, C.; Wilson, M.; Liang, Y.; Grant, J.; et al. T3DB: The toxic exposome database. *Nucleic Acids Res.* **2015**, *43*, D928–D934. [CrossRef]
44. ContaminantDB v1.0, TMIC, University of Alberta, Canada. Available online: http://contaminantdb.ca/ (accessed on 28 March 2019).
45. FooDB v1.0, TMIC, University of Alberta, Canada. Available online: http://foodb.ca/ (accessed on 28 March 2019).
46. Sajed, T.; Marcu, A.; Ramirez, M.; Pon, A.; Guo, A.C.; Knox, C.; Wilson, M.; Grant, J.R.; Djoumbou, Y.; Wishart, D.S. ECMDB 2.0: A richer resource for understanding the biochemistry of *E. coli*. *Nucleic Acids Res.* **2016**, *44*, D495–D501. [CrossRef]
47. Ramirez-Gaona, M.; Marcu, A.; Pon, A.; Guo, A.C.; Sajed, T.; Wishart, N.A.; Karu, N.; Feunang, Y.D.; Arndt, D.; Wishart, D.S. YMDB 2.0: A significantly expanded version of the yeast metabolome database. *Nucleic Acids Res.* **2017**, *45*, D440–D445. [CrossRef]
48. Sawada, Y.; Nakabayashi, R.; Yamada, Y.; Suzuki, M.; Sato, M.; Sakata, A.; Akiyama, K.; Sakurai, T.; Matsuda, F.; Aoki, T.; et al. RIKEN tandem mass spectral database (ReSpect) for phytochemicals: A plant-specific MS/MS-based data resource and database. *Phytochemistry* **2012**, *82*, 38–45. [CrossRef]
49. Dodder, N.G. Organic/Biological Mass Spectrometry Data Analysis. Available online: https://cran.r-project.org/web/packages/OrgMassSpecR/index.html (accessed on 28 March 2019).
50. Djoumbou-Feunang, Y.; Fiamoncini, J.; Gil-de-la-Fuente, A.; Greiner, R.; Manach, C.; Wishart, D.S. BioTransformer: A comprehensive computational tool for small molecule metabolism prediction and metabolite identification. *J. Cheminform.* **2019**, *11*. [CrossRef]

© 2019 by the authors. Licensee MDPI, Basel, Switzerland. This article is an open access article distributed under the terms and conditions of the Creative Commons Attribution (CC BY) license (http://creativecommons.org/licenses/by/4.0/).

 *metabolites*

Article

R-MetaboList 2: A Flexible Tool for Metabolite Annotation from High-Resolution Data-Independent Acquisition Mass Spectrometry Analysis

Manuel D. Peris-Díaz [1,2], Shannon R. Sweeney [3,4], Olga Rodak [5], Enrique Sentandreu [2,6,*] and Stefano Tiziani [3,4,*]

1. Department of Chemical Biology, Faculty of Biotechnology, University of Wrocław, J.Curie 14a, 50-383 Wrocław, Poland; manuel.perisdiaz@uwr.edu.pl
2. Unidad Analítica, Instituto de Investigación Sanitaria La Fe (IIS La Fe), 46026 Valencia, Spain
3. Dell Pediatric Research Institute (DPRI), University of Texas at Austin, Austin, TX 78723, USA; ssweeney@utexas.edu
4. Institute for Cellular and Molecular Biology, The University of Texas at Austin, Austin, TX 78723, USA
5. Department of Reproduction and Clinic of Farm Animals, Faculty of Veterinary Medicine, Wrocław University of Environmental and Life Sciences, 50-366 Wrocław, Poland; olga.rodak@upwr.edu.pl
6. Instituto de Agroquímica y Tecnología de Alimentos (IATA-CSIC), Paterna, 46980 Valencia, Spain
* Correspondence: infusoriosentandreu@gmail.com (E.S.); tiziani@austin.utexas.edu (S.T.)

Received: 7 August 2019; Accepted: 12 September 2019; Published: 17 September 2019

Abstract: Technological advancements have permitted the development of innovative multiplexing strategies for data independent acquisition (DIA) mass spectrometry (MS). Software solutions and extensive compound libraries facilitate the efficient analysis of MS^1 data, regardless of the analytical platform. However, the development of comparable tools for DIA data analysis has significantly lagged. This research introduces an update to the former MetaboList R package and a workflow for full-scan MS^1 and MS/MS DIA processing of metabolomic data from multiplexed liquid chromatography high-resolution mass spectrometry (LC-HRMS) experiments. When compared to the former version, new functions have been added to address isolated MS^1 and MS/MS workflows, processing of MS/MS data from stepped collision energies, performance scoring of metabolite annotations, and batch job analysis were incorporated into the update. The flexibility and efficiency of this strategy were assessed through the study of the metabolite profiles of human urine, leukemia cell culture, and medium samples analyzed by either liquid chromatography quadrupole time-of-flight (q-TOF) or quadrupole orbital (q-Orbitrap) instruments. This open-source alternative was designed to promote global metabolomic strategies based on recursive retrospective research of multiplexed DIA analysis.

Keywords: liquid chromatography high-resolution mass spectrometry; data-independent acquisition; all ion fragmentation; targeted analysis; untargeted analysis; metabolomics; R programming; full-scan MS/MS processing; R-MetaboList 2

1. Introduction

Liquid chromatography high-resolution mass spectrometry (LC-HRMS) technology makes it feasible to simultaneously apply qualitative and quantitative approaches to the metabolite profiling of biological samples [1–6]. During the last decade, technological advances in electronics and hardware design have expanded multiplexing capacities, sensitivity and specificity of detectors, and facilitated the development of innovative scan options to address the needs of global metabolomics research [7]. Thus, traditional data-dependent acquisition (DDA), which requires the predetermined selection of precursors for MS/MS research, has been complemented by untargeted data-independent acquisition

(DIA) approaches, such as all ion fragmentation (AIF) analysis [8–10]. This precursor-free strategy was initially introduced by Thermo Scientific in early Exactive benchtop Orbitraps for small-molecule applications in order to ameliorate the constraints of targeted analysis performed on triple-quadrupole (QQQ) detectors [9]. This operation mode was later adapted for modern hybrid quadrupole-Orbitrap (Thermo Q Exactive and Fusion Tribrid) and time-of-flight (q-TOF) detectors under different synonyms, such as all ion MS/MS, MS^{ALL}, and MS^E, depending on the manufacturer [11]. The flexibility of full-scan MS/MS analysis for targeted/untargeted-quantitative/qualitative research combined with high-throughput capacity of modern LC-HRMS detectors created a gap between hardware capabilities and licensed programs for in-depth automated processing of data from DIA analysis. While MS^1 processing solutions are widely available and easily implementable [12–14], alternatives that address bulky AIF data processing are mainly limited to recently released open-source programs. This is the case for MS-DIAL, which was initially proposed for lipidomic research using a triple-TOF device [15], and later MetDIA, a solution with stated superior features for small molecule analysis while using the same detector [16]. Recently, the suitability of MS-DIAL for small molecule research assessed by quadrupole-Orbitrap AIF analysis has been shown [17]. However, the ability of these programs to reliably extract data from bulky DIA-MS files has not been demonstrated for small molecule research ($m/z < 400$).

Recently, the R-package MetaboList was proposed as an accurate, flexible, and highly customizable alternative for full-scan MS/MS data processing [10]. The authors demonstrated the suitability of this approach for the study of metabolites with $m/z < 250$ while considering a mass tolerance of 5 ppm for both MS^1 and MS/MS analyses collected by a quadrupole-Orbitrap detector. Interestingly, this study demonstrated how data analysis with R-MetaboList could be easily enhanced by continuous customization from users. From this, the suitability of R-MetaboList for small molecule research utilizing multiplexed full-scan MS-MS/MS experiments being performed on different LC-HRMS systems deserves further investigation.

This research aims to demonstrate the flexibility and improved efficiency of an upgraded version of the previously released open-source R package MetaboList for metabolite research supported by LC full-scan MS^1 and DIA-MS/MS analyses. A highly diluted human urine sample was analyzed in positive ionization mode by an LC-qTOF device that merged full-scan experiments at different collision-induced dissociation (CID) energies of 0, 5, 10, and 20 eV. Similarly, myeloid leukemia cells and medium extracts were studied by full-scan analyses on an LC q-Orbitrap system operating in fast polarity switching mode at 0% and 30% higher-energy collisional dissociation (HCD) energies. Automated processing of full-scan MS and MS/MS data for both HRMS instruments was carried out by R-Metabolist 2. Here, we demonstrate the utility of this data processing solution for the retrospective interrogation of DIA approaches to facilitate new insights for addressing global metabolomics of biological samples.

2. Results and Discussion

The R-MetaboList 2 package was developed in the R environment and it can be freely downloaded from the CRAN repository (https://CRAN.R-project.org/package=MetaboList) for automated targeted data extraction and the annotation of full-scan MS^1 and/or MS/MS DIA spectra generated by LC-HRMS analysis. Figure 1 illustrates the workflow pipeline that was followed in this research and indicates the functions that are included in the R-MetaboList 2 package. In comparison with the previous version [10], the updated R-MetaboList 2 incorporates the following new features:

(1) Processing workflow for full-scan MS^1 analysis (Figure 1A) independent of full-scan MS/MS analysis. The previous version did not include the processing of full-scan MS^1 data outside the scope of the associated MS/MS data.
(2) Simultaneous processing of full-scan MS/MS data generated under different instrumental conditions (Figure 1B).

(3) Incorporation of scoring functions to evaluate metabolite annotation of both full-scan MS^1 and MS/MS approaches (Figure 1B).
(4) Improved graphical representation of the results.
(5) Incorporation of a batch job function for compilation of full-scan MS^n reports from multiple samples for high-throughput applications.

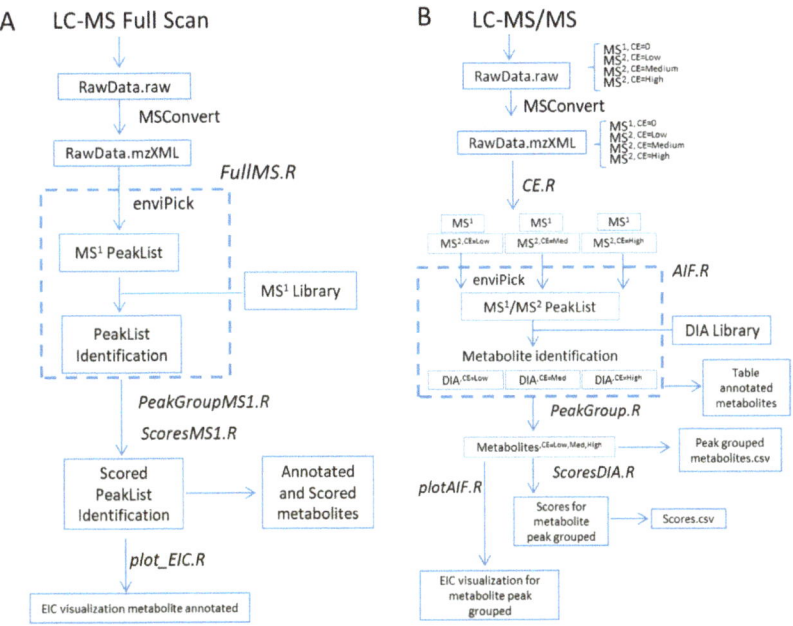

Figure 1. Overview of the R-MetaboList 2 workflow pipeline. (**A**) Initially, the raw data from an LC-MS full-scan experiment is converted to an .mzXML file format using MSConvert or other software. The file converted is processed by the *FullMS.R* function which performs a peak picking with the embedded enviPick algorithm to generate a peak list. A metabolite library consisting of neutral masses with optional retention time annotations is used by the *FullMS.R* function to provide a list of annotations that are grouped by metabolite assignment by the *PeakGroupMS1.R* function. Finally, the function *ScoresMS1.R* evaluates the isotope peak intensity ratio (IPIR), peak-to-peak Pearson correlation (PPC), and peak-to-peak shape (PPS) scores for each given metabolite. Finally, visualization of the extracted ion chromatogram (EIC) for the annotated metabolite is produced by the *plot_EIC.R* function. (**B**) Raw data from LC-MS/MS full-scan experiment is converted to an .mzXML file format which is further separated by collision energy (*CE.R*). MS^1 at CE 0 and one MS^2 per CE are processed by the *AIF.R* function, which performs a targeted extraction and putative annotation when an MS/MS library is provided. Peak grouping across CE values is performed with the *PeakGroup.R* function followed by scoring with the *ScoresDIA.R* function to evaluate the annotation confidence.

2.1. Metabolite Profiling of Samples from Full-Scan MS^1 Analysis

Metabolites annotation was initially addressed by R-MetaboList 2 through the processing of full-scan MS^1 data from q-TOF and q-Orbitrap systems. Next, preliminary lists of tentative assignments that were generated by theoretical monoisotopic mass matching within a 5 ppm window were subsequently refined by full-scan MS/MS analysis. Peak picking of the underivatized urinary sample (q-TOF analysis) and targeted metabolite extraction by the *FullMS.R* function while considering the in-house neutral library utilized in this research (detailed in materials and methods section) yielded a total of 68 tentative metabolite assignments (Table S1). The tentative list of metabolites was grouped according to metabolite assignment and was exported in .csv file format (*PeakGroupMS1.R* function). Figure S1A,B illustrate the output style of the *plot_EIC.R* function (from *FullMS.R* function analysis) of [M+H]$^+$ and [M+NH$_4$]$^+$ glutamine adducts in urine (qTOF), both annotated with less than 1 ppm mass deviation and a peak asymmetry factor of 1.5. The function (*plot_EIC.R*) produces a quality control plot that shows the *m/z* deviation for each scan forming the annotated peak (Figure S1C). Moreover, we designed a function named *ScoresMS1.R*, which incorporates the isotope peak intensity ratio (IPIR), peak-to-peak Pearson correlation (PPC), and peak-to-peak shape (PPS) scores (Detailed information in Section 3.3). Evaluation of the [M+H]$^+$ and [M+NH$_4$]$^+$ glutamine adducts by the *ScoresMS1.R* function yielded a null PPC coefficient score revealing the absence of co-elution between both adducts. Similarly, urinary phenylacetylglutamine was detected in positive mode ([M+H]$^+$) and the isotopic profile was resolved for the first isotopologue with a mass error lower than 5 ppm for both cases. The R package includes an IPIR score to increase the confidence of metabolite annotations. For metabolites with an absence of S or Br in the molecular formula, the IPIR should be greater than one. The extracted ion chromatogram (EIC) was plotted by the *plot_EIC.R* function and was evaluated by the *ScoresMS1.R* function which yielded a PPC score, IPIR, and asymmetry peak ratio of 0.99, 8.2, and 0.84, respectively (Figure 2A).

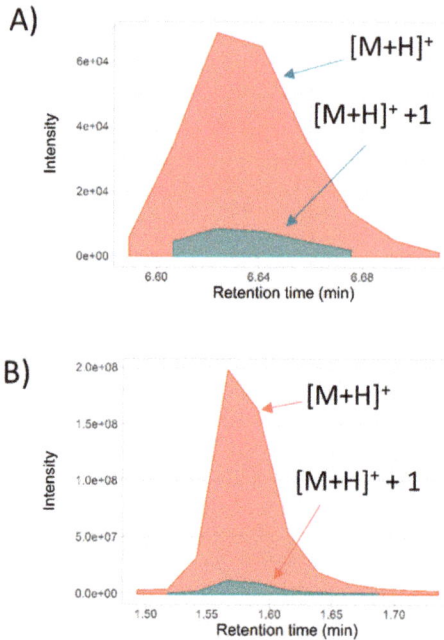

Figure 2. Graphical output generated by the *ScoresMS1.R* function. (**A**) Coelution extracted ion chromatograms (EIC) (extracted ion chromatogram) profile for phenylacetylglutamine detected in positive ionization mode with [M+H]$^+$ and [M+H]$^+$ +1 isotope for urine sample analyzed by LC-qTOF. (**B**) Coelution EIC profile for betaine detected in positive ionization mode with [M+H]$^+$ and [M+H]$^+$ +1 isotope putative identified in cell sample analyzed by LC-q-Exactive Orbitrap.

Similarly, peak picking followed by the targeted feature extraction of cell and medium samples (q-Orbitrap analysis) led to 181 and 123 putative assignments, respectively (ESI, Tables S2 and S3 .csv). As an example of tentative assignments from cell and medium extracts using the q-Orbitrap instrument, betaine was found as [M+H]$^+$ and its naturally occurring [M+H]$^+$ +1 isotopologues in the cell sample with a mass accuracy below 1.5 ppm for both cases and peak asymmetry of 2.4 and 2.2, respectively (Figure 2B). Evaluation of both peaks by the *ScoresMS1.R* function resulted in a PPC score, IPIR, and asymmetry peak ratio of 0.99, 17, and 0.94, respectively. Overall, the workflow implemented for LC-MS full-scan analysis in the R-Metabolist 2 package generates a preliminary list of metabolites that can be confirmed by MS/MS analysis and/or retention time matching.

2.2. Metabolites Annotation by Full-Scan MS/MS Approach

Preliminary metabolite assignments that were achieved by the *FullMS.R* function in the urine sample analyzed by LC-qTOF were assessed by the *AIF.R* and *Filter_AIF.R* functions while using full-scan MS/MS data processing and loading the in-house MS/MS library detailed in Table S4A (positive ionization mode). Tentative MS/MS assignments were subsequently grouped by the *PeakGroup.R* function according to the appropriated CID assayed. Tables S5–S7 detail the tentative assignments achieved by peak grouping (alignment) of precursors and respective MS/MS fragments listed in Table S4 (positive ionization) at CID 5, 10, and 20 eV, respectively. Tentative assignments varied according to the CID assayed, although in all cases the mass error remained below 10 ppm and the retention time window for alignment was less than 0.1 min. Thus, 16, 20, and 23 metabolites were tentatively identified aligning the molecular mass with one (1 parent-fragment pair) of the respective fragment ions for CID 5, 10, and 20 eV, respectively. When considering alignment of molecular masses with their respective all fragment ions as a requisite for tentative assignments, there were annotated 11, 14, and 16 metabolites for CID 5, 10, and 20 eV, respectively. Election of the number of fragments that are required for tentative assignment was controlled by *Filter_AIF.R* functions embedded in R-MetaboList 2 and it can be customized by the user.

Data acquisition speed has a preponderant role in the sensitivity that is achieved by q-TOF analyzers, since higher scan rates decrease the accumulation time of ions. This is critical for low abundance species since high velocities can compromise detection. In contrast, scanning activity that is too slow permits the detection of minor compounds, but compromises the definition of the chromatographic response of all compounds (major and minor) by reducing the number of scans across each peak. An insufficient number of scans across any given peak results in increasing peak asymmetry, thus hindering quantitative analysis, as stated in a former version of R-MetaboList [10]. Moreover, there are numerous instrumental parameters that affect signal intensity, and thus optimization is required to increase the performance of MS detectors [18]. In this study, we focused on the suitability of the MS device for obtaining high-quality qualitative data without sacrificing quantitative analysis. An intermediate acquisition time of 250 ms was selected as a good compromise for multiplexed analyses (four scan events) of highly diluted samples.

Moreover, it should be highlighted that the simultaneous calculation of signal intensities (Tables S5–S7) achieved at different collision energies (CE) greatly facilitates the election of appropriate breakdown energy according to the desired fragment being analyzed [19]. For example, the experimental glutamine peak group was formed by MS^1 at 147.0764 *m/z* and two MS/MS fragments at 130.0499 and 84.0445 *m/z* (Table S8). At CE 5 and 10 eV both 130.0499 and 84.0445 *m/z* ([M+H]$^+$) fragments were detected while at 20 eV only 84.0445 *m/z* fragment was found, revealing CE 5 and 10 eV as more suitable conditions for glutamine. Similarly, phenylacetylglutamine analyzed at CE 20 eV resulted in the absence of the 147.0763 *m/z* ion, whereas at CE 5 and 10 eV fragments at 84.0444, 130.0499, 136.0756, and 147.0763 *m/z* were observed (Table S8). On the other hand, for phenylalanine the optimum CID was found at CE 20 eV, in which both fragment ions, 103.0543 and 120.0808 *m/z*, appeared (Table S8). Overall, these results demonstrate minimal mass deviations and clearly indicate different optimal CID energies for maximized response of considered AIF fragments, depending on the molecule being studied (Table S5–S7).

Targeted metabolite extraction of full-scan MS/MS for cell extract analyzed by q-Orbitrap yielded a total of 53 and 51 tentative assignments (Table S9) when the alignment of molecular masses with one or all of their respective fragments (detailed in Table S4) was considered as an assignment constraint, respectively. Similarly, 29 and 26 metabolites were annotated in the medium sample (Table S10) when the alignment of molecular masses with one or all of their respective fragments, as listed in Table S4, is used as an assignment constraint.

The limited number of tentative assignments that were found in this study arose from the use of an early stage in-house AIF library listing 68 compounds and the analysis of highly diluted samples (mainly in the case of the urinary extract). More annotations can be achieved through the analysis of less diluted samples and/or the curation and use of a more extensive MS/MS AIF library that can be continuously expanded by users. In any case, these results demonstrate the flexibility of R-MetaboList 2 for processing multiplexed data generated by different LC-HRMS systems. The high-throughput capacity of such analytical platforms generates massive amounts of raw data that require the appropriate, customizable processing workflow to maximize the flexibility and reliability of biological data analysis. The manual handling of full-scan MS^1 and MS/MS experiments is tedious and time-consuming. To ameliorate this problem, this research implemented a script (*AIF_Batch.R*, Supplementary Materials) that enables batch job processing of reports following parameter optimization.

2.3. Selectivity for Metabolite Annotation by LC-DIA-MS: Quality Control and Scores Test

Once a full-scan MS^1-MS/MS peak group is generated, further evaluation by statistical analyses can increase the confidence of the metabolite assignments. R-MetaboList 2 includes score tests based on the PPC score and PPS ratio for both quality control and product/precursor ion intensity ratios featured by the *ScoresDIA.R* function [20]. From our experience, a PPS value between 0.3 and 3 reflects acceptable similarity in chromatographic peak shape, however this parameter is defined by the discretion of the user. It should be noted that the PPC score is based on correlation coefficients and it can be overestimated when the EIC peaks are defined by an insufficient number of scans. It is recommended that 0.7 be set as the PPC cutoff for precursor-product scoring. To control potential overfitting, the function returns an intensity coelution plot of the scans shared by precursor/fragment peaks, as well as the correlation coefficient calculated by Pearson and *p*-value achieved by the fitting. The intensity co-elution plot also enables the inspection of the number of scans forming the peaks from precursor/fragment pairs.

Evaluating the feature previously annotated in urine as glutamine, scores were generated with the *ScoresDIA.R* function. The PPC was higher than 0.8 in all cases (Table 1). The fragment 84.0444 *m/z* that was obtained at CE 5 eV resulted in a PPS of 0.2 and a product/precursor ion intensity ratio of 0.2 and, thus, its annotation was not scored positively. However, this fragment was positively scored at CE 10 eV and 20 eV, in which the PPS was 0.67 for both and the product/precursor ion ratios were 0.74 and 0.99, respectively. Regarding the fragment 130.0499 *m/z*, at both CE 5 and 10 eV, all of the scores were satisfactory. Thus, we can conclude that glutamine analyzed at CE 10 eV produced fragment ion that can be most confidently annotated (Figure 3).

For phenylacetylglutamine, at CE 5 eV only 84.0444 and 130.0499 *m/z* fragments were found that coeluted with the respective precursor. However, the PPC score for the first fragment was too low and it was discarded as a positive annotation (Table 1). At CE 10 eV, a whole set of product ions were observed but with different PPC scores in comparison with their counterparts that were observed at CE 20 eV (Table 1). Product ion 136.0756 *m/z* $[M+H]^+$ at CE 10 eV scored lower than the aforementioned recommended cutoff of 0.7, making the product-precursor association unreliable. As observed, CE 20 eV yielded the best results. Figure 4 shows the co-elution plot for the phenylacetylglutamine precursor and the product ions at 20 eV.

Table 1. Statistical evaluation of peak groups for glutamine, phenylacetylglutamine, and phenylalanine performed by *ScoresDIA.R* function. Analysis performed on an LC-qTOF instrument. The recommended cut-off for PPC is ≥ 0.7. Good chromatographic similarity is indicated by PPS scores between 0.3 and 3. Abbreviations used: CE, Collision Energy; PPC, peak-to-peak Pearson correlation; PPS, peak-to-peak shape ratio.

	Experimental Fragment [M+H]$^+$ (m/z)	CE (eV)	PPC	PPS	[a] Product/Precursor Ion Ratio
Glutamine					
	84.0444	5	0.93	0.22	0.23
	130.0499	5	0.97	1.00	0.72
	84.0444	10	0.87	0.67	0.74
	130.0499	10	0.87	0.67	0.74
	84.0444	20	0.87	0.67	0.99
Phenylacetylglutamine					
	84.0444	5	0.39	0.80	0.04
	130.0499	5	0.76	0.60	0.20
	84.0444	10	0.72	0.40	0.07
	130.0499	10	0.91	0.80	0.54
	136.0756	10	0.67	0.40	0.06
	147.0762	10	0.80	0.40	0.06
	84.0444	20	0.89	0.40	0.13
	130.0499	20	0.95	0.40	0.54
	136.0757	20	0.89	0.40	0.06
	147.0762	20	0.97	0.40	0.04
Phenylalanine					
	120.0809	5	0.60	3.00	0.77
	120.0809	10	0.87	1.50	1.39
	103.0543	20	0.76	2.00	0.43
	120.0809	20	0.93	1.50	1.05

[a] Experimental intact mass of the precursor ion detailed in Table S4A (MS^1 level).

Regarding phenylalanine, the precursor ion at 166.0862 *m/z* was grouped with the AIF ion at 120.0809 *m/z* at the three CE voltages assayed and the scores were evaluated. The fragment ion that was obtained at CE 5 eV did not score above the cutoff threshold for PPC and scored in the upper limit for PPS, in contrast to CE 10 and 20 eV, which showed scores within the recommended values (Table 1). Moreover, the fragment ion 103.0543 *m/z* was also detected at CE 20 eV.

To illustrate the results that were achieved by the q-Orbitrap approach, glutathione found in cell sample was statistically evaluated by the *ScoresDIA.R* function after its annotation with the *AIF.R* function. As observed in Table S9, all of the product ions were detected and coeluted with the [M+H]$^+$ precursor ion 308.0903 *m/z*. In all cases, the PPC and PPS scores were within the cut-off thresholds (Table 2). Another scoring example was performed for methionine, which showed positive scoring except for the 133.0315 *m/z* fragment, which exhibited a PPS lower than 0.2 (Table 2). As previously commented, an insufficient number of scans across metabolite peaks can result in overestimated PPC scores, but also the opposite effect for PPS and, from this, the visualization of co-eluted precursor/fragments peaks is highly recommended. Extracted ion chromatograms (Figure S2) of the precursor (blue line) and the fragment 133.0315 *m/z* (red line) demonstrate co-elution and, thus, the low PPS scored is due to the low intensity of the fragment and number of scans per peak. Tyrosine is an example in which in all cases scores were within the recommended thresholds, indicating optimal parameters for the detection, fragmentation, and annotation of this metabolite (Table 2).

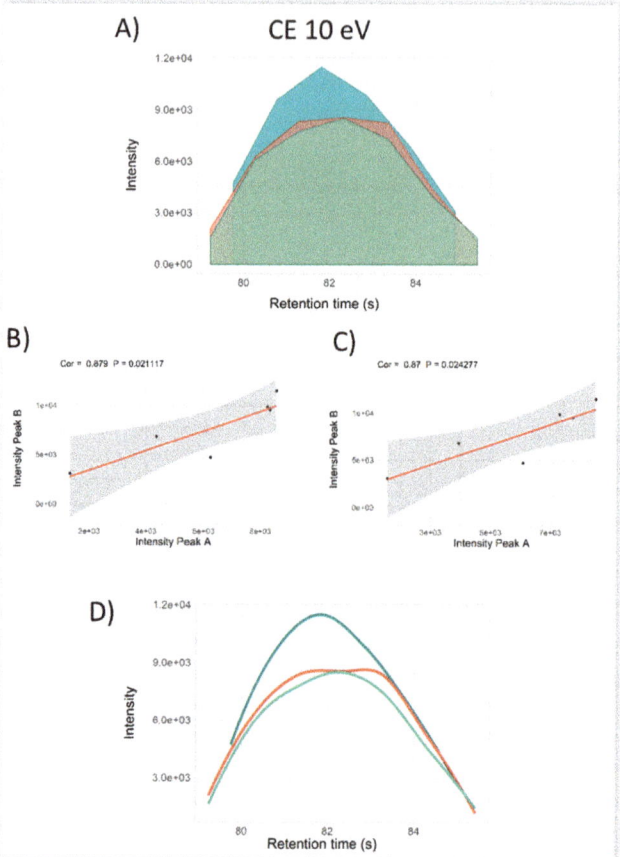

Figure 3. Peak visualization and statistical evaluation of glutamine characterized by LC-qTOF data independent acquisition (DIA)-MS/MS with the *ScoresDIA.R* function. Coelution profile for the EIC (extracted ion chromatogram) generated is plotted and followed by analysis of the peak-to-peak Pearson correlation (PPC) and peak-to-peak shape (PPS) ratio for the product/precursor ions. (**A**) Coelution profile for the precursor 147.0764 *m/z* and fragments 130.0499 *m/z* and 84.0444 *m/z* annotated as glutamine $[M+H]^+$ obtained at 10 eV. (**B**) Peak-to-peak Pearson correlation analysis for 84.0444 *m/z* fragment with precursor ion. (**C**) Peak-to-peak Pearson correlation analysis for 130.0499 *m/z* fragment with precursor ion. (**D**). Smoothed coelution plot for PPC and PPS analysis.

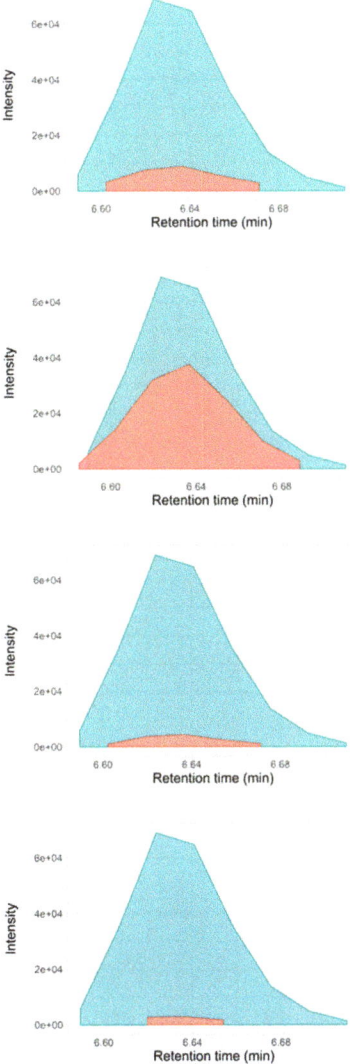

Figure 4. Extracted ion chromatograms (EIC) of phenylacetylglutamine precursor and fragment ions detected by LC-DIA-MS/MS at CE 20 eV generated with the *ScoresDIA.R* function. Figure shows coelution plots for each of the precursor-product pair ions from top to bottom: 84.0444 *m/z*, 130.0499 *m/z*, 136.0756 *m/z*, and 147.0763 *m/z*.

Table 2. Statistical evaluation of glutathione, methionine, and tyrosine peak groups performed by *ScoresDIA.R* function. Extracted from data acquired on an LC-Q-Exactive Hybrid Quadrupole-Orbitrap device. Recommended values for PPC are ≥ 0.7. Good chromatographic similarity is indicated by 0.3 ≥ PPS ≥ 3. Abbreviations used: CE, Collision Energy; PPC, peak-to-peak Pearson correlation; PPS, peak-to-peak shape ratio.

	Experimental Fragment [M+H]$^+$ (m/z)	CE (eV)	PPC	PPS	[a] Product/Precursor Ion Ratio
Glutathione					
	76.0214	30	0.99	0.79	0.44
	116.0163	30	0.99	0.30	0.08
	144.0112	30	0.99	0.35	0.08
	162.0217	30	0.99	0.40	0.17
	179.0482	30	0.99	0.25	0.04
	233.0585	30	0.99	0.20	0.02
	130.0497	30	0.99	0.60	0.08
	84.0443	30	0.99	0.60	0.15
Methionine					
	133.0315	30	0.98	0.17	0.02
	104.0526	30	0.96	0.49	0.03
	61.0107	30	0.99	1.25	0.30
	56.0497	30	0.99	0.49	0.22
Tyrosine					
	147.0438	30	0.99	0.50	0.015
	136.0754	30	0.99	0.49	0.16
	123.0439	30	0.99	0.99	0.40
	119.0490	30	0.99	1.25	0.22
	95.0490	30	0.99	0.99	0.19
	91.0541	30	0.99	0.99	0.40

[a] Experimental intact mass of the precursor ion detailed in Table S4A (MS^1 level).

3. Materials and Methods

3.1. Chemicals and Sample Preparation

LC-MS grade methanol (MeOH), formic acid (FA), and acetonitrile (ACN) were from Fisher Scientific (Pittsburgh, PA, USA). Water was of ultrapure grade (EMD Millipore Co., Billerica, MA, USA). Two different batches of deuterated internal standards were prepared to be spiked as internal standards (IS) in samples that were separately studied by the approaches considered. Stable isotope-labeled D5-glutamic acid and D5-phenylalanine constituted the q-TOF IS mix. The q-Orbitrap IS mix contained D2-Fumaric acid, D3-DL-Glutamic acid, D3-Malic acid, D4-Citric acid, D4-succinic acid, D2-Cysteine, D5-Glutamine, D3-Serine, D3-Aspartic acid, and D5-L-Tryptophan. Labelled standards were purchased from Cambridge Isotope (Cambridge Isotope Laboratories Inc., Tewksbury, MA, USA). Deuterated standards were in the 98–99% and 97–99% chemical and isotopologue purity ranges, respectively. Internal standards were dissolved in 0.2% FA, diluted to a final concentration of 2 ppm, and the aliquots were kept at −80 °C until analysis. Commercial negative/positive calibration and reference (lock masses) solutions specific for the q-TOF device were purchased from Agilent (Agilent Technologies, Santa Clara, CA, USA). Positive and negative calibration solutions for the q-Orbitrap detector were from Thermo Scientific (Thermo Sci., San Jose, CA, USA).

The underivatized 24-hour urine sample assayed was from a healthy human volunteer. It was centrifuged at 22,000 g at 4 °C for 15 min. An aliquot of the supernatant was diluted 1:1000 with ultrapure water, spiked with the q-TOF IS mix (final IS concentration in sample was 0.2 ppm), and filtered through a 0.2 µm nylon membrane. Aliquots of 150 µL were transferred to LC-MS vials and stored at −80 °C until analysis.

The cell and medium samples were prepared from acute myeloid leukemia cells (MOLM-13) cultured in RPMI-1640 medium supplemented with 10% characterized fetal bovine serum (FBS) and 2 mM L-glutamine (GE Healthcare Biosciences, Pittsburgh, PA, USA). Cells were incubated under standard conditions at 37 °C with 5% CO_2 and maintained at a concentration range of 200,000 to 2×10^6 cells/mL. Medium and cells were collected following a 24-hour incubation period. Suspension cells and medium were aspirated and centrifuged. Supernatant (conditioned medium) was snap frozen in liquid nitrogen. Prior to LC-MS analysis, medium was thawed, ultrafiltered (Nanosep centrifugal devices with Omega membrane, Pall Corporation, Port Washington, New York, USA), diluted 1:500 with ultrapure water, and then spiked with the q-Orbitrap IS mix (final IS concentration in sample was 0.2 ppm). Cells were washed twice with phosphate buffered solution (GE Healthcare Biosciences), harvested by centrifugation, and snap frozen in liquid nitrogen. Metabolite extraction was performed by modified Bligh-Dyer, as previously reported [10]. In brief, cell pellets were extracted with 1:1 water:methanol and equal parts chloroform. Following mixing and centrifugation, the polar fraction was transferred to Eppendorf tubes and then dried at 4 °C (Vacuum Concentrator, LabConco Corporation, Kansas City, MO, USA). Metabolites were resuspended in ultrapure water containing the q-Orbitrap IS mix (final IS concentration in sample was 0.2 ppm) and ultrafiltered before being transferred into LC-MS vials.

3.2. LC-MS/MS Analysis

Chromatographic separation of the underivatized urine sample was carried out on an Agilent 1290 Infinity II (Agilent Technologies, Santa Clara, CA, USA) HPLC system that was equipped with a quaternary pump, vacuum degasser, and an autosampler with a temperature controller coupled to an Agilent 6550 q-TOF mass analyzer equipped with an electrospray ionization (ESI) source with Jet Stream Technology. Metabolite separation was achieved on a 150 mm × 2.1 mm, 4 µm particle size Synergi-Hydro C18 column (Phenomenex Inc., Torrance, CA, USA) under the following separation conditions: solvent A, water/FA (99.8:0.2 v:v); solvent B, ACN; separation gradient, initially 1% B, held for 2 min., and then linear 1–80% B in 8 min, washing with 98% B for 2 min., and column equilibration with 1% B for 7 min.; total run time, 19 min.; flow rate, 0.25 mL/min; injection volume, 5 µL. Autosampler and column temperatures were set at 6 °C and 23 °C, respectively. Column flow was directed into the mass analyzer in the time range of 0.7–12 min., diverting the rest of the run time to waste. The samples were analyzed in positive ionization conditions operating in high-resolution full-scan MS mode with the settings: gas temperature, 130 °C; drying gas, 14 L/min.; nebulizer, 30 psig; sheath gas, 10 L/min.; isolation width, narrow (1.3 m/z); nozzle voltage, 500 V; fragmentor, 380 V; octapole 1 RF, 400V; capillary voltage, 3500 V; lock masses, 121.0509 m/z and 922.0098 m/z; data acquisition, centroid mode. Injections merged four full-MS analyses with CID collision energies of 0, 5, 10, and 20 eV with an acquisition rate of four spectra/s and 250 ms/spectrum as accumulation time. Polarity switching was not considered in this research because the mass deviations achieved by the MS device used were above 100 ppm regarding molecules at $m/z < 250$. Before analysis, the MS device was tuned and calibrated in the low mass range and high-resolution mode (4 GHz) to maximize the mass accuracy of detection (considered mass tolerance was 10 ppm at all times). Additionally, the peak area ratio of D5-glutamic/D5-phenylalanine in the sample analyzed were compared to that observed in an aqueous model solution of IS at 0.2 ppm to confirm the absence of significant matrix effects.

The analysis of cell and media extracts was performed on a Thermo Accela HPLC system equipped with a quaternary pump, vacuum degasser, and an open autosampler with a temperature controller (Thermo Scientific, San José, CA, USA). Chromatographic separation of metabolites was achieved by the same reverse phase column described above with the following separation conditions: solvent A, water/FA (99.8:0.2); solvent B, MeOH; separation gradient, initially 5% B, held for two minutes and then linear 30–80% B in eight minutes, washing with 98% B for 10 min and column equilibration with 5% B for 10 min; flow rate, 0.25 mL/min.; injection volume, 5 µL; total run time, 30 min.; autosampler and column temperatures were set at 6 °C and 22 °C, respectively. Column flow was directed into the mass analyzer in the time range of 1–15 min. and diverted to waste outside this period. Mass spectrometry analysis was carried out on a Thermo Q Exactive Hybrid Quadrupole-Orbitrap benchtop detector that was equipped with an electrospray (ESI) source simultaneously operating in fast positive/negative polarity switching mode (Thermo Scientific, Bremen, Germany). Multiplexed full-scan MS^1 (full-MS) and MS/MS (AIF) experiments had the following settings: microscans, 1; AGC target, 1e^6; maximum injection time, 100 ms; mass resolution, 35,000 FWHM at m/z 200 for full-MS analysis whereas AIF scan conditions were microscans, 1; AGC target, 3e^6; maximum injection time, 1000 ms; mass resolution, 70,000 FWHM at m/z 200; HCD energy, 30. In both cases, the instrument was set to spray voltage, 4.0 kV; capillary temperature, 300 °C; sheath gas, 55 (arbitrary units); auxiliary gas, 30 (arbitrary units); m/z range, 50–750; data acquisition, centroid mode. The accuracy of Orbitrap analysis was ensured by calibrating the detector while using the commercial calibration solutions that were provided by the manufacturer, followed by a customized adjustment for small molecular masses. Masses at m/z 87.00877 (Pyruvic acid); 117.01624 (D2-Fumaric acid); 149.06471 (D3-Glutamic acid); 265.14790 (Sodium dodecyl sulfate); and, 514.288441 (Sodium taurocholate) were used for the negative ionization mode, whereas masses at m/z 74.09643 (n-Butylamine), 138.06619 (Caffeine fragment), 195.08765 (Caffeine), and 524.26496 (Met-Arg-Phe-Ala tetrapeptide, MRFA) were used to adjust the mass accuracy of the positive ionization mode. Maximal mass tolerance was 5 ppm at all times. The LC-MS platform of analysis was controlled by a PC operating the Xcalibur v. 2.2 SP1.48 software package (Thermo Scientific, San Jose, CA, USA). Again, the ratios among spiked IS in samples and in an aqueous model solution at same concentration confirmed the absence of matrix effects.

3.3. Automated Data Processing by R-MetaboList 2

Agilent and Thermo experimental data files (extension .d and .raw, respectively) were converted into .mzXML files by the MSconvert option embedded in the freely available Proteowizard application (http://proteowizard.sourceforge.net/). Full-scan MS^1 and MS/MS data were separated according to CID (0, 5, 10, and 20 eV for q-TOF) and HCD (0 and 30% for q-Orbitrap), and simultaneously assayed while using the *CE.isolation.R* function included in R-MetaboList 2. Peak picking of MS^1 and MS/MS data was performed in the background by the enviPick algorithm embedded in the software in a stepped process [21] (Figure 1).

A preliminary full-MS (intact molecule) analysis of samples was carried out by R-MetaboList 2 loading an in-house neutral mass library (.csv format) of 320 underivatized metabolites (m/z < 650) commonly found in biological samples. The targeted peak picking extraction of MS^1 data was performed by the *FullMS.R* function using 5 ppm and 0.005 Da as mass tolerance and m/z interval window as constraints, respectively, for general peak grouping and library interrogation. Ion polarity (neutral/negative/positive) and retention time are optional constraints that can be selected by users according to the customized library employed. The output generates a results list that includes the type of isotope or adduct annotated and the score that is reached by the peak shape based on the asymmetry factor (f) defined, as follows:

$$f = (t_{Rf} - t_{Rmax})/(t_{Rmax} - t_{Ri}), \qquad (1)$$

where t_{Rmax} represents the retention time for the scan with the highest intensity at a given EIC and t_R, t_{Rf} represents the retention time for the final scan, and t_{Ri} represents the retention time for the initial scan that together define the limits of the EIC. Therefore, f values that are closer to 1 indicate better peak symmetry. Where calculation of such factor was not feasible for chromatographic peaks below three scans across peak, and/or maximum signal intensity appeared as first or last scan (zero value in Tables).

Matched peaks were smoothed (cubic or smoothing spline) and evaluated regarding to their isotope peak intensity ratio (IPIR), peak-to-peak Pearson correlation (PPC), and peak-to-peak shape (PPS) ratios. The IPIR score was calculated according to the rule indicating that, in the absence of S or Br in the molecular formula, the ratio between monoisotopic and/or next isotopologues considered must be greater than one. Thus, IPIR was calculated, as follows:

$$\text{IPIR} = \frac{I_k}{I_{k+1}} \qquad (2)$$

where I_k and I_{k+1} are the intensity of the monoisotopic peaks or the former and latter isotopologues.

The PPC score, based on Pearson correlation, was calculated with the following equation [22,23]:

$$\text{PPC} = \frac{\sum_{i=1}^{n}(I_{Pi} - \widetilde{I_P})(I_{Fi} - \widetilde{I_F})}{\sqrt{\sum_{i=1}^{n}(I_{Pi} - \widetilde{I_P})^2}\sqrt{\sum_{i=1}^{n}(I_{Fi} - \widetilde{I_F})^2}} \qquad (3)$$

where P and F are peaks "A" and "B", I_{Pi} and I_{Fi} represents the intensity of a particular scan from a smoothed peak, $\widetilde{I_P}$ and $\widetilde{I_F}$ refer to the intensity sum for all scans forming the peak. The recommended cut-off value is PPC ≥ 0.7.

Lastly, peak-to-peak shape (PPS) was defined as the ratio between the asymmetry factors from features within the same peak group (i.e. ions from the same metabolite), as follows [22,23]:

$$\text{PPS} = \frac{f_{k1}}{f_{k2}} \qquad (4)$$

where f_{k1} and f_{k2} are the asymmetry factors calculated with Equation (1) for a peak k1 and peak k2. Asymmetry factor ratios for features within the same peak group can be used as an indication of similarity due to the mandatory chromatographic elution behavior. Values of PPS below 0.3 and above 3 might reflect low similarity, in which case the metabolite with this considered precursor-product association should be discarded. IPIR, PPC, and PPS scores are implemented in the *ScoresMS1.R function* and graphical inspection of tentative assignments can be performed with the *plot_EIC.R* function.

Exploratory MS^1 analysis was refined by R-MetaboList 2 through full-scan MS/MS data processing loading an upgraded AIF library (.csv format) that was previously released to study melanoma tissue and leukemia cell extracts while using a q-Orbitrap device [10]. In our case, MS/MS information of some underivatized metabolites commonly found in human urinary samples not considered in the aforementioned original library were additionally included (Table S4A for positive and S4B for negative ionization modes, respectively) following similar guidelines previously stated [10]. From these new urinary metabolites, accurate masses from fragments above 20% of relative abundance in the 0 to 30 eV CID range that is detailed in the mzCloud database populated the updated library used. Moreover, metabolites largely found in urine, cell, and medium samples with AIF fragments below m/z < 50 (i.e. urea and lactic acid) or assignments supported by only one ubiquitous ion (i.e. fragment at m/z 72.0444 from alanine) were discarded. Protocols to elaborate high-quality mass spectral libraries are described in the literature and can be readily used as an input for the MetaboList software [24]. AIF data analysis used 5 ppm and 0.08 min. as m/z and retention time tolerances as the main constraints, respectively, for proper peak alignment of precursors and their respective MS/MS fragments listed in Table S4A,B. Targeted data extraction was performed with a precursor-fragment ion mass-to-mass matching and having at least one fragment or all fragment ion (N) included in the MS/MS library matched as a minimum co-elution requirement. From assignments, the aligned EICs from MS^1 and

MS/MS were grouped and subsequently evaluated by the *ScoresDIA.R* function while using PPC, PPS, and product/precursor ion intensity ratio, with the last being defined as:

$$F/PIon\ ratio = \frac{I_{max,F}}{I_{max,P}} \quad (5)$$

where $I_{max,F}$ and $I_{max,P}$ are the maximum EIC intensities corresponding to the fragment and precursor ion, respectively.

4. Conclusions

This study demonstrates the efficiency of R-MetaboList 2 for the simultaneous processing of multiplexed full-scan MS^1 and MS/MS data from small molecule analysis. The complete flexibility of the methodology proposed facilitates the clear visualization and exhaustive quality assessment of findings from LC-HRMS data that were acquired by both q-TOF and q-Orbitrap devices analyzing underivatized human urine and myeloid leukemia cell and medium samples, respectively. Continuous upgradability of this strategy by users allows for the adaptation of a previously released in-house full-scan MS/MS q-Orbitrap library for R-MetaboList 2 analysis of data from both instrumental approaches considered. The flexibility of this approach permits the improvement of functions that were implemented in the previous R-MetaboList version as well as the incorporation of the new functions outlined above. Thus, detailed and accurate metabolite (mostly with m/z <250) profiling of samples was achieved, despite the complexity of merged full-scan analyses evaluated. Moreover, R-MetaboList 2 can facilitate quantitative studies and the election of the optimal collision energy for specific MS/MS fragments through the concurrent analysis of multiple fragmentation experiments. The proposed methodology represents a customizable and complementary alternative to the existing approaches to the automated processing of untargeted/targeted data dependent/independent MS/MS analyses, thus promoting global metabolomic strategies that are supported by recursive retrospective interrogation of multiplexed DIA data.

Supplementary Materials: The following are available online at http://www.mdpi.com/2218-1989/9/9/187/s1, Figure S1. Output generated by the plot_EIC.R function for glutamine as detected by LC-qTOF. (A) Coelution profile for glutamine [M+H]+ and [M+NH4]+ adducts with a graphical abstract of the scores evaluated. Peak-to-peak Pearson correlation (PPC) was null whereas peak shape and mass accuracy acceptable for both peaks. (B) Extracted ion chromatogram (EIC) for the glutamine adducts found with dots indicating the scans forming the EIC and blue line the peak smoothed. (C) Quality control (QC) for the mass accuracy for each scan forming the EIC. Figure S2. Co-elution for extracted ion chromatograms for methionine precursor (blue line) and fragment at 133.0315 m/z (red line). The EICs show that these ions co-elute, indicating a low PPS (peak-to-peak shape ratio) due to the low intensity of the fragment ion and number of scans per peak. Table S1. Tentative assignments based on full-MS analysis in urine sample by LC-qTOF approach. Rt, retention time. Table S2. Tentative assignments based on full-MS analysis in cell sample by LC-Q-Exactive approach. Table S3. Tentative assignments based on full-MS analysis in medium sample by LC-Q-Exactive approach. Rt, retention time. Table S4. (A) In-house MS/MS library in positive ionization mode. (B) In-house MS/MS library in negative ionization mode. Table S5. Metabolites annotated by full-scan MS/MS of the urinary sample assayed with LC-qTOF device at CIDs of 5 eV. Rt, retention time. Table S6. Metabolites annotated by full-scan MS/MS of the urinary sample assayed with LC-qTOF device at CIDs of 10 eV. Rt, retention time. Table S7. Metabolites annotated by full-scan MS/MS of the urinary sample assayed with LC-qTOF device at CIDs of 20 eV. Rt, retention time. Table S8. Peak grouping for glutamine, phenylacetylglutamine and phenylalanine analyzed in urine by LC-qTOF at the three CE assayed. Rt, retention time; CE, collision energy. Table S9. Metabolites annotated by full-scan MS/MS analysis of the leukemia cell extract analyzed by q-Orbitrap. Rt, retention time. Table S10. Metabolites annotated by full-scan MS/MS analysis of the leukemia cell medium extract analyzed by q-Orbitrap. Three data sets converted to mzXML format for LC-qTOF and q-Exactive analysis of human urinary, leukemia cell and cell medium samples. Two R-scripts to reproduce results obtained in this research (AIF_Batch.R; Script_MetabolitesJournal.R).

Author Contributions: Conceptualization: M.D.P.-D., E.S. and S.T.; Methodology: M.D.P.-D., S.R.S, E.S. and S.T.; Software: M.D.P.-D.; Validation: M.D.P.-D., S.R.S, O.R. and E.S.; Formal Analysis: M.D.P.-D., S.R.S, O.R. and E.S.; Investigation: M.D.P.-D. and E.S.; Data Curation: M.D.P.-D., S.R.S, O.R. and E.S.; Writing (original draft): M.D.P.-D. and E.S.; Writing (review and editing): M.D.P.-D., S.R.S, E.S. and S.T. Supervision: E.S. and S.T.

Funding: This research was partially supported by R01 CA206210-R01 CA189623 (National Institutes of Health, NIH) and CPRIT RP180309 (Cancer Prevention & Research Institute of Texas). Research supported in part by National Science Center of Poland (NCN) for financial support of M.D.P.D. (Preludium Grant no. 2018/31/N/ST4/01909).

Acknowledgments: Enrique Sentandreu thanks support from his current host group at IATA-CSIC to complete this research.

Conflicts of Interest: Authors declare no conflict of interest.

Financial Disclosure Statement: No financial disclosures were reported the authors.

References

1. Rochat, B. Quantitative and Qualitative LC-High-Resolution MS: The Technological and Biological Reasons for a Shift of Paradigm. In *Recent Advances in Analytical Chemistry*; IntechOpen: London, UK, 2018.
2. Bouatra, S.; Aziat, F.; Mandal, R.; Guo, A.C.; Wilson, M.R.; Knox, C.; Bjorndahl, T.C.; Krishnamurthy, R.; Saleem, F.; Liu, P.; et al. The Human Urine Metabolome. *PLoS ONE* **2013**, *8*, e73076. [CrossRef] [PubMed]
3. Psychogios, N.; Hau, D.D.; Peng, J.; Guo, A.C.; Mandal, R.; Bouatra, S.; Sinelnikov, I.; Krishnamurthy, R.; Eisner, R.; Gautam, B.; et al. The Human Serum Metabolome. *PLoS ONE* **2011**, *6*, e16957. [CrossRef] [PubMed]
4. Wishart, D.S.; Jewison, T.; Guo, A.C.; Wilson, M.; Knox, C.; Liu, Y.F.; Djoumbou, Y.; Mandal, R.; Aziat, F.; Dong, E.; et al. HMDB 3.0-The Human Metabolome Database in 2013. *Nucleic Acids Res.* **2013**, *41*, D801–D807. [CrossRef] [PubMed]
5. Fiehn, O. Metabolomics—The link between genotypes and phenotypes. *Plant Mol. Boil.* **2002**, *48*, 155–171. [CrossRef]
6. Patti, G.J.; Yanes, O.; Siuzdak, G. Metabolomics: The apogee of the omic triology. *Nat. Rev. Mol. Cell Boil.* **2012**, *13*, 263–269. [CrossRef]
7. Forcisi, S.; Moritz, F.; Kanawati, B.; Tziotis, D.; Lehmann, R.; Schmitt-Kopplin, P. Liquid chromatography–mass spectrometry in metabolomics research: Mass analyzers in ultra high pressure liquid chromatography coupling. *J. Chromatogr. A* **2013**, *1292*, 51–65. [CrossRef] [PubMed]
8. Eliuk, S.; Makarov, A. Evolution of Orbitrap Mass Spectrometry Instrumentation. In *Annual Review of Analytical Chemistry*; Cooks, R.G., Pemberton, J.E., Eds.; Annual Reviews: Palo Alto, CA, USA, 2015; Volume 8, pp. 61–80.
9. Bateman, K.P.; Kellmann, M.; Muenster, H.; Papp, R.; Taylor, L. Quantitative-qualitative data acquisition using a benchtop orbitrap mass spectrometer. *J. Am. Soc. Mass Spectrom.* **2009**, *20*, 1441–1450. [CrossRef]
10. Sentandreu, E.; Peris-Díaz, M.D.; Sweeney, S.R.; Chiou, J.; Muñoz, N.; Tiziani, S. A Survey of Orbitrap All Ion Fragmentation Analysis Assessed by an R-MetaboList Package to Study Small-Molecule Metabolites. *Chromatographia* **2018**. [CrossRef]
11. Gillet, L.C.; Navarro, P.; Tate, S.; Röst, H.; Selevsek, N.; Reiter, L.; Bonner, R.; Aebersold, R. Targeted Data Extraction of the MS/MS Spectra Generated by Data-independent Acquisition: A New Concept for Consistent and Accurate Proteome Analysis. *Mol. Cell. Proteom.* **2012**, *11*. [CrossRef]
12. Pluskal, T.; Castillo, S.; Villar-Briones, A.; Orešič, M. MZmine 2: Modular framework for processing, visualizing, and analyzing mass spectrometry-based molecular profile data. *BMC Bioinform.* **2010**, *11*, 395. [CrossRef]
13. Shulaev, V. Metabolomics technology and bioinformatics. *Briefings Bioinform.* **2006**, *7*, 128–139. [CrossRef] [PubMed]
14. Smith, C.A.; Want, E.J.; O'Maille, G.; Abagyan, R.; Siuzdak, G. XCMS: Processing Mass Spectrometry Data for Metabolite Profiling Using Nonlinear Peak Alignment, Matching, and Identification. *Anal. Chem.* **2006**, *78*, 779–787. [CrossRef] [PubMed]
15. Tsugawa, H.; Cajka, T.; Kind, T.; Ma, Y.; Higgins, B.; Ikeda, K.; Kanazawa, M.; VanderGheynst, J.; Fiehn, O.; Arita, M. MS-DIAL: Data Independent MS/MS Deconvolution for Comprehensive Metabolome Analysis. *Nat. Methods* **2015**, *12*, 523–526. [CrossRef] [PubMed]
16. Cai, Y.; Zhu, Z.-J.; Li, H.; Guo, Y.; Chen, F. MetDIA: Targeted Metabolite Extraction of Multiplexed MS/MS Spectra Generated by Data-Independent Acquisition. *Anal. Chem.* **2016**, *88*, 8757–8764.
17. Zhou, J.; Li, Y.; Chen, X.; Zhong, L.; Yin, Y. Development of data-independent acquisition workflows for metabolomic analysis on a quadrupole-orbitrap platform. *Talanta* **2017**, *164*, 128–136. [CrossRef]

18. Peris-Díaz, M.D.; Rodak, O.; Sweeney, S.R.; Krężel, A.; Sentandreu, E. Chemometrics-assisted optimization of liquid chromatography-quadrupole-time-of-flight mass spectrometry analysis for targeted metabolomics. *Talanta* **2019**, *199*, 380–387. [CrossRef] [PubMed]
19. Naz, S.; Gallart-Ayala, H.; Reinke, S.N.; Mathon, C.; Blankley, R.; Chaleckis, R.; Wheelock, C.E. Development of a Liquid Chromatography–High Resolution Mass Spectrometry Metabolomics Method with High Specificity for Metabolite Identification Using All Ion Fragmentation Acquisition. *Anal. Chem.* **2017**, *89*, 7933–7942. [CrossRef]
20. Ipsen, A.; Want, E.J.; Lindon, J.C.; Ebbels, T.M.D. A Statistically Rigorous Test for the Identification of Parent–Fragment Pairs in LC-MS Datasets. *Anal. Chem.* **2010**, *82*, 1766–1778. [CrossRef]
21. Loos, M.; Singer, H. Nontargeted homologue series extraction from hyphenated high resolution mass spectrometry data. *J. Cheminformatics* **2017**, *9*, 12. [CrossRef]
22. Senan, O.; Aguilar-Mogas, A.; Navarro, M.; Capellades, J.; Noon, L.; Burks, D.; Yanes, O.; Guimerà, R.; Sales-Pardo, M. CliqueMS: A computational tool for annotating in-source metabolite ions from LC-MS untargeted metabolomics data based on a coelution similarity network. *Bioinformatics* **2019**. [CrossRef]
23. Kuhl, C.; Tautenhahn, R.; Böttcher, C.; Larson, T.R.; Neumann, S. CAMERA: An integrated strategy for compound spectra extraction and annotation of liquid chromatography/mass spectrometry data sets. *Anal. Chem.* **2012**, *84*, 283–289. [CrossRef] [PubMed]
24. Bruderer, T.; Varesio, E.; Hidasi, A.O.; Duchoslav, E.; Burton, L.; Bonner, R.; Hopfgartner, G. Metabolomic spectral libraries for data-independent SWATH liquid chromatography mass spectrometry acquisition. *Anal. Bioanal. Chem.* **2018**, *410*, 1873–1884. [CrossRef] [PubMed]

© 2019 by the authors. Licensee MDPI, Basel, Switzerland. This article is an open access article distributed under the terms and conditions of the Creative Commons Attribution (CC BY) license (http://creativecommons.org/licenses/by/4.0/).

 *metabolites*

Article

MolNetEnhancer: Enhanced Molecular Networks by Integrating Metabolome Mining and Annotation Tools

Madeleine Ernst [1,2,*], Kyo Bin Kang [1,3], Andrés Mauricio Caraballo-Rodríguez [1], Louis-Felix Nothias [1], Joe Wandy [4], Christopher Chen [1], Mingxun Wang [1], Simon Rogers [5], Marnix H. Medema [6], Pieter C. Dorrestein [1,7,8] and Justin J.J. van der Hooft [1,6,*]

1. Collaborative Mass Spectrometry Innovation Center, Skaggs School of Pharmacy and Pharmaceutical Sciences, University of California San Diego, La Jolla, CA 92093, USA
2. Department of Congenital Disorders, Center for Newborn Screening, Statens Serum Institut, 2300 Copenhagen, Denmark
3. Research Institute of Pharmaceutical Sciences, College of Pharmacy, Sookmyung Women's University, Seoul 04310, Korea
4. Glasgow Polyomics, University of Glasgow, Glasgow G12 8QQ, UK
5. School of Computing Science, University of Glasgow, Glasgow G12 8QQ, UK
6. Bioinformatics Group, Department of Plant Sciences, Wageningen University, 6708 PB Wageningen, The Netherlands
7. Department of Pediatrics, University of California San Diego, La Jolla, CA 92093, USA
8. Center for Microbiome Innovation, University of California San Diego, La Jolla, CA 92093, USA
* Correspondence: maet@ssi.dk (M.E.); justin.vanderhooft@wur.nl (J.J.J.v.d.H.)

Received: 29 May 2019; Accepted: 11 July 2019; Published: 16 July 2019

Abstract: Metabolomics has started to embrace computational approaches for chemical interpretation of large data sets. Yet, metabolite annotation remains a key challenge. Recently, molecular networking and MS2LDA emerged as molecular mining tools that find molecular families and substructures in mass spectrometry fragmentation data. Moreover, in silico annotation tools obtain and rank candidate molecules for fragmentation spectra. Ideally, all structural information obtained and inferred from these computational tools could be combined to increase the resulting chemical insight one can obtain from a data set. However, integration is currently hampered as each tool has its own output format and efficient matching of data across these tools is lacking. Here, we introduce MolNetEnhancer, a workflow that combines the outputs from molecular networking, MS2LDA, in silico annotation tools (such as Network Annotation Propagation or DEREPLICATOR), and the automated chemical classification through ClassyFire to provide a more comprehensive chemical overview of metabolomics data whilst at the same time illuminating structural details for each fragmentation spectrum. We present examples from four plant and bacterial case studies and show how MolNetEnhancer enables the chemical annotation, visualization, and discovery of the subtle substructural diversity within molecular families. We conclude that MolNetEnhancer is a useful tool that greatly assists the metabolomics researcher in deciphering the metabolome through combination of multiple independent in silico pipelines.

Keywords: chemical classification; in silico workflows; metabolite annotation; metabolite identification; metabolome mining; molecular families; networking; substructures

1. Introduction

Metabolomics has matured into a research field generating increasing amounts of metabolome profiles of complex metabolite mixtures aiming to provide biochemical insights. Mass spectrometry has become the workhorse of metabolomics and typical untargeted experiments currently result in qualitative and semiquantitative information on several thousands of molecular ions across tens to hundreds of samples. Technical advances in the last decade have allowed researchers to fragment increasing amounts of mass peaks that result in mass fragmentation spectra (MS/MS or MS2). Metabolite annotation and identification tools have benefited from these advances as now more MS2 spectra per sample can be queried in reference libraries in order to find candidate structures or submitted to in silico tools that propose a putative structure [1–9].

Despite these tremendous advances, a key challenge remaining for metabolomics researchers is to biochemically interpret large-scale untargeted metabolomics studies due to the complexity of the metabolomes represented by mass fragmentation spectra to which actual chemical structures need to be assigned, and for which reference spectra are not available. In biological samples, many metabolites share molecular substructures and form structurally related molecular families (MFs) of various chemical classes, which has inspired metabolome mining tools exploiting these biochemical relationships. Based on the assumption that structurally similar molecules (analogs) generate similar mass spectrometry fragmentation spectra, one can group analogs by comparing their fragmentation spectra resulting in the construction of molecular families. To do this on a larger scale, computational tools have been developed such as molecular networking (MN) [7]. However, to actually annotate structural information additional sources are usually needed such as library matches, candidate structures from libraries or chemical class annotations.

Indeed, since the molecular networking approach was proposed in 2012 [10], numerous complementary metabolome mining workflows as well as annotation and classification tools have been introduced including SIRIUS [3], CSI:FingerID [4], MetFusion [11], MetFamily [12], and many others of which some also use molecular networks as basis [1,2,7,8,13–24] and their combined use for natural product discovery was very recently reviewed [25]. Where tandem mass spectral molecular networking efficiently can group molecular features in molecular families [10], MS2LDA can discover substructures, not only based on common fragment peaks but also common neutral losses, which can aid in further annotation of subfamilies and shared modifications [14]. These metabolome mining tools typically take MS/MS spectra as input, such as the open formats Mascott Generic Format (MGF), the mzML, or mzXML format, and generate tables where a fragmented mass feature is linked to other fragmented mass features or substructure patterns. Reference fragmentation spectra in public repositories are still very few. Thus, on average only 2–5% percent of MS2 spectra acquired in a typical LC–MS/MS experiment can be matched to known molecules [26]. Complementary to library matching, in silico tools such as Network Annotation Propagation (NAP) [8], DEREPLICATOR [1], VarQuest [2], or SIRIUS+CSI:FingerID [4] predict fragmentation spectra in silico from known structures and allow for effective searching in chemical databases for candidate structures. These metabolome annotation tools also take MS/MS spectra as input and typically use precursor masses to find candidate structures in compound databases followed by a ranking of those structures based on the similarity of the predicted and experimental MS/MS data. The output is typically a table with candidate structures found for each mass feature and associated score. These tools typically differ in the compound databases they use to query for candidate structures, or the processing of mass spectrometry data. For example, SIRIUS+CSI:FingerID first builds annotated fragmentation trees before searching molecular structures in large compound databases. DEREPLICATOR and VarQuest are annotation tools that match structures from a large database of Peptidic Natural Products to MS/MS spectra, whereby DEREPLICATOR looks for exact matches and VarQuest also allows for one modified amino acid. It is important to realize that each tool has its own set of parameters that will affect the number of annotated features.

The outputted structural information for each mass feature can be mapped on a molecular network, for example, to show for which mass features library matches or in silico predicted structural matches are available. The recently introduced Network Annotation Propagation (NAP) also exploits the network topology to rerank candidate structure lists based on neighboring matches within molecular families [8]. Furthermore, when using multiple annotation tools, the structural information they provide may support each other increasing confidence in the annotation.

To assess whether molecular families are of particular interest for your research question, knowing their chemical class may provide sufficient information. The recently proposed ClassyFire tool [16] takes molecular descriptors as SMILES or InchiKeys as input and outputs hierarchical chemical ontology terms. Thus, the candidate structures outputted for each mass feature by the metabolome annotation tools mentioned above can now be automatically chemically classified. When that is done at larger scale for an entire molecular family, one can combine those chemical class terms and assess whether particular terms are enriched.

Taken together, all these recent developments enable the discovery of relations between millions of spectra and the listing of candidate structures from various spectral libraries or alternatively from compound libraries using in silico approaches.

Whilst each of those tools produce useful structural information, their combined application has been hampered by the use of different file formats, platforms, and the challenge to match molecular features across the outputs of these tools. We postulate that whilst each tool provides complementary insights, their combined use allows an increased level of biochemical interpretation, i.e., the sum becomes greater than the individual parts. Furthermore, it would be practically advantageous to combine all these results in one place. We have previously described the integration of Mass2Motifs and chemical classifications with molecular networks to assess the chemical diversity within a subset of species of the plant genus *Euphorbia* [27] and the plant family Rhamnaceae [28]. However, in those studies, integration was achieved using custom in-house scripts in R, hampering adoption by the community. Moreover, the results of the peptide annotation tools DEREPLICATOR and VarQuest were not included in those custom scripts.

Here, we introduce MolNetEnhancer a software package available in Python and R that unites the output of many of the above-mentioned metabolome mining and annotation tools (GNPS molecular networking, MS2LDA substructure discovery, and in silico annotation tools) independent of what dataset it processes, thus making the algorithm accessible in an easy-to-use format to the community (Figure 1). MolNetEnhancer discovers molecular families (MFs), subfamilies, and subtle structural differences between family members. The workflow enhances the currently available molecular networking methods based on either MS-Cluster [29] (classical) or MZmine2 [30] (also called "feature-based molecular networking") and results in annotated molecular networks that can be explored in Cytoscape [31]. We applied MolNetEnhancer to publicly available mass spectrometry fragmentation data ranging from marine-sediment and nematode-related bacteria, to *Euphorbia* and Rhamnaceae plants. Illustrated by four case studies, we demonstrate how our integrative workflow discovers dozens of MFs in large-scale metabolomics studies of these plant and bacterial extracts. Moreover, discovered MFs can be divided into subfamilies using the mapped MS2LDA results. Structural annotation of Mass2Motifs is facilitated by having chemical and structural annotations at hand, for example by recognizing substructures in peptidic molecules. We conclude that our workflow provides chemical refinement of metabolomics results beyond spectral matches through large-scale MF and substructure discovery and annotation by integrating outputs of various tools in one place allowing for enhanced visualization. This also guides the metabolomics researcher in prioritizing MFs to explore and in structurally annotating molecules.

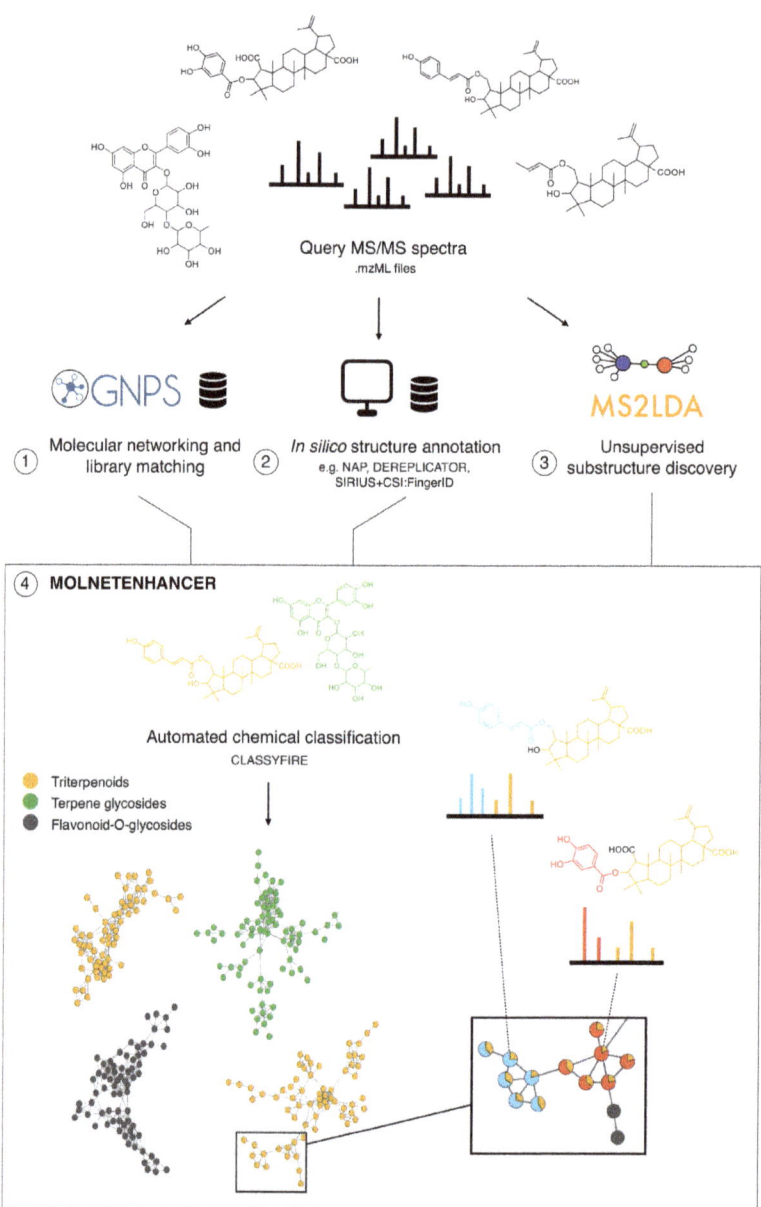

Figure 1. Schematic overview of the MolNetEnhancer workflow. Starting with mass spectrometry data in the mzML format obtained from complex metabolic mixtures the user creates (**1**) mass spectral molecular networks in GNPS, (**2**) performs in silico structure annotation (e.g., through NAP, DEREPLICATOR or SIRIUS+CSI:FingerID), and (**3**) performs unsupervised substructure discovery through MS2LDA. Steps 1–3 are performed prior to the MolNetEnhancer workflow within the respective platforms. MolNetEnhancer is then used in (**4**) to map information layers obtained from all three platforms independently on top of each other resulting in network-wide chemical class information and more detailed substructure information within molecular families (as exemplified for the organic acid conjugates in the enlarged part of the triterpenoid molecular family on the right).

2. Materials and Methods

MolNetEnhancer is a software package available in Python and R that unites the output of several metabolome mining and annotation tools, including mass spectral molecular networking through GNPS, unsupervised substructure discovery through MS2LDA and in silico structure annotation, for example through NAP, DEREPLICATOR, or SIRIUS+CSI:FingerID (Figure 1). Before using the MolNetEnhancer workflow, the user will run each metabolome mining tool separately:

1. Perform mass spectral molecular networking analysis through the Global Natural Products Social Molecular Networking platform (https://gnps.ucsd.edu).
2. Perform in silico chemical structural annotation using for example Network Annotation Propagation (NAP) and DEREPLICATOR through the GNPS platform. Alternatively, other in silico tools for putative chemical structural annotation (e.g., SIRIUS+CSI:FingerID) [3,4] can also be used.
3. Perform unsupervised substructure discovery using MS2LDA (http://ms2lda.org).

For documentation of steps 1–3 the user is referred to the original publications and guidelines for each tool [1,2,7,8,14]. Section 8 contains links to tutorials of the analysis tools used in this study. Functions implemented in the MolNetEnhancer workflow can then be used to combine the outputs created in step 1–3 such that

a   Substructure information retrieved through MS2LDA is integrated with mass spectral molecular networks.
b   Most abundant chemical classes per molecular family are retrieved based on GNPS structural library hits and in silico chemical structural annotation and integrated within the mass spectral molecular networks.

MolNetEnhancer is freely available on GitHub at https://github.com/madeleineernst/pyMolNetEnhancer and https://github.com/madeleineernst/RMolNetEnhancer. Interactive Jupyter example notebooks and a step by step tutorial guide the user to build enhanced mass spectral molecular networks, which are outputted in the graphml format for visualization in Cytoscape.

Currently, two distinct methods from raw data to MNs exist. One method takes all MS2 spectra found in the input files and uses MS-Cluster to prepare a set of representative "consensus" MS2 spectra for molecular networking, and the other method uses MZmine2 for data preprocessing, which performs molecular feature detection at the MS1 level and associates each MS1 feature with its respective MS2 spectra to send off to GNPS Molecular Networking. The here proposed MolNetEnhancer workflow can enrich both these molecular networking methods with Mass2Motif presence and chemical class annotations.

Substructural information retrieved through MS2LDA is integrated in two ways within the mass spectral molecular networks. Shared substructures or motifs between two molecular features are visualized as multiple edges connecting the nodes. Furthermore, motifs found within a molecular feature can be visualized as pie charts, where the relative abundance of each motif represents the overlap score, a score measuring how much of the motif is present in the spectrum [32]. Furthermore, for each molecular family, the x most shared motifs are shown, where x is defined by the user. An example of such a molecular family with motifs mapped is shown in Figure 6 in the results section.

To retrieve the most abundant chemical classes per molecular family, all chemical structures obtained through GNPS library matching, and in silico chemical structural annotation are submitted to automated chemical classification and taxonomy structure using ClassyFire [16]. This retrieves chemical classes for each of the putative structures submitted organized in five hierarchical levels of a chemical taxonomy (kingdom, superclass, class, subclass, and direct parent). For each level of the chemical ontology, a score is calculated, which represents the most abundant chemical class found for the structural matches within the molecular family. It is important to note that a high score does not represent a higher confidence in the true identity of the chemical structures found within the molecular family, but indicates more consistency as more structural matches obtained for this molecular family fall within the same chemical class. Figure 2 exemplifies how the score is calculated. Given a molecular family consisting of six molecular features (nodes), the percentage of nodes classified as cinnamaldehydes, coumarins and derivatives, flavonoids and macrolactames at the chemical class level respectively is calculated. Each molecular feature can have multiple structural matches with multiple (e.g., node 2) or identical (e.g., node 3) chemical classes. A majority of the structural matches obtained in the network shown in Figure 2 were classified as flavonoids (2.25 out of six nodes), thus the molecular family is classified as flavonoids with a chemical classification score at the class level of 0.375 (2.25/6). For single nodes (molecular features which show no spectral similarity with any other molecular features found in the dataset) the chemical classes are retrieved analogously, however, it should be noted that single nodes often result in a very high score, as only one structural match is retrieved, corresponding to a score of 1 (1 node out of 1).

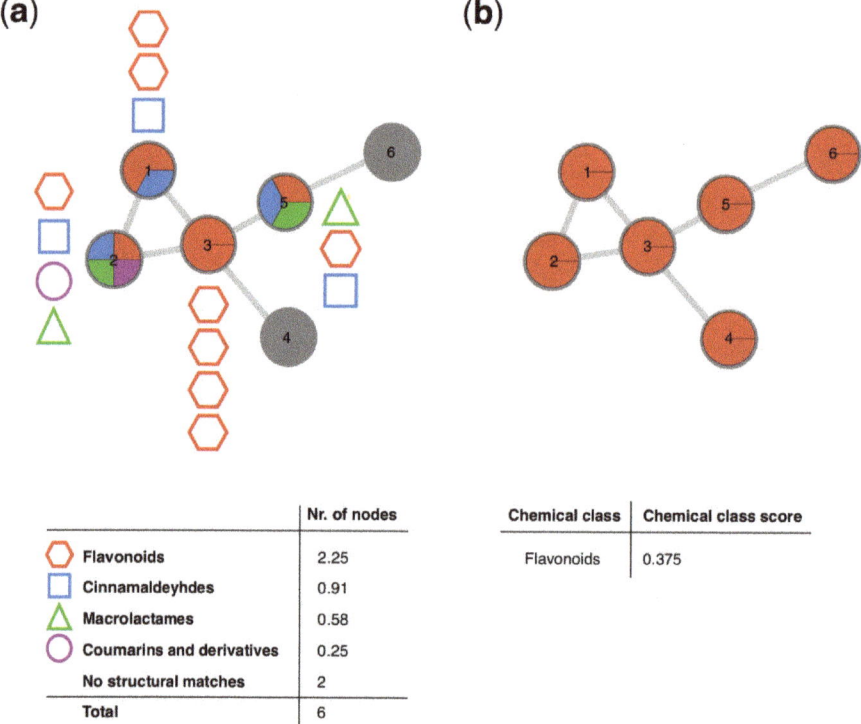

Figure 2. Schematic overview of how the chemical classification score is calculated and visualized within a molecular family. (a) Schematic overview of hypothetical structural annotations within a molecular family consisting of 6 nodes. Out of the 6 nodes, chemical structural information could be retrieved for 4, where each node can consist of structural annotations to multiple different (e.g., node 2) or identical (e.g., node 3) chemical classes. The total number of nodes per chemical class retrieved is calculated and the most abundant chemical class is assigned to the molecular family, resulting in (b). Schematic overview of the molecular family shown in (a), classified as 'flavonoids' at the chemical class level by MolNetEnhancer, with a score of 0.375, translating to the majority of the putative structural annotations within this molecular family (2.25) belong to the flavonoid structural class.

3. Results

3.1. MolNetEnhancer Workflow

MolNetEnhancer requires inputs from independent metabolome mining tools including mass spectral molecular networking through GNPS, unsupervised substructure discovery through MS2LDA and in silico structure annotation, for example through NAP, DEREPLICATOR or SIRIUS+CSI:FingerID (Figure 1). Provided with these inputs, MolNetEnhancer consists of two independent steps. During the first step, molecular substructures detectable by co-occurring fragment ions or neutral losses, so called Mass2Motifs, are mapped onto a Molecular Network. Each node in the network represents a molecular feature, whereas Mass2Motifs represent substructural features. Most fragmented mass peaks (precursor ions) represent molecular ions, although fragmented mass peaks may also represent adducts of one and the same molecule, in source fragments or doubly-charged peaks [33]. For simplicity, we will refer to any fragmented mass peak as molecular feature throughout the manuscript. Mass2Motifs contained within each molecular feature can be visualized as pie charts on the nodes. Alternatively, Mass2Motifs shared across multiple molecular features can be visualized as multiple lines (edges) connecting the nodes. In a second step, most abundant chemical classes per molecular family based on candidate structures from in silico annotation tools as well as GNPS library matches can be mapped through chemical classification using ClassyFire [16]. A chemical classification score is calculated representing what percentage of nodes within a molecular family are attributed to a given chemical class (see Section 2 and Figure 2 therein). In Sections 3.2–3.5 we show how MolNetEnhancer can accelerate and enrich chemical information retrieval in 4 case studies, comprising two plant and two bacterial publicly accessible datasets. The MolNetEnhancer workflow results in one graphml network file that contains all the structural information obtained from the individual tools. Such a file can be easily imported into network visualization tools such as Cytoscape [31], an environment where additional metadata on the molecular features can be added. In addition, all structural information is also available as tab delimited text files.

3.2. Case Study 1: Annotation of Euphorbia Specialized Metabolites Using MolNetEnhancer

With more than 2000 species worldwide, the plant genus *Euphorbia* is among the most species-rich and diverse flowering plants on earth [34,35]. Besides exhibiting an extreme diversity in its growth forms and habitat types, the genus has also attracted interest within natural products drug discovery [36,37]. *Euphorbia* species are chemically highly diverse, particularly within macro- and polycyclic diterpenoids, biosynthetically derived from a head-to-tail cyclization of the tetraprenyl pyrophosphate precursor, which have been found to exhibit a range of biological activities with pharmaceutical interest, such as antitumor, antimicrobial or immunomodulatory activity [36]. Ingenol mebutate for example, a diterpenoid originally isolated from *Euphorbia peplus* L. is marketed for the topical treatment of actinic keratosis, a precancerous skin condition [38], however production through plant extraction or chemical synthesis is inefficient and expensive [39,40].

A key interest is therefore to find species within the genus producing higher quantities of ingenol mebutate or other close diterpenoid analogs exhibiting biological activities with pharmaceutical interest. We have previously assessed chemical diversity within a representative subset of species of the plant genus *Euphorbia* [27]. A major challenge is the rapid identification of known and unknown *Euphorbia* diterpenoid structures. Using MolNetEnhancer, we were able to significantly accelerate manual annotation of diterpenoids and retrieve chemical structural information, even for molecular families with no structural matches in the GNPS spectral libraries.

An example of how MolNetEnhancer increases chemical structural information throughout two molecular families is highlighted in Figure 3. Using GNPS spectral library matching, chemical structural information for only one molecular feature was obtained, and manual propagation of the annotation throughout molecular family (i) was limited given that the annotated ion exhibited one neighbor only.

No structural information could be retrieved for family (ii), where no chemical structural information was retrieved through GNPS library matching (Figure 3a).

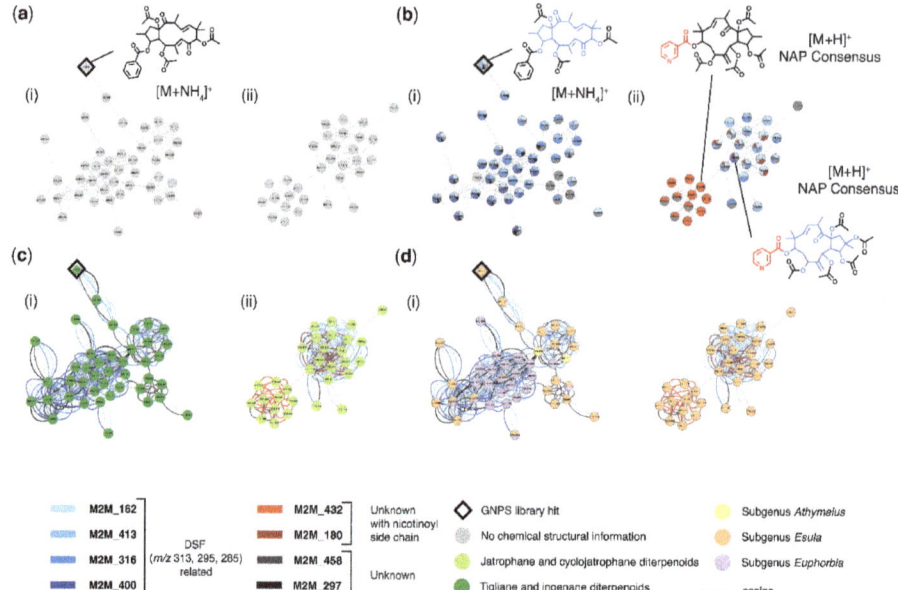

Figure 3. MolNetEnhancer increases chemical structural information obtained for *Euphorbia* specialized metabolites. (**a**) Mass spectral molecular network showing two molecular families of *Euphorbia* specialized metabolites. Using GNPS library matching only one molecular feature could be putatively annotated. Manual annotation propagation is limited for family (i) and impossible for family (ii). (**b**) Using MolNetEnhancer, substructural Mass2Motifs can be visualized within the network; both molecular family (i) and (ii) contain Mass2Motifs related to a *Euphorbia* diterpene spectral fingerprint (DSF) and molecular family (ii) contains Mass2Motifs related to a nicotinoyl side chain. Mass2Motifs are mapped on the nodes as pie charts with an area proportional to their overlap score, a score measuring how much of the Mass2Motif is present in the spectrum, whereas dotted lines connecting the nodes represent features with a MS2 spectral similarity of a cosine score over 0.6 (**c**) Most chemical structures retrieved for molecular family (i) and (ii) are diterpenoids of the jatrophane, tigliane or ingenane type, which both can result in a DSF with m/z 313, 295, or 285. Substructures with mass fragments characteristic of these *Euphorbia* DSFs were also found within the Mass2Motifs. Node colors represent most abundant chemical classes, colored lines connecting the nodes represent shared Mass2Motifs, and dotted lines connecting the nodes represent features with a MS2 spectral similarity of a cosine score over 0.6 (**d**) *Euphorbia* diterpenoid skeletons of the jatrophane, deoxy tigliane, or ingenane ester type are found within all *Euphorbia* subgeneric clades, whereas nicotinoyl sidechain modifications are unique to subgenus *Esula*. Node colors represent summed peak area per *Euphorbia* subgeneric clade, colored lines connecting the nodes represent shared Mass2Motifs, and dotted lines connecting the nodes represent features with a MS2 spectral similarity of a cosine score over 0.6.

Using MolNetEnhancer however, we were able to highlight substructural Mass2Motifs within both molecular families (Figure 3b). Substructural Mass2Motifs, putatively annotated as a *Euphorbia* diterpenoid backbone skeleton with mass peaks at m/z 313, 295, and 285 were found both in molecular families (i) and (ii) (Figure 3b). Manual annotation of these Mass2Motifs was possible by comparing mass fragments of the library spectrum to mass fragments contained in the Mass2Motifs. A mirror plot comparing the GNPS reference spectrum to the unknown spectrum found in our samples is shown in Supplementary Figure S1. The exact *Euphorbia* backbone skeleton type could not be identified unambiguously, as many *Euphorbia* diterpenoid skeletons are isomeric and their respective MS2 spectra are identical or very similar. A *Euphorbia* backbone skeleton with masses at *m/z* 313, 295, 285 can either result from a jatrophane, deoxy tigliane, or ingenane ester like skeleton [41,42]. Furthermore, we were able to see that molecular family (ii) contains substructural Mass2Motifs related to a nicotinoyl side chain. Manual annotation of these Mass2Motifs was possible by comparing chemical structures retrieved through NAP in silico structure annotation with mass fragments found in the Mass2Motifs. Motifs 432 and 180 were both found to contain mass peaks at *m/z* 106 and 124, possibly resulting from a nicotinoyl side chain and a hydroxylation (Figure 3b). Chemical structures retrieved through in silico annotation or library matching can aid the manual annotation of Mass2Motifs and vice versa annotated Mass2Motifs can aid the propagation of chemical structural information throughout the network. Additionally, chemical structural hypotheses can be reinforced by taking into consideration both substructural information as well as chemical class information obtained through in silico annotation and library matching. Most chemical structures retrieved for molecular family (i) and (ii) were diterpenoids of the jatrophane, tigliane or ingenane type and substructures related to these *Euphorbia* diterpenoid backbone skeletons were also found within the Mass2Motifs (Figure 3c).

In conclusion, using MolNetEnhancer we were able to significantly increase chemical structural annotations obtained from retrieving chemical structural information of one molecular feature through GNPS library matching (Figure 3a), to retrieving chemical structural information at an annotation level 3 (putatively characterized compound classes) according to the Metabolomics Standard Initiative's reporting standards [43] of two molecular families comprising 73 molecular features (Figure 3b–d). Finally, this information allowed us to conclude that within the investigated subset of molecular families *Euphorbia* diterpenoid skeletons of the jatrophane, deoxy tigliane, or ingenane ester type are found within all *Euphorbia* subgeneric clades, whereas nicotinoyl sidechain modifications are unique to subgenus *Esula* (Figure 3d).

3.3. Case Study 2: Annotation of Rhamnaceae Specialized Metabolites

Another case where we demonstrate the efficiency of MolNetEnhancer for enhancing the chemical annotation of metabolomics data is our previous study on the plant family Rhamnaceae [28]. Rhamnaceae is a cosmopolitan family including about 900 species, and Rhamnaceae species are known for their exceptional morphological and genetic diversity, which are thought to be caused by the wide geographic distribution and different habitats [44]. We applied an MS2-based untargeted metabolomics approach to get insights on the metabolomic diversity of this highly-diversified family, and MolNetEnhancer was used as a key to provide fundamental annotations for MS2 spectra.

As shown in Figure 4a, MolNetEnhancer provided the putative chemical classification of molecular families within the Rhamnaceae molecular network. After combining this chemical class annotations with taxonomic information of each molecular feature, the normalized distribution pattern of different classes of metabolites were analyzed. This revealed that the taxonomic clade Rhamnoid exhibits more diversified flavonoids, carbohydrates, and anthraquinones, while the Ziziphoid clade produces various triterpenoids and triterpenoid glycosides [28].

MolNetEnhancer allowed us to visualize and discover the subtle substructural diversity within the molecular families. In the molecular family of triterpenoid esters, for example, substructural differences of phenolic moieties such as protocatchuate, vanillate, and coumarate were easily recognized by analyzing the distribution of Mass2Motifs 28, 117, 120, and 191 (Figure 4b). Two flavonoid aglycone substructures, kaempferol and quercetin, were also distinguished by analyzing the distribution of Mass2Motifs 86, 130, and 149 in the molecular family of flavone 3-*O*-glycosides (Figure 4c). Mass2Motif 130 contained mass peaks at *m/z* 284, 255, and 227, while Mass2Motifs 86 and 149 covered mass peaks at *m/z* 300, 271, and 255. These fragment ions are well-known as characteristic fragments of kaempferol 3-*O*-glycosides and quercetin 3-*O*-glycosides [45–47], so these Mass2Motifs could be easily annotated. This case study shows how MolNetEnhancer facilitates the interpretation process and our knowledge on MS2 fragmentation, previously mainly applied manually by experts.

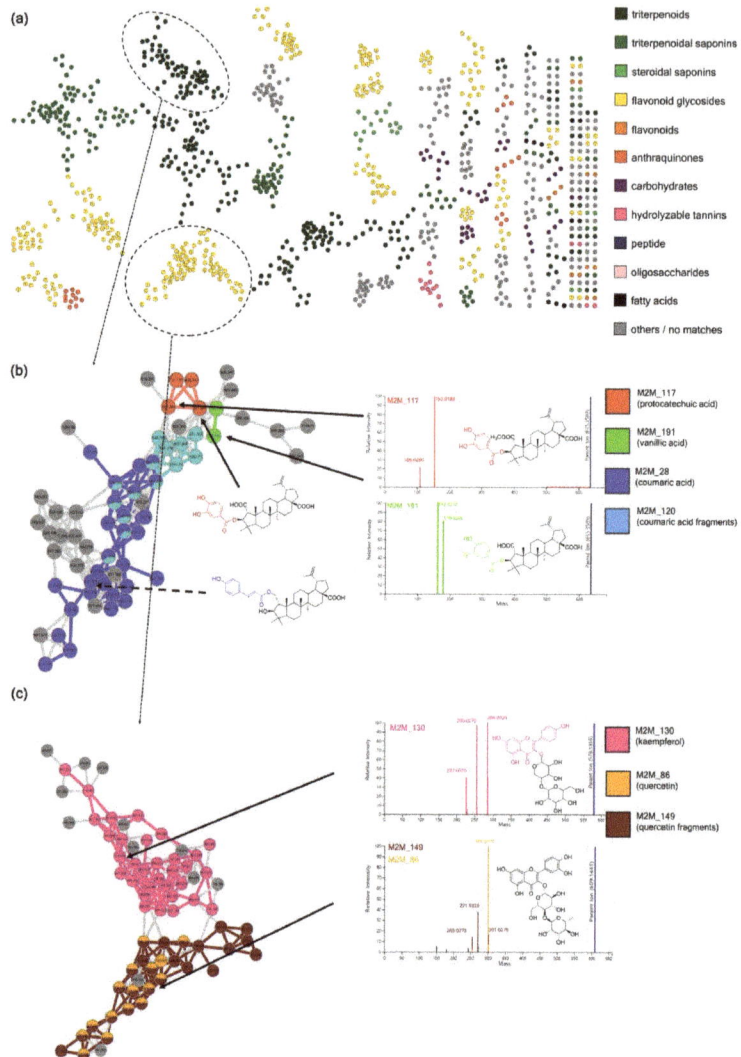

Figure 4. MolNetEnhancer increases chemical structural information obtained for Rhamnaceae specialized metabolites. (**a**) Structural annotation for molecular families was suggested based on consensus-based classification of NAP in silico structure annotation. (**b**) Subtle chemical differences of phenolic acid moieties can be visualized within the molecular family of triterpenoid esters based on Mass2Motifs. (**c**) Molecular family annotated as flavonoid glycosides reveals two subfamilies by Mass2Motif mapping: the pink Mass2Motif is related to the kaempferol core structure, whereas the orange and brown Mass2Motifs are related to the quercetin core structure—two related yet distinct flavonoid structures.

3.4. Case Study 3: Large Chemical Diversity Uncovered by Annotating Specialized Metabolites in Marine Sediment Streptomyces and Salinispora Bacterial Extracts

The MolNetEnhancer workflow was also applied to bacterial data sets to gain more detailed insights into their chemical richness. Crüsemann and coworkers created a molecular network of extracts of the marine sediment bacteria *Salinispora* and *Streptomyces* that formed the basis for this case study [48]. Figure 5 displays the molecular network colored by the most prevalent chemical class annotations. Whilst we can observe that the bacteria also produce a structurally diverse arsenal of molecules, its composition is clearly different from that of the Rhamnaceae plants in Figure 4a. The most prevalent chemical class annotations are "Carboxylic acid and derivatives" and "Prenol lipids" with the first containing peptide-related molecules and the latter containing terpenoid molecules. Both these classes of molecules are known to be produced by *Salinispora* and *Streptomyces* bacteria. The chemical classification scores (see Section 2) for the ClassyFire class and kingdom terms are presented in Supplementary materials Figure S2. These scores aid in assessing chemical novelty and also provide information on the consistency of the chemical class annotations of the structural candidates.

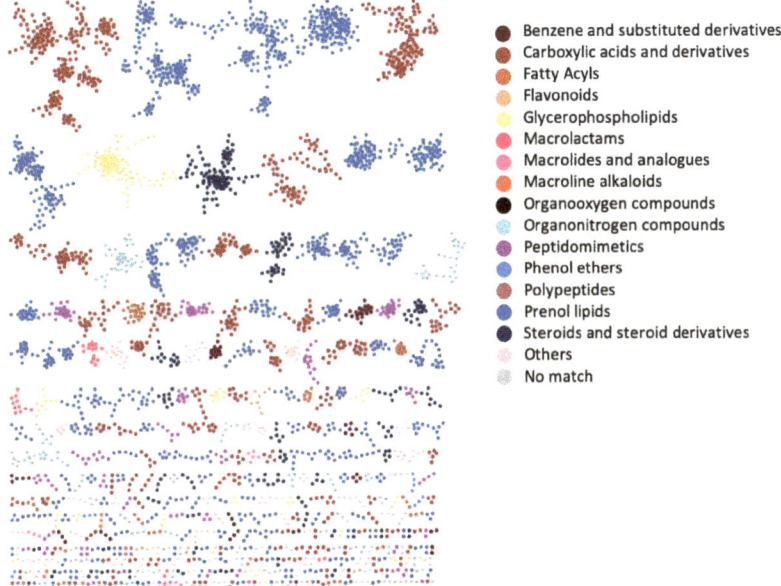

Figure 5. Marine sediment *Salinispora/Streptomyces* molecular network colored by 15 selected chemical class terms as indicated in the legend. In total, 50 different class terms were annotated in the network using MolNetEnhancer, indicating that the metabolic output of the *Salinispora/Streptomyces* strains is chemically very diverse. We can observe that the larger molecular families are mostly annotated with prenol lipids (blue) and carboxylic acids and derivatives (red). Furthermore, for a couple of MFs no chemical class annotations were obtained as no candidate structures were retrieved through any of the annotation tools.

From the 5930 network nodes, we discovered 300 Mass2Motifs using MS2LDA. From those, we could annotate 40 with structural information at various levels of structural details gained from spectral matching with the GNPS libraries or from the in silico annotation tools NAP, DEREPLICATOR, and VarQuest. For example, we could annotate an amino sugar-related Mass2Motif with fragment ions related to two known N,N-dimethyl amino sugars present in known specialized molecules from the bacteria studied [48]: dimethylamino-β-D-xylo-hexopyranoside (rosamicin) and N,N-dimethyl-pyrrolosamine (lomaiviticin) which have overlapping fragment ions and are therefore characterized by the same Mass2Motif. With a frequency of more than 70 throughout the entire molecular network (using probability and overlap score thresholds of 0.1 and 0.3, respectively, for the molecular feature—Mass2Motif connections), the amino sugar Mass2Motif can be used as a handle to identify known and potential novel natural products throughout network. Indeed, the Mass2Motif was found in all members of the Rosamicin MF (Figure 6a) and the Lomaiviticin MF (Supplementary materials Figure S3a). Moreover, the same amino sugar-related Mass2Motif was also found in all members of two yet unknown MFs (Figure 6b, Supplementary materials Figure S3b). In addition, the Mass2Motif was also found in a number of singletons not connected to any MF, often in combination with Mass2Motif 66 as well like we see for the rosamicin-related MF. Mass2Motif 66 represents the presence of an m/z 116 fragment which is likely also generated by the dimethylated amino sugar; in fact it may point to the dimethylamino-β-D-xylo-hexopyranoside moiety or something very similar as this fragment is absent in spectra from the lomaiviticin MF which contains the different dimethylated amino sugar N,N-dimethyl-pyrrolosamine. In most singletons, no other Mass2Motifs were discovered that could provide clues on the complete structures of these molecules; however, given the presence of the amino sugar moiety they are likely natural products and not core metabolites or contaminants—something that we could not confidently state without using the MolNetEnhancer workflow.

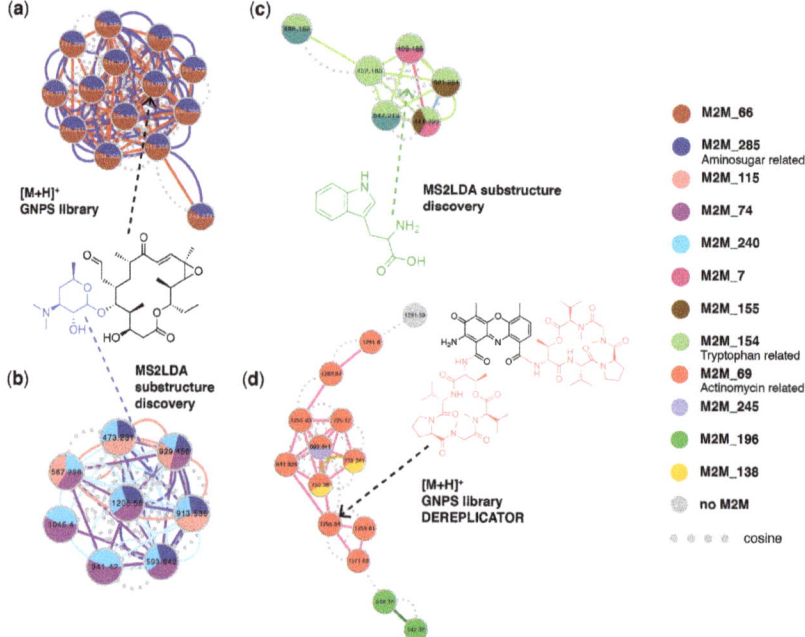

Figure 6. Molecular families from marine sediment bacteria with color coded Mass2Motif substructure information mapped on them, with (**a**) rosamicin-related molecular family found through GNPS library hits where all members contain an amino sugar-related motif as colored in blue in its depicted structure—substructures or motifs found within each molecular feature are mapped on the nodes as pie charts, where the relative abundance of each motif represents the overlap score, a score measuring how much of the motif is present in the spectrum. Furthermore, motifs shared between two nodes are visualized as colored continuous lines (edges) connecting the nodes whereas dashed lines (edges) represent a cosine score of over 0.6, (**b**) Yet unknown molecular family that shares an amino sugar-related motif connecting this MF to (**a**) by sharing a substructure, (**c**) tryptophan-related molecular family sharing the Tryptophan Mass2Motif, and (**d**) actinomycin-related molecular family—found through GNPS library hits and further validated with help of DEREPLICATOR results—sharing an Actinomycin related motif across most of its members. The actinomycin D (Daptomycin) structure is depicted with the Mass2Motif substructure highlighted in color: the peptide lactone ring present twice in the molecule. In all MFs, nodes are colored based on Mass2Motif overlap scores and the edges show if cosine score-connected nodes share similar Mass2Motifs. It can be seen that in all families multiple motifs are shared across some of its members.

Another MF displayed in Figure 6c did not return any GNPS library hits; however, all its members shared Mass2Motif 154. Due to its indicative fragment ions, we could annotate this Mass2Motif as tryptophan-related, indicating that all these molecules contain a tryptophan core structure. Based on their shared Mass2Motif, the masses of the molecular features, and their fragmentation patterns, with the help of MolNetEnhancer we could now tentatively annotate this MF as tryptophan-related containing molecules such as small peptides or N-acyltryptophans. Figure 6d shows the peptidic MF of actinomycin-related molecules. The annotation of this MF was guided by DEREPLICATOR and VarQuest annotations as well as the Mass2Motif that 10 of its members shared. We could annotate this Mass2Motif as the peptide lactone ring (depsipeptide moiety) present twice in actinomycins using reference data from literature [49]. The unique combination of four actinomycin-related mass fragments was only present in the 10 MF members, thereby reinforcing the DEREPLICATOR and VarQuest annotations.

Furthermore, mapping the Mass2Motifs on the molecular network means that we can more easily track neutral loss-based motifs such as the loss of an acetyloxy group that was only found in *Streptomyces* MFs. Moreover, inspection of the MFs without annotated chemical classes revealed that they contained some Mass2Motifs with relatively low frequency throughout the data set—something that could point to a unique substructure or scaffold possibly from a unique biosynthesis enzymatic function. For example, Mass2Motif 35 has a frequency of 43 and was present in all four members of the MF in Supplementary materials Figure S3c. It is a mass-fragment-based Mass2Motif and with masses of 142, 100, and 58 Da it could be related to a polyamine-like structural feature. Finally, the MF in Supplementary materials Figure S3d shares the two still unknown loss-based Mass2Motifs 250 and 261 that have frequencies of 26 and 50, respectively. These are examples of Mass2Motifs representing potential novel chemistry that can now be easily tracked in the molecular network.

3.5. Case Study 4: Annotating Peptidic Motifs in Peptide-Rich Xenorhabdus/Photorhabdus Extracts

Xenorhabdus and *Photorhabdus* are Gammaproteobacteria that live in symbiotic association with soil-dwelling nematodes of the genus *Steinernema* [50,51]. Eventually as a consequence thereof, they spend a large amount of their resources to the production of specialized metabolites, in particular nonribosomal peptides and polyketides. Tobias and coworkers recently published metabolomics data of 25 *Xenorhabdus* and five *Photorhabdus* strains to explore metabolic diversity amongst these strains [50]. Here, we applied MolNetEnhancer on this publicly available molecular networking data to further probe the chemical diversity previously found. The 6228 network nodes were analyzed with MS2LDA to discover 300 Mass2Motifs. Furthermore, we also submitted the *Xenorhabdus/Photorhabdus* molecular networking data to NAP, DEREPLICATOR, and VarQuest to run the MF chemical class annotation pipeline. By far the majority of the 46 annotated motifs were peptide, amino acid, or likely to be peptidic-related which fits with the ClassyFire predicted peptide-related MFs present in the *Xenorhabdus/Photorhabdus* extracts with "Carboxylic acids and derivatives" and "Peptidomimetics" as most frequently occurring annotations (see Figure 7, with corresponding chemical classification scores in Supplementary materials Figure S4). We could also annotate an indole-related Mass2Motif which can be part of peptides/amino acids. An exception is the ethylphenyl-related Mass2Motif that was found in 478 molecules (out of 6228 nodes, corresponding to 7.7%) of the *Xenorhabdus/Photorhabdus* extracts. This can be explained by the reported production of phenylethylamines, dialkylresorcinoles, and cyclohexadions derivatives by the studied strains [52].

Annotations included Mass2Motifs that form peptidic substructures related to well-known *Xenorhabdus* peptidic families such as the commonly found bioactive rhabdopeptides and the related xenortides [52,53]. We could annotate two rhabdopeptide-related motifs with frequencies of 231 and 186 (3.7% and 3.0% of nodes, respectively). Compared to the structurally less diverse xentrivalpeptides [54] which the Mass2Motif had a frequency of 28, corresponding to 0.45% of the nodes, we can conclude that rhabdopeptide-related molecules are widespread in the *Xenorhabdus/Photorhabdus* extracts. The PAX peptides constitute another well-known *Xenorhabdus/Photorhabdus* lysine-rich peptide class [55].

The corresponding MF consisted of 13 members; indeed, they shared a Mass2Motif related to lysine (lys) and lys–lys fragments. Similarly, a leucine-leucine Mass2Motif was found in molecules annotated as xenobovid. This motif occurred in 110/6228 (1.8%) nodes pointing to several peptidic families that contain this amino acid motif—in contrast to the lys–lys amino acid motif that is very wide-spread in *Xenorhabdus/Photorhabdus* molecules, being present in 1500 (24%) nodes. In total, using the MolNetEnhancer workflow we could annotate 32 peptidic motifs of which we could link 11 to peptides known to be produced by *Xenorhabdus/Photorhabdus* strains whilst the other 21 Mass2Motifs represent substructures not yet elucidated. The peptidic nature of these Mass2Motifs was assessed by recognition of typical fragment ion patterns as seen for known peptides as well as doubly charged precursor ions that are often a sign of peptides in these extracts.

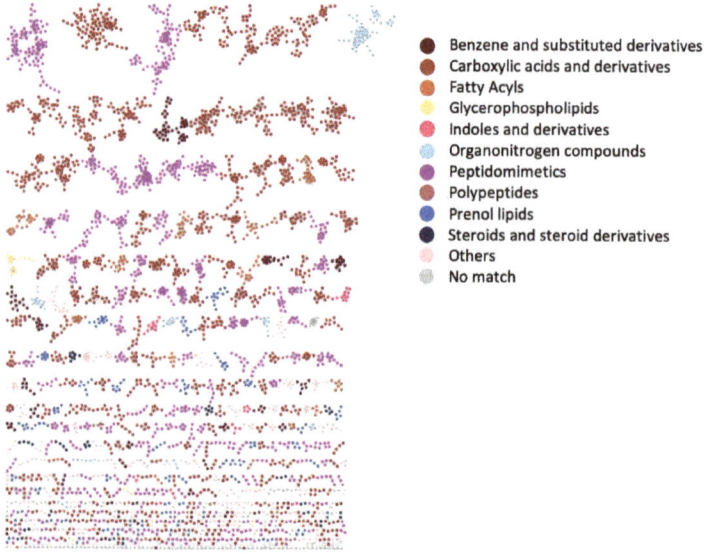

Figure 7. Nematode symbionts *Photorhabdus/Xenorhabdus* network colored by 10 selected chemical class terms as indicated in the legend. In total, 49 different class terms were annotated in the network using MolNetEnhancer. We can observe that the larger molecular families as well as many smaller molecular families are mostly annotated with peptidomimetics (purple) and carboxylic acids and derivatives (red). This is consistent with earlier findings that these nematode symbionts produce a wide array of peptidic products.

With the help of the integrative display of DEREPLICATOR and VarQuest annotation results, we could also annotate two xenoamicin-related peptidic MFs (Figure 8a,b). Xenoamicins are known to be produced by *Xenorhabdus* and eight variants have been described in detail with variants A and B present in peptidic databases [56]. Xenoamicin is a cyclic peptide consisting of a peptidic ring and peptidic tail (see Figure 8d). Interestingly, in one of the annotated MFs, not one but two Mass2Motifs were shared between most of its members (see Figure 8a). With help of DEREPLICATOR-predicted annotations of the fragment ions, we could annotate the Mass2Motif shared by almost the entire MF as being related to the xenoamicin A peptidic ring, whereas the other more abundant Mass2Motif was related to the xenoamicin peptidic tail (Figure 8c, and Supplementary materials Figure S5a,b). These Mass2Motifs are quite specific as we observed that 9 and 6 mass fragments, respectively, were consistently present in more than 75% of the molecular features to which the ring and tail Mass2Motifs were linked. A third Mass2Motif could be putatively annotated as xenoamicin B peptidic ring-related as its masses are +14 Da as compared to the ring A motif and xenoamicin B differs from A with an isobutyl replacing an isopropyl group. Based on the Mass2Motif presence/absence analysis in the larger MF of 32 members, we observe that 4 have links (overlap score > 0.3) to both ring A and tail motifs, 10 just have the ring A motif, three have only links to the peptidic tail motif, two share both ring A and putative ring B together with the tail Mass2Motif, and two share the putative ring B with the tail Mass2Motif (Figure 8a). Thus, this indicates how MolNetEnhancer increases the resolution in molecular networks by highlighting structural differences in between MF members.

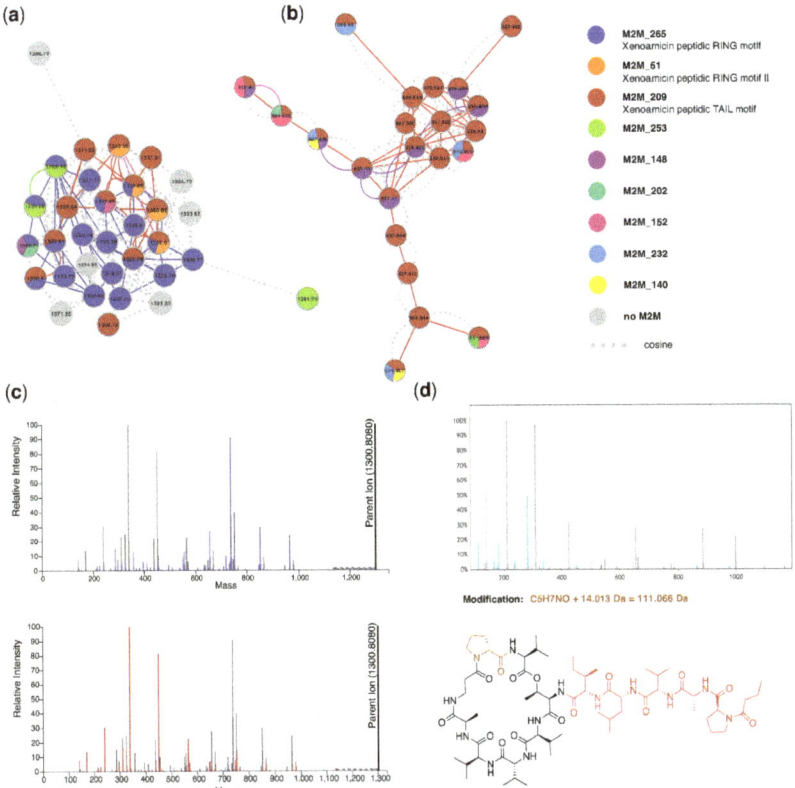

Figure 8. Xenoamicin-related molecular families annotated by MolNetEnhancer with (**a**) MF of 32 nodes of which 23 were annotated with at least one xenoamicin modified structure (xenoamicin A or B) by either VarQuest or DEREPLICATOR with VarQuest using 0.005 Da fragment binning assigning most xenoamicin structures (FDRs mostly < 2.5). This MF also contains nodes sharing all Mass2Motifs related to xenoamicin structures with two ring and tail-related Mass2Motifs. Mass2Motif 265 contains mass fragments related to xenoamicin A, whereas masses in Mass2Motif 51 are shifted with 14 Da pointing towards xenoamicin B. The MF consists of singly charged molecular features. (**b**) Related MF of which 20 out of 22 nodes were annotated with xenoamicin modified structures (FDRs mostly < 2.5). This MF only shares the Mass2Motif annotated as xenoamicin tail-related and consists of doubly-charged precursor ions. (**c**) Xenoamicin A spectrum in the ms2lda.org environment with (top) ring-related Mass2Motif highlighted and (bottom) tail-related Mass2Motif highlighted with the corresponding blue and red colors as in (**a**) and (**b**). (**d**) VarQuest annotation of xenoamicin modified peptide where a ring proline indicated in brown is likely methylated. All light blue peaks in the mass spectrum were annotated by VarQuest. The red part in the xenoamicin structure corresponds to the selected fragment of *m/z* 537.348, which includes the tail part, whereas the light blue amino acid is annotated to be modified with a mass shift of 14.013 Da that likely corresponds to a methylation. Indeed, the Mass2Motif related to the xenoamicin tail is found in this fragmentation spectrum, whereas the ring Mass2Motif is absent.

We could also find additional MFs and singletons in which the xenoamicin ring or tail Mass2Motif was present, pointing to related peptidic molecules not linked through the modified cosine score. Further inspection with help of VarQuest annotations strengthened these annotations as VarQuest annotated modified amino acids in both rings (Figure 8, Supplementary materials Figure S5e,f) and the tail region (Supplementary materials Figure S5c,d) of xenoamicin many of which, to our knowledge, have not been reported yet, such as the one highlighted in Figure 8d where the ring-proline is likely methylated (the ring A motif is not linked to this molecular feature). In fact, xenoamicin A was annotated as variant from xenoamicin B (Supplementary materials Figure S5f) where the modified amino acid (demethylation) corresponds to previous literature findings [56], further increasing our trust in these *in silico* approaches. The smaller MF of 22 nodes consisted of doubly-charged precursor ions where no ring-related Mass2Motifs were assigned. Some members like xenoamicin A appeared in both MFs as singly and doubly charged precursor ions; the differences in motif distributions between the two MFs indicates that the initial charge has an impact on the fragmentation pathways and thus the acquired spectra given that we know the ring A is part of xenoamicin A.

Altogether, this example highlights how the MolNetEnhancer approach facilitates fragmentation based metabolomics analysis workflows by increasing the "structural resolution", the discovery of more xenoamicin variants than previously described, and highlighting previously unseen connections between MFs and molecules. Furthermore, the integrative approach enabled straightforward annotation of Mass2Motifs found in the xenoamicin MF by using the VarQuest fragment ion annotations as guide for Mass2Motif feature annotation. Both Mass2Motif and VarQuest results strengthened each other since when predicted amino acid changes occurred in the peptidic ring, the corresponding ring-related Mass2Motif was absent, and vice versa—made possible by combining the outputs of several *in silico* tools together.

4. Discussion

Although significant advances have been made in molecular mining workflows, chemical annotation as well as classification tools [1–4,7,8,10,14–16], chemical structural annotation remains the major and most challenging bottleneck in mass spectrometry-based metabolomics as most of our biological interpretations rely on annotated structures [8,26,57]. MolNetEnhancer is a workflow that combines chemical structural information retrieved from different *in silico* tools, thus increasing structural information retrieved and enhancing biological interpretation. Here, we have chosen a representative number of *in silico* tools covering mining, annotation, and chemical annotation to provide the user with different chemical insights. Although we used DEREPLICATOR and NAP to exemplify *in silico* annotation tools here, MolNetEnhancer is platform independent, meaning that chemical structures retrieved from any *in silico* annotation platform could be used given the molecular feature identities correspond across all molecular mining and annotation tools.

Particularly in natural products research, the rapid annotation of known (i.e., dereplication) as well as unknown specialized metabolites from complex metabolic mixtures hinders interpretation in an ecological, agricultural or pharmaceutical context. Many specialized metabolites from natural sources are used as pharmaceuticals [58], in agriculture [59], or nutrition [60]; however, their discovery is inherently slow due to the above-mentioned limitations. To highlight how MolNetEnhancer can accelerate chemical structural annotation in complex metabolic mixtures from natural sources, we exemplified its use on four plant and bacterial datasets.

In the plant genus *Euphorbia*, we were able to retrieve chemical structural information of previously described pharmaceutically highly valuable diterpenoid skeletons corresponding to an annotation level 3 according to the Metabolomics Standard Initiative's reporting standards [43]. The use of different tools combined in one data format with MolNetEnhancer allowed both for the retrieval of complementary information as well as the reinforcement of putative annotations, in cases where two independent tools pointed to the same chemical structural conclusion. Used separately, none of the tools were able to retrieve as much chemical structural information as when combined in MolNetEnhancer.

Likewise, MolNetEnhancer allowed for the annotation of triterpenoids chemistries with several distinct phenolic acid modifications (e.g., vanillate, protocatechuate) in the plant family Rhamnaceae. In *Salinispora* and *Streptomyces* bacterial extracts, MolNetEnhancer aided the annotation of a previously unreported tryptophan-based MF, and a xenoamycin-related MF in the Gammaproteobacteria of the genus *Xenorhabdus* and *Photorhabdus* could be studied in more detail than in previous studies.

It is of utmost importance to note that results retrieved from MolNetEnhancer summarize results retrieved from third-party software and manual inspection and validation of all structural hypotheses remain essential. However, MolNetEnhancer significantly aids the manual inspection and validation process conducted by the expert, by making substructural as well as chemical class information readily available and visible within one data resource. As exemplified in the case studies, MolNetEnhancer can for example help in prioritizing molecular families within a molecular network, which consists of many hundreds to thousands of molecular features, be it by highlighting different chemical classes of interest or molecular families, for which only very few structural hypotheses could be retrieved, potentially highlighting novel chemistry.

Limitations introduced through data acquisition on different mass spectrometric instrument types do also apply to MolNetEnhancer. Acquiring data on different instruments can cause different MS2 fragmentation patterns, thus in some cases leading to different structural hypotheses through library matching or *in silico* structure prediction [61]. Also, the presence of low quality and/or chimeric MS2 spectra is a challenge for mass spectrometry annotation tools as the one described here, and methods that are capable of filtering-out these spectra before proceeding with *in silico* annotation tools will improve our confidence in *in silico* spectral annotation [62].

These limitations highlight the importance of good practices during data acquisition and processing to minimize the time spent analyzing mass spectrometry artefacts and improving the confidence in any downstream annotations. Here, the use of feature-based molecular networking could also help to focus the analysis on those molecular features that are very likely molecular ions [63]—and it has the added benefit that MS1 differential abundance information from LC–MS peak picking is available on the molecular features as well.

Apart from limitations caused by experimental conditions, analysis bias can be introduced for structural predictions based on chemical structures available in public databases, which are still limited especially for particular compound classes. This is particularly true for the chemical class annotations provided through ClassyFire, which rely on collecting correct or structurally closely related candidate structures from compound databases. The chemical annotation score was implemented to guide the researcher in assessing how consistent the chemical annotations are and for how many molecular features at least one candidate structure is found. The peptidic annotations by DEREPLICATOR and VarQuest come with scores, *p*-values, and false discovery rates to assess confidence in the annotations. Using MolNetEnhancer, it is now also possible to explore the consistency in peptidic annotations within MFs, along with their associated Mass2Motifs, which also assist in improving confidence in the annotations, as we have shown for the xenoamicin MFs in the nematode symbiont bacteria where the majority of the MFs were annotated with xenoamicin variants.

One limitation of the use of MS2LDA on the bacterial datasets is that most noncyclic peptidic molecular families do not share any motifs as typically analogues differ by modifications such as methylation or hydroxylation causing a shift in *m/z* in most of their mass fragment peaks. Incorporation of amino acid-related mass differences as features for MS2LDA could be a route to also discover Mass2Motifs for noncyclic peptides. As it is, cyclic peptides do often contain one or more Mass2Motifs and peptides containing positively charged amino acids such as lysine and leucine have this structural information represented by Mass2Motifs. Furthermore, many Mass2Motifs are currently still unannotated, which hampers fast structural analysis. To partially solve this bottleneck, MotifDB (www.ms2lda.org/motifdb) was recently introduced [64] and the here annotated Mass2Motif sets from the four case studies are made available through MotifDB for matching against Mass2Motifs found in other MS2LDA experiments. Furthermore, this will allow to use a combination of "supervised" (annotated) Mass2Motifs and "unsupervised" (free) Mass2Motifs in future MS2LDA experiments on data of related samples thereby accelerating structural annotation since part of the motifs already discovered do not need to be reannotated.

Despite the limitations discussed above, MolNetEnhancer assists in metabolite annotations by its combined analysis of chemical class annotations, structural annotations, and Mass2Motif annotations. If these annotations support each other, as for example for the actinomycin MF in the marine sediment bacteria, there is more confidence that these in silico annotations will indeed be correct. It is noteworthy that the modularity of MolNetEnhancer allows for complementary sources of structural information to be added on in future. We showed that MolNetEnhancer is a practical tool to annotate the chemical space of complex metabolic mixtures using a panel of complementary in silico annotation tools for mass spectrometry based metabolomics experiments. Although we have highlighted the use of MolNetEnhancer using two plant and bacterial datasets, MolNetEnhancer is sample type-independent and may be used for any mass spectrometry-based metabolomics experiment, where chemical structural annotation and interpretation is of interest. Future work will focus on making the complete MolNetEnhancer workflow available within the GNPS platform in order to further increase its user friendliness. Currently, the chemical classification workflow is available to run within the GNPS framework directly outputting an annotated network (see URL in code availability Section 7). Furthermore, the integration of other existing and future metabolome mining and annotation tools in the output of MolNetEnhancer is also planned to extend on the initial set of in silico tools that it currently can combine.

5. Conclusions

MolNetEnhancer is a powerful tool to accelerate chemical structural annotation within complex metabolic mixtures through the combined use of mass spectral molecular networking, substructure discovery, in silico annotation as well as chemical classifications provided by ClassyFire. The MolNetEnhancer workflow is presented both as an open source Python module and R package, allowing easy access and usability by the community as well as the possibility for customization and further development by integration into future collaborative modular tools and by integration of other existing or future metabolome mining and annotation tools. Whilst its use was showcased using natural product examples, we expect that MolNetEnhancer will also enhance biological and chemical interpretations in other scientific fields such as clinical and environmental metabolomics.

6. Data Availability

Publicly available mass spectrometry fragmentation data sets from four studies were used for this study. Details on how samples and data were collected can be found in the original studies [27,28,48,50]. Here, we list links to the different analyses that were done on each of the studies. Through these links, all used settings and parameters can be retrieved.

Data from case studies 1 & 2 illustrating MolNetEnhancer applied to feature-based molecular networking are publicly accessible through the links listed below.

Case study 1: *Euphorbia* study—combined analysis of 43 *Euphorbia* plant extracts

- MASSIVE: MSV000081082 https://massive.ucsd.edu/ProteoSAFe/dataset.jsp?task=c9f09d31a24c475e87a0a11f6e8889e7
- GNPS Molecular Networking job: https://gnps.ucsd.edu/ProteoSAFe/status.jsp?task=26326c233918419f8dc80e8af984cdae
- GNPS NAP jobs: https://proteomics2.ucsd.edu/ProteoSAFe/status.jsp?task=2cfddd3b8b1e469181a13e7d3a867a6f and https://proteomics2.ucsd.edu/ProteoSAFe/status.jsp?task=184a80db74334668ae1d0c0f852cb77c
- MS2LDA experiment: http://ms2lda.org/basicviz/summary/390

Case study 2: Rhamnaceae study—combined analysis of 71 Rhamnaceae plant extracts

- MASSIVE: MSV000081805 https://massive.ucsd.edu/ProteoSAFe/dataset.jsp?task=36f154d1c3844d31b9732fbaa72e9284
- GNPS Molecular Networking job: https://gnps.ucsd.edu/ProteoSAFe/status.jsp?task=e9e02c0ba3db473a9b1ddd36da72859b
- GNPS NAP job: https://proteomics2.ucsd.edu/ProteoSAFe/status.jsp?task=6b515b235e0e4c76ba539524c8b4c6d8
- MS2LDA experiment: http://ms2lda.org/basicviz/summary/566

GNPS example study used in Jupyter notebook to show MolNetEnhancer based on feature-based molecular networking—subset of American Gut Project:

- MASSIVE: MSV000082678 https://massive.ucsd.edu/ProteoSAFe/dataset.jsp?task=de2d18fd91804785bce8c225cc94a44
- GNPS Molecular Networking job: https://gnps.ucsd.edu/ProteoSAFe/status.jsp?task=b817262cb6114e7295fee4f73b22a3ad
- GNPS NAP job: https://proteomics2.ucsd.edu/ProteoSAFe/status.jsp?task=c4bb6b8be9e14bdebe87c6ef3abe11f6
- MS2LDA experiment: http://ms2lda.org/basicviz/summary/907

Data from case studies 3 & 4 illustrating MolNetEnhancer applied to classical molecular networking are publicly accessible through the links listed below.

Case study 3: Marine-sediment bacteria study—combined analysis of 120 *Salinospora* and 26 *Streptomyces* bacterial strain extracts

- MASSIVE: MSV000078836, MSV000078839 https://massive.ucsd.edu/ProteoSAFe/dataset.jsp?task=9277186021274990a5e646874a435c0d https://massive.ucsd.edu/ProteoSAFe/dataset.jsp?task=a507232a787243a5afd69a6c6fa1e508
- GNPS Molecular Networking job: http://gnps.ucsd.edu/ProteoSAFe/status.jsp?task=c36f90ba29fe44c18e96db802de0c6b9
- GNPS NAP job: https://proteomics2.ucsd.edu/ProteoSAFe/status.jsp?task=60925078e0c148cbaba3593569e983d6
- GNPS DEREPLICATOR 0.005 job: https://gnps.ucsd.edu/ProteoSAFe/status.jsp?task=0ad6535e34d449788f297e712f43068a
- GNPS DEREPLICATOR 0.05 job: https://gnps.ucsd.edu/ProteoSAFe/status.jsp?task=e494a63be6d34747a4b8cdfb838ef96e
- GNPS VARQUEST 0.005 job: https://gnps.ucsd.edu/ProteoSAFe/status.jsp?task=f1f00c1c20ba4f61ad471d340066df76
- GNPS VARQUEST 0.05 job: https://gnps.ucsd.edu/ProteoSAFe/status.jsp?task=f5ffcc8f63ab4e6f96a97caabc11048b
- MS2LDA annotation experiment: http://ms2lda.org/basicviz/summary/551
- MS2LDA MolNetEnhancer workflow experiment: http://ms2lda.org/basicviz/summary/912

Case study 4: Nematode symbionts study—combined analysis of 25 *Xenorhabdus* and 5 *Photorhabdus* bacterial strain extracts

- MASSIVE: MSV000081063 https://massive.ucsd.edu/ProteoSAFe/dataset.jsp?task=dcc30b777c344d668a5626d01f26c9a0
- GNPS Molecular Networking job: https://gnps.ucsd.edu/ProteoSAFe/status.jsp?task=aaff4721951b4d92b54ecbd2fe4b9b4f

- GNPS NAP job: http://gnps.ucsd.edu/ProteoSAFe/status.jsp?task=677f076eb04b4518958ca8cd56b4c753
- GNPS DEREPLICATOR 0.005 job: http://gnps.ucsd.edu/ProteoSAFe/status.jsp?task=338b422483d1432e82afd1bf848f1292
- GNPS DEREPLICATOR 0.05 job: http://gnps.ucsd.edu/ProteoSAFe/status.jsp?task=83bca3c45665470891d41ead275dcae7
- GNPS VARQUEST 0.005 job: http://gnps.ucsd.edu/ProteoSAFe/status.jsp?task=20cfb9af4a244feea102aa9c9da2651c
- GNPS VARQUEST 0.05 job: http://gnps.ucsd.edu/ProteoSAFe/status.jsp?task=a4ffda169823476a9b1e81616aeccbda
- MS2LDA annotation experiment: http://ms2lda.org/basicviz/summary/570
- MS2LDA MolNetEnhancer workflow experiment: http://ms2lda.org/basicviz/summary/917

GNPS example study used in Jupyter notebook to show MolNetEnhancer based on classical molecular networking—drug metabolism in set of sputum samples:

- MASSIVE: MSV000081098 https://gnps.ucsd.edu/ProteoSAFe/result.jsp?task=7c4b25d21a6348df9a6942d3071a4b1f&view=advanced_view
- GNPS Molecular Networking job: https://gnps.ucsd.edu/ProteoSAFe/status.jsp?task=b76dd5a123e54a7eb42765499f9163a5
- GNPS NAP job: https://proteomics2.ucsd.edu/ProteoSAFe/status.jsp?task=cb63770fe307410492468f62f9edb8f3
- VarQuest job: https://gnps.ucsd.edu/ProteoSAFe/status.jsp?task=4d971b8162644e869a68faa35f01b915
- DEREPLICATOR job: https://gnps.ucsd.edu/ProteoSAFe/status.jsp?task=c62d3283752f4f98b1720d0a6d1ee65b
- MS2LDA experiment: http://ms2lda.org/basicviz/summary/909

7. Code Availability

The MolNetEnhancer package in R including Jupyter notebooks with an exemplary analysis workflow for mapping Mass2Motifs and chemical class annotations onto classical and feature-based molecular networks is publicly accessible at https://github.com/madeleineernst/RMolNetEnhancer and the MolNetEnhancer package in Python including Jupyter notebooks with an exemplary analysis workflow for mapping Mass2Motifs and chemical class annotations onto classical and feature-based molecular networks is publicly accessible at https://github.com/madeleineernst/pyMolNetEnhancer. A beta version of the MolNetEnhancer workflow is also available from within GNPS: https://gnps.ucsd.edu/ProteoSAFe/index.jsp?params=%7B%22workflow%22:%22MOLNETENHANCER%22%7D. This currently outputs the chemical class annotated molecular network by user provided task ids to the individual jobs run within GNPS.

8. Tutorials

Tutorials to get familiar with individual tools from which the output is combined with MolNetEnhancer can be found here.

GNPS molecular networking:
https://ccms-ucsd.github.io/GNPSDocumentation/networking
DEREPLICATOR/VarQuest:
https://ccms-ucsd.github.io/GNPSDocumentation/dereplicator
Network annotation propagation:
https://ccms-ucsd.github.io/GNPSDocumentation/nap

ClassyFire:

http://classyfire.wishartlab.com

MS2LDA:

https://ccms-ucsd.github.io/GNPSDocumentation/ms2lda/

http://ms2lda.org/user_guide

MolNetEnhancer workflow tutorials in both R and Python can be found here:

https://github.com/madeleineernst/pyMolNetEnhancer

https://github.com/madeleineernst/RMolNetEnhancer

Supplementary Materials: The following are available online at http://www.mdpi.com/2218-1989/9/7/144/s1, Figure S1: Mirror plot comparing molecular feature with m/z 614.30 and RT 373.17 (black) to GNPS reference spectrum of a jatrophane diterpenoid (green), Figure S2: (a) Marine sediment *Salinispora/Streptomyces* molecular network colored by chemical classification scores for annotated chemical class terms and (b) same molecular network colored by chemical classification scores for annotated chemical kingdom terms. Light gray means no database matches were found. The higher the class score, the more consistent the chemical annotations are. The kingdom scores represent the database coverage of nodes across a molecular family with scores closer to zero representing families with fewer nodes that have at least one database hit. Whilst most MFs do have database matches for all or most nodes, the consistency in chemical class annotations is—apart from some exceptions—less (indicated by the more orange/pink colors in the left panel). This indicates that for many MF family members the right molecular structures might not yet be present in the structural databases used, Figure S3: Molecular families from marine sediment bacteria with color coded Mass2Motif substructure information mapped on them, with (a) lomaiviticin-related molecular family where all members contain an amino sugar related motif, (b) yet unknown molecular family that shares an amino sugar related motif, (c) yet unknown molecular family sharing an unknown fragment-based motif occurring 0.7% in the marine sediment data set, and (d) yet unknown molecular family sharing unknown loss-based motifs occurring 0.4% (Mass2Motif 250) and 0.8% (Mass2Motif 261) in the marine sediment data. In all MFs, nodes are colored based on motif overlap scores and the edges present similar colors to show if cosine score-connected nodes share similar Mass2Motifs. It can be seen that in most families multiple motifs are shared across some of its members, Figure S4: (a) Nematode symbionts *Photorhabdus/Xenorhabdus* network colored by chemical classification scores for annotated chemical class terms, and (b) same molecular network colored by chemical classification scores for annotated chemical kingdom terms. Light gray means no database matches were found. The higher the class score, the more consistent the chemical annotations are. The kingdom scores represent the database coverage of nodes across a molecular family with scores closer to zero representing families with fewer nodes that have at least a database hit. We observe database coverages of close to 1 for most molecular families; however, some molecular families have a lower coverage with a few nodes that return candidate structures. Furthermore, we observe that the chemical class annotation is not always consistent indicating that manual inspection and validation of those hits remains essential, Figure S5: Xenoamicin Mass2Motif mass feature frequency plots for (a) Mass2Motif related to xenoamicin peptidic ring and (b) xenoamicin peptidic tail. It can be observed that many mass fragments are present in at least 75% of the associated molecular features (9 and 6 for ring and tail Mass2Motif, respectively) with a few mass fragments present in nearly all associated molecular features. (c,d) Examples of annotated xenoamicin A modified structures in which only the ring Mass2Motif was found. Indeed, we observe that VarQuest annotates a modified amino acid (addition and loss of) in the tail region of xenoamicin A indicated in orange. (e,f) Examples of annotated xenoamicin B modified structures in which only the ring Mass2Motif was found. Indeed, we observe that VarQuest annotates a modified amino acid (double water addition, loss of methyl) in the ring region of xenoamicin B indicated in orange. The structures of xenoamicin A and B differ in one methyl group on the amino acid highlighted in orange in (f) where B has an isobutyl group and A an isopropyl group. In fact, the structure of xenoamicin A is correctly annotated by VarQuest to this fragmented doubly charged ion.

Author Contributions: Conceptualization, M.E., S.R. and J.J.J.v.d.H.; methodology, J.J.J.v.d.H. and M.E.; software M.E., C.C., M.W., J.W. and S.R.; validation, J.J.J.v.d.H., K.B.K., A.M.C.-R. and L.-F.N.; formal analysis, J.J.J.v.d.H., M.E. and K.B.K.; supervision, J.J.J.v.d.H.; writing—original draft preparation, J.J.J.v.d.H. and M.E.; writing—review and editing, J.J.J.v.d.H., M.E., K.B.K., A.M.C.-R., L.-F.N., J.W., C.C., M.W., S.R., M.H.M. and P.C.D.; visualization, M.E., J.J.J.v.d.H. and K.B.K.; funding acquisition, J.J.J.v.d.H., P.C.D. and M.H.M.

Funding: J.J.J.v.d.H. was funded by an ASDI eScience grant, ASDI.2017.030, from the Netherlands eScience Center—NLeSC. K.B.K. was supported by the National Research Foundation of Korea (NRF) grant funded by the Korea government (MIST) (No. 2019R1F1A1058068). A.M.C.R. and P.C.D. were supported by USA National Science Foundation grant IOS-1656481. S.R. and J.W. were supported by EPSRC EP/R018634/1. SR was supported by BBSRC BB/R022054/1.

Acknowledgments: The authors thank all research groups that made their metabolomics data publicly available so it could be reused in the current study. Yannick Djoumbou Feunang (University of Alberta, Canada) is thanked for his support with the use of ClassyFire and Ricardo da Silva (UCSD, USA) for scientific discussions and feedback on the methodology and workflow.

Conflicts of Interest: The authors declare no conflicts of interest.

References

1. Mohimani, H.; Gurevich, A.; Mikheenko, A.; Garg, N.; Nothias, L.-F.; Ninomiya, A.; Takada, K.; Dorrestein, P.C.; Pevzner, P.A. Dereplication of peptidic natural products through database search of mass spectra. *Nat. Chem. Biol.* **2017**, *13*, 30–37. [CrossRef] [PubMed]
2. Gurevich, A.; Mikheenko, A.; Shlemov, A.; Korobeynikov, A.; Mohimani, H.; Pevzner, P.A. Increased diversity of peptidic natural products revealed by modification-tolerant database search of mass spectra. *Nat. Microbiol.* **2018**, *3*, 319–327. [CrossRef] [PubMed]
3. Dührkop, K.; Fleischauer, M.; Ludwig, M.; Aksenov, A.A.; Melnik, A.V.; Meusel, M.; Dorrestein, P.C.; Rousu, J.; Böcker, S. SIRIUS 4: A rapid tool for turning tandem mass spectra into metabolite structure information. *Nat. Methods* **2019**, *16*, 299–302. [CrossRef] [PubMed]
4. Dührkop, K.; Shen, H.; Meusel, M.; Rousu, J.; Böcker, S. Searching molecular structure databases with tandem mass spectra using CSI:FingerID. *Proc. Natl. Acad. Sci. USA* **2015**, *112*, 12580–12585. [CrossRef] [PubMed]
5. Allen, F.; Pon, A.; Wilson, M.; Greiner, R.; Wishart, D. CFM-ID: A web server for annotation, spectrum prediction and metabolite identification from tandem mass spectra. *Nucleic Acids Res.* **2014**, *42*, W94–W99. [CrossRef] [PubMed]
6. Djoumbou-Feunang, Y.; Pon, A.; Karu, N.; Zheng, J.; Li, C.; Arndt, D.; Gautam, M.; Allen, F.; Wishart, D.S. CFM-ID 3.0: Significantly Improved ESI-MS/MS Prediction and Compound Identification. *Metabolites* **2019**, *9*, 72. [CrossRef]
7. Wang, M.; Carver, J.J.; Phelan, V.V.; Sanchez, L.M.; Garg, N.; Peng, Y.; Nguyen, D.D.; Watrous, J.; Kapono, C.A.; Luzzatto-Knaan, T.; et al. Sharing and community curation of mass spectrometry data with Global Natural Products Social Molecular Networking. *Nat. Biotechnol.* **2016**, *34*, 828–837. [CrossRef]
8. Da Silva, R.R.; Wang, M.; Nothias, L.-F.; van der Hooft, J.J.J.; Caraballo-Rodríguez, A.M.; Fox, E.; Balunas, M.J.; Klassen, J.L.; Lopes, N.P.; Dorrestein, P.C. Propagating annotations of molecular networks using in silico fragmentation. *PLoS Comput. Biol.* **2018**, *14*, e1006089. [CrossRef]
9. Ridder, L.; van der Hooft, J.J.J.; Verhoeven, S.; de Vos, R.C.H.; Vervoort, J.; Bino, R.J. In silico prediction and automatic LC-MS(n) annotation of green tea metabolites in urine. *Anal. Chem.* **2014**, *86*, 4767–4774. [CrossRef]
10. Watrous, J.; Roach, P.; Alexandrov, T.; Heath, B.S.; Yang, J.Y.; Kersten, R.D.; van der Voort, M.; Pogliano, K.; Gross, H.; Raaijmakers, J.M.; et al. Mass spectral molecular networking of living microbial colonies. *Proc. Natl. Acad. Sci. USA* **2012**, *109*, E1743–E1752. [CrossRef]
11. Gerlich, M.; Neumann, S. MetFusion: Integration of compound identification strategies. *J. Mass Spectrom.* **2013**, *48*, 291–298. [CrossRef] [PubMed]
12. Treutler, H.; Tsugawa, H.; Porzel, A.; Gorzolka, K.; Tissier, A.; Neumann, S.; Balcke, G.U. Discovering Regulated Metabolite Families in Untargeted Metabolomics Studies. *Anal. Chem.* **2016**, *88*, 8082–8090. [CrossRef] [PubMed]
13. Van der Hooft, J.J.J.; Padmanabhan, S.; Burgess, K.E.V.; Barrett, M.P. Urinary antihypertensive drug metabolite screening using molecular networking coupled to high-resolution mass spectrometry fragmentation. *Metabolomics* **2016**, *12*, 125. [CrossRef] [PubMed]
14. Van der Hooft, J.J.J.; Wandy, J.; Barrett, M.P.; Burgess, K.E.V.; Rogers, S. Topic modeling for untargeted substructure exploration in metabolomics. *Proc. Natl. Acad. Sci. USA* **2016**, *113*, 13738–13743. [CrossRef] [PubMed]
15. Wandy, J.; Zhu, Y.; van der Hooft, J.J.J.; Daly, R.; Barrett, M.P.; Rogers, S. Ms2lda.org: web-based topic modelling for substructure discovery in mass spectrometry. *Bioinformatics* **2018**, *34*, 317–318. [CrossRef]
16. Feunang, Y.D.; Eisner, R.; Knox, C.; Chepelev, L.; Hastings, J.; Owen, G.; Fahy, E.; Steinbeck, C.; Subramanian, S.; Bolton, E.; et al. ClassyFire: Automated chemical classification with a comprehensive, computable taxonomy. *J. Cheminform.* **2016**, *8*, 61. [CrossRef] [PubMed]
17. Olivon, F.; Elie, N.; Grelier, G.; Roussi, F.; Litaudon, M.; Touboul, D. MetGem Software for the Generation of Molecular Networks Based on the t-SNE Algorithm. *Anal. Chem.* **2018**, *90*, 13900–13908. [CrossRef]
18. Ma, Y.; Kind, T.; Yang, D.; Leon, C.; Fiehn, O. MS2Analyzer: A software for small molecule substructure annotations from accurate tandem mass spectra. *Anal. Chem.* **2014**, *86*, 10724–10731. [CrossRef]

19. Laponogov, I.; Sadawi, N.; Galea, D.; Mirnezami, R.; Veselkov, K.A. ChemDistiller: an engine for metabolite annotation in mass spectrometry. *Bioinformatics* **2018**, *34*, 2096–2102. [CrossRef]
20. Edmands, W.M.B.; Petrick, L.; Barupal, D.K.; Scalbert, A.; Wilson, M.J.; Wickliffe, J.K.; Rappaport, S.M. compMS2Miner: An Automatable Metabolite Identification, Visualization, and Data-Sharing R Package for High-Resolution LC–MS Data Sets. *Anal. Chem.* **2017**, *89*, 3919–3928. [CrossRef]
21. Ruttkies, C.; Schymanski, E.L.; Wolf, S.; Hollender, J.; Neumann, S. MetFrag relaunched: incorporating strategies beyond in silico fragmentation. *J. Cheminform.* **2016**, *8*, 3. [CrossRef] [PubMed]
22. Naake, T.; Gaquerel, E. MetCirc: Navigating mass spectral similarity in high-resolution MS/MS metabolomics data. *Bioinformatics* **2017**, *33*, 2419–2420. [CrossRef] [PubMed]
23. Beauxis, Y.; Genta-Jouve, G. MetWork: A web server for natural products anticipation. *Bioinformatics* **2019**, *35*, 1795–1796. [CrossRef] [PubMed]
24. Guijas, C.; Montenegro-Burke, J.R.; Domingo-Almenara, X.; Palermo, A.; Warth, B.; Hermann, G.; Koellensperger, G.; Huan, T.; Uritboonthai, W.; Aisporna, A.E.; et al. METLIN: A Technology Platform for Identifying Knowns and Unknowns. *Anal. Chem.* **2018**, *90*, 3156–3164. [CrossRef] [PubMed]
25. Fox Ramos, A.E.; Evanno, L.; Poupon, E.; Champy, P.; Beniddir, M.A. Natural products targeting strategies involving molecular networking: Different manners, one goal. *Nat. Prod. Rep.* **2019**. [CrossRef] [PubMed]
26. Da Silva, R.R.; Dorrestein, P.C.; Quinn, R.A. Illuminating the dark matter in metabolomics. *Proc. Natl. Acad. Sci. USA* **2015**, *112*, 12549–12550. [CrossRef] [PubMed]
27. Ernst, M.; Nothias, L.-F.; van der Hooft, J.J.J.; Silva, R.R.; Saslis-Lagoudakis, C.H.; Grace, O.M.; Martinez-Swatson, K.; Hassemer, G.; Funez, L.A.; Simonsen, H.T.; et al. Assessing Specialized Metabolite Diversity in the Cosmopolitan Plant Genus *Euphorbia* L. *Front. Plant Sci.* **2019**, *10*, 846. [CrossRef]
28. Kang, K.B.; Ernst, M.; van der Hooft, J.J.J.; da Silva, R.R.; Park, J.; Medema, M.H.; Sung, S.H.; Dorrestein, P.C. Comprehensive mass spectrometry-guided phenotyping of plant specialized metabolites reveals metabolic diversity in the cosmopolitan plant family Rhamnaceae. *Plant J.* **2019**. [CrossRef]
29. Frank, A.M.; Bandeira, N.; Shen, Z.; Tanner, S.; Briggs, S.P.; Smith, R.D.; Pevzner, P.A. Clustering millions of tandem mass spectra. *J. Proteome Res.* **2008**, *7*, 113–122. [CrossRef]
30. Pluskal, T.; Castillo, S.; Villar-Briones, A.; Orešič, M. MZmine 2: Modular framework for processing, visualizing, and analyzing mass spectrometry-based molecular profile data. *BMC Bioinform.* **2010**, *11*, 395. [CrossRef]
31. Shannon, P.; Markiel, A.; Ozier, O.; Baliga, N.S.; Wang, J.T.; Ramage, D.; Amin, N.; Schwikowski, B.; Ideker, T. Cytoscape: A Software Environment for Integrated Models of Biomolecular Interaction Networks. *Genome Res.* **2003**, *13*, 2498–2504. [CrossRef] [PubMed]
32. Van der Hooft, J.J.J.; Wandy, J.; Young, F.; Padmanabhan, S.; Gerasimidis, K.; Burgess, K.E.V.; Barrett, M.P.; Rogers, S. Unsupervised Discovery and Comparison of Structural Families Across Multiple Samples in Untargeted Metabolomics. *Anal. Chem.* **2017**, *89*, 7569. [CrossRef] [PubMed]
33. Kuhl, C.; Tautenhahn, R.; Böttcher, C.; Larson, T.R.; Neumann, S. CAMERA: An integrated strategy for compound spectra extraction and annotation of liquid chromatography/mass spectrometry data sets. *Anal. Chem.* **2012**, *84*, 283–289. [CrossRef] [PubMed]
34. Govaerts, R.; Fernández Casas, F.J.; Barker, C.; Carter, S.; Davies, S.; Esser, H.-J.; Gilbert, M.; Hoffmann, P.; Radcliffe-Smith, A.; Steinmann, V.; et al. World Checklist of Euphorbiaceae. Facilitated by the Royal Botanic Gardens, Kew. Available online: http://apps.kew.org/wcsp/ (accessed on 25 July 2014).
35. Horn, J.W.; van Ee, B.W.; Morawetz, J.J.; Riina, R.; Steinmann, V.W.; Berry, P.E.; Wurdack, K.J. Phylogenetics and the evolution of major structural characters in the giant genus *Euphorbia* L. (Euphorbiaceae). *Mol. Phylogenet. Evol.* **2012**, *63*, 305–326. [CrossRef] [PubMed]
36. Vasas, A.; Hohmann, J. Euphorbia Diterpenes: Isolation, Structure, Biological Activity, and Synthesis (2008–2012). *Chem. Rev.* **2014**, *114*, 8579–8612. [CrossRef] [PubMed]
37. Shi, Q.-W.; Su, X.-H.; Kiyota, H. Chemical and pharmacological research of the plants in genus Euphorbia. *Chem. Rev.* **2008**, *108*, 4295–4327. [CrossRef] [PubMed]
38. Berman, B. New developments in the treatment of actinic keratosis: Focus on ingenol mebutate gel. *Clin. Cosmet. Investig. Dermatol.* **2012**, *5*, 111–122. [CrossRef] [PubMed]

39. Luo, D.; Callari, R.; Hamberger, B.; Wubshet, S.G.; Nielsen, M.T.; Andersen-Ranberg, J.; Hallström, B.M.; Cozzi, F.; Heider, H.; Møller, B.L.; et al. Oxidation and cyclization of casbene in the biosynthesis of Euphorbia factors from mature seeds of *Euphorbia lathyris* L. *Proc. Natl. Acad. Sci. USA* **2016**, *113*, E5082–E5089. [CrossRef] [PubMed]
40. Appendino, G. Ingenane Diterpenoids. In *Progress in the Chemistry of Organic Natural Products 102*; Springer: Berlin/Heidelberg, Germany, 2016; pp. 1–90.
41. Nothias-Scaglia, L.-F.; Schmitz-Afonso, I.; Renucci, F.; Roussi, F.; Touboul, D.; Costa, J.; Litaudon, M.; Paolini, J. Insights on profiling of phorbol, deoxyphorbol, ingenol and jatrophane diterpene esters by high performance liquid chromatography coupled to multiple stage mass spectrometry. *J. Chromatogr. A* **2015**, *1422*, 128–139. [CrossRef]
42. Nothias, L.-F.; Boutet-Mercey, S.; Cachet, X.; De La Torre, E.; Laboureur, L.; Gallard, J.-F.; Retailleau, P.; Brunelle, A.; Dorrestein, P.C.; Costa, J.; et al. Environmentally Friendly Procedure Based on Supercritical Fluid Chromatography and Tandem Mass Spectrometry Molecular Networking for the Discovery of Potent Antiviral Compounds from *Euphorbia semiperfoliata*. *J. Nat. Prod.* **2017**, *80*, 2620–2629. [CrossRef]
43. Sumner, L.W.; Amberg, A.; Barrett, D.; Beale, M.H.; Beger, R.; Daykin, C.A.; Fan, T.W.; Fiehn, O.; Goodacre, R.; Griffin, J.L.; et al. Proposed minimum reporting standards for chemical analysis. *Metabolomics* **2007**, *3*, 211–221. [CrossRef] [PubMed]
44. Onstein, R.E.; Carter, R.J.; Xing, Y.; Richardson, J.E.; Linder, H.P. Do Mediterranean-type ecosystems have a common history?–insights from the Buckthorn family (Rhamnaceae). *Evolution* **2015**, *69*, 756–771. [CrossRef] [PubMed]
45. March, R.E.; Lewars, E.G.; Stadey, C.J.; Miao, X.-S.; Zhao, X.; Metcalfe, C.D. A comparison of flavonoid glycosides by electrospray tandem mass spectrometry. *Int. J. Mass Spectrom.* **2006**, *248*, 61–85. [CrossRef]
46. Van der Hooft, J.J.J.; Vervoort, J.; Bino, R.J.; de Vos, R.C.H. Spectral trees as a robust annotation tool in LC–MS based metabolomics. *Metabolomics* **2012**, *8*, 691–703. [CrossRef]
47. Van der Hooft, J.J.J.; Vervoort, J.; Bino, R.J.; Beekwilder, J.; de Vos, R.C.H. Polyphenol identification based on systematic and robust high-resolution accurate mass spectrometry fragmentation. *Anal. Chem.* **2011**, *83*, 409–416. [CrossRef] [PubMed]
48. Crüsemann, M.; O'Neill, E.C.; Larson, C.B.; Melnik, A.V.; Floros, D.J.; da Silva, R.R.; Jensen, P.R.; Dorrestein, P.C.; Moore, B.S. Prioritizing Natural Product Diversity in a Collection of 146 Bacterial Strains Based on Growth and Extraction Protocols. *J. Nat. Prod.* **2017**, *80*, 588–597. [CrossRef] [PubMed]
49. Crnovčić, I.; Semsary, S.; Vater, J.; Keller, U. Biosynthetic rivalry of o-aminophenol-carboxylic acids initiates production of hemi-actinomycins in Streptomyces antibioticus. *RSC Adv.* **2014**, *4*, 5065. [CrossRef]
50. Tobias, N.J.; Wolff, H.; Djahanschiri, B.; Grundmann, F.; Kronenwerth, M.; Shi, Y.-M.; Simonyi, S.; Grün, P.; Shapiro-Ilan, D.; Pidot, S.J.; et al. Natural product diversity associated with the nematode symbionts Photorhabdus and Xenorhabdus. *Nat. Microbiol.* **2017**, *2*, 1676. [CrossRef]
51. Shi, Y.-M.; Bode, H.B. Chemical language and warfare of bacterial natural products in bacteria–nematode–insect interactions. *Nat. Product Rep.* **2018**, *35*, 309–335. [CrossRef]
52. Tobias, N.; Parra-Rojas, C.; Shi, Y.-N.; Shi, Y.-M.; Simonyi, S.; Thanwisai, A.; Vitta, A.; Chantratita, N.; Hernandez-Vargas, E.A.; Bode, H.B. Focused natural product elucidation by prioritizing high-throughput metabolomic studies with machine learning. *bioRxiv* **2019**, 535781.
53. Zhao, L.; Kaiser, M.; Bode, H.B. Rhabdopeptide/Xenortide-like Peptides from Xenorhabdus innexi with Terminal Amines Showing Potent Antiprotozoal Activity. *Org. Lett.* **2018**, *20*, 5116–5120. [CrossRef] [PubMed]
54. Zhou, Q.; Dowling, A.; Heide, H.; Wöhnert, J.; Brandt, U.; Baum, J.; ffrench-Constant, R.; Bode, H.B. Xentrivalpeptides A–Q: Depsipeptide Diversification in Xenorhabdus. *J. Nat. Prod.* **2012**, *75*, 1717–1722. [CrossRef] [PubMed]
55. Fuchs, S.W.; Proschak, A.; Jaskolla, T.W.; Karas, M.; Bode, H.B. Structure elucidation and biosynthesis of lysine-rich cyclic peptides in Xenorhabdus nematophila. *Org. Biomol. Chem.* **2011**, *9*, 3130–3132. [CrossRef] [PubMed]
56. Zhou, Q.; Grundmann, F.; Kaiser, M.; Schiell, M.; Gaudriault, S.; Batzer, A.; Kurz, M.; Bode, H.B. Structure and biosynthesis of xenoamicins from entomopathogenic Xenorhabdus. *Chemistry* **2013**, *19*, 16772–16779. [CrossRef] [PubMed]
57. Metabolomics: Dark matter. *Nature* **2008**, *455*, 698. [CrossRef] [PubMed]

58. Newman, D.J.; Cragg, G.M. Natural Products as Sources of New Drugs from 1981 to 2014. *J. Nat. Prod.* **2016**, *79*, 629–661. [CrossRef] [PubMed]
59. Crupi, P.; Antonacci, D.; Savino, M.; Genghi, R.; Perniola, R.; Coletta, A. Girdling and gibberellic acid effects on yield and quality of a seedless red table grape for saving irrigation water supply. *Eur. J. Agron.* **2016**, *80*, 21–31. [CrossRef]
60. Pan, A.; Chen, M.; Chowdhury, R.; Wu, J.H.Y.; Sun, Q.; Campos, H.; Mozaffarian, D.; Hu, F.B. α-Linolenic acid and risk of cardiovascular disease: A systematic review and meta-analysis. *Am. J. Clin. Nutr.* **2012**, *96*, 1262–1273. [CrossRef]
61. Oberacher, H.; Reinstadler, V.; Kreidl, M.; Stravs, M.A.; Hollender, J.; Schymanski, E.L. Annotating Nontargeted LC-HRMS/MS Data with Two Complementary Tandem Mass Spectral Libraries. *Metabolites* **2018**, *9*, 3. [CrossRef]
62. Scheubert, K.; Hufsky, F.; Petras, D.; Wang, M.; Nothias, L.-F.; Dührkop, K.; Bandeira, N.; Dorrestein, P.C.; Böcker, S. Significance estimation for large scale metabolomics annotations by spectral matching. *Nat. Commun.* **2017**, *8*, 1494. [CrossRef]
63. Olivon, F.; Grelier, G.; Roussi, F.; Litaudon, M.; Touboul, D. MZmine 2 Data-Preprocessing To Enhance Molecular Networking Reliability. *Anal. Chem.* **2017**, *89*, 7836–7840. [CrossRef] [PubMed]
64. Rogers, S.; Ong, C.W.; Wandy, J.; Ernst, M.; Ridder, L.; van der Hooft, J.J.J. Deciphering complex metabolite mixtures by unsupervised and supervised substructure discovery and semi-automated annotation from MS/MS spectra. *Faraday Discuss.* **2019**. [CrossRef] [PubMed]

© 2019 by the authors. Licensee MDPI, Basel, Switzerland. This article is an open access article distributed under the terms and conditions of the Creative Commons Attribution (CC BY) license (http://creativecommons.org/licenses/by/4.0/).

 *metabolites*

Article

In Silico Optimization of Mass Spectrometry Fragmentation Strategies in Metabolomics

Joe Wandy [1,†], Vinny Davies [2,†], Justin J. J. van der Hooft [3], Stefan Weidt [1], Rónán Daly [1] and Simon Rogers [2,*]

[1] Glasgow Polyomics, University of Glasgow, Glasgow G61 1BD, UK; joe.wandy@glasgow.ac.uk (J.W.); stefan.weidt@glasgow.ac.uk (S.W.); ronan.daly@glasgow.ac.uk (R.D.)
[2] School of Computing Science, University of Glasgow, Glasgow G12 8RZ, UK; vinny.davies@glasgow.ac.uk
[3] Bioinformatics Group, Department of Plant Sciences, Wageningen University, Wageningen 6780 PB, The Netherlands; justin.vanderhooft@wur.nl
* Correspondence: Simon.Rogers@Glasgow.ac.uk
† These authors contributed equally to this work.

Received: 28 August 2019; Accepted: 2 October 2019; Published: 9 October 2019

Abstract: Liquid chromatography (LC) coupled to tandem mass spectrometry (MS/MS) is widely used in identifying small molecules in untargeted metabolomics. Various strategies exist to acquire MS/MS fragmentation spectra; however, the development of new acquisition strategies is hampered by the lack of simulators that let researchers prototype, compare, and optimize strategies before validations on real machines. We introduce Virtual Metabolomics Mass Spectrometer (ViMMS), a metabolomics LC-MS/MS simulator framework that allows for scan-level control of the MS2 acquisition process in silico. ViMMS can generate new LC-MS/MS data based on empirical data or virtually re-run a previous LC-MS/MS analysis using pre-existing data to allow the testing of different fragmentation strategies. To demonstrate its utility, we show how ViMMS can be used to optimize N for Top-N data-dependent acquisition (DDA) acquisition, giving results comparable to modifying N on the mass spectrometer. We expect that ViMMS will save method development time by allowing for offline evaluation of novel fragmentation strategies and optimization of the fragmentation strategy for a particular experiment.

Keywords: liquid chromatography–mass spectrometry (LC/MS); fragmentation (MS/MS); data-dependent acquisition (DDA); simulator; in silico

---

1. Introduction

Liquid chromatography (LC) tandem mass spectrometry (MS/MS) is commonly used to identify small molecules in untargeted metabolomics. In this setup, chemicals elute through the liquid chromatographic column at different retention times (RTs) before entering the mass spectrometer and potentially undergoing fragmentation. Fragmentation produces distinct patterns of fragment peaks at different mass-to-charge ratios (m/zs) that can be used to annotate chemical structures [1,2]. The choice of fragmentation strategy, which determines how precursor ions are selected for further fragmentation in tandem mass spectrometry, is an important factor affecting the coverage and quality of MS/MS spectra available for subsequent analysis. Many strategies exist to perform fragmentation, including data-independent acquisition (DIA) and data-dependent acquisition (DDA), and new and improved fragmentation strategies are constantly being introduced [3,4]. However, evaluating and comparing different strategies is challenging since the chemicals present in the samples in untargeted metabolomics studies are generally unknown, making it hard to judge whether a certain strategy leads to optimal MS/MS coverage. Currently, this is usually done by trying different fragmentation settings on the instrument followed by manual inspection for the samples of interest.

An appealing alternative way to evaluate fragmentation strategies is using a simulator, which can replicate the underlying LC-MS/MS processes and allow researchers to prototype and compare strategies before validation on the actual MS instrument. Although some mass spectrometry simulators exist they are typically focused on proteomics and do not include simulation of the MS2 acquisition strategy within a chromatographic run [5–10]. Additionally, existing simulators do not allow for real-time control of scan events (such as programmatically determining which m/z ranges to scan at a particular retention time), a crucial function for developing novel fragmentation strategies that can be controlled through libraries available with modern mass spectrometers, e.g., using the Instrument Application Programming Interface (API) available for Thermo Tribrid instruments [11] that has begun to generate interest within the mass spectrometry community (e.g., [12]).

In this work, we introduce Virtual Metabolomics Mass Spectrometer (ViMMS) a modular LC-MS/MS simulator for metabolomics that allows for real-time scan-level control of the MS2 acquisition process in silico. ViMMS works by creating a set of chemical objects, each with its own chromatogram, RT and intensity, fragmentation spectra and propensity to generate particular adducts. These can be created from a list of known metabolites (for example from the Human Metabolome Database, HMDB [13]) or from chromatographic peaks extracted in experimental .mzML files. A selection of controllers that implement different fragmentation strategies are available, including standard Top-N strategies but also MS1-only simulation as they also form a part of LC-MS/MS experiments. Using the appropriate controllers, users can benchmark and test different strategies and obtain simulated results in mzML format (the entire simulator state can also be saved for inspection later).

The idea of ViMMS is to offer the functionality of simulating MS1 and MS2 generation processes, but also to be modular enough that additional features are easily integrated in the framework. The development of a simulator such as ViMMS makes it possible to optimize MS/MS acquisition in silico without having to use valuable instrument time. Please note that our proposed tool is not a new acquisition strategy itself, but rather a framework that makes the development, testing, and benchmarking of such acquisition strategies easier. All code and examples are available at https://github.com/sdrogers/vimms and demonstrate how our simulator framework can be used in an interactive setting via Jupyter Notebooks. We demonstrate the utility of ViMMS with two examples: first we perform an experiment to vary N (the number of precursor peaks selected for fragmentation in standard Top-N DDA fragmentation strategy) in silico as well as the dynamic exclusion window (DEW) that is used to exclude ions from fragmentation for a certain time and evaluate how changing those parameter settings affects fragmentation coverage and the quality of MS1 peak picking. We then validate these results by comparing the ViMMS output against experimental data when both N and dynamic exclusion window parameters are varied. Secondly, we use the simulator to reproduce key results from a novel fragmentation strategy, data-set-dependent acquisition (DsDA) [4], demonstrating how ViMMS can be used to compare fragmentation strategies before implementation in an actual MS instrument.

2. Materials and Methods

2.1. LC-MS/MS Materials and Methods

2.1.1. Samples

Beer and urine samples (labelled *multi-beer* and *multi-urine*) from a previously published study [14] are used in our experiments. Here we briefly summarize the sample preparation and analytical platform for the *multi-beer* and *multi-urine* in [14]. 19 different beers were collected from bottles over a period of 5 months and frozen immediately after sampling. 22 urine samples were obtained from a clinical trial of an anonymized cohort of elderly hypertensive patients who were administered several drugs, including antihypertensives. 5 µL of beer/urine was extracted in 200 µL of chloroform/methanol/water (1:3:1) at

4 °C, vortexed for 5 min at 4 °C and centrifuged for 3 min (13,000 g) at 4 °C. The resulting supernatant was stored at −80 °C until analysis, and a pooled aliquot of the 22 selected urine samples and 19 beer samples were prepared prior to LC-MS/MS runs.

On top of the existing *multi-beer* and *multi-urine* samples, we also introduce newly generated beer data in this study. One beer extract (labelled *BeerQCB*) was selected for repeated and reproducible sampling across this experiment. An English premium bitter (Black Sheep Ale, 4.4 %) was purchased from a local supermarket. Beer metabolites were extracted by addition of chloroform and methanol to the ratio of 1:1:3 ($v/v/v$), as previously described, except for the total volume being scaled up to 100 mL. The solution was thoroughly mixed using a vortex mixer, before protein and other precipitates removed by centrifuging at 14,000 rpm at 4 °C for 10 min. The supernatant was removed, and aliquots stored at −80 °C until needed.

2.1.2. Liquid Chromatography

All samples underwent liquid chromatography separation under the following experimental conditions: a Thermo Scientific UltiMate 3000 RSLC liquid chromatography system was used for HILIC separation with a SeQuant ZIC-pHILIC column using a gradient elution with (A) 20 mM ammonium carbonate and (B) acetontrile. 10 μL of each sample was injected onto the column with initial conditions of 80% (B). A linear gradient from 80% to 20% (B) over 15 min, a wash of 5% (B) for 2 min, before re-equilibration at 80% (B) for 7 min (QE) or 9 min (Fusion). A constant flow rate of 300 μL/min was used. The column oven was maintained at a constant temperature of 25 °C (QE) or 40 °C (Fusion). Blank runs, quality control samples and three standard mixes were prepared according to the standard procedures at Glasgow Polyomics [14,15].

2.1.3. Mass Spectrometer Acquisition

The *multi-beer* and *multi-urine* datasets were acquired using a Q-Exactive orbitrap mass spectrometer for LC-MS/MS. All full-scan spectra were acquired in positive ion mode only, with a fixed resolution of 70,000, with mass range 70–1050 m/z. Ions were isolated with 1.0 m/z width and fragmented with stepped HCD collision energy of 25.2, 60, 94.8% for both positive and negative ion modes. Fragmentation spectrum were acquired with the orbitrap mass analyzer with resolution of 17,500. Top 10 ions with an intensity threshold $\geq$1.3E5 were selected for fragmentation and then added to a dynamic exclusion window for 15 s. For more mass spectrometer acquisition details, we refer to [14].

The new validation dataset (*BeerQCB*) to simulate fragmentation performance in Section 3.4 was generated using an orbitrap fusion tribrid-series mass spectrometer. All full-scan spectra were acquired in positive ion mode only, with a fixed resolution of 120,000, with mass range 70–1000 m/z. To investigate the instrument performance with differing Top-N and dynamic exclusion windows, filters such as intensity threshold and monoisotopic peak determination were not used. This allowed for a consistent number tandem MS scans to be acquired under varying Top-N parameters and dynamic exclusion window (DEW), for $N = (1, 2, 3, 4, 5, 10, 15, 20, 35, 50)$ and $DEW = (15, 30, 60, 120)$. Ions were isolated with 0.7 m/z width and fragmented with fixed HCD collision energy of 25%. Fragmentation spectrum were acquired with the orbitrap mass analyzer with resolution of 7500.

2.1.4. Data Transformation

Raw files from acquisition were converted into mzML format using MSconvert (Proteowizard). In the evaluation of the Top-N controller in Sections 3.2 and 3.3, two of the *multi-beer* samples (labelled *multi-beer-1* and *multi-beer-2*) and two of the *multi-urine* samples (labelled *multi-urine-1* and *multi-urine-2*) are used. In Section 3.5 to evaluate DsDA, all *multi-beer* and *multi-urine* samples are used. Section 3.4 uses only the *BeerQCB* samples.

2.2. Computational Methods

2.2.1. Overall Framework

The overall schematic for ViMMS can be found in Figure 1. ViMMS works by first creating *chemical objects* which represent the possible metabolites in a sample (Section 2.2.2). These objects contain information which defines how each chemical appears when scanned by the virtual mass spectrometer (yellow box in Figure 1). To get the information to fill the chemical objects, we create a database of spectral features from experimental data from which we can sample (Section 2.2.3). Regions of interest (ROIs) representing groups of mass traces that could potentially form chromatographic peaks are also extracted from experimental files and assigned to chemicals (Section 2.2.4). Unlike other simulators, e.g., [5–9], chemical objects can also be associated with fragment spectra that could themselves be extracted from spectral databases or generated using *in silico* fragment prediction methods (Section 2.2.5). *In silico* scan simulation in ViMMS (yellow box in Figure 1) proceeds as follows. A virtual mass spectrometer takes the list of chemical objects as input and generates MS1 and MS2 scans at appropriate RTs (Section 2.2.6). Scan parameters are determined by a controller that implements a particular fragmentation strategy. (Section 2.3). The proposed framework is designed to be completely modular such that a variety of situations and different fragmentation strategies can be tested. Finally, using the psims library [16] simulated results can be written as mzML files for further analysis in other tools. The entire state of the simulator over time can also be saved for inspections using the built-in pickle function in Python.

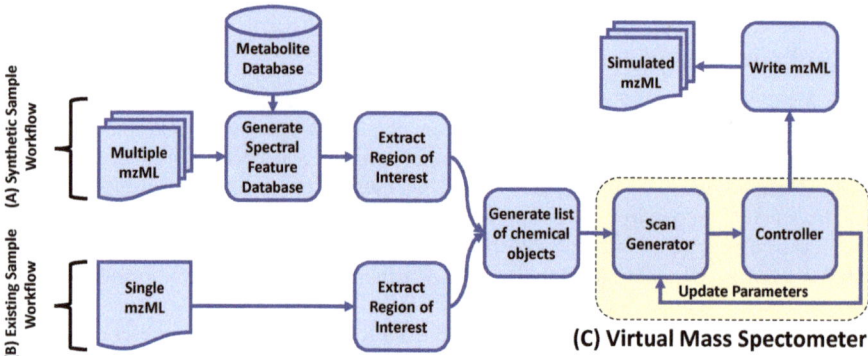

Figure 1. An overall schematic of ViMMS. (**A**) Synthetic Sample Workflow: Chemical objects in ViMMS can be created by sampling for compound formulae, mz, RT, and intensity values from the spectral feature database. (**B**) Existing Sample Workflow: alternatively, chemical objects can be created by extracting regions of interest from a single mzML file and converting them to chemical objects. (**C**) Yellow box: chemical objects are processed in the virtual mass spectrometer during in silico scan simulations. A controller performs parameter updates on the mass spectrometer depending on the fragmentation strategy implemented in the controller. Simulated results can be written as mzML files.

2.2.2. Chemical Objects

Chemical objects in ViMMS can be created in two ways—by sampling chemical formulae from a relevant database and then associating them with chromatographic peaks, or by re-running an existing analysis. In the first method, formulae are first sampled from a metabolite database such as HMDB [13] (Synthetic Sample Workflow in Figure 1). Each chemical is given a starting RT (the first RT at which they will appear when scanned) and a maximum intensity value by sampling from the spectral feature database in Section 2.2.3. Based on the spectral information they contain, the chemical objects are able to generate MS1 peaks for the relevant adducts and isotopes, with the intensity of the chemical object split between the various adduct and isotope combinations and the m/z values being calculated based on the chemical's assigned formula. Distributions over adduct intensities can be specified by the user. Finally, an ROI with a similar maximum intensity to the chemical is chosen (Section 2.2.4), and fragment peaks assigned (Section 2.2.5). It is also possible to generate multiple related samples of chemicals, whether biological or technical replicates. To do this we introduce independent Gaussian noise to the maximum intensity values and allow chemicals to be excluded from samples with a certain dropout probability.

When real data is available and the user wishes to re-run the same data under different fragmentation strategies, chemicals can also be extracted from an existing mzML file (Existing Sample Workflow in Figure 1). Here ROIs in the file are extracted and converted to chemical objects (we make the simplifying assumption that each ROI corresponds to a single unknown chemical). Unknown chemicals created in this manner will generate a single trace in the output (as opposed to multiple traces where multiple adducts and isotopes are generated.

2.2.3. Spectral Feature Database

To generate data, we create a database of spectral features extracted from actual experimental data. This database is used to sample the features associated with a chemical including the m/z, RT, and maximum intensity values of observed MS1 and MS2 peaks, as well the number of fragment peaks found for typical scans. During simulation, the database is also used by the controller to sample for the duration of each scan (Section 2.2.6). To construct this database, users provide their data in mzML format. pymzML [17] is then used to load the input mzML files, extract the necessary features and construct the database which is stored as Python pickled format. In the case of Synthetic Sample Workflow in Figure 1, the database also stores information on the small molecules extracted from an external metabolite database such as HMDB.

2.2.4. ROI Extraction and Normalization

ROIs are extracted using our Python [18] re-implementation of the ROI extraction procedure of XCMS's CentWave algorithm [19] originally available in the R programming language [20], although ROIs could have easily been extracted with alternative software such as MZmine [21]. First, spectra in an mzML file are loaded using pymzML. Then the ROI extraction algorithm loops over all scans, extracting the raw traces (recorded in centroid mode) from observed spectra. This results in a list of peak features of (m/z, RT, intensity) values. Features are first filtered to remove any that have an intensity below some user-defined threshold. The current m/z value is matched to find existing ROIs that it could fall into within a mass tolerance window, defined as the window above and below the mean m/z of the ROI. If no match exists, then this feature forms its own ROI and gets added to the list of existing ROIs. ROIs that are not added to are closed and put aside. ROIs that contain fewer data points than a user-defined threshold parameter are discarded. Finally, ROIs are normalized so their m/z values are centered around 0, RT values start at 0, and intensity values are scaled to have a maximum of 1, such that they can be assigned to chemicals.

2.2.5. MS2 Scan Generation

The MS2 scan generation process in ViMMS is modular and allows for different methods to be selected for generating and associating MS2 fragments to chemical objects. In our current implementation, two baseline methods are provided. The first is to assign m/z and intensity values to fragment peaks by randomly sampling from the spectral feature database in Section 2.2.3. This works for experiments where we can make the simplifying assumptions that fragment peaks are completely independent across scans. To reflect a more realistic scenario where groups of fragment peaks may co-occur in multiple fragmentation spectra [22], we provide a second method of assigning MS2 peaks in a fragmentation scan by following a truncated Chinese Restaurant Process (CRP) [23]. This allows for a fragment peak to have a greater likelihood to be selected again if it has been selected before in previous scans. The truncated CRP process follows the standard process of a CRP, but prevents the same MS2 peak being assigned to the same fragmentation spectra more than once. The modular nature of ViMMS means that it would be straightforward to incorporate MS2 prediction methods such as CFM-ID [24,25] or NEIMS [26].

2.2.6. Scan Time

For accurate simulation of duty cycles, we sample scan durations of MS1 and MS2 scans from the spectral feature database in Section 2.2.3. Based on the MS level of the previous scan, as well as that of the scan about to be undertaken, the time for the scan about to take place is drawn from the times of those scans in the database which represent the relevant scan transition. The only time that this is not the case is when the DsDA controller is used (Section 2.3.3) as we have a fixed timing schedule. Scan times sampled in this manner will almost always not correspond to values observed in the original files from which the ROIs were extracted. This causes some difficulty with determining the intensity and m/z values of the chemicals that would be observed at this time, as they will not have previously been observed. To overcome this, we use a simple interpolation scheme (the trapezium rule) between the two nearest scans, which gives us estimates of the intensity and m/z values that would be expected for any chemical object at the previously unobserved RT.

2.3. Controllers

ViMMS is designed to be flexible, and to achieve this aim, we separate the simulation of mass spectrometer (generating spectra from chemicals) and the fragmentation strategy (determining which precursors to fragment) in the framework. Generating spectra from chemicals is implemented inside a virtual mass spectrometer, while different fragmentation strategies are implemented as controllers. To simulate a scan, the virtual MS iterates through chemical objects that each generate MS1 or MS2 peaks depending on the current RT and the MS level requested by the controlled. The virtual MS is also responsible for broadcasting events, such as when a new scan is generated or when acquisition is started or has been finished. Controllers can subscribe to these events and act upon them, for example by directing the virtual MS to perform different scans according to the current fragmentation strategy (yellow box in Figure 1). It is relatively straightforward to implement various controllers that perform different fragmentation strategies. Each controller is designed such that it is separate from the virtual mass spectrometer, allowing controllers to interact with either the virtual MS or with an actual MS instrument through an application programming interface as a future work.

2.3.1. MS1 Controller

The MS1 controller is designed to replicate the process of generating MS1 full scans by a mass spectrometer. Given a start and end RT range, the MS1 controller steps through time and generates scans from chemicals. A scan therefore consists of m/z and intensity pairs for those chemicals that are currently eluting. The timings of the scans are determined based on experimental data by sampling from the spectral feature database, as described in Section 2.2.6. Scan results can be exported as an mzML file and viewed in standard programs such as TOPPView [27].

2.3.2. Top-N DDA Controller

The Top-N controller performs standard DDA acquisition. In each duty cycle, the controller first performs an MS1 scan to establish the most intense precursor ions, followed by up to N fragmentation scans depending on the number of precursor ions selected for further fragmentation. To generate fragmentation scans, the Top-N precursor ions (in descending order of intensities) in the initial MS1 scan are isolated and fragmented. A dynamic exclusion window (DEW) is used to prevent precursor ions that have recently been analyzed from being fragmented again. In the controller, we also provide a threshold on the minimum MS1 intensity for a precursor ion to be selected for fragmentation.

2.3.3. DsDA Controller

The DsDA [4] controller attempts to optimize fragmentation strategy over several similar samples. DsDA keeps track of which precursor ions have been fragmented in previous samples, and prioritizes those that have high MS1 intensity and have either not been fragmented, or have been fragmented producing low quality MS/MS spectra.

Implementing the full DsDA analysis pipeline in ViMMS requires the following process. First the DsDA controller, written in Python, calls the Top-N controller to perform an initial DDA analysis (for the first sample) using a fixed timing schedule. Once the initial DDA analysis is complete, the resulting mzML file is analyzed using the original DsDA scan prioritization algorithm written in R (available from https://github.com/cbroeckl/DsDA). This involves picking peaks and comparing the picked peaks to what has previously been fragmented. This information is used to determine at what m/z and RT locations new fragmentation scans should be performed. The prioritization algorithm attempts to get the highest quality MS/MS spectra for as many different precursor ions as possible. To avoid missing novel precursor ions that may not have appeared before, DsDA also includes an option called 'MaxDepth' which increases the probability of sampling rare features that the prioritization algorithm was originally designed to devalue. The resulting schedule is used for the analysis of the next sample using the Python-based DsDA controller, a process that is automatically repeated until all the samples have been analyzed.

3. Results

3.1. MS1 Simulations

To demonstrate the ability of ViMMS to simulate MS1 scans generated by chemicals from a metabolite database, we create a sample consisting of 6500 chemicals from HMDB and use the 19 full-scan experimental beer data from the *multi-beer* dataset to generate the spectral feature database (Synthetic Sample Workflow in Figure 1). The MS1 controller (Section 2.3.1) in ViMMS is used to perform a full-scan MS1 simulation. Simulation results are exported as an .mzML file and loaded into Jupyter Notebook for further analysis (all example notebooks can be found in our code repository).

Figure 2 shows examples of snapshots of full-scan chromatograms in TOPPView [27] for the actual experimental *multi-beer-1* sample (Figure 2A) and a simulated sample created in ViMMS (Figure 2B). The resulting spectra show similar characteristics to each other in terms of the shapes of the peaks and how they are observed in a full-scan samples. Individually the peaks appear at the different locations and with different profiles as a result of the simulation process, with the aim here not to directly copy the real beer sample, but create a sample with similar overall properties. A further demonstration of the similarity of the samples can be seen in boxplots of the XCMS picked peaks characteristics (RT, m/z, log intensity) shown in Figure 1 of the supplementary materials. A user could also produce similar results with alternative peak picking algorithms such as MZmine.

3.2. Top-N Simulations

We now show an example of using the Top-N controller, available from ViMMS (described in Section 2.3.2). This controller accepts as input a list of chemicals objects and performs MS2 fragmentation simulation by isolating precursor (MS1) ions and producing scans containing product (MS2) peaks. To check that our Top-N simulation processes reflect reality, we conduct an experiment where existing chromatographic peaks from the *multi-beer-1* fragmentation file are loaded into the simulator (Existing Sample Workflow in Figure 1). Top-10 DDA fragmentation is performed using the Top-N controller and the resulting output compared to the original input file. The aim here is to assess how much our simulated file differs from the actual fragmentation file given the same input ROIs and similar fragmentation parameters ($N=10$, DEW=15 s). A visual snapshot of resulting spectra in TOPPView can be found in Figure 2 of the supplementary materials and a comparison of when and where the fragmentation events occurred can be seen in Figure S3 of the Supplementary Materials.

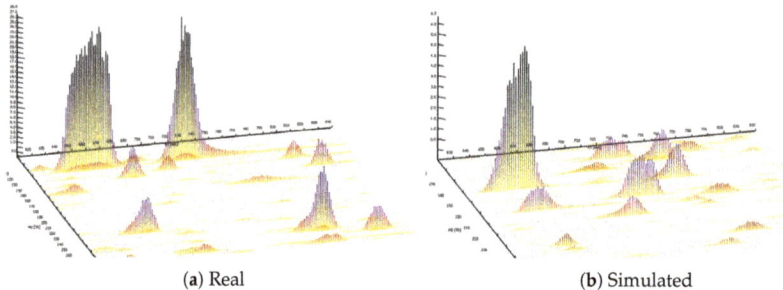

(a) Real   (b) Simulated

Figure 2. Real and simulated example outputs. (a) A region from the *beer-multibeers-1* LC/MS data. (b) A region from an LC/MS datafile generated by randomly generating peaks (mz, RT, intensity, chromatographic shape) from a database of peaks extracted from all *multi-beer* data.

Figure 3a shows the number of MS1 and MS2 scans completed over time for the true and simulated scenarios. The total number of scans is very similar in both cases, as can also be seen in Table S1 in the Supplementary Materials. Figure 3b shows that the situations in which the simulator and actual data do not match typically involve low intensity precursors. Investigating the differences between the simulation and the real data in detail, we observe what seems to be unpredictable behavior from the mass spectrometer. For example, in some cases it fragments 9 instead of 10 ions (even when other ions are present above the minimum intensity that should not be excluded due to a previous fragmentation event), and on some occasions it fragments ions despite them being below the minimum intensity threshold. These differences might be due to our handling of the data in centroid mode (and the real MS controller operating in profile mode), and there will also be a small difference due to our randomly sampled scan times. Overall, however, we are confident that the behavior of the simulator is close enough to reality and that our Top-N controller captures the most important fragmentation events and can be used for further experiments in subsequent sections.

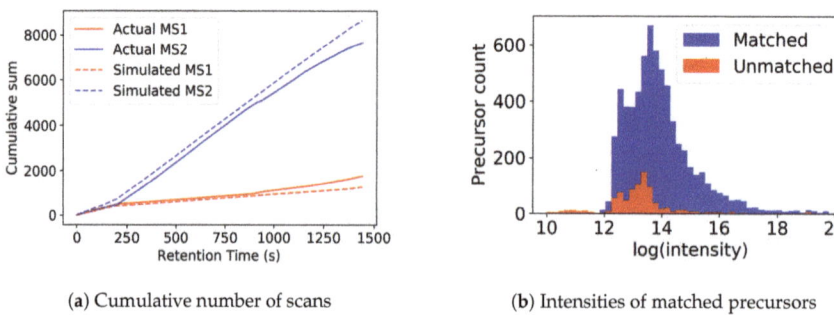

(a) Cumulative number of scans   (b) Intensities of matched precursors

Figure 3. Figures showing (a) the cumulative number of MS1 and MS2 scans over time for real and simulated data, and (b) matched precursors from the actual *multi-beer-1* data to the simulated data. Most precursors that could be matched (blue) have higher intensities than those that cannot be matched (red).

3.3. Varying N in Top-N Simulations

Choosing N in DDA is a critical part of method development. Increasing N ought to give better MS/MS coverage as more ions are fragmented. However, increasing N too far will result in many ions being fragmented below their minimum intensity threshold (even if they were above the minimum during the initial MS1 scan). In addition, larger N reduces the frequency of MS1 scans, which will have a detrimental effect on MS1 peak picking. ViMMS allows us to objectively investigate this trade-off, providing a strong evidence base for method development.

Consider a typical scenario where within an experimental batch, only Top-N DDA is performed and no full-scan data are available (an alternative scenario where both full-scan and Top-N data are acquired is also considered in Section S3 of the Supplementary Material). In this case, it is standard to use only peaks picked from the MS1 scans (which we call *MS1 features*) in the DDA fragmentation files for further analysis. As already mentioned, increasing N could result in greater fragmentation coverage since more precursor ions are fragmented but also potentially fewer MS1 features from the fragmentation file due to fewer MS1 data points available for peak picking. Evaluating the best Top-N parameter that results in an optimal trade-off between fragmentation coverage and peak picking performance can be challenging on real data, but it is possible in a simulated environment such as ViMMS.

To perform this simulated experiment, first an existing full-scan file is loaded into ViMMS. The Top-N DDA controller (Section 2.3.2) can be run with a variety of different Ns and the results evaluated. Based on these results we can choose the best N for future experiments on similar samples for that mass spectrometer. Given actual experimental full-scan MS1 files, the effect of varying N to simulated fragmentation coverage and peak picking quality can be evaluated with respect to the ground truth MS1 features found in both the full-scan and fragmentation files. For evaluation, the following definition of positive and negative instances (illustrated in Figure 4) is proposed:

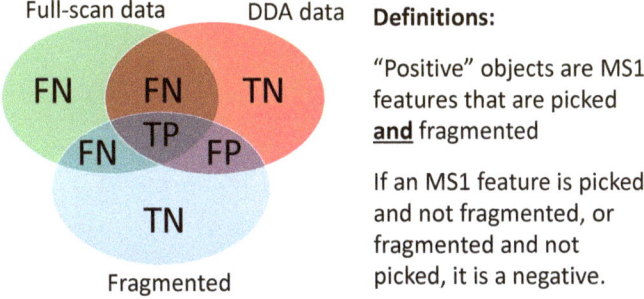

Figure 4. Definitions of True Positives (TP), False Positives (FP), True Negatives (TN) and False Negatives (FN) for performance evaluation of Top-N DDA fragmentation strategy. The blue circle in the Venn diagram refers to all MS1 features that are fragmented above the minimum MS1 intensity threshold, the green circle refers to all MS1 features found by XCMS' CentWave from the full-scan file, while the red circle refers to all MS1 features found by CentWave from the fragmentation file.

True Positives (TP): MS1 features from ground truth (found in both fragmentation and full-scan files) that are fragmented above the minimum intensity threshold.
False Positives (FP): MS1 features not from ground truth (found in fragmentation file but not in full-scan file) that are fragmented above the minimum intensity threshold.
False Negatives (FN): MS1 features not from ground truth (not found in fragmentation file but found in full-scan file) that are not fragmented or fragmented below the minimum intensity threshold.
True Negatives (TN): MS1 features not from ground truth (found in fragmentation file but not found in full-scan file) that are not fragmented or fragmented below the minimum intensity threshold.

It is worth noting that this evaluation strategy uses picked peaks as a ground truth. Peak picking is a process known to not be entirely accurate, although we believe that this represents a meaningful evaluation metric given the widespread use of peaking picking in metabolic analyses.

In our experiment, four existing Top-10 DDA files from the *multi-beer* and *multi-urine* samples are loaded into ViMMS using the Existing Sample Workflow in Figure 1. For each sample (labelled *multi-beer-1*, *multi-beer-2*, *multi-urine-1* and *multi-urine-2* respectively), DDA fragmentation is simulated using the Top-N controller in ViMMS. The parameter N for Top-N is varied in the range $N = (1, 2, 3, 4, 5, 6, 7, 8, 9, 10, 15, 20, 25, \ldots, 100)$ in the simulator, while other parameters are fixed following Section 3.2. In this experiment we also fix the dynamic exclusion window (DEW) to 15 s and the minimum MS1 intensity to fragment to 1.75×10^5 based on the actual parameters that were used to generate the data. Our results are evaluated in terms of precision, recall, numbers of peaks picked and F_1 score ($Precision = TP/(TP+FP)$, $Recall = TP/(TP+FN)$, $F_1 = (2 * Precision * Recall)/(Precision + Recall)$). To obtain the ground truth for evaluation, we performed peak picking using XCMS' CentWave on both the full-scan and simulated fragmentation files using the parameters in [14].

Using the simulator, we observe that increasing N produces an initial increase followed by a decrease in precision (Figure 5a), suggesting that with greater N, more peaks in the ground truth are being fragmented but this benefit is rapidly cancelled out by a fast increase in the number of false positives. Similarly, recall increases with N initially but decreases (Figure 5b), suggesting that with greater N, more precursor ions from ground truth MS1 features are fragmented—up to the point when all possible precursor ions above the minimum intensity threshold of 1.75×10^5 are selected. We can explain this trade-off between precision and recall due to the fact that as fragmentation coverage increases (with greater N), fewer ground truth peaks are detected from the fragmentation files (Figure 5c). The quality of MS1 chromatographic peak shapes in the fragmentation file becomes poorer since more duty cycle time is spent performing MS2 than MS1 scans, reducing the number of good-quality MS1 features that can be found by XCMS from the fragmentation files. Assessing the F_1 score (Figure 5d), which is the harmonic average of precision and recall and is representative of overall fragmentation performance, we see that the best F_1 score can be found at $N = 10$. This is the same as the actual value of N used to generate the data ($N = 10$) obtained by expert judgement. The results here demonstrate how a simulated environment such as ViMMS can be used to quantify the trade-off between fragmentation coverage and peak picking performance.

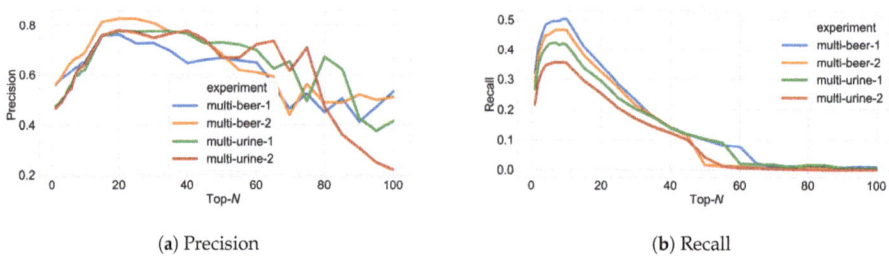

(a) Precision (b) Recall

Figure 5. *Cont.*

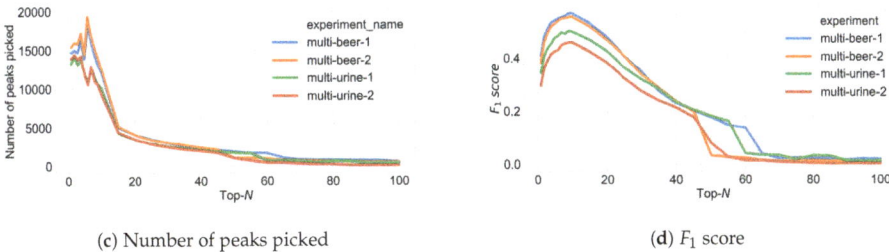

(c) Number of peaks picked (d) F_1 score

Figure 5. Figures showing (**a**) precision, (**b**) recall, (**c**) the number of peaks picked, and (**d**) F_1 score for peak picking performance as N changes in Top-N DDA experiments in ViMMS based on the classification specifications given in Figure 4.

3.4. Varying Multiple Parameters in Top-N Simulations

To validate the use of ViMMS for Top-N method development, we now show how ViMMS compares to data generated at a wide range of N and DEW times. In the previous Section 3.3 DEW is fixed to 15 s for all values of N; however our hypothesis is that the best fragmentation performance can be obtained by optimizing both parameters simultaneously. Here we evaluate the ability of ViMMS to suggest the parameter combinations that provide the best fragmentation performance and compare the results to actual experimental data.

To validate simulated results, we generated a large real dataset in which the same sample, *BeerQCB* (introduced in Section 2.1) was fragmented using all combinations of $N = (1, 2, 3, 4, 5, 10, 15, 20, 35, 50)$ and $DEW = (15, 30, 60, 120)$. The minimum MS1 intensity threshold to fragment was completely disabled for this experiment to allow a consistent number of MS scans to be acquired under the different scenarios (see Section 2.1.3). To generate simulated data in ViMMS, we extracted ROIs from a full-scan MS1 analysis of the *BeerQCB* sample using the Existing Sample Workflow in Figure 1. These ROIs were used as input to the Top-N controller using the same ranges of parameters for N and DEW as the real data. For evaluation, peak picking using XCMS was performed on the full-scan and fragmentation mzML files, and fragmentation performance was computed on both real and simulated data following Section 3.3.

Inspecting parameter combinations in the heatmaps of Figure 6 we see a high level of agreement between the performance obtained from the simulated data, and that obtained from the real measurements. Optimal performance is observed in both cases for $N = 20$ and $DEW = 30s$ although regions of high performance for both real and simulated results can be found at $N = (10, 15, 20)$ and $DEW = (15, 30, 60)$. Ranges of N that are either too large or too small demonstrate decreased performance in Figure 6a,b. Please note that the difference in optimum value in this experiment when compared with the previous one is explainable due to the use of a different MS platform (Q-Exactive orbitrap versus Fusion Tribid orbitrap).

Overall our findings demonstrate that ViMMS can be used to optimize Top-N acquisition methods in silico before actually running the experiment on a real MS instrument—something of great benefit to the community. Additional results are given in Section 4 of the supplementary materials.

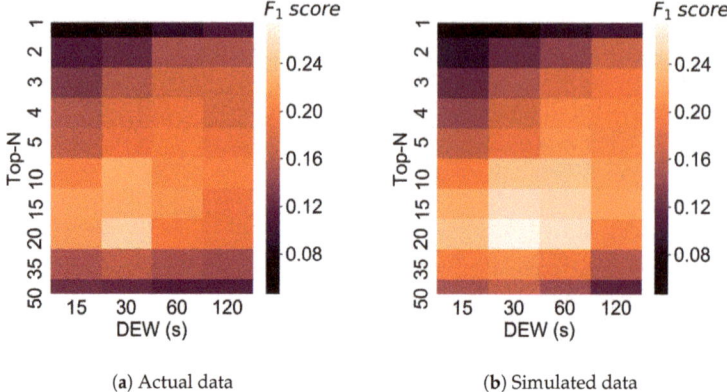

(a) Actual data (b) Simulated data

Figure 6. Fragmentation performance in terms of F_1 score for (**a**) an actual *BeerQCB* sample, (**b**) simulated results from ViMMS.

3.5. DsDA Simulations

Finally, we show how ViMMS can be used to benchmark fragmentation strategies that work on multiple samples, such as DsDA [4] (Section 2.3.3). To benchmark DsDA using ViMMS, we generate synthetic data where samples are almost identical using the Synthetic Sample Workflow in Figure 1. To do this, 6500 chemical objects are generated by sampling formulae from HMDB (the *multi-beer* data is used to construct the spectral feature database). 20 samples are created from these chemical objects by adding independent Gaussian noise (with standard deviation set to 10,000) to the maximum intensities of the chemicals in the original sample. These 20 samples will have peaks in the same RT and m/z locations but with a slight variation in how intense they are. We compare the results from DsDA, DsDA MaxDepth and Top-4 DDA fragmentation strategies ($N = 4$ was chosen as that is the default option for DsDA). Following the original DsDA study, performance is evaluated in terms of how many of the aligned peaks found by XCMS are successfully fragmented above a minimum intensity of 1.75×10^5. Our experiment shows that DsDA and DsDA MaxDepth clearly outperform Top-4 DDA strategy in terms of how many chemicals they successfully fragment (Figure 7a). This is consistent with the results from the original DsDA study.

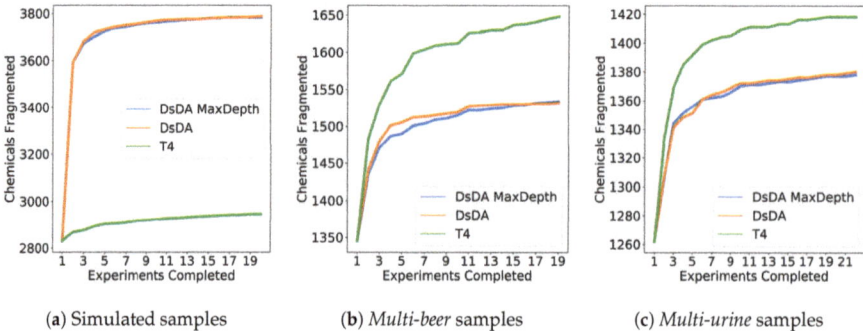

(a) Simulated samples (b) *Multi-beer* samples (c) *Multi-urine* samples

Figure 7. Top 4, DsDA and DsDA MaxDepth performance for in terms of the number of chemicals fragmented for (**a**) the simulated samples, (**b**) the *multi-beer* samples and (**c**) the *multi-urine* samples.

As a further investigation, we also compare the methods on the *multi-beer* and *multi-urine* data using the Existing Samples Workflow in Figure 1. ROIs are extracted from the full-scan mzML files of the two datasets and converted into chemical objects allowing us to virtually re-run the data under the DsDA fragmentation strategy using real chromatographic peaks. The result in Figure 7b,c shows that unlike previous results on synthetic data, here Top-4 DDA fragmentation strategy clearly gives the best performance in fragmenting the most peaks picked by XCMS, and no difference can be observed between DsDA and DsDA MaxDepth. Since DsDA prioritizes precursor peaks to fragment in a run based on previously seen runs, we explain the results here by the fact that the beer and urine samples are not similar enough for the DsDA strategy to be effective.

To confirm this, we return to our synthetic data and investigate the performance of the different methods as increasing numbers of chemicals are randomly removed from each sample. We consider scenarios where we randomly remove 0%, 5%, 10%, 15%, 20%, 25%, 30%, 35%, 40%, 45%, 50% of chemicals from each samples, meaning that on average samples will become less similar. In these samples, a given chemical object will appear in any two samples with a probability of 1, 0.90, 0.81, 0.72, 0.64, 0.56, 0.49, 0.42, 0.36, 0.30 and 0.25, respectively. In all cases, we generate 5 samples to run through the DsDA analysis. Figure 8 shows the number of chemicals fragmented above a minimum intensity of 1.75E5 after all five samples are processed by both the DsDA and Top-4 DDA fragmentation strategies in the different scenarios. The results show that DsDA performs well when the samples are similar, but as the samples becomes less similar the performance drops and DsDA is comfortably outperformed by the Top-4 DDA fragmentation strategy. Hence, as samples become more different, a Top-4 strategy should be preferred, but where samples are very similar (e.g., technical replicates), DsDA is likely to be more efficient.

Such experiments would be very challenging to do in reality. This example demonstrates how ViMMS can provide insight into the scenario in which a certain fragmentation strategy will be successful.

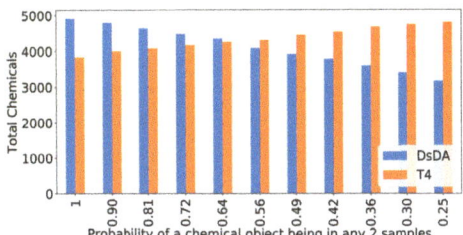

Figure 8. DsDA and Top 4 DDA performance in terms of the number of chemicals fragmented over multiple simulated datasets with varying dropout. In each scenario a percentage of chemicals are dropped from the sample (0%, 5%, 10%, 15%, 20%, 25%, 30%, 35%, 40%, 45%, 50%), meaning that on average samples will become less similar. In these samples, a given chemical object will appear in any two samples with a probability of 1, 0.90, 0.81, 0.72, 0.64, 0.56, 0.49, 0.42, 0.36, 0.30 and 0.25, respectively.

4. Discussion and Conclusions

In this paper, we introduce ViMMS, the first simulator specifically targeted at mass spectrometry fragmentation-based metabolomics that is modular, easily extensible, and can be used for the development, testing, and benchmarking of different fragmentation strategies. Processing MS2 data (particularly identifying spectra) is generally considered to be more challenging in metabolomics than in proteomics [28]. An in silico simulator such as ViMMS, which can be used to generate realistic-looking full-scan and fragmentation spectra based on either existing data or by sampling from a database of known metabolites, can be used to alleviate this problem. In this work, our experiments show how our proposed simulator can be used to help optimize acquisition methods in silico through two examples: Top-N DDA fragmentation, and DsDA. It is also important to note that our simulator could be used to create datasets on which novel data processing methods could be benchmarked.

The results from our experiments show that the spectral data generated from ViMMS have a strong resemblance to data produced from MS instruments. Our experiments with the Top-N and DsDA controllers in Sections 3.2–3.5 demonstrate that despite some minor differences in output, the proposed simulator framework can be useful in investigating, understanding and comparing the characteristics of different fragmentation strategies. Furthermore, we provide insights in when best to use Top-N and DsDA fragmentation methods; something that is not that easily and cheaply done using experimental data.

When developing acquisition methods, selecting the N that provides the highest fragmentation performance and number of detected peaks can be challenging, particularly in the typical scenario where the full-scan data is assumed to be absent and peak picking quality from fragmentation files is therefore important for subsequent analysis. We demonstrated how ViMMS can be used to suggest N for use for similar future samples on the MS instrument. Our results show how ViMMS can be used to explore parameter combinations for a particular fragmentation strategies in silico for existing data, virtually re-run existing data under an alternative strategy and benchmark existing fragmentation strategies (like DsDA) with minimal modifications under the proposed framework. This is a capability not available from other simulators [5–10]. On top of fragmentation data, ViMMS can also be used to benchmark and perform comparative evaluation of different LC-MS data processing algorithm, such as peak picking and retention time alignment [29] in a more controlled manner. In each of these cases, ViMMS also has the potential to help develop new methods by allowing them to be evaluated in a scenario where the ground truth is known, and little machine time needed.

The modular nature of ViMMS means that as future work, we can extend it with different and improved noise models and test noise reduction approaches, additional improvement to MS1/MS2 spectral data generations through incorporating fragmentation spectra prediction methods such as CFM-ID [24,25] or NEIMS [26], as well as retention time predictions from chemical structures [15]. Expanding the capabilities in ViMMS by us or others (all code is open source) in the future will further enhance its utility. The target users of ViMMS are currently algorithmic and LC-MS/MS method developers. ViMMS is available as a Python package that can be accessed from Python scripts and interactive environments such as Jupyter Notebook from where users can point to their own spectral files or compound lists to start using ViMMS on their own data. However, for end-users who are not comfortable with scripting, we aim to build an easy-to-use graphical user interface on top of ViMMS. Finally, we plan to use the proposed framework to develop and evaluate novel model-based fragmentation strategies that produces the highest coverage of MS1 and MS2 fragmentation in real time.

Supplementary Materials: A variety of additional text, tables and figures are available online at http://www.mdpi.com/2218-1989/9/10/219/s1.

Author Contributions: Conceptualization, S.R.; methodology, J.W., V.D., R.D. and S.R.; software, J.W. and V.D.; validation, J.W., V.D., J.J.J.v.d.H., S.W., R.D. and S.R.; data curation, J.J.J.v.d.H. and S.W.; writing–original draft preparation, J.W. and V.D.; writing–review and editing, J.W., V.D., J.J.J.v.d.H., S.W., R.D. and S.R.; supervision, R.D. and S.R.

Funding: EPSRC project EP/R018634/1 on 'Closed-loop data science for complex, computationally and data-intensive analytics'.

Conflicts of Interest: The authors declare no conflict of interest.

References

1. Dührkop, K.; Fleischauer, M.; Ludwig, M.; Aksenov, A.A.; Melnik, A.V.; Meusel, M.; Dorrestein, P.C.; Rousu, J.; Böcker, S. SIRIUS 4: A rapid tool for turning tandem mass spectra into metabolite structure information. *Nat. Methods* **2019**, *16*, 299. [CrossRef] [PubMed]
2. Ernst, M.; Kang, K.B.; Caraballo-Rodríguez, A.M.; Nothias, L.F.; Wandy, J.; Wang, M.; Rogers, S.; Medema, M.H.; Dorrestein, P.C.; Van Der Hooft, J.J. MolNetEnhancer: Enhanced molecular networks by integrating metabolome mining and annotation tools. *Metabolites* **2019**, *9*, 144. [CrossRef] [PubMed]
3. Kaufmann, A.; Walker, S. Nested data independent MS/MS acquisition. *Anal. Bioanal. Chem.* **2016**, *408*, 5031–5040. [CrossRef] [PubMed]

4. Broeckling, C.D.; Hoyes, E.; Richardson, K.; Brown, J.M.; Prenni, J.E. Comprehensive Tandem-Mass-Spectrometry Coverage of Complex Samples Enabled by Data-Set-Dependent Acquisition. *Anal. Chem.* **2018**, *90*, 8020–8027. [CrossRef] [PubMed]
5. Noyce, A.B.; Smith, R.; Dalgleish, J.; Taylor, R.M.; Erb, K.C.; Okuda, N.; Prince, J.T. Mspire-Simulator: LC-MS shotgun proteomic simulator for creating realistic gold standard data. *J. Proteome Res.* **2013**, *12*, 5742–5749. [CrossRef]
6. Smith, R.; Prince, J.T. JAMSS: Proteomics mass spectrometry simulation in Java. *Bioinformatics* **2014**, *31*, 791–793. [CrossRef]
7. Schulz-Trieglaff, O.; Pfeifer, N.; Gröpl, C.; Kohlbacher, O.; Reinert, K. LC-MSsim–a simulation software for liquid chromatography mass spectrometry data. *BMC Bioinform.* **2008**, *9*, 423. [CrossRef]
8. Bielow, C.; Aiche, S.; Andreotti, S.; Reinert, K. MSSimulator: Simulation of mass spectrometry data. *J. Proteome Res.* **2011**, *10*, 2922–2929. [CrossRef]
9. Awan, M.G.; Saeed, F. MaSS-Simulator: A Highly Configurable Simulator for Generating MS/MS Datasets for Benchmarking of Proteomics Algorithms. *Proteomics* **2018**, *18*, e1800206. [CrossRef]
10. Goldfarb, D.; Wang, W.; Major, M.B. MSAcquisitionSimulator: Data-dependent acquisition simulator for LC-MS shotgun proteomics. *Bioinformatics* **2015**, *32*, 1269–1271. [CrossRef]
11. Bailey, D.J.; Grosse-Coosmann, F.; Doshi, M.; Song, Q.; Canterbury, J.D.; Wan, Q.; Senko, M.W. Real-Time Instrument Control of the Orbitrap Tribrid Mass Spectrometer. 2016. Available online: http://tools.thermofisher.com/content/sfs/posters/PN-64748-Orbitrap-Tribrid-Mass-Spectrometer-ASMS2016-PN64748-EN.pdf (accessed on 8 October 2019).
12. Schweppe, D.K.; Eng, J.K.; Bailey, D.; Rad, R.; Yu, Q.; Navarrete-Perea, J.; Huttlin, E.L.; Erickson, B.K.; Paulo, J.A.; Gygi, S.P. Full-featured, real-time database searching platform enables fast and accurate multiplexed quantitative proteomics. *bioRxiv* **2019**. [CrossRef]
13. Wishart, D.S.; Feunang, Y.D.; Marcu, A.; Guo, A.C.; Liang, K.; Vázquez-Fresno, R.; Sajed, T.; Johnson, D.; Li, C.; Karu, N.; et al. HMDB 4.0: The human metabolome database for 2018. *Nucleic Acids Res.* **2017**, *46*, D608–D617. [CrossRef] [PubMed]
14. van der Hooft, J.J.J.; Wandy, J.; Young, F.; Padmanabhan, S.; Gerasimidis, K.; Burgess, K.E.V.; Barrett, M.P.; Rogers, S. Unsupervised discovery and comparison of structural families across multiple samples in untargeted metabolomics. *Anal. Chem.* **2017**, *89*, 7569–7577. [CrossRef] [PubMed]
15. Creek, D.J.; Jankevics, A.; Breitling, R.; Watson, D.G.; Barrett, M.P.; Burgess, K.E. Toward global metabolomics analysis with hydrophilic interaction liquid chromatography–mass spectrometry: Improved metabolite identification by retention time prediction. *Anal. Chem.* **2011**, *83*, 8703–8710. [CrossRef]
16. Klein, J.; Zaia, J. psims-A declarative writer for mzML and mzIdentML for Python. *Mol. Cell. Proteom.* **2019**, *18*, 571–575. [CrossRef]
17. Kösters, M.; Leufken, J.; Schulze, S.; Sugimoto, K.; Klein, J.; Zahedi, R.; Hippler, M.; Leidel, S.; Fufezan, C. pymzML v2. 0: Introducing a highly compressed and seekable gzip format. *Bioinformatics* **2018**, *34*, 2513–2514. [CrossRef]
18. Van Rossum, G.; Google, Inc. Python Programming Language. In Proceedings of the USENIX Annual Technical Conference, Santa Clara, CA, USA, 17–22 June 2007; Volume 41, p. 36.
19. Tautenhahn, R.; Boettcher, C.; Neumann, S. Highly sensitive feature detection for high resolution LC/MS. *BMC Bioinform.* **2008**, *9*, 504. [CrossRef]
20. Ihaka, R.; Gentleman, R. R: A language for data analysis and graphics. *J. Comput. Graph. Stat.* **1996**, *5*, 299–314.
21. Pluskal, T.; Castillo, S.; Villar-Briones, A.; Orešič, M. MZmine 2: Modular framework for processing, visualizing, and analyzing mass spectrometry-based molecular profile data. *BMC Bioinform.* **2010**, *11*, 395. [CrossRef]
22. van Der Hooft, J.J.J.; Wandy, J.; Barrett, M.P.; Burgess, K.E.; Rogers, S. Topic modeling for untargeted substructure exploration in metabolomics. *Proc. Natl. Acad. Sci. USA* **2016**, *113*, 13738–13743. [CrossRef]
23. Griffiths, T.L.; Jordan, M.I.; Tenenbaum, J.B.; Blei, D.M. Hierarchical topic models and the nested Chinese restaurant process. *Adv. Neural Inf. Process. Syst.* **2004**, 17–24.
24. Allen, F.; Pon, A.; Wilson, M.; Greiner, R.; Wishart, D. CFM-ID: A web server for annotation, spectrum prediction and metabolite identification from tandem mass spectra. *Nucleic Acids Res.* **2014**, *42*, W94–W99. [CrossRef] [PubMed]

25. Allen, F.; Greiner, R.; Wishart, D. Competitive fragmentation modeling of ESI-MS/MS spectra for putative metabolite identification. *Metabolomics* **2015**, *11*, 98–110. [CrossRef]
26. Wei, J.N.; Belanger, D.; Adams, R.P.; Sculley, D. Rapid Prediction of Electron–Ionization Mass Spectrometry Using Neural Networks. *ACS Cent. Sci.* **2019**, *5*, 700–708. [CrossRef] [PubMed]
27. Sturm, M.; Kohlbacher, O. TOPPView: An open-source viewer for mass spectrometry data. *J. Proteome Res.* **2009**, *8*, 3760–3763. [CrossRef]
28. Smith, R.; Mathis, A.D.; Ventura, D.; Prince, J.T. Proteomics, lipidomics, metabolomics: A mass spectrometry tutorial from a computer scientist's point of view. *BMC Bioinform.* **2014**, *15*, S9. [CrossRef]
29. Smith, R.; Ventura, D.; Prince, J.T. LC-MS alignment in theory and practice: A comprehensive algorithmic review. *Briefings Bioinform.* **2013**, *16*, 104–117. [CrossRef]

Sample Availability: The original 19 *multi-beer* data from [14] are available from GNPS MassIVE MSV000081119 (https://massive.ucsd.edu/ProteoSAFe/dataset.jsp?task=3d3801965ccb4b269a3c8547115c544b), while the original *multi-urine* data from [14] are available from GNPS MassIVE MSV000081118 (https://massive.ucsd.edu/ProteoSAFe/dataset.jsp?task=17813156319b488f9b3351c440ac8d92). The *BeerQCB* data alongside converted mzML files that can be readily used by ViMMS for the *multi-beer* and *multi-urine* data can be found at http://dx.doi.org/10.5525/gla.researchdata.870.

© 2019 by the authors. Licensee MDPI, Basel, Switzerland. This article is an open access article distributed under the terms and conditions of the Creative Commons Attribution (CC BY) license (http://creativecommons.org/licenses/by/4.0/).

Article

Annotating Nontargeted LC-HRMS/MS Data with Two Complementary Tandem Mass Spectral Libraries

Herbert Oberacher [1,*], Vera Reinstadler [1], Marco Kreidl [1], Michael A. Stravs [2], Juliane Hollender [2,3] and Emma L. Schymanski [2,4,*]

[1] Institute of Legal Medicine and Core Facility Metabolomics, Medical University of Innsbruck, 6020 Innsbruck, Austria; vera.reinstadler@i-med.ac.at (V.R.); marco.kreidl@uibk.ac.at (M.K.)
[2] Eawag, Swiss Federal Institute of Aquatic Science and Technology, 8600 Dübendorf, Switzerland; michael.stravs@eawag.ch (M.A.S.); juliane.hollender@eawag.ch (J.H.)
[3] Institute of Biogeochemistry and Pollutant Dynamics, ETH Zurich, 8092 Zurich, Switzerland
[4] Luxembourg Centre for Systems Biomedicine (LCSB), University of Luxembourg, 4367 Belvaux, Luxembourg
* Corresponding authors: herbert.oberacher@i-med.ac.at (H.O.); emma.schymanski@uni.lu (E.L.S.); Tel.: +43-512-9003-70639 (H.O.); +352-46-66-44-5612 (E.L.S.)

Received: 4 December 2018; Accepted: 21 December 2018; Published: 23 December 2018

Abstract: Tandem mass spectral databases are indispensable for fast and reliable compound identification in nontargeted analysis with liquid chromatography–high resolution tandem mass spectrometry (LC-HRMS/MS), which is applied to a wide range of scientific fields. While many articles now review and compare spectral libraries, in this manuscript we investigate two high-quality and specialized collections from our respective institutes, recorded on different instruments (quadrupole time-of-flight or QqTOF vs. Orbitrap). The optimal range of collision energies for spectral comparison was evaluated using 233 overlapping compounds between the two libraries, revealing that spectra in the range of CE 20–50 eV on the QqTOF and 30–60 nominal collision energy units on the Orbitrap provided optimal matching results for these libraries. Applications to complex samples from the respective institutes revealed that the libraries, combined with a simple data mining approach to retrieve all spectra with precursor and fragment information, could confirm many validated target identifications and yield several new Level 2a (spectral match) identifications. While the results presented are not surprising in many ways, this article adds new results to the debate on the comparability of Orbitrap and QqTOF data and the application of spectral libraries to yield rapid and high-confidence tentative identifications in complex human and environmental samples.

Keywords: nontarget analysis; liquid chromatography mass spectrometry; compound identification; tandem mass spectral library; forensics; wastewater

---

1. Introduction

Tandem mass spectral databases are indispensable for fast and reliable compound identification in nontargeted analysis with liquid chromatography–high resolution tandem mass spectrometry (LC-HRMS/MS) [1–7]. These databases have been applied in diverse fields, including forensics, environmental analysis, food analysis, and metabolomics. They are usually applied for target and suspect analysis [8–11], and enable fast and automated annotation of components [12,13]. Database searching can yield identifications at a high confidence level. According to the scheme introduced by Schymanski et al. [14], a Level 2a identification (probable structure via spectral match) can immediately be reached with sufficient match to a library spectrum. Even Level 1 (structure confirmed by a reference compound) can be achieved when the library spectrum and associated retention time (or index) match with data acquired on the same analytical set-up as in the sample. This identification scheme was designed specifically for HRMS/MS data and is applied in the current manuscript. However, in the context of this article, these levels do not differ markedly from the Metabolomics Standard Initiative levels (MSI) 1 (Identified compounds) and 2 (Putatively identified compounds based upon spectral similarity with spectral libraries) [15].

Tandem mass spectral databases consist of two integral parts: (1) the collection of tandem mass spectral data accompanied by chemical information on the corresponding compounds, and (2) a database management system with diverse search functions. Tandem mass spectra are usually produced by collision-induced dissociation (CID) or higher-energy collision dissociation (HCD). The instruments most commonly applied for the acquisition of reference spectra are quadrupole time-of-flight (QqTOF) and iontrap/quadrupole-Orbitrap. Before storage, spectra are usually curated and cleaned employing multiple steps, which can include some or all of noise and artefact removal, peak annotation and recalibration, testing and benchmarking, as well as expert reviewing [16–21].

A challenge limiting tandem spectral database development has been the variability in observed fragmentation reactions caused by limited standardization and harmonization of experimental conditions. To cope with these reproducibility issues, state-of-the-art libraries contain multiple spectra per compound [17,22–24]. This is usually accomplished by comprehensive coverage of compound-specific breakdown curves via stepwise increase of applied collision energies. Combining these libraries with appropriate tailor-made search algorithms [25–27] enables reliable and robust identification. Such databases are characterized by false positive rates and false negative rates below 5% [3].

Tandem mass spectral libraries are constantly growing. The total number of compounds covered by tandem mass spectral databases is already in the range of several tens of thousands [1,2]. However, the overlap between libraries is still relatively limited [1]. While the results of extensive testing and benchmarking experiments will provide guidance for database selection [20], as has recently been investigated for genome-wide metabolic networks [28], such data is not available for the majority of established databases in an environmental context. A further complication is the fact that databases were established on either single or multiple instruments (i.e., QqTOF and various Orbitrap hybrid instruments). There are a range of scientific opinions on whether Orbitrap databases with HCD (and sometimes CID) spectra and QqTOF databases with CID spectra offer complementary identification possibilities. Initial findings suggest that HCD MS/MS spectra yield acceptable matches in CID mass spectral databases [29]. However, a thorough evaluation of the complementarity of these two important types of tandem mass spectral databases has not been accomplished yet.

Here, we use two specialized collections to investigate the complementarity of QqTOF and Orbitrap libraries, where the Orbitrap library contains both HCD and ion trap CID spectra. First, we investigate the comparability of the spectra in the two libraries, one created on a QqTOF in a forensic-toxicological context, the other a subset of Orbitrap spectra from MassBank compiled in an environmental context. We then use both libraries for mining nontarget Orbitrap and QqTOF data. While more extensive collections are available, we have limited this investigation deliberately to these specialized collections, as both the libraries and nontarget data were generated under relatively consistent conditions at the respective institutes of the coauthors, allowing greater intuitive interpretation of the results beyond other, more extensive collections where this institutional background knowledge is missing.

2. Results and Discussion

2.1. Testing and Benchmarking of the Tandem Mass Spectral Libraries

In the first evaluation approach, the performance of the two well-established tandem mass spectral libraries was evaluated. The first collection was the "Wiley Registry of Tandem Mass Spectral Data", hereafter termed WRTMD, developed on QqTOF instruments. The second library was the Eawag collection part of MassBank, developed on Orbitrap instruments (for more details see the "Materials and Methods" section). Overall, 14,693 QqTOF spectra representing 1349 compound species (i.e., including some compounds with multiple entries due to different precursor ions such as abundant isotopes, adducts, and in-source fragments) and 7415 Orbitrap spectra representing 744 compounds were available. For the QqTOF spectra, fragmentation was accomplished by CID at various collision energies. Out of the entire set of Orbitrap spectra, 321 spectra were acquired with CID at 35 NCE (nominal collision energy units), and 7094 spectra with HCD at various collision energies.

The WRTMD collection of 14,693 CID QqTOF spectra of 1349 compounds has been investigated in multiple studies and the reliability of the search expressed as sensitivity and specificity has been demonstrated [3,16,20,24,25,27,29]. Although the database was tested with spectra acquired on all common types of tandem mass spectral instrumentation, the observed error rate was typically below 5%. This proven track record renders the WRTMD highly suitable for benchmarking experiments.

The Eawag collection of 7415 Orbitrap spectra (321 CID, 7094 HCD), representing 744 compounds, has a proven record of success in application work [8–10,30,31]. As described above, the library spectra are filtered and recalibrated [18]. This level of data curation also renders the Eawag collection suitable for quality tests. The influence of recalibration and cleanup of library spectra on database searching is shown in Table 2 of Stravs et al. [18].

Investigating the overlap of the two libraries tested revealed 233 compounds present in both collections. These 233 compounds represented 17.3% of the WRTMD (2840 QqTOF spectra) and 31.3% of the Eawag collection (2405 Orbitrap spectra).

As described in the "Materials and Methods" section, the 'MSforID Search' was used for spectral matching to obtain *amp*- and *ramp*-values. The thresholds (see "Materials and Methods") are deduced from quality tests and represent a compromise between sensitivity and specificity [20,25].

Firstly, the compatibility of the Eawag collection with the spectral matching via 'MSforID Search' was evaluated. The true positive rate obtained by matching each individual spectrum of the Eawag collection to the entire library was determined. Sensitivity (= true positive rate) was found to be 99.5%. The same test with the WRTMD yielded a sensitivity value of 99.7%. Secondly, each library was used as test set to characterize the reliability of a match to the other collection. For statistical evaluation, libraries were divided into positive and negative controls. By querying the WRTMD with the Orbitrap spectra, sensitivity was 88.0% (2405 test spectra) and specificity (= true negative rate) was 97.7% (5010 test spectra). Querying the QqTOF spectra against the Eawag collection gave a true positive rate of 91.5% (2840 test spectra) and a true negative rate of 98.0% (11,853 test spectra). The observed specificities correlated well to values observed with other test sets [3]. However, the observed sensitivities fell short of expectations. Based on previous results [29], matching Orbitrap spectra to WRTMD was expected to yield a true positive rate closer to 100%.

As a result, the impact of the collision energy on the true positive rate was investigated to determine whether this could cause the reduced sensitivity (see Figure 1). For the majority of compounds, the collision energy ranges 20–50 eV on the QqTOF and 30–60 nominal collision energy units (NCE) on the Orbitrap seem to enable the acquisition of comparable reference and sample spectra. In these cases, substantial overlap between compound-specific spectra acquired on QqTOF and Orbitrap was observed. For the spectra acquired under these conditions, sensitivity values were 95.1–98.4%. For the QqTOF spectra acquired at very low collision energies (5 and 10 eV), sensitivity values fell below 81%. Similarly, for the Orbitrap spectra acquired at collision energies above 90, sensitivity values decreased to 21–61%. The 'MSforID Search' considers the similarity of the sample spectrum to the entire series of compound-specific reference spectra, such that the outcome is not a one-to-one match with a single reference spectrum. Thus, these results of this performance evaluation study indicate that to use these two libraries in a complementary manner in nontargeted LC-MS/MS identification, optimal sensitivity will be achieved for matching to both libraries if the nontarget data is acquired with collision energies in the range of 20–50 eV on a QqTOF or 30–60 NCE on an Orbitrap instrument, which was the case for the application cases presented below.

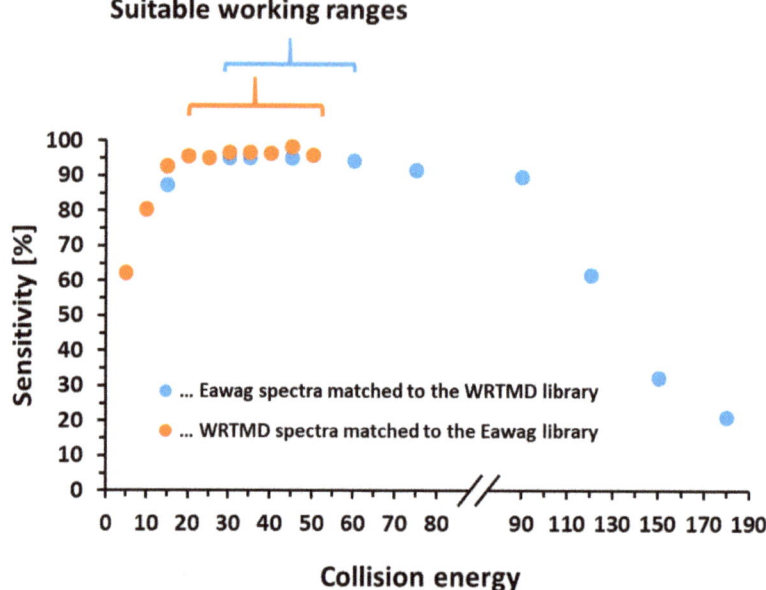

Figure 1. Evaluation of the reliability of a match in the WRTMD and the Eawag library illustrated by plots of sensitivity vs. collision energy applied during spectra acquisition.

2.2. Compound Annotation Workflow for Application Samples

As discussed above, tandem mass spectral libraries are valuable for mining nontargeted LC-MS/MS data and can rapidly yield either Level 2a (library match) or Level 1 (in-house reference standard match) identifications.

Workflows for mining nontargeted LC-MS/MS data usually involve diverse steps of feature detection, feature annotation, and compound identification. A feature detected by nontargeted LC-MS/MS is characterized by the m/z and retention time and, where available, the isotopic pattern of the precursor ion, any additional adduct species, and the corresponding fragmentation pattern. Particularly in environmental analysis and metabolomics, peak picking and extracted ion chromatograms (XICs) often play a key role in data processing. However, the data mining approach used for the plasma and wastewater sample here is different. All features containing information on the m/z of the precursor ion and the fragmentation pattern are matched directly to the tandem mass spectral library. This approach is suitable for complex data when searching using tandem mass spectral databases with high sensitivity. It also avoids the loss of matching compounds that may not have been detected by peak picking algorithms.

2.3. Application Work

2.3.1. Application 1: Systematic Toxicological Analysis of Human Plasma Samples

Forensic toxicology is an important field of application for nontargeted LC-MS/MS [3,5]. Although the WRTMD has a proven record of success in forensic toxicological analysis [3], this library does not cover the full range of compounds principally observable in human samples and should therefore be complemented by other databases. To evaluate the impact of applying multiple libraries for compound annotation, 10 human plasma samples were submitted to systematic toxicological analysis involving nontargeted LC-MS/MS with data-dependant acquisition (DDA) on a QqTOF instrument. Tandem mass spectra were acquired at 35 eV with a collision energy spread of 10 eV. This

CE is well within the working range defined above. The obtained data sets were then matched to the WRTMD and Eawag collections. False positive matches were sorted out by expert reviewing, which involved visual inspection of the spectral match.

In the 10 samples analyzed, a total number of 132 compounds were identified (Figure 2a, Supplementary Table S1). The number of identifications obtained for the individual samples ranged from 41 to 68. In each sample, a considerable number of endogenous compounds were detected. These biomolecules observed included amino acids, biogenic amines, steroids, nucleosides, and vitamins, which are only covered by WRTMD. Several nutritional compounds were observed, including caffeine, nicotine, and piperine, as well as their corresponding metabolites. A third group of observed compounds represented industrial chemicals. While some of these were also detected in the blank and thus may represent impurities and contaminants introduced after sample collection, there were nine compounds that were only observed in patient samples. These included the vulcanization accelerators 2-mercaptobenzothiazole and dibenzothiazyldisulfide, the corrosion inhibitor 2-hydroxybenzothiazole, the cosmetic ingredients ethylparabene, propylparabene, and octocrylene, the plasticiser benzyl butyl phthalate, as well as phenylurea and neocuproine. Detection of these industrial chemicals suggests that nontargeted LC-MS/MS techniques will be an important approach to detect unexpected compounds in human biomonitoring [32]. The fourth group of compounds detected were pharmaceutical compounds and corresponding metabolites. In total, 58 different species were detected. In accordance with previous findings [33], a high number of psychoactive drugs were observed, and these included 12 compounds belonging to the group of benzodiazepines and 8 to the group of opioids. Thirteen antidepressants and six antipsychotics were also identified. The last group of observed compounds represented illegal drugs and corresponding metabolites. Their detection provided evidence for cannabis consumption by four patients, cocaine consumption by six patients, and heroin consumption by one patient. There were three patient samples without any illegal drug detected. Further information about the identified compounds, including chemical identifiers, is given in the Supplementary Materials (Tables S1 and S4).

An important aspect of this study was the evaluation of the number of compounds identified with the two libraries employed in the context of forensic toxicological analysis (Figure 2b). Out of the 570 identifications obtained, 384 (67.4%) were only obtained with the WRTMD, 22 (3.9%) only with the Eawag collection, and 164 (28.8%) with both libraries tested. Obviously for forensic samples, searching the Eawag collection enables verification of a considerable number of matches to the WRTMD, but it only provided a limited number of unique matches. This observation is quite reasonable taking into account that the Eawag library was initially built for environmental applications. The 164 identifications obtained with both libraries corresponded to 39 reference compounds. All other identifications involved compounds that were only included in one of the two libraries applied (85 compounds of the WRTMD and 9 compounds of the Eawag collection).

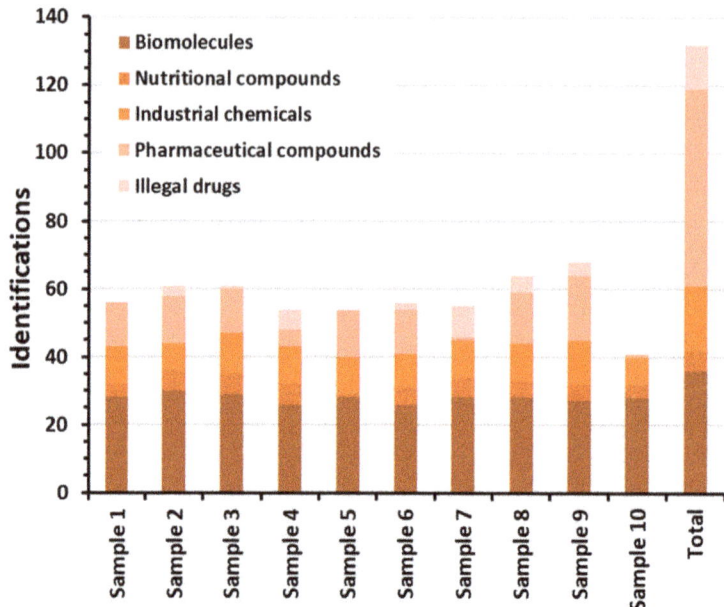

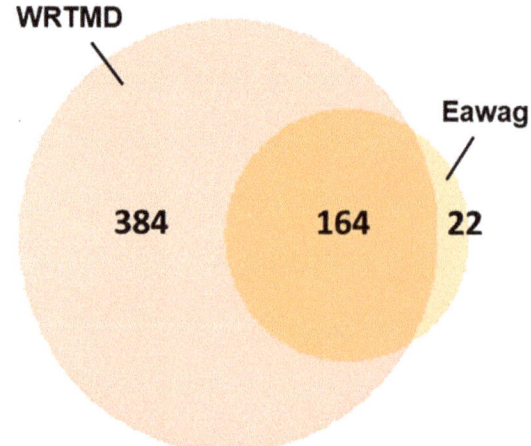

Figure 2. Application of the two tandem mass spectral libraries to systematic toxicological analysis of 10 authentic plasma samples. Nontargeted LC-MS/MS data was acquired on a QqTOF instrument using DDA. (**a**) Overview on the number of compounds identified in different compound classes via the combined use of the two libraries tested, and (**b**) the Venn diagram illustrating the number of identified compounds obtained with the two libraries tested.

2.3.2. Application 2: Comprehensive Compound Identification in Wastewater Influent Samples Collected in a Local Wastewater Treatment Plant (WWTP)

Environmental analysis is another important field of application for nontargeted LC-MS/MS workflows [8–11,30,31]. Particularly in water analysis, the Eawag collection has a proven record of success. Recently, it has been demonstrated that the WRTMD is applicable for that purpose as well [34]. To evaluate the coverage of the two libraries, samples collected at the WWTP Rossau from 1–10 April 2016, were submitted for nontargeted LC-MS/MS analysis with DDA on a QqTOF instrument. Tandem mass spectra were acquired at 35 eV with a collision energy spread of 10 eV. This CE was well within the working range defined above. The obtained data sets were matched to the WRTMD and Eawag collections. False positive matches were sorted out by expert reviewing.

In the 10 influent samples, 149 different compounds were identified (Figure 3a, Supplementary Table S2). Pharmaceutical compounds and their metabolites represented the largest group of compounds detected ($N = 96$). Diverse antipsychotics, anticonvulsants, antidepressants, hypnotics and sedatives, hypoglycaemic agents, anti-inflammatory agents, cardiovascular agents, analgesics, and antibiotics were present. Clearly, wastewater analysis yields a comprehensive overview on medical prescription and consumption practices. Other important classes of compounds observed included biomolecules ($N = 21$) and industrial chemicals ($N = 16$). The groups of nutritional compounds ($N = 8$) and illegal drugs ($N = 8$) provide some insights into lifestyle of the community monitored. It provides evidence for the consumption of caffeine and tobacco, as well as of cocaine, amphetamine, MDMA, and heroine.

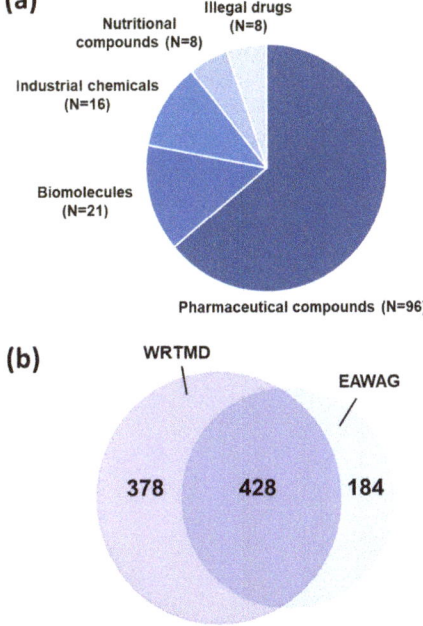

Figure 3. Application of the two tandem mass spectral libraries to the analysis of wastewater samples collected at the WWTP in Innsbruck. Ten influent samples were analyzed. The nontargeted LC-MS/MS data was acquired on a QqTOF instrument using DDA. (**a**) Overview on the number of compounds identified in different compound classes, as well as (**b**) a Venn diagram characterizing the number of identified compounds obtained with the two libraries tested are provided.

A total of 990 identifications were obtained (Figure 3b) with the two libraries. The WRTMD produced 806 identifications, and the Eawag collection 612 identifications. Of these, 378 identifications (38.2%) were solely obtained by the WRTMD, 184 identifications (18.6%) solely by the Eawag collection, and 428 identifications (43.2%) by both libraries tested. This clearly proves that the two libraries complement each other in wastewater analysis. Thus, for more comprehensive compound identification (at Level 2a), the combined use of the two libraries is recommended.

False negative rates were determined using the 449 identifications corresponding to compounds that were available in both libraries tested. The WRTMD produced 8 (1.8%), and the Eawag collection 13 false negative identifications (2.9%). In the majority of cases, the false negatives matched the corresponding reference compounds but were sorted out during data evaluation based on match probability values below the defined thresholds or during the final expert reviewing. Thus, when using stringent thresholds, the combined use of two or more libraries is recommended. The lower false negative rate for the WRTMD is most likely due to the fact that the acquisition data better matched the original library data.

2.3.3. Application 3: Retrospective Compound Identification in LC-MS/MS Data Acquired from Swiss Wastewater Effluent Samples

The third set of experimental data was selected to evaluate the compatibility of data mining workflow presented here with Orbitrap data. The test sets were obtained from analysing nine Swiss wastewater effluent samples by nontargeted LC-MS/MS with DDA [30]. Tandem mass spectra were acquired at CID 35 and HCD 60. These CE values were within the working range defined above.

In the nine samples analyzed, 82 different compounds were identified (Supplementary Table S3). These included 54 pharmaceutical compounds, 24 industrial compounds, 3 nutritional compounds, and 1 illegal drug. Identifications per sample ranged from 45 to 58, leading to a total number of 458 identifications (Figure 4). Only 7.0% of the identifications were obtained with the WRTMD, 27.5% with the Eawag collection, and 65.5% with both collections. As each institution generally develops their reference standard collection (and thus libraries) for the local conditions and studies of interest, it is not surprising that the Eawag library results in more % identifications for the Swiss data set, and the WRTMD for the Austrian data sets.

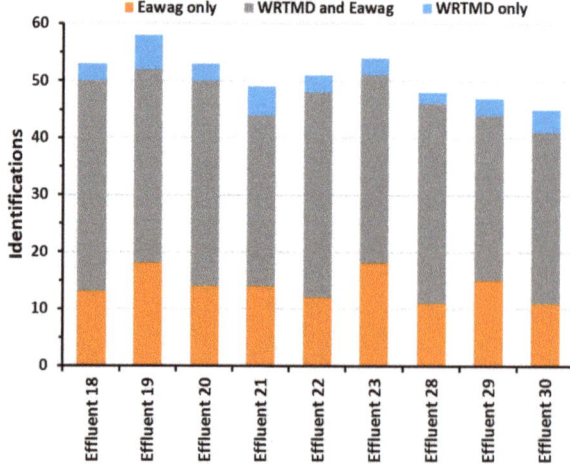

Figure 4. Application of the two tandem mass spectral libraries to the analysis of wastewater samples collected at the effluent of nine Swiss WWTP. The target and nontargeted LC-MS/MS data was acquired on an Orbitrap instrument using DDA. The column chart visualises the number of identifications obtained with the WRTMD and/or the Eawag library for each sample analyzed.

With the 492 identifications corresponding to compounds that were available in both libraries tested, false negative rates were determined. The WRTMD produced 20 (4.1%) and the Eawag collection 14 false negative identifications (2.8%). As above, in the majority of cases, negatively identified compounds matched to the corresponding reference compounds but were sorted out during data evaluation based on match probability values below the defined thresholds or during the final expert reviewing. The lower false negative rate for the Eawag collection in this case supports the conclusion above that fewer false negatives can be expected when the sample acquisition matches the library acquisition. Nonetheless, it is clear that libraries acquired on different instruments can provide valuable additional information in many cases.

As part of the initial study for this data set, a comprehensive quantitative target analysis was performed [30]. This analysis detected 73 compounds in positive mode. With the retrospective data analysis performed here, 58 of these targets were detected and identified. The identification of the remaining 15 targeted compounds was not reproduced. For six of these false negatives, the tandem mass spectral library search did not produce any evidence for their occurrence in the tested data sets (i.e., no fragmentation information was available). For the remaining eight compounds, at least one match was obtained, but in all cases, the spectral similarity was insufficient for a positive match (Figure 5). The observed discrepancies between the results obtained by target analysis and the suspect screening approach applied here can be explained by the different working principles of the two identification workflows. The suspect screening workflow relies on tandem mass spectral information for identification, such that compounds without fragments will not be detected—six compounds in this case, which were identified with retention time and exact mass and a correspondingly lower "identification point (IP) score" (2 IP vs 4.5 IP for targets with reported matching fragments) in the original study [30]. This means that some low-abundance but well-known compounds will be missed with a spectral library search approach.

The most interesting cases are those that failed due to low spectral similarity values (see Figure 5). This is perhaps not surprising when querying spectra recorded in complex samples, as impurities are likely to occur even in MS/MS fragment information obtained using DDA [12]. This indicates some potential to apply a partial cleanup such as that performed in RMassBank prior to querying spectral libraries. A simple subformula or mass defect filter based on the precursor mass will potentially eliminate several interfering peaks that may correspond with different (coeluting) precursors that are still within the DDA window. Furthermore, this problem could be exacerbated with the increasing popularity of data-independent acquisition data (without precursor isolation and thus potentially more spectral interferences), increasing the need for deconvolution [12] and alternative data-processing approaches (e.g., [35]).

Another interesting result is that the retrospective data analysis performed in this study produced 67 additional tentative identifications corresponding to 24 compounds that were in WRTMD only and thus not obtained in the original investigation (with either target, suspect, or nontarget approaches) [30]. Two of these compounds (O-desmethyltramadol and tri(butoxyethyl)phosphate) were found to be among the thirty most abundant species observed in positive ion mode LC-MS/MS analysis.

Very recently, the Swiss wastewater data sets used here were included in a proof-of-concept study that demonstrated the potential of a global emerging contaminant early warning network to rapidly assess the spatial and temporal distribution of contaminants of emerging concern in environmental samples through performing retrospective data analysis [36]. The data sets were screened for 156 compounds included in the NORMAN Early Warning System (NormaNEWS) suspect list (http://comptox.epa.gov/dashboard/chemical_lists/normanews). With the data acquired in positive ion mode, 40 compounds were tentatively identified with the NormaNEWS method. For 31 of these compounds, reference spectra were available in the WRTMD and/or the Eawag collection and thus amenable to identification with the tandem mass spectral library search approach applied here. However, out of these 31 compounds detected in the wastewater samples, only 16 were successfully matched to the libraries with the approach used here. In the remaining cases, either no (N = 12) or only low-quality tandem mass spectra (N = 3) were available in the data sets (Figure 5), rendering confident compound identification (Level 2a or better) nearly impossible. This reinforces the need for high-quality spectral searching to provide additional evidence to increase the confidence of identification in nontarget screening efforts beyond the levels achieved with exact mass and retention time matches and, where available, selected fragment masses. As discussed above and as shown in Figure 5, the issue of interferences in the spectra extracted from complex samples played a role in the poor-quality spectra in many cases and a future investigation could look into whether spectral cleanup steps may improve these results.

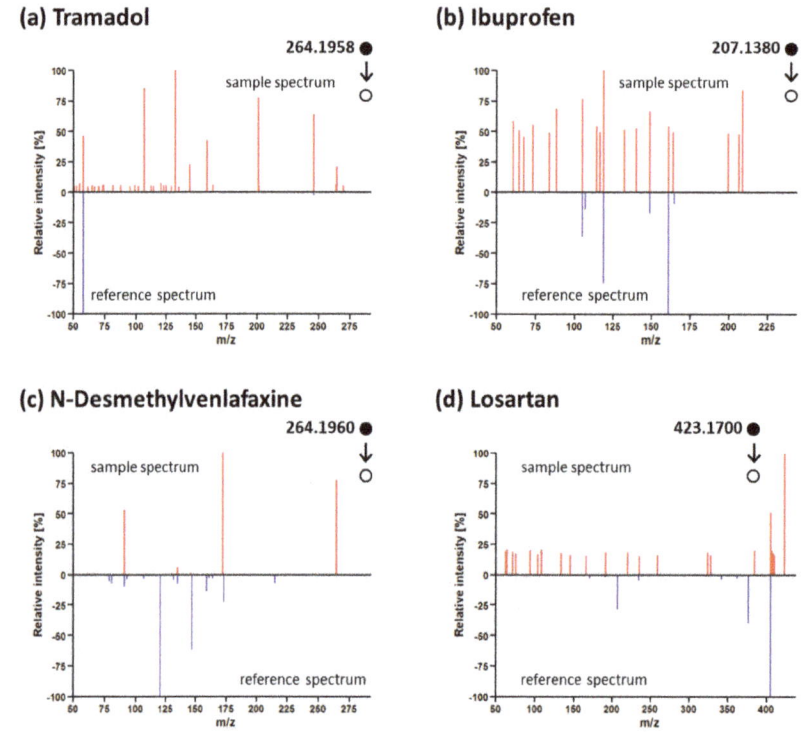

Figure 5. Examples of tandem mass spectra obtained from analysing wastewater samples with Orbitrap that showed insufficient spectral similarity to reference spectra of (**a**) tramadol (interfering peaks), (**b**) ibuprofen (noisy sample spectrum), (**c**) N-desmethylvenlafaxine (noise and/or interfering peaks), and (**d**) losartan (noisy spectrum and interfering peaks) stored in the Eawag collection. Black dots indicate precursor mass that triggered the MS/MS spectra (hollow dot).

3. Materials and Methods

3.1. Tandem Mass Spectral Libraries

Two libraries were tested: the WRTMD (Wiley, Hoboken, NJ, USA) [37] and the Eawag collection in MassBank [18,23].

Tandem mass spectral data stored in the WRTMD were acquired on QqTOF instruments (Qstar XL or TripleTOF 5600+, Sciex, Framingham, MA, USA). For each reference compound, 10 or more product-ion spectra were acquired at different collision energy levels (resolution >10,000) to comprehensively cover compound-specific breakdown curves. Low-abundance and unspecific signals were removed from reference spectra by filtering [16,17]. For this study, a library version containing

1349 entries with 14,693 spectra was used. A more detailed description of the mass spectral library is provided on www.msforid.com.

The Eawag library used for this study contained 7415 MS/MS spectra corresponding to 744 compounds. Reference spectra of 321 compounds were acquired on a LTQ-Orbitrap XL (Thermo Fisher Scientific, Waltham, MA, USA). For each of these compounds, HCD product-ion spectra were acquired at six different collision energy levels (HCD 15, 30, 45, 60, 75, 90) and a CID spectrum at one collision energy level (CID 35) to comprehensively cover compound-specific breakdown curves. The MS/MS spectra for each collision energy were recorded at two resolutions (7500 and 15,000). Reference spectra for a further 423 compounds were acquired on a QExactive Orbitrap (Thermo Fisher Scientific). For each of these reference compounds, HCD product-ion spectra were acquired at six different collision energy levels (HCD 15, 30, 45, 60, 75, 90). For a subset of 216 compounds, the collision energy range was extended to include HCD product-ion spectra at the collision energy levels 120, 150, and 180. MS/MS spectra were recorded at a resolution of 35,000. In all cases, the R package RMassBank was used to perform recalibration and cleanup of all spectra [18]. RMassBank can be downloaded from BioConductor, at http://bioconductor.org/packages/RMassBank/. The curated spectra (records published prior to 2018) are available at https://github.com/MassBank/MassBank-data/tree/master/Eawag. Listings of the chemicals available in MassBank.EU and WRTMD used in this investigation (beyond those detected and presented in the Supplementary Information) are given on the NORMAN Suspect Exchange (https://www.norman-network.com/?q=node/236) and CompTox Chemicals Dashboard (https://comptox.epa.gov/dashboard/chemical_lists).

3.2. Tandem Mass Spectral Library Search

The library search was accomplished using the 'MSforID Search' [17,25]. The search algorithm determines the similarity between a sample spectrum and library spectra. The estimation of similarity starts with the identification of fragment ions that are present in both of the spectra being compared. These ions are called "matching fragments". The spectral information retrieved is used to calculate the "reference spectrum specific match probability" (*mp*). As the mass spectral libraries contain multiple spectra per reference compound, multiple *mp* values per reference compound are obtained. To combine all these compound-specific *mp* values to one value that specifies the similarity between the unknown and the specific reference compound, the compound-specific *mp* values are averaged and normalized to yield the compound-specific "average match probability" (*amp*) and "relative average match probability" (*ramp*), respectively. These values range between 0 and 100. High compound-specific *amp* and *ramp* values indicate high similarity between the unknown and the reference compound. The substance with the highest *amp* and *ramp* value is considered to be the best match to the unknown compound.

Automated MSforID search was performed with a program written in Pascal using Delphi 6 for Windows (Borland Software Corporation, Scotts Valley, CA, USA; now Embarcadero Technologies, Inc., San Francisco, CA, USA) using the following search parameters: mass-to-charge ratio (*m/z*) tolerance of ±0.01, intensity cut-off factor of 0.01. The following criteria were used to classify obtained search results as tentatively correct positive results: precursor ion mass tolerance of ±0.01, *amp* > 1.0–10.0 and *ramp* > 30–50. The thresholds were determined using quality tests and represent a compromise between sensitivity and specificity [17,25]. The correctness of tentative identifications was checked by expert reviewing, which included visual inspection and comparison of tandem mass spectral data.

3.3. Performance Evaluation

The performance of the two libraries (WRTMD, Eawag) was evaluated using two approaches.

In the first approach, the libraries were searched against each other. Either library was used as reference or sample set. The spectra of compounds covered in both libraries served as positive controls. All other spectra represented negative controls. The positive controls were further grouped according to the collision energy settings used to acquire the individual spectra. For each test set, the number of positive identifications and the number of negative identifications were counted and used to calculate the statistical parameters sensitivity (= true positive rate) and specificity (= true negative rate).

The second evaluation approach involved the analysis of forensic casework and environmental samples. Here, the focus was on evaluating the number and type of identifications obtained with the two libraries. The first set of samples analyzed represented 10 plasma samples collected as evidence in forensic casework at the Institute of Legal Medicine of the Medical University Innsbruck. The second set consisted of wastewater samples collected on 10 consecutive days (1–10 April 2016) at the WWTP Rossau (Innsbrucker Kommunalbetriebe AG, Innsbruck, Austria). The wastewater samples represented 24-h average samples of the influent [34]. The two sample sets were submitted to nontargeted LC-MS/MS on a QqTOF instrument (TripleTOF 5600+, Sciex, Framingham, MA, USA). Details of the analytical workflows employed are provided in the Electronic Supplementary File 1. The third set of samples consisted of nine Swiss WWTP effluent samples that had been analyzed by target and nontargeted LC-MS/MS on an Orbitrap instrument (LTQ Orbitrap XL, Thermo Fisher Scientific, Waltham, MA, USA). Details of the analytical workflow have been published previously [30]. Raw data files for the Swiss study are available at ftp://massive.ucsd.edu/MSV000079601. The remaining files cannot be uploaded for legal reasons, but can be made available to interested researchers upon request.

Data mining involved the extraction of the tandem mass spectra and a subsequent database search. Raw data files were converted to Mascot Generic Format (.mgf) files with the MSConvert from ProteoWizard [38]. The MS/MS spectra part of the .mgf files were extracted with a program written in ActivePerl 5.6.1 (Active State Corporation, Vancouver, Canada) to yield all MS/MS spectra as plain text (ASCII) files containing peak list information. These spectra were then submitted to the tandem mass spectral library search as described above.

4. Conclusions

This article demonstrates the applicability of tandem mass spectral library searching to complex environmental and toxicological samples and reveals a wide range of comparability between collision energies of different tandem mass spectral instruments over a diverse range of compounds. For complementary use of the two libraries tested, the collision energy ranges 20–50 eV on the QqTOF and 30–60 NCE on the Orbitrap represented suitable working ranges. The results of the applications are in many ways unsurprising, that is, that searching in two libraries instead of one reveals more hits and that entries without fragmentation or with poor fragmentation information are not found. However, this article documents additional investigations to add to the debate on the comparability between QqTOF and Orbitrap instruments. This comparability is of utmost importance to achieve the desired goal of developing a unified and universally applicable tandem mass spectral database. Library development is laborious, time-consuming, and expensive, and this enormous effort is a serious hurdle for individual and isolated labs interested in contributing to accomplishing this mammoth task. Compatibility of libraries will enable the building of strong and dynamic consortia within scientific communities that will significantly increase the number of available reference spectra by sharing the connected workload. Further conclusions from this work are that the data mining approach used here could possibly be improved in the future through the application of some basic spectral cleanup to remove clear matrix interferences as well as the consideration of additional information such as isotope patterns/adduct and retention behavior.

Supplementary Materials: The following are available online at http://www.mdpi.com/2218-1989/9/1/3/s1. Supplementary File 1: Experimental settings for nontargeted LC-MSMS analysis with QqTOF; Supplementary File 2: Excel spreadsheet containing the following tables: Supplementary Table S1: Overview of compounds identified by systematic toxicological analysis of ten authentic plasma samples; Supplementary Table S2: Overview of compounds identified by nontargeted LC-MS/MS in ten wastewater samples collected at the influent of the WWTP in Innsbruck; Supplementary Table S3: Overview of compounds identified by target and nontargeted LC-MS/MS in nine wastewater samples collected at the effluent of Swiss WWTPs; Supplementary Table S4: Additional chemical information for all compounds mentioned in Table S1 to S3.

Author Contributions: Conceptualization, H.O. and E.L.S.; Data curation, H.O., V.R., M.K., M.A.S., and E.L.S.; Formal analysis, H.O., V.R., M.K., M.A.S., and E.L.S.; Funding acquisition, H.O. and J.H.; Investigation, H.O. and E.L.S.; Methodology, H.O., V.R., M.K., M.A.S., and E.L.S.; Project administration, H.O. and J.H.; Resources, H.O.; Software, H.O., M.A.S., and E.L.S.; Supervision, H.O. and J.H.; Validation, H.O., V.R., M.K., and E.L.S.; Visualization, H.O.; Writing—original draft, H.O. and E.L.S.; Writing—review & editing, H.O., V.R., M.K., M.A.S., J.H., and E.L.S.

Funding: H.O. acknowledges financial support by the HBM4EU project. HBM4EU has received funding from the European Union's Horizon 2020 research and innovation programme under grant agreement No 733032. E.L.S. acknowledges funding from the Luxembourg National Research Fund (FNR) for project 12341006. J.H., and E.L.S. were supported by the European Union Seventh Framework Program project SOLUTIONS under grant agreement number 603437, J.H. and M.A.S. by the Swiss Federal Office for the Environment and by the Swiss National Science Foundation under grant number 205320165935.

Acknowledgments: The authors thank Klemens Geiger and Michael Schlapp (Innsbrucker Kommunalbetriebe, Innsbruck, Austria) for providing wastewater samples. The authors gratefully acknowledge colleagues at the Uchem department involved in the Swiss Wastewater study and in acquiring the MassBank spectra, as well as Antony J. Williams (US EPA) for his efforts in mapping WRTMD and MassBank compounds to the CompTox Chemicals Dashboard.

Conflicts of Interest: The authors declare that they have no conflict of interest.

References

1. Vinaixa, M.; Schymanski, E.L.; Neumann, S.; Navarro, M.; Salek, R.M.; Yanes, O. Mass spectral databases for LC/MS- and GC/MS-based metabolomics: State of the field and future prospects. *TrAC-Trend. Anal. Chem.* **2016**, *78*, 23–35. [CrossRef]
2. Kind, T.; Tsugawa, H.; Cajka, T.; Ma, Y.; Lai, Z.J.; Mehta, S.S.; Wohlgemuth, G.; Barupal, D.K.; Showalter, M.R.; Arita, M.; et al. Identification of small molecules using accurate mass MS/MS search. *Mass Spectrom. Rev.* **2018**, *37*, 513–532. [CrossRef] [PubMed]
3. Oberacher, H.; Arnhard, K. Current status of non-targeted liquid chromatography-tandem mass spectrometry in forensic toxicology. *TrAC-Trend. Anal. Chem.* **2016**, *84*, 94–105. [CrossRef]
4. Blazenovic, I.; Kind, T.; Ji, J.; Fiehn, O. Software tools and approaches for compound identification of LC-MS/MS data in metabolomics. *Metabolites* **2018**, *8*, 31. [CrossRef] [PubMed]
5. Oberacher, H.; Arnhard, K. Compound identification in forensic toxicological analysis with untargeted LC-MS-based techniques. *Bioanalysis* **2015**, *7*, 2825–2840. [CrossRef] [PubMed]
6. Milman, B.L.; Zhurkovich, I.K. Mass spectral libraries: A statistical review of the visible use. *TrAC-Trend. Anal. Chem.* **2016**, *80*, 636–640. [CrossRef]
7. Stein, S. Mass spectral reference libraries: An ever-expanding resource for chemical identification. *Anal. Chem.* **2012**, *84*, 7274–7282. [CrossRef]
8. Krauss, M.; Singer, H.; Hollender, J. LC-high resolution MS in environmental analysis: From target screening to the identification of unknowns. *Anal. Bioanal. Chem.* **2010**, *397*, 943–951. [CrossRef]
9. Chiaia-Hernandez, A.C.; Schymanski, E.L.; Kumar, P.; Singer, H.P.; Hollender, J. Suspect and nontarget screening approaches to identify organic contaminant records in lake sediments. *Anal. Bioanal. Chem.* **2014**, *406*, 7323–7335. [CrossRef]
10. Gago-Ferrero, P.; Schymanski, E.L.; Bletsou, A.A.; Aalizadeh, R.; Hollender, J.; Thomaidis, N.S. Extended suspect and non-target strategies to characterize emerging polar organic contaminants in raw wastewater with LC-HRMS/MS. *Environ. Sci. Technol.* **2015**, *49*, 12333–12341. [CrossRef]
11. Zedda, M.; Zwiener, C. Is nontarget screening of emerging contaminants by LC-HRMS successful? A plea for compound libraries and computer tools. *Anal. Bioanal. Chem.* **2012**, *403*, 2493–2502. [CrossRef] [PubMed]
12. Arnhard, K.; Gottschall, A.; Pitterl, F.; Oberacher, H. Applying 'Sequential Windowed Acquisition of all Theoretical Fragment Ion Mass Spectra' (SWATH) for systematic toxicological analysis with liquid chromatography-high-resolution tandem mass spectrometry. *Anal. Bioanal. Chem.* **2015**, *407*, 405–414. [CrossRef] [PubMed]
13. Oberacher, H.; Schubert, B.; Libiseller, K.; Schweissgut, A. Detection and identification of drugs and toxicants in human body fluids by liquid chromatography-tandem mass spectrometry under data-dependent acquisition control and automated database search. *Anal. Chim. Acta* **2013**, *770*, 121–131. [CrossRef] [PubMed]

14. Schymanski, E.L.; Jeon, J.; Gulde, R.; Fenner, K.; Ruff, M.; Singer, H.P.; Hollender, J. Identifying small molecules via high resolution mass spectrometry: Communicating confidence. *Environ. Sci. Technol.* **2014**, *48*, 2097–2098. [CrossRef] [PubMed]
15. Sumner, L.W.; Amberg, A.; Barrett, D.; Beale, M.H.; Beger, R.; Daykin, C.A.; Fan, T.W.; Fiehn, O.; Goodacre, R.; Griffin, J.L.; et al. Proposed minimum reporting standards for chemical analysis: Chemical Analysis Working Group (CAWG) Metabolomics Standards Initiative (MSI). *Metabolomics* **2007**, *3*, 211–221. [CrossRef] [PubMed]
16. Oberacher, H.; Pavlic, M.; Libiseller, K.; Schubert, B.; Sulyok, M.; Schuhmacher, R.; Csaszar, E.; Kofeler, H.C. On the inter-instrument and inter-laboratory transferability of a tandem mass spectral reference library: 1. Results of an Austrian multicenter study. *J. Mass Spectrom.* **2009**, *44*, 485–493. [CrossRef]
17. Pavlic, M.; Libiseller, K.; Oberacher, H. Combined use of ESI-QqTOF-MS and ESI-QqTOF-MS/MS with mass-spectral library search for qualitative analysis of drugs. *Anal. Bioanal. Chem.* **2006**, *386*, 69–82. [CrossRef]
18. Stravs, M.A.; Schymanski, E.L.; Singer, H.P.; Hollender, J. Automatic recalibration and processing of tandem mass spectra using formula annotation. *J. Mass Spectrom.* **2013**, *48*, 89–99. [CrossRef]
19. Yang, X.Y.; Neta, P.; Stein, S.E. Quality control for building libraries from electrospray ionization tandem mass spectra. *Anal. Chem.* **2014**, *86*, 6393–6400. [CrossRef]
20. Oberacher, H.; Weinmann, W.; Dresen, S. Quality evaluation of tandem mass spectral libraries. *Anal. Bioanal. Chem.* **2011**, *400*, 2641–2648. [CrossRef]
21. Shahaf, N.; Rogachev, I.; Heinig, U.; Meir, S.; Malitsky, S.; Battat, M.; Wyner, H.; Zheng, S.N.; Wehrens, R.; Aharoni, A. The WEIZMASS spectral library for high-confidence metabolite identification. *Nat. Commun.* **2016**, *7*, 12423. [CrossRef] [PubMed]
22. Smith, C.A.; O'Maille, G.; Want, E.J.; Qin, C.; Trauger, S.A.; Brandon, T.R.; Custodio, D.E.; Abagyan, R.; Siuzdak, G. Metlin: A metabolite mass spectral database. *Ther. Drug. Monit.* **2005**, *27*, 747–751. [CrossRef] [PubMed]
23. Horai, H.; Arita, M.; Kanaya, S.; Nihei, Y.; Ikeda, T.; Suwa, K.; Ojima, Y.; Tanaka, K.; Tanaka, S.; Aoshima, K.; et al. Massbank: A public repository for sharing mass spectral data for life sciences. *J. Mass Spectrom.* **2010**, *45*, 703–714. [CrossRef] [PubMed]
24. Oberacher, H.; Whitley, G.; Berger, B. Evaluation of the sensitivity of the 'Wiley Registry of Tandem Mass Spectral Data, MSforID' with MS/MS data of the 'NIST/NIH/EPA mass spectral library'. *J. Mass Spectrom.* **2013**, *48*, 487–496. [CrossRef]
25. Oberacher, H.; Pavlic, M.; Libiseller, K.; Schubert, B.; Sulyok, M.; Schuhmacher, R.; Csaszar, E.; Kofeler, H.C. On the inter-instrument and the inter-laboratory transferability of a tandem mass spectral reference library: 2. Optimization and characterization of the search algorithm. *J. Mass Spectrom.* **2009**, *44*, 494–502. [CrossRef] [PubMed]
26. Mylonas, R.; Mauron, Y.; Masselot, A.; Binz, P.A.; Budin, N.; Fathi, M.; Viette, V.; Hochstrasser, D.F.; Lisacek, F. X-Rank: A robust algorithm for small molecule identification using tandem mass spectrometry. *Anal. Chem.* **2009**, *81*, 7604–7610. [CrossRef]
27. Oberacher, H.; Whitley, G.; Berger, B.; Weinmann, W. Testing an alternative search algorithm for compound identification with the 'Wiley Registry of Tandem Mass Spectral Data, MSforID'. *J. Mass Spectrom.* **2013**, *48*, 497–504. [CrossRef]
28. Frainay, C.; Schymanski, E.L.; Neumann, S.; Merlet, B.; Salek, R.M.; Jourdan, F.; Yanes, O. Mind the gap: Mapping mass spectral databases in genome-scale metabolic networks reveals poorly covered areas. *Metabolites* **2018**, *8*, 51. [CrossRef]
29. Oberacher, H.; Pitterl, F.; Siapi, E.; Steele, B.R.; Letzel, T.; Grosse, S.; Poschner, B.; Tagliaro, F.; Gottardo, R.; Chacko, S.A.; et al. On the inter-instrument and the inter-laboratory transferability of a tandem mass spectral reference library. 3. Focus on ion trap and upfront CID. *J. Mass Spectrom.* **2012**, *47*, 263–270. [CrossRef]
30. Schymanski, E.L.; Singer, H.P.; Longree, P.; Loos, M.; Ruff, M.; Stravs, M.A.; Vidal, C.R.; Hollender, J. Strategies to characterize polar organic contamination in wastewater: Exploring the capability of high resolution mass spectrometry. *Environ. Sci. Technol.* **2014**, *48*, 1811–1818. [CrossRef]
31. Schymanski, E.L.; Singer, H.P.; Slobodnik, J.; Ipolyi, I.M.; Oswald, P.; Krauss, M.; Schulze, T.; Haglund, P.; Letzel, T.; Grosse, S.; et al. Non-target screening with high-resolution mass spectrometry: Critical review using a collaborative trial on water analysis. *Anal. Bioanal. Chem.* **2015**, *407*, 6237–6255. [CrossRef] [PubMed]

32. Andra, S.S.; Austin, C.; Patel, D.; Dolios, G.; Awawda, M.; Arora, M. Trends in the application of high-resolution mass spectrometry for human biomonitoring: An analytical primer to studying the environmental chemical space of the human exposome. *Environ. Int.* **2017**, *100*, 32–61. [CrossRef] [PubMed]
33. Pitterl, F.; Kob, S.; Pitterle, J.; Steger, J.; Oberacher, H. Applying LC with low resolution MS/MS and subsequent library search for reliable compound identification in systematic toxicological analysis. *LC GC Eur.* **2016**, *29*, 419–427.
34. Steger, J.; Arnhard, K.; Haslacher, S.; Geiger, K.; Singer, K.; Schlapp, M.; Pitterl, F.; Oberacher, H. Successful adaption of a forensic toxicological screening workflow employing nontargeted liquid chromatography-tandem mass spectrometry to water analysis. *Electrophoresis* **2016**, *37*, 1085–1094. [CrossRef] [PubMed]
35. Li, H.; Cai, Y.; Guo, Y.; Chen, F.; Zhu, Z.-J. MetDIA: Targeted metabolite extraction of multiplexed MS/MS spectra generated by data-independent acquisition. *Anal. Chem.* **2016**, *88*, 8757–8764. [CrossRef] [PubMed]
36. Alygizakis, N.A.; Samanipour, S.; Hollender, J.; Ibanez, M.; Kaserzon, S.; Kokkali, V.; van Leerdam, J.A.; Mueller, J.F.; Pijnappels, M.; Reid, M.J.; et al. Exploring the potential of a global emerging contaminant early warning network through the use of retrospective suspect screening with high-resolution mass spectrometry. *Environ. Sci. Technol.* **2018**, *52*, 5135–5144. [CrossRef] [PubMed]
37. Oberacher, H. *The Wiley Registry of Tandem Mass Spectral Data, MSforID*, 1st ed.; John Wiley & Sons: Hoboken, NJ, USA, 2012; ISBN 978-1-118-03744-7.
38. Kessner, D.; Chambers, M.; Burke, R.; Agusand, D.; Mallick, P. ProteoWizard: Open source software for rapid proteomics tools development. *Bioinformatics* **2008**, *24*, 2534–2536. [CrossRef] [PubMed]

© 2018 by the authors. Licensee MDPI, Basel, Switzerland. This article is an open access article distributed under the terms and conditions of the Creative Commons Attribution (CC BY) license (http://creativecommons.org/licenses/by/4.0/).

Article

Mind the Gap: Mapping Mass Spectral Databases in Genome-Scale Metabolic Networks Reveals Poorly Covered Areas

Clément Frainay [1], Emma L. Schymanski [2,3], Steffen Neumann [4,5], Benjamin Merlet [1], Reza M. Salek [6], Fabien Jourdan [1,*] and Oscar Yanes [7,8,*]

1. Toxalim (Research Centre in Food Toxicology), Université de Toulouse, INRA, ENVT, INP-Purpan, UPS, 31555 Toulouse, France; Clement.Frainay@inra.fr (C.F.); Benjamin.Merlet@inra.fr (B.M.)
2. Eawag: Swiss Federal Institute for Aquatic Science and Technology, Überlandstrasse 133, 8600 Dübendorf, Switzerland; emma.schymanski@uni.lu
3. Luxembourg Centre for Systems Biomedicine (LCSB), University of Luxembourg, 7, avenue des Hauts-Fourneaux, L-4362 Esch-sur-Alzette, Luxembourg
4. Leibniz Institute of Plant Biochemistry, Department of Stress and Developmental Biology, Weinberg 3, 06120 Halle, Germany; Sneumann@ipb-halle.de
5. German Centre for Integrative Biodiversity Research (iDiv), Halle-Jena-Leipzig Deutscher Platz 5e, 04103 Leipzig, Germany
6. The International Agency for Research on Cancer (IARC), 150 Cours Albert Thomas, 69372 Lyon CEDEX 08, France; SalekR@iarc.fr
7. Metabolomics Platform, IISPV, Department of Electronic Engineering, Universitat Rovira i Virgili, Avinguda Paisos Catalans 26, 43007 Tarragona, Spain
8. Spanish Biomedical Research Center in Diabetes and Associated Metabolic Disorders (CIBERDEM), Monforte de Lemos 3-5, 28029 Madrid, Spain
* Correspondence: Fabien.Jourdan@inra.fr (F.J.); oscar.yanes@urv.cat (O.Y.); Tel.: +33-582-066-395 (F.J.); +34-977-776-617 (O.Y.)

Received: 18 July 2018; Accepted: 7 September 2018; Published: 15 September 2018

Abstract: The use of mass spectrometry-based metabolomics to study human, plant and microbial biochemistry and their interactions with the environment largely depends on the ability to annotate metabolite structures by matching mass spectral features of the measured metabolites to curated spectra of reference standards. While reference databases for metabolomics now provide information for hundreds of thousands of compounds, barely 5% of these known small molecules have experimental data from pure standards. Remarkably, it is still unknown how well existing mass spectral libraries cover the biochemical landscape of prokaryotic and eukaryotic organisms. To address this issue, we have investigated the coverage of 38 genome-scale metabolic networks by public and commercial mass spectral databases, and found that on average only 40% of nodes in metabolic networks could be mapped by mass spectral information from standards. Next, we deciphered computationally which parts of the human metabolic network are poorly covered by mass spectral libraries, revealing gaps in the eicosanoids, vitamins and bile acid metabolism. Finally, our network topology analysis based on the betweenness centrality of metabolites revealed the top 20 most important metabolites that, if added to MS databases, may facilitate human metabolome characterization in the future.

Keywords: metabolic networks; mass spectral libraries; metabolite annotation; metabolomics data mapping

1. Introduction

Metabolomics, or the comprehensive characterization and quantification of metabolites, complements upstream biochemical information obtained from genes, transcripts, and proteins, widening current genomic reconstructions of metabolism and improving our understanding of biological and environmental processes [1]. Metabolomics is thus finding applications that span almost the full width of natural sciences, ranging from human [2,3], plant [4] and microbial biochemistry [5–7] to organism-environment interactions [8,9]. Despite the high research interest, identifying and characterizing the structure of metabolites has become a major obstacle for converting raw mass spectrometry (MS) data into biological knowledge. In this regard, open and commercial MS-based databases play an important role in identifying and characterizing the structure of metabolites by matching mass spectral features of the measured metabolites to curated spectra of reference standards [10]. Despite attempts to increase and improve the content of mass spectral databases in recent years, these are still far from containing experimental data of the known compounds. For instance, the widely used METLIN database [11] and the Human Metabolome Database (HMDB version 4.0) [12] now provide links and information for >900,000 and >110,000 compounds, respectively. However, barely 5% of these known small molecules have experimental spectral data from pure standards [13]. Equally important, the biochemical roles and metabolic activity of such small percentage of known and chemically well characterized metabolites is still lacking. Many compounds in mass spectral databases are exogenous drugs or chemical structures that are mainly laboratory based. Hence, it is important to elucidate how many and which compounds in mass spectral databases are involved in metabolic transformations encoded by the genome of prokaryotic and eukaryotic cells. Answering this question is central to investigate and improve the biochemical landscape of metabolomics databases, and assess their usability for reconstructing comprehensive mechanistic scenarios in cell metabolism.

Here, we use genome-based reconstructions of metabolism, also called genome-scale metabolic networks [14,15], to investigate their coverage by existing mass spectral libraries. Genome-scale metabolic networks are manually curated models that best describe our understanding of the metabolic processes occurring in an organism, acting as an indispensable tool to gain biological insight from metabolomic data. Genome-scale metabolic networks enable in-depth mechanistic interpretation through metabolic flux simulation and network analysis.

By analysing the coverage of metabolic networks, we have computationally deciphered which parts of the human metabolic network are poorly covered by mass spectral libraries and have identified metabolite gaps that, if added to MS databases, may enhance human metabolome characterization in the future, and consequently, provide a better understanding of cell metabolism.

2. Material and Methods

2.1. Chemical Library

Only compounds with measured mass spectra were used. *In silico* predicted MS/MS spectra available in certain public databases [12] were not considered in our study. A merged list of InChIKeys was initially created from public and commercial datasets published by Vinaixa et al. 2016 [13]. This list was further updated with new entries and resources [16,17] yielding: 9419 InChIKeys of compounds from the METLIN database [18] provided by Agilent Technologies; 399 InChIKeys from ReSpect [19]; 1171 InChIKeys from the Wiley MS for ID database provided by Herbert Oberacher; 3401 InChIKeys from the GNPS [20]; 11,009 InChIKeys from MassBank [21]; 3480 InChIKeys from mzCloud provided by Robert Mistrik (21 June 2016); 1034 InChIKeys from the HMDB [12] (downloaded on 21 June 2016); and 242,463 InChIKeys from NIST 14 provided by Stephen Stein and Dmitrii Tchekhovskoi. These InChIKey lists (which often contained duplicated entries) were merged for a total of 261,330 non-redundant InChIKey, containing 253,927 non-redundant InChIKey first-block.

The InChIKey mapping was performed using the first block of the string, thus not taking into account charge or stereochemistry.

2.2. Human Metabolic Network and Graph Construction

Recon2 [22] was used to map our chemical library of 253,927 non-redundant first block InChIKeys [23]. The original Recon 2 network provided 968 InChIKeys, which was supplemented with additional InChIKeys from other compound identifiers in Recon2, using a combination of web services from PubChem [24], HMDB [25] and ChEBI [26] and home-made parsers (Supplementary File 1). We removed generic compounds (e.g., substrates denoting a set of possible compounds, often by using R-groups, such as an alcohol or sugar) with no proper structure or InChI, and peptides or other macro molecules that are too big to have their structure represented by a single string. We also discarded compounds without any external database reference, as the lack thereof prevents the retrieval of molecular descriptors through the aforementioned web services. Redundancy caused by compounds present in several compartments was avoided by merging all compartments into one single cell-scale model. We created a metabolite network (Compound graph, see Figure 1) where two metabolites are connected if there is at least one reaction producing one and consuming the other, with at least one carbon atom shared between the two metabolites. This allows not taking into account spurious connections involving side compounds like water. Inorganic carbonated compounds, such as CO_2, were manually removed to complete this task. Some small sub-networks were disconnected from the rest of the network due to missing InChIs or incomplete annotations in Recon2 (network is provided in GML (Graph Modelling Language) format in Supplementary file 2).

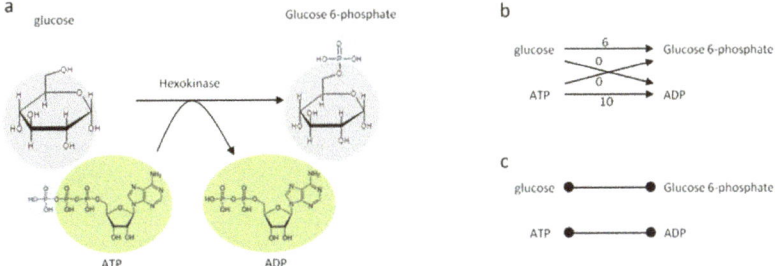

Figure 1. Graph reconstruction process. (a) Hexokinase reaction as described in the Recon2 database. Colored circles provide information on shared substructures between substrates and products. (b) Compound graph: each substrate is connected to each product of the reaction. Edges are weighted by the number of carbon atoms shared between each substrate to each product. (c) Final graph: transitions that do not involve the preservation of at least one carbon atom between the source and the target were removed.

2.3. Network Topology Analysis

After the creation of the undirected compound graph, we identified parts of the network that were less covered by mass spectral libraries. For this, we used the Label Propagation Algorithm (LPA) [27], which aims at finding communities within a network. The nodes in the network initially carry a label that denotes the two communities they belong to: the "well covered" (mapped metabolites in the chemical library) or the "poorly covered" (unmapped metabolites in the chemical library). The algorithm then diffuses the labels throughout the network by changing membership in both communities based on the labels that the neighbouring nodes (i.e., metabolites) possess. This process is applied to a network where the direction of metabolic reactions is not considered. In a biochemical context, this means that if a mapped metabolite is mostly surrounded by unmapped metabolites, the LPA will switch this metabolite from a 'well covered' to a 'poorly covered' community. The reasons for it being that measuring such metabolite will likely provide little biochemical information.

In contrast, if one unmapped metabolite is mostly surrounded by mapped metabolites, the LPA will switch it from a 'poorly covered' to a 'well covered' community, so that the absence of this metabolite from mass spectral databases may be counterbalanced by the identification of its neighbouring metabolites. Consequently, densely connected groups of nodes reach a common community label quickly. Such steps were conducted iteratively until all label assignments were stable. We ran the analysis 1000 times and aggregated the results to obtain a final assignment taking into account different ties resolutions scenario (R code is provided in Supplementary File 3).

To identify key missing nodes (i.e., metabolites) in mass spectral libraries, we used a network topology measure called centrality. Centrality is a very well-studied field in network science which aims at identifying important actors in a network. Among the numerous centrality indices, we chose the betweenness as the criterion for metabolite prioritisation. The betweenness centrality quantifies the number of times a node acts as a bridge along the shortest path between two other nodes in the network [28]. The betweenness, therefore, provides a solution to identify metabolites with the greatest potential for bridging the gap between other metabolites, leading to a more cohesive view of the metabolism through metabolomics data.

2.4. Publication Mapping

Beside topological measure, we also characterised metabolites through their prominency in scientific literature. We used the PubChem REST API [29] to obtain PubChem identifiers (CID) from our InChIKey list. We then used the API to retrieve PubMed article identifiers (PMID) referenced from an entry accessed through its CID. We compared the number of associated articles between mapped and non-mapped metabolites using Wilcoxon rank sum test with continuity correction and a significance level of $\alpha = 0.001$. We evaluated the association for a metabolite of having at least one associated article and being mapped using Fisher's Exact Test, with a significance level of $\alpha = 0.001$.

3. Results

3.1. Coverage of Genome-Scale Metabolic Networks by Mass Spectral Libraries

We mapped the chemical library containing 253,927 non-redundant first block InChIKeys onto 38 different genome-scale metabolic networks, including relevant organisms such as *Escherichia coli*, *Arabidopsis thaliana*, *Saccharomyces cerevisiae* (yeast), *Mus musculus* (mouse) or *Homo sapiens* (human). Figure 2 shows the coverage of all the metabolic networks investigated (see Supplementary Files 4 and 5).

Two significant findings can be drawn from a closer analysis of Figure 2. First, the coverage of mapped metabolites in genome-scale metabolic models by mass spectral libraries is relatively low, and coverage varies from 20–60% depending on the species. In the case of model organisms, with extensively characterized genomes and annotated metabolic networks, such as *Mus musculus*, *Escherichia coli* and *Arabidopsis thaliana*, only 52–60% of their metabolomes could be potentially characterized by confronting MS data with all existing mass spectral information from pure standards (which are not currently accessible from a single resource). For human (*Homo sapiens*), this number drops to 42.2% and 30.5% in the case of the KEGG and Recon2 metabolic models, respectively. Second, the annotation level, i.e., specification of chemical identifiers, in genome-scale metabolic models is still very limited. Models such as *Homo sapiens* (Recon2 and HumanCyc) and different plants (PlantCyc) contain a large number of compounds with no compound identifier other than its name, resulting in fewer compounds than expected with associated InChIKey (an unambiguous identifier of chemical substances): 48.7% for Recon2, 48.6% for PlantCyc, and 35.7% for HumanCyc. On average, 63.2% of compounds in our metabolic models have InChIKey, which constitutes an obstacle for reliably mapping experimental metabolomics data onto metabolic models.

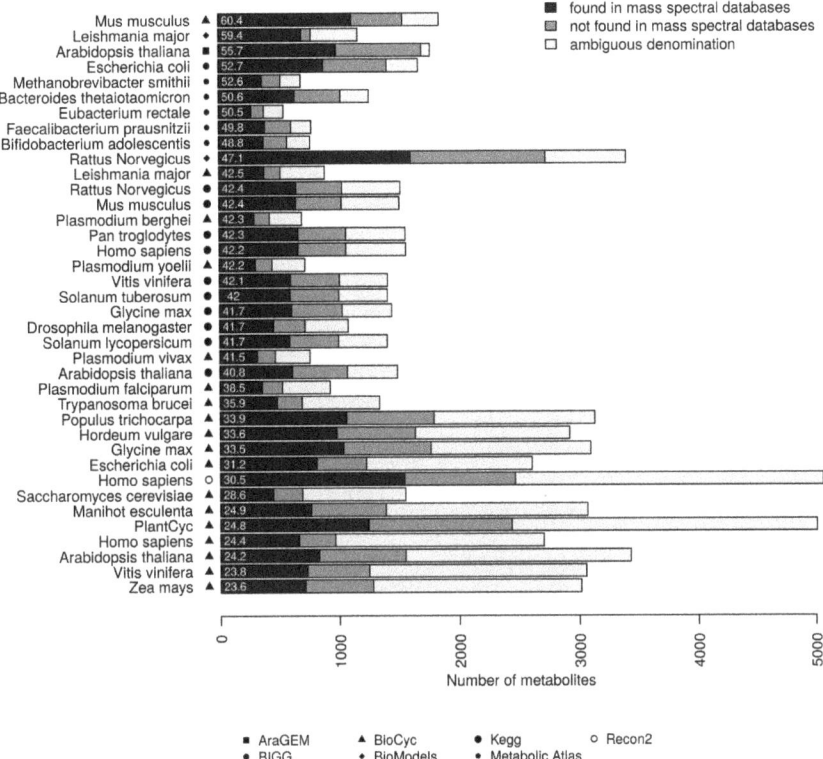

Figure 2. Coverage of prokaryotic and eukaryotic metabolic networks by mass spectral libraries. The genome-scale metabolic models are listed according to an increasing percentage of metabolites covered by mass spectral libraries. The percentage from 60.4 down to 23.6 is displayed to the left of each bar. "Found in mass spectral databases" refers to metabolites that can be mapped in at least one mass spectral database. "Not found in mass spectral databases" refers to compounds with an InChI from metabolic models that could not be matched with any compound in any mass spectral databases. "Ambiguous denomination" refers to compounds with undefined structures or insufficient information to retrieve the unambiguous InChIKey identifier; these compounds were not mapped.

Additional to the above analysis, we have also assessed the coverage of individual mass spectral databases in metabolic models (see Supplementary Files 6 and 7). Figure 3 shows, for each spectral library, the percentage of compounds that could be mapped in each network. Overall, databases with the largest number of compounds (by InChIKey), such as NIST and MassBank, showed the best coverage, however these databases also include many exogenous compounds or chemical structures that could not be matched in the genome-scale metabolic models. GNPS covers the smallest percentage of metabolic networks since, at the date of the analysis, the database was mainly focused on secondary metabolites that are not well covered and annotated by genome-scale metabolic networks. The small coverage of MS for ID was also explained by its specificity towards forensic and toxicology related small molecules.

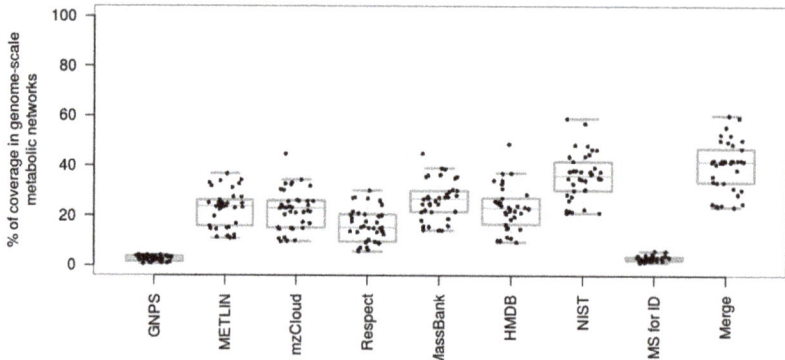

Figure 3. Coverage of prokaryotic and eukaryotic metabolic networks by individual mass spectral databases. HMDB and NIST include MS^2 and electron ionization (EI)-MS spectral information. Box plots show the distribution of the percentages of coverage in 38 different genome-scale metabolic networks.

3.2. Deciphering Poorly Covered Parts of the Human Metabolic Network

As a priority, coverage of the human metabolic network by existing MS databases was investigated. Figure 4 shows the graph built based on Recon 2.03 human genome-scale metabolic network (see methods section), where the mapped and unmapped metabolites are represented as blue and white nodes, respectively. The number of nodes in the graph has been reduced by eliminating compounds without InChIs, compounds without carbons, and duplicated compounds in different cellular compartments. Inorganic compounds such as CO_2 were manually removed. Out of 1597 resulting nodes in the metabolic network, 890 metabolites (55.7%) were mapped (see Supplementary File 8).

Next, we analysed which parts of the human network are poorly covered by experimental data present in MS databases. To do so, we used the LPA for community detection [27] (see Methods for details) and neighbourhood coverage analysis. The results reveal that 61% of connected metabolites in our network have at least half of their neighbours mapped in MS databases, and 80% have at least one mapped neighbour (Figure 5), which indicates that, despite the low coverage of genome-scale metabolic networks by MS databases, they can still broadly cover the human network without leaving large areas with uncovered metabolites. However, some poorly covered regions were evident in the network. About 293 compounds, of which 216 are not covered, have 90–100% of their neighbours not covered by MS databases either. This may be linked to the existence of metabolic gaps that represents around 18% of the overall network (considering only compounds annotated with InChIKeys). These poorly covered parts of the network identified by LPA are composed of small-size components (Figure 6), supporting the idea that most parts of the known human metabolism are covered in a broad sense. Some metabolic pathways nevertheless appear especially poorly covered, including eicosanoids, vitamins, heme and bile acid metabolism.

Figure 4. Coverage of the human metabolic network. Blue nodes: Covered by MS databases. White nodes: not covered by MS databases. Isolated nodes have been removed for easy viewing of the metabolic network.

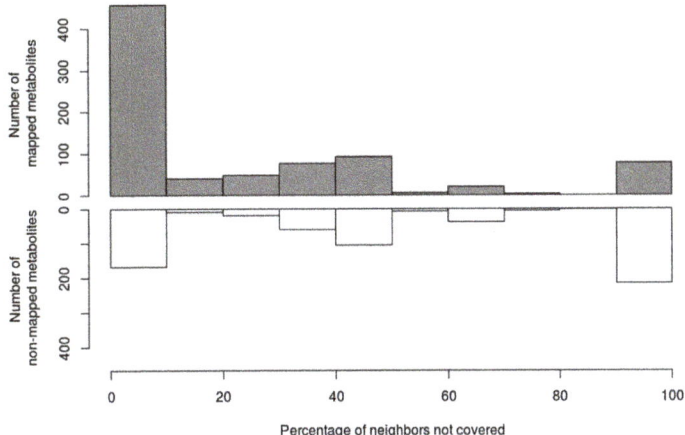

Figure 5. Relative coverage of metabolites' neighborhood. Metabolites are categorized according to the coverage of their neighborhood, from fully covered to 90–100% uncovered. The Y-axis represents the number of metabolites in each category, with mapped metabolites displayed in grey, and non-mapped metabolites displayed in white.

Figure 6. The 'dark side' of Human metabolism. The least covered subgraph of Recon 2.03 obtained from LPA using mapping status as the initial state. White circles: Non-mapped metabolites. Blue circles: mapped metabolites. Edges: Substrate-product relationships. Metabolites with ambiguous identifier have been removed. Colored Hulls: Pathways overrepresented in the poorly mapped area of the human metabolic network Recon 2.03. Right-tailed Fisher exact test with Benjamini-Hochberg correction, $\alpha = 0.05$.

We also explored the topological characteristics of poorly covered parts in the human metabolic network. The most relevant aspect is a lower average clustering coefficient (i.e., nodes often have their neighbours poorly connected, as an indicator of low local density) in the poorly covered areas relative to metabolites from the well-covered areas (Figure 7A). The few links shared between the two parts (Figure 7B) also suggest that the poorly covered areas are virtually disconnected from the rest of the network. Overall, our results indicate that poorly covered areas tend to be located in sparsely connected spaces of the metabolic network. The sparsity of metabolic reactions in the poorly covered areas could describe few and very specific linear pathways, or it may also reveal missing metabolic reactions due to a lack of biochemical knowledge or sporadic activities in scientific investigation in those regions. We have attempted to tackle this issue by analysing the number of publications associated with each metabolite. We have linked metabolites in the networks to publications by retrieving the cross-referenced PubMed articles in their PubChem entry. The non-mapped metabolites (and the sparse regions in the network analysis) tend to have fewer publications than the mapped compounds (Figure 8a). The distribution of publications is heavily skewed, and as a result, we were not able to retrieve any article using PubMed CID query for 588 metabolites, while 53 metabolites exceeded 10,000 articles. The metabolites without associated publications are significantly enriched in non-mapped areas (Figure 8b). Note that 7% of the metabolites were excluded from our query in PubMed because no entry was found for them in PubChem. These missing compounds are also significantly enriched in poorly covered areas of the human network. Overall, this analysis suggests that metabolites not covered by spectral databases are less prominent in the scientific literature.

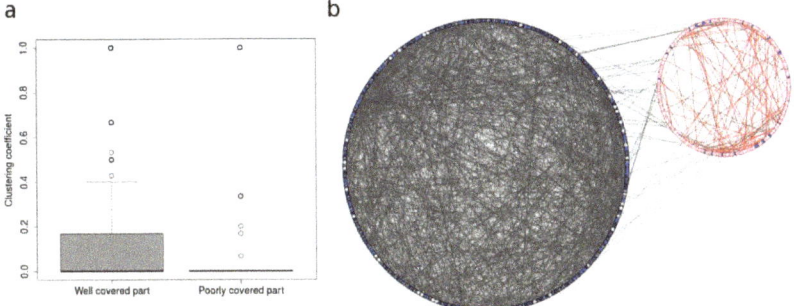

Figure 7. Topological analysis of the least covered areas. (**a**) Clustering coefficient distribution in well covered and poorly covered parts of human metabolism. Only the main component of the whole human metabolic network is considered. (**b**) Well-covered area vs. poorly-covered area in the human metabolic network. Blue nodes: mapped; white nodes: unmapped. Left: Well-covered group; right: poorly covered group. The poorly covered group appears quite small and sparsely connected compared to the well-covered one. Also, there are few connections (i.e., biochemical transformation with some carbon backbone conservation) between the two groups.

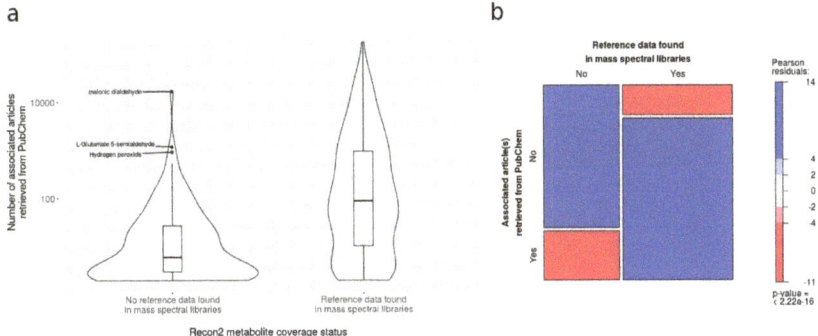

Figure 8. Relationship between the coverage status of Recon2 metabolites and the scientific literature. (**a**) Violin plots showing the distribution of the number of articles associated with mapped and non-mapped metabolites in Recon2. Y axis shows the number of articles (logarithmic scale) obtained from PubMed references in PubChem entries. Only metabolites with at least one associated article are considered. (**b**) Mosaic plot showing the proportion of Recon2 metabolites with PubMed references. Only metabolites with PubChem CID annotation were considered. The area of the tiles is proportional to the number of metabolites within each category. The color and shade of the tiles correspond to the sign and magnitude of the Pearson residuals. The Pearson residuals represent the contribution of the tile to the chi-squared statistics, assessing whether the two variables are independent or not. Red tiles indicate the proportion of under-represented metabolites, namely, metabolites with a smaller number of PubMed references than expected if the two variables (i.e., an entry in spectral libraries and a PubMed article in PubChem) were independent, while blue tiles indicate over-represented metabolites, namely, metabolites with a greater number of PubMed references than expected.

3.3. Filling Gaps in Poorly Covered Areas of Human Metabolism

Recently, Aguilar-Mogas et al., systematically demonstrated that neighbouring metabolites in a metabolic network share structural similarities and have similar MS/MS spectra [30]. On this basis, our network topology analysis provides an opportunity to identify the most important reference mass spectra to acquire in order to cover the largest number of structurally similar unmapped metabolites in the human metabolic network. Both machine learning algorithms for mass spectra prediction [31,32] and the biochemical interpretation of metabolomics results would benefit from filling these gaps.

In order to identify the most important metabolites currently missing in the MS databases, we performed a centrality analysis. Table 1 shows the top 20 metabolites with the highest betweenness centrality (see the Methods section) from the poorly mapped areas of human metabolism. These high betweenness metabolites are key chemical structures [33], hence adding their mass spectra to reference libraries, as training data for machine learning algorithms and other identification approaches, will greatly improve prediction of the mass spectra of their unmapped neighbour metabolites. In turn, these metabolites are more likely biochemically affected by the propagation of metabolic perturbations due to their crossroad status, and therefore a must-have in metabolism monitoring.

Table 1. Top 20 metabolites with the highest overall betweenness centrality from the poorly mapped area of human network. PubChem CIDs were obtained using the Chemical Translation Service (http://cts.fiehnlab.ucdavis.edu/) with the name as presented in the first column.

Name (from Network)	PubChem CID	InChIKey
(25R)-3alpha,7alpha,12alpha-trihydroxy-5beta-cholestan-26-oyl-CoA(4-)	15942889	MNYDLIUNNOCPHG-FJWDCHQMSA-N
12-oxo-c-LTB3	122164853	ZFHPYBQKHVEFHO-LECUDPRGSA-N
3alpha,7alpha,12alpha-Trihydroxy-5beta-cholestanoate	440460	CNWPIIOQKZNXBB-SQZFNYHNSA-N
3alpha,7alpha,12alpha-trihydroxy-5beta-cholestan-26-al	193321	XJZGNVBLVFOSKJ-XZULNKEGSA-N
12-oxo-leukotriene B4	5280876	SJVWVCVZWMJXOK-NOJHDUNKSA-N
20-CoA-20-oxo-leukotriene B4	53481505	WLWKYZHFLKRKEU-WCOJVGLOSA-J
5beta-cholestane-3alpha,7alpha,12alpha,26-tetrol	439479	USFJGINJGUIPSY-XZULNKEGSA-N
(4R,5S)-4,5,6-trihydroxy-2,3-dioxohexanoate	440390	GJQWCDSAOUMKSE-STHAYSLISA-N
20-carboxy-leukotriene-B4	5280877	SXWGPVJGNOLNHT-VFLUTPEKSA-N
5beta-cholestane-3alpha,7alpha,12alpha-triol	160520	RIVQQZVHIVNQFH-XJZYBRFWSA-N
3-oxo-tetracosa-12,15,18,21-all-cis-tetraenoyl-CoA	131769900	HPMVBGKWFWCZAY-JDTXFHFDSA-N
6-pyruvoyl-5,6,7,8-tetrahydropterin	128973	WBJZXBUVECZHCE-UHFFFAOYSA-N
Hydroxymethylbilane	788	WDFJYRZCZIUBPR-UHFFFAOYSA-N
5beta-cholestane-3alpha,7alpha,12alpha,25-tetrol	160520	RIVQQZVHIVNQFH-XJZYBRFWSA-N
3(S)-hydroxy-tetracosa-12,15,18,21-all-cis-tetraenoyl-CoA	53477712	NTIXPPFPXLYJCT-OWOWEXKPSA-N
Uroporphyrinogen III	1179	HUHWZXWWOFSFKF-UHFFFAOYSA-N
12-oxo-20-hydroxy-leukotriene B4	53481459	CZWPUWRHQBAXJS-PABROBRYSA-N
3-oxo-all-cis-6,9,12,15,18-tetracosapentaenoyl-CoA	131769894	UQPANOGFYCZRAV-UWOIJHEUSA-N
all-cis-10,13,16,19-docosatetraenoyl-CoA	71627222	BEEQBBPNTYBGDP-BUSXXEPMSA-J
kinetensin	53481569	PANUJGMSOSQAAY-HAGIGRARSA-N

4. Discussion

Here we have combined cheminformatics and network analysis methods to investigate the coverage of public and commercial mass spectral databases in the metabolism of prokaryotic and eukaryotic organisms, particularly taking a closer look at human metabolism. For this, we have used genome-scale metabolic reconstructions, which are considered the most comprehensive and annotated models of metabolism in multiple organisms. Genome-scale metabolic networks contain information both on metabolites and their reactions with corresponding genes and proteins. However, most genome-scale metabolic networks are reconstructed from genomic sequences and literature, and rarely incorporate new and rapidly evolving metabolomic data. This has resulted in some of the constraints and mismatches encountered in our study.

Our computational approach has revealed that many metabolites are missing from mass spectral libraries. For example, 44% of compounds with an InChIKey in Recon2 could not be matched in any mass spectral database. Our results, therefore, provide an essential resource to improve the biochemical landscape of mass spectral databases, and highlights the pressing need for standards to prioritise on to fill these gaps. However, the apparent "low metabolic content" of mass spectral libraries may also be a consequence of insufficient annotation of genome-scale metabolic models. These models (available in SBML format) were initially built for constraint-based computational studies (e.g., Flux Balance Analysis), where the chemical structure of small molecules is not necessarily required for computation. Therefore, most of these models contain a substantial number of metabolites with only short and ambiguous names but no other standard identifiers, which represent a serious obstacle for mapping metabolomics data onto genome-scale metabolic models. Metabolites without proper identifiers can result from the lack of cross-references during their annotation by the scientific community, making computational tools unable to reach the information needed to make correspondences between mass spectral libraries and metabolic networks. One common and useful identifier in this regard is the InChI, which is directly built from the chemical structure of compounds and the hash of the structure, the InChIKey, enabling both the computational analysis performed here, as well as much broader searching of other resources. Unfortunately, we have noticed that most metabolic models often refer to classes of compounds (instead of single chemical species with accurate structures) in order to represent the enzymatic promiscuity of substrates or to describe generic biochemical reactions. Consequently, when the metabolic networks are generated, nodes without chemical structures cannot be mapped on to the mass spectral libraries. Automated approaches to enumerate potentially matching structures to generic representations are required to capture these substances in future studies [34]. Metabolic models may also include some macromolecules that cannot be encoded into all resources due to its string length, although these are likely to be out of the mass range of mass spectrometry in a typical metabolomics experiment. Finally, metabolic models also often contain some entries that do not describe metabolites and therefore cannot be labelled with an InChIKey. For example, most prokaryotic models contain an entry named "biomass", which provide a convenient way of defining an objective function for constraint-based modelling. The common lack of proper System Biology Ontology (SBO) term annotations and the rare usage of SBML packages allowing different entry types prevent the specific selection of metabolites in models.

The difficulty of mapping metabolomics data onto metabolic networks can also stem from the different scale between models and measures: different stereoisomers may be encoded in the network but are often indistinguishable in a MS experiment (see Figure 1 in Schymanski & Williams 2017 [34]). Furthermore, when no distinction is made between stereoisomers, or between the acid and base form of a compound, one of them can be arbitrarily chosen for setting the name and the annotations of the entry in the model. This could lead to false negatives in the coverage results. To overcome this issue, we used the first InChIKey block, which reduces the structures from the libraries and the networks to a "stereochemistry neutral" or a simplified version of the "MS-ready" form. This can lead to mismatches resulting from tautomers and other substances where different InChIKey first blocks can occur (e.g., monosaccharide compounds in networks, which can be labelled with both the cyclic (PubChem CID:5793) or the linear form (PubChem CID:10954115)). There is thus a strong need to coordinate cheminformaticians with the field of systems biology in order to improve the annotation of metabolic models and develop InChIs and InChIKeys for less defined structures. This would greatly facilitate data exchange and the integration of metabolomics data in the context of metabolic networks.

Eventually, comparing coverages between organisms can be misleading due to differences in size, quality, and completeness of metabolic models. Plant models, for instance, contain the largest number of metabolites among eukaryote organisms, yet they seem to have the poorest coverage by spectral data. While our work focused on human metabolism, the same workflow could be implemented by experts in plant metabolism to reveal metabolite gaps. On the other hand, incomplete and small metabolic models with a relatively good coverage may hide a 'streetlight effect', since these models are mainly annotated with well-known reactions and compounds, which are more likely to be present in mass spectral libraries. Since spectral databases and metabolic models are so dynamic, we present the data "as calculated" to describe the first use of LPA to detect dense blind spots in the coverage of a metabolic network.

Also significant is the striking number of compounds in the spectral databases that did not match with any of our 38 genome-scale networks, namely 251.763 compounds, that is, ~99% in the merged database. Possible causes may include a very large number of exogenous compounds and secondary metabolites in spectral databases, synthetic compounds not found in nature, the annotation in other organisms that were not included in our list of genome-scale networks, and non-enzymatically produced compounds.

Finally, it should be emphasized the continuous growth of mass spectral databases with the addition of new spectra. Since performing this analysis, the latest NIST2017 has been released with spectra from 15,243 compounds, while mzCloud has grown to contain spectra from 7249 compounds (just to name two examples). The methods proposed in this article are sufficiently generic to be applied to updated datasets and/or in-house spectral libraries. It will also be possible to apply this approach to updated versions of metabolic networks. As a matter of fact, a new version of the human metabolic network Recon has been released concurrently to our work [35]. Our preliminary analysis indicates that Recon3D has considerably more annotated compounds with associated InChI than Recon2, however, the coverage of mapped metabolites remains roughly the same. We think, however, that further analyses and improvements of metabolic networks should be considered on the basis of Recon3D.

Supplementary Materials: The following are available online at http://www.mdpi.com/2218-1989/8/3/51/s1, Supplementary File 1: Supp1-Recon2.v03_noCompartment_extra-annotations.xml. Supplementary File 2: Supp2-Recon2_compound-graph.gml. Supplementary File 3: Supp3-label-propagation-script.r. Supplementary File 4. Supp4-merge_mapping.csv. Supplementary File 5. Supp5-merge_mapping_barplot.r. Supplementary File 6: Supp6-model_vs_lib.csv. Supplementary File 7: Supp7-model_vs_lib_boxplot.r. Supplementary File 8: Supp8-recon_mapping_status.csv. Supplementary File 9: Supp9-recon_CID_and_publication_count.tab.

Author Contributions: O.Y. and F.J. designed the study. E.L.S., O.Y. and S.N. collected, processed and formatted chemical library files. B.M. implemented the automatic mapping of libraries onto metabolic models. C.F. performed network analysis (implementation and interpretations). C.F. performed mapping result analysis. All authors contributed to discussion on results. All authors participated in the writing.

Funding: O.Y. thanks the following bodies for funding: Ministerio de Economia y Competitividad (MINECO) (BFU2014-57466-P) and the Spanish Biomedical Research Centre in Diabetes and Associated Metabolic Disorders (CIBERDEM), an initiative of Instituto de Investigacion Carlos III (ISCIII). C.F., B.M. and F.J. were supported by the French Ministry of Research and National Research Agency as part of the French MetaboHUB (Grant ANR-INBS-0010). S.N., R.M.S., B.M. and F.J. were supported by PhenoMeNal project, European Commission's Horizon 2020 programme, grant agreement number 654241. This study was supported in part by the SOLUTIONS project, which received funding from the European Union's Seventh Framework Programme for research, technological development, and demonstration under Grant Agreement No. 603437.

Acknowledgments: The authors express their gratitude to Don Li and Emma Rennie from Agilent Technologies, Stephen Stein and Dmitrii Tchekhovskoi from NIST, Robert Mistrik from mzCloud, Mingxun Wang from UCSD (GNPS), Herbert Oberacher (MSforID, sold byWiley), and Tobias Schulze (UFZ, massbank.eu) for providing their compound lists for the spectral overlap calculations, as well as all contributors to open access data.

Conflicts of Interest: Authors declare no conflict of interest.

References

1. Patti, G.J.; Yanes, O.; Siuzdak, G. Innovation: Metabolomics: The apogee of the omics trilogy. *Nat. Rev. Mol. Cell Biol.* **2012**, *13*, 263. [CrossRef] [PubMed]
2. Panopoulos, A.D.; Yanes, O.; Ruiz, S.; Kida, Y.S.; Diep, D.; Tautenhahn, R.; Herrerías, A.; Batchelder, E.M.; Plongthongkum, N.; Lutz, M.; et al. The metabolome of induced pluripotent stem cells reveals metabolic changes occurring in somatic cell reprogramming. *Cell Res.* **2012**, *22*, 168–177. [CrossRef] [PubMed]
3. Slebe, F.; Rojo, F.; Vinaixa, M.; García-Rocha, M.; Testoni, G.; Guiu, M.; Planet, E.; Samino, S.; Arenas, E.J.; Beltran, A.; et al. FoxA and LIPG endothelial lipase control the uptake of extracellular lipids for breast cancer growth. *Nat. Commun.* **2016**, *7*, 11199. [CrossRef] [PubMed]
4. Jorge, T.F.; Rodrigues, J.A.; Caldana, C.; Schmidt, R.; van Dongen, J.T.; Thomas-Oates, J.; António, C. Mass spectrometry-based plant metabolomics: Metabolite responses to abiotic stress. *Mass Spectrom. Rev.* **2016**, *35*, 620–649. [CrossRef] [PubMed]
5. Barkal, L.J.; Theberge, A.B.; Guo, C.-J.; Spraker, J.; Rappert, L.; Berthier, J.; Brakke, K.A.; Wang, C.C.C.; Beebe, D.J.; Keller, N.P.; et al. Microbial metabolomics in open microscale platforms. *Nat. Commun.* **2016**, *7*, 10610. [CrossRef] [PubMed]

6. Garg, N.; Wang, M.; Hyde, E.; da Silva, R.R.; Melnik, A.V.; Protsyuk, I.; Bouslimani, A.; Lim, Y.W.; Wong, R.; Humphrey, G.; et al. Three-Dimensional Microbiome and Metabolome Cartography of a Diseased Human Lung. *Cell Host Microbe* **2017**, *22*, 705–716. [CrossRef] [PubMed]
7. Baran, R.; Brodie, E.L.; Mayberry-Lewis, J.; Hummel, E.; Da Rocha, U.N.; Chakraborty, R.; Bowen, B.P.; Karaoz, U.; Cadillo-Quiroz, H.; Garcia-Pichel, F.; et al. Exometabolite niche partitioning among sympatric soil bacteria. *Nat. Commun.* **2015**, *6*, 8289. [CrossRef] [PubMed]
8. Hollender, J.; Schymanski, E.L.; Singer, H.P.; Ferguson, P.L. Nontarget Screening with High Resolution Mass Spectrometry in the Environment: Ready to Go? *Environ. Sci. Technol.* **2017**, *51*, 11505–11512. [CrossRef] [PubMed]
9. Navarro-Reig, M.; Jaumot, J.; Piña, B.; Moyano, E.; Galceran, M.T.; Tauler, R. Metabolomic analysis of the effects of cadmium and copper treatment in Oryza sativa L. using untargeted liquid chromatography coupled to high resolution mass spectrometry and all-ion fragmentation. *Metallomics* **2017**, *9*, 660–675. [CrossRef] [PubMed]
10. Kind, T.; Tsugawa, H.; Cajka, T.; Ma, Y.; Lai, Z.; Mehta, S.S.; Wohlgemuth, G.; Barupal, D.K.; Showalter, M.R.; Arita, M.; et al. Identification of small molecules using accurate mass MS/MS search. *Mass Spectrom. Rev.* **2017**, *37*, 513–532. [CrossRef] [PubMed]
11. Zhu, Z.-J.; Schultz, A.W.; Wang, J.; Johnson, C.H.; Yannone, S.M.; Patti, G.J.; Siuzdak, G. Liquid chromatography quadrupole time-of-flight mass spectrometry characterization of metabolites guided by the METLIN database. *Nat. Protoc.* **2013**, *8*, 451–460. [CrossRef] [PubMed]
12. Wishart, D.S.; Feunang, Y.D.; Marcu, A.; Guo, A.C.; Liang, K.; Vázquez-Fresno, R.; Sajed, T.; Johnson, D.; Li, C.; Karu, N.; et al. HMDB 4.0: The human metabolome database for 2018. *Nucleic Acids Res.* **2017**, *46*, D608–D617. [CrossRef] [PubMed]
13. Vinaixa, M.; Schymanski, E.L.; Neumann, S.; Navarro, M.; Salek, R.M.; Yanes, O. Mass spectral databases for LC/MS- and GC/MS-based metabolomics: State of the field and future prospects. *TrAC-Trends Anal. Chem.* **2016**, *78*, 23–35. [CrossRef]
14. Henry, C.S.; DeJongh, M.; Best, A.A.; Frybarger, P.M.; Linsay, B.; Stevens, R.L. High-throughput generation, optimization and analysis of genome-scale metabolic models. *Nat. Biotechnol.* **2010**, *28*, 977. [CrossRef] [PubMed]
15. McCloskey, D.; Palsson, B.Ø.; Feist, A.M. Basic and applied uses of genome-scale metabolic network reconstructions of Escherichia coli. *Mol. Syst. Biol.* **2013**, *9*, 661. [CrossRef] [PubMed]
16. Kim, S.; Thiessen, P.A.; Bolton, E.E.; Chen, J.; Fu, G.; Gindulyte, A.; Han, L.; He, J.; He, S.; Shoemaker, B.A.; et al. PubChem Substance and Compound databases. *Nucleic Acids Res.* **2015**, *44*, D1202–D1213. [CrossRef] [PubMed]
17. Pence, H.E.; Williams, A. ChemSpider: An Online Chemical Information Resource. *J. Chem. Educ.* **2010**, *87*, 1123–1124. [CrossRef]
18. Smith, C.A.; Maille, G.O.; Want, E.J.; Qin, C.; Trauger, S.A.; Brandon, T.R.; Custodio, D.E.; Abagyan, R.; Siuzdak, G. METLIN: A Metabolite Mass Spectral Database. *Ther. Drug Monit.* **2005**, *27*, 747–751. [CrossRef]
19. Sawada, Y.; Nakabayashi, R.; Yamada, Y.; Suzuki, M.; Sato, M.; Sakata, A.; Akiyama, K.; Sakurai, T.; Matsuda, F.; Aoki, T.; et al. RIKEN tandem mass spectral database (ReSpect) for phytochemicals: A plant-specific MS/MS-based data resource and database. *Phytochemistry* **2012**, *82*, 38–45. [CrossRef] [PubMed]
20. Wang, M.; Carver, J.J.; Phelan, V.V.; Sanchez, L.M.; Garg, N.; Peng, Y.; Nguyen, D.D.; Watrous, J.; Kapono, C.A.; Luzzatto-Knaan, T.; et al. Sharing and community curation of mass spectrometry data with Global Natural Products Social Molecular Networking. *Nat. Biotechnol.* **2016**, *34*, 828. [CrossRef] [PubMed]
21. Horai, H.; Arita, M.; Kanaya, S.; Nihei, Y.; Ikeda, T.; Suwa, K.; Ojima, Y.; Tanaka, K.; Tanaka, S.; Aoshima, K.; et al. MassBank: A public repository for sharing mass spectral data for life sciences. *J. Mass Spectrom.* **2010**, *45*, 703–714. [CrossRef] [PubMed]
22. Thiele, I.; Swainston, N.; Fleming, R.M.T.; Hoppe, A.; Sahoo, S.; Aurich, M.K.; Haraldsdottir, H.; Mo, M.L.; Rolfsson, O.; Stobbe, M.D.; et al. A community-driven global reconstruction of human metabolism. *Nat. Biotechnol.* **2013**, *31*, 419–425. [CrossRef] [PubMed]
23. Haraldsdóttir, H.S.; Thiele, I.; Fleming, R.M. Comparative evaluation of open source software for mapping between metabolite identifiers in metabolic network reconstructions: Application to Recon 2. *J. Cheminform.* **2014**, *6*, 2. [CrossRef] [PubMed]

24. Wang, Y.; Xiao, J.; Suzek, T.O.; Zhang, J.; Wang, J.; Bryant, S.H. PubChem: A public information system for analyzing bioactivities of small molecules. *Nucleic Acids Res.* **2009**, *37*, W623–W633. [CrossRef] [PubMed]
25. Wishart, D.S.; Tzur, D.; Knox, C.; Eisner, R.; Guo, A.C.; Young, N.; Cheng, D.; Jewell, K.; Arndt, D.; Sawhney, S.; et al. HMDB: The Human Metabolome Database. *Nucleic Acids Res.* **2007**, *35*, D521–D526. [CrossRef] [PubMed]
26. Degtyarenko, K.; de Matos, P.; Ennis, M.; Hastings, J.; Zbinden, M.; McNaught, A.; Alcántara, R.; Darsow, M.; Guedj, M.; Ashburner, M. ChEBI: A database and ontology for chemical entities of biological interest. *Nucleic Acids Res.* **2008**, *36*, D344–D350. [CrossRef] [PubMed]
27. Raghavan, U.N.; Albert, R.; Kumara, S. Near linear time algorithm to detect community structures in large-scale networks. *Phys. Rev. E Stat. Nonlinear Soft Matter Phys.* **2007**, *76*, 036106. [CrossRef] [PubMed]
28. Frainay, C.; Jourdan, F. Computational methods to identify metabolic sub-networks based on metabolomic profiles. *Brief. Bioinform.* **2017**, *18*, 43–56. [CrossRef] [PubMed]
29. Kim, S.; Thiessen, P.A.; Bolton, E.E.; Bryant, S.H. PUG-SOAP and PUG-REST: Web services for programmatic access to chemical information in PubChem. *Nucleic Acids Res.* **2015**, *43*, W605–W611. [CrossRef] [PubMed]
30. Aguilar-Mogas, A.; Sales-Pardo, M.; Navarro, M.; Guimerà, R.; Yanes, O. iMet: A network-based computational tool to assist in the annotation of metabolites from tandem mass spectra. *Anal. Chem.* **2017**, *89*, 3474–3482. [CrossRef] [PubMed]
31. Allen, F.; Pon, A.; Wilson, M.; Greiner, R.; Wishart, D. CFM-ID: A web server for annotation, spectrum prediction and metabolite identification from tandem mass spectra. *Nucleic Acids Res.* **2014**, *42*, W94–W99. [CrossRef] [PubMed]
32. Dührkop, K.; Shen, H.; Meusel, M.; Rousu, J.; Böcker, S. Searching molecular structure databases with tandem mass spectra using CSI:FingerID. *Proc. Natl. Acad. Sci. USA* **2015**, *112*, 12580–12585. [CrossRef] [PubMed]
33. Wohlgemuth, G.; Haldiya, P.K.; Willighagen, E.; Kind, T.; Fiehn, O. The Chemical Translation Service—A web-based tool to improve standardization of metabolomic reports. *Bioinformatics* **2010**, *26*, 2647–2648. [CrossRef] [PubMed]
34. Schymanski, E.L.; Williams, A.J. Open Science for Identifying "Known Unknown" Chemicals. *Environ. Sci. Technol.* **2017**, *51*, 5357–5359. [CrossRef] [PubMed]
35. Brunk, E.; Sahoo, S.; Zielinski, D.C.; Altunkaya, A.; Dräger, A.; Mih, N.; Gatto, F.; Nilsson, A.; Preciat-Gonzalez, G.A.; Aurich, M.K.; et al. Recon3D enables a three-dimensional view of gene variation in human metabolism. *Nat. Biotechnol.* **2018**, *36*, 272–281. [CrossRef] [PubMed]

© 2018 by the authors. Licensee MDPI, Basel, Switzerland. This article is an open access article distributed under the terms and conditions of the Creative Commons Attribution (CC BY) license (http://creativecommons.org/licenses/by/4.0/).

Article

Mass Spectrometry Data Repository Enhances Novel Metabolite Discoveries with Advances in Computational Metabolomics

Hiroshi Tsugawa [1,2,*,†], Aya Satoh [1,†], Haruki Uchino [2,3], Tomas Cajka [4,5], Makoto Arita [2,3,6] and Masanori Arita [1,7,*]

1. Metabolome informatics research team, RIKEN Center for Sustainable Resource Science, Yokohama 230-0045, Japan; aya.hayaishi@riken.jp
2. Laboratory for metabolomics, RIKEN Center for Integrative Medical Sciences, Yokohama 230-0045, Japan; haruki-uchino@keio.jp (H.U.); makoto.arita@riken.jp (M.A.)
3. Division of Physiological Chemistry and Metabolism, Graduate School of Pharmaceutical Sciences, Keio University, Minato-ku, Tokyo 105-8512, Japan
4. Department of Metabolomics, Institute of Physiology of the Czech Academy of Sciences, Videnska 1083, 14220 Prague, Czech Republic; tomas.cajka@fgu.cas.cz
5. Department of Translational Metabolism, Institute of Physiology of the Czech Academy of Sciences, Videnska 1083, 14220 Prague, Czech Republic
6. Cellular and Molecular Epigenetics Laboratory, Graduate School of Medical Life Science, Yokohama City University, Tsurumi, Yokohama 230-0045, Japan
7. National Institute of Genetics, Mishima 411-8540, Japan
* Correspondence: hiroshi.tsugawa@riken.jp (H.T.); arita@nig.ac.jp (M.A.); Tel.: +81-45-503-9491 (H.T.); +81-45-503-9491 (M.A.)
† These authors contributed equally to this work.

Received: 20 May 2019; Accepted: 19 June 2019; Published: 24 June 2019

Abstract: Mass spectrometry raw data repositories, including Metabolomics Workbench and MetaboLights, have contributed to increased transparency in metabolomics studies and the discovery of novel insights in biology by reanalysis with updated computational metabolomics tools. Herein, we reanalyzed the previously published lipidomics data from nine algal species, resulting in the annotation of 1437 lipids achieving a 40% increase in annotation compared to the previous results. Specifically, diacylglyceryl-carboxyhydroxy-methylcholine (DGCC) in *Pavlova lutheri* and *Pleurochrysis carterae*, glucuronosyldiacylglycerol (GlcADG) in *Euglena gracilis*, and *P. carterae*, phosphatidylmethanol (PMeOH) in *E. gracilis*, and several oxidized phospholipids (oxidized phosphatidylcholine, OxPC; phosphatidylethanolamine, OxPE; phosphatidylglycerol, OxPG; phosphatidylinositol, OxPI) in *Chlorella variabilis* were newly characterized with the enriched lipid spectral databases. Moreover, we integrated the data from untargeted and targeted analyses from data independent tandem mass spectrometry (DIA-MS/MS) acquisition, specifically the sequential window acquisition of all theoretical fragment-ion MS/MS (SWATH-MS/MS) spectra, to increase the lipidomic annotation coverage. After the creation of a global library of precursor and diagnostic ions of lipids by the MS-DIAL untargeted analysis, the co-eluted DIA-MS/MS spectra were resolved in MRMPROBS targeted analysis by tracing the specific product ions involved in acyl chain compositions. Our results indicated that the metabolite quantifications based on DIA-MS/MS chromatograms were somewhat inferior to the MS^1-centric quantifications, while the annotation coverage outperformed those of the untargeted analysis of the data dependent and DIA-MS/MS data. Consequently, integrated analyses of untargeted and targeted approaches are necessary to extract the maximum amount of metabolome information, and our results showcase the value of data repositories for the discovery of novel insights in lipid biology.

Keywords: data repository; computational metabolomics; reanalysis; lipidomics; data processing

1. Introduction

Many studies using mass spectrometry (MS)-based untargeted metabolomics have provided novel insights in biology, and the importance of metabolomics data repositories has been recognized [1]. In addition to the international data repositories, including Metabolomics Workbench [2], MetaboLights [3], and GNPS MassIVE [4], institute-oriented repositories such as RIKEN DropMet (http://prime.psc.riken.jp/) are available for sharing raw MS data. MS repositories aim to (A) increase the transparency and reproducibility of MS-centric metabolomics studies, (B) provide a benchmark for testing new analytical and computational methodologies, (C) share the results of metabolome analyses for providing opportunities for data-driven hypothesis generation, and (D) reanalyze published data with continuous identification efforts to obtain novel insights and discover novel metabolites. Nevertheless, few studies have demonstrated the value of MS repositories except for the first purpose. Case studies showing remarkable results toward the other three purposes would facilitate data sharing by researchers and academic journals [5].

We published nine algal lipidomics datasets in 2015 which are available on the RIKEN DropMet. According to previous reports, 1023 lipids were annotated by integrating the results of data-dependent MS/MS acquisition (DDA-MS/MS) and data-independent MS/MS acquisition (DIA-MS/MS) with an in-silico MS/MS spectral library of lipids to assign the algal phylogenetic tree based on lipid properties [6]. Although comprehensive lipid analysis has been achieved by these previous methodologies, the coverage of algal lipids can be improved by two major methodological updates. First, the count of annotated lipids can be increased by updating the in-silico spectral library with continuous data curation efforts, where 1,051,894 spectra of 525,947 molecules from 90 lipid classes are currently registered in MS-DIAL (version 3.68), while 122,844 spectra of 61,422 molecules from 24 lipid classes were registered in the first version of MS-DIAL (version 1.82) [6–8]. Herein, the characterization of 10 newly incorporated lipid classes including lysophosphatidylserine (LPS), lysophosphatidylglycerol (LPG), phosphatidylmethanol (PMeOH), glucuronosyldiacylglycerol (GlcADG), diacylglyceryl-carboxyhydroxy-methylcholine (DGCC), and its lyso-type form (LDGCC), as well as oxidized fatty acids containing phosphatidylcholine (OxPC), phosphatidylethanolamine (OxPE) phosphatidylglycerol (OxPG), and phosphatidylinositol (OxPI) are highlighted for algal lipid profiling. Second, the peak capacity in LC-MS/MS data could be increased by the integrated analyses of MS-DIAL-based untargeted [6,9] and MRMPROBS-based targeted analyses [10,11] for DIA-MS/MS data. In DIA-MS/MS data, MS-DIAL uses the MS^1 chromatogram trace for metabolite quantification and the deconvoluted MS/MS spectrum for metabolite annotation. Therefore, the program does not completely resolve co-eluted metabolites, as only a singlet MS^1 chromatogram peak from mixed metabolite ions can be obtained [12]. On the other hand, MRMPROBS can use either the MS^1 or MS/MS chromatogram for metabolite quantification and metabolite diagnostics is performed by the integrated score of the peak groups from the user-defined precursor-product transitions library [10]. Notably, co-eluted metabolites in the MS^1 chromatogram trace can be resolved using the MS/MS chromatograms which differ based on the unique product ions from the lipid structure, resulting in increased peak capacity, i.e., increased deconvolution efficiency, in the LC-MS/MS dataset.

Herein, we showcase novel lipid discoveries using algal lipidomics data as a benchmark. We discovered novel lipid classes which have never been reported in the algal species using updated in-silico MS/MS libraries. Moreover, we demonstrate increased annotated lipid coverage by integrating the pipelines of the MS-DIAL and MRMPROBS programs. Although the integrated pipeline can be executed using other state-of-the-art program combinations, such as XCMS [13] and MZmine 2 [14], for untargeted analysis and MetDIA for targeted analysis [15], the selected programs support the direct link from untargeted to targeted analyses with a user-friendly graphical user interface (GUI) where manual peak-picking required for targeted approaches is acceptable. This study highlights the importance of mass spectrometry data repositories to deepen our understanding of lipids in algal species.

2. Materials and Methods

2.1. Overview of Data Analysis Workflow

Since the MetaboLights database and repository was launched in 2012 by the European Bioinformatics Institute (EMBL-EBI) as the first repository for metabolomics data, data submission has continuously increased (~2.5 TB data was available in June 2019), and accessibility and awareness have been enhanced through the efforts of MetabolomeXchange (http://www.metabolomexchange.org) and OmicsDI [16]. RIKEN DropMet (http://prime.psc.riken.jp/menta.cgi/prime/drop_index) has also been launched in 2009 to share MS-based metabolomics data from RIKEN, in which ~300 GB of data from 29 studies are currently available; a part of this repository, i.e., the algae lipidomics data, was used in this study.

On the other hand, data processing tools like MS-DIAL [6,9], XCMS [13], and MZmine 2 [14] have continuously been updated with database curations like Metlin [17] in XCMS. Since the LipidBlast library was released in 2013 as the first public in-silico library for lipids [18], the fork libraries for quadrupole/time-of-flight mass spectrometry (QTOF-MS) with collision-induced dissociation (CID) and orbital ion trap MS with higher-energy collisional dissociation (HCD) data have been developed in MS-DIAL [6,7] owing to the continuous effort. The annotation described in this study can be executed in the MS-DIAL version 3.66 or higher. All programs, i.e., MS-DIAL, MRMPROBS, and the related spectral libraries are available on the RIKEN PRIMe website (http://prime.psc.riken.jp/).

2.2. Mass Spectrometry Data

The DDA and DIA lipidomics data obtained in positive and negative ion modes of nine algal species were downloaded from the RIKEN DropMet website (http://prime.psc.riken.jp/menta.cgi/prime/drop_index; ID, DM0022). Briefly, the extraction of algal lipids was performed using a biphasic solvent system of cold methanol, methyl *tert*-butyl ether (MTBE), and water followed by lipid separation via reversed-phase liquid chromatography. Both DDA and DIA data were acquired using a QTOF mass spectrometer (TripleTOF 5600+, SCIEX). For DIA (SWATH-MS/MS), a 21 Da isolation window was used for selecting precursor ions shifting over an m/z 100–1250 mass range. Further details are provided in the previous study [6].

2.3. Software Programs

MS-DIAL version 3.06 and MRMPROBS version 2.44 were used herein. All programs including the latest version are freely available on the RIKEN PRIMe website (http://prime.psc.riken.jp/).

The same parameters in MS-DIAL were used for DDA and DIA data analyses: retention time begin, 0 min; retention time end, 100 min; mass range begin, 0 Da; mass range end, 5000 Da; accurate mass tolerance (MS1), 0.01 Da; MS2 tolerance, 0.025 Da; maximum charge number, 2; smoothing method, linear weighted moving average; smoothing level, 3; minimum peak width, 5 scan; minimum peak height, 1000; mass slice width, 0.1 Da; sigma window value, 0.5; MS2Dec amplitude cut-off, 0; exclude after precursor, true; keep isotope until, 0.5 Da; keep original precursor isotopes, false; exclude after precursor, true; retention time tolerance for identification, 4 min; MS1 for identification, 0.01 Da; accurate mass tolerance (MS2) for identification, 0.05 Da; identification score cut-off, 70%; using retention time for scoring, true; relative abundance cut off, 0; top candidate report, true; retention time tolerance for alignment, 0.05 min; MS1 tolerance for alignment, 0.015 Da; peak count filter, 0; remove feature based on peak height fold-change, true; sample max/blank average, 5; keep identified and annotated metabolites, true; keep removable features and assign the tag for checking, true; replace true zero values with 1/10 of the minimum peak height over all samples, false. Lipid annotation was performed automatically using the in-silico MS/MS spectral library described below, and the result was manually curated with the confirmation of the characteristic product ions and neutral losses to reduce false-positive annotations.

The parameters in MRMPROBS were set as follows: MS1 tolerance, 0.01 Da; MS2 tolerance, 0.025 Da; smoothing method, linear weighted moving average; smoothing level, 1; minimum peak width, 5 scan; minimum peak height, 200; retention time tolerance for identification, 0.1 min; amplitude tolerance for identification, 15%; minimum posterior, 70%; the abundance ratios in reference library were automatically generated by MS-DIAL. The results of metabolite annotation and peak picking were manually curated using the graphical user interface of MRMPROBS.

2.4. In-Silico MS/MS Spectral Libraries

The diagnostic ions used to characterize lipid classes were determined using authentic standards, experimental MS/MS spectra of biological samples, or MS/MS spectral information reported in the literature. The MS/MS spectra of PMeOH, LPS, and LPG were confirmed using the standard compounds PMeOH 16:0–16:0, LPG 18:1, and LPS 18:1 (Avanti Polar Lipids, Inc., Alabaster, AL, USA). The DGCC and LDGCC spectra were examined in the DDA-MS/MS data of *Pavlova lutheri* because these lipids were previously discovered in *P. lutheri* [19] and the corresponding literature's MS/MS spectrum was utilized to create an in-silico MS/MS library [20]; the MS/MS spectra that have electronically been described in a peer-review journal but not recorded in publicly and commercially available spectral databases such as MassBank and NIST are referred to as the literature's MS/MS. The in-silico MS/MS spectral libraries for oxidized phospholipids were developed considering our previously published data [21]. The library creation for GlcADG was based on the literature's MS/MS spectrum [22]. Information regarding ion abundances in the MS/MS spectral libraries was based on our LC-MS/MS experimental conditions and the detailed analytical conditions were described in a previous study [7]. Briefly, the MS data were acquired in information-dependent mode (IDA), i.e., DDA, using SCIEX TripleTOF 5600+ or 6600 systems. The mass range, collision energy, and collision energy spread were set to m/z 70–1250, 45 V, and 15 V, respectively.

3. Results and Discussion

3.1. Novel Lipid Characterizations in Algae with Enriched In-Silico Spectral Libraries

The global lipid profiling of nine algal lipids was achieved in 2015 and 15 lipid classes were characterized [6]. These classes include free fatty acid (FFA), di- and triacylglycerols (DAG and TAG), seven phospholipid classes (phosphatidylcholine, PC; phosphatidylethanolamine, PE; phosphatidylglycerol, PG; phosphatidylinositol, PI; phosphatidylserine, PS; lysophosphatidylcholine, LPC; and lysophosphatidylethanolamine, LPE), mono- and digalactosyldiacylglycerol (MGDG and DGDG), sulfoquinovosyldiacylglycerol (SQDG), diacylglyceryltrimethylhomoserine (DGTS), and its lyso-type form (LDGTS). Of these, the most common lipid classes in the photosynthetic membranes of plants, cyanobacteria, and algae, which include PG, SQDG, MGDG, and DGDG, have been characterized in all algal species. In contrast, N,N,N-trimethylammonium cation-containing lipids, i.e., PC and DGTS, were characterized as species-specific lipid classes. For example, *Chlamydomonas reinhardtii* only contains DGTS, while Chlorella species only contain PC as their characteristic positively charged membrane lipids. Since the specificity of lipid metabolism is highly influenced by genetics, evolution, and the environment of living organisms, increasing lipidomics coverage is an emerging requirement in biology.

Herein, 17 lipid classes were newly characterized in algal species using enriched MS/MS spectral libraries and include LPS, LPG, oxidized phospholipids (OxPC, OxPE, OxPG, OxPI), seven ceramide classes (Cer-NS, Cer-NDS, Cer-AP, Cer-NP, Cer-AS, Cer-ADS, and HexCer-AP), PMeOH, GlcADG, DGCC, and LDGCC (Table 1). The diagnostic ions are summarized in Table 2, and the annotation strategy and nomenclature of the ceramides are reported elsewhere [7]. The phytoceramide species, Cer-AP and Cer-NP, were characterized in all algal species, while several lipid classes were determined to be algal species-specific (Figure 1).

Table 1. Summary of annotated lipids.

Super Class	Class	Auxenochlorella protothecoides	Chlorella sorokiniana	Chlorella variabilis	Chlamydomonas reinhardtii	Dunaliella salina	Euglena gracilis	Nannochloropsis oculata	Pavlova lutheri	Pleurochrysis carterae	Total
Fatty acids	FA	5	5	5	5	4	9	6	6	9	11
Glycerolipids	DAG	13	18	21	16	2	61	27	5	13	100
Glycerolipids	TAG	91	80	144	97	152	481	231	126	121	622
Phospholipids	PC	25	21	26	0	10	33	42	1	0	75
Phospholipids	PE	12	18	19	5	5	14	16	4	1	46
Phospholipids	PG	12	16	13	9	9	9	13	8	1	28
Phospholipids	PS	3	2	3	0	0	1	0	0	0	6
Phospholipids	PI	8	8	9	8	6	7	14	8	1	19
Phospholipids	PMeOH	0	0	0	0	0	29	0	0	0	29
Phospholipids	LPC	4	8	6	0	0	1	6	0	0	10
Phospholipids	LPE	2	6	2	1	0	0	3	0	0	8
Phospholipids	LPG	0	2	1	2	0	1	0	0	0	2
Phospholipids	LPS	0	1	1	0	0	0	0	0	0	1
Oxidized lipids	OxPC	0	0	3	0	0	0	0	0	0	3
Oxidized lipids	OxPE	0	0	3	0	0	0	0	0	0	3
Oxidized lipids	OxPG	0	2	6	0	1	0	0	0	0	7
Oxidized lipids	OxPI	0	0	3	0	0	0	0	0	0	3
Algal lipids	LDGTS/LDGTA	0	0	0	14	4	9	21	1	3	34
Algal lipids	DGTS/DGTA	0	0	0	68	12	12	68	14	4	134
Algal lipids	LDGCC	0	0	0	0	0	0	0	7	14	16
Algal lipids	DGCC	0	0	0	0	0	0	0	35	38	47
Plant lipids	MGDG	25	40	35	26	16	42	18	24	27	82
Plant lipids	DGDG	19	22	28	23	15	39	26	12	28	64
Plant lipids	SQDG	16	15	10	20	8	25	22	16	24	41
Plant lipids	GlcADG	0	0	0	0	0	3	0	1	4	5
Ceramides	Cer-AP	8	8	8	7	8	8	8	8	8	10
Ceramides	Cer-NP	8	7	8	7	6	6	10	7	6	10
Ceramides	Cer-NS	0	0	0	0	0	1	4	0	2	5
Ceramides	Cer-NDS	1	2	4	1	2	3	4	2	2	6
Ceramides	Cer-AS	1	1	1	1	1	3	1	2	1	4
Ceramides	Cer-ADS	0	0	3	0	0	1	0	0	0	4
Ceramides	HexCer-AP	0	0	0	0	0	0	0	2	0	2
Total		253	282	362	310	261	798	540	289	307	1437

The count of annotated lipids is provided for each lipid class and algal species. DGTS/DGTA indicates that these lipid classes are annotated using the same characteristic ions.

Table 2. Diagnostic ions for lipid characterizations.

Lipid Class	Ion Mode	Adduct Type	Example	Diagnostic Ions (Lipid Class)	Diagnostic Ions (Acyl Chains)
LDGCC	Positive	$[M+H]^+$	LDGCC 18:0	m/z 104.107 $C_5H_{14}NO^+$, m/z 132.102 $C_6H_{14}NO_2^+$	-
DGCC	Positive	$[M+H]^+$	DGCC 18:0-20:4	m/z 104.107 $C_5H_{14}NO^+$, m/z 132.102 $C_6H_{14}NO_2^+$	NL of SN1 (m/z 538.374 $C_{30}H_{52}NO_7+$), NL of SN1+H_2O (m/z 520.363 $C_{30}H_{50}NO_6+$), NL of SN2 (m/z 518.405 $C_{28}H_{56}NO_7+$), NL of SN2+H_2O (m/z 500.395 $C_{28}H_{54}NO_6+$)
OxPC	Negative	$[M+HCOO]^-$	OxPC 18:0-20:4+2O	NL of HCOO+CH3 (m/z 826.56 $C_{45}H_{81}NO_{10}P^-$)	SN1 (m/z 283.264 $C_{18}H_{35}O_2^-$), SN2 (m/z 335.223, $C_{20}H_{31}O_4^-$), SN2−H_2O (m/z 317.212 $C_{20}H_{29}O_3^-$) *SN2−$2H_2O$ (m/z 299.202 $C_{20}H_{27}O_2^-$)
OxPE	Negative	$[M-H]^-$	OxPE 18:0-20:4+2O	m/z 196.038 $C_5H_{11}NO_5P^-$	SN1 (m/z 283.264 $C_{18}H_{35}O_2^-$), SN2 (m/z 335.223, $C_{20}H_{31}O_4^-$), SN2−H_2O (m/z 317.212 $C_{20}H_{29}O_3^-$) *SN2−$2H_2O$ (m/z 299.202 $C_{20}H_{27}O_2^-$)
OxPG	Negative	$[M-H]^-$	OxPG 18:0-20:4+2O	m/z 152.995 $C_3H_6O_5P^-$	SN1 (m/z 283.264 $C_{18}H_{35}O_2^-$), SN2 (m/z 335.223, $C_{20}H_{31}O_4^-$), SN2−H_2O (m/z 317.212 $C_{20}H_{29}O_3^-$) *SN2−$2H_2O$ (m/z 299.202 $C_{20}H_{27}O_2^-$)
OxPI	Negative	$[M-H]^-$	OxPI 18:0-20:4+2O	m/z 297.038 $C_9H_{14}O_9P^-$, m/z 241.012 $C_6H_{10}O_8P^-$	SN1 (m/z 283.264 $C_{18}H_{35}O_2^-$), SN2 (m/z 335.223, $C_{20}H_{31}O_4^-$), SN2−H_2O (m/z 317.212 $C_{20}H_{29}O_3^-$) *SN2−$2H_2O$ (m/z 299.202 $C_{20}H_{27}O_2^-$)
PMeOH	Negative	$[M-H]^-$	PMeOH 18:0-20:4	m/z 167.012 $C_4H_8O_5P^-$, m/z 110.985 $CH_4O_4P^-$	SN1 (m/z 283.264 $C_{18}H_{35}O_2^-$), SN2 (m/z 303.233 $C_{20}H_{31}O_2^-$)
GlcADG	Negative	$[M-H]^-$	GlcADG 18:0-20:4	m/z 249.062 $C_9H_{13}O_7$	SN1 (m/z 283.264 $C_{18}H_{35}O_2^-$), SN2 (m/z 303.233 $C_{20}H_{31}O_2^-$)
LPG	Negative	$[M-H]^-$	LPG 18:0	m/z 152.995 C3H6O5P$^-$	SN1 ‖ SN2 (m/z 283.264 $C_{18}H_{35}O_2^-$)
LPS	Negative	$[M-H]^-$	LPS 18:0	NL of C3H6NO2 (m/z 437.267 C21H42O7P$^-$)	SN1 ‖ SN2 (m/z 283.264 $C_{18}H_{35}O_2^-$)

The product ion m/z or neutral loss information is summarized. In this study, LDGCC and DGCC are characterized in positive ion mode and the other lipid classes are characterized in negative ion mode. The example lipid molecule is used for the showcase of fragment ions. The term "20:4" describes the fatty acid moiety of lipids including 20 carbons and 4 double bonds. The asterisk denotes a minor fragment ion that is rarely detected under our experimental conditions.

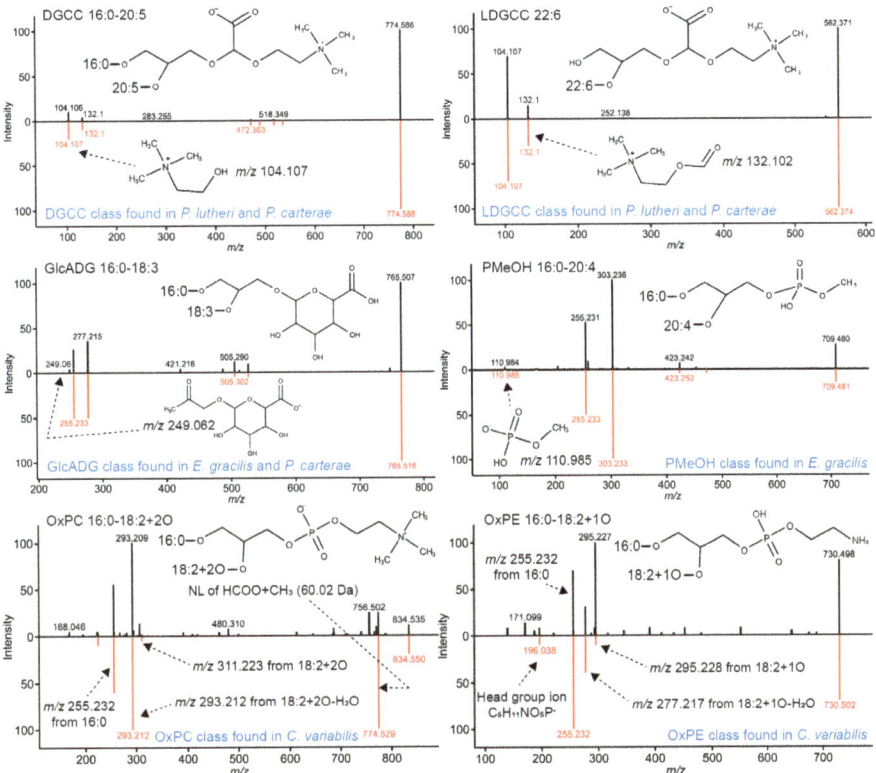

Figure 1. Lipid characterization using enriched in-silico MS/MS spectral libraries. The in-silico MS/MS characterizations for phosphatidylmethanol (PMeOH), glucuronosyldiacylglycerol (GlcADG), oxidized fatty acids containing phosphatidylcholine (OxPC) and phosphatidylethanolamine (OxPE), diacylglyceryl-carboxyhydroxy-methylcholine (DGCC), and its lyso-type form (LDGCC) are showcased. The upper- and bottom spectra show the experimental and in-silico MS/MS spectra, respectively. The string character indicates the abbreviation of fatty acids, and the ester link of the fatty acids is also described by string characters. NL refers to neutral loss. The algal species where the classified lipids are observed is also highlighted.

For example, DGCC and LDGCC lipids were only characterized in *Pavlova lutheri* and *Pleurochrysis carterae*. DGCC is well-known as a major betaine lipid of non-plastid membranes in *P. lutheri* [19], while this lipid class has never been reported in *P. carterae*. Thus, further investigation in *P. carterae* is required to define its exact stereochemistry. The MS-based lipidomics platform does not resolve the stereochemistry of acyl chains and sometimes lipid classes cannot uniquely be assigned, although a large variety of lipid molecules can be covered by tracing the lipid class-specific product ions and neutral losses. For example, DGTS and diacylglyceryl hydroxymethyl-N,N,N-trimethyl-β-alanine (DGTA), the major lipid class in *P. lutheri*, are characterized by the same diagnostic ions (m/z 144.102 and m/z 236.149) [23] under our experimental conditions, so the annotation must be determined by considering the genetic background in mass spectrometry-based metabolite annotations [9]. GlcADG, also known as diacylglyceryl glucuronide (DGGA), was observed in *Euglena gracilis*, *P. lutheri*, and *P. carterae*. GlcADG is known to be accumulated in response to phosphorus starvation in *Arabidopsis thaliana* and *Oryza sativa* [24], and this lipid class is commonly observed in several algal species. A previous study has also reported its existence in *P. lutheri*. Furthermore, the rare phospholipid

PMeOH class was characterized in *E. gracilis*, although it could also be detected as an artifact of extraction [25]. Finally, several oxidized fatty acid-containing phospholipids, including OxPC, OxPE, OxPG, and OxPI, were characterized in *Chlorella variabilis*. Although further investigation of these discovered lipids is required to determine whether the lipid class is endogenously biosynthesized in a specific algal species [26], our results indicated that the reanalysis of the published data with the updated annotation workflow could provide new insights and hypotheses not previously reported.

3.2. Strategy to Link Untargeted- and Targeted Analyses for Increasing Lipid Coverage

We further demonstrated the increased lipid profiling coverage by integrating untargeted and targeted analysis approaches (Figure 2). Although MS-DIAL involves a deconvolution algorithm, MS2Dec, to process the DIA-MS/MS data, MS2Dec requires at least two data point peak-top differences of co-eluted peaks for chromatogram deconvolution [6,12]. Moreover, MS-DIAL uses MS^1 chromatogram traces for metabolite quantification, while the MS/MS chromatogram can effectively be used to annotate and quantify the target metabolite in DIA-MS/MS data [15]. Therefore, the MRMPROBS program was used, in which the user-friendly GUI was available for data curation in addition to its favorable algorithm aspects [10,11], to compensate for the shortcomings of the MS-DIAL program. First, both DDA- and DIA-MS/MS data were analyzed using MS-DIAL. Second, all spectrometrically 'matched' candidates to an MS/MS spectrum were obtained and the function was newly developed. In this study, we utilized the DDA-MS/MS spectral data to examine the co-eluted metabolite profile because of the better spectrum quality than that of the DIA-MS/MS spectra. Third, the reference format file, which contains (1) metabolite name (2) retention time, (3) precursor ion *m/z*, and product ion *m/z* list, and (4) ion abundance ratios, was generated to cover all matched candidates. Finally, the DIA-MS/MS data were analyzed by MRMPROBS using the reference library where the peak left and right edges of the metabolite peak in each MS/MS chromatogram trace were manually refined.

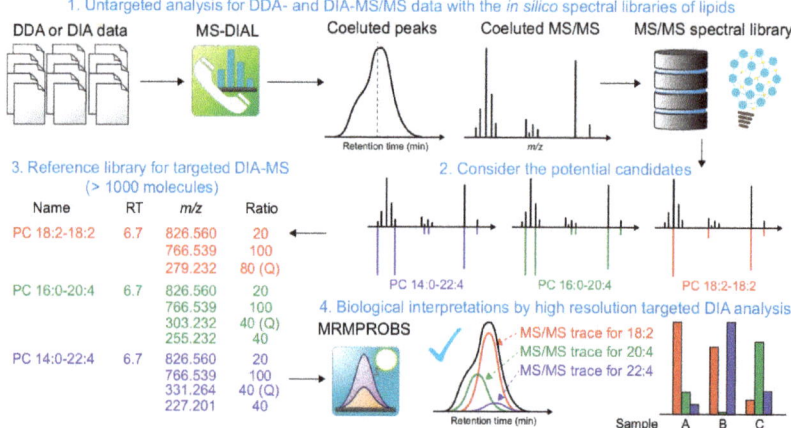

Figure 2. Integrated strategy of untargeted and targeted analyses to increase the coverage of annotated lipids. First, the data dependent (DDA) and independent (DIA) acquisition data are analyzed using the untargeted analysis pipeline where peak-picking, MS/MS assignment, and peak alignment are performed. Second, all potential lipid candidates that exceeded the cut-off of mass spectral similarity are obtained. Third, a reference library containing the target metabolite name, retention time, precursor ion *m/z*, product ion *m/z* list, and ion abundance ratios is automatically generated. In our study, the ratio "100" indicates that the trace is used to quantify the metabolite, and the diagnostic ion for characterizing the metabolite is described by "Q". Finally, the MS/MS chromatograms are analyzed by the targeted analysis pipeline where the chromatogram traces are evaluated with the reference libraries combined with manual curations.

Importantly, smoothing level 1 was used in the MRMPROBS program and it was set to 3 in the MS-DIAL program. The higher smoothing level allows for the determination of peak left and right edges in the automated data analysis pipeline owing to the reduced noise level. Therefore, the higher smoothing value was used in the untargeted analysis. Conversely, the co-eluted peaks are often merged as a single peak. Because all chromatogram peaks could manually be checked and modified in the GUI, the lower smoothing value was used in the targeted analysis software.

3.3. Showcase of Newly Resolved Lipid Profiles by MS/MS-Centric Data Analysis

We showcased the methodology by profiling three co-eluted lipid molecules, DGDG 16:2–18:1, DGDG 16:1–18:2, and DGDG 16:0–18:3, with the same precursor m/z and similar retention times (Figure 3a). In the analysis of *E. gracilis*, only DGDG 16:2–18:1 was annotated correctly in MS-DIAL based on the spectral match score, while the MS/MS spectrum was partially interpreted as DGDG 16:1–18:2 and 16:0–18:3. Using the principles of MS-DIAL, the spectra of co-eluted metabolites are annotated using the representative metabolite with the highest spectral matching score, although it could be manually modified. Therefore, MS-DIAL generated the MRMPROBS reference format for the three lipid candidates, and the lipids were quantified using the MRMPORBS program. As a result, DGDG 16:0–18:3 was determined to be the major component of the co-eluted lipids in *Chlamydomonas reinhardtii*, *Auxenochlorella prototothecoides*, *C. sorokiniana*, *C. variabilis*, and *Dunaliella salina*, DGDG 16:2–18:1 the major component in *E. gracilis*, and DGDG 16:1–18:2 in *Nannochloropsis oculate* and *P. carterae* (Figure 3b), where the lipid differences clearly reflected the differences in the phylum. Importantly, these differences could not be resolved using MS-DIAL untargeted analysis (Figure 3c) because the program uses MS^1-centric peak quantification, i.e., the red traces in the chromatograms shown in Figure 3b. This indicated that the DIA-MS/MS data enabled the increased coverage of metabolic profiling, as described elsewhere [27], and the two program suites MS-DIAL and MRMPROBS provided a solution to fully utilize the information-rich MS/MS spectral data for comprehensive metabolome analyses.

3.4. Comparison of Untargeted- and Targeted Analysis Results

We characterized 1437 molecules in nine algal species, and the total count of annotated lipids was 40% higher than that (1023) of the lipids annotated using the previously developed methodology (Figure 4a, Table 1, Supplementary Data 1, 2, and 3). Moreover, we examined correlations among the quantification methods, including MS^1-centric peak height in DDA and DIA-MS/MS data, and MS/MS-centric peak height and area in the DIA-MS/MS data. As expected, the correlation between peak height and area in DIA-MS/MS data were high (Figure 4b, right-bottom), but the correlation between peak heights in DDA and DIA-MS/MS data could be affected by the mass spectrometry settings [6] where the total scan cycle times were different in DDA (650 ms) and DIA-MS/MS (730 ms) data acquisition (Figure 4b, top-left). These differences were also caused by different LC-MS analysis days, where the MS sensitivities differed for each lipid class. Surprisingly, our results indicated that the correlations between MS^1 and MS/MS chromatograms were highly dependent on the lipid classes. This indicates that the sensitivity of the product ions is different for each lipid class, and the correlation value is high when abundances are compared within each lipid class. The dynamic range using MS/MS chromatograms was narrower than that of the MS^1 chromatograms, and the saturation behavior was observed in the correlation plots, especially for TAG lipids, between MS^1- and MS/MS-centric quantifications. In fact, the SWATH-MS/MS channels of the TripleTOF 5600+ instrument have a lower linear dynamic range compared to MS^1. These results suggest that MS^1-centric metabolite quantification is slightly superior to that of the MS/MS-centric quantification, while the annotation coverage in MS/MS-centric analyses outperformed the untargeted analysis pipeline.

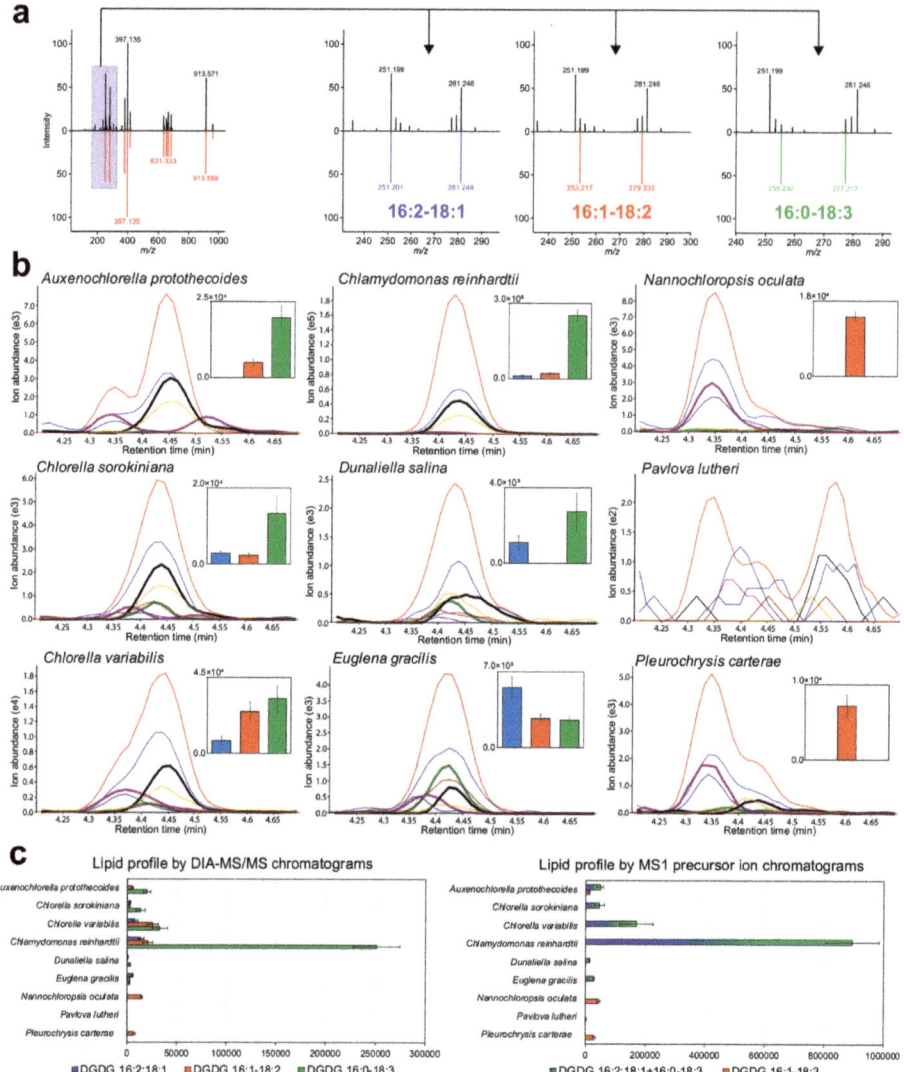

Figure 3. Showcase of the MS/MS-centric lipid quantifications. (**a**) The co-eluted MS/MS spectra of digalactosyldiacylglycerol (DGDG) 16:2–18:1, DGDG 16:1–18:2, and DGDG 16:0–18:3. (**b**) The red and blue traces in the chromatograms for each algal species show the extracted ion chromatograms of the precursor and product ions of m/z 397.135 used for the lipid class diagnostics, respectively. The bold green, black, and purple traces show the extracted ion MS/MS chromatograms of the m/z 251.201, m/z 253.217, and m/z 255.232 ions for fatty acids 16:2, 16:1, and 16:0, respectively. (**c**) The three molecules are quantified by the traces of unique product ion chromatograms in the targeted analysis pipeline, while two are not resolved in the MS^1 chromatogram traces.

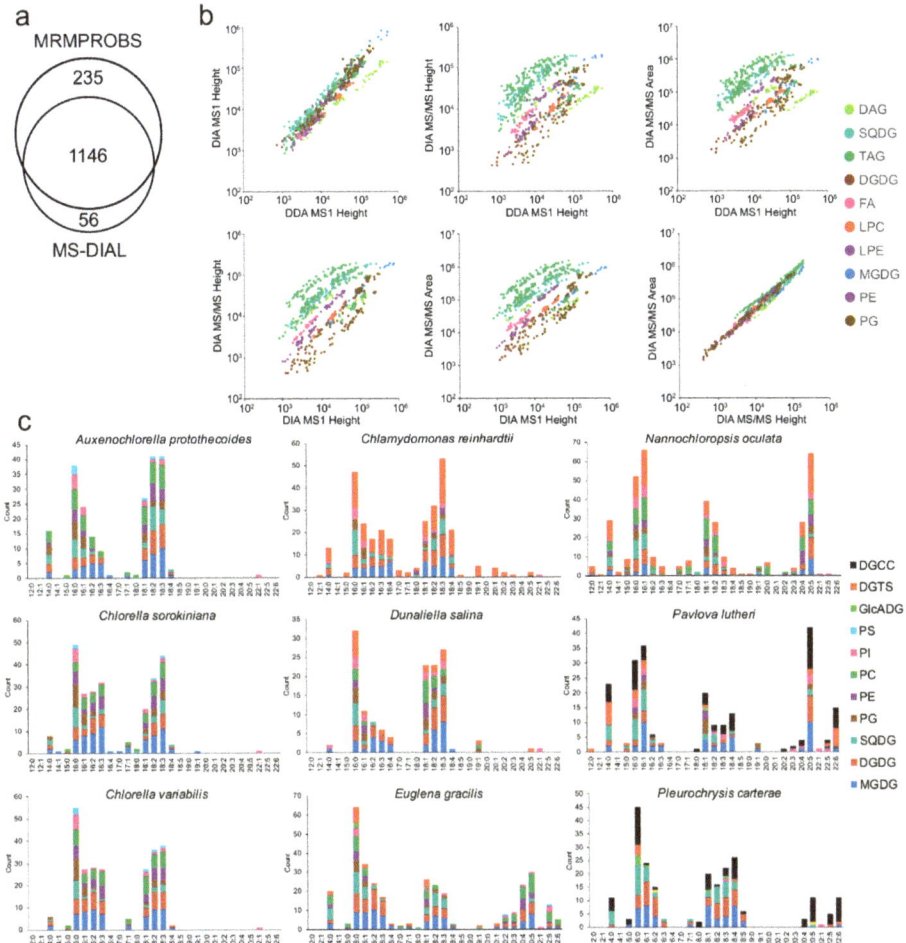

Figure 4. Summary of lipid annotations and comparison of MS^1- and MS/MS-centric peak quantifications. (**a**) Counts of the annotated lipids in untargeted (MS-DIAL) and targeted (MRMPROBS) analyses. (**b**) The correlations of ion abundances where the MS^1-centric peak heights in the DDA and DIA data and MS/MS-centric peak height and area are examined. (**c**) The statistics of acyl chains in all lipid classes except for triacylglycerol (TAG) for each algal species. The x- and y-axis shows the fatty acid information and frequency, respectively. The TAG lipids are not used for the counts because many combinations are observed in a single MS/MS spectrum, which may include false-positive identifications.

Finally, a detailed investigation of fatty acid properties revealed the uniqueness of the acyl chains in each algal species (Figure 4c). Importantly, we used the fatty acid counts included in the lipid classes instead of the ion abundances because lipid ionization efficiency is highly dependent on the lipid class and retention time. In Plantae, 16:0, 16:1, 16:2, 16:3, 18:0, 18:1, 18:2, and 18:3 are known to be major acyl chains [28], while 16:4 and 18:4 are highly distributed in Chlorophyceae including *C. reinhardtii* and *D. salina* compared to Trebouxiophyceae including *Chlorella* species. Moreover, the acyl chain of 18:0 is not often observed in glycerolipids and glycerophospholipids in nine algal species. In Chromista and Protozoa, polyunsaturated fatty acids (PUFAs) are enriched in addition to the common 16 and 18 carbon length series. These results show that various PUFAs, such as 20:4, 20:5, 22:5, and 22:6, were observed in *E. gracilis* while 20:5 and 22:6 were enriched in *P. lutheri*, and 20:4 and 20:5 in the lipids of *N. oculate*. These observations were achieved using the MS/MS chromatogram traces for lipid quantification, and the approach is effective for investigating lipid profiles in living organisms to deepen our understanding of lipid metabolism and its connection with gene expression and enzyme activities.

In general, untargeted analysis searches are conducted for as many metabolites as possible to generate hypotheses in biology, though the rate of false-positive annotations becomes higher than that in targeted analysis; therefore, data analysts should devote much time and effort in curating annotation results. On the other hand, the targeted analysis focuses on a limited number of metabolites with less false-positive rate, though curation is still needed to modify the peak-picking results. Although the automated pipelines with the estimation of false discovery rate (FDR) in annotations have also been developed in metabolomics [29–31] for large-scale datasets like cohort studies, data analysts should recognize the pitfall in annotations that may be mentioned as false-positive metabolites in the metabolome and lipidome data sheet for statistical analyses. Therefore, the integrated analysis by untargeted and targeted techniques is important to reduce misleading results in biological studies. In fact, the metabolites of interest obtained from the integrated results must be validated using authentic standard compounds and further biological experiments to compensate for the lack of current MS instruments and informatic techniques providing limited stereochemical and isomer information.

4. Conclusions

Consequently, the reanalysis of published data was demonstrated where 17 lipid classes were newly characterized in nine algal species in addition to the 15 lipid classes annotated previously. In effect, the coverage of lipid classes was doubled by updating the computational mass spectrometry techniques and mass spectral libraries, and our reanalysis indicates the value of MS data repositories where the raw data could be utilized as a benchmark for new software programs and data-driven hypothesis generation. The lipidomics workflow is also executable with hydrophilic interaction chromatography (HILIC) [32] or supercritical fluid chromatography (SFC) [33], in which the molecules can be separated based on the specific chemical properties of each lipid class, enabling efficient exclusion of false-positive annotations from incorrect lipid classes. Ion mobility MS provides another diagnostic criterion, viz. collision cross-section (CCS), to increase the confidence in lipid annotation [34]. Although we only showcased the increase in lipid profiling coverage, this strategy could also be applied to more diverse metabolites with experimentally acquired spectral libraries. There are three types of spectral databases: (1) completely open-access, i.e., all records are browsable and downloadable (e.g., MassBank [35], PlaSMA [9], Fiehnlib [36], and GNPS [4]), (2) limited access, i.e., browsable but not downloadable (e.g., Metlin [17] and mzCloud (https://www.mzcloud.org/)), and (3) licensed databases such as NIST and Wiley, and the integrated databases cover the MS/MS spectra of approximately 12,000 unique metabolites [9,26]. Importantly, all these databases have increasingly been updated by the continuous effort of mass spectrometrists; therefore, success similar to that obtained herein is achievable by reanalyzing public data using the upgraded databases.

In conclusion, the science of metabolomics and lipidomics now enters a new era owing to state-of-the-art analytical techniques and informatics platforms where metabolic profiling is semi-automatically executable [37]. Therefore, MS data repositories will become increasingly important to reach a 'standard' in genomics and transcriptomics data sciences. Our computational workflow could be used as a pipeline for metabolomics and lipidomics data processing and the understanding of metabolism is deepened by advances in computational metabolomics.

Supplementary Materials: The following are available online at http://www.mdpi.com/2218-1989/9/6/119/s1. Supplementary Data 1. MS-DIAL original output for DIA-MS/MS data. The peak height is exported. The representative SMILES and InChIKey codes are also exported although the stereochemistry is not determined spectrometrically; Supplementary Data 2. MS-DIAL original output for DDA-MS/MS data. The peak height is exported. The representative SMILES and InChIKey codes are also exported although the stereochemistry is not determined spectrometrically; Supplementary Data 3. MRMPROBS output for DIA-MS/MS data. The peak height- and area values are exported.

Author Contributions: H.T., T.C., M.A. (Makoto Arita) and M.A. (Masanori Arita) designed the research. H.T. wrote all source codes for MS-DIAL and MRMPROBS. H.T. and H.U. analyzed standard compounds and created in-silico MS/MS spectral library. A.S. performed the reanalysis of the algal lipidomics data. H.T. wrote the manuscript, and all authors helped to improve the manuscript.

Funding: This work was partially supported by JSPS KAKENHI (15H05897, 15H05898, 17H03621, 18H02432, 18K19155) and JST National Bioscience Database Center (NBDC).

Conflicts of Interest: The authors declare no conflict of interest.

References

1. Haug, K.; Salek, R.M.; Steinbeck, C. Global Open Data Management in Metabolomics. *Curr. Opin. Chem. Biol.* **2017**, *36*, 58–63. [CrossRef] [PubMed]
2. Sud, M.; Fahy, E.; Cotter, D.; Azam, K.; Vadivelu, I.; Burant, C.; Edison, A.; Fiehn, O.; Higashi, R.; Nair, K.S.; et al. Metabolomics Workbench: An International Repository for Metabolomics Data and Metadata, Metabolite Standards, Protocols, Tutorials and Training, and Analysis Tools. *Nucleic Acids Res.* **2016**, *44*, D463–D470. [CrossRef] [PubMed]
3. Kale, N.S.; Haug, K.; Conesa, P.; Jayseelan, K.; Moreno, P.; Rocca-Serra, P.; Nainala, V.C.; Spicer, R.A.; Williams, M.; Li, X.; et al. MetaboLights: An Open-Access Database Repository for Metabolomics Data. *Curr. Protoc. Bioinform.* **2016**, *53*, 14.13.1–14.13.18.
4. Wang, M.; Carver, J.J.; Phelan, V.V.; Sanchez, L.M.; Garg, N.; Peng, Y.; Nguyen, D.D.; Watrous, J.; Kapono, C.A.; Luzzatto-Knaan, T.; et al. Sharing and Community Curation of Mass Spectrometry Data with Global Natural Products Social Molecular Networking. *Nat. Biotechnol.* **2016**, *34*, 828–837. [CrossRef] [PubMed]
5. Spicer, R.A.; Steinbeck, C. A Lost Opportunity for Science: Journals Promote Data Sharing in Metabolomics but Do Not Enforce It. *Metabolomics* **2018**, *14*. [CrossRef] [PubMed]
6. Tsugawa, H.; Cajka, T.; Kind, T.; Ma, Y.; Higgins, B.; Ikeda, K.; Kanazawa, M.; VanderGheynst, J.; Fiehn, O.; Arita, M. MS-DIAL: Data-Independent MS/MS Deconvolution for Comprehensive Metabolome Analysis. *Nat. Methods* **2015**, *12*, 523–526. [CrossRef] [PubMed]
7. Tsugawa, H.; Ikeda, K.; Tanaka, W.; Senoo, Y.; Arita, M.; Arita, M. Comprehensive Identification of Sphingolipid Species by in Silico Retention Time and Tandem Mass Spectral Library. *J. Cheminform.* **2017**, *9*, 19. [CrossRef]
8. Tsugawa, H.; Ikeda, K.; Arita, M. The importance of bioinformatics for connecting data-driven lipidomics and biological insights. *Biochim. Biophys. Acta Mol. Cell Biol. Lipids* **2017**, *1862*, 762–765. [CrossRef]
9. Tsugawa, H.; Nakabayashi, R.; Mori, T.; Yamada, Y.; Takahashi, M.; Rai, A.; Sugiyama, R.; Yamamoto, H.; Nakaya, T.; Yamazaki, M.; et al. A Cheminformatics Approach to Characterize Metabolomes in Stable-Isotope-Labeled Organisms. *Nat. Methods* **2019**, *16*, 295–298. [CrossRef]
10. Tsugawa, H.; Arita, M.; Kanazawa, M.; Ogiwara, A.; Bamba, T.; Fukusaki, E. MRMPROBS: A Data Assessment and Metabolite Identification Tool for Large-Scale Multiple Reaction Monitoring Based Widely Targeted Metabolomics. *Anal. Chem.* **2013**, *85*, 5191–5199. [CrossRef]
11. Tsugawa, H.; Kanazawa, M.; Ogiwara, A.; Arita, M. MRMPROBS Suite for Metabolomics Using Large-Scale MRM Assays. *Bioinformatics* **2014**, *30*, 2379–2380. [CrossRef] [PubMed]
12. Lai, Z.; Tsugawa, H.; Wohlgemuth, G.; Mehta, S.; Mueller, M.; Zheng, Y.; Ogiwara, A.; Meissen, J.; Showalter, M.; Takeuchi, K.; et al. Identifying Metabolites by Integrating Metabolome Databases with Mass Spectrometry Cheminformatics. *Nat. Methods* **2017**, *15*, 53–56. [CrossRef] [PubMed]
13. Mahieu, N.G.; Genenbacher, J.L.; Patti, G.J. A Roadmap for the XCMS Family of Software Solutions in Metabolomics. *Curr. Opin. Chem. Biol.* **2016**, *30*, 87–93. [CrossRef] [PubMed]
14. Pluskal, T.; Castillo, S.; Villar-Briones, A.; Oresic, M. MZmine 2: Modular Framework for Processing, Visualizing, and Analyzing Mass Spectrometry-Based Molecular Profile Data. *BMC Bioinform.* **2010**, *11*, 395. [CrossRef] [PubMed]
15. Li, H.; Cai, Y.; Guo, Y.; Chen, F.; Zhu, Z.J. MetDIA: Targeted Metabolite Extraction of Multiplexed MS/MS Spectra Generated by Data-Independent Acquisition. *Anal. Chem.* **2016**, *88*, 8757–8764. [CrossRef] [PubMed]

16. Perez-Riverol, Y.; Bai, M.; da Veiga Leprevost, F.; Squizzato, S.; Park, Y.M.; Haug, K.; Carroll, A.J.; Spalding, D.; Paschall, J.; Wang, M.; et al. Discovering and Linking Public Omics Data Sets Using the Omics Discovery Index. *Nat. Biotechnol.* **2017**, *35*, 406–409. [CrossRef] [PubMed]
17. Koellensperger, G.; Guijas, C.; Benton, H.P.; Huan, T.; Wolan, D.W.; Warth, B.; Aisporna, A.E.; Hermann, G.; Domingo-Almenara, X.; Spilker, M.E.; et al. METLIN: A Technology Platform for Identifying Knowns and Unknowns. *Anal. Chem.* **2018**, *90*, 3156–3164.
18. Kind, T.; Liu, K.-H.; Lee, D.Y.; DeFelice, B.; Meissen, J.K.; Fiehn, O. LipidBlast in Silico Tandem Mass Spectrometry Database for Lipid Identification. *Nat. Methods* **2013**, *10*, 755–758. [CrossRef]
19. Eichenberger, W.; Gribi, C. Lipids of *Pavlova Lutheri*: Cellular Site and Metabolic Role of DGCC. *Phytochemistry* **1997**, *45*, 1561–1567. [CrossRef]
20. Schleyer, G.; Shahaf, N.; Ziv, C.; Dong, Y.; Meoded, R.A.; Helfrich, E.J.N.; Schatz, D.; Rosenwasser, S.; Rogachev, I.; Aharoni, A.; et al. In Plaque-Mass Spectrometry Imaging of a Bloom-Forming Alga during Viral Infection Reveals a Metabolic Shift towards Odd-Chain Fatty Acid Lipids. *Nat. Microbiol.* **2019**, *4*, 527–538. [CrossRef]
21. Aoyagi, R.; Ikeda, K.; Isobe, Y.; Arita, M. Comprehensive Analyses of Oxidized Phospholipids Using a Measured MS/MS Spectra Library. *J. Lipid Res.* **2017**, *58*, 2229–2237. [CrossRef] [PubMed]
22. Okazaki, Y.; Otsuki, H.; Narisawa, T.; Kobayashi, M.; Sawai, S.; Kamide, Y.; Kusano, M.; Aoki, T.; Hirai, M.Y.; Saito, K. A New Class of Plant Lipid Is Essential for Protection against Phosphorus Depletion. *Nat. Commun.* **2013**, *4*, 1510. [CrossRef] [PubMed]
23. Li, Y.; Lou, Y.; Mu, T.; Xu, J.; Zhou, C.; Yan, X. Simultaneous Structural Identification of Diacylglyceryl-N-Trimethylhomoserine (DGTS) and Diacylglycerylhydroxymethyl-N, N, N-Trimethyl-β-Alanine (DGTA) in Microalgae Using Dual Li$^+$/H$^+$ Adduct Ion Mode by Ultra-Performance Liquid Chromatography/Quadrupole Time-Of-Flight Mass Spectrometry. *Rapid Commun. Mass Spectrom.* **2017**, *31*, 824. [PubMed]
24. Okazaki, Y.; Nishizawa, T.; Takano, K.; Ohnishi, M.; Mimura, T.; Saito, K. Induced accumulation of glucuronosyldiacylglycerol in tomato and soybean under phosphorus deprivation. *Physiol. Plant.* **2015**, *155*, 33–42. [CrossRef] [PubMed]
25. Roughan, P.G.; Slack, C.R.; Holland, R. Generation of phospholipid artefacts during extraction of developing soybean seeds with methanolic solvents. *Lipids* **1978**, *13*, 497–503. [CrossRef]
26. Reis, A.; Spickett, C.M. Chemistry of Phospholipid Oxidation. *Biochim. Biophys. Acta-Biomembr.* **2012**, *1818*, 2374–2387. [CrossRef]
27. Bonnera, R.; Hopfgartner, G. SWATH data independent acquisition mass spectrometry for metabolomics. *TrAc Trends Anal. Chem.* **2018**. [CrossRef]
28. Ohlrogge, J.; Browse, J. Lipid Biosynthesis. *Plant Cell* **2007**, *7*, 957–970. [CrossRef]
29. Matsuda, F.; Tsugawa, H.; Fukusaki, E. Method for Assessing the Statistical Significance of Mass Spectral Similarities Using Basic Local Alignment Search Tool Statistics. *Anal. Chem.* **2013**, *85*, 8291–8297. [CrossRef]
30. Palmer, A.; Phapale, P.; Chernyavsky, I.; Lavigne, R.; Fay, D.; Tarasov, A.; Kovalev, V.; Fuchser, J.; Nikolenko, S.; Pineau, C.; et al. FDR-Controlled Metabolite Annotation for High-Resolution Imaging Mass Spectrometry. *Nat. Methods* **2016**, *14*, 57–60. [CrossRef] [PubMed]
31. Scheubert, K.; Hufsky, F.; Petras, D.; Wang, M.; Nothias, L.-F.; Dührkop, K.; Bandeira, N.; Dorrestein, P.C.; Böcker, S. Significance Estimation for Large Scale Metabolomics Annotations by Spectral Matching. *Nat. Commun.* **2017**, *8*, 1494. [CrossRef] [PubMed]
32. Pham, T.H.; Zaeem, M.; Fillier, T.A.; Nadeem, M.; Vidal, N.P.; Manful, C.; Cheema, S.; Cheema, M.; Thomas, R.H. Targeting Modified Lipids during Routine Lipidomics Analysis Using HILIC and C30 Reverse Phase Liquid Chromatography Coupled to Mass Spectrometry. *Sci. Rep.* **2019**, *9*. [CrossRef] [PubMed]
33. Lísa, M.; Holčapek, M. High-Throughput and Comprehensive Lipidomic Analysis Using Ultrahigh-Performance Supercritical Fluid Chromatography-Mass Spectrometry. *Anal. Chem.* **2015**, *87*, 7187–7195. [CrossRef] [PubMed]
34. Blaženović, I.; Shen, T.; Mehta, S.S.; Kind, T.; Ji, J.; Piparo, M.; Cacciola, F.; Mondello, L.; Fiehn, O. Increasing Compound Identification Rates in Untargeted Lipidomics Research with Liquid Chromatography Drift Time-Ion Mobility Mass Spectrometry. *Anal. Chem.* **2018**, *90*, 10758–10764. [CrossRef] [PubMed]
35. Horai, H.; Arita, M.; Kanaya, S.; Nihei, Y.; Ikeda, T.; Suwa, K.; Ojima, Y.; Tanaka, K.; Tanaka, S.; Aoshima, K.; et al. MassBank: A Public Repository for Sharing Mass Spectral Data for Life Sciences. *J. Mass Spectrom.* **2010**, *45*, 703–714. [CrossRef] [PubMed]

36. Kind, T.; Wohlgemuth, G.; Lee, D.Y.; Lu, Y.; Palazoglu, M.; Shahbaz, S.; Fiehn, O. FiehnLib: Mass Spectral and Retention Index Libraries for Metabolomics Based on Quadrupole and Time-of-Flight Gas Chromatography/Mass Spectrometry. *Anal. Chem.* **2009**, *81*, 10038–10048. [CrossRef]
37. Tsugawa, H. Advances in Computational Metabolomics and Databases Deepen the Understanding of Metabolisms. *Curr. Opin. Biotechnol.* **2018**, *54*, 10–17. [CrossRef]

© 2019 by the authors. Licensee MDPI, Basel, Switzerland. This article is an open access article distributed under the terms and conditions of the Creative Commons Attribution (CC BY) license (http://creativecommons.org/licenses/by/4.0/).

Article

Visualization and Interpretation of Multivariate Associations with Disease Risk Markers and Disease Risk—The Triplot

Tessa Schillemans [1,†], Lin Shi [2,†], Xin Liu [3], Agneta Åkesson [1], Rikard Landberg [2,4] and Carl Brunius [2,*]

1. Cardiovascular and Nutritional Epidemiology, Institute of Environmental Medicine, Karolinska Institutet, SE-171 77 Stockholm, Sweden
2. Department of Biology and Biological Engineering, Chalmers University of Technology, SE-412 96 Gothenburg, Sweden
3. Department of Epidemiology and Biostatistics, School of Public Health, Xi'an Jiaotong University Health Science Center, SE-710049 Xi'an, China
4. Department of Public Health and Clinical Medicine, Umeå University, SE-901 87 Umeå, Sweden
* Correspondence: carl.brunius@chalmers.se; Tel.: +46-70-4834385
† These authors contributed equally to this work.

Received: 18 June 2019; Accepted: 3 July 2019; Published: 6 July 2019

Abstract: Metabolomics has emerged as a promising technique to understand relationships between environmental factors and health status. Through comprehensive profiling of small molecules in biological samples, metabolomics generates high-dimensional data objectively, reflecting exposures, endogenous responses, and health effects, thereby providing further insights into exposure-disease associations. However, the multivariate nature of metabolomics data contributes to high complexity in analysis and interpretation. Efficient visualization techniques of multivariate data that allow direct interpretation of combined exposures, metabolome, and disease risk, are currently lacking. We have therefore developed the 'triplot' tool, a novel algorithm that simultaneously integrates and displays metabolites through latent variable modeling (e.g., principal component analysis, partial least squares regression, or factor analysis), their correlations with exposures, and their associations with disease risk estimates or intermediate risk factors. This paper illustrates the framework of the 'triplot' using two synthetic datasets that explore associations between dietary intake, plasma metabolome, and incident type 2 diabetes or BMI, an intermediate risk factor for lifestyle-related diseases. Our results demonstrate advantages of triplot over conventional visualization methods in facilitating interpretation in multivariate risk modeling with high-dimensional data. Algorithms, synthetic data, and tutorials are open source and available in the R package 'triplot'.

Keywords: triplot; metabolomics; multivariate risk modeling; environmental factors; disease risk

1. Introduction

Environmental factors, such as diet, smoking, and pollutants, are associated with risk of developing non-communicable diseases (NCDs), including obesity, type 2 diabetes (T2D), and cardiovascular disease [1], which together constitute the leading cause of morbidity, mortality, and high healthcare costs worldwide. The role of lifestyle factors in development and progression of NCDs has often been studied in prospective cohorts or case-controlled studies, where associations of specific exposures with health outcomes or intermediate risk markers of NCDs (e.g., blood pressure, lipid profiles, and body weight) are assessed. Several challenges exist in the research on exposure–health relationships, including the measurement of environmental factors and the lack of understanding of underlying molecular mechanisms that are affected by the exposures [2].

Metabolomics is the comprehensive assessment of metabolites in biological samples, which enables investigation of physiological and biological states at the molecular phenotype level, reflecting both exogenous and endogenous exposures. Thus, metabolomics could potentially advance the understanding of associations between exposures and health status [3–5]. For example, using metabolomics to identify metabolite biomarkers objectively reflecting dietary exposures could provide a complement to self-reported dietary assessments that are known to suffer from large systematic and random measurement errors [6]. Metabolomics can also be used to link exposures to outcomes [7,8] by detecting endogenous changes in response to exposures [3]. However, in addition to these advantages, application of metabolomics in epidemiologic research makes interpretation and visualization of the results more complex due to the high dimensionality of the data.

Both multivariate analysis (e.g., reduced rank/component-based techniques) and univariate analysis are routinely used in metabolomics studies to extract meaningful information from complex datasets and thus provide biological knowledge of the research question under investigation [9]. Univariate analyses allow both for simultaneous investigation of multiple study factors, time series data, as well as adjustment for potential covariates or confounders. In general, univariate methods also provide more straightforward interpretation of results compared to multivariate analyses, which on the other hand make use of all variables simultaneously and are well-equipped to deal with high collinearity, which is often a challenge in epidemiological studies [10]. However, they offer limited options to investigate several study factors simultaneously, i.e., analyze data from time series or adjust for potential covariates or confounders.

Results from metabolomics studies aiming to investigate exposure–disease relationships are often using a combination of figures to illustrate the findings. Observation scores and metabolite loadings from latent variable (LV) modeling (e.g., principal component analysis (PCA), factor analysis (FA), or partial least squares (PLS)) can be shown, e.g., in a biplot (Figure 1a), to identify outliers, to visualize separation of individuals into subgroups, and to examine how individual metabolites contribute to the LVs. Correlations between individual metabolites or LV scores and exposures are then frequently visualized using heatmaps (Figure 1b). Finally, individual metabolites or LV scores can be used as independent variables to model disease outcome or intermediate risk markers. Associated risk can then be visualized as odds ratios (ORs) or beta coefficients from logistic or linear regressions in a forest plot (Figure 1c). However, the lack of effective tools for direct interpretation of the relationship between exposures, metabolome, and outcome measure by visualization of combined data makes interpretation and communication of findings difficult.

We therefore developed the novel 'triplot' tool to facilitate visualization and interpretation of multivariate risk modeling, which enables a global, combined overview of information representing the metabolome (or other types of multivariate data), exposures, or environmental factors of interest and associated health outcomes (i.e., disease outcomes or intermediate risk factors) (Figure 1d). We present the workflow of the triplot package and demonstrate its applicability using two synthetic datasets that were simulated from a case-controlled study nested within the Swedish prospective Västerbotten Intervention Programme cohort [11] and from a cross-sectional study of Carbohydrate Alternatives and Metabolic Phenotypes in Chinese young adults [12].

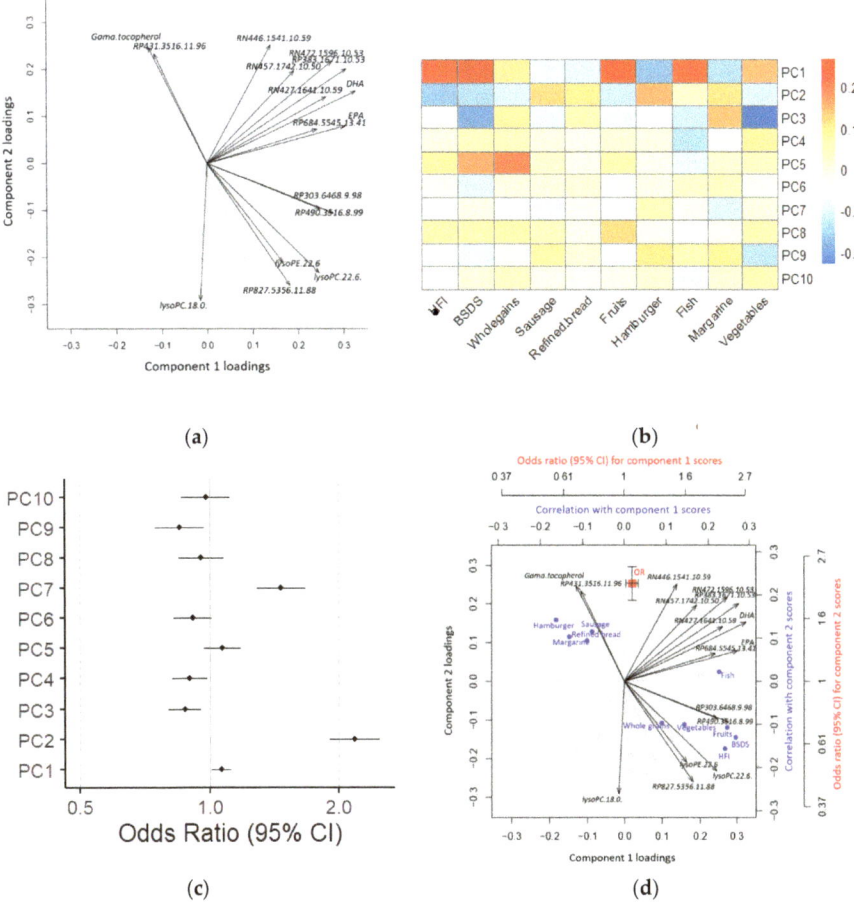

Figure 1. Using metabolomics data to investigate the relationship between exposures and disease risk. In a standard approach, latent variable (LV) modeling (**a**) is used to achieve a reduced rank approximation of the metabolomics data. Correlation heatmaps (**b**) and forest plots (**c**) are then used to associate observation scores with exposures and risks, respectively. For more direct interpretation, LV modeling, and their associations with exposures and risks can be visualized jointly in a triplot (**d**). HFI: Healthy Food Index; BSDS: Baltic Sea Diet Score; PC: Principal Component; OR: Odds Ratio; CI: Confidence Interval. lysoPC: Lysophosphatidylcholine; lysoPE: Lysophosphoethanolamine; EPA: Eicosapentaenoic acid; DHA: Docosahexaenoic acid; RP: reverse phase chromatography positive mode ionization; RN: reverse phase chromatography negative mode ionization.

2. Materials and Methods

2.1. Synthetic Data

'HealthyNordicDiet': This synthetic dataset was simulated from data used in a case-controlled study nested within the Swedish prospective Västerbotten Intervention Programme (VIP) cohort [8]. The entire study protocol was approved by the Regional Ethics Committee in Uppsala, Sweden (registration number 2014/011). The original study material was used to investigate how the plasma metabolome and the risk of developing T2D were related to compliance to a Healthy Nordic Diet [8]. Detailed information on study design and metabolomics data acquisition is provided elsewhere [7,8]. In brief, the original dataset included 421 participants from VIP at baseline (median time of 7 years before T2D diagnosis). Each case was individually matched to one nondiabetic participant on age, gender, sampling date, and sample storage time. Untargeted liquid chromatography quadrupole time-of-flight mass spectrometry (LC-qTOF-MS) metabolomics was performed on plasma samples using reverse phase and hydrophilic interaction chromatography in both positive and negative electrospray ionization modes. In total, 31 plasma metabolites related to a priori-defined healthy Nordic dietary indices, i.e., the Baltic Sea Diet Score (BSDS) and Healthy Nordic Food Index (HNFI), were selected using a random forest algorithm incorporated into a repeated double cross-validation framework with unbiased variable selection [8,13]. Subsequently, associations were investigated between the 31 dietary index-related metabolites, dietary intakes, and T2D risk [8].

The simulated data contains three data frames: Baseline characteristics of participants (*BaselineData*, 11 variables), identified metabolites associated with healthy Nordic diet (*MetaboliteData*, 31 variables), and food items associated with Healthy Nordic Diet (*FoodData*, 17 variables). The data frames are row-wise matched by observation and consist of 1000 synthetic observations that correspond to 500 case-controlled pairs matched by gender and age.

CAMP: This synthetic dataset was simulated from real data used in a cross-sectional study of carbohydrate alternatives and metabolic phenotypes [12]. The study was approved by the ethical committee of Xi'an Jiaotong University Health Science Center, and all participants provided written informed consent. The original data were obtained from fasting plasma samples from 86 men and women that were between 18–35 years of age. Samples were analyzed by untargeted LC-qTOF-MS metabolomics using reverse phase chromatography in both positive and negative electrospray ionization modes. Associations were investigated between an optimal selection of plasma metabolites predictive of BMI and dietary intakes as well as several clinical measurements.

The simulated data contains three data frames: Clinical measurements (*ClinData*, 11 variables), plasma metabolites predictive of BMI (*MetaboliteData*, 20 variables), and dietary intake as measured by food frequency questionnaires (*FoodData*, 11 variables). The data frames are row-wise matched by observation and consist of 300 synthetic observations.

2.2. Algorithm Description

The 'triplot' is a novel tool that simultaneously integrates three levels of information, effectively providing interpretable visualization of multivariate associations between exposures, metabolome, and disease risk by superimposing LVs from multivariate modeling of, e.g., metabolomics data with correlations of exposures (or other correlations) and associations with disease risk or intermediate risk markers (Figure 2). An overview of the functions and workflow of the triplot package is presented in Table 1.

In the first layer of the triplot, LV modeling is performed on a high-dimensional dataset, generated from, e.g., metabolomics, proteomics or other omics, to reduce the data dimensionality, and to aggregate correlated variables into LVs. The choice of LV modeling method depends on the preference of the user, the data, and the analytical question. The triplot algorithm accepts input from any LV modeling that conforms to reporting observation scores and variable loadings. Frequently used LV algorithms include unsupervised PCA and FA as well as supervised PLS analyses. PCA and FA are used to describe the total variability among the observed (metabolomics) variables using a lower number of LVs called principal components or factors, respectively. PLS is conceptually similar but identifies components that are instead optimized for covariation between the observed (independent) variables and an outcome (dependent) variable [14,15].

There are several methods to determine the number of LVs to retain in unsupervised LV modeling, i.e., PCA and FA [16]. Among them, a scree plot, which shows how much variation each factor or principal component captures from the data, and very simple structure analysis are commonly used [17]. For supervised modeling like PLS, the number of LVs should be optimized by cross validation. Out of several cross-validation approaches, repeated double cross validation has shown advantages in estimation of the optimum number of PLS components and estimations of prediction errors over several other commonly used validation approaches, such as k-fold and leave-n-out [13,18,19].

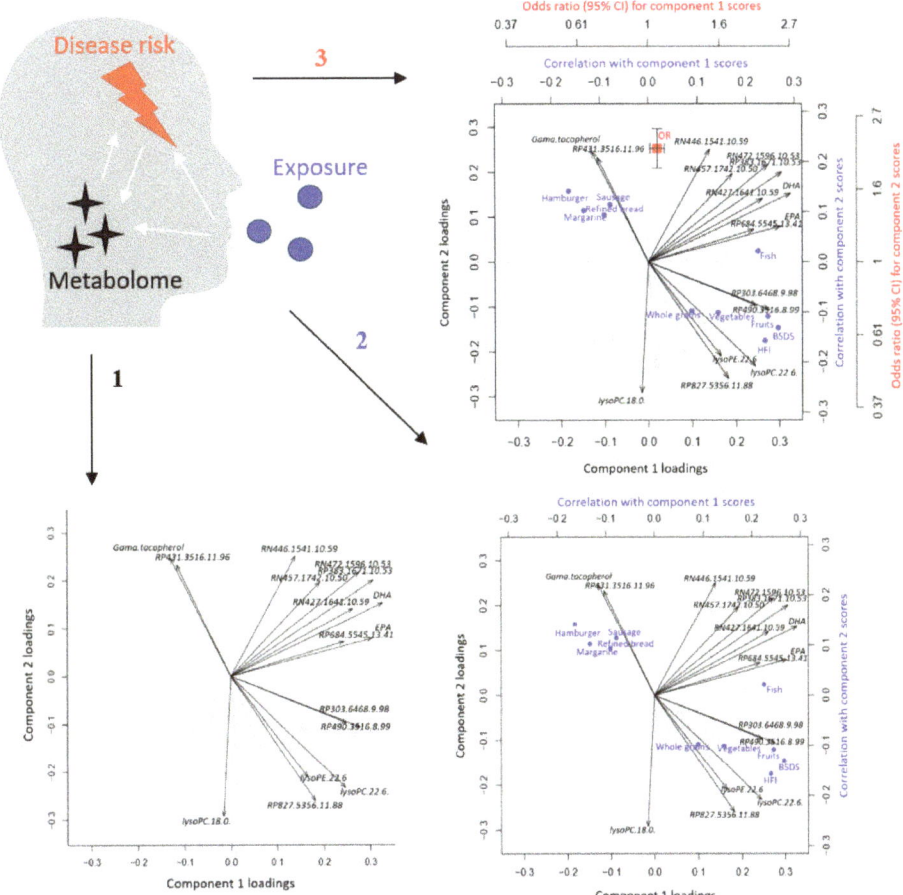

Figure 2. Link between exposures, metabolome, and disease risk as presented in the triplot. The first step consists of latent variable modeling of metabolomics data providing scores and loadings. The second step superimposes correlations between component scores and exposures (or covariates). The third step superimposes risk of outcome associated with the component scores.

A second layer presents correlations between LV observation scores and single or multiple exposures, such as self-reported dietary intakes. Correlation coefficients can be obtained by any correlation methodology that is suitable for the data structure, such as the Pearson method for linear correlations, the Spearman method for non-linear (rank) correlations, or polychoric/polyserial correlation methods for ordinal variables [20]. In order to adjust the correlation results for confounders, users can also apply partial correlations [21].

Associations between the LV observation scores and disease risk or intermediate risk factors are added in a third layer. Users can define risk associations suitable for different study designs, such as ORs of disease risk calculated using (conditional) logistic regression in case-controlled studies, hazard ratios of disease risk calculated using cox regression in prospective cohorts, or beta coefficients of intermediate risk markers calculated using linear regression in cross-sectional studies.

Associated correlations and risk estimates are added to the LV modeling in a modular, easy-to-use workflow, and a summarized overview in the form of a heatmap can then be generated to assist in selecting LVs to investigate using the triplot function.

Table 1. Overview of the workflow and main functions in the 'triplot' R package.

Function	Description
	First layer: Latent variable (LV) modeling
Custom [a]	Perform LV modeling of high-dimensional (metabolomics) data.
makeTPO() [a]	Initiate a triplot object (TPO) from LV model
	Second layer: Correlations
makeCorr() or custom [b]	Perform correlation analysis between LV observation scores and exposures or covariates.
addCorr()	Add correlation results to the TPO.
	Third layer: Associated risk
crudeCLR(), crudeLR(), or custom [c]	Calculate risk associations (i.e., odds ratio or hazard ratio) in (conditional) logistic regression or association with intermediate risk markers (i.e., beta coefficient) in linear regression.
addRisk()	Add risk associations to the TPO.
	Visualizations
checkTPO()	Generate a heatmap visualizing correlations and risk associations to identify relevant LVs for the triplot visualization.
triplot()	Create a triplot containing LV analysis results, correlations, and risk associations.

[a] Actual LV modeling is purposely omitted from the triplot package to give the user the choice of LV method, such as PCA, FA, or PLS. The *makeTPO()* function will accept any input that conforms to scores and loadings. [b] *makeCorr()* constitutes a convenience function for standard correlation analysis (Pearson, Spearman, Kendall). Partial correlation requires custom scripts and is covered in the tutorial. [c] *crudeLR()* and *crudeCLR()* constitute convenience functions for (conditional) logistic regression. Adjusting associations for covariates requires custom scripts and is covered in the tutorial.

2.3. Software and Implementation

The triplot algorithm is publicly available in an open source R implementation (https://gitlab.com/CarlBrunius/triplot). The repository provides the 'triplot' R package, installation instructions, synthetic data, and a tutorial that covers the case studies described in this manuscript in a high level of detail, as well as several additional case studies.

3. Results and Discussion

We applied various analyses on the two simulated datasets available from the package to demonstrate the wide applicability of the triplot. Disease risk (discrete outcome) is modeled using the 'HealthyNordicDiet' dataset and intermediate risk markers (continuous outcomes) are modeled using the 'CAMP' dataset.

3.1. HealthyNordicDiet

The original study was set up to explore plasma metabolites that could objectively reflect healthy Nordic dietary patterns in a matched case-controlled study and to assess associations between such patterns and later development of T2D [8]. The processing pipeline for the generation and visualization of the original data is described in Supplementary Materials Figure S1. A global overview of intercorrelations between plasma metabolites related to the healthy Nordic diet, dietary intake variables, as well as T2D risk is shown in Figure 3 (Tutorial—Example 1). PC1 constituted a metabolite profile, which directly reflected the healthy Nordic dietary indices and individual food components of the indices and was not associated with T2D risk after adjustment for lifestyle-related factors. PC2 instead, while it was negatively correlated with the healthy Nordic dietary indices, it was predominantly correlated with foods not part of the indices, e.g., margarine, sausages, and poultry, and also more strongly associated with risk of developing T2D, even after adjustment for BMI and lifestyle-related factors (smoking status, education, physical activity, and total energy intake). Results from different risk modeling approaches can easily be incorporated into the triplot framework, e.g., using normal logistic regression, which achieved similar OR estimates as conditional logistic regression (Figure 3, Tutorial—Example 2).

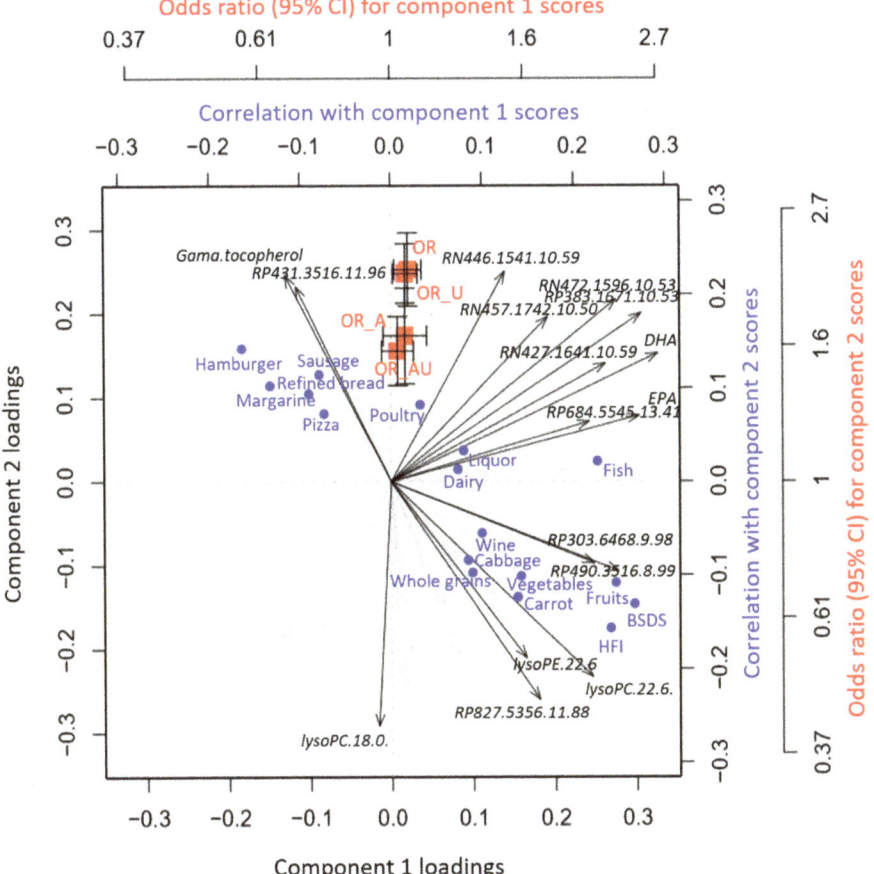

Figure 3. A PCA-based triplot visualizing the inter-correlation between plasma metabolites related to healthy Nordic diet and dietary intake variables as well as association with type 2 diabetes (T2D) risk. Odds ratios of T2D were calculated using conditional logistic regression with or without adjusting for BMI and lifestyle-related confounders (smoking status, education, physical activity, and total energy intake) (OR_A and OR, respectively). Risk associations were calculated similarly using unconditional logistic regression (OR_AU and OR_U, respectively). Correlations between PCA components and dietary intakes were calculated using partial Pearson method, adjusted for case-controlled status, gender, age, BMI, and lifestyle-related confounders (smoking status, education, and physical activity). Only metabolite feature loadings > 0.25 and dietary intake variables significantly correlated with the PCA components are shown.

Importantly, all information incorporated in the triplot visualization could have been obtained using conventional tools, such as separate PCA biplots, heatmaps, and forest plots for risk estimates (Figure 1). However, such an approach presents results scattered across different tables and/or figures, which impedes the direct interpretation of the results. The triplot algorithm instead provides an integrated overview of metabolites as well as associated exposures and risk estimates, which intuitively and clearly presents relevant biological information: The results obtained from synthetic data, i.e., that the metabolite profile related to healthy Nordic diet is not associated with T2D whereas that of more unhealthy dietary choices is, effectively mirror those that were obtained from authentic data [8].

3.2. CAMP

Obesity has been associated with increased morbidity and mortality from NCDs, and high BMI has also been associated with the intake of unhealthy food, i.e., fast food and red/processed meat [22,23]. The cross-sectional study of Carbohydrate Alternatives and Metabolic Phenotypes in Chinese young adults was therefore designed to assess relationships between diet, metabolic profiles, and risk factors of metabolic diseases, using both traditional epidemiological approaches and metabolomics techniques [12].

Intercorrelations between BMI-related plasma metabolites, dietary intakes, and metabolic traits are shown in Figure 4 (Tutorial—Example 3). The PCA-based triplot shows that the metabolite profile predicting BMI was strongly associated with liver enzyme activity, i.e., gamma-glutamyltransferase (GGT), alanine aminotransferase (ALT), and aspartate aminotransferase (AST) (Figure 4), and also with several other health-related metabolic traits, including fasting glucose, triglycerides, total cholesterol, as well as high- (HDL) and low-density lipoprotein (LDL) cholesterol (data not shown), in line with previous studies [24–27]. PC1 reflected metabolites that were positively associated with BMI and also correlated with a high intake of meat and refined grains and negatively with seafood intake, in agreement with observational studies [28–30]. We also found that a high intake of fruits correlated with BMI-related metabolites and other metabolic traits (Figure 4). Fruit consumption is widely considered an important part of a healthy diet, which may provide a host of beneficial nutrients, i.e., vitamins and minerals, dietary fiber, and polyphenols, and aid in the reduction of energy intake and body weight. However, conflicting results exist regarding associations between fruit intake and risk factors of NCDs, including BMI [31,32], as supported by the present investigation. Moreover, PC2 contained high negative loadings of, e.g., phosphatidylcholines containing the marine polyunsaturated fatty acid (C22:6), which in turn correlated positively with seafood intake. From the direct associations of PC2 with liver enzyme activity we then may speculate that the results support the benefits of seafood intake, rich in omega-3 polyunsaturated fatty acids, on human health [33–36].

Of note, the triplot can also be easily constructed based on components derived from supervised modeling of multivariate data (Tutorial—Example 4). To illustrate the wide applicability of the triplot, we performed PLS modeling on the BMI-related metabolites and assessed associations between PLS-derived metabolite components with dietary intakes and metabolic traits, which resulted in similar results as the PCA analysis (Supplementary Materials, Figure S2). The overall direction of the associations obtained using synthetic data was comparable to the results that were obtained from authentic data, although the association between PC1 and high intake of meat was not significant in either synthetic or authentic data (Supplementary Materials, Figure S3).

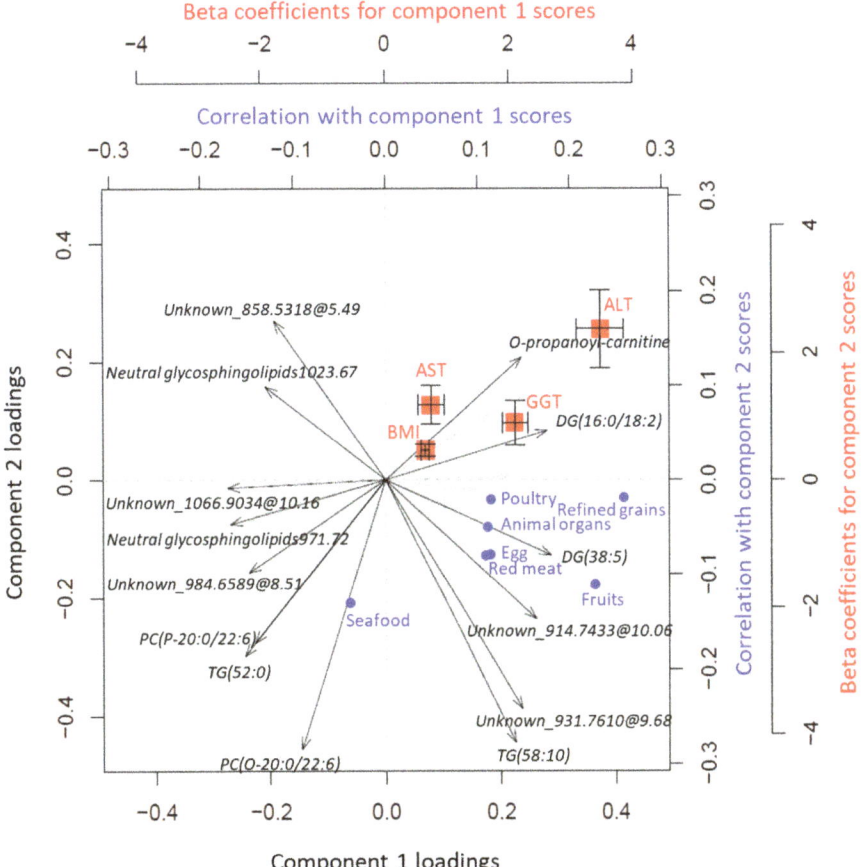

Figure 4. A PCA-based triplot visualizing the inter-correlations between plasma metabolites predicting BMI, dietary intake variables, and metabolic traits, after adjusting for age and gender. Correlations between PCA components and dietary intakes estimated from food frequency questionnaires were calculated using the partial Spearman method. Associations of PCA components with metabolic traits were assessed using linear regression. Only metabolite feature loadings > 0.25, significant correlations, as well as correlations with animal derived foods and metabolic traits with strongest associations are shown. ALT: alanine aminotransferase; AST, aspartate aminotransferase; GGT: gamma-glutamyltransferase.

4. Conclusions

In this work, we have proposed a novel tool, the 'triplot', which can be effectively used to visualize and interpret multivariate risk modeling with high-dimensional data. The framework for integration of metabolomics data, analyzed using either unsupervised or supervised LV modeling, with dietary intakes and disease risk or intermediate risk factors was illustrated using two synthetic datasets representing different study designs. Moreover, our results demonstrate how the triplot could provide advantages over conventional methods in terms of visualization and interpretation of modeling results and thus has the potential to assist in extracting biological meaning from complex data.

Supplementary Materials: The following are available online at http://www.mdpi.com/2218-1989/9/7/133/s1, Figure S1: Overall workflow for generation of the data in the original *HealthyNordicDiet* study. Figure S2: A PLS-based triplot visualizing the intercorrelations between plasma metabolites predicting BMI, dietary intake variables, and metabolic traits, adjusting for age and gender in synthetic 'CAMP' data. Figure S3: A PCA-based triplot visualizing the intercorrelations between plasma metabolites predicting BMI, dietary intake variables, and metabolic traits, adjusting for age and gender in authentic 'CAMP' data.

Author Contributions: Conceptualization: T.S., L.S., R.L., and C.B.; methodology, formal analysis, and investigation: T.S., L.S., and C.B.; data curation: L.S., T.S., X.L., and C.B.; writing—original draft preparation: T.S., L.S., and C.B.; writing—review and editing: T.S., L.S., X.L., A.Å., R.L., and C.B.; supervision: A.Å., R.L., and C.B.; project administration: C.B.; funding acquisition: R.L. and C.B.

Funding: This work was supported by the Swedish Research Council, Swedish Research Council FORMAS, the Dr. Håkanssons Foundation, the Chinese Nutrition Society nutrition research foundation, and the DSM Research Fund.

Conflicts of Interest: The authors declare no conflict of interest.

References

1. Nishtar, S.; Niinistö, S.; Sirisena, M.; Vázquez, T.; Skvortsova, V.; Rubinstein, A.; Mogae, F.G.; Mattila, P.; Ghazizadeh Hashemi, S.H.; Kariuki, S.; et al. Time to deliver: Report of the WHO Independent High-Level Commission on NCDs. *Lancet* **2018**, *392*, 245–252. [CrossRef]
2. Kuras, E.R.; Richardson, M.B.; Calkins, M.M.; Ebi, K.L.; Hess, J.J.; Kintziger, K.W.; Jagger, M.A.; Middel, A.; Scott, A.A.; Spector, J.T.; et al. Opportunities and Challenges for Personal Heat Exposure Research. *Environ. Health Perspect.* **2017**, *125*, 085001. [CrossRef] [PubMed]
3. Scalbert, A.; Brennan, L.; Manach, C.; Andres-Lacueva, C.; Dragsted, L.O.; Draper, J.; Rappaport, S.M.; van der Hooft, J.J.; Wishart, D.S. The food metabolome: A window over dietary exposure. *Am. J. Clin. Nutr.* **2014**, *99*, 1286–1308. [CrossRef] [PubMed]
4. Wild, C.P. Complementing the genome with "an exposome": The outstanding challenge of environmental exposure measurement in molecular epidemiology. *Cancer Epidemiol. Biomark. Prevent. A Publ. Am. Assoc. Cancer Res. Cosponsored Am. Soc. Prevent. Oncol.* **2005**, *14*, 1847–1850. [CrossRef] [PubMed]
5. Rattray, N.J.W.; Deziel, N.C.; Wallach, J.D.; Khan, S.A.; Vasiliou, V.; Ioannidis, J.P.A.; Johnson, C.H. Beyond genomics: Understanding exposotypes through metabolomics. *Hum. Genom.* **2018**, *12*, 4. [CrossRef]
6. Gibbons, H.; Brennan, L. Metabolomics as a tool in the identification of dietary biomarkers. *Proc. Nutr. Soc.* **2017**, *76*, 42–53. [CrossRef]
7. Shi, L.; Brunius, C.; Lehtonen, M.; Auriola, S.; Bergdahl, I.A.; Rolandsson, O.; Hanhineva, K.; Landberg, R. Plasma metabolites associated with type 2 diabetes in a Swedish population: A case-control study nested in a prospective cohort. *Diabetologia* **2018**, *61*, 849–861. [CrossRef]
8. Shi, L.; Brunius, C.; Johansson, I.; Bergdahl, I.A.; Lindahl, B.; Hanhineva, K.; Landberg, R. Plasma metabolites associated with healthy Nordic dietary indexes and risk of type 2 diabetes-a nested case-control study in a Swedish population. *Am. J. Clin. Nutr.* **2018**, *108*, 564–575. [CrossRef]
9. Saccenti, E.; Hoefsloot, H.C.J.; Smilde, A.K.; Westerhuis, J.A.; Hendriks, M.M.W.B. Reflections on univariate and multivariate analysis of metabolomics data. *Metabolomics* **2014**, *10*, 361–374. [CrossRef]
10. Alonso, A.; Marsal, S.; Julià, A. Analytical methods in untargeted metabolomics: State of the art in 2015. *Front. Bioeng. Biotechnol.* **2015**, *3*, 23. [CrossRef]
11. Norberg, M.; Wall, S.; Boman, K.; Weinehall, L. The Västerbotten Intervention Programme: Background, design and implications. *Glob. Health Act.* **2010**, *3*. [CrossRef] [PubMed]
12. Liu, X.; Liao, X.; Gan, W.; Ding, X.; Gao, B.; Wang, H.; Zhao, X.; Liu, Y.; Feng, L.; Abdulkadil, W.; et al. Inverse Relationship Between Coarse Food Grain Intake and Blood Pressure Among Young Chinese Adults. *Am. J. Hypertens.* **2018**, *32*, 402–408. [CrossRef] [PubMed]
13. Shi, L.; Westerhuis, J.A.; Rosen, J.; Landberg, R.; Brunius, C. Variable selection and validation in multivariate modelling. *Bioinformatics* **2019**, *35*, 972–980. [CrossRef] [PubMed]
14. Worley, B.; Powers, R. Multivariate Analysis in Metabolomics. *Curr. Metab.* **2013**, *1*, 92–107. [CrossRef]
15. Madsen, R.; Lundstedt, T.; Trygg, J. Chemometrics in metabolomics—A review in human disease diagnosis. *Anal. Chim. Acta* **2010**, *659*, 23–33. [CrossRef] [PubMed]
16. Revelle, W. Psych: Procedures for Personality and Psychological Research, Northwestern University, Evanston, Illinois, USA. Version=1.8.12. 2018. Available online: https://CRAN.R-project.org/package=psych (accessed on 1 July 2019).

17. Revelle, W.; Rocklin, T. Very Simple Structure: An Alternative Procedure For Estimating the Optimal Number of Interpretable Factors. *Multivar. Behav. Res.* **1979**, *14*, 403–414. [CrossRef] [PubMed]
18. Filzmoser, P.; Liebmann, B.; Varmuza, K. Repeated double cross validation. *J. Chemom.* **2009**, *23*, 160–171. [CrossRef]
19. Westerhuis, J.A.; Hoefsloot, H.C.J.; Smit, S.; Vis, D.J.; Smilde, A.K.; van Velzen, E.J.J.; van Duijnhoven, J.P.M.; van Dorsten, F.A. Assessment of PLSDA cross validation. *Metabolomics* **2008**, *4*, 81–89. [CrossRef]
20. Olsson, U. Maximum likelihood estimation of the polychoric correlation coefficient. *Psychometrika* **1979**, *44*, 443–460. [CrossRef]
21. Zuo, Y.; Yu, G.; Tadesse, M.G.; Ressom, H.W. Biological network inference using low order partial correlation. *Methods* **2014**, *69*, 266–273. [CrossRef]
22. Heerman, W.J.; Jackson, N.; Hargreaves, M.; Mulvaney, S.A.; Schlundt, D.; Wallston, K.A.; Rothman, R.L. Clusters of Healthy and Unhealthy Eating Behaviors Are Associated With Body Mass Index Among Adults. *J. Nutr. Educ. Behav.* **2017**, *49*, 415–421.e1. [CrossRef] [PubMed]
23. Newby, P.; Muller, D.; Hallfrisch, J.; Qiao, N.; Andres, R.; Tucker, K.L. Dietary patterns and changes in body mass index and waist circumference in adults. *Am. J. Clin. Nutr.* **2003**, *77*, 1417–1425. [CrossRef] [PubMed]
24. Ahn, M.B.; Bae, W.R.; Han, K.D.; Cho, W.K.; Cho, K.S.; Park, S.H.; Jung, M.H.; Suh, B.K. Association between serum alanine aminotransferase level and obesity indices in Korean adolescents. *Korean J. Pediatr.* **2015**, *58*, 165–171. [CrossRef] [PubMed]
25. Salvaggio, A.; Periti, M.; Miano, L.; Tavanelli, M.; Marzorati, D. Body mass index and liver enzyme activity in serum. *Clin. Chem.* **1991**, *37*, 720–723. [PubMed]
26. Cirulli, E.T.; Guo, L.; Leon Swisher, C.; Shah, N.; Huang, L.; Napier, L.A.; Kirkness, E.F.; Spector, T.D.; Caskey, C.T.; Thorens, B.; et al. Profound Perturbation of the Metabolome in Obesity Is Associated with Health Risk. *Cell Metab.* **2019**, *29*, 488–500.e2. [CrossRef] [PubMed]
27. Ho, J.E.; Larson, M.G.; Ghorbani, A.; Cheng, S.; Chen, M.-H.; Keyes, M.; Rhee, E.P.; Clish, C.B.; Vasan, R.S.; Gerszten, R.E.; et al. Metabolomic Profiles of Body Mass Index in the Framingham Heart Study Reveal Distinct Cardiometabolic Phenotypes. *PLoS ONE* **2016**, *11*, e0148361. [CrossRef] [PubMed]
28. Liaset, B.; Oyen, J.; Jacques, H.; Kristiansen, K.; Madsen, L. Seafood intake and the development of obesity, insulin resistance and type 2 diabetes. *Nutr. Res. Rev.* **2019**, *32*, 146–167. [CrossRef]
29. Wang, Y.; Beydoun, M.A. Meat consumption is associated with obesity and central obesity among US adults. *Int. J. Obes.* **2009**, *33*, 621–628. [CrossRef]
30. Vatanparast, H.; Whiting, S.; Hossain, A.; Mirhosseini, N.; Merchant, A.T.; Szafron, M. National pattern of grain products consumption among Canadians in association with body weight status. *BMC Nutr.* **2017**, *3*, 59. [CrossRef]
31. Ham, E.; Kim, H.-J. Evaluation of fruit intake and its relation to body mass index of adolescents. *Clin. Nutr. Res.* **2014**, *3*, 126–133. [CrossRef]
32. Charlton, K.; Kowal, P.; Soriano, M.M.; Williams, S.; Banks, E.; Vo, K.; Byles, J. Fruit and vegetable intake and body mass index in a large sample of middle-aged Australian men and women. *Nutrients* **2014**, *6*, 2305–2319. [CrossRef] [PubMed]
33. Hosomi, R.; Yoshida, M.; Fukunaga, K. Seafood consumption and components for health. *Glob. J. Health Sci.* **2012**, *4*, 72–86. [CrossRef] [PubMed]
34. Lee, D.-H.; Steffen, L.M.; Jacobs, D.R., Jr. Association between serum γ-glutamyltransferase and dietary factors: The Coronary Artery Risk Development in Young Adults (CARDIA) Study. *Am. J. Clin. Nutr.* **2004**, *79*, 600–605. [CrossRef] [PubMed]
35. Qin, Y.; Zhou, Y.; Chen, S.H.; Zhao, X.L.; Ran, L.; Zeng, X.L.; Wu, Y.; Chen, J.L.; Kang, C.; Shu, F.R.; et al. Fish Oil Supplements Lower Serum Lipids and Glucose in Correlation with a Reduction in Plasma Fibroblast Growth Factor 21 and Prostaglandin E2 in Nonalcoholic Fatty Liver Disease Associated with Hyperlipidemia: A Randomized Clinical Trial. *PLoS ONE* **2015**, *10*, e0133496. [CrossRef]

36. Gupta, V.; Mah, X.J.; Garcia, M.C.; Antonypillai, C.; van der Poorten, D. Oily fish, coffee and walnuts: Dietary treatment for nonalcoholic fatty liver disease. *World J. Gastroenterol.* **2015**, *21*, 10621–10635. [CrossRef] [PubMed]

© 2019 by the authors. Licensee MDPI, Basel, Switzerland. This article is an open access article distributed under the terms and conditions of the Creative Commons Attribution (CC BY) license (http://creativecommons.org/licenses/by/4.0/).

 *metabolites*

Article

Comparison of Bi- and Tri-Linear PLS Models for Variable Selection in Metabolomic Time-Series Experiments

Qian Gao [1], Lars O. Dragsted [1] and Timothy Ebbels [2],*

[1] Department of Nutrition, Exercise and Sports, University of Copenhagen, 1958 Frederiksberg, Denmark; qian@nexs.ku.dk (Q.G.); ldra@nexs.ku.dk (L.O.D.)
[2] Computational and Systems Medicine, Department of Surgery and Cancer, Imperial College London, London SW7 2AZ, UK
* Correspondence: t.ebbels@imperial.ac.uk; Tel.: +44-2075943160

Received: 3 March 2019; Accepted: 8 May 2019; Published: 9 May 2019

Abstract: Metabolomic studies with a time-series design are widely used for discovery and validation of biomarkers. In such studies, changes of metabolic profiles over time under different conditions (e.g., control and intervention) are compared, and metabolites responding differently between the conditions are identified as putative biomarkers. To incorporate time-series information into the variable (biomarker) selection in partial least squares regression (PLS) models, we created PLS models with different combinations of bilinear/trilinear **X** and group/time response dummy **Y**. In total, five PLS models were evaluated on two real datasets, and also on simulated datasets with varying characteristics (number of subjects, number of variables, inter-individual variability, intra-individual variability and number of time points). Variables showing specific temporal patterns observed visually and determined statistically were labelled as discriminating variables. Bootstrapped-VIP scores were calculated for variable selection and the variable selection performance of five PLS models were assessed based on their capacity to correctly select the discriminating variables. The results showed that the bilinear PLS model with group × time response as dummy **Y** provided the highest recall (true positive rate) of 83–95% with high precision, independent of most characteristics of the datasets. Trilinear PLS models tend to select a small number of variables with high precision but relatively high false negative rate (lower power). They are also less affected by the noise compared to bilinear PLS models. In datasets with high inter-individual variability, bilinear PLS models tend to provide higher recall while trilinear models tend to provide higher precision. Overall, we recommend bilinear PLS with group x time response **Y** for variable selection applications in metabolomics intervention time series studies.

Keywords: time series; PLS; NPLS; variable selection; bootstrapped-VIP

1. Introduction

Metabolomics is a widely applied technology for capturing the perturbations of metabolites in biological systems and for discovery of dietary and health biomarkers. Liquid chromatography–mass spectrometry (LC-MS), nuclear magnetic resonance spectroscopy (NMR), and gas chromatography–mass spectrometry (GC-MS) are most commonly employed in metabolomics studies providing information-rich, high throughput data [1]. Such data contains information on hundreds or even thousands of metabolites, resulting in challenges for both data pre-processing and statistical analysis [2].

Biomarker discovery in metabolomic studies consists of several stages: collection of biological samples under different conditions; application of analytical techniques for characterising the "unknown" metabolome; extraction of information from raw analytical data; statistical analysis to select putative biomarkers with the capacity to discriminate the samples from different conditions; and further studies to validate the performance of selected biomarkers [3]. Selection of variables (putative biomarkers) plays an important role in the process as it determines the scale and outcome of later validation studies [4]. It is crucial to keep the number of selected variables at a reasonable level without compromising the number of true positives.

Time-series design has been adopted in many metabolomic studies for both biomarker discovery and validation stages. It is advantageous because it allows discovery of biomarkers responding to an intervention and provides time response information of biomarkers, which is of importance to select the best time window for sampling [5]. Figure 1 shows eight different types of temporal profiles typically seen in response to intervention in acute metabolomic studies (<24 h). Metabolites responding differently between the groups in such studies may vary in their temporal response profiles as seen in (a)–(f). Other metabolites (g)–(h) show no difference in response between control and intervention, or vary randomly over time, which is often the case for the majority of metabolites.

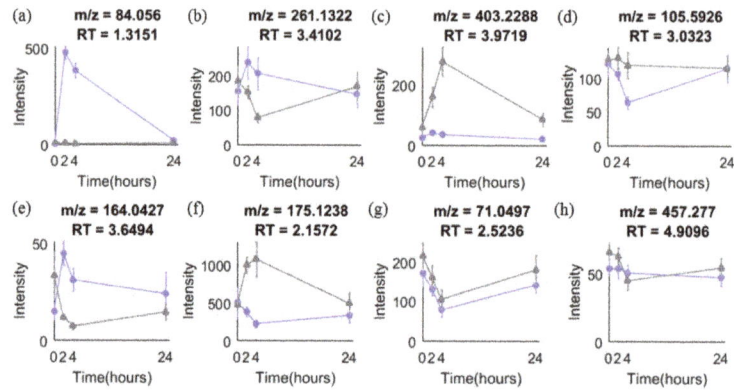

Figure 1. Typical temporal profiles of metabolites observed in metabolomics data from our onion study with a time-series design. (a)–(h) are temporal profiles of eight metabolites in control (grey) and intervention (purple) group. More details are explained in Text S1.

A time-series design yields more information but also leads to more complex data. Not only are the variables correlated but also temporal autocorrelation exists between time points. The classical supervised multivariate approach adopted in many metabolomic studies is PLSDA followed by variable (biomarker) selection [6]. PLSDA is a classification method based on classical PLS regression where the response variable, **y**, is categorical and represents which treatment group each sample belongs to [7]. Normally the model is built on the data acquired from a single time point, from combined time points or on pooled samples. However, in this case, only treatment group information is used while all the time response information is ignored.

Some attempts have been made to take time-series information into account during PLS modelling. One approach is to use time of sampling or maturity of the process as the response variable, **y**, [8] which has been applied in a small number of metabolomic studies [9,10]. The problem with this method is that it works well only when there is a linear relation between variables and time, which is often not the case (see Figure 1). Another approach is piecewise Orthogonal Projections to Latent Structures (OPLS), which uses a set of sub-models to describe the changes between successive time points [11]. This does not assume any linear trend between data and time, which makes it suitable for the analysis of non-linear response over time. However, the time-series information is distributed in a range of sub-models which hinders interpretation. A variety of non-PLS methods could also be adopted for modelling metabolomics time-series data but there are some limitations. Autoregressive moving average with exogenous inputs models (ARMAX) or space-state models can be used to describe the temporal profiles, but typically requires more time points (>10) [12]. Smoothness or its combination with dimension reduction method have also been developed and applied for time-series data [13]. However, all the methods above mainly focus on predicting response to a treatment over time instead of selecting important variables which discriminate between different treatments. More investigation of time-series models using PLS for metabolomics analyses is therefore needed, especially with respect to variable selection, in order to provide better guidance on optimal data analysis of such datasets. Conventionally, metabolomic time series data are constructed into a two-way structure (Sample × Metabolite) in PLS modelling where the time response information is overlooked. To incorporate such information into the data structure, time can be considered as the third mode. In this study, five different bi- and tri-linear PLS models were used to identify important variables contributing to the difference between groups in intervention response metabolomics studies with a time-series design. The variable selection performance of the five models were evaluated on both simulated and real datasets to provide insight into the most appropriate modelling approach for intervention response time series experiments.

2. Materials and Methods

2.1. PLS and NPLS

PLS is a latent variable based multivariate linear regression between predictor variables (X) and dependent variables (Y), which aims at maximizing the covariance between the X and response Y [14]. N-PLS is an extension of PLS to multiway data [15] where X is an array with more than two dimensions (also referred to as ways or modes). Compared to PLS, N-PLS provides simpler models with relatively few parameters and avoids the interference between information from different modes [16]. Metabolomic data with a time-series design can be structured as a two-way table of dimensions $I \times J$, where $I = S \times T$ (S = number of subjects; T = number of time points), J = number of metabolites. During the analysis, such data is divided into subsets according to time points for further analysis separately or analysed as a whole. In either case, the time-series information is not used by the model and correlation between samples collected at different time points from the same subject is lost. To make use of this autocorrelation between samples, we transformed the metabolomics time-series data into a three-way array with a size of $S \times J \times T$ and analysed it using N-PLS. In the current paper, both two-way PLS and N-PLS models are used to analyse metabolomic time-series data and they are referred to as bi-PLS (bilinear-PLS) and tri-PLS (trilinear-PLS) models, respectively.

2.2. PLS-DA and Dummy Y

In standard PLSDA, class labels indicating the group membership of each sample are used as dependant Y (dummy Y), e.g., y for the intervention group sample is 1 and for the control group sample is 0 or −1. However, samples obtained from different time points can be very different within the same class causing large variation within classes and consequently lead to poor predictions. Dividing the data and building separate models for each time point can reduce this problem but in this case, there are fewer observations for each comparison, and most importantly, the time response information is not modelled. To include such variation into the dependent Y and provide more guidance on the separation of samples, we created a new 'time response' dummy Y to reflect how the metabolites respond to the intervention with time. Specifically, for the target metabolites (Figure 1a–f), their excretion experiences an increase and a decrease within a certain time frame i.e., their intensities are higher or lower in the middle of the time-series than that at the beginning or at the end of the time-series. Therefore, we assign the samples acquired from the middle of the time-series capturing the high intensities of the target metabolites to a 'response class' and samples acquired from the first and last time point to a 'no-response class'. Samples from these two classes are labelled with 10 and 1 respectively, which would be subsequently used as dummy Y in further PLSDA modelling. In our experiments, the model performance improved with increasing magnitude of the 'time response class' until it reached around 10. Therefore, 10 was used as the label for 'response class' in this paper. The value of the time response should be a user-defined value and it can be adjusted by testing with a range of values to find out the optimal one achieving the best predictive performance (Q^2 or area under the ROC curve) of the model.

2.3. Comparison of Variable Selection by Five PLS Models

In order to take advantage of the time-series data structure and to make use of both group and time response information, we combined different PLS models (bi-PLS or tri-PLS) with different dummy **Y**s (group or time response labels) as shown in Figure 2. Models 1–3 are bi-PLS models built on a two-way matrix **X** of size $ST \times J$. Model 4–5 are tri-PLS models built on a three-way array $\underline{\mathbf{X}}$ of size $S \times J \times T$. For models 1–4, group labels, time response labels or their products are used as a one-way dummy **Y**. Model 5 uses a two-way dummy **Y** with group label as the first mode and time response label as the second mode. We note that model 1 only addresses group differences, while model 2 only addresses time response changes. Since we are interested in both group and time responses, we included these two basic models against which to compare the more complex models 3–5. The five PLS models were applied on the same datasets and their performances were compared.

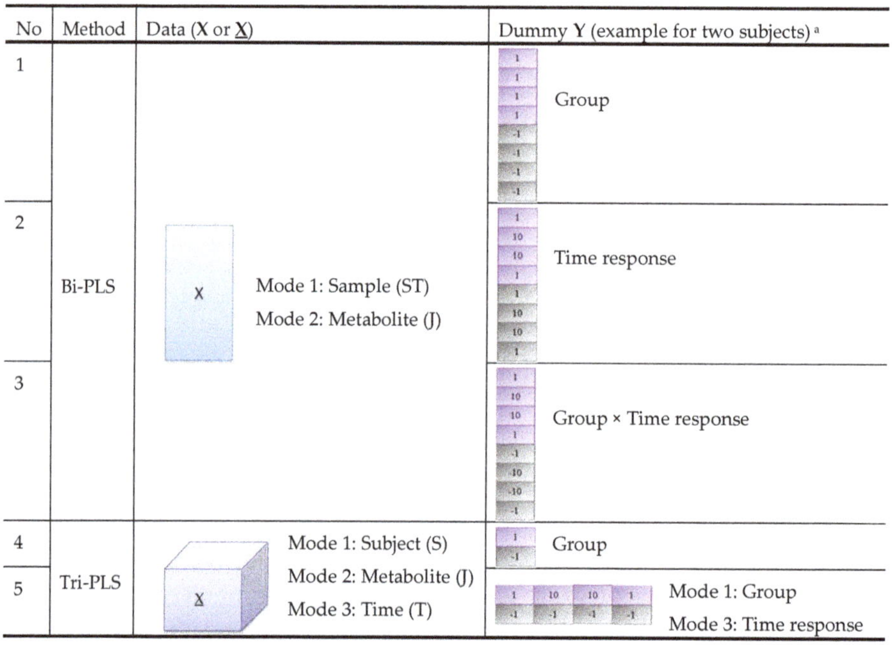

No	Method	Data (**X** or $\underline{\mathbf{X}}$)		Dummy **Y** (example for two subjects) [a]	
1	Bi-PLS	**X**	Mode 1: Sample (ST) Mode 2: Metabolite (J)		Group
2					Time response
3					Group × Time response
4	Tri-PLS	$\underline{\mathbf{X}}$	Mode 1: Subject (S) Mode 2: Metabolite (J) Mode 3: Time (T)		Group
5					Mode 1: Group Mode 3: Time response

Figure 2. Structure of five PLS models for comparison. [a] The dummy **Y** in this figure is an example for data obtained from eight samples collected from two subjects at four time points (0, 2, 4, 24 h after intervention). Dummy **Y** in purple and grey colour corresponds to samples collected from Subject 1 (from intervention group) and Subject 2 (from the control group), respectively.

The focus of this paper is on the ability of the models to highlight variables important to the time-treatment response. In PLS regression, variable selection is used to improve model performance to provide better predictions [17]. It identifies variables with large influence on the model, which could be used to interpret the model and to be investigated as potential biomarkers in further studies. In the current paper, VIP scores were calculated to identify the relevant variables and a bootstrap procedure was adopted to estimate VIP uncertainty.

2.4. Datasets

2.4.1. Simulated Datasets

In order to assess the variable selection performance of the five PLS models, a data simulation procedure is proposed to simulate the time-series metabolomic dataset. For a simulated dataset, we generated J variables and for each variable j, the observations for a subject s in group g are generated according to the following equation:

$$x_{sg} = \mu_g \circ (b_s + w_s + \varepsilon_s)$$

where $\circ$ denotes the entry-wise product and $\mu_g = c + at^\alpha e^{-\beta t}$. μ_g is the vector containing the values of the mean curve for the group g, of dimension $1 \times T$ and t is the time. c, a, α, β are generated from uniform distributions, the intervals of which are adjusted to create different temporal profiles, as shown in Figure 1a–h for both intervention and control groups (see Figure S1). The $1 \times T$ vector b_s controls inter-individual variability, which follows a normal distribution with zero mean and covariance matrix $\sigma_b^2 \mathbf{1}_T$, where $\mathbf{1}$ denotes a matrix with all entries equal to 1, with σ_b^2 being the inter-individual variance. The intra-individual variability denoted by the 1xT vector w_s is taken to be multivariate normally distributed with zero mean and covariance D_w. D_w is a first-order autoregression covariance matrix of dimension $T \times T$ with entries being $D_w(i,j) = \sigma_w^2 \rho^{|i-j|}$, where σ_w^2 is the intra-individual variance and ρ is the autocorrelation coefficient between two consecutive time points. The noise ε_s is normally distributed with zero mean and covariance matrix $\sigma_\varepsilon^2 \mathbf{1}_T$, of dimension $T \times T$.

Sixteen datasets with different numbers of subjects, numbers of variables, inter-individual variability, intra-individual variability and number of time points were generated with the above simulation method. In each of the sixteen datasets, eighty discriminating variables were simulated. Table S1 provides an overview of the characteristics of all the datasets.

In the simulated dataset, the variables with the temporal profiles, (**a**)–(**f**) in Figure 1, were considered as discriminating variables, which are the target of variable selection while avoiding selection of variables with profiles (**g**)–(**h**) in Figure 1.

2.4.2. Onion Intervention Data

This data is taken from a randomized controlled trial with a crossover design, where participants were assigned to either an onion consuming group or a control group. Untargeted UPLC-qTOF-MS was applied to measure the metabolites in urine samples at four time points (0, 2, 4, 24 h after intervention) for six subjects per group [18]. The resulting raw data consists of 48 samples.

2.4.3. Coffee Intervention Data

This data is generated from a randomized controlled trial with a crossover design, where urine samples were collected at 0, 0.5, 1, and 2 h after intervention with coffee or control drink (water) from 11 subjects per group. A total of 88 samples were analysed with untargeted UPLC-qTOF-MS [18].

Both onion and coffee raw data were converted to NetCDF files using DataBridge (Waters, Manchester, UK) and analysed with MZmine 2.19 for data peak detection, alignment and quantification [19]. The preprocessed data were imported into MATLAB and feature reduction was applied to remove unreliable variables due to compounds with extreme retention times, variables not detected in more than 70% of the samples in each subgroup and variables with a coefficient of variation (CV) in pooled quality control samples higher than 0.7 [20]. The resulting onion and coffee data sets had dimensions (samples x variables) of 48 × 3209 and 88 × 2321, respectively.

For onion and coffee intervention data, true discriminating variables are not known *a priori*. However, to enable evaluation of the variable selection performance on this real data, 'truly' discriminating variables were determined by two methods. First, visual inspection was applied to identify variables exhibiting profiles similar to (**a**)–(**f**) in Figure 1. Second, a t-test was applied at each timepoint and the variable flagged if at least one time point was significant with a nominal $p < 0.05$. Variables were considered discriminating if both methods indicated a difference, and were the object of variable selection procedures.

2.5. Workflow

The assessment of the variable selection of the five PLS models was performed on the simulated datasets as well as real datasets. The workflow is outlined in Figure 3 and explained in the following sections.

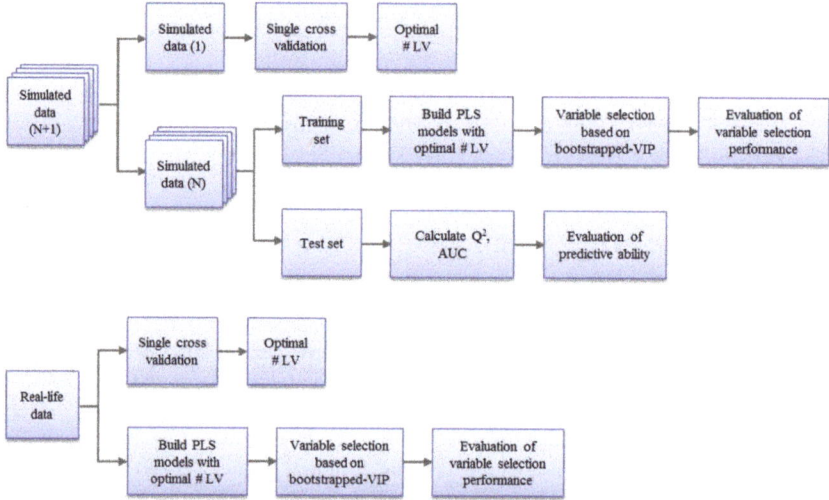

Figure 3. Workflow for the evaluation of variable selection performance of five PLS models on simulated datasets (top) and real datasets (bottom). For the simulated datasets, a single cross validation was applied on one of them to determine the optimal number of latent variables, which was then applied to all the similar simulated datasets for building the PLS models and variable selection. For real datasets, the optimal number of latent variables was obtained based on a single cross validation on the whole dataset and the PLS models were built on the whole dataset for variable selection.

2.5.1. Pre-Processing of Data

Centring and scaling are commonly applied prior to the regression modelling and have a critical influence on the performance of the model. Centring is performed to shift the mean of the data to zero and scaling is used to adjust the relative influence of variables with different variability. Centring across the first mode (samples or subjects) is a widely accepted step for both two-way and three-way data while scaling is more complicated. Scaling within one mode may disturb other modes [21,22]. In the current study, centring across the first mode was applied for both two-way and three-way data. For the two-way data, the values for each variable (column) were scaled to unit variance. On the three-way data, single-slab scaling within the metabolite mode was applied, as recommended by Gurden et al. [23]. (A slab is a single layer of the three-way array, here corresponding to a single variable). In single-slab scaling, each variable in the jth slab is scaled to unit root-mean-square of the slab (RMS_j):

$$RMS_j = \sqrt{\frac{\sum_{s=1}^{S} \sum_{t=1}^{T} x_{sjt}^2}{ST}}$$

$$x_{sjt}^* = \frac{x_{sjt}}{RMS_j}$$

where x_{sjt} is the intensity of metabolite j in the sample acquired from subject s at time point t, x^*_{sjt} is the single-slab scaled data.

2.5.2. Model Optimization and Evaluation

For both simulated and real data, a single cross validation scheme was implemented, and the optimal number of latent variables was decided as the smallest number at which the decrease in root mean squared error in cross validation (RMSECV) between consecutive models was less than 2%. Due to the similarity of the repeated simulations using the same parameters, for the same type of PLS model, the number of latent variables was determined on one dataset and adopted for all the other repeats.

A two-stage procedure was used to evaluate the performance of different models on simulated datasets. Each simulated dataset was divided into training and test sets. First, variable selection performance was evaluated on the training set. Next, the model's predictive ability was evaluated on the test set.

(1). Evaluation of Variable Selection Performance with Training Sets

Balanced bootstrapping was performed to resample B bootstrap datasets [24,25]. Various values of B were tested and B = 200 was chosen as the smallest value providing consistent results (data not shown). PLS models with an optimal number of latent variables were built on each bootstrap subset and the Variable Importance in Projection (VIP) was calculated for each variable [26,27]. For each variable, the mean (VIP*) and standard deviation (σ_{VIP}) of the B VIP values were obtained. The variable was selected if the lower-bound of the one standard deviation error bar was above 1 (i.e., $VIP^* - \sigma_{VIP} > 1$).

To evaluate the variable selection performance of the five models, "Variable Selection ROC curves" were created. Since the discriminating variables are known, the model selecting the higher number of discriminating variables and lower number of non-discriminating variables is considered to have better variable selection performance. After the selected variables were obtained for each model, the number of variables considered as true positives, false positives, true negatives and false negatives were calculated according to Table 1. The comparison between convention ROC curve and Variable Selection ROC curve are shown in Figure S2.

Table 1. Variable selection confusion matrix.

		True Condition	
	Total Variables	Discriminating Variables	Non-Discriminating Variables
Predicted Condition	Selected variables	True positive (TP)	False positive (FP)
	Unselected variables	False negative (FN)	True negative (TN)

The area under the variable selection ROC curve (AUVSC) was calculated to provide an evaluation of the overall variable selection performance of each model. The following scores were calculated:

Recall = TP/(TP + FN)
Precision = TP/(TP + FP)
F_1-score = $(\beta^2+1)\times$ Precision $\times$ Recall/$\beta^2\times$ (Precision + Recall)

Recall reflects the model's capacity to select all the discriminating variables. Precision expresses the ability of the model to avoid the selection of non-discriminating variables. The F_1-score is an overall assessment of the model's performance on recall and precision, assessing the effectiveness of the model to identify all the discriminating variables without selecting too many non-discriminating variables. β is set to 1 to emphasize the importance of both recall and precision for a reasonable selection of variables.

(2). Evaluation of predictive ability with test sets

The models with the optimal number of latent variables determined on the training sets were applied (using all variables) to the corresponding test sets. Predictive variance explained Q^2, and area under the conventional ROC curve (AUC, using all variables) were calculated to evaluate the predictive ability of the model.

For real datasets, stage (1) evaluation of variable selection performance was performed on the whole dataset. Stage (2) evaluation was not applied because the numbers of subjects are too small in the real datasets to obtain an independent test set. Instead, a permutation test was performed to evaluate the validity of the model.

2.6. Evaluation of the Influence of Characteristics of the Dataset on the Model Performance

Characteristics of metabolome vary, e.g., between different human studies, from humans to animals, and from studies on diets or drugs thereby leading to different characteristics of the datasets potentially influencing the performance of the statistical methods. To evaluate such influences and to provide guidelines for the use of different models, all five PLS models were applied on all sixteen simulated datasets as shown in Table S1. The results from different datasets were compared to assess the influence of characteristics on the model performance. The datasets used to compare the evaluation of different characteristics are shown in Table S2.

All the calculations were performed in MATLAB Version R2015b (8.6.0.267246) (The Mathworks, Inc, Natick, MA, USA) using scripts modified from N-way toolbox [28] and multiway VIP package [27]. The code for building the five PLS models and performing variable selection is available at https://github.com/qian-gao/PLSvar_sel. Simulated dataset 3 and anonymised onion intervention data are provided as examples for testing.

3. Results

3.1. Assessment of Variable Selection Performance on Simulated Data

3.1.1. Overall Evaluation

The overall evaluation of the variable selection, prediction and classification performance of the five PLS models was performed on Dataset 3 (10 subjects, 3000 variables, 4 time points) and the results are shown in Table 2 and Figure 4. Dataset 3 was chosen for the overall evaluation because it has the characteristics that are most similar to those of the real dataset. As expected, bi-PLS models resulted in a higher number of latent variables than tri-PLS models indicating higher model complexity. Model 3 showed the best variable selection performance in that it provides the highest number of true positives with a relatively small number of selected variables, consequently leading to the highest precision. Model 1, 4 and 5 selected similar numbers of true positives while model 1 selected a higher number of false positives showing low precision. Model 2 showed the best prediction with highest Q^2 but, as expected, provided a poor classification of the samples according to group. Unsurprisingly, only a few true positive variables were selected together with a large number of false positives resulting in the poorest precision. The number of latent variables did not have a strong influence on performance. Restricting all models to two latent variables (see Table S3), showed that the performance was not markedly different from that of those presented in Table 2.

Table 2. Performance of five PLS models evaluated on simulated datasets with the optimal number of latent variables.

Model	Data (X or X)	Dummy Y	# LV[a]	Predictive Ability		Variable Selection Performance	
				Q^2	AUC	# Varsel[b]	# TP[c]
1	Mode 1: Sample	Group	3	0.57 (0.02)	0.93 (0.06)	249.3 (11.2)	53.6 (4)
2	Mode 2: Metabolite	Time response	5	1 (0)	0.58 (0.08)	591.1 (16)	12.8 (3.9)
3		Group × Time response	5	0.83 (0.01)	0.75 (0)	194.5 (9.1)	77.3 (1.6)
4	Mode 1: Subject Mode 2: Metabolite Mode 3: Time	Group	1	0.6 (0.01)	1 (0)	165.9 (11.4)	53 (4.1)
5		Mode 1: Group Mode 3: Time	1	0.6 (0.02)	0.75 (0)	166.7 (13.5)	53.9 (4.3)

[a] # LV, number of latent variables; [b] # Varsel, number of selected variables; [c] # TP, number of true positives. Values reported are mean and standard deviation across 100 repeats.

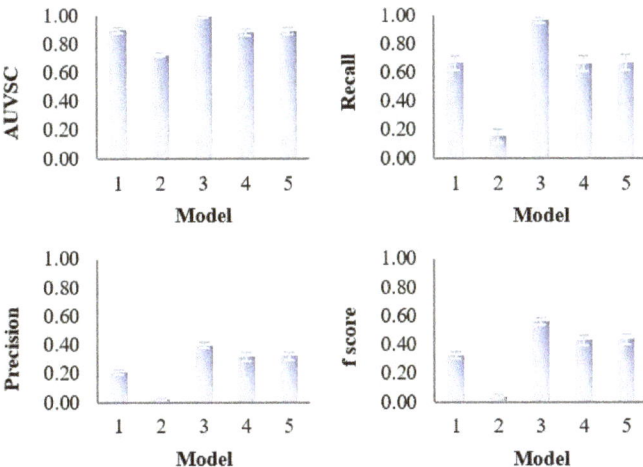

Figure 4. Evaluation of the variable selection performance of five PLS models on 100 simulated datasets. The variable selection performance consists of four criteria—area under the ROC curve (AUVSC), recall, precision, F_1- score, which were calculated based on the variable selection confusion matrix.

Although the variable selection performances of the five models vary, the majority of discriminating variables were selected by at least two models, and variables selected by model 3 included approximate all the variables selected by other models (Figure 5). Beyond that, model 3 selected about eight unique true positives which were selected by none of the other models. The discriminating variables also had higher ranks in model 3 than the other models indicating its efficiency in variable selection (Figure 6). Model 4 and 5 resulted in low overall level of VIP scores and relatively larger variation, which caused a higher number of false negatives.

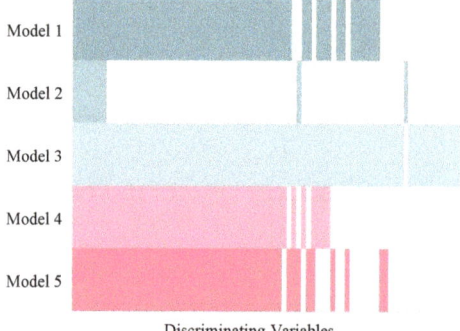

Figure 5. Comparison among discriminating variables selected by five PLS models in simulated Dataset 3. The coloured and white strips represent true positives (selected discriminating variables) and false negatives (unselected discriminating variables), respectively. The discriminating variables were arranged in order so that the variables selected by all five models were on the left side and the variables selected only by one model were on the right side.

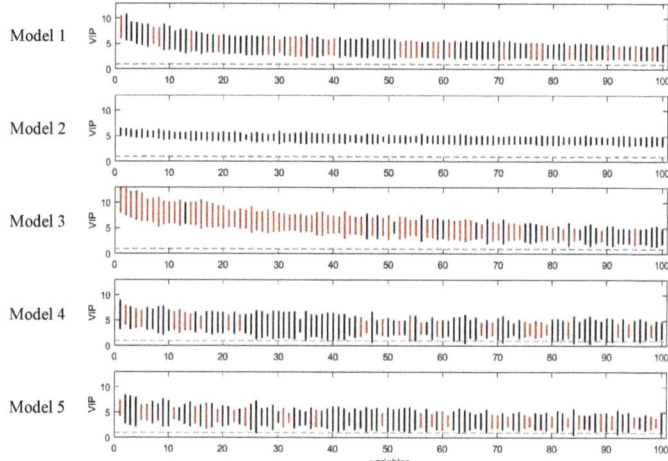

Figure 6. Rank of VIP scores for the discriminating variables in five PLS models on simulated Dataset 3. Bootstrapped VIP scores for all the variables were ranked according to their mean VIP scores in descending order. Bars show the mean +/- one standard deviation. Red and black represent the variables which are discriminating or non-discriminating, respectively. The horizontal blue dash line corresponds to VIP = 1.

3.1.2. Influence of Characteristics of the Dataset on the Performance of the Five PLS Models

The influence of number of subjects, number of variables, inter-individual variability, intra-individual variability and number of time points was assessed with the simulated datasets and the results are shown in Figure 7, Table 3, Table 4, Figure S3 and Figure S4.

As expected, variable selection performance (recall and precision) of all models was improved with increasing number of subjects (Figure 7). Notably, model 3 was only slightly affected by the number of subjects as it maintained its good recall and precision throughout all datasets, suggesting good robustness to this parameter.

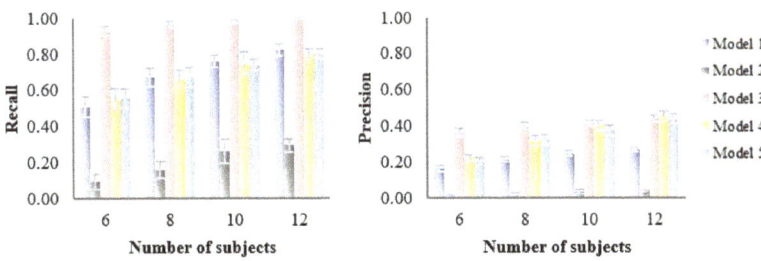

Figure 7. Influence of number of subjects (6–12) on the variable selection performance of five PLS models on simulated datasets. Recall and precision were calculated based on the variable selection confusion matrix.

Table 3. Influence of the number of variables on variable selection performance of the five models on simulated data.

	Number of Variables (No. Discriminating Variables Kept at 80 in All Cases).							
Model.	1000		3000		5000		7000	
	# Varsel[a]	# TP[b]	# Varsel	# TP	# Varsel	# TP	# Varsel	# TP
1	105 (5.2)	51.7 (3.1)	249.3 (11.2)	53.6 (4)	396.3 (12.2)	53.9 (4)	540.4 (20.3)	53.3 (4.4)
2	189.8 (6.9)	15.1 (3.9)	591.1 (16)	12.8 (3.9)	983.1 (19.8)	15.8 (3.7)	1379.1 (22.1)	13.7 (2.1)
3	95.7 (4.6)	74.3 (1.8)	194.5 (9.1)	77.3 (1.6)	304.7 (14.8)	77.1 (2.2)	409.3 (18.2)	77.5 (1.4)
4	86.2 (7.1)	58 (3.6)	165.9 (11.4)	53 (4.1)	243.8 (18.8)	50.2 (4.1)	325.8 (21.7)	49.6 (2.9)
5	89 (5.2)	58.4 (3.8)	166.7 (13.5)	53.9 (4.3)	247.4 (14.8)	51.7 (2.8)	325.2 (15.6)	51.3 (3.3)

[a] # Varsel, number of selected variables; [b] # TP, number of true positives. Values reported are mean and standard deviation across 100 repeats.

Table 4. Influence of inter-individual variability on variable selection performance of five models on simulated data.

	Inter-Individual Variability							
Model	0.1		0.3		0.5		0.7	
	# Varsel[a]	# TP[b]	# Varsel	# TP	# Varsel	# TP	# Varsel	# TP
1	153.5 (8.2)	75.1 (1.9)	249.3 (11.2)	53.6 (4)	301 (11.5)	39.2 (3.8)	323 (11.1)	34.2 (3.3)
2	681.5 (17.6)	2.7 (1.4)	591.1 (16)	12.8 (3.9)	513.5 (15.3)	19.4 (3)	493 (18.3)	19.2 (3.6)
3	143.5 (4.5)	79.9 (0.3)	194.5 (9.1)	77.3 (1.6)	216.5 (14.4)	72.2 (2.5)	243.1 (13.3)	68.3 (3.5)
4	173.9 (12.1)	78.7 (1.2)	165.9 (11.4)	53 (4.1)	155.2 (11.6)	35.9 (4.3)	165.9 (15.8)	27 (2.5)
5	177.5 (12.5)	79.2 (0.9)	166.7 (13.5)	53.9 (4.3)	158.8 (12.7)	35.4 (3.4)	170.1 (13.4)	28.1 (5)

[a] # Varsel, number of selected variables; [b] # TP: number of true positives. Values reported are mean and standard deviation across 100 repeats.

Not surprisingly, the increased number of noisy variables in the data led to a higher number of selected variables and most of the extra selected variables are false positives (Table 3). The number of true positives in model 1–3 was not affected by the noisy variables while Model 4 and 5 selected fewer true positives but also fewer false positives under the influence of noise.

Variable selection performances of the five models were strongly affected by inter-individual variability in that all the models except model 2 selected fewer true positives with larger inter-individual variability (Table 4). When the inter-individual variability increased, bi-PLS models tended to maintain their recall by sacrificing the precision; tri-PLS models tended to maintain the precision by keeping a stable number of selected variables. Overall, model 3 was less affected by inter-individual variability than other models showing a good trade-off between recall and precision.

Intra-individual variability had little influence on the variable selection performance of five PLS models (Figure S3). As expected, a higher number of time points led to better recall of all the five models and model 1 benefited most from the extra temporal information (Figure S4).

3.2. Assessment of Variable Selection Performance on Real Data

The five PLS models were applied on the onion intervention data to discover variables discriminating the control and intervention groups and the results are shown in Figures 8 and 9. Similar to the simulated dataset, Model 3 provided the best recall and precision resulting in around 28 more true positives than the second best, model 1. Again, most of the discriminating variables had high ranks in model 3. Model 4 and model 5 were not capable of selecting many true positives in this more challenging real dataset, perhaps due to their tendency to maintain precision by keeping a low number of selected variables when dealing with data having large inter-individual variability. The low overall level of VIP scores and relatively large variation could also be the reason why so few variables were selected in Model 5. Interestingly, when variables were selected according to loading weights (instead of VIP), the performance of model 4 and 5 was improved, and was similar to the performance of model 1, but still not better than Model 3 (see Figure S6). A permutation test was performed which showed that Model 3 was significant at $p < 0.001$ (Figure S9).

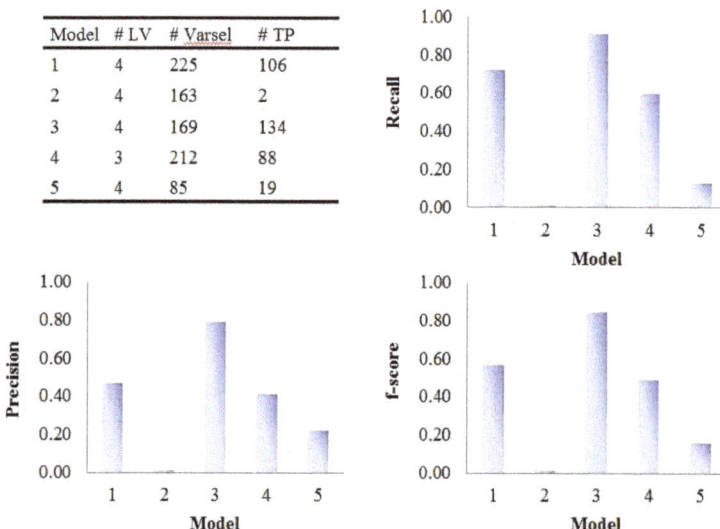

Figure 8. Evaluation of the variable selection performance of five PLS models on onion study data. Recall, precision and F_1-score were calculated based on the variable selection confusion matrix. # LV, number of latent variables; # Varsel, number of selected variables; # TP, number of true positives.

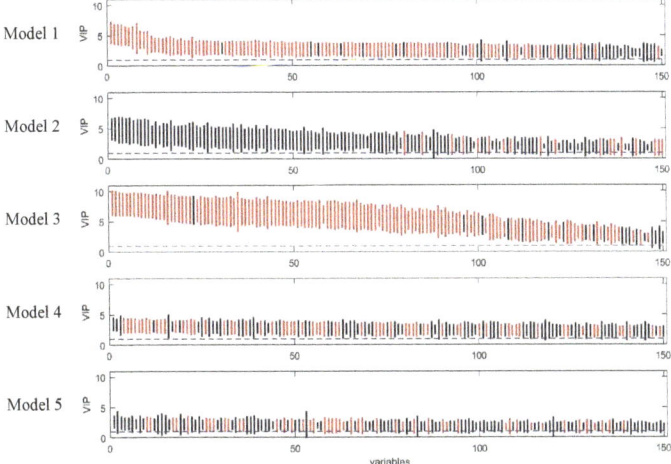

Figure 9. Rank of VIP scores for the discriminating variables in five PLS models on onion study dataset. Bootstrapped VIP scores for all the variables were ranked according to their mean VIP scores in descending order. Red and black represent the variables which are discriminating or non-discriminating, respectively. The horizontal blue dash line corresponds to VIP = 1.

3.2.1. Coffee Intervention Study

In coffee intervention study, urine samples were collected at 0, 0.5, 1, and 2 h after intervention. Due to the short sample collection period, the temporal profiles of metabolites were incomplete as shown in Figure S7. In this case, the time response class was labelled as 1 for the samples collected at 0 h and 10 for the samples collected at 0.5, 1, and 2 h after intervention. The performances of the five PLS models on coffee intervention data were similar to that for simulated data and the results were shown in Figures 10 and 11. Model 3 gave the highest number of true positives with a reasonable number of selected variables. It also provided the most comprehensive list of selected variables; its selection of true positives included almost all the true positives found in all the other models (see Figure S8). The permutation test (Figure S9) indicated Model 3 was significant at $p < 0.001$ confirming that it was not overfitted and therefore its good variable selection performance was valid. Tri-PLS models were very conservative in that they selected fewer variables but gave very high precision. In fact, the discriminating variables had better ranks in tri-PLS models than in Model 1, so that if we lower the threshold for bootstrapped-VIP scores, model 4 and 5 would outperform model 1.

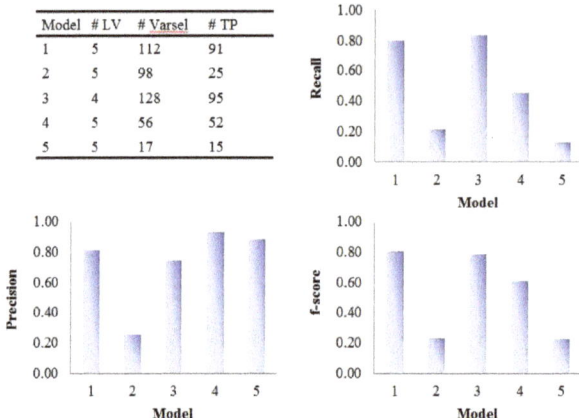

Figure 10. Evaluation of the variable selection performance of five PLS models on coffee study data. Recall, precision and F_1-score were calculated based on the variable selection confusion matrix. # LV, number of latent variables; # Varsel, number of selected variables; # TP, number of true positives.

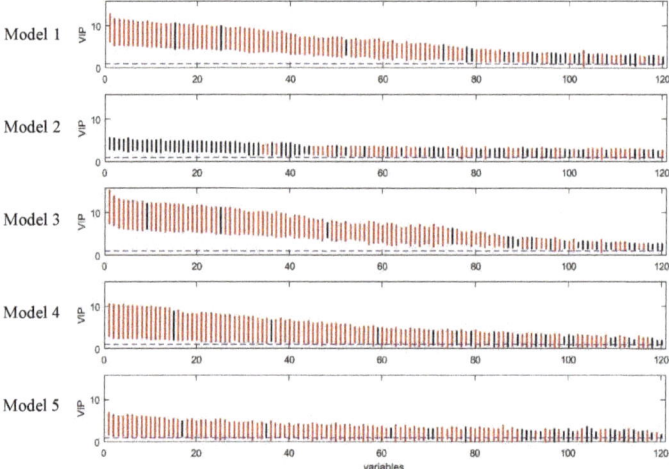

Figure 11. Rank of VIP scores for the discriminating variables in five PLS models on coffee study dataset. Bootstrapped VIP scores for all the variables were ranked according to their mean VIP scores in descending order. Red and black represent the variables which are discriminating or non-discriminating, respectively. The horizontal blue dash line corresponds to VIP = 1.

4. Discussion

In this paper, five PLS modelling approaches for metabolomic time series data were evaluated with simulated and real data with the objective of identifying variables showing discriminatory temporal patterns. The variable selection performance of the models was compared on simulated datasets based on their capacity to select discriminating variables while avoiding non-discriminating variables. The influence on model performance of five factors (number of subjects, number of variables, inter-individual variability, intra-individual variability and number of time points) was assessed to provide additional information on the application of suitable models for different scenarios of data.

Several issues have been considered regarding the development of these models. Bootstrapped-VIP scores were calculated to evaluate the importance of variables in the current paper. This approach was shown in previous studies [4,29,30] to be sensitive and precise in selecting relevant variables. However, we are aware that it might not always be the optimal approach for all models or datasets. For example, in the analysis of the onion intervention study, the loading weight for the first component was a more powerful selection tool for N-PLS models. This might be due to the fact that loading weight for the first component directly reflects the covariance between **X** and **Y**. Additional components that are found in the residuals after removal of previous components from **X** might be influenced by irrelevant information in **X** [31]. Therefore, the inclusion of the information from extra components does not necessarily result in better variable selection performance of the model. This may also explain why no strong difference in variable selection performance was observed between the models with different number of latent variables.

Another issue is the applicability of the proposed model to data with incomplete temporal profiles, where metabolite levels may not return to pre-intervention levels. For example, the coffee intervention study collected data at 0 h and 0.5, 1, and 2 h after intervention which means the whole excretion profile of the metabolites might not be recorded since the sampling period was too short (Figure S7). Our results from the coffee study indicate that incomplete temporal profiles can still provide information for the identification of discriminating variables as long as the 'response class' and 'non-response class' (i.e., responding and nonresponding time points) are accurately assigned.

The resulting models were assessed on both simulated and real data and our results were consistent in showing that 1) The bi-PLS model with combined time response and group information as **Y** (model 3) had the best variable selection performance and the most comprehensive list of true positives for all datasets tested. 2) The tri-PLS models tested both tend to maintain high precision by sacrificing recall, however they show robust performance on data with a high number of noise variables. 3) In datasets with high inter-individual variability, bi-PLS models tend to provide higher recall while tri-PLS models tend to provide higher precision. As expected, the bi-PLS model with time response as **Y** (model 2) performed most poorly under all conditions confirming that time response alone is not enough to discriminate samples from different classes.

Discovery, identification and validation of biomarkers in metabolomic studies is difficult and time-consuming. The goal is often to provide a list of discriminating variables with as many true positives and as few false positives as possible. Based on this goal and our comparison between the five models, Model 3 provided both good recall and precision and therefore represents a good choice for suitable datasets with time response profiles in two treatment groups. When the time dependant response is not recorded, model 1 and 4 may be adopted as the best general approach and they can be selected in different situation depending on the purpose of the study. For instance, Model 1 would be a good choice for exploring the data and collecting as many relevant variables as possible since it tends to keep high recall at any costs. For studies aiming at finding biomarkers with potential to classify new samples, model 4 has the potential to select the most suitable metabolites because of its good precision.

Time-series designs are widely used in life science research and the purpose is to observe the response of a biological system to a certain challenge over a defined time period. Although this work is demonstrated with LC-MS metabolomic data, it is applicable also to other types of multivariate time-series data, such as RNA-seq experiments aiming to detect the gene expression differences between experimental groups. Several methods have been proposed previously to deal with this type of time-series data. Bar-Joseph et al. [32] describes gene expression over time as a continuous curve and identifies genes showing significant temporal expression differences based on the difference between the curves. To accurately fit the curve representing the temporal profile, this method usually requires relatively long time series and homogeneous data which is not often available due to limitations of the study design or high inter-individual variability. Compared to this method, in our study Model 3 successfully dealt with short time series data and maintained high recall and precision even in the presence of high inter-individual variability. Regression-based methods have also been developed where gene expression is described as a function of time and regression coefficients of each gene from different experimental groups are compared using ANOVA [33]. Compared to this method, our Model 3 and 5 retain the multivariate structure and thus take correlations between variables into account. ANOVA-simultaneous component analysis (ASCA) is another popular method that can be applied to time-series data [34]. The data is separated into the variations that contributed by different experimental design factors such as time, dose of intervention, and their interactions using ANOVA equation. Simultaneous component analysis is then applied to different variations to approximate the scores and loadings in each sub-model. ASCA is efficient in separating design factors and exploring the data correspondingly. However, it is not able to select variables with specific response profiles (e.g., (a)–(f)) as our models do but only indicate if there is an overall difference. Moreover, these five models have low computational cost.

In summary, both simulated and real data demonstrate that bilinear PLS model with group × time response as dummy **Y** is a powerful method for variable selection in time-series experiments. It maintains good performance in the presence of noise and high inter-individual variability. In general, bi-PLS models tend to provide higher recall while tri-PLS models tend to provide higher precision.

Supplementary Materials: The following are available online at http://www.mdpi.com/2218-1989/9/5/92/s1. Figure S1: Temporal profiles of metabolites in simulated data with a time-series design. Figure S2: Convention ROC curve and Variable Selection ROC curve (VSROC) for a. model 1 and b. model 3 in simulated Dataset 3. Figure S3: Influence of intra-individual variability (0.1–0.4) on the variable selection performance of five PLS models on simulated datasets. Figure S4: Influence of number of time points (3–6) on the variable selection performance of five PLS models on simulated datasets. Figure S5: Comparison among discriminating variables selected by five PLS models in onion study data. Figure S6: Comparison between the variable selection performances based on loading weight (green) and VIP (blue) of five PLS models on onion study data. Figure S7: Temporal profiles of metabolites observed in our coffee data with a time-series design. Figure S8: Comparison among discriminating variables selected by five PLS models in coffee study data. Figure S9: Area under the ROC curve (AUC) calculated on permuted **Y** data for model 3 (histogram, 1000 permutations) and original data (red dot) generated on samples obtained from onion (left) and coffee (right) studies. Table S1: Characteristics of sixteen simulated datasets. Table S2: Datasets used to compare for the evaluation of different factors. Table S3: Performance of five PLS models evaluated on simulated dataset with same number of latent variables. Table S4: Parameters used for pre-processing the onion study data in MZmine2. Table S5: Parameters used for pre-processing the coffee study data in MZmine2.

Author Contributions: Q.G., L.O.D. and T.E. designed the study. Q.G. and T.E. developed the strategy of data simulation and statistical analyses and Q.G. conducted the study. Q.G. and T.E. were responsible for the interpretation of the results. Q.G drafted the manuscript. All the authors reviewed the final manuscript.

Funding: The work was funded by a grant from the China Scholarship Council (201506350127) to Q.G. T.E. acknowledges support from National Institutes of Health (grants R01HL135486 and R01HL133932).

Acknowledgments: We express our gratitude to Camilla T. Damsgaard, Eduvigis Roldán-Marín, Concepción Sánchez-Moreno, M. Pilar Cano, Birgitte Borg and Lars O. Dragsted for performing the onion study and generously allowing us to use the data. We would like to thank Elin Rakvaag and Lars O. Dragsted for their work in the coffee study and kindly giving us the permission to use the data.

Conflicts of Interest: The authors declare no conflict of interest. The funders had no role in the design of the study; in the collection, analyses, or interpretation of data; in the writing of the manuscript, or in the decision to publish the results.

References

1. Rezzi, S.; Ramadan, Z.; Fay, L.B.; Kochhar, S. Nutritional metabonomics: applications and perspectives. *J. Proteome Res.* **2007**, *6*, 513–525. [CrossRef]
2. Broadhurst, D.I.; Kella, D.B. Statistical strategies for avoiding false discoveries in metabolomics and related experiments. *Metabolomics* **2008**, *4*, 81–89. [CrossRef]
3. Brennan, L. Metabolomics in nutrition research: current status and perspectives. *Biochem. Soc. Trans.* **2013**, *41*, 670–673. [CrossRef]
4. Christin, C.; Hoefsloot, H.C.J.; Smilde, A.K.; Hoekman, B.; Suits, F.; Bischoff, R.; Horvatovich, P. A critical assessment of feature selection methods for biomarker discovery in clinical proteomics. *Mol. Cell. Proteom.* **2013**, *12*, 263–276. [CrossRef] [PubMed]

5. Dragsted, L.O.; Gao, Q.; Scalbert, A.; Vergères, G.; Kolehmainen, M.; Manach, C.; Brennan, L.; Afman, L.A.; Wishart, D.S.; Andres-Lacueva, C.; Garcia-Aloy, M.; Verhagen, H.; Feskens, E.J.M.; Praticò, G. Validation of biomarkers of food intake: critical assessment of candidate biomarkers. *Genes Nutr.* **2018**, *13*, 1–14. [CrossRef] [PubMed]
6. Szymańska, E.; Saccenti, E.; Smilde, A.K.; Westerhuis, J.A. Double-check: validation of diagnostic statistics for PLS-DA models in metabolomics studies. *Metabolomics* **2012**, *8*, 3–16. [CrossRef]
7. Barker, M.; Rayens, W. Partial least squares for discrimination. *J. Chemom.* **2003**, *17*, 166–173. [CrossRef]
8. Wold, S.; Kettaneh, N.; Fridén, H.; Holmberg, A. Modelling and diagnostics of batch processes and analogous kinetic experiments. *Chemom. Intell. Lab. Syst.* **1998**, *44*, 331–340. [CrossRef]
9. Antti, H.; Bollard, M.E.; Ebbels, T.; Keun, H.; Lindon, J.C.; Nicholson, J.K.; Holmes, E. Batch statistical processing of 1H NMR-derived urinary spectral data. *J. Chemom.* **2002**, *16*, 461–468. [CrossRef]
10. Jonsson, P.; Stenlund, H.; Moritz, T.; Trygg, J.; Sjöström, M.; Verheij, E.R.; Lindberg, J.; Schuppe-Koistinen, I.; Antti, H. A strategy for modelling dynamic responses in metabolic samples characterized by GC/MS. *Metabolomics* **2006**, *2*, 135–143. [CrossRef]
11. Rantalainen, M.; Cloarec, O.; Ebbels, T.M.D.; Lundstedt, T.; Nicholson, J.K.; Holmes, E.; Trygg, J. Piecewise multivariate modelling of sequential metabolic profiling data. *BMC Bioinform.* **2008**, *9*, 1–13. [CrossRef]
12. Kusalik, A.J. State-space model with time delays for gene regulatory networks. *J. Biol. Syst.* **2004**, *12*, 483–500.
13. Smilde, A.K.; Westerhuis, J.A.; Hoefsloot, H.C.J.; Bijlsma, S.; Rubingh, C.M.; Vis, D.J.; Jellema, R.H.; Pijl, H.; Roelfsema, F.; van der Greef, J. Dynamic metabolomic data analysis: a tutorial review. *Metabolomics* **2010**, *6*, 3–17. [CrossRef]
14. Wold, S.; Sjöström, M.; Eriksson, L. PLS-regression: a basic tool of chemometrics. *Chemom. Intell. Lab. Syst.* **2001**, *58*, 109–130. [CrossRef]
15. Bro, R. Multiway calibration. Multilinear PLS. *J. Chemom.* **1996**, *10*, 47–61. [CrossRef]
16. Rubingh, C.M.; Bijlsma, S.; Jellema, R.H.; Overkamp, K.M.; Van Der Werf, M.J.; Smilde, A.K. Analyzing longitudinal microbial metabolomics data. *J. Proteome Res.* **2009**, *8*, 4319–4327. [CrossRef]
17. Andersen, C.M.; Bro, R. Variable selection in regression-a tutorial. *J. Chemom.* **2010**, *24*, 728–737. [CrossRef]
18. Barri, T.; Holmer-Jensen, J.; Hermansen, K.; Dragsted, L.O. Metabolic fingerprinting of high-fat plasma samples processed by centrifugation-and filtration-based protein precipitation delineates significant differences in metabolite information coverage. *Anal. Chim. Acta* **2012**, *718*, 47–57. [CrossRef]
19. Gürdeniz, G.; Kristensen, M.; Skov, T.; Dragsted, L.O. The effect of LC-MS data preprocessing methods on the selection of plasma biomarkers in fed vs. *fasted rats*. *Metabolites* **2012**, *2*, 77–99. [CrossRef]
20. Gürdeniz, G.; Jensen, M.G.; Meier, S.; Bech, L.; Lund, E.; Dragsted, L.O. Detecting beer intake by unique metabolite patterns. *J. Proteome Res.* **2016**, *15*, 4544–4556. [CrossRef]
21. Smilde, A.; Bro, R.; Geladi, P. *Multi-way Analysis: Applications in the Chemical Sciences*; John Wiley & Sons: Hoboken, NJ, USA, 2005; ISBN 0470012102.
22. Kiers, H.A.L.; Van Mechelen, I. Three-way component analysis: Principles and illustrative application. *Psychol. Methods* **2001**, *6*, 84–110. [CrossRef] [PubMed]
23. Gurden, S.P.; Westerhuis, J.A.; Bro, R.; Smilde, A.K. A comparison of multiway regression and scaling methods. *Chemom. Intell. Lab. Syst.* **2001**, *59*, 121–136. [CrossRef]
24. Gosselin, R.; Rodrigue, D.; Duchesne, C. A Bootstrap-VIP approach for selecting wavelength intervals in spectral imaging applications. *Chemom. Intell. Lab. Syst.* **2010**, *100*, 12–21. [CrossRef]
25. Gleason, J.R. Algorithms for balanced bootstrap simulations. *Am. Stat.* **1988**, *42*, 263–266. [CrossRef]
26. Wold, S.; Johansson, E.; Cocchi, M. *3D QSAR in Drug Design: Theory, Methods and Applications*; ESCOM: Leiden, The Netherlands, 1993; pp. 523–550.
27. Favilla, S.; Durante, C.; Vigni, M.L.; Cocchi, M. Assessing feature relevance in NPLS models by VIP. *Chemom. Intell. Lab. Syst.* **2013**, *129*, 76–86. [CrossRef]
28. Andersson, C.A.; Bro, R. The N-way Toolbox for MATLAB. *Chemom. Intell. Lab. Syst.* **2000**, *52*, 1–4. [CrossRef]
29. Chong, I.-G.; Jun, C.-H. Performance of some variable selection methods when multicollinearity is present. *Chemom. Intell. Lab. Syst.* **2005**, *78*, 103–112. [CrossRef]
30. Alves, A.C.; Li, J.V.; Garcia-Perez, I.; Sands, C.; Barbas, C.; Holmes, E.; Ebbels, T.M.D. Characterization of data analysis methods for information recovery from metabolic 1H NMR spectra using artificial complex mixtures. *Metabolomics* **2012**, *8*, 1170–1180. [CrossRef]

31. Gidskehaug, L.; Anderssen, E.; Flatberg, A.; Alsberg, B.K. A framework for significance analysis of gene expression data using dimension reduction methods. *BMC Bioinform.* **2007**, *8*, 346. [CrossRef]
32. Bar-Joseph, Z.; Gerber, G.; Simon, I.; Gifford, D.K.; Jaakkola, T.S. Comparing the continuous representation of time-series expression profiles to identify differentially expressed genes. *Proc. Natl. Acad. Sci. USA* **2003**, *100*, 10146–10151. [CrossRef]
33. Berk, M.; Ebbels, T.; Montana, G. A statistical framework for biomarker discovery in metabolomic time course data. *Bioinformatics* **2011**, *27*, 1979–1985. [CrossRef] [PubMed]
34. Smilde, A.K.; Jansen, J.J.; Hoefsloot, H.C.J.; Lamers, R.J.A.N.; van der Greef, J.; Timmerman, M.E. ANOVA-simultaneous component analysis (ASCA): A new tool for analyzing designed metabolomics data. *Bioinformatics* **2005**, *21*, 3043–3048. [CrossRef] [PubMed]

© 2019 by the authors. Licensee MDPI, Basel, Switzerland. This article is an open access article distributed under the terms and conditions of the Creative Commons Attribution (CC BY) license (http://creativecommons.org/licenses/by/4.0/).

Article

rMSIKeyIon: An Ion Filtering R Package for Untargeted Analysis of Metabolomic LDI-MS Images

Esteban del Castillo [1,†], Lluc Sementé [1,†], Sònia Torres [1,2], Pere Ràfols [1,2,*], Noelia Ramírez [1,2], Manuela Martins-Green [3], Manel Santafe [4] and Xavier Correig [1,2]

1. Department of Electronic Engineering, Rovira i Virgili University, IISPV, 43007 Tarragona, Spain
2. Spanish Biomedical Research Centre in Diabetes and Associated Metabolic Disorders (CIBERDEM), 28029 Madrid, Spain
3. Department of Molecular, Cell and Systems Biology, University of California, Riverside, CA 92521, USA
4. Unit of Histology and Neurobiology, Department of Basic Medical Sciences, Faculty of Medicine and Health Sciences, Rovira i Virgili University, Carrer St. Llorenç, No. 21, 43201 Reus, Spain
* Correspondence: pere.rafols@urv.cat
† These authors contributed the same.

Received: 7 June 2019; Accepted: 30 July 2019; Published: 2 August 2019

Abstract: Many MALDI-MS imaging experiments make a case versus control studies of different tissue regions in order to highlight significant compounds affected by the variables of study. This is a challenge because the tissue samples to be compared come from different biological entities, and therefore they exhibit high variability. Moreover, the statistical tests available cannot properly compare ion concentrations in two regions of interest (ROIs) within or between images. The high correlation between the ion concentrations due to the existence of different morphological regions in the tissue means that the common statistical tests used in metabolomics experiments cannot be applied. Another difficulty with the reliability of statistical tests is the elevated number of undetected MS ions in a high percentage of pixels. In this study, we report a procedure for discovering the most important ions in the comparison of a pair of ROIs within or between tissue sections. These ROIs were identified by an unsupervised segmentation process, using the popular k-means algorithm. Our ion filtering algorithm aims to find the up or down-regulated ions between two ROIs by using a combination of three parameters: (a) the percentage of pixels in which a particular ion is not detected, (b) the Mann–Whitney U ion concentration test, and (c) the ion concentration fold-change. The undetected MS signals (null peaks) are discarded from the histogram before the calculation of (b) and (c) parameters. With this methodology, we found the important ions between the different segments of a mouse brain tissue sagittal section and determined some lipid compounds (mainly triacylglycerols and phosphatidylcholines) in the liver of mice exposed to thirdhand smoke.

Keywords: mass spectrometry imaging; metabolomics imaging; biostatistics; ion selection algorithms

1. Introduction

Mass Spectrometry Imaging (MSI) is a label-free analytical technique that can locate chemical compounds (metabolites, peptides, lipids, or proteins) directly in a biological sample and give their concentration for every pixel. The most common analytical strategy is MALDI due to its soft ionization, fast analysis, high throughput, versatility, and selectivity [1]. Other techniques, like desorption electrospray ionization (DESI), are becoming more popular because of the simplicity of their sample preparation [2]. MSI is currently used in the fields of drug discovery and toxicology [3,4]. In most experiments, researchers use a targeted strategy, which consists of visualizing and (sometimes) quantifying the concentration of a particular compound, or a reduced set of compounds throughout the tissue. Many MSI software packages have been released [5]. However, none of them provides an automated workflow for untargeted MSI applications since the end-user has to approach each MSI experiment data analysis in its unique manner.

Besides annotating and identifying the MS ions, one of the main challenges in untargeted MSI analysis is to determine the statistically differentiating ions in different regions of interest (ROIs) of the same tissue section or in different tissues of case versus control experiments. These key ions could be associated with biomarker candidates of disease or treatment efficacy. Previous studies have successfully used segmentation processes to find these key ions between clusters [6,7]. Most of these studies identify the key ions associated with a certain region by analysing the ions that most influence the segmenting process. In [8], the authors applied a Non-negative Matrix Factorization multivariate analysis to select a reduced group of lipid MS signals associated with the metabolite profile of each component. The t-test associated with segmentation with Spatial Shrunken Centroids can find the enriched and absent MS peaks for a particular region in a segmented image [9,10]. A technique based on deep unsupervised neural networks and parametric t-SNE was used to detect metabolic hidden sub-regions [11]. The same algorithm, linked to a significance analysis of microarrays (SAM), detected the protein subpopulations that can differentiate between t-SNE segments in a dataset of breast cancer samples; interestingly, they used the selected ions for a kNN second segmentation step [12]. Gorzolka et al. [13] studied the space-time profiling of the barley germination process by carrying out an unsupervised joint segmentation of a high number of images and found the ion-associated profile for every segment. The Algorithm for MSI Analysis by Semi-supervised Segmentation (AMASS) was used to segment leech embryo samples [14] and there is a complete analysis of the ions associated to every region according to its weighting factors. In all these references, no statistical significance test was conducted on the key ions found.

Another common strategy in MSI data analysis is to manually define the ROIs to be compared, guided by an annotated histology image [15–18]. In general, the ions are selected by means of statistical hypothesis testing and the fold change (FC) calculation of the ion concentrations between ROIs. These parameters are usually represented as volcano plots. By way of example, Hong et al. [19] studied the global changes of phospholipids in brain samples from a mouse model of Alzheimer disease by performing ANOVA tests of ion concentrations in ROI. A common problem that MSI has in calculating statistical significance is that the p-values are generally extremely low [16]. This is because there are a large number of pixels within each ROI, which gives this parameter a low discrimination power.

Additionally, the statistical hypothesis testing (such as the t-test) fails when is applied to compare the concentration of an ion between ROIs. The existence of morphological areas in the images is the responsible of a high pixel autocorrelation. This violates the assumption of observation independence necessary for statistical hypothesis testing. In order to find statistically significant ions between ROIs, Conditional Autoregressive (CAR) models, which take into account the auto-correlated nature of ion distribution concentration in MS image ROIs, are calculated to correct the p-values [20]. Nevertheless, the difficulty of calculating the autocorrelation models and the complexity of the computational approach hampers the inclusion of this strategy in a MSI workflow.

Another common situation in MS imaging is the elevated intensity differences of the ions' concentration between pixels, due to the existence of several morphologic regions with different metabolic profiles [21] and the ion shielding phenomena which takes place in MSI. It is also common to find a high proportion of pixels where a certain ion is not detected, for a given signal to noise ratio. This influences to a large extend the calculation of the p-values and the FC.

In this study, we describe the development of an ion filtering algorithm that is used in a workflow for the untargeted analysis of metabolomic MALDI-MS images. The workflow consists of a segmentation step, followed by the ion filtering procedure, independent of the segmentation process, that detects the up/down regulated ions between image segments. Our algorithm calculates and combines three parameters: (a) the Mann–Whitney U statistical test of the ion concentration between segments [22]; (b) the FC in the ion concentration between segments; and (c) a new parameter that accounts for the proportion of pixels with undetected ions between segments. In addition, the data from which parameters (a) and (b) are derived is obtained by previously filtering out the undetected MS signals (null values). With this methodology, we can find the key ions between any segment pair in MSI datasets, from single or multiple tissue sections. We successfully applied this workflow to the analysis of mouse brain tissue sample and to study fatty liver disease in mice liver tissue samples.

2. Results

The rMSIKeyIon package, written in R, is able to find the key ions in a pair of ROIs within or between images. The ions are selected according to the similarity parameters calculated in Appendix A and ordered following the contrast parameter, described in Appendix B. In Figure 1, there is a description of the data processing workflow, showing the main steps implemented in the rMSIKeyIon package. The spectra preprocessing and image segmentation has to be performed before and independently to the rMSIKeyIon execution. The resulting list of selected ions is related to the key metabolites exhibiting biological difference between tissue regions and reducing the candidates to identify.

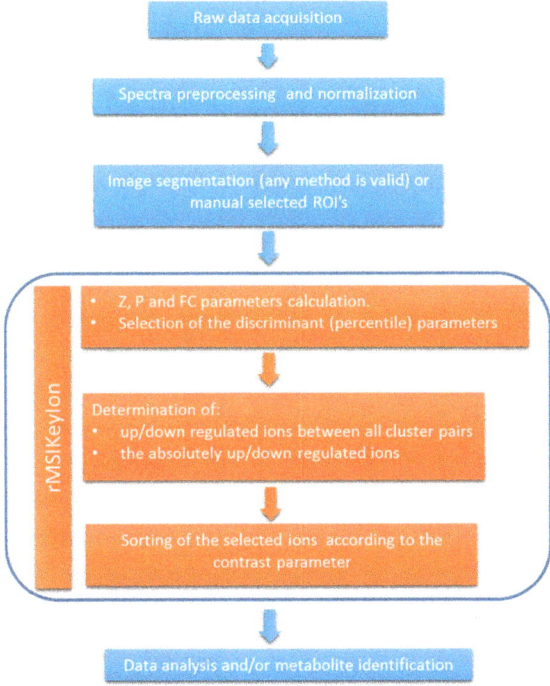

Figure 1. Workflow of the data processing, indicating the steps performed by the rMSIKeyIon package.

In the next section, we will describe the results of the package in the analysis of a sagittal brain mouse sample, which has been segmented by k-means algorithm (Section 2.1). In particular, we will illustrate the up or down regulated ions resulting of the comparison of two clusters and the up/down regulated ions when comparing one cluster with the rest.

In the Section 2.2, we will apply the package in the identification of the fat areas in control liver samples and liver samples exposed to thirdhand smoke (THS).

2.1. Results of the Brain Mouse Sample

Figure 2 shows the number of up and down-regulated ions associated with the comparison of one particular cluster with each of the others (columns 1 to 6) in the segmented image of the brain slice tissue of C57BL/6 mouse using the k-means algorithm (n = 7 clusters). Cluster 7, identified as non-tissue section areas, has not participated in the comparisons. In column "All" appear the ions that are up-regulated (or down-regulated) in a cluster as a result of the comparison between this cluster and the rest of clusters, called "absolutely up-regulated ions" (or "absolutely down-regulated ions"). The *m/z* values resulting from comparisons can be available at the GitHub repository of the package (https://github.com/LlucSF/rMSIKeyIon).

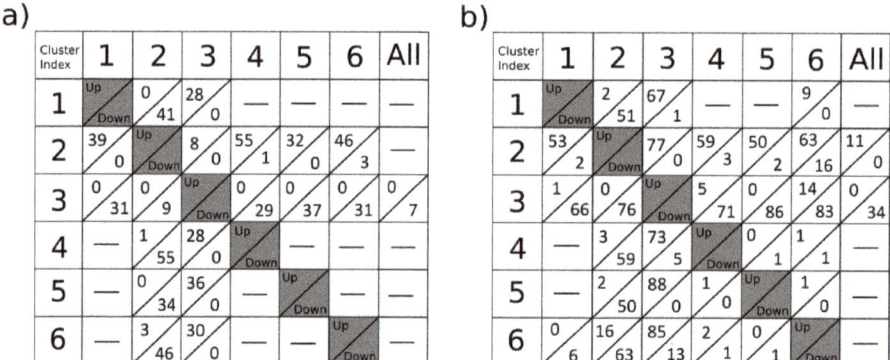

Figure 2. Number of up or down-regulated ions associated with the comparison of one particular cluster with each of the others (columns 1 to 6) and the ions that are up-regulated (or down-regulated) in a cluster as a result of the comparison between this cluster and the rest of clusters, called "absolutely up-regulated ions" (or "absolutely down-regulated ions"). The image is composed by 6898 pixels and the number of detected ions is 277. The percentile value used for the selection of the ions is 1% for the null concentration parameter (Z) and 10% for the Mann–Whitney U (V) test and for the concentration fold change (FC). The intensity threshold for the ions is 2.5×10^{-4} over the normalized spectra matrix. The small lack of symmetry observed in the table is a consequence of the lack of symmetry in the distributions considered. In (**a**), the up-down regulated ions are calculated following the classical procedure, while in (**b**) the ions are calculated according the procedure described in section methods, that considers that the null values are not taken into account.

For each cluster comparison, an associated figure gives information about the resulting up or down-regulated ions, and the number of null and non-null parameters defined in the section Ion analysis and filtering (see below). The ions on the list are ordered in terms of the value of the "contrast parameter", calculated with Equation (A4) in Appendix B.

Figure 2a shows the results obtained by the classical procedure, where null values do not have a special treatment. Figure 2b corresponds to the case in which the null values are treated separately. Although both cases make use of the same processing parameters, the results are very different. Figure 2b shows a higher abundance of up-down regulated ions versus Figure 2a. In addition, the ions find in Figure 2b are of higher relevance, as can be seen in Figure S1. Figure S1 shows the two ions with the highest contrast value from the volcano plot when comparing clusters 2 and 6. Figure S1a corresponds to the classic test, and Figure S1b corresponds to the separation of the null values.

A slightly asymmetry is displayed in the tables present in Figure 2. Each parameter has its own set of discriminant values. They are obtained from the evaluation of each parameter on all the pairs of clusters without repetition. The distribution generated by the set of all these values may not be symmetric. By applying the same percentile on both tails of the distribution, non-symmetric discriminant values may arise.

2.1.1. Comparison of C2 & C6

By way of example, the comparison of clusters C2 and C6 showed 63 up-regulated ions in C2 versus C6 and 16 down-regulated ions in C2 versus C6.

As an example, Figure S2 shows the volcano plot of the ions resulting from the comparison of C2 and C6. The ions at the top right and top left are selected by the ion filtering algorithm (see the caption to Figure S2 for more details).

Figure S3a shows the histogram of the concentration of the up-regulated ion with the highest contrast parameter (m/z 198.076) in C6, and Figure S3b shows the histogram of the up-regulated ion (m/z 848.636) in C2 also with the highest contrast parameter.

Figure 3a shows the segmented brain image (n = 7), and Figure 3b,c shows the concentration intensity plot of the ions mentioned above. In these intensity maps, the contrast intensity between both ions and clusters is clear, and the intensity of m/z 848.636 is much higher in C2 than in C6 and vice-versa for m/z 198.076.

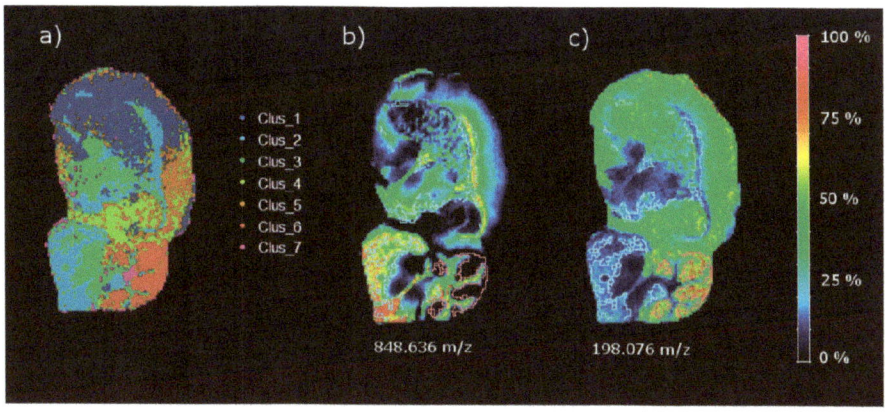

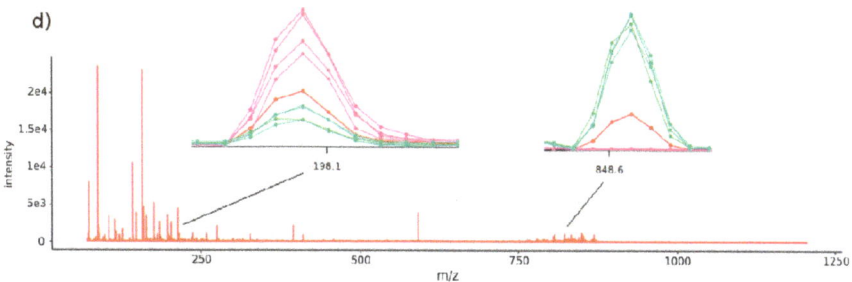

Figure 3. (**a**) Mouse brain segmentation using k-means (n = 7 clusters), (**b**) intensity map of ion m/z 848.636 (the up-regulated ion in C2 versus C6 with the highest contrasting parameter extracted from the null concentration parameter) and (**c**) intensity map of ion m/z 198.076, the down-regulated ion with the highest contrast parameter after comparing C2 and C6, extracted from the volcano plot. The highlighted areas in (**b**,**c**) represent C2 (white contour) and C6 (red contour). (**d**) Mean spectrum (red), spectra from C2 pixels (green), and spectra from C6 pixels (pink) near m/z 848.636 and m/z 198.076. The spectra show the up-regulated and down-regulated behaviour of the ions. See also the optical image of the same brain tissue section stained with a Hematoxilyn in Figure S4.

2.1.2. Absolutely Up and Down-Regulated Ions in Brain

According to the results in Figure 2b, there are 11 absolutely up-regulated ions in C2, and 34 absolutely down-regulated ions in C3. Figure 4 shows the concentration intensity plot of the two up-regulated ions (m/z 835.656 and m/z 806.633) in C2, and Figure 5 shows two down-regulated ions (m/z 868.459 and m/z 853.471) in C3 with the highest contrast parameter. There is an evident similarity between the images of the two up-regulated ions for one hand and two down-regulated ones for the other one. A comparison of the images in Figure 4 with the distribution of C2 in the brain are clearly similar. And the same is true of a comparison of the images in Figure 5 with the distribution of C3 in the brain.

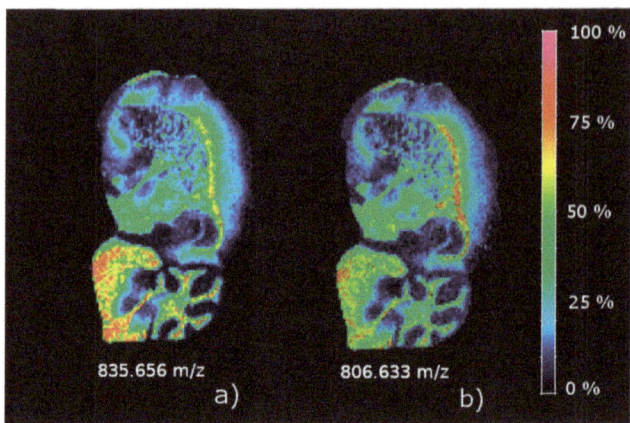

Figure 4. Concentration images of the two absolutely up-regulated ions in C2. (**a**) m/z 835.656; (**b**) m/z 806.633.

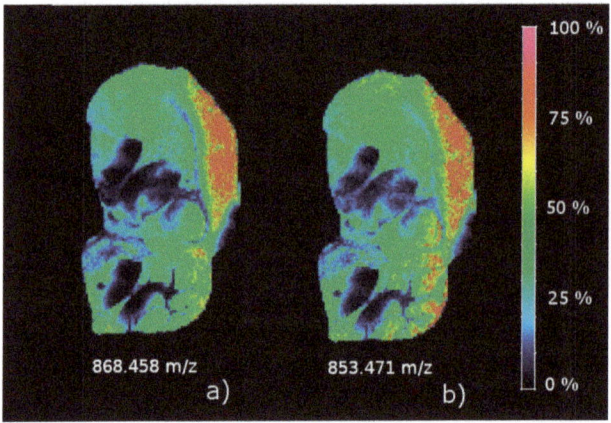

Figure 5. Concentration images of two absolutely down-regulated ions in C3. (**a**) m/z 868.458; (**b**) m/z 853.471.

2.2. Results of the Liver Samples

The methodology used in this article has been applied to the study of non-alcoholic fatty liver disease in mice exposed to thirdhand tobacco smoke (TBS) [23]. We have taken a total of six images from the liver samples (three from a control mouse and three from a THS-exposed mouse). The images has been segmented using the k-means algorithm (n = 6 clusters). The results of rMSIKeyIon algorithm showed that cluster 2 (C2) has an elevated number of ions in the lipid mass range that are absolutely up-regulated, and we hypothesized that this cluster represents the lipid droplet areas characteristic of the fatty livers (see Figure 6) and the full segmented image (see Figure S5). The THS exposed mouse has the largest area, while the control animals have the smallest, in accordance with Martins-Green et al. [23]. In addition, the Figure S6 is an optical image of a selected area of a tissue section of a control and a THS exposed mouse stained with an Oil Red O protocol. It can also be observed the higher density of lipid droplets in the THS exposed sample.

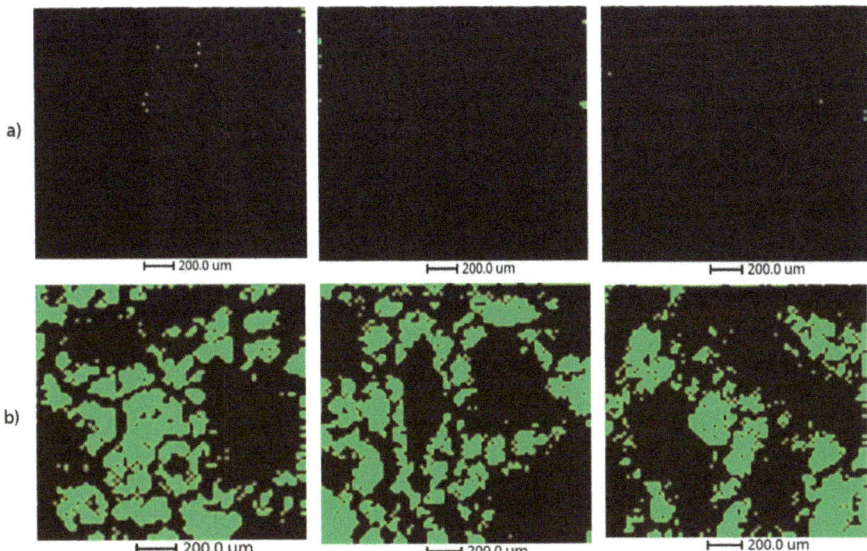

Figure 6. Representation of cluster 2 of the six liver samples: (**a**) the three analytical replicates of a control mouse and (**b**) the three replicates of a thirdhand smoke (THS)-exposed mouse.

Table S1 shows the compounds in C2 putatively identified after a manual curation process. As can be observed, most of them are putatively identified as triglycerides or phosphatidylcholine. In Figure S6, there is the intensity map of the triacylglycerol (50:30), which is highly similar to the geometry of C2.

3. Discussion

Here, we developed a new methodology for the untargeted analysis of MS images that can be used coupled with any segmentation process and an ion filtering algorithm based on the combination of three parameters: (a) The ratio of ions with a null concentration between the regions, (b) the U Mann–Whitney U Test, calculated by segregating the non-detected ions from the distribution, and (c) the FC between the medians of the distribution (the non-detected ions were also segregated from the distribution). This methodology has proved to be efficient at finding the up/down-expressed ions in an intra-image analysis or in the comparative analysis of groups of images. The presented workflow is different to previously released software tools due to two main reasons: (a) it is flexible and independent to the segmentation process, so the ion selection process can be applied to any clustering algorithm or manually drawn ROIs. (b) Our methodology provides a completely automated ion filtering approach enabling the fast detection of a morphological region characteristic ions.

The results on the sagittal mouse brain sample show that an unsupervised clustering process followed by the rMSIKeyIon algorithm is able to select the (possible) up/down-regulated ions between any pair of clusters, in a holistic approach, and between one cluster and the rest. The concentration maps of the selected ions, ordered by the contrast parameter, depicts faithfully the morphology of the brain. These ions are probably biologically relevant and could be interesting to identify.

Using the described methodology, we have been able to detect the regions containing the lipid droplets in the liver samples from mouse exposed to THS. The putative identification of the key up-regulated ions in the cluster 2, mainly triglycerides and phosphatidylcholines, confirm that THS exposure conducts to the apparition of fatty liver disease in mice [23].

Untargeted metabolomics data analysis workflows are associated to standard analytical platforms (LC-MS, GC-MS, and NMR) [24]. These analyses compare the concentrations of chemical compounds in a CASE and a CONTROL group in order to discover features that they express differently and which could be used as biomarkers or in biological pathway analysis. In general, the number of samples (n) of each experimental group are similar, the distribution is normal (for large n values), and the principle of independent measures is assumed. However, in spatial metabolomics, the number of samples in every group (i.e., the number of pixels in an ROI) is not determined a priori, as in metabolomics studies.

Untargeted image analysis has two main applications:

(a) The comparison of two regions inside the same tissue section (intra-image analysis) to find the relevant ions. This could be used to discover cancer biomarkers by comparing the ion profile of the tumorous area with a non-tumorous area from the same sample. In general, the areas to be compared are determined by a histopathologist annotating a consecutive tissue section. The size of the ROIs in which we will compare the ions is determined manually.

(b) For several reasons, the analysis of morphologically equivalent regions in different tissues in a case-control experiment is much more complicated. First of all, the tissue samples to be compared between groups are equivalent but not similar because of the biological differences between the animals and the intrinsic difficulty of achieving identical tissue sections. Consequently, it is not straightforward to delimit the areas to be compared. The ROIs to be compared can be determined by histological annotation (supervised process), or automatically by means of a segmentation process (unsupervised process). In both cases, there are not established rules, and the following steps in the statistical analysis of the ions between ROIs can be highly affected by this fact.

In both cases, it is very common to find skewed ion distributions and a high percentage of null values, a high degree of autocorrelation between pixels, and a very high number of observations (pixels). This leads to extremely low p-values when classical parametric or non-parametric statistical tests are used [25], so these tests are not appropriate for this kind of analysis. For all the above reasons, the untargeted analysis of images remains a challenge. However, the results shown by rMSIKeyIon R package have been revealed to be very useful to find the most differential ions between ROIs. The biological relevance of these ions has been validated in a fatty liver study with animal models.

4. Materials and Methods

4.1. Materials

Indium tin oxide (ITO)-coated glass slides were obtained from Bruker Daltonics (Bremen, Germany). The gold target used for sputtering coating was obtained from Kurt J. Lesker Company (Hastings, England) with a purity grade higher than 99.995%. HPLC grade xylene was supplied by Sigma–Aldrich (Steinheim, Germany), and ethanol (96% purity) was supplied by Scharlau (Sentmenat, Spain).

4.2. Methods

4.2.1. Sample Preparation

Mice models were developed at the Department of Molecular, Cell, and Systems Biology at the University of California Riverside [23]. Animal experimental protocols were approved by the University of California, Riverside, Institutional Animal Care and Use Committee (IACUC). The animal use protocol is A3400-01. The suitability of the workflow presented here to determine significant ions between ROIs from the same tissue was tested in a brain sample from a 6-month-old C57BL/6 mouse feed with a standard chow diet (percent calories: 58% carbohydrates, 28.5% protein, and 13.5% fat). To test the suitability of the method in different tissue sections in a case versus control experiment, we used liver samples from mice exposed to THS—the residual particles and gases from tobacco smoke that remain in dust and surfaces—from weaning (three weeks of age) to 24 weeks, without exposure to secondhand smoke (SHS) at any time during the study, and compared them with liver samples of mice that had not been exposed to THS (control group) [26]. Brain and liver samples were snap frozen at −80 °C after collection and stored and shipped at this temperature until analysis.

For MSI acquisition, the tissues were sectioned at −20 °C in slices 10 µm thick using a Leica CM-1950 cryostat (Leica Biosystems, Nussloch, Germany) located at the Centre for Omics Sciences (COS) of the Rovira i Virgili University and mounted on ITO slides by directly placing the glass slide onto the section at ambient temperature. To remove residual humidity, samples were dried in a desiccator under vacuum for 15 min after tissue mounting.

4.2.2. Deposition of Au Nanolayers for LDI-MS Imaging

Gold nanolayers were deposited on the 10 µm tissue sections using an ATC Orion 8-HV sputtering system (AJA International, N. Scituate, MA, USA) [27]. Briefly, an argon atmosphere with a pressure of 30 mTor was used to create the plasma in the gun. The working distance of the plate was set to 35 mm. Sputtering conditions for MS were ambient temperature, and RF mode at 60 W for 50 s. The argon ion current was adjusted to 20 mL min $^{-1}$.

4.2.3. LDI-MS Acquisition

One image of a sagittal brain tissue section and six liver tissue sections (three slices from a control animal and three sections from a THS-exposed animal) were acquired using a MALDI TOF/TOF UltrafleXtreme instrument with SmartBeam II Nd:YAG/355 nm laser from Bruker Daltonics, also at the COS facilities. Raster sizes of 80 and 20 µm were used for the brain and liver tissue sections, respectively. The TOF spectrometer operated in reflectron positive mode with the digitizer set at a sample rate of 1.25 GHz in a mass range between 70 and 1200 Da. The spectrometer was calibrated prior to tissue image acquisitions using [Au]$^+$ cluster MS peaks as internal mass references [27].

4.2.4. MSI Data Processing and Image Segmentation

The MSI data acquired with Bruker's FlexImaging 3.0 software was exported to XMASS data format using instrument manufacturer software packages (FlexImaging and Compass export). The raw data was loaded using the in-house rMSI package [28]. This package provides a data storage format based on segmented matrices and optimized for processing large MSI datasets in R language. Next, we applied our complete MSI pre-processing workflow consisting of spectral smoothing, alignment, mass recalibration, peak detection and peak binning [29] with the default parameters: Savitzky–Golay kernel size of 7, peak detection threshold SNR of 5, and peak binning tolerance of 6 scans with 5% filter. At this point, we obtained a peak matrix object of each MSI dataset: the brain tissue sagittal section and the liver tissue sections. These peak matrix objects are highly reduced, robust, and accurate representations of all the MSI data and can be used to perform complex statistical analyses on the huge amount of data generated in the MSI experiment. ROIs were generated by means of a k-means process. Finally, we applied the rMSIKeyIon workflow using the peak matrices as the input data.

4.2.5. Ion Analysis and Filtering

The procedure used for identifying statistically different ions compared the concentration distributions of the ions in all possible pairs of ROIs in which the tissue (or tissues) had been segmented.

In general, the total number of pixels in each ROI is different and the probability density function of the ion concentrations is not normal. We used the Mann–Whitney U test [22] because it can test the null hypothesis (both sets of samples come from the same distribution) of two non-normal distributions that have a different number of observations.

In addition, in non-normal distributions of different sample sizes, there is usually a singular element: In some ROIs, there is a considerable possibility that the distribution of some ions will have small concentration values. Figure S8 represents the percentage of non-detected ions in the segmented brain image, using the k-means algorithm with n = 7 clusters. It can be observed that for some clusters (i.e., cluster 7) the percentage is very high.

For purposes of illustration, Figure S9 shows a simulated histograms of an ion in two different clusters with samples taken from normal distributions, with different average values, to which significant amounts of null values have been added. In total, there are 200 samples for both cases. Both distributions appear to be very different and the Mann–Whitney U test yields a very high p-value (0.38). The idea we have worked on here is to segregate the values obtained from non-detected ions (null values) from the rest of the distribution so that they can be treated separately. Thus, we obtain a very small p-value (of the order of 1×10^{-43}). On the other hand, the percent of null values in each ROI also provides valuable information. For these reasons, we decided to segregate the null values from the ion matrix and use them to calculate a parameter (null concentration parameter), as will be explained below.

The calculation of the null concentration parameter, as well as the non-null parameters (Mann–Whitney U distribution and FC), are described in Appendix A.

Once the ions were selected using the two procedures described above, they were ordered in terms of the contrast generated by every ion between one ROI and the set of other ROIs. The procedure is described in Appendix B.

The ion filtering algorithm described in this section has been implemented in the R package named rMSIKeyIons, accessible at (https://github.com/LlucSF/rMSIKeyIon). The software's source code was written in C++ and requires the GNU Scientific Library (GSL) (https://www.gnu.org/software/gsl). Later, it was ported to R using the Rcpp R package. As input, the function requires an rMSIproc peak matrix, a previously calculated segmentation and the percentiles for each parameter, and as output, the function returns a list containing the ions for each comparison between all pair of clusters and the data related with those ions.

4.2.6. Metabolite Identification

The obtained list of up regulated lipids for mice liver samples in cluster 2 was matched with the HMDB 4.0 [30] database within a tolerance of 20 ppm and the possible ion adducts: H, Na, K, and NH4. Results were filtered using the biological information of molecules provided by the HMDB, thus metabolites with no biological origin or not likely to be found in liver were discarded.

5. Conclusions

In this study, we developed the ion filtering R package rMSIKeyIon. It is open source, publicly available, and based on the combination of three parameters: the non-detected ion concentration ratio, the Mann–Whitney U ion concentration test, and the FC in the ion concentration. The null values were discarded before computing the last two parameters.

We demonstrated that our tool is very effective at discovering up or down-regulated ions between clusters using an unsupervised k-means procedure. The ions selected are the candidates that, subsequently, have to be identified. This package is a valuable tool for the untargeted analysis of MALDI images and is an important advance in this area because, at present, there are no tools available.

Supplementary Materials: The following are available online at http://www.mdpi.com/2218-1989/9/8/162/s1. The brain dataset, the used clustering and a R script containing instructions about the installation and the testing of the package accompanied with a document containing illustrative figures. Also the results of the method are included.

Author Contributions: X.C. and E.d.C. designed and conducted the research. M.M.-G. designed the animal model experiments, and generated and collected the mice samples, and M.S. processed the liver and brain samples. P.R. acquired the images and processed the data, N.R. supervised the biological interpretation and S.T. worked on the putative identification of the metabolites in the liver samples. E.d.C. and L.S. programmed the ion filtering routine software. E.d.C., X.C. and N.R. wrote the article and L.S. was in charge of the illustrations. All the authors revised the manuscript for important intellectual content and read and approved the final manuscript.

Funding: This study has been supported by the Spanish Ministry of Economy and Competitiveness through projects TEC2015-69076-P and RTI2018-096061-B-I00, PR's predoctoral grant No. BES-2013-065572 and the General Directorate of Research of the Government of Catalonia through project 2017 SGR 1119. Animal model development was funded by the Tobacco Research Disease Related Program (TRDRP) of the University of California under projects 22RT-0121 and 23DT-0103.

Conflicts of Interest: The authors declare no conflict of interest.

Appendix A Calculation of the Similarity Parameters between ROIs

In order to determine the ions that are expressed differently in two given ROIs, we calculate three parameters:

(a) The null concentration parameter (Z parameter)

The Z_{ijk} parameter is calculated according to Equation (A1):

$$Z_{ijk} = \frac{\frac{Nz_{ij}}{N_j}}{\frac{Nz_{ik}}{N_k}} \forall i \in I; \forall j, k \in S_p, \tag{A1}$$

where Z_{ijk} is the parameter that accounts for the null values (i.e., the non-detected values) of the i ion when comparing the j and k ROIs; Nz_{ij} and Nz_{ik} are the number of pixels with null values of the i ion in j and k ROIs, respectively; N_j and N_k are the total number of ROI pixels in j and k, respectively; I is the set of ions and Sp is the set of ROIs.

The equation calculates the ratio between the null values of a particular ion in the two ROIs. A value of $Z_{ijk} > Z_{high}$ (Z_{high} being a positive value greater than 1) means that the i ion is more expressed in k ROI than in j ROI, while $Z_{ijk} < Z_{low}$ (Z_{low} being a positive value much lower than 1) means that the i ion is less expressed in k ROI than in j ROI.

The importance of this parameter is assessed in Figure S7. For clusters 1 to 7, we plotted, the percentage of pixels that have null concentration for every ion.

The Z_{high} and Z_{low} values are calculated by following these steps:

(1) The Z values of all ions, for all cluster-pairs, are calculated according to Equation (A1).
(2) An ordered rank list of all the Z values is created.
(3) Z_{low} is determined considering that this value is a certain percentile P_Z of the rank list of Z values.
(4) Z_{high} is determined considering that this value is a certain percentile $100 - P_Z$ of the rank list of Z values.

(b) Non-null concentration parameters (V parameters)

Provided that the distribution of the ions concentration is non-normal, we considered the U Mann–Whitney U test and the concentration FC between two ROIs, as a non-null concentration parameters.

Generally speaking, if N_j and N_k are high, the random variable U can be regarded as normally distributed [22]. The U_{ijk} parameter is then normalized following Equation (A2):

$$V_{ijk} = \frac{U_{ijk} - m_u}{\sigma_u}, \tag{A2}$$

where m_u and σ_u are the average and standard deviation of zero U_{ijk} and V_{ijk} is a random variable with a normalized Gaussian distribution. If V has values close to 1 the similarity between the distributions is high, while values close to zero indicate disparate distributions. The value obtained for V indicates the similarity between the distributions of two ROIs for an ion.

Another parameter often used to compare sets of magnitudes is the FC, defined as the ion median concentration quotient between two ROIs Equation (A3):

$$FC_{ijk} = \frac{M_{ij}}{M_{ik}}, \qquad (A3)$$

where M_{ij} is the distribution median of the i ion in j ROI and M_{ik} is the same for k ROI. For every i ion, the FC_{ijk} parameter is calculated between the j and k ROIs. For a pair of ROIs, a Volcano plot [31] can be drawn from the V and FC parameters.

In this representation, the position occupied by the ions is important: the ions located in the top corners generate very different distributions in the two ROIs. The ions at the top left are under-expressed ($V_{ijk} < V_{high} \wedge Fc_{ijk} < Fc_{low}$) and the ions at the top right are over-expressed ($V_{ijk} < V_{high} \wedge Fc_{ijk} > Fc_{high}$).

The values V_{high}, Fc_{high} and Fc_{low} are calculated following the same steps as for Z_{high} and Z_{low}, but with a difference in the percentile value. The ions located in the areas of interest must satisfy the probability of being within a range associated with two random variables; that is to say: $P(V_{ijk} \leq V_{high}, Fc_{ijk} \leq Fc_{low})$ for under-expressed ions and $P(V_{ijk} \leq V_{high}, Fc_{ijk} \geq Fc_{high})$ for over-expressed ions. Assuming that these are independent random variables, we obtain $P(V_{ijk} \leq V_{high}) = P(Fc_{ijk} \leq Fc_{low}) = P(Fc_{ijk} \geq Fc_{high}) = \sqrt{P_z/100}$. That is, the percentile that has to be used to determine the cutoff values in the volcano plot should be $P_V = 10 \cdot \sqrt{P_Z}$

Appendix B Determination of the Discriminating Figure Values and Generation of the Discriminant Ions Lists

The contrast parameter $C_{ij \vee S_p}$ of the i ion between the j ROI and all the ROIs (set S_p is calculated according to Equation (A4)):

$$C_{ij \vee S_p} = \frac{\frac{1}{N_j} \sum_{p=1}^{N_j} m_{ip}^j}{\frac{1}{N} \sum_{k=0}^{N_{S_p}} \sum_{p=1}^{N_k} m_{ip}^k}, \qquad (A4)$$

where N is the total number of pixels in S_p, N_j and N_k are the number of pixels in the j and k ROIs respectively. N_{S_p} is the total number of ROIs in set S_p, m_{ip}^j and m_{ip}^k are the magnitude of the i ion in pixel p of the j and k ROI, respectively. The list is ordered according to the $C_{ij \vee S_p}$, assuming that high values mean high contrast and vice-versa.

References

1. Karas, M.; Hillenkamp, F. Laser desorption ionization of proteins with molecular masses exceeding 10,000 daltons. *Anal. Chem.* **1988**, *60*, 2299–2301. [CrossRef] [PubMed]
2. Wiseman, J.M.; Ifa, D.R.; Song, Q.; Cooks, R.G. Tissue imaging at atmospheric pressure using Desorption Electrospray Ionization (DESI) mass spectrometry. *Angew. Chem. Int. Ed.* **2006**, *45*, 7188–7192. [CrossRef] [PubMed]
3. Morosi, L.; Zucchetti, M.; D'Incalci, M.; Davoli, E. Imaging mass spectrometry: Challenges in visualization of drug distribution in solid tumors. *Curr. Opin. Pharmacol.* **2013**, *13*, 807–812. [CrossRef] [PubMed]
4. Greer, T.; Sturm, R.; Li, L. Mass spectrometry imaging for drugs and metabolites. *J. Proteom.* **2011**, *74*, 2617–2631. [CrossRef] [PubMed]
5. Ràfols, P.; Vilalta, D.; Brezmes, J.; Cañellas, N.; del Castillo, E.; Yanes, O.; Ramírez, N.; Correig, X. Signal preprocessing, multivariate analysis and software tools for MA(LDI)-TOF mass spectrometry imaging for biological applications. *Mass Spectrom. Rev.* **2018**, *37*, 281–306. [CrossRef] [PubMed]
6. Alexandrov, T. MALDI imaging mass spectrometry: Statistical data analysis and current computational challenges. *BMC Bioinform.* **2012**, *13*, S11. [CrossRef] [PubMed]
7. Jones, E.A.; Deininger, S.O.; Hogendoorn, P.C.; Deelder, A.M.; McDonnell, L.A. Imaging mass spectrometry statistical analysis. *J. Proteom.* **2012**, *75*, 4962–4989. [CrossRef]

8. Lee, D.Y.; Platt, V.; Bowen, B.; Louie, K.; Canaria, C.A.; McMurray, C.T.; Northen, T. Resolving brain regions using nanostructure initiator mass spectrometry imaging of phospholipids. *Integr. Biol.* **2012**, *4*, 693–699. [CrossRef]
9. Bemis, K.D.; Harry, A.; Eberlin, L.S.; Ferreira, C.R.; van de Ven, S.M.; Mallick, P.; Stolowitz, M.; Vitek, O. Probabilistic Segmentation of Mass Spectrometry (MS) Images Helps Select Important Ions and Characterize Confidence in the Resulting Segments. *Mol. Cell. Proteom.* **2016**, *15*, 1761–1772. [CrossRef]
10. Bemis, K.D.; Harry, A.; Eberlin, L.S.; Ferreira, C.; van de Ven, S.M.; Mallick, P.; Stolowitz, M.; Vitek, O. Cardinal: An R package for statistical analysis of mass spectrometry-based imaging experiments. *Bioinformatics* **2015**, *31*, 2418–2420. [CrossRef]
11. Inglese, P.; McKenzie, J.S.; Mroz, A.; Kinross, J.; Veselkov, K.; Holmes, E.; Takats, Z.; Nicholson, J.K.; Glen, R. Deep learning and 3D-DESI imaging reveal the hidden metabolic heterogeneity of cancer. *Chem. Sci.* **2017**, *8*, 3500–3511. [CrossRef] [PubMed]
12. Abdelmoula, W.M.; Balluff, B.; Englert, S.; Dijkstra, J.; Reinders, M.J.; Walch, A.; McDonnell, L.A.; Lelieveldt, B.P. Data-Driven Identification of Prognostic Tumor Subpopulations Using Spatially Mapped t-SNE of Mass Spectrometry Imaging Data. *Proc. Natl. Acad. Sci. USA* **2016**, *113*, 12244–12249. [CrossRef] [PubMed]
13. Gorzolka, K.; Kölling, J.; Nattkemper, T.W.; Niehaus, K. Spatio-Temporal metabolite profiling of the barley germination process by MALDI MS imaging. *PLoS ONE* **2016**, *11*, e0150208. [CrossRef] [PubMed]
14. Bruand, J.; Alexandrov, T.; Sistla, S.; Wisztorski, M.; Meriaux, C.; Becker, M.; Salzet, M.; Fournier, I.; Macagno, E.; Bafna, V. AMASS: Algorithm for MSI analysis by semi-supervised segmentation. *J. Proteome Res.* **2011**, *10*, 4734–4743. [CrossRef] [PubMed]
15. Moreno-Gordaliza, E.; Esteban-Fernández, D.; Lázaro, A.; Aboulmagd, S.; Humanes, B.; Tejedor, A.; Linscheid, M.W.; Gómez-Gómez, M.M. Lipid imaging for visualizing cilastatin amelioration of cisplatin-induced nephrotoxicity. *J. Lipid Res.* **2018**, *59*, 1561–1574. [CrossRef] [PubMed]
16. Yajima, Y.; Hiratsuka, T.; Kakimoto, Y.; Ogawa, S.; Shima, K.; Yamazaki, Y.; Yoshikawa, K.; Tamaki, K.; Tsuruyama, T. Region of Interest analysis using mass spectrometry imaging of mitochondrial and sarcomeric proteins in acute cardiac infarction tissue. *Sci. Rep.* **2018**, *8*, 7493. [CrossRef] [PubMed]
17. Wang, X.; Han, J.; Hardie, D.B.; Yang, J.; Pan, J.; Borchers, C.H. Metabolomic profiling of prostate cancer by matrix assisted laser desorption/ionization-Fourier transform ion cyclotron resonance mass spectrometry imaging using Matrix Coating Assisted by an Electric Field (MCAEF). *Biochim. Biophys. Acta Proteins Proteom.* **2017**, *1865*, 755–767. [CrossRef]
18. Otsuka, Y.; Satoh, S.; Naito, J.; Kyogaku, M.; Hashimoto, H. Visualization of cancer-related chemical components in mouse pancreas tissue by tapping-mode scanning probe electrospray ionization mass spectrometry. *J. Mass Spectrom.* **2015**, *50*, 1157–1162. [CrossRef]
19. Hong, J.H.; Kang, J.W.; Kim, D.K.; Baik, S.H.; Kim, K.H.; Shanta, S.R.; Jung, J.H.; Mook-Jung, I.; Kim, K.P. Global changes of phospholipids identified by MALDI imaging mass spectrometry in a mouse model of Alzheimer's disease. *J. Lipid Res.* **2016**, *57*, 36–45. [CrossRef]
20. Cassese, A.; Ellis, S.R.; Ogrinc Potočnik, N.; Burgermeister, E.; Ebert, M.; Walch, A.; Van Den Maagdenberg, A.M.; McDonnell, L.A.; Heeren, R.M.; Balluff, B. Spatial Autocorrelation in Mass Spectrometry Imaging. *Anal. Chem.* **2016**, *88*, 5871–5878. [CrossRef]
21. Chernyavsky, I.; Nikolenko, S.; von Eggeling, F.; Alexandrov, T.; Becker, M. Analysis and Interpretation of Imaging Mass Spectrometry Data by Clustering Mass-to-Charge Images According to Their Spatial Similarity. *Anal. Chem.* **2013**, *85*, 11189–11195. [CrossRef]
22. Mann, H.B.; Whitney, D.R. On a Test of Whether one of Two Random Variables is Stochastically Larger than the Other. *Ann. Math. Stat.* **1947**, *18*, 50–60. [CrossRef]
23. Martins-Green, M.; Adhami, N.; Frankos, M.; Valdez, M.; Goodwin, B.; Lyubovitsky, J.; Dhall, S.; Garcia, M.; Egiebor, I.; Martinez, B.; et al. Cigarette smoke toxins deposited on surfaces: Implications for human health. *PLoS ONE* **2014**, *9*, e86391. [CrossRef] [PubMed]
24. Patti, G.J.; Yanes, O.; Siuzdak, G. Metabolomics: The apogee of the omics trilogy. *Nat. Rev. Mol. Cell Biol.* **2012**, *13*, 263–269. [CrossRef] [PubMed]
25. Fagerland, M.W. t-tests, non-parametric tests, and large studies—A paradox of statistical practice? *BMC Med. Res. Methodol.* **2012**, *12*, 78. [CrossRef] [PubMed]

26. Adhami, N.; Starck, S.R.; Flores, C.; Green, M.M. A health threat to bystanders living in the homes of smokers: How smoke toxins deposited on surfaces can cause insulin resistance. *PLoS ONE* **2016**, *11*, e0149510. [CrossRef]
27. Ràfols, P.; Vilalta, D.; Torres, S.; Calavia, R.; Heijs, B.; McDonnell, L.A.; Brezmes, J.; del Castillo, E.; Yanes, O.; Ramírez, N.; et al. Assessing the potential of sputtered gold nanolayers in mass spectrometry imaging for metabolomics applications. *PLoS ONE* **2018**, *13*, e0208908. [CrossRef] [PubMed]
28. Ràfols, P.; Torres, S.; Ramírez, N.; Del Castillo, E.; Yanes, O.; Brezmes, J.; Correig, X. rMSI: An R package for MS imaging data handling and visualization. *Bioinformatics* **2017**, *33*, 2427–2428. [CrossRef] [PubMed]
29. Ràfols, P.; del Castillo, E.; Yanes, O.; Brezmes, J.; Correig, X. Novel automated workflow for spectral alignment and mass calibration in MS imaging using a sputtered Ag nanolayer. *Anal. Chim. Acta* **2018**, *1022*, 61–69. [CrossRef] [PubMed]
30. Wishart, D.S.; Feunang, Y.D.; Marcu, A.; Guo, A.C.; Liang, K.; Vázquez-Fresno, R.; Sajed, T.; Johnson, D.; Li, C.; Karu, N.; et al. HMDB 4.0: The human metabolome database for 2018. *Nucleic Acids Res.* **2018**, *46*, D608–D617. [CrossRef]
31. Mak, T.D.; Laiakis, E.C.; Goudarzi, M.; Fornace, A.J. MetaboLyzer: A Novel Statistical Workflow for Analyzing Postprocessed LC–MS Metabolomics Data. *Anal. Chem.* **2014**, *86*, 506–513. [CrossRef] [PubMed]

© 2019 by the authors. Licensee MDPI, Basel, Switzerland. This article is an open access article distributed under the terms and conditions of the Creative Commons Attribution (CC BY) license (http://creativecommons.org/licenses/by/4.0/).

MDPI
St. Alban-Anlage 66
4052 Basel
Switzerland
Tel. +41 61 683 77 34
Fax +41 61 302 89 18
www.mdpi.com

Metabolites Editorial Office
E-mail: metabolites@mdpi.com
www.mdpi.com/journal/metabolites

www.ingramcontent.com/pod-product-compliance
Lightning Source LLC
LaVergne TN
LVHW070509100526
838202LV00014B/1822